Sociology

301
Sol

132875

DATE DUE

WITHDRAWN

Sociology: A Descriptive Approach

Jeffrey E. Nash and James P. Spradley
Macalester College

Rand McNally College Publishing Company/Chicago

Rand McNally Sociology Series

76 77 78 10 9 8 7 6 5 4 3 2 1

Copyright © 1976 by Rand McNally College Publishing Co.
All Rights Reserved
Printed in U.S.A.
Library of Congress Catalog Card Number 75-20658

Preface

Robert Park, the famous Chicago sociologist, frequently admonished his graduate students to "get the seat of your pants dirty with research." He wanted to be sure that the new generation of social scientists would produce accurate, firsthand accounts of the *lived-in* and *lived-through* world of real people. He hoped that participation in the everyday life of society would temper their scholarly work. Some thirty years later, modern sociology has only partially heeded his advice. Like the medieval scholastics, many sociologists are shocked by the suggestion that they should go out and experience the social world rather than analyze, debate, and speculate about its nature. Sociology has an abundance of theories, data banks, statistics, and treatises about virtually every aspect of social behavior. Yet, most of these studies are based on second- and thirdhand information or on indirect measures of what the sociologists judge to be important aspects of societal life. Although such research makes an important contribution to building a science of society, it neglects the fundamental feature of firsthand description.

Description is not the end of sociological research but the beginning. Anyone who seeks to understand and explain human society must start with this task. We offer this book of readings to provide the beginning student with studies that preserve the wholeness and vividness of social life. We believe that an early saturation in the descriptive literature of sociology enables students to understand more fully the conceptual and theoretical aspects of the discipline. To reverse this process puts the cart before the horse, places the general before the particular, the abstract before the concrete. We often take it for granted that most people already know what everyday life in society is like; therefore, our task is merely to analyze, generalize, and explain. But such is not the case, if only because our culture and society remain at the tacit level of awareness.

The descriptive approach is not simply another "school" of sociological thought. It is a cornerstone of all sociology. Descriptive information consists of accurate data gathered on the scene and experienced by the observer. It involves the activities of watching people, talking to people, and participating with people in their daily lives. It requires a "watch and wonder" attitude. Instead of abstracting neatly defined bits of information about classes of people and types of institutions, descriptive sociology seeks to record what actually occurs in a restricted social setting. It is one thing to know how many auto thefts occur each year in a particular city, for example, but quite another to describe the strategies and activities of an organized gang of car thieves. Both kinds of information are important, but they cannot be substituted for each other. Another example of this difference in outlook can be seen in the way that the descriptive approach is more concerned with the complex interactions and activities that go on during surgery in an operating room than with the social class and median income of surgeons.

Descriptive sociology is empirical. It is based on knowledge about society derived from observation and experience rather than from abstract statistical or theoretical concepts. The studies that make up this book are grounded in the cognitive and emotional experiences of persons living in the real and imagined presence of others. As empirical information, the fruits of description can be used as evidence to test many different theories and concepts about the nature of society. We contend, however, that sociology is an immature discipline. It suffers from a dearth of the kind of rich, descriptive accounts needed to provide the discipline with the impetus and data for growth and development.

The descriptive articles in this book also share an implicit assumption that society is much like a puzzle. To appreciate the picture one must begin by observing the characteristics of each piece, noticing the shape and pattern that makes it distinctive. Then, to discover how one part fits into the scheme of things, you must become aware of how it is different from all the rest in the minute detail of form and structure. As a few related pieces fit together, a small part of the picture comes into view and takes on significance. Understanding grows in direct proportion to our ability to see the context of each piece, each cluster of related pieces, and finally the entire picture.

Descriptive sociology takes seriously the maxim that reality is "socially constructed." The everyday lives of people in society are profoundly affected by what W. I. Thomas called their "definition of the situation." As students, we must know what people actually think about the matters they deem significant in their daily lives. We need basic information about how they actually conduct their affairs on a day-to-day basis. We need to stand in the places of third-grade pupils, taxi drivers, waitresses, bus riders, mothers, fathers, salesmen, teachers, and a host of others in modern society and see the social world from their perspectives. Our appraisals will ring with authenticity when we know of and appreciate the realities that people construct and live in. Descriptions of the life-situations in which the members of a society work, play, and suffer are necessary to the more general task of conceptual understanding.

We think that the studies presented here, and descriptive accounts in general, make another important contribution. As our society becomes more complex, two opposing trends occur. On the one hand, the opportunities for varied lifestyles and forms of social existence increase. On the other hand, we find that once we have found a particular social niche, we become more isolated than ever from the rich diversity around us. A particular social position, such as policeman, professor, farmer, or bricklayer, demands an increasing amount of time and energy; it influences who we associate with and in subtle ways dominates the way we interpret all of life. The temptation to view others with a kind of ethnocentric bias affects all of us, sociologist as well as construction worker. The lawyer who becomes preoccupied with legal studies may begin to think of the whole world in terms of precedent and cases. Thus, at a time when society is immensely complex and variegated, we become limited in our views, narrowed in perspective according to our niches in the complex whole. Descriptions of the way others live and think, of their life situations, can inform us and enable us to avoid this kind of one-dimensionality. Description can allow a luxury of vicariously experiencing many lifestyles and world views that our particular position in society does not allow. When it is impossible to experience directly and when such experience is prerequisite to achieving intersubjective understanding, vicarious experience is the next best thing. Such experience is especially important for the beginning student in sociology.

Finally, when we ignore or depart from the descriptive approach, it creates the impression that sociology is remotely abstract and far removed from everyday life. Many people see sociology as simply an elaboration and confusion of commonsense knowledge, at best a pseudoscience. The goal of a *descriptive* sociology is to understand the world of commonsense knowledge as it is known by those who use it. In order to achieve this objective, researchers must present accounts of that "real world" in clear, straightforward language. These descriptions then become the basis for developing typologies and ordered observations.

In selecting articles for this book, we looked for papers that preserved a sense of participation in society. Each article describes the firsthand experience of those involved in an action scene. Although many articles are written from a particular viewpoint within sociology, we are not attempting to present a theory of society. Our hope is that these papers communicate the descriptive stance.

Jeffrey E. Nash
James P. Spradley
January, 1976

Contents

Part One: Culture

1. Culture: The Hidden Dimension   3
   The Sounds of Silence
   Edward T. Hall and Mildred R. Hall

2. The Culture of Everyday Places   15
   Pinball Occasions
   William B. Sanders

3. Perspectives on Culture   31
   The Martian and the Convert: Ontological Polarities in Social Research
   Fred Davis

Part Two: Society

4. Organizing New Forms   43
   Bus Riding: Community on Wheels
   Jeffrey Nash

5. Organizing Work   64
   The Social Structure of the Restaurant
   William Foote Whyte

6. Organizing Everyday Life   79
   Learning to Live with Lines
   Leon Mann

Part Three: Socialization

7. The Everyday World of Childhood   101
   Child's-Eye Views of Life in an Urban Barrio
   Mary Ellen Goodman and Alma Beman

8. **Entering Adulthood** — 120
The Dance Party as a Socialization Mechanism for Black Urban Pre-adolescents and Adolescents
R. Milton Clark

9. **Learning an Occupation** — 135
On the Job
Arthur Niederhoffer

10. **Acquiring New Identities** — 161
The Short and the Long of It: Legitimizing Motives for Running
Jeffrey Nash

Part Four: Differentiation and Stratification

11. **Division of Labor** — 185
Teamwork in the Operating Room
Robert N. Wilson

12. **Little Ways to Show Big Differences** — 199
Sociology of Christmas Cards
Sheila K. Johnson

13. **When High Meets Low** — 207
Janitors Versus Tenants: A Status Income Dilemma
Ray Gold

14. **The Law and The Poor** — 220
Beating the Drunk Charge
James P. Spradley

Part Five: Sex Roles

15. **Woman's Work in a Man's World** — 231
Division of Labor
James P. Spradley and Brenda J. Mann

16. **The Female Gender** — 262
Growing Up Female
Alan Graebner

17. **Sex Roles in Everyday Life** — 272
The Changing Door Ceremony: Notes on the Operation of Sex Roles
Laure Richardson Walum

18. **Sex Role Games** — 281
The Doctor-Nurse Game
Leonard I. Stein

Part Six: The Family

19. Society as Drama — 293
The Family as a Company of Players
Annabella B. Motz

20. Selecting Spouses — 301
Sororities and the Husband Game
John Finley Scott

21. "Normal" Family Forms — 311
Reform-School Families
Barbara Carter

22. Domesticated Singles — 324
Tuesdays and Saturdays: A Preliminary Study of the Domestic Patterns of Young Urban Singles
Mimi Rodin

Part Seven: Education

23. Everyday Life in the Classroom — 347
Learning the Student Role: Kindergarten as Academic Boot Camp
Harry L. Gracey

24. Managing Everyday Disruptions — 362
Guided Options as a Pattern of Control in a Head Start Program
Carol Dixon

25. Schedules for Students — 374
Getting it Done: Notes on Student Fritters
Stan Bernstein

26. Negotiated Interaction in the Classroom — 388
Observations in a Bilingual Classroom: The Role of the Interpreter
Anedith Nash

Part Eight: Religion

27. Civil Religion — 407
An American Sacred Ceremony
W. Lloyd Warner

28. Religion and Self — 425
The Jesus People: An Identity Synthesis
David Gordon

Contents

29.	The Function of Religion *Urban Witches* Edward J. Moody	442

Part Nine: Economics

30.	Selling the Culture *The Encyclopedia Game* Lynn M. Buller	457
31.	Sociology for Selling *The Social Base of Sales Behavior* Stephen J. Miller	473
32.	Core Values in Everyday Economics *The Flea Market as an Action Scene* Robert Maisel	486

Part Ten: Bureaucracy and Power

33.	Informal Law *Dispute Settlement in an Urban Supermarket* Spencer MacCullum	503
34.	The Life of an Organization *The Reluctant Organization and the Aggresive Environment* John Maniha and Charles Perrow	511
35.	The Structure of Power *Oil in Santa Barbara and Power in America* Harvey Molotch	528

Part Eleven: Social Change

36.	New Kinds of Neighbors *The Function of Neighboring for the Middle-Class Male* Ruth Hill Useem, John Useem, and Duane L. Gibson	559
37.	A Changing Social Scene *Surfing: The Natural History of an Urban Scene* John Irwin	581
38.	Modern Reasons for Preserving the Past *Fear and Loathing in Mass Society: The Strategic Negotiation of Social Change* Armin Sebran	605

PART ONE
Culture

In our daily lives we often use the word *culture* to refer to artistic endeavors and to the end result of painting, composing music, and writing. In the world of the science laboratory, culture refers to mold or bacteria growing in a small dish. Although these things are all parts of our culture, they are not culture per se, at least not according to the way we talk when playing the game of sociology. In the social sciences the concept is used in a specific, analytic way, and it refers to a very general phenomenon common to all people.

Culture distinguishes humans from the other animals. As a species, we have lost the automatic, involuntary, and unlearned way of accomplishing the task of living that characterizes the rest of the animal kingdom. We must learn virtually everything to survive, even how to give birth to our offspring! Aside from a few reflexes, we come into the world without knowledge and without skills. Immediately, we begin to acquire information about the world, and we go on learning for the rest of our lives. We learn the language spoken around us; we pick up the beliefs of our parents and friends; we acquire the appropriate ways to feel, to walk, and even to think. Within a very short period, we display the sounds, actions, and attitudes that characterize "our group of people." We have become members of our culture. We know how to produce appropriate actions, to understand ourselves and others, and to deal with the social world in which we live. We have come to think of ourselves as members of our group and to believe that others think we are members.

Culture refers to the general phenomenon of patterned actions and beliefs. Culture consists of rules for understanding and generating forms of action, for perceiving the world, for making up our minds, for deciding what we should do, and even for knowing who we are. We all employ cultural rules every day in connection with the circumstances in which we find ourselves. Culture takes the place of instincts in human beings, but culture does not operate like instincts. It is much less precise and demanding. Cultures change from one generation to the next. None of the members learn and understand their culture in exactly the same way. We learn and share ideas, beliefs, and knowledge, to be sure, but we also apply our skills, memories, and practices in different ways.

When we stand back and try to observe our collective actions, we can discern patterns, trends, and adaptations. We can see how our lives follow careers, that culture provides us with the capabilities necessary for beginning social life, carrying it through, ending it, even thinking of it as never ending. Therefore, whenever we observe differences in these life processes among people, we can say that there are boundaries that mark off one way of living from another, one culture from another. Within a single culture, we can observe variations in these processes that are subtle, not dramatic. When such intracultural differences result in systematic and distinguishable differences in people's perceptions, knowledge, and beliefs, we say we have identified a subculture.

Culture, then, is learned, and shared to the extent that we can presume similar backgrounds and learning experiences; it changes and adapts to its surroundings; it is patterned and identifiable. Culture is a human phenomenon, both our blessing and our curse. It gives humans extreme flexibility in adapting to different environments, but it also holds us to established patterns. It is our link to the past and to the future.

In this section, we will explore the many subtleties and patterns of American culture. We will look at the unspoken and the spoken versions of it, and, in particular, we will look for it in out-of-the-way places that we all take for granted—our everyday lives.

1
Culture: the Hidden Dimension

We are born into a social world that is varied and complex. As observers, we can concentrate on all-encompassing patterns of behavior, or we can focus on minute details. Culture involves both general and detailed designs for living. By varying our stances, moving our hands, or changing our facial expressions ever so slightly, we can add another dimension to our verbal statements. But even these small and often unconscious actions follow widely held cultural rules. In this article Edward and Mildred Hall give a vivid and detailed description of the meanings and consequences of social encounters. They demonstrate numerous ways in which the culture we have learned to use in our everyday lives remains on the edge of consciousness, outside our awareness.

The Sounds of Silence
Edward T. Hall and Mildred R. Hall

Bob leaves his apartment at 8:15 A.M. and stops at the corner drugstore for breakfast. Before he can speak, the counterman says, "The usual?" Bob nods yes. While he savors his Danish, a fat man pushes onto the adjoining stool and overflows into his space. Bob scowls, and the man pulls himself in as much as he can. Bob has sent two messages without speaking a syllable.

Henry has an appointment to meet Arthur at 11:00 A.M.; he arrives at 11:30. Their conversation is friendly, but Arthur retains a lingering

From *Playboy Magazine* (1971). Reprinted by permission.

hostility. Henry has unconsciously communicated that he doesn't think the appointment is very important or that Arthur is a person who needs to be treated with respect.

George is talking to Charley's wife at a party. Their conversation is entirely trivial, yet Charley glares at them suspiciously. Their physical proximity and the movements of their eyes reveal that they are powerfully attracted to each other.

José Ybarra and Sir Edmund Jones are at the same party, and it is important for them to establish a cordial relationship for business reasons. Each is trying to be warm and friendly, yet they will part with mutual distrust, and their business transaction will probably fall through. José, in Latin fashion, moves closer and closer to Sir Edmund as they speak, and this movement is being miscommunicated as pushiness to Sir Edmund, who keeps backing away from this intimacy, which in turn is being miscommunicated to José as coldness. The silent languages of Latin and English cultures are more difficult to learn than their spoken languages.

In each of these cases, we see the subtle power of nonverbal communication. The only language used throughout most of the history of humanity (in evolutionary terms, vocal communication is relatively recent), it is the first form of communication you learn. You use this preverbal language, consciously and unconsciously, every day to tell other people how you feel about yourself and them. This language includes your posture, gestures, facial expressions, costume, the way you walk, even your treatment of time and space and material things. All people communicate on several different levels at the same time but are usually aware of only the verbal dialogue and don't realize that they respond to nonverbal messages. But when a person says one thing and really believes something else, the discrepancy between the two can usually be sensed. Nonverbal communication systems are much less subject to the conscious deception that often occurs in verbal systems. When we find ourselves thinking, "I don't know what it is about him, but he doesn't seem sincere," it's usually this lack of congruity between a person's words and his behavior that makes us anxious and uncomfortable.

Few of us realize how much we all depend on body movement in our conversation or are aware of the hidden rules that govern listening behavior. But we know instantly whether or not the person we're talking to is "tuned in," and we're very sensitive to any breach in listening etiquette. In white middle-class American culture, when someone wants to show he is listening to someone else, he looks either at the other person's face or, specifically, at his eyes, shifting his gaze from one eye to the other.

If you observe a person conversing, you'll notice that he indicates he's listening by nodding his head. He also makes little "Hmm" noises. If he agrees with what's being said, he may give a vigorous nod. To show pleasure or affirmation, he smiles; if he has some reservations, he looks skeptical by raising an eyebrow or pulling down the corners of his mouth. If a participant wants to terminate the conversation, he may start shifting his body position, stretching his legs, crossing or uncrossing them, bobbing his foot, or diverting his gaze from the speaker. The more he fidgets, the more the speaker becomes aware that he has lost his audience. As a last measure, the listener may look at his watch to indicate the imminent end of the conversation.

Talking and listening are so intricately intertwined that a person cannot do one without the other. Even when one is alone and talking to oneself, there is part of the brain that speaks while another part listens. In all conversations, the listener is positively or negatively reinforcing the speaker all the time. He may even guide the conversation without knowing it, by laughing or frowning or dismissing the argument with a wave of his hand.

The language of the eyes—another age-old way of exchanging feelings—is both subtle and complex. Not only do men and women use their eyes differently, but there are class, generation, regional, ethnic, and national cultural differences. Americans often complain about the way foreigners stare at people or hold a glance too long. Most Americans look away from someone who is using his eyes in an unfamiliar way because it makes them self-conscious. If a man looks at another man's wife in a certain way, he's asking for trouble, as indicated earlier. But he might not be ill-mannered or seeking to challenge the husband. He might be a European in this country who hasn't learned our visual mores. Many American women visiting France or Italy are acutely embarrassed because, for the first time in their lives, men really look at them—their eyes, hair, nose, lips, breasts, hips, legs, thighs, knees, ankles, feet, clothes, hairdo, even their walk. These same women, once they have become used to being looked at, often return to the United States and are overcome with the feeling that "No one ever really looks at me anymore."

Analyzing the mass of data on the eyes, it is possible to sort out at least three ways in which the eyes are used to communicate: dominance vs. submission, involvement vs. detachment, and positive vs. negative attitude. In addition, there are three levels of consciousness and control, which can be categorized as follows: (1) conscious use of the eyes to communicate, such as the flirting blink and the intimate nose-wrinkling squint; (2) the very extensive category of unconscious but learned behavior governing where the eyes are directed and when (this unwritten set of rules dictates how and under what circumstances the sexes, as well as people of all status categories, look at each other); and (3) the response of the eye itself, which is completely outside both awareness and control—changes in the cast (sparkle) of the eye and the pupillary reflex.

The eye is unlike any other organ of the body, for it is an extension of the brain. The unconscious pupillary reflex and the cast of the eye have been known by people of Middle Eastern origin for years—although most are unaware of their knowledge. Depending on the context, Arabs and others look either directly at the eyes or deeply *into* the eyes of their interlocutor. We became aware of this in the Middle East several years ago while looking at jewelry. The merchant suddenly started to push a particular bracelet at a customer and said, "You buy this one." What interested us was that the bracelet was not the one that had been consciously selected by the purchaser. But the merchant, watching the pupils of the eyes, knew what the purchaser really wanted to buy. Whether he specifically knew *how* he knew is debatable.

A psychologist at the University of Chicago, Eckhard Hess, was the first to conduct systematic studies of the pupillary reflex. His wife remarked one evening, while watching him reading in bed, that he must be very interested in the text because his pupils were dilated. Following up on this, Hess slipped some pictures of nudes into a stack of photographs that he gave to his male assistant. Not looking at the photographs but watching his assistant's pupils, Hess was able to tell precisely when the assistant came to the nudes. In further experiments, Hess retouched the eyes in a photograph of a woman. In one print, he made the pupils small, in another, large; nothing else was changed. Subjects who were given the photographs found the woman with the dilated pupils much more attractive. Any man who has had the experience of seeing a woman look at him as her pupils widen with reflex speed knows that she's flashing him a message.

The eye-sparkle phenomenon frequently turns up in our interviews of couples in love. It's apparently one of the first reliable clues in the other person that love is genuine. To date, there is no scientific data to explain eye sparkle; no investigation of the pupil, the cornea, or even the white sclera of the eye shows how the sparkle originates. Yet we all know it when we see it.

One common situation for most people involves the use of the eyes in the street and in public. Although eye behavior follows a definite set of rules, the rules vary according to the place, the needs and feelings of the people, and their ethnic background. For urban whites, once they're within definite recognition distance (sixteen to thirty-two feet for people with average eyesight), there is mutual avoidance of eye contact—unless they want something specific: a pickup, a handout, or information of some kind. In the West and in small towns generally, however, people are much more likely to look and greet one another, even if they're strangers.

It's permissible to look at people if they're beyond recognition distance, but once inside this sacred zone, you can only steal a glance at strangers. You *must* greet friends, however; to fail to do so is insulting. Yet, to stare too fixedly even at them is considered rude and hostile. Of course, all of these rules are variable.

A great many blacks, for example, greet each other in public even if they don't know each other. To blacks, most eye behavior of whites has the effect of giving the impression that they aren't there, but this is due to white avoidance of eye contact with *anyone* in the street.

Another very basic difference between people of different ethnic backgrounds is their sense of territoriality and how they handle space. This is the silent communication, or miscommunication, that caused friction between Mr. Ybarra and Sir Edmund Jones in our earlier example. We know from the research that everyone has around himself an invisible bubble of space that contracts and expands depending on several factors: his emotional state, the activity he's performing at the time, and his cultural background. This bubble is a kind of mobile territory that he will defend against intrusion. If he is accustomed to close personal distance between himself and others, his bubble will be smaller than that of someone who's accustomed to greater personal distance. People of northern European heritage—English, Scandinavian, Swiss, and German—tend to avoid contact. Those whose heritage is Italian, French, Spanish, Russian, Latin American, or Middle Eastern like close personal contact.

People are very sensitive to any intrusion into their spatial bubble. If someone stands too close to you, your first instinct is to back up. If that's not possible, you lean away and pull yourself in, tensing your muscles. If the intruder doesn't respond to these body signals, you may then try to protect yourself, using a briefcase, umbrella, or raincoat. Women—especially when traveling alone—often plant their pocketbooks in such a way that no one can get very close to them. As a last resort, you may move to another spot and position yourself behind a desk or a chair that provides screening. Everyone tries to adjust the space around himself in a way that's comfortable for him; most often, he does this unconsciously.

Emotions also have a direct effect on the size of a person's territory. When you're angry or under stress, your bubble expands and you require more space. New York psychiatrist Augustus Kinzel found a difference in what he calls body-buffer zones between violent and nonviolent prison inmates. Dr. Kinzel conducted experiments in which each prisoner was placed in the center of a small room, and then Dr. Kinzel slowly walked toward him. Nonviolent prisoners allowed him to come quite close, while prisoners with a history of violent behavior couldn't tolerate his proximity and reacted with some vehemence.

Apparently, people under stress experience other people as looming larger and closer than they actually are. Studies of schizophrenic patients have indicated that they sometimes have a distorted perception of space, and several psychiatrists have reported patients who experience their body boundaries as filling up an entire room. For these patients, anyone who comes into the room is actually inside their body, and such an intrusion may trigger a violent outburst.

Unfortunately, there is little detailed information about normal people who live in highly congested urban areas. We do know, of course, that the noise, pollution, dirt, crowding, and confusion of our cities induce feelings of stress in most of us, and stress leads to a need for greater space. The man who's packed into a subway, jostled in the street, crowded into an elevator, and forced to work all day in a bull pen or in a small office without auditory or visual privacy is going to be very stressed at the end of his day. He needs places that provide relief from constant overstimulation of his nervous system. Stress from overcrowding is cumulative, and people can tolerate more crowding early in the day than later; note the increased bad temper during the evening rush hour as compared with the morning melee. Certainly one factor in people's desire to commute by car is the need for privacy and relief from crowding (except, often, from other cars); it may be the only time of the day when nobody can intrude.

In crowded public places, we tense our muscles and hold ourselves stiff, and thereby communicate to others our desire not to intrude on their space and, above all, not to touch them. We also avoid eye contact, and the total effect is that of someone who has "tuned out." Walking along the street, our bubble expands slightly as we move in a stream of strangers, taking care not to bump into them. In the office, at meetings, in restaurants, our bubble keeps changing as it adjusts to the activity at hand.

Most white middle-class Americans use four main distances in their business and social relations: intimate, personal, social, and public. Each of these distances has a near and a far phase and is accompanied by changes in the volume of the voice. Intimate distance varies from direct physical contact with another person to a distance of six to eighteen inches and is used for our most private activities—caressing another person or making love. At this distance, you are overwhelmed by sensory inputs from the other person—heat from the body, tactile stimulation from the skin, the fragrance of perfume, even the sound of breathing—all of which literally envelop you. Even at the far phase, you're still within easy touching distance. In general, the use of intimate distance in public between adults is frowned on. It's also much too close for strangers, except under conditions of extreme crowding.

In the second zone—personal distance—the close phase is one and a half to two and a half feet; it's at this distance that wives usually stand from their husbands in public. If another woman moves into this zone, the wife will most likely be disturbed. The far phase—two and a half to four feet—is the distance used to "keep someone at arm's length" and is the most common spacing used by people in conversation.

The third zone—social distance—is employed during business transactions or exchanges with a clerk or repairman. People who work together tend to use close social distance—four to seven feet. This is also the distance for conversation at social gatherings. To stand at this distance from someone who is seated has a dominating effect (e.g., teacher to pupil, boss to secretary). The far phase of the third zone—seven to twelve feet—is where people stand when someone says, "Stand back so I can look at you." This distance lends a formal tone to business or social discourse. In an executive office, the desk serves to keep people at this distance.

The fourth zone—public distance—is used by teachers in classrooms or speakers at public gatherings. At its farthest phase—twenty-five feet and beyond—it is used for important public figures. Violations of this distance can lead to serious complications. During his 1970 U.S. visit, the president of France, Georges Pompidou, was harassed by pickets in Chicago, who were permitted to get within touching distance. Since pickets in France are kept behind barricades a block or more away, the president was outraged by this insult to his person, and President Nixon was obliged to communicate his concern as well as offer his personal apologies.

It is interesting to note how American pitchmen and panhandlers exploit the unwritten, unspoken conventions of eye and distance. Both take advantage of the fact that once explicit eye contact is established, it is rude to look away, because to do so means to brusquely dismiss the other person and his needs. Once having caught the eye of his mark, the panhandler then locks on, not letting go until he moves through the public zone, the social zone, the personal zone and, finally, into the intimate sphere, where people are most vulnerable.

Touch also is an important part of the constant stream of communication that takes place between people. A light touch, a firm touch, a blow, a caress are all communications. In an effort to break down barriers among people, there's been a recent upsurge in group-encounter activities, in which strangers are encouraged to touch one another. In special situations such as these, the rules for not touching are broken with group approval, and people gradually lose some of their inhibitions.

Although most people don't realize it, space is perceived and distances are set not by vision alone but with all the senses. Auditory space is perceived with the ears, thermal space with the skin, kinesthetic space with the muscles of the body, and olfactory space with the nose. And, once again, it's one's culture that determines how his senses are programmed—which sensory information ranks highest and lowest. The important thing to remember is that culture is very persistent. In this country, we've noted the existence of culture patterns that determine distance between people in the third and fourth generations of some families, despite their prolonged contact with people of very different cultural heritages.

Whenever there is great cultural distance between two people, there are bound to be problems arising from differences in behavior and expectations. An example is the American couple who consulted a psychiatrist about their marital problems. The husband was from New England and had been brought up by reserved parents who taught him to control his emotions and to respect the need for privacy. His wife was from an Italian family and had been brought up in close contact with all the members of her large family, who were extremely warm, volatile, and demonstrative.

When the husband came home after a hard day at the office, dragging his feet and longing for peace and quiet, his wife would rush to him and smother him. Clasping his hands, rubbing his brow, crooning over his weary head, she never left him alone. But when the wife was upset or anxious about her day, the husband's response was to withdraw completely and leave her alone. No comforting, no affectionate embrace, no attention—just solitude. The woman became convinced her husband didn't love her, and in desperation she consulted a psychiatrist. Their problem wasn't basically psychological but cultural.

Why has man developed all these different ways of communicating messages without words? One reason is that people don't like to spell out certain kinds of messages. We prefer to find other ways of showing our feelings. This is especially true in relationships as sensitive as courtship. Men don't like to be rejected, and most women don't want to turn a man down bluntly. Instead, we work out subtle ways of encouraging or discouraging each other that save face and avoid confrontations.

How a person handles space in dating others is an obvious and very sensitive indicator of how he or she feels about the other person. On a first date, if a woman sits or stands so close to a man that he is acutely conscious of her physical presence—inside the intimate-distance zone—the man usually construes it to mean that she is encouraging him. However, before the man starts moving in on the woman, he should be sure what message she's really sending; otherwise, he risks bruising his ego. What is close to someone of northern European background may be neutral or distant to someone of Italian heritage. Also, women sometimes use space as a way of misleading a man, and there are few things that put men off more than women who communicate contradictory messages, such as women who cuddle up and then act insulted when a man takes the next step.

How does a woman communicate interest in a man? In addition to such familiar gambits as smiling at him, she may glance shyly at him, blush, and then look away. Or she may give him a real come-on look and move in very close when he approaches. She may touch his arm and ask for a light. As she leans forward to light her cigarette, she may brush him lightly, enveloping him in her perfume. She'll probably continue to smile at him, and she may use what ethologists call preening gestures—touching the back of her hair, thrusting her breasts forward, tilting her hips as she stands, or crossing her legs if she's seated, perhaps even exposing one thigh or putting a hand on her thigh and stroking it. She may also stroke her wrists as she converses or show the palm of her hand as a way of gaining his attention. Her skin may be unusually flushed or quite pale, her eyes brighter, the pupils larger.

If a man sees a woman whom he wants to attract, he tries to present himself by his posture and stance as someone who is self-assured. He moves briskly and confidently. When he catches the eye of the woman, he may hold her glance a little longer than normal. If he gets an encouraging smile, he'll move in close and engage her in small talk. As they converse, his glance shifts over her face and body. He, too, may make preening gestures—straightening his tie, smoothing his hair, or shooting his cuffs.

How do people learn body language? The same way they learn spoken language—by observing and imitating people around them as they're growing up. Little girls imitate their mothers or an older female. Little boys imitate their fathers or a respected uncle or a character on television. In this way, they learn the gender signals appropriate for their sex. Regional, class, and ethnic patterns of body behavior are also learned in childhood and persist throughout life.

Such patterns of masculine and feminine body behavior vary widely from one culture to another. In America, for example, women stand with their thighs together. Many walk with their pelvis tipped slightly forward and their upper arms close to their body. When they sit, they cross their legs at the knee, or, if they are well past middle age, they may cross their ankles. American men hold their arms away from their body, often swinging them as they walk. They stand with their legs apart (an extreme example is the cowboy, with legs apart and thumbs tucked into his belt). When they sit, they put their feet on the floor with legs apart, and, in some parts of the country, they cross their legs by putting one ankle on the other knee.

Leg behavior indicates sex, status, and personality. It also indicates whether or not one is at ease or is showing respect or disrespect for the other person. Young Latin American males avoid crossing their legs. In their world of *machismo*, the preferred position for young males when with one another (if there is no older dominant male present to whom they must show respect) is to sit on the base of their spine with their leg muscles relaxed and their feet wide apart. Their respect position is like our military equivalent: spine straight, heels and ankles together—almost identical to that displayed by properly brought up young women in New England in the early part of this century.

American women who sit with their legs spread apart in the presence of males are *not* normally signaling a come-on—they are simply (and often unconsciously) sitting like men. Middle-class women in the presence of other women to whom they are very close may on occasion throw themselves down on a soft chair or sofa and let themselves go. This is a signal that nothing serious will be taken up. Males, on the other hand, lean back and prop their legs up on the nearest object.

The way we walk similarly indicates status, respect, mood, and ethnic or cultural affiliation. The many variants of the female walk are too well known to go into here, except to say that a man would have to be blind not to be turned on by the way some women walk—a fact that made Mae West rich before scientists ever studied these matters. To white Americans, some French middle-class males walk in a way that is both humorous and suspect. There is a bounce and looseness to the French walk, as though the parts of the body were somehow unrelated. Jacques Tati, the French movie actor, walks this way; so does the great mime, Marcel Marceau.

Blacks and whites in America—with the exception of middle- and upper-middle-class professions of both groups—move and walk very differently from each other. To the blacks, whites often seem incredibly stiff, almost mechanical in their movements. Black males, on the other hand, have a looseness and coordination that frequently makes whites a little uneasy; it's too different, too integrated, too alive, too male. Norman Mailer has said that squares walk from the shoulders, like bears, but blacks and hippies walk from the hips, like cats.

All over the world, people walk not only in their own characteristic way but have walks that communicate the nature of their involvement with whatever it is they're doing. The purposeful walk of northern Europeans is an important component of proper behavior on the job. Any male who has been in the military knows how essential it is to walk properly (which makes for a continuing source of tension between blacks and whites in the service). The quick shuffle of servants in the Far East in the old days was a show of respect. On the island of Truk, when we last visited, the inhabitants even had a name for the respectful walk that one used when in the presence of a chief or when walking past a chief's house. The term was *sufan,* which meant to be humble and respectful.

The notion that people communicate volumes by their gestures, facial expressions, posture, and walk is not new; actors, dancers, writers, and psychiatrists have long been aware of it. Only in recent years, however, have scientists begun to make systematic observations of body motions. Ray L. Birdwhistell of the University of Pennsylvania is one of the pioneers in body-motion research and coined the term kinesics to describe this field. He developed an elaborate notation system to record both facial and body movements, using an approach similar to that of the linguist, who studies the basic elements of speech. Birdwhistell and other kinesicists such as Albert Sheflen, Adam Kendon, and William Condon take movies of people interacting. They run the film over and over again, often at reduced speed for frame-by-frame analysis, so that they can observe even the slightest body movements not perceptible at normal interaction speeds. These movements are then recorded in notebooks for later analysis.

To appreciate the importance of nonverbal communication systems, consider the unskilled inner-city black looking for a job. His handling of time and space alone is sufficiently different from the white middle-class pattern to create great misunderstandings on both sides. The black is told to appear for a job interview at a certain time. He arrives late. The white interviewer concludes from his tardy arrival that the black is irresponsible and not really interested in the job. What the interviewer doesn't know is that the black time system (often referred to by blacks as C.P.T.—colored people's time) isn't the same as that of whites. In the words of a black student who had been told to make an appointment to see his professor: "Man, you *must* be putting me on. I never had an appointment in my life."

The black job applicant, having arrived late for his interview, may further antagonize the white interviewer by his posture and his eye behavior. Perhaps he slouches and avoids looking at the interviewer; to him, this is playing it cool. To the interviewer, however, he may well look shifty and sound uninterested. The interviewer has failed to notice the actual signs of interest and eagerness in the black's behavior, such as the subtle shift in the quality of the voice—a gentle and tentative excitement—an almost imperceptible change in the cast of the eyes and a relaxing of the jaw muscles.

Moreover, correct reading of black-white behavior is continually complicated by the fact that both groups are comprised of individuals—some of whom try to accommodate and some of whom make it a point of pride *not* to accommodate. At present, this means that many Americans, when thrown into contact with one another, are in the precarious position of not knowing which pattern applies. Once identified and analyzed, nonverbal communications systems can be taught, like a foreign language. Without this training, we respond to nonverbal communications in terms of our own culture; we read everyone's behavior as if it were our own, and thus we often misunderstand it.

Several years ago in New York City, there was a program for sending children from predominantly black and Puerto Rican low-income neighborhoods to summer school in a white upper-class neighborhood on the East Side. One morning, a group of young black and Puerto Rican boys raced down the street, shouting and screaming and overturning garbage cans on their way to school. A doorman from an apartment building nearby chased them and cornered one of them inside a building. The boy drew a knife and attacked the doorman. This tragedy would not have occurred if the doorman had been familiar with the behavior of boys from low-income neighborhoods, where such antics are routine and socially acceptable and where pursuit would be expected to invite a violent response.

The language of behavior is extremely complex. Most of us are lucky to have under control one subcultural system—the one that reflects our sex, class, generation, and geographic region within the United States. Because of its complexity, efforts to isolate bits of nonverbal communication and generalize from them are in vain; you don't become an instant expert on people's behavior by watching them at cocktail parties. Body language isn't something that's independent of the person, something that can be donned and doffed like a suit of clothes.

Our research and that of our colleagues has shown that, far from being a superficial form of communication that can be consciously manipulated, nonverbal communication systems are interwoven into the fabric of the personality and, as sociologist Erving Goffman has demonstrated, into society itself. They are the warp and woof of daily interactions with others, and they influence how one expresses oneself, how one experiences oneself as a man or a woman.

Nonverbal communications signal to members of your own group what kind of person you are, how you feel about others, how you'll fit into and work in a group, whether you're assured or anxious, the degree to which you feel comfortable with the standards of your own culture, as well as deeply significant feelings about the self, including the state of your own psyche. For most of us, it's difficult to accept the reality of another's behavioral system. And, of course, none of us will ever become fully knowledgeable of the importance of every nonverbal signal. But as long as each of us realizes the power of these signals, this society's diversity can be a source of great strength rather than a further—and subtly powerful—source of division.

2
The Culture of Everyday Places

There are different levels of involvement and membership in any cultural scene. Each level has its characteristic demeanor and mental states, and a participant may choose among various styles and degrees of membership in any cultural activity. William Sanders describes one scene, a poolhall, where one of the main activities is playing the pinball machines. A player himself, he describes the nature of the game, its social context, and the levels of involvement available to the participant. Some play for fun; others find the game a serious activity, an arena in which their competence is displayed and put to the test. Human emotions, thoughts, and feelings are dramatically exhibited during these occasions, and this description captures their sociological significance.

Pinball Occasions
William B. Sanders

Participants in social occasions are expected to involve themselves in such a manner as to preserve the sanctity of the occasion (Goffman 1963). In most situations the proper allocation of involvement can at least be presented by participants even though they do not feel what they present. That is, they can fake engrossment, both cognitive and affective, and as long as they appear to be appropriately involved, the integrity of the occasion has not been violated (Goffman 1959).

Some situations, however, require a special kind of involvement that

From *People in Places: The Sociology of the Familiar,* ed. Arnold Bierenbaum and Edward Sagarin (New York: Praeger, 1973).

is not easily faked. A bomb defuser, for example, must display a calm, steady hand while he detaches wires and fuses from explosive packages. His actions function in two importantly different ways. On the one hand, shaky movements may set off the bomb, and, on the other hand, such nervousness reveals a weakness of character (Goffman 1967, p. 217). In either case the trembling defuser blows his performance, pointing to an instrumental as well as an expressive stake in acting calmly. Moreover, the instrumental and expressive aspects of the performance are linked. The risky commitment happens simultaneously with the resolution requirements.

However, not all risks are so linked. In horse racing, for instance, the bettor places his bet in an act that is divorced from the requirement for him to win. Once he has committed himself, the racing fan can tear his hair and bite his nails, but while these actions may show weakness of character, they in no way jeopardize or enhance his chances of winning (Scott 1968). His commitment move, then, is separated from the resolution requirement. However, in the case of the bomb defuser, as well as in cases of poker playing, skiing, surfing, and similar activities where composure is a technical requirement, the actor's performance after the commitment move is fatefully linked to the outcome.

The interest in such activities concerns the two issues of social control and social evaluation. Social control can best be seen in those situations where an individual's inner state contradicts his outward appearance. Just as a bomb defuser would be blown to bits if he followed an inner urge to rip apart a bomb package, so too would social occasions be wrecked if the participants followed inner urges to do what they felt (Goffman 1961, p. 51).

A final interest centers around how and why social members spend their time as they do. Involvements of various sorts are found on various occasions, and one interesting occasion where people spend time is pinball. What happens in these occasions in terms of the actors' involvements will be the focus of the following discussion.

Methodology

In order to come to terms with the world of pinball, I spent three months observing players in a West Coast poolhall where several pinball machines were located. The poolhall was in a student community located adjacent to a public university. Separated from a nearby city, the community is unique in that it is composed almost wholly of college-age youth, most of whom are students, but it also includes many nonstudents in its population of 13,000.

The observation period spanned a time from early March to the beginning of June; thus, the study took place while school was in session and the students, most of whom moved away during the summer, were in residence. Even though the average income of the students' families is in excess of $20,000, the character of the community lacks the flavor of most middle- and upper-middle-class communities. Composed of inexpensively built apartments, residence halls, and a few houses, the community is transient and youth oriented. From early 1970 to the present, there have been annual riots, and the students have what would be considered a radical lifestyle, which includes, for example, drug use, left-wing politics (in the 1970 statewide election, the Peace and Freedom party candidates received more votes than the Republicans), and heterosexual unmarried cohabitation.

Observational procedures and recording had to be tailored to the setting. It was decided that all data would be collected unobtrusively to control researcher contamination (Webb et al. 1966, p. 138), and interviewing was done in such a manner that it was not seen to be "interviewing" by the subjects; in other words, questions concerning features and practices were asked in normal conversations. The observations were conducted from the stations of a "loiterer" and a "game watcher," two normal roles in the setting (Gold in Denzin 1970, p. 373).

Because it was an unobtrusive study and I could find no way to take notes in the setting without drawing attention to myself, I waited until I returned home to write up the findings. It was a five-minute walk from where I lived to the poolhall; thus, there was a minimum amount that was forgotten or left out. Observation time lasted from fifteen minutes to an hour and a half, covering all days of the week and all hours that the establishment was open for business.

Characteristics

The Setting

The setting where the pinball machines are located is a poolhall, but the area reserved for pool tables is clearly set off from the pinball area. In addition to pinball and pool, there are two "Foosball"[1] tables located

---

[1] "Foosball" is a machine game similar to hockey but using a table-tennis ball as a puck. It is not a pinball game, although it is often found in the same locales as pinball machines.

in the area formed by the two legs of the "L" formed by the pinball machines, giving the pinball and pool areas an even more distinct border. Business hours are not regular, or at least not strictly so, but the establishment usually does not close until two in the morning and opens around ten or eleven in the morning. If business is good, however, the place sometimes stays open longer, as the following observation illustrates:

> 4/22: When I walked in, I asked the guy at the counter how late they stayed open. He asked how late I wanted it to, and I told him I just wanted to know if they had a particular hour they closed. He said that as long as there was enough business, he would stay open.

The setting was used for other than "business" purposes, however. Activities such as looking for people, looking for money (either by panhandling or by checking the coin return slots), talking to the cashier, talking to one another, watching the pinball players, smoking marijuana (generally outside of the building, in front of the door), waiting for friends or drug contacts, and simply loitering took place in and around the setting. The following are some instances:

> 3/6: Two girls about high school age came in and began panhandling without much success. One came up to me and asked for a penny, which I gave her. She put it in one of the candy machines.
> 4/14: A girl walked in, looked around, then left.
> 4/15: A guy asked me for spare change. I told him that my last dime was in the machine and he walked away. Later, I saw him standing by the window looking out.
> 4/22: A couple of girls with a baby were talking with Rick at the counter.
> 4/28: A guy walked in and gave Roberta the peace sign, and she said hello. He talked by the two guys at the juke box and one of them said something to him, and he went over and talked to them. After the music stopped, they left together.

There are, however, limitations as to activities on the scene. The cashier and owner admonish children when they pound on the pinball machines, even if they are spending money. Also, a bystander is obliged to move away from a pinball machine if someone wishes to play. Furthermore, if all of the machines are being used, there is nothing other than the juke box and the "Foosball" machines to lean on while watching a game of pinball, and, because neither of these provide a good vantage point, people may be forced to leave. That is, even if one wishes to loiter, the spatial arrangements make it extremely difficult to loiter if certain strategic niches in the setting are taken.

Patrons

People who enter the pinball scene can be divided into "regulars" and "occasionals" (Cavan 1966, p. 65; Scott 1968, pp. 81–112, 113–16). Regulars are those who normally include the setting in their daily round of activities. Some of the regulars are pool players, some are street people who come to see if anything interesting is happening (for example, if friends are present), some are friends of the cashier who come to visit him, and some are pinball players. I will focus on the pinball regulars.

The regulars who come primarily to play pinball can be divided into three age groups. First, there are the "little kids," aged between nine and junior-high or early high-school age. This group is there mostly in the afternoon and early evening, and although it includes some very good pinball players, they are treated as nonserious players, merely coming in to "play" the way kids "play." Second, there is a group aged from late high-school to late college age whom I will refer to as the "regulars." (Almost all of the "kids" are regulars, but for simplicity, I will use the terms "kids" and "regulars" to differentiate between the two groups.) A third set is the "tennyboppers," or the young adolescents; however, the members of this group are more likely to be treated as "kids" if they are younger and as "regulars" if they are more mature.

Most of the pinball regulars are young men, and the only girls who can be considered pinball regulars are those who come in with their boyfriends; however, there are only a few pinball players who bring their girlfriends. On any given day, while it would not be unusual to see girls on the scene, it is not very common to see them playing pinball. No girls come in who are not accompanied by boys who are pinball regulars.

The pinball occasionals consist of pool players who shoot a game of pinball every now and then, street people who are passing through, students who wander in, and others who drop in on an irregular basis. Other than the pool players, the occasionals do not generally know one another or the people who work in the establishment. In general, their presence is "in" the setting but not "of" the setting.

A final note of interest concerning both regulars and occasionals involves their dress and general appearance. On a continuum from "straight" to "hippie," every gradation of appearance could be observed in the setting. For reasons that will become apparent later, an individual's appearance is simply not relevant to playing pinball or to the other activities in the setting.

Pinball Encounters

Getting Started

I will assume that a person who wants to play pinball knows enough to activate a pinball machine by putting a coin in the coin slot, but I would like to discuss the various means of getting started in a game of pinball. Machines have signs indicating that one game can be played for a dime and three for a quarter. Thus, for ten cents, the player can shoot five balls, the game beginning with the first ball and ending when the last ball rolls out of play.

However, there are other ways to get started. First, people sometimes leave free games on the machine, and all the next person has to do to play is press the replay button. Another way of getting free games is to be invited by the person who is playing. The following happened in the course of my observations:

> 4/19: When I first came in, three guys were playing the "Baseball" machine. As I began watching, two of the players left the player who appeared to be winning most of the games. He asked me if I wanted to play. I shot two games, lost both of them, and he shot some more. Finally, he said, "I'm tired of playing. You can have them." He left me four games, which I played out.

On other occasions, I have been invited to play or been given free games. "Giving away games," however, is apparently somewhat peculiar to this setting, as I learned from one informant.

> 5/5: A young player who is around a lot was given three games by a couple of players. He thanked them and started to play. I commented on their giving the games to him, and he said this was the only place he knew of where that happened and indicated that he appreciated it a great deal.

Free games are also "hustled" by the kids. The above-mentioned player who was given free games was observed flattering players, including myself, in the hope that he would be given some games.

> 4/21: As I began playing, the observer commented on what a good player I was after the first ball. I had only scored 3,000 points out of 30,000 needed for a free game and I commented that I hadn't done too well. He looked up and said, "I thought you had done better with all the bells ringing," and agreed that I was not doing too well.

This form of hustling does not include the type practiced by pool players, whereby they attempt to win money (Polsky 1967, pp. 41–44). Moreover, it is usually done only by the kids, and unlike pool hustling, where the player's hustling activity increases with age and skill, the pinball player's decreases as he grows up and gets better.

A final way of getting started in a pinball game is to "buy" games from players. This happens when a player has won a number of games and would rather sell them to someone than play them himself. For instance:

> 4/19: I was watching a player winning several games on a machine. When he had four games left, he asked me if I wanted to buy them for "two dimes." I told him I did not, and he went on playing. When he was down to two games, I offered to buy them for a dime and he agreed. As he backed away from the machine he let out a sigh of relief and said he had been at the machine for an hour and a half. When I started to play, I noticed it was extremely warm around the flipper buttons.
>
> 5/23: A kid came over and asked if I wanted to buy four games for a dime, and I told him I did. When I finished shooting my game, I went over and asked if they had change for a quarter. They did not and suggested asking the cashier. When I came back I asked them if they'd take a nickel so that I could use my two dimes on other games. They agreed, and so I got four games for a nickel.

As can be seen from the above examples, there are no set prices in buying and selling games. However, it should be pointed out that a player always pays less for games he buys from other players than he would pay a machine.

Before going on to playing pinball, I would like to briefly mention money and pinball players. Early in my observations, I began evaluating my change in terms of the number of pinball games I could buy at machine prices. Later, I found this to be true of many regular pinball players. In a previous example, a player offered to sell games for "two dimes." He could have said "twenty cents," but in the reality of the pinball occasion, "twenty cents" meant less than "two dimes," because the latter represents what can be put in the machine. The following also illustrates counting money in terms of the tokens the machine will accept.

> 5/9: I had been watching a player who had been losing several games. When he finally began winning, I commented on the wins, and he said, "Yeah, but it cost me two quarters and two dimes."

Thus, he told me that he had spent money on eight games—three apiece for the two quarters and one apiece for the two dimes. If he had said "seventy cents," he would not have given the same information, and if he had spent any other combination that would have added up to seventy cents, he would have reported it in terms of the number of tokens dropped in the machine. Similarly, the cashiers always give pinball players tokens that can be used in the machine without asking the players to specify what they need. They know what it takes to play and need not be told.

Playing

In pinball, as in other games, the players attempt to win, but "winning" in pinball, unlike other games, does not involve beating an opponent. To get more points than another player may constitute winning for some occasional players, but for the regulars, winning is to receive the number of points or other play conditions needed for a free game. This is crucial for understanding pinball and pinball players, for unlike many games where winning routinely entails beating a human opponent, winning at pinball constitutes beating the machine.

Linked with the lack of competition in the setting studied was also a lack of gambling among pinball players. However, this cannot be accounted for by any lack of gambling ethic either in the establishment or among its patrons. The following observations point to this:

> 4/29: I was trying to get the cashier to talk about payoffs or gambling by saying that I had heard of certain bars paying off pinball players for winning a certain number of games. In response, he told me that there was a "Bowl-O" game in the Las Vegas bus station that paid off in cash for wins and that he had a friend who won a good deal of money playing it.
> 4/30: Rick said that he had lost $3.00 playing pool. I asked if he ever saw pinball players gambling, and he said he had. When I told him I had never seen it, he said it was extremely rare.
> 4/20: Two boys about sixteen or seventeen were playing "Paul Bunyan," taking turns on a one-player game. One had just won a game on the fourth ball and the other shot the fifth. "You blew it," the one said to the second when he failed to score enough points to win a second game.

The conversation with the cashier, Rick, indicates that, while gambling is common in the building, pinball players are not generally gamblers, at least in the setting studied. The two boys who were taking turns shooting were not trying to get more points than one another, but they were trying to beat the machine, that is, win a free game. A player who was trying to sell his games further illustrates that competition is against the machine and not against human opponents.

> 5/9: A guy told me that he believed that people would not buy the seventeen games he was trying to sell because the machine had already been beaten and there was no challenge left.

The pinball player who is serious about playing will attempt to win a game with some belief that, if he concentrates, he can do so. The most common type of win entails getting a certain number of points that are electroncially recorded and displayed when the ball hits or rolls over various devices on the sloped surface of the machine.

Besides winning by getting the needed number of points, some games have "specials" that also give the player a free game for meeting specified requirements. For example, one game has a special win if numbers in a series from one to twelve are hit. When all twelve numbers are hit, one of the numbers lights up, and if the player hits that number again, he wins a game.

A final way of receiving a free game is by a "match." This is not considered "winning," nor is the player considered to have beaten the machine. A match occurs at the end of the game. If a player's last number or last two numbers match the number or numbers that light up on the upright board of the machine, he gets a free game. Matches are considered matters of luck and are not believed to reflect the player's ability to play.

To begin playing, the player shoots the ball up a corridor by means of a spring-loaded plunger. Some players consider shooting important, especially if a special is pending on one of the scoring devices at the top of the machine; however, it is generally considered the least important of the skills involved in playing pinball. Sometimes the kids will go around and ask to "hit the ball up" for a player, and because this aspect is relatively unimportant, the players usually let the kids do it.

Once the ball is in play, the pinball player's skill in using the flippers and shaking the machine comes to the fore. The flippers are two arms at the bottom of the machine that pivot on pins and flip upward when the flipper buttons are pressed. Depending upon when the player presses the flipper buttons in relation to the position of the ball, the ball will be hit, missed, go where he wants it to go, or go where he does not want it to go. Hence, the player's skill rests on his ability to press the buttons at the most opportune moment. The inexperienced player will frantically start flapping the flipper buttons, and hits and misses become random. The better player will catch the ball on the rail with the flipper button, letting the ball roll down the flipper to the point he wants, and then press the button, sending the ball where he wants it to go. Or else he will simply hit it at the right moment to keep it in play if it is moving too fast to catch or slow enough for him to hit it correctly without stopping it.

Likewise, shaking the machine requires an artful touch. If the machine is shaken too hard or incorrectly, it will indicate "tilt," and the player will receive no more points for the ball in play or, on some machines, for the entire game. One very good player explained it to me:

4/19: "You don't push it or it'll tilt. You shake it hard, quick."

Another player who did not shake it explained:

4/22: "I put the machine right up against the wall and don't jiggle it. I don't have the touch."

The object, of course, in working the flippers and shaking the machine, is to get points to win the game or to get the special. To do this while the ball keeps rolling downward to a hole near the front of the machine requires some self-control. Goffman (1967, p. 225) refers to the ability to think clearly under circumstances that may muddle the brain as "presence of mind," and Lyman and Scott (1970, p. 145) define "coolness" as the ability to keep calm under pressure. These attributes are essential for good pinball playing, for as was pointed out at the beginning of this discussion, the resolution requirement, that is, hitting the ball so that it will score points, occurs after the commitment and before the outcome. Thus, the sign of good pinball playing, namely, winning free games, is also a sign of strong character, for in order to meet the resolution requirements, the player has to maintain a clear head as well as his "cool."

The pressure and actions under pressure are in the structure of the pinball situation. In every game there are five balls, and in every series of games, there is a first and a last game. When the player puts money in the machine and begins to play, it is his "first game." On any given occasion, he may have several "first games," depending on how often he has to put money in the machine. If the player has only put a dime in the machine, he will either have to win a game, get a match, or put more money in the machine; hence, there is added pressure to win. One player who always put a quarter in the machine explained that he always got nervous on the first game and could never win. If he lost, he knew he had two more games, and because of this knowledge, he relaxed more and consequently did better.

The "last game," on the other hand, is the last of whatever series of games is played before more money has to be spent, and as in the first game of a dime's play, there is added pressure. One player told me he always "blew it" on the last game because of this. There can be several last games in a series, because whenever the game counter reaches "zero" the game being played is the "last game." If the player wins games, the game counter will register the number of games won, and the game no longer is the last one.

As with games, there are "balls to be played," but it is only the last, the fifth, ball, under certain conditions, that creates added pressure. As soon as the player has the number of points needed for at least one free game, he can relax to some extent because, no matter what happens, he will have another game. However, it is not uncommon for the player to find himself in a situation where he has shot four balls and is short of the needed number of points for a free game. If it happens to be the last ball of his last game and he is "within range" of a free game, the pressure is multiplied. (By "within range" I mean that the player can expect to get the needed number of points with close attention to the game.) The player who calmly shakes the machine without tilting it and catches the ball, and then shoots it off the tip of the flipper on the last ball of his last game, when he still needs points to win, is considered cool indeed.

Pinball Relationships

Most players have a single machine or a limited number of machines that they play. The choice of a machine by a player is not determined so much by its being fun to play as by the player's ability to beat the game. For example, I found "Jive Time" more fun than "On Beam," simply because I liked the spinner on "Jive Time," but I rarely won playing "Jive Time," so I usually played "On Beam." Other players have similar sentiments and know a good deal about the machine they usually play.

> 4/28: After a while a guy came over and started watching and said, "This is the only machine I can win on." I told him there was a whirling sound every now and then, and I had to wait a long time for the ball to come out. He told me that the last time it happened there was an "Out of Order" sign on it the next time he came in after hearing the same sound.

"Getting to know" the machine means becoming accustomed to the various specials, point-scoring systems, and other quirks of the machine.

For example, one machine has a left flipper button that sticks slightly, and it is necessary to hit the button before one normally would to strike the ball properly. The list of idiosyncrasies for almost any machine is quite long and deals with so many variables that even a player who is well acquainted with a machine may not understand all of the machine's characteristics. Concerning one machine, even the proprietor had problems figuring out how the points were scored.

> 5/11: I was talking with Roberta about the broken glass on the "Student Prince" machine and we got to talking about playing the various machines. Discussed "On Beam." Roberta said that she thought that if the space ship and the space station came together on the same beam, the special would be activated, but she said she had to watch the place and was unable to concentrate on the game enough to figure it out.

Nevertheless, a player who has his "own" machine has considerably more knowledge about that machine than one who only occasionally uses the same machine.

Sustained playing of the same machine or same group of machines usually leads to a form of acquaintanceship with other players who use the same machine. In getting to know a machine, the player also gets to know those who regularly play it. Regular players will inform other players as to the machine's characteristics and how best to play the machine in order to get a replay. One of the kids, for example, told me to hit the shooter as hard as I could on the "Paul Bunyan" machine so the ball would go through a 500-point gate at the top of the machine. Players are advised by regulars of another machine to shake the table when the ball comes back out between the flippers on the special. Thus, in discussing the machine, "pinball relationships" develop.

The relationships between pinball players appear to be strictly situational and formal. Players who strike up these situational acquaintanceships do not seem to maintain them beyond the boundaries of the setting; even knowing the other's name does not seem to be important. Each will acknowledge the other's presence when he comes over to watch or play a game, but the talk does not go beyond discussion about playing pinball and how the particular machine has been behaving.

> 5/9: When I came in, the guy who had been playing "On Beam" earlier was still there. He had been having difficulty when I left, but now he had twenty games on the counter. He said that the most he had ever seen on the counter was twenty-three and he was trying for twenty-four. We discussed the machine and how it was not responding well earlier. He said that the "D" slot was a bad one

to get, because the ball would go through it and head straight for the flippers without getting any points on the way. He let me shoot three games, and I won only one. Also, he mentioned that he had once gotten 94,000 and was trying to get the point counter back to zero so that he could get more free games by working it back up to 30,000 or more.

The difference between a "pinball acquaintanceship" and two players who come in together can be seen in the way the people treat each other. The pinball acquaintances will be very circumspect and never deride the player for losing or handling the ball poorly. Friends, on the other hand, will tease one another about their play, take turns shooting the same game, and stand closer to the machine and player. Friends may even jostle one another in a playful attempt to make the other lose. Pinball acquaintances, while they may let one another take turns on games or give a series of games to one another, will rarely take turns shooting the same game. In general, pinball acquaintances watch one another shoot, make comments about the machine or about techniques for beating the machine, and formally console the player if he muffs a ball or loses a game.

In getting to know a pinball acquaintance, the "knowing" has to do with his style of play, his ability to win the game, and his general knowledge of pinball. For example, some pinball players sit when they play and some stand, some are tense and some are loose, some can beat only one game and some can beat several. The players also have a variety of personal habits. However, the acquaintanceship is thoroughly occasioned in terms of the pinball situation, and the knowing does not extend beyond that occasion.

Even though pinball acquaintances may talk with one another readily, a player does not have to have sustained copresence with other players to initiate conversation. Because most of the talk is about pinball, it takes a minimum of contact to engage in discussions. One player I had met for the first time was asking me about the game he was playing and the characteristics of various other games. When he had finished playing, I asked him to hold the machine for me while I went to get change, and he obliged. On other occasions I have been invited to play some games, been engaged in conversations, and been asked advice by players I had never seen before. Like the relationships between horse players, pinball relationships are temporary and diffuse, being an emergent property of the pinball setting and not necessarily the primary reason for players' coming there (Scott 1968, p. 115).

To some extent, then, the pinball setting is an "open region" in that "any two persons, acquainted or not, have a right to initiate face engagement" (Goffman 1963, p. 132). However, it is not the case, as it is in bars, for example, that face engagements have priority over other forms of involvement (Cavan 1966, p. 156). For instance, if an observer came up to watch a game being played and began commenting on the play, the machine, or anything else to a player he did not know, his right to engage in such talk would not be questioned, but the player would not be expected to take his attention away from the game to make small talk with the observer. Between balls, the player might say something or look over at the observer, but even this much attention is not demanded or expected from someone who is playing. If the player is very close to winning a game and is on his last ball, or even appears to be concentrating very hard, little talk is offered by the observer or the player, and talking observers have been heard to stop in midsentence on seeing that a tense situation is developing. Exceptions to this rule occur among occasionals and kids, but regulars adhere to it, and in all my observations I never saw regulars break it.

Conclusion

A player's style of play is linked very closely to the features of involvement of the pinball occasion. Unlike the case in settings where pinball is a subordinate involvement, pinball is the dominant involvement, for the most part, for those who come to the pinball area. By certain players, such as pool players who shoot a game of pinball between games of pool, pinball is treated as a subordinate involvement, but on the whole, it is the dominant one for the people in that part of the building.

The extent to which a player treats the play as serious determines the amount of concentration he will give the task of winning and the amount he is expected to give it by others (Goffman 1961, p. 17). The less serious the endeavor, the less the concentration and the less the player is expected to win. Thus, a player whose body idiom is loose and casual, who looks around while the ball is in play, and pays a considerable amount of attention to an observer or friend, can claim he is playing for "fun." Of course, if a player is losing more or less consistently, he may claim post facto that all along he was playing for fun. Such a claim by an occasional is believable because he is not expected to win except by luck, anyway, but for a regular to make such a claim requires a special set of circumstances. If, for example, a regular finds that his machine is occupied, he may play another, which he does not expect to beat, until his machine is free. Under such circumstances, he may claim that he was playing the machine for fun; however, even under these conditions, a regular will give the play more concentration and effort than would an occasional who plays for fun.

The move from casual to serious play usually takes place when the player realizes that he has a good chance of winning. As this happens, the tension increases, along with the attention given by the player. In this way, playing pinball is transformed from an idle pastime to serious business.

As the serious concern with winning increases, engrossment to the point of shakiness or "overinvolvement" (Goffman 1963, p. 62) occurs. With this overinvolvement, the player's self-control decreases, and he increases the chances of tilting the machine and misjudging flipper shots. (Players have been observed to hit and break the glass on a machine as a result of such overinvolvement.) It is one thing for the kids who play to jump up and down and shout while they play, because they are not expected to demonstrate control over the situation, but for a person who wishes to communicate dignity, composure, and presence of mind in a tense situation, it is altogether another matter. Likewise, for a player who sees that he is going to lose the game, barring a small miracle, it is not too difficult to maintain calmness and poise. The true test of pinball character comes when the player tacitly indicates that he is a serious player but can remain unruffled and clearheaded when the last ball of the last game rolls dizzily toward the flippers.

These attributes are recognized by players, and a good player who maintains his dignity while shooting a tight game is well thought of. Some players believe that they can play better when they smoke marijuana, and if marijuana has a calming effect, it probably does help. Thus, the presentation of a calm, cool, dignified front, while problematic in a tense situation in pinball, can be maintained, if not through strength of character, by other means.

Finally, it should be noted that the maintenance of character and preservation of grace and face among pinball players are joint efforts (Goffman 1967, p. 27-31). As mentioned earlier, pinball acquaintanceships are formal and circumspect, and pinball acquaintances never make derogatory remarks about a player they are watching and will often attempt face-saving remarks by blaming the loss on ill fortune and not on the player. Observers will give the player all the room he needs by not leaning on the machine and by not creating other distractions, for while a player is operating a machine, his play is the center of attention, and the player on stage is trying to win against an impersonal force. If he wins, the observers will help him celebrate his victory, and if he loses, they will help him lessen his defeat (Goffman 1952).

References

Cavan, S. 1966. *Liquor License: An Ethnography of Bar Behavior.* Chicago: Aldine.

Goffman, E. 1967. *Interaction Ritual: Essays on Face-to-Face Behavior.* Garden City, N. Y.: Doubleday.

———.1963. *Behavior in Public Places: Notes on the Social Organization of Gatherings.* New York: Free Press.

———.1961. *Encounters: Two Studies in the Sociology of Interaction.* Indianapolis: Bobbs-Merrill.

———.1959. *The Presentation of Self in Everyday Life.* Garden City, N. Y.: Doubleday.

———.1952. "On Cooling the Mark Out: Some Aspects of Adaptation to Failure." *Psychiatry* 15 (November):451–63.

Gold, R. L. 1970. "Roles in Sociological Field Observations." In *Sociological Methods: A Sourcebook,* ed. Norman K. Denzin. Chicago: Aldine, pp. 370–80.

Lyman, S. M., and M. B. Scott. 1970. *A Sociology of the Absurd.* New York: Appleton-Century-Crofts.

Polsky, N. 1967. *Hustlers, Beats and Others.* Garden City, N. Y.: Doubleday.

Scott, M. B. 1968. *The Racing Game.* Chicago: Aldine.

Webb, E. J., D. T. Campbell, R. Schwartz, and L. Sechrest. 1966. *Unobtrusive Measures: Nonreactive Research in the Social Sciences.* Chicago: Rand McNally.

3
Perspectives on Culture

How does one know what to observe in order to make a valid sociological description? The way in which we answer this question will often direct the type of study that we conduct and the observations we make. In this article Fred Davis suggests a way to clarify some of the implications of this question. He asks us to imagine two extreme positions: that of the Martian and that of the Convert. The Martian, having come from another world, attempts to observe without reliance on his own experiences or dependence on his own ways of knowing and feeling. He wants to see this new world with freshness and without contamination from his own world. The Convert, on the other hand, tries diligently to use his experiences in order to see the world the same way those whom he studies see it. In his conclusion the author offers both a challenge and a concession to the problem he raises.

The Martian and the Convert: Ontological Polarities in Social Research
Fred Davis

A perennial, if often submerged, concern of what are loosely termed the cultural sciences revolves around the core epistemological issue of "How can we know?" With what eyes, thoughts, feelings, acts, assumptions, and cognitions is the cultural scientist to approach and engage the human subjects of his inquiry so as to be able, in the end, to render

From *Urban Life and Culture* 2 (1973):333–343. Reprinted by permission. This is a slightly expanded version of a paper presented at the Pacific Sociological Meetings, Scottsdale, Arizona, May 3–5, 1973. I am much indebted to Lyn Lofland and Jack Douglas who, at different times and in different places, patiently indulged me in many hours of stimulating, if at times ethereal, discussion of epistemological issues in the social sciences. A fair number of the ideas appearing in this paper first saw the dim dawn of recognition in those discussions.

as valid and felicitous an account of their being and doing as science, or perhaps art, will allow?

As in the broader discussion of this overarching philosophical question, that dealing with the problem of knowledge in general, the cultural sciences have, since their beginnings in the eighteenth and nineteenth centuries, come up with a range of parallel and equally conflicting answers. These have varied, at one extreme, from highly astringent forms of objectivistic positivism ("we can know nothing of our fellow humans other than those sense data which their actions register upon our standard measuring instruments") through a number of materialistic-naturalistic approaches ("there is a concrete social reality out there which exists independent of our being and can be explained in its own terms") to, at the other extreme, several subtypes of subjectivistic idealism, some of which verge on the solipsistic ("what we know of our fellow man is in the last analysis wholly locked in our own minds and, hence, is incapable of generalization"). Needless to say, none of these putative "answers" has at any time proved sufficiently satisfactory to a large enough body of social scientists to lay further methodological controversy to rest. Also, needless to say, the gnawing persistence of this fundamental epistemological issue appears in no way to have diminished the ever-swelling tide of studies and professional publications that purport, often with a heady cocksureness, to describe, analyze, and explain this or that slice of social reality. Whether this attests to some inherent robustness of the cultural sciences, an *élan vital* which recoils from the sickly pale of philosophical speculation, or more to a state of rampant mindlessness, I leave for others to judge. Here I wish only to draw out and explicate to a degree two contrary ontological-epistemological tendencies found among cultural scientists and oftentimes as well within the same cultural scientist, depending on the kind of research problem at hand. Rather, though, than attempt to distinguish these contrasting, at times polarized, tendencies with the now almost conventional language in which they are discussed in that somewhat nebulous realm known as the philosophy of the social sciences, I have chosen here instead to resort to the metaphors of the *Martian* and the *Convert*. I do so out of the conviction that when faced with the concrete problem of studying this or that about our fellow human beings, these metaphors can better capture the epistemological dilemma (and subjective anxiety) of the cultural scientist than can the more formal language of philosophy.[1] It should, perhaps, also be stated that although my remarks will relate mainly to the situation of the participant-observer field-worker, they per-

---

[1] On the social scientist's use of metaphor, see Severyn T. Bryn, *The Human Perspective in Sociology* (Englewood Cliffs, N.J.: Prentice-Hall, 1966), pp. 133–42.

tain at a level once or twice removed almost equally to other modes of social science inquiry as well, for example, questionnaire surveys, interview studies, demographic research, and historical inquiries of various kinds.[2]

The Martian

The underlying attitude of the Martian, assuming even he is prepared to acknowledge something so intangible as an attitude, is one of intransigent and unremitting doubt toward everything the members of a group, organization, or society may tell him, or even show him, concerning their motives, purposes, values, plans for everyday action, and so forth. This is not to say the Martian would for a moment deny that members' accounts of themselves and of their actions were not meaningful, necessary, or relevant *for themselves.* On the contrary, he is more than ready to allow that were it not for these more or less standardized, commonsensical accounts of "why what is done is done the way it is," social life would be impossible; that is, society could not exist. The crucial point for the Martian, however, lies in the recognition that *all such accounts* are by their very nature more or less unexamined *social constructions.* And, for him, the overriding aim of social-science inquiry is to get beyond the literal substance of members' constructions of their social lives to the most basic elements and processes whereby such constructions take shape in the first place. That is, he aims to dissect the *constructed* character of social life rather than merely to elaborate, classify, or otherwise "rationally reorder" that which a society's members tell him about their world, their world being a socially constructed one within which, as he sees it, they are cognitively imprisoned and, hence, incapable of doing more than replicating its taken-for-granted dimensions in self-confirming ways.

The Martian, then, yearns to grasp the human situation with wholly fresh or, better yet, strange eyes in a blush of wonderment, as it were. In order to do this he wants to divest himself completely of the vast array of unwitting cultural assumptions, rules of thumb, modes of sensibility, and—were it somehow possible—the very language, which com-

[2] The rendering of these other modes of inquiry within the same metaphorical scheme is not to deny that each cannot in its own right be differentially classified as partaking more of one tendency than of the other. Thus, for example, whereas I would be inclined to locate conventional demographic studies near the Martian end of the continuum, we cannot rule out the presence of certain epistemological assumptions and cognitions in demographic studies which partake more of the Convert stance.

prise the "cognitive stuff" of our everyday worlds and beings. In keeping with that version of radical empiricism associated with Husserlian phenomenology, he seeks to free himself as far as possible from *all* presuppositions that touch on his inquiry.[3] While, perhaps, not going so far as to fancy himself the *tabula rasa* of Lockean philosophy, he does, nevertheless, envisage the possibility of some distinctive order of intelligence which would permit him to see through, around, and behind the perceptual and cognitive constructs operative in the world of everyday life. Only then is there a chance for their workings to be revealed. Moreover, this is an intelligence which would in no way derive from that of everyday life but would attain a status wholly independent of it; hence, an intelligence which is not sullied through "translation" back into the world of everyday life. (It would not be *traduced*, in the original, pejorative sense of that term.)

Our true Martian fantasizes invisibility as well. Not only would this spare him the pain of participatory pretense, but invisibility would also serve to eliminate the danger of having his pristine, presuppositionless intelligence contaminated through contact with the cognitively corrupted characters he wishes to study in their native habitat and natural state, as it were. How marvelous to be the omnipresent ghost in the family closet, to witness firsthand and in utter unobtrusiveness the anguish of the boudoir and the bestiality of the playroom! Would such freedom and power, at long last, not make for a social science? Whether the Martian (or some merely perverse mortal) could in fact so drastically distantiate himself from the immediate concerns and involvements of those he studies and yet manage to *understand* them is a question we shall consider later.[4] For now let us simply record his profound conviction that it is only by so transcending the encrusted givenness of everyday life, however this is to be accomplished, that a truly valid and objective science of society becomes possible; a science which, precisely because it chooses rigorously to suspend the assumptions of the commonsense world, can furnish us knowledge of the constituent character of that world without itself being reduced to mere commonsensicality.

---

[3] Marvin Farber, *The Aims of Phenomenology* (New York: Harper, 1966), pp. 36–38.
[4] See, however, Schutz's unusually sensitive discussion of this problem in his essay "The Stranger," in Alfred Schutz, *Collected Papers, Volume II* (The Hague, Martinus Nijhoff, 1964).

The Convert

The Convert, too, starts from the conviction that the human's social world is a wholly constructed one and not something given in nature or through outside agency. Paradoxically, however, he draws a very different conclusion from this axiom than does the Martian. Because, in the first instance, he knows himself to be an outsider and not a natural member of the group he wishes to study, he takes it as an article of faith that the lives, views, and aspirations of natural members (including, perhaps, the very ways they perceive, organize, and interpret their constructed worlds) must differ in *significant*, if not in all, respects from his own. The main methodological objective of his inquiry, therefore, is to reduce as far as possible the estrangement he feels from his subjects so that he may begin to perceive, experience, and interpret their world as they do. The fact that he may share a language and numerous taken-for-granted mundane assumptions with his subjects is not viewed by him, as it is by the Martian, as a source of *cognitive entrapment*. On the contrary, the fact of such sharing is evaluated positively inasmuch as it affords a basis for gaining more rapid entrée into the group and achieving greater intimacy with its members. For only then, of course, does the Convert's goal of experiencing his subjects' world as they do stand some chance of realization; and this, in turn, is absolutely essential, as he sees it, if he is to ever produce a valid, *objective* account of their subjective world. Put somewhat tritely, his guiding principle is but a variant of the familiar everyday adage "unless you've been in my shoes, you cannot know whereof you speak." In contrast to the Martian's desire to escape and stand wholly outside the social ontological frame of his subjects in order to see how the frame is constructed, the Convert's overriding impulse is to immerse himself ever more deeply *within* the frame so that the distinctive subjective currents of the group may forcibly and directly reveal themselves to him.

It is, perhaps, superfluous by this point to explain why I have chosen to label the possessor of this ontological stance the *Convert*. Suffice it to suggest that so thoroughly to divest oneself—even if only temporarily "until the study is over"—of one's customary sense of self for a passionate identification with the life scheme of others is closely to approximate what the social psychologist would term a *conversion experience,* that is, a radical, relatively discontinuous transformation of identity. An important difference, of course, is that whereas the religious or political convert does not (consciously, at least) plan on getting converted—deeply unsettling and revelatory experiences *move him* toward conversion—the anthropologist or sociologist may all but explicitly plot his conversion upon entering the field. (Is a consciously engineered conversion a genuine conversion, one might ask?) In any case, the number of field-workers who enter the field as Martians and exit as Converts is, I would guess, far greater than the other way around.[5]

Discussion

Surely, by now the reader may well object: there is no such person, much less social scientist, like the Martian or Convert. Indeed, the more one contemplates these crude, cardboard cutouts, the more outlandish does their existence seem. No one, be he steeplejack, stockbroker, or sociologist, goes about—wittingly or unwittingly—perceiving and engaging the world about him in ways approximating either of the ontological stances drawn in the preceding pages. In short, these types are existential impossibilities.

With these objections I have no quarrel. On the contrary, I could not agree with them more. But to quickly assent to the empirical impossibility of such fictional characters is to retreat too soon from the more interesting question of what it is about the cultural scientist's actual being-in-the-world which makes for the types' impossibility in the first place. And, to raise this question involves something more than the facile erection of straw men. For, as we all know, there are innumerable methodological writings in the cultural sciences as well as a much word-of-mouth "professional wisdom," which tacitly, if not always consistently, enjoins the student to conduct himself in the field in ways closely resembling a Martian or Convert stereotype. By inquiring into the existential bases for the Martian's and Convert's impossibility, we are also pointing to the dangers of such "advice."

I can here only allude to, rather than fully explicate, some of the considerations underlying the impossibility of these types in their pure form.

As regards the Martian, we must consider the following:

1. Is it possible even remotely to attain—through meditation, drugs,

---

[5]Indeed, a considerable body of at times conscience-stricken, conversion-sensitive literature has accumulated in the cultural sciences in recent years; see, for example, P. Hammond, ed., *Sociologists at Work* (New York: Basic Books, 1964); A. J. Vidich et al., eds., *Reflections on Community Studies* (New York: John Wiley, 1964); R. Redfield, *Human Nature and the Study of Society*, vol. 1 (Chicago: University of Chicago Press, 1962); J. Seeley, *The Americanization of the Unconscious* (Philadelphia: International Science Press, 1967); H. Powdermaker, *Stranger and Friend* (New York: W. W. Norton, 1966); G. Sjoberg, ed., *Ethics, Politics and Social Research* (Cambridge, Mass.: Schenkman, 1967). Also see the extraordinarily well informed novel on the "culture" of sociological field work by Alison Lurie, *Imaginary Friends* (New York: Coward-McCann, 1967).

or sheer phenomenological gall—the presuppositionless universe that the Martian-in-principle strives for? My own hunch is that, beyond some probably unspecifiable point, as the social researcher begins to approximate the extreme ontological stance of pure Martianhood, to that degree does he come to understand less rather than more about the constitutive world of his subjects. To see the world with pure eyes unsullied by prior experience or assumption is, in other words, to see nothing at all, simply because without prior experience we don't know what to look for or what we see.

2. This is not to deny that the Martian's attempt to make the commonplace and taken-for-granted seem uncommon and problematic—a sociological version of Bertold Brecht's *verfremdungseffekt*[6]—is not a useful heuristic device. To think of being as "presentation of self," of becoming as "socialization," of a person as an "actor," of what he does as his "role," of what others customarily expect of him as his "status," and so forth, through the whole glossary of key social-science terms, can, of course, prove of much help in conceptualizing our data and pointing up connections among them that we might otherwise have missed. But, Erving Goffman notwithstanding, to assume or even talk "as if" the *verfremdungseffekt* of the observer-analyst is what is *actually* seen, felt, or thought by those he studies—in other words, that the shoe clerk really thinks of the fitting bench as "front stage" and the stockroom as "backstage"—is, finally, seriously to falsify and distort this subjective world. This variant of what Alfred North Whitehead[7] once termed "the fallacy of misplaced concreteness" summons to mind the still charming and ever instructive spoof of Horace Miner, "Body Ritual Among the Nacirema."[8] Here Miner pokes somewhat obvious fun at the health practices of Americans but much more subtle fun at the explanatory style of his own guild, the anthropologists, wherein the accepted jargon of the craft evokes in those who are being written about that queasy intellectual feeling of cognitive seasickness; the world as described seems accurate enough in its gross features but somehow terribly skewed and off-center in its particularities. To wit, bathroom sinks are not experienced by Americans as ritual fonts nor hospital nurses as vestal virgins.

3. Finally, even if we grant a certain validity to the Martian's metaphoric constructions of everyday experience, to the degree that these succeed at all they come peculiarly to negate themselves. Thus, for the layman to come to conceive of an inchoate sense of disconnectedness

---

[6] See Peter Winch, *The Idea of a Social Science* (London: Routledge and Kegan Paul, 1958), pp. 118–19.
[7] A. N. Whitehead, *Science and the Modern World* (New York: Macmillan, 1925).
[8] H. Miner, "Body Ritual Among the Nacirema," *American Anthropologist* 58(1956):503–7.

as "alienation" or a hypersensitivity to others' opinions as "other-directedness" is to transmute the very experience which the sociological concept was meant to comprehend in the first place. Put differently, to assimilate such concepts into one's being is to make a different social object of the self than existed prior to the act. Fresh possibilities for avoiding, affirming, rejecting, or revising the identity implications of the construct are thereby opened to the actor and thus drain the construct of its erstwhile descriptive éclat and predictive power. And, in this modern world of rapid media popularization of social science concepts, and given the highly self-conscious and ideologically manipulative use that radical and other protest groups have come to make of the social science armamentarium, the likelihood of any pristine Martian construct remaining phenomenologically uncontaminated for long, as it were, is drastically diminished. Ironically, it can, perhaps, now be said of social science that *nothing flaws like success.*

So much, for here, for the Martian. As for the Convert we must consider such matters as these:

(1) As I have already implied, in what sense is the somewhat studied and planned immersion of the Convert into the culture of the group the equivalent of a more naive and forthright conversion experience? And if, as we have reason to suspect, these are not the same thing—indeed there is a pronounced quality of disingenuousness about the whole business—could this not also account for the passionate zealotry with which many an ethnographer Convert takes up the cudgels for the group he has studied after leaving the field? It is almost as if the insincerity of the ethnographer's conversion experience per se generates so large a burden of guilt, he can only dissipate it through an excess of ideological partisanship in favor of the group studied.

(2) More pointedly, can the ethnographer's *acquired* intersubjective view of his informants' world ever be the same as that of the informants themselves? One may doubt this, if only for the reason that the ethnographer can assume and renounce affiliation with the group he studies in a way that is foreclosed to members themselves. And, does this freedom of nonmembership not impart to the ethnographic account certain peculiar emphases, niceties, and rigidities which are absent from the members' own experiences of their lived world *(lebenswelt)?* In the end William Whyte could write about the "status hierarchy" significance of bowling scores for the boys of Cornerville in a way that, at best, "translates" or reifies the bowling experiences of the boys themselves. Not that I am for a moment suggesting that there is anything inadequate or flawed about Whyte's account; on the contrary, *Street Corner Society* endures as one of the best ethnographic works of modern social science. It is only that it, too, must ultimately encounter the epistemological para-

doxes inherent in humans trying to study and objectify their fellow humans.

3. Thus, even if there were no grounds for questioning the correspondence of subjective orientation resulting from the ethnographer's immersion in his subjects' world with the actual intersubjective constitution of that world, the prior epistemological question (one which positivists take positive relish in) of whether a *verstehen* account can ever be a wholly accurate, or even adequate, one remains far from resolved.

Conclusion

Clearly, then, there is for social research no easy reconciliation or resolution of the contradictions represented by a Martian as against a Convert stance toward our topics of inquiry. And even though much more could be said about the scope and content of the debate, I think most of us would still be inclined ultimately to opt, perhaps Pollyannaishly and with the smug wisdom of Goldilocks, for some middle ground—to wit, that we need both the Martian and Convert strains in our research, preferably with both echoed in the same researcher if at all possible, as I believe it is. For, in the end, the capacity to experience the world freshly from the outside and knowingly from the inside is part of the great duality of intelligent social life itself. To replicate in our sociological research this duality through an ongoing interior dialogue which constantly counterposes the stark epiphanies of the one to the intimate knowingness of the other moves us nearer, I would suggest, to a more felicitous account of humans' actual lived world than can either stance by itself.

PART TWO
Society

Society is made up of people, but numbers of people are not sufficient to make up a society. In many respects a society may be thought of as the enactment of its culture; it is defined and constructed from the principles, rules, and meanings of that culture. It is composed of commonsense understandings derived from the categories of thought that are given by the culture. Every society consists of an elaborate network of relationships among different kinds of knowledge, such as commonsense, technical, expert, and vocational. These systems produce typical ways of thinking about the nature of the social world. At the most general level, knowledge schemes, interrelationships among them, and the courses of plausible action given by these states of affairs are what we usually refer to as the society.

However, within the general patterns, there is latitude, or freedom of movement. Each person and each group of people have a cultural background, and they find themselves bound by the past enactments of the culture which we often refer to as the "way things are." Through collective action, immediate changes can be effected in the society; the culture, on the other hand, changes in a much slower and more indirect fashion. Within the limits set by the culture and the society as we have it given to us, there are varying degrees of freedom for working out with others mutually acceptable meanings for thought and action. American society is rich in variation. It provides opportunities for negotiation and renegotiation of the enactments of the culture.

Our tendency to stress the historically predetermined forms of the society may mislead us into thinking that the society compels us to think and behave in a characteristic fashion. Although it is true that the products of the application of cultural knowledge may have constraining effects, the constraint represents the outcomes of negotiated relationships among people of varying motives and intentions but of one culture. The society effects the future, to be sure, but never in a one-to-one, causal fashion. The society is essentially a creation of the mind; its permanency and its effectiveness depend on the continuing redefinition of its members, redefinitions in which the appropriateness of the particular outcomes are reaffirmed and reestablished as morally correct.

Such processes of continuing the social order are not smooth and uniform throughout the society. There are many different ways to be a member of a society, many different ways to enact the culture. The following articles describe how these collective enactments result in organized phenomena, relationships among phenomena, and typical understandings of the meaning of typical actions.

4

Organizing New Forms

Whatever form a society takes, membership in that society includes a sense of belonging. In the past this sense of togetherness was ensured by identification with a place of lifelong residence, face-to-face interaction with the same people, and traditional patterns of thought and action. Today members of American society are mobile; we move when our jobs require it, when we tire of a place, or when a new locale seems to offer a fresh opportunity. Kinsmen and friends are left behind as we take up residence in a new community. All these considerations mean that a feeling of *belongingness* to the collective society is accomplished in new ways. It may come from a uniting effect, joining with others in some common purpose, being caught in the same predicament, or simply from occupying the same place on a regular basis. In this article Jeffrey Nash shows how the ordinary daily bus ride can provide a sense of membership under certain conditions. He describes the feelings and conditions that engender this sense of community.

Bus Riding: Community on Wheels

Jeffrey E. Nash

Bus riding seems an unlikely setting for feelings and thoughts ordinarily associated with communities or stable groups. Keyes's provocative analysis of modern urban life, however, has suggested that within anonymous, impersonal, and lonely environs "community" assumes different forms; as the context varies, so vary the forms or manifestations of communitylike phenomena.[1] Thus, Git and Go's, 7-11's, and shopping

---

[1] R. Keyes, *We, the Lonely People: Searching for a Community* (New York: Harper and Row, 1973).

From *Urban Life and Culture* 4 (1975): 99–124. Reprinted by permission. Urban Life, 4, 1 (April 1975) © 1975 Sage Publications, Inc.

centers replace kinship and geographically specific tribal locations. Instead of interpreting the shift from *gemeinschaft* to *gesellschaft* that urban settings with their mobility, anonymity, and estrangement work against the development of a sense of community, the expectation is formulated that *gemeinschaftlich* mentalities and encounters are modified by the urban settings but not obviated by them. This realization, coupled with recent analyses such as Goffman's description of interguises of the microstructure of everyday urban life,[2] suggests that settings such as bus riding are often more complex and social psychologically relevant than their specific, rapid, and impersonal surface characteristics would indicate.

By analyzing bus riding as an arena where a high degree of intimate and continuous ambiguity is changed into recognizable occurrences that involve a mentality of membership, several objectives may be accomplished. The requisites necessary for generating appropriate bus-riding behavior may be uncovered; variation in the contexts of those requisites may appear, and some generalizations about factors of the setting that affect the acquisition and character of being a rider may be presented. A portrayal of a peculiar urban form of belongingness emerges, a kind of "community on wheels."[3]

---

[2] E. Goffman, *Relations in Public: Microstudies of the Public Order* (New York: Basic Books, 1971).

[3] Ethnographic descriptions of similar phenomena include Cavan's analysis of home-based bars, S. Cavan, *Liquor License: An Ethnography of Bar Behavior* (Chicago: Aldine, 1966). Although the bus rider's territory is much more flexible than the bar's location, claims of a public area as belonging to regulars occur among bus riders. The defense and management of the territory are less dramatic on the bus since crowdedness and "unfocused gatherings" are common; nevertheless, riders do claim bus space as personal space and subsequent social organization around that space is documented in the present analysis, see also E. Goffman, *Encounters: Two Studies in the Sociology of Interaction* (Indianapolis: Bobbs-Merrill, 1961). Henslin's discussion of cab drivers notes that some riders become known to drivers and mutual trust characterizes this relationship. The relationship then often becomes the basis for further encounters such as contacts with prostitutes and gamblers. "Charge customers" and "personals" are examples of regular riders, see J. M. Henslin, "What Makes for Trust?" in *Down to Earth Sociology*, ed. J. M. Henslin (New York: Free Press, 1972), pp. 20-32, 410. J. P. Spradley and B. J. Mann have identified the way in which language used to order a drink in a bar has meanings that vary with the degree of "belongingness" or "competency" in the social world of the bar in *The Cocktail Waitress: Woman's Work in a Man's World* (New York: John Wiley, 1975). Bar behavior and cab riding, among regulars, appear to have many communitylike features.

the years of skeleton operation, years during which they made lasting acquaintances with regular riders. New drivers, of course, are those added after expansion of service. They are broken in by old-timers, i.e., shown the routes, given instruction on passenger treatment, and so on. However, new drivers can be seen, on careful observation, to possess mannerisms and stances toward the passengers that are obtrusive when compared to those of the old-timers. They don't know the "lay of the land" to the same degree as old-timers. They see their job differently. They have a matter-of-fact, "do my job" mentality as contrasted with the old-timers' service-for-the-rider mentality. Characteristic interaction among the four types will be described with the emphasis placed on riders. These types must not be construed as exhaustive of the phenomena of riding and driving. They are characterizations of these phenomena insofar as the observer is interested in knowing the scene from the rider's vantage point.

The Decision to Ride and Subsequent Problems

No doubt the enumeration of "because motives" for riding the bus would require extensive cataloging. That task is not pertinent to the analysis at hand. Whether motivated by "civic mindedness" in response to the energy crisis, "ecological awareness" (a theme displayed on the side of MTTA buses), or just "financial necessity," entrance into the world of riding buses presents a set of common problems for negotiation.

Timing the Bus

Regardless of the finer distinctions that could possibly be introduced along a continuum of motivation, the first problem is to render the schedule recognizable, i.e., learning to read the schedule and its sister problem, timing the bus. Perhaps few things are so foreboding on first glance as a bus schedule. The MTTA schedule is no exception. A sheet of paper seventeen inches by nine inches is filled with column headings of bureaucratic terms standing guard over mysterious-looking columns of times, e.g., Sub-Acres, leaves 6th Bost 5:40, 5:55, 6:10, 6:25, . . . , n.

In addition to activating stocks of knowledge regarding how to read a schedule—find the appropriate heading then read downward—the potential bus rider must bring to a schedule a backlog of information extraneous to the schedule itself, now rendered relevant to the successful reading of the schedule. The bus rider must know locations along spacial and temporal dimensions. In other words, one must know where the point of initial timing is in relation to where one wishes to catch the bus. Further the rider must be aware of considerations that will affect the movement of the bus. Some of these considerations are: (1) the nature of the roads—fast or slow, four lane or two lane; (2) traffic conditions—heavy or light; (3) the time of the day and the day of the week, not in a calendar sense, but in the city-scene (what activities take place at that particular time); (4) construction on the roads and crucial places, e.g., intersections that force a detour or a delay for a left turn.

With these bits of knowledge at hand, the rider hypothesizes an estimated time of arrival; the bus is timed. The regular rider will be able to explain a missed bus in terms of erroneous timing due to ignorance of some of the above considerations, the particular idiosyncracies of an old-timer driver, or the advent of a new driver. For example, new drivers are often either late or early. If a regular rider knows beforehand of a driver change, the margin of safety is established by showing up early and waiting. Old-timer drivers are "on time." On time, of course, may not be schedule time, but rather the routine or ordinary arrival for that driver; i.e., she is always here at twenty after, and so on. According to how the route is negotiated, the time of arrival will vary within a fifteen-minute "clock-time" interval.

The following is an example of a method of timing the bus. East 15th bus leaves 6th and Boston downtown at 3:13 P.M. and leaves 6th and Denver at 3:18 P.M. This means that the bus makes the downtown loop at the time of day before rush-hour traffic, and with the absence of construction that blocks or slows the route, the bus will head out on 15th Street more or less on schedule. This route has an old-timer driver. He maintains the required 20 mph speed, but only after clearing the downtown area. Since 15th Street is straight with stop lights on an average of every half mile, the bus should arrive at the intersection of Harvard and 15th within fifteen minutes, plus or minus five minutes, of departure of the downtown area. All of this leads to the conclusion that the bus will arrive at the stop about 3:30 P.M.

Of course, several other options are open to neophyte riders. One is simply to go out and wait. Depending on luck, this could mean anywhere from a few minutes to an hour. Also, if you have cowaiters or coriders, this may provide the opportunity to act on surface features only; i.e., just ask a cowaiter, a regular, when the bus usually comes by. Such an option does not require the degree of competency being discussed in this analysis. Of course, the results of both options are the same, namely, getting on the bus. However, there is a crucial difference. With intermittence of bus runs there is a corresponding requirement of competency in timing. The obverse of this is that as service

Why Study the MTTA?

The observations for this report were made while riding several bus lines of the Metropolitan Tulsa Transit Authority over a two-year period.[4] During that time the MTTA experienced a dramatic increase both in numbers of people riding the bus and in service expansion. As in many cities, the bus service had declined through the 1960s as the city became more suburban and oriented toward the private automobile. By the 1970s all that was left of the old M, K, and O service was a city-owned and -operated skeleton service, used mostly by domestic servants, the unemployed, the elderly, and school children. The buses were few and far between along the routes, the riders were regulars, and the drivers were those whose seniority enabled them to survive the many layoffs and cutbacks.

Beginning in about 1972, interest in the bus line became more pronounced. A new director was hired with an eye to rejuvenating the system. Much of the early impetus for invigorated bus service came from the elderly with whom the new director was acutely sympathetic. Finally, with the "energy crisis" and the subsequent increased cost of gasoline, commuters were lured or forced into riding buses.

This profile indicates a setting where drivers with years of experience and regular riders are rather suddenly inundated with changes. New riders—those riding for the first time, others riding for the first time in years—are now back on buses. The times have changed. Now the city is suburban. Street patterns are not downtown block and grid. Schedules are complicated, and the lines traverse many miles. Also, there are many new drivers who are equally neophytes in the habits and customs of the world of bus riding. All of this provides a scene which is highly ambiguous but negotiable. In short, riding the MTTA buses constitutes a strategic arena for social encounters.

---

[4]The fieldwork for this paper was conducted from fall 1971 to spring 1974. Notes were taken in a systematic fashion. While on the bus, I took no notes. This was done to avoid drawing attention and affecting the ongoing interaction. Efforts to stay out of encounters were made, but in some cases this was impossible. Nevertheless, most observations were made from the vantage point of a passive involvement, i.e., riding on the bus and observing the encounters of others. Immediately after getting off the bus, I took notes in as complete a form as possible. The length of the rides was usually short, fifteen to thirty minutes, and recall was a relatively simple matter. Some observations in the present analysis were secondhand, through interviews with other bus riders and, in one case, as reported in the local newspaper. The study is, however, primarily participant observation.

Finding One's Way in the World of Buses

For the purposes of ordering a series of observations, the following analytic scheme is introduced. Those persons who have ridden the bus long enough to have negotiated a routine of riding are called regulars. They have been riding the bus as a principal means of transportation for several years, although routine knowledge is usually acquired in about six months to a year. These persons ride the same line, know the drivers, and are generally knowledgeable concerning bus-related matters. Newcomer riders are those people who either have never been on a bus or are returning to riding after a long absence. This type includes commuting businessmen, some students, and occasionally housewives. The main distinction between these two types is along a competency continuum. Regulars "know the ropes"; they can "time" the bus, find stops, make transfers, and engage in "bus conversation." Newcomers flounder in a world of "not knowing" what comes next. They often request advice, make mistakes in terms of hailing buses, and are generally inept at bus etiquette. In short, they do not have a well-developed bus-riding *lebenswelt*.[5]

A similar delineation can be introduced for drivers. The primary focus of this paper is not on drivers.[6] However, it is necessary to introduce a rudimentary distinction between types of drivers so that observations on riding can be placed in a more complete context. The types of drivers that can be found in the employ of the MTTA are old-timers and new drivers. Old-timers are vestiges of earlier days. They are usually males in their fifties. Several have years numbering in double figures of driving services. These drivers remember a day when buses played an integral part in the transportation of the city. They also drove through

---

[5] *Lebenswelt*, or life-world, is used here to refer to the sphere of experiences that characterize a set of individuals circumscribed by objects, persons, and events encountered in the pursuit of the pragmatic objectives of bus riding. It is a world in which an individual is "wide awake" and which asserts itself as the "paramount reality" of his life associated with this particular activity. Schutz provides examples of analyses of *lebenswelten* in his book on strangers, homecomers, and Tiresias. All can be found in A. Schutz, *Collected Papers II: Studies in Social Theory* (The Hague: Martinus Nijhoff, 1971).

[6] Slosar has written an ethnographic account of bus drivers. He identified features of the drivers' behavior and attitudes through a detailed analysis of the language of the "society of bandits." He notes the designation of "old-timer" in reference to a driver's seniority and ability to run "hot," meaning the ability to manipulate conformity to transit authority rules to stay ahead of the schedule, see J. A. Slosar, Jr., "Ogre, Bandit and Operating Employee: The Problems and Adaptations of the Metropolitan Bus Driver," *Urban Life and Culture* (January 1973): 344-46. Some of the practices identified by Slosar do affect the riders. For example, timing the bus depends on knowing whether the driver is "hot" or not, and the hailing of the bus will be more or less dramatic depending on the schedule time of the driver.

improves or the frequencies of buses along the lines increase, less competency is required to successfully ride the bus. This does not necessarily mean that the phenomenon of rider membership ceases to exist. It does mean, however, that some settings are more or less conducive to the knowledge of timing buses and, hence, provide a variable opportunity for "membership" as a bus rider.

Where the Bus Stops: Corners or Signs?

After a sufficient degree of competency at "timing," the next problem involves where to wait for the bus. Of course, most cities offer at least one well-marked central area of bus service. In Tulsa the downtown business district is dotted with signs bearing the MTTA designation. These markers constitute bus stops. However, out on the lines few, if any, of these signs can be found. A noticeable exception is South Lewis Street where signs can be observed lining both sides of the streets for about a three-mile stretch. South Lewis in this particular area is quite fashionable and, incidentally, is the general residential area of most city officials. This display of bus stops, no doubt, has both political and economic purposes, the latter referring to the custom of employing domestic servants from the predominantly black north side who must ride buses to work on the south side.

When out on the line and wishing to stop a bus, the rider must "discover" a place where the bus might stop. There is an official regulation known to all drivers and some riders that the bus will stop at every corner or at designated stops if a rider is standing at the location. In other words, buses do not stop unless hailed. Out of necessity the drivers must make the best possible time in the outer regions of their route. Here there are long stretches of road where they can travel 40 to 50 mph to make up for lost time in the denser downtown and main-street traffic. There is a driver practice that should be reported here. Old-timers and new drivers are very much aware of the difficulty of "keeping on time." The old-timer drivers develop coping tactics. These tactics entail knowledge of who rides and where they wait for the bus. The outer reaches of the routes provide few contacts with the casual or one-time-only rider. Drivers will "know" that no one is ever on a particular stretch of the run. They will, as a matter of course, "cut" off that part to make up time. Often, if the bus is carrying several passengers, the driver will ask, "Anyone get off between here and 21st?" (or whatever location). With no reply or a negative reply from the riders, the driver then proceeds to "shortcut." New drivers often display an unwarranted amount of élan with this practice. For example, they will shortcut without adequate knowledge of regular riders waiting at stops and thus leave them

50 Organizing New Forms

stranded. A regular rider who will have a backlog of success at timing arrivals will surmise that "something is wrong." On occasion the rider will report to the downtown office that a bus did not show along a particular section of the route. Repercussions of this then get back to the drivers. This can be a serious matter, since the neophyte driver's incompetencies call into question at official levels the entire practice of shortcutting. Hence, old-timer drivers are reluctant to inform new drivers of the tactic. Instead, new drivers are allowed to find out for themselves how to stay on time and not to irritate regular riders. Of course, this means learning not only the routes but also the riders on the routes.

The problematic nature of stopping the bus should now be well established, and a full description of "where the bus stops" is now possible. Many regular riders will define a location as a corner. Over a period of time, this location will become a stop. For instance, driveways leading into apartment houses, shopping areas, or food stores are not actually intersections of streets, a legalistic definition of a corner. However, a curved curb is present, and if a known regular rider waits there, the bus will stop. The problem of what constitutes a corner is subjectively real as is illustrated by the common observance of riders, even regulars, walking several blocks to select an obvious stop, which might be either a clear case of a street intersection or a marked stop. Regular riders and old-timer drivers, of course, may suspend the "corner or stop" rule. If the driver knows the pedestrian to be a rider, he will stop regardless of the presence of a corner, curved curbs, or marked stops. On the other hand, new drivers will run past the regular rider to an obvious stop and force the rider to walk a few yards in order to establish the official recognition of a stop. On a few rare occasions the new driver may pass the regular rider altogether. However, this is an infrequent circumstance, since the regular rider has available a repertoire of "hailing behaviors" which may stop the bus regardless of the corner or stop rules.

Hailing a Bus

Even casual observation of taxi riders demonstrated that a sophisticated array of hailing behaviors exists for "getting a cab."[7] The bus rider,

"What Makes for Trust?", p. 22, treats how the driver determines whether an individual can be trusted to become his passenger or not in terms of interaction among three sets of considerations: (1) setting, (2) appearance, and (3) the manner of the performer. Bus drivers do not exercise as much discretion in the decision to stop or not as do cab drivers. The focus of the present analysis is on the riders' efforts to get the attention of the driver and to appear as a potential rider. Although there is a degree of "trust" in this decision, it is much more limited than in the cab-riding situation. The buses observed in this analysis operated only during the daylight hours and were highly visible in the however, faces a different situation since stopping the bus involves interactive outcomes of location (corner or stops) and hailing gestures. Where stops are designated, e.g., in the downtown area, a rider may hail the bus only to see it pass him and halt at the next bus sign. In unmarked stretches of the routes, the rider may stand motionless at an appropriate location only to watch the bus pass him. Hence, it is the interaction between location and hailing that serves as the sufficient situation to actualize the interpretive procedure on the part of a driver: "This is a rider; stop the bus."

Another way to think about the rider's problem is to say that potential riders must be at an appropriate location and assume the appearance of a rider; i.e., one must look like one wants to ride. There are several typical solutions to the appearance assumption. These may be construed as typical of hailing behaviors. Perhaps the most common is simply to move toward the street. Again, moving toward the street is not always sufficient to stop the bus. One must be at a stop or corner or be a recognized regular rider. Moving toward the street may vary from a slight head-downward gesture toward the street to a gait of several yards. There are slight variations on the basic move. If a handbag, briefcase, shopping bag, or other item is being carried, then it can be placed on the ground while waiting and picked up with a move toward the street on sighting the bus. Coat collars can be manipulated while moving toward the street. A shuffle, step, or just a nod—all of these manifestations contain a common element: movement toward the street.

Another common hailing behavior is the raised hand. This can occur in combination with the movement toward the street or independently of any total bodily disposition. The raised hand ordinarily entails an upward movement of the hand not exceeding the top of the head. Some regular riders will indicate this hailing with a slight upward movement of the fingers, a kind of slow "brush-off." Other less confident riders will raise the hand completely over the head in a magnified circle.

One of the most dramatic hails involves a gesture marking the exact stop for the bus. Usually this occurs simultaneously with the movement toward the street. Here the would-be rider points to an imaginary stop on the ground as if to say to the driver, "stop here." Needless to say, this gesture is often interpreted by drivers as definite. Although the bus will stop, rarely does it stop at the precise point signified.

The surest way to hail the bus, a hail which can often stop a bus at inappropriate locations, is the obvious display of the "bus pass."

sense that they traveled on or near heavy trafficked roads only. Thus, the problem of stopping the bus is not so much one of winning trust but of getting attention and assuming a rider's stance.

Riders may purchase for five dollars a yellow pass, which entitles them to twenty-five rides. Each ride is punched in the pass by the driver. The card is about two inches by four inches and usually is carried in a billfold or purse. The card is visible to the approaching driver. The common form of hailing with the card is to simply hold the card up. Also, a gesture in the direction of fetching the card will signify that the card display is about to take place. The actual display of the card is not always necessary to hail the bus. Often the fetching gesture will suffice. A variation of the card display is the mundane fare-fetching posture. Here the would-be rider assumes a posture that will be interpreted by the driver as "getting fare." A man, for example, will place his hand in his pants pocket, or a woman will open her purse. Whether fare or a bus pass is retrieved is irrelevant for this hail. On some rare occasions, the display of the fare can be observed. However, since quarters are far less visible than the yellow pass, the display of the fare is regarded by the driver as superfluous and, perhaps, as indicative of overwroughtness on the part of the rider. The display of the card, though, is an effective tactic for hailing whenever the rider is caught in an inappropriate location.

These are several considerations of appearance, independent from discrete hailing tactics, that can bear on the driver's halting the bus. In other words, if certain types of people are viewed along the roadside, the driver will slow, often even stop the bus without any ostensible hailing displays. This phenomenon may be observed mostly on the part of old-timer drivers. For them, the following situations appear sufficient for slowing or stopping: (1) any elderly person at any location along an unmarked route at any time of the day; (2) middle-aged women, black or white, whose manner and appearances are interpretable as "cleaning ladies," at any location along an unmarked route at any time of the day in a fashionable part of town; (3) blacks of any age or sex, with the possible exception of young blacks (to be discussed later), at any location in a predominantly white section of town at any time of day; (4) a well-dressed white person in white sections of town during times of morning and afternoon commuting; (5) school-aged children during morning and early afternoon when school is in session; and (6) any regular rider known to the driver. This last category has the effect of superseding all other categories and becoming the taken-for-granted knowledge of the driver about who rides the bus. However, the regular rider usually does conform to categories one through five.

Partial confirmation of the validity of the above characteristics comes from mistakes that drivers make in their judgment of a potential rider. The categories that appear to have greatest likelihood of error are young, male blacks and school-aged children. A driver will slow, but there is noticeable difference in his degree of readiness to brake when these people are involved. School-aged children may look as if they intend to ride the bus but then wave off the driver or just ignore the stopped bus. Drivers do not like to waste a stop and often comment on the empty-headedness or lack of purpose on the part of youngsters in general. Typically the children appear surprised or just unaffected by the stopped bus. Sometimes, on unmarked stretches of routes young male blacks can be observed "putting on the man" by working this commonsense rendition of where the bus stops. For example, they may stroll along the roadway and allow the driver to stop but then wave him off without any indication of intention to board the bus. Occasionally, the black may even gesture almost imperceptibly in what might appear to the driver as a hail and then wave him off as the bus approaches. The most common form of this behavior involves movement toward the street.

Where to Sit?

On the bus a new field of existential choices is presented to the rider. The selection of a seat can represent a serious commitment to a social encounter. There are identifiable aspects of this situation which bear on seat selection. The overriding consideration is the number of people on the bus. If the bus is crowded, as it is during commuter hours, one simply sits where he can. All other rules regarding significance of the seat location are suspended. Thus, a well-dressed businessman may sit next to an attractive high-school or college-aged girl, a move which on a less crowded bus might be viewed with some suspicion by other riders. The strategic setting for selecting a seat, then, takes place on buses that are less than full passenger capacity.

Where seat selection is virtually unimpeded by crowds, the following patterns emerge: first, sitting behind or close to the driver. Although some old-timers will initiate the talks, ordinarily the rider starts the conversation. Old-timers and regulars converse over a wide range of topics. In fact, topics are secondary to style of conversing. Games of naming and timing the buses that are passing by ("that's the Ridgeway bus and he's on time") are common. Discussion of new buses, problems of transfering, and just small talk frequently occur. Second, if the rider does not intend such conversations, then seat selection in the middle of the bus is made, and the double seat is marked as personal space[8] by placing a handbag, briefcase, or other personal item on the opposite seat, or by just sitting close to the aisle with the window seat left vacant. Third,

---

[8] Goffman, *Relations in Public*, pp. 41–42.

seat selection in the rear of the bus is typical of what Goffman calls "withs," i.e., persons together, usually more than two, claiming a group priority while sitting in the back of the bus.[9] Most commonly, the "withs" are school-aged children, male blacks, or coworkers. Regular riders characteristically sit slightly forward of the middle of the bus. This is done to space oneself or to distance oneself from any possible "with" that might board and to close off the opportunity for conversation backward and across seats. In other words, conversation is rarely initiated from the front to the back of the bus. Rather, casual talk is across seats, across aisles, or forward talk to the driver. By positioning oneself slightly forward of the middle, the likelihood is that anyone sitting forward or parallel to the rider will be a "single" and often another regular. This seating tactic tends to isolate "withs" and newcomer riders and to congregate regulars.

Exiting the bus may be seen as a consequence or correlative with seating location. Sitting forward means exiting forward, and exiting forward means parting ritual exchanges between rider and driver, e.g., "see you tomorrow," "have a nice day," and so forth. Of course, these patterns are not unchangeable. In fact, they are more often than not impeded by uncontrollable events, such as a newcomer having already selected the prime seat without fully appreciating its significance, a "with" that selected the middle of the bus, or the intentional use of the bus for rituals that have meaning wider than the scope of bus riding. For example, an encounter between a white driver and a black rider was observed that glossed the entire domain of seat selection and subsequent exiting. In a sense this episode may be viewed as a denigration ceremony with two distinct, consequent reactions.

A poorly dressed, elderly black woman, a regular rider, tries to exit at the back door, an event which must receive approval from the driver since he controls the lock from his panel and an event which is uncharacteristic of regular riders. The woman pushes repeatedly at the door without success. The bus driver refuses to release the lock. He states in a typical toward-the-back-of-the-bus official tone, "I believe you owe me a nickel." He is referring to the woman's purchase of a transfer. Apparently, she was allowed a transfer without paying on the expectation that she would pay on exiting, an option sometimes allowed regular riders. After the driver repeats himself a few times without recognition from the woman, a white woman moves forward and pays the nickel. The driver releases the lock, and the woman exits. A black "with" consisting of two adult males is located in the back of the bus and observes the entire scene. A few blocks further down the line, they move to exit from the back door, standing turned toward the driver in anticipation

[9]Goffman, *Relations in Public*, pp. 19–27.

of his action. Ordinarily, back exiting does not entail this posture. A person usually would stand facing the door as if waiting for it to open. By facing the driver, the members of the "with" indicate that they have full knowledge of the mechanism for the control of the door and that challenge is being offered—in effect, "Try that on me, honkey." The driver, in this case, released the door, and the blacks exited, thereby reestablishing that backdoor exiting is appropriate and does not involve the necessity of exchanging parting amenities with the driver.

That this exiting scene was embedded with this meaning was further evidenced when, not more than two miles down the line, the driver stops to pick up two young black boys. They are not standing on an appropriate location, nor do they hail the bus. However, this area of the route is in a white section of town near a number of schools. The time is early afternoon, and blacks, regardless of other factors of appearance, are potential riders under these circumstances. One boy has a Coke in a paper cup in his hand. The driver remarks after coming to a stop, "Boy, can't let you on with that." A few moments of uncertainty pass while the hopeful rider decides what is meant. (There is an official rule, frequently violated, that no eating or drinking of any kind can take place on the bus.) The driver comments, "I will wait." This sentence has the general meaning that if you can drink the Coke fast, i.e., this instant, then you can board and thereby avoid a long wait for the next bus. The boy comprehends, gulps the drink, and discards the cup on the street as he boards the bus.

The driver is able to renegotiate his control over passengers on the bus by selectively enforcing a rule of bus behavior. On this occasion racial undertones are obvious. The driver, who on other occasions with white riders has been observed relaxing the eating and drinking prohibition, was able to recoup his domain as controller of the bus after having been outruled by the "with."

Encounters

Once on the bus and riding, the bus can become stage for the enactment of dramatic exchanges among drivers and riders, and riders and riders.[10] The following are characterizations of some of these exchanges.

[10] Encounters on the bus refer to types of social arrangements that occur when persons are in one another's immediate physical presence. They involve a focus of attention, and " 'we rationale' is likely to emerge, that is, a sense of the single thing that we are doing together at the time. . . .Such encounters provide a communication base for a circular flow of feelings among the participants as well as corrective compensation for deviant acts" (Goffman, *Encounters*, p. 18).

Regular Riders and Newcomer Riders

Not knowing the rules of the setting, the newcomer rider will often inadvertently position himself within conversational proximity to a regular rider. The first few rides are often accompanied by a kind of wide-eyed innocence that leads to engagement of anyone in talk. The scene is "Oh, I haven't been on the bus in years," or "This is little Jimmie's first ride ever; isn't this exciting?" "I used to ride when. . . ." If the newcomer is lucky, one word or short answers will be elicited, such as "that's nice," "a fine boy you have there," "okay," "fine," and so on. However, some riders use the bus not only for transportation but also for the opportunity bus riding affords for conversation. The observer has the impression that, perhaps, no one will listen to them anywhere else. For example, a long-haired young girl in blue jeans gets on. She takes out knitting, smiles the wide-eyed first-timer's smile, and soon has the little old lady behind her rolling yarn. An Indian woman with three children in tow offers suggestions, and the hitherto quiet man across the aisle watches with great interest. The newcomer asks the man, "Do you knit?" Now any regular knows that that sort of question is an extremely dangerous, leading utterance to address to a rider who has caught your eye, especially if you had observed that he rides the bus to and from the library. The man is a regular, dressed in used khaki with old, black lace-up shoes, and a crew cut in military fashion. "Do you knit?" is an opener for the biographical unveiling. The man proceeds to unfold his life for all to hear. He was a marine, is now retired, and his story begins with boot camp. The girl, after an uncommonly short ride within the downtown loop, usually not considered worth the fare, gathers up her knitting and exits, with a strange look of one who is older but wiser.

There are tactics available to the newcomer or to one who wishes not to become a regular for avoiding this sort of exchange. To avoid life stories, never sit on the wall seats near the driver, one is far too accessible; never sit on the first seats facing the wall seats; never sit in the back of the bus, the place for community gatherings; choose a seat one or two seats behind the first ones, and never catch anyone's eye. Sometimes this requires techniques of direct avoidance because the life-story teller or bus-story teller is often persistent and will stare at you for long periods of time, hoping to catch you off guard. Then it is probably best to stare out the window for the rest of the trip.

Newcomer Riders and Old Drivers

In addition to encounters between riders, rider-driver encounters can constitute major portions of the drama of the bus. The old-timer driver is a pivotal character to entrance into the world of bus riding. In a sense, he is like a gatekeeper who can simply operate the bus or provide information and background knowledge essential to one becoming a regular rider. If a first-time rider is fortunate enought to ride with an old-timer driver, then opportunities for expanded horizons are available. The driver can offer information on schedules and tips on how to make a transfer. Which lines are likely to connect and which are not is crucial information to transferring successfully. However, connection depends on being on time, which, as already indicated, depends on many extra-schedule factors. An old-timer driver knows the routes, the drivers for the day, and the road conditions along the line. He also knows which lines belong to other old-timer drivers. Thus, if a neophyte rider wishes to transfer, an old-timer driver can be immensely helpful. For example, he will know if a new driver is on the route of transfer or if an old-timer has chosen that route. (Drivers select routes on the basis of seniority. The attractive routes, i.e., the most direct or ones with many regular riders, are usually selected by the old-timers.) This kind of information is readily at hand to the old-timer.

The rider, however, must be minimally congenial with the driver before this aid is rendered. For instance, initial exchanges of greeting may suffice for acceptance and subsequent aid. The rider will be recognized by the driver on the second or third ride. This recognition can manifest itself in stopping the bus without necessary hailing. On one occasion, this observer, who had just begun to ride but who was on good terms with a particular driver, was waiting for the bus at a location used several times before. Standing back from the street, under a canopy, reading a book at an unmarked location, I easily could have been passed by the bus. However, the bus pulled to a stop unnoticed by me. The driver opened the door and remarked, "Almost didn't see you standing back there."

The relationships between old drivers and new riders, however, can be tenuous. On one occasion this observer was the only passenger on the bus. The old-timer driver was busily narrating all sorts of details about buses he had driven, commenting on the quality of the newly purchased buses as compared with the old ones he had operated for years. Along an industrial stretch on the line, he stopped the bus, picked up his water jug, and walked to the rear door. He urinated out the back door, washing the urine from the doorway with water from his drinking jug. He casually commented that the SOB's downtown have the route timed so tightly that there is no time for "restroom stops." He then continued evaluating the relative merits of new versus old style buses.

On later rides with this driver, he began to peddle tickets to a square-dance exhibition in which he and his wife were to participate.

58   Organizing New Forms

No matter what was the subject of conversation, the square-dance tickets emerged, and a pitch was forthcoming. I used the excuse of being short on money and repeatedly declined the tickets. The date of the event passed, and over the next several rides there was only mention of the dance exhibition to the effect that "you really missed a good show." However, after this the driver became less and less helpful. Before, he had saved new or discarded copies of schedules for me and had offered to sell me bus passes. (Drivers do not ordinarily sell passes. In fact, there are official prohibitions against doing so.) Failure to purchase a ticket affected all these practices, and thereafter conversation stayed pretty much at the level usually reserved for first time or nonregular riders.

Regular Riders and New Drivers

Undoubtedly, one of the most strategic encounters takes place between regular riders and new drivers. Here it is the rider who is a member of the bus community and the driver who is a fledgling. Of course, the driver has operating control over the scene in the sense that he can stop and start the bus and vary speed and direction. Nevertheless, often the rider exerts surprising influence on even these matters. These events were observed in this setting. An old lady rang the buzzer to indicate intent to exit at a general location known to all regulars on this line as a place where old people board. The location is an elongated stop of about three hundred yards fronting on apartments that are exclusively for the elderly. Normally, a bus will stop anywhere along this stretch. On this occasion the driver passed the place where the lady buzzed to what appeared to be a driveway entrance into the street. The lady had to walk approximately twenty yards to return to the location signified by the buzz. She was obviously irritated. "I thought you were supposed to stop back there." The driver replied, "I didn't know that was a stop." The old lady: "Oh, I will call to see if I can get a bus stop back there. It's awfully hard on *us* to walk that far when you carry *us* past."

When the driver demonstrates that he either does not have sufficient knowledge of the nature of the route or refuses to behave like an old-timer, the regular rider's advantage over the ordinary or casual rider disappears. There is no recourse except to formal procedure. A sign, in this instance, would equalize riders, i.e., relieve the necessity for knowing that this is a location for elders. To date, no signs have been posted along that stretch.

Another similar episode involved a lady known to be a veteran of fifteen years of bus riding in this town, a fact announced during the encounter. The woman is obese. She and I were cowaiters at a stop.

We boarded. The driver was obviously new. His uniform was not complete, and he was known to neither of us, both regulars on this line. The woman had difficulty navigating the doorway and the steps at the front-door entrance. She commented, "You should have helped me; most drivers do." No response came from the driver, just an expression of disgust. Aiding passengers to board is clearly not "part of the job." "After all," remarked another new driver on a different occasion, "we are not operating a taxi here."

Newcomer Riders and New Drivers

The resort to formal procedures is most pronounced when strangeness characterizes the situation of both parties, a point made many years ago by Toennies.[11] Here there can be no presumption of commonsense knowledge of an intimate or special nature. The only commonly available, shared information is the formal rule. However, this situation is actually transitory. No bus line operates exclusively at this level. When untoward events occur, their accounting is usually outside the scope of the formal procedure. An "exact-change" rule encounter illustrates this point.

During the years of skeleton operation and active years prior to the 1960s, drivers customarily made change for riders. However, an innovation recently introduced and one that is fairly standard throughout transit systems is the exact-change rule. Drivers will not provide change, and the rider must have a quarter or smaller denominations of coins to equal twenty-five cents. Of course, regulars often use the bus pass. Newcomers, however, use money as fare. A girl who had already ridden on this bus for a while wished to buy a transfer and asked the driver for change. He invoked the exact-change rule. The girl explained that she must have a transfer or be stranded miles from her destination. The driver said nothing; the girl stood motionless. The bus was stopped in the middle of a busy street at the entrance to a busy intersection, and there was a green light. After what seemed an interminable period of time, a regular rider came to the girl's rescue and paid the extra fare for the transfer. The girl quietly exited to make connection with the other bus. A few blocks farther down the line, another regular rider offered to pay half of the extra fare to the rider who purchased the transfer for the girl. The driver said nothing throughout this entire episode. Repeated observations of the behavior of old-timer drivers in similar cases provide interesting contrast. Most old-timer drivers have developed tactics of coping with the consequences of the exact-change rule. First

---

[11] Ferdinand Toennies, *Community and Society,* trans. C. P. Loomis (East Lansing: Michigan State University Press, 1957).

they will routinely invoke the rule, and then ask passengers on the bus if they have change. If no one volunteers from among the riders, most drivers carry two to four dollars worth of quarters with them for the purpose of making change, which they will do as a last resort.

Structural Factors that Affect the Characteristics of the Bus Scene

That a lack of competency, or the absence of detailed and mutual *lebenswelten*, results in reliance on formal or institutional procedures has already been discussed. The same point should be presented now in a different context. There are certain features of the bus-riding scene that produce structures variably conducive to rider membership. New lines, crowded buses, new riders, and new drivers combine to produce an eyes-straight-ahead or gazing-out-the-window/no-talking riding posture. Encounters that take place can be analyzed without reference to membership concepts; i.e., the mentality and action of a *gemeinschaftlich* nature are not ordinarily observed. What is typically observed under these conditions might be termed the "commuter stance." The commuter stance is highly institutionalized and involves the negotiation of private space or territory within the public domain.[12] The commuter, by preference, shares a physical environment, but he does not intentionally go about displaying through his behavior the communality of his action. Rather his task is to preserve his individuality against great structural odds. Even if the bus environs are not structurally conducive to the commuter stance, the absence of competency on the part of either participant in the scene is sufficient to elicit this behavior.

The MTTA has routes during rush hours that are "standing room only," punctuated by frequent stops and highly standardized with regard to verbal and paralinguistic encounters. However, a theme of this paper has been that even these scenes, under certain conditions, may admit of *gemeinschaftlich* characteristics. There are three interrelated structural conditions that bear on the character of action in the bus-riding scene: (1) the degree of competency possessed by the actors as riders and drivers, respectively; (2) the number of people on the bus; and (3) "riding time," which refers to the clock time duration of the ride.

None of these conditions should be interpreted as determining the emergence of bus membership. Rather, they are structural states of affairs, interrelationships among some objective features of bus riding, that set

[12] See Goffman, *Relations in Public*.

scenes or stages which vary in conduciveness to mental states of membership. No single condition or combination of conditions necessarily precludes membership. Lack of competency on the part of one participant is transitory and often a prelude to full membership. The competent member can serve as guide or teacher, thereby providing entrance to competency. In fact, as already discussed, such encounters are ordinary means of entrance. Thus, the last two conditions are more salient with regard to impeding or enhancing membership.

All of the observations reported so far were made on buses with two to fifteen occupants (including the driver). Having few riders allows for maneuvering for seating placements and is conducive to conversation with the option of engaging the driver. MTTA buses are ridden infrequently between rush or commuter hours. The world of regular riders primarily exists in this lull. At these times there is room for interaction even if the ride is relatively short. Talking throughout the entire space of the bus is possible. However, when the bus begins to fill and the stops are often and regular, across-aisle talk, talk with the driver, and the maintenance of "withs" becomes difficult. Often a "with" will dissolve when its members are forced to take available seats. The business of opening and closing doors, watching traffic, and spotting potential riders occupies the attention of the driver. Repeated observations have confirmed that major shifts in the character of the interaction on the bus occur when the number of passengers surpasses fifteen. There is a transformation from the intimate world of the rider to the stance of commuting. Buses that are crowded and have a rapid turnout of passengers simply provide no time for sociability other than the formal and routine variety.

There is an extenuating circumstance. Crowdedness is apparently not sufficient to obviate the intimate world of riding, provided the ride's length of time is enough to allow patterns of behavior that include the scope of the bus to emerge. The crucial consideration is whether or not what transpires on the bus is segmentalized into pairs, co-occupants of seats or standers and sitters, in short adjacent interactions and encounters or bus-wide patterns. Before the intimate world of riding can emerge, all on the bus must enter into interactions that have parameters encompassing the revelation of biographies, feelings, and knowledge, i.e., displays of competency in emotions and knowledge that can be judged by others on the bus as appropriate to a bus rider. This circumstance is structurally possible when the rider is in the company of other riders for a long time.

Such a setting exists on the commuter express runs. The MTTA, in an effort to serve the outlying suburban areas of the city, has several routes that operate only during the rush hours and are express, meaning that they do not stop at locations between the suburbs and downtown. These buses depart the downtown area empty. They have a direct route to a suburban area, usually using a freeway. A load of passengers is picked up within the suburban region, and then the bus heads directly for downtown. These express buses are started only when sufficient interest is shown in such service. The impetus for the express often comes from a single business located downtown or groups of such businesses that are all centered in the central city. Many employees, in fact most, reside in the outlying areas. They are often centralized in a few suburbs, which makes the express bus a viable alternative to car pooling or single-car commuting. Many expresses began experimentally and continued only after the MTTA was convinced that there was demand enough to justify the expense of the express. Some expresses have been markedly successful, with typical runs of full or near capacity. These buses provide the setting in which a bus rider *lebenswelt* may develop.

One such express recently received newspaper notoriety. The No. 1 Broken Arrow Express is a standing-room-only bus and apparently is quite ordinarily commuter in the quality of the interactions on the bus. The No. 2 Express of the same line is less crowded, but still near capacity, and has a regular set of passengers and an old-timer driver. The No. 2 bus has a social organization *gemeinschaftlich* in nature. For example, there is the "Green Dragon crew," men who wait for the No. 2 bus in a bar from which they derived their name. The "Green Dragon dirty dozen divided by three" is strictly men only. After boarding the bus and several beers, they sit in the back of the bus and constitute the nucleus of the X-rated section, so rated on the basis of the jokes told there. The front of the bus, G-rated, is composed of women. The middle of the bus is a GP group. Over a period of time, however, there was a shifting of membership in these groups. Some women started as G and slowly worked their way back, or down depending on perspective, to the X-rated section.

The driver of this bus once started the route early in order to purchase coffee and donuts for the passengers. This practice has since been institutionalized into a sharing of this function, with each row purchasing on a rotating basis, e.g., the first row gets donuts today. The driver will stop the bus so that a representative from the row of the day can get off and make the purchase. One passenger, known as the "hostess with the mostess," serves as the purchasing coordinator.

The camaraderie extends to the driver. On his birthday a radio (prohibited by bus regulations) out of a corner of the bus reports that No. 2 has just suffered a flat tire. Then the radio broadcaster announces "happy birthday" to the driver and plays the birthday song. At the same time, outside the bus a regular rider who had "missed" the bus that day rides past on a motorcycle carrying a banner bearing birthday wishes.[13]

Of course, the level of community on this express is not usually equaled on other buses. However, its existence and perseverance are noteworthy. In a less dramatic fashion encounters of an intimate nature are common on buses throughout the city. Bus riding can be considered a strategic arena and can reveal a great deal about the taken-for-granted knowledge and membership feelings of participants within a particular urban setting. Often the quality of *lebenswelt* is much more *gemeinshaftlich* than previously thought. Depending on the interrelationships among objective conditions of the scene, there is a degree of conduciveness to the acquisition of community in the phenomenon of bus riding.

[13] Tulsa *Daily World*, December 16, 1973.

5

Organizing Work

Although the organization of social life varies greatly from setting to setting, it is often possible to discover types of organizations and their characteristics. After repeated observations and the discovery of patterns, some researchers draw conclusions about the relationship between organization and behavior. In a now-classic article, William Whyte specifies the characteristics of the restaurant as it expands and grows. He identifies some problems of interaction that the structure produces and draws far-reaching conclusions for our understanding of organizations. As the communication system of the restaurant becomes more mechanical, the problems of coordination become much more complex. In this description the author presents some of the unanticipated consequences of this process.

The Social Structure of the Restaurant

William Foote Whyte

While research has provided a large and rapidly growing fund of knowledge concerning the social organization of a factory, studies of other industrial and business structures are only beginning. Sociologists who are concerned with working out the comparative structures of economic organizations must therefore look beyond as well as into the factory. This paper represents one effort in that direction. It grows out of a four-

From *American Journal of Sociology,* 54 (1949): 302–10. Reprinted by permission.

teen-month study of restaurants.[1] We do not claim to have studied a representative sample of restaurants. In an industry having so many types of operations and sizes of units, such a task would have taken years. We did aim to find out, at least in a general way, what sort of structure a restaurant is and what human problems are found within it.

Here I shall present a schematic picture of the findings as they bear upon problems of social structure. I am also using the discussion of research findings to illustrate certain points of theory and methodology in studies of social structures. Discussions of theory and methodology, divorced from the research data upon which the theory and methods are to be used, are generally fruitless. In a brief paper, discussion of our research findings must necessarily be sketchy, but that will provide a basis for at least tentative conclusions.

Characteristics of the Restaurant

The restaurant is a combination production and service unit. It differs from the factory, which is solely a production unit, and also from the retail store, which is solely a service unit.

The restaurant operator produces a perishable product for immmediate sale. Success requires a delicate adjustment of supply to demand and skillful coordination of production with service. The production and service tie-up not only makes for difficult human problems of coordinating action but adds a new dimension to the structure of the organization: the customer-employee relationship.

The contrast between factory and restaurant can be illustrated by this simple diagram [Figure 5-1], representing the direction of orders in the two structures.[2]

The problems of coordination and customer relations are relatively simple in the small restaurant, but they become much more difficult as

---

[1] The research was financed by the National Restaurant Association. The field work was done by Margaret Chandler, Edith Lentz, John Schaefer, and William Whyte. We made interview or participant-observation studies of twelve restaurants in Chicago and did some brief interviewing outside Chicago. From one to four months was spent upon each Chicago restaurant. In *Human Relations in the Restaurant Industry* (New York: McGraw-Hill, 1948), I report the study in detail. Since the book is primarily addressed to restaurant operators and supervisors, the sociological frame of reference given here does not duplicate the more detailed publication.

[2] This is, of course, an oversimplified picture, for many factory workers interact also with inspectors, engineers, time-study men, etc., but the frequency of such interaction does not compare with what we observe between customers and waiters or waitresses in a restaurant.

66   Organizing Work

FIGURE 5-1.   Factory and restaurant organizational structure

Factory
Foreman
↓
Worker

Restaurant
Supervisor ⇄ Customer
↕
Worker

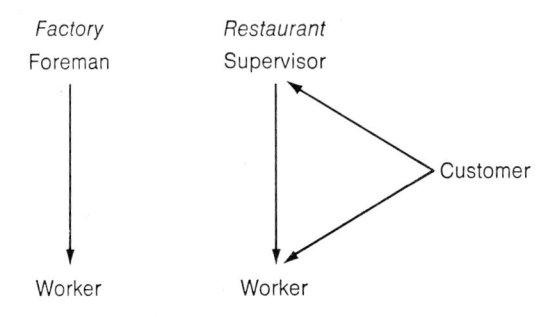

FIGURE 5-2.   Restaurant organizational structure: stages 1 and 2

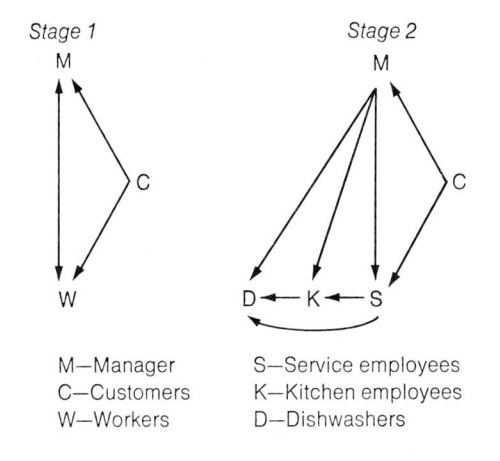

Stage 1
M ⇅ C
W

Stage 2
M
↕
D ← K ← S   C

M—Manager
C—Customers
W—Workers

S—Service employees
K—Kitchen employees
D—Dishwashers

the organization grows. This may be illustrated structurally in terms of five stages of growth [Figure 5-2].[3]

In the first stage, we have a small restaurant where the owner and several other employees dispense short orders over the counter. There is little division of labor. The owner and employees serve together as cooks, countermen, and dishwashers.

In the second stage, the business is still characterized by the informality and flexibility of its relationships. The boss knows most customers and all his employees on a personal basis. There is no need for formal controls and elaborate paper work. Still, the organization has grown in complexity as it has grown in size. The volume of business is such that it becomes necessary to divide the work, and we have dishwashers and

---

[3] I am indebted to Donald Wray for the particular structural approach presented here.

kitchen employees, as well as those who wait on the customers. Now the problems of coordination begin to grow also, but the organization is still small enough so that the owner-manager can observe directly a large part of its activities and step in to straighten out friction or inefficiency.

As the business continues to expand, it requires a still more complex organization as well as larger quarters. No longer able to supervise all activities directly, the owner-manager hires a service supervisor, a food production supervisor, and places one of his employees in charge of the dishroom as a working supervisor. He also employs a checker to total checks for his waitresses and see that the food is served in correct portions and style.

FIGURE 5-3. Restaurant organizational structure: stage 3

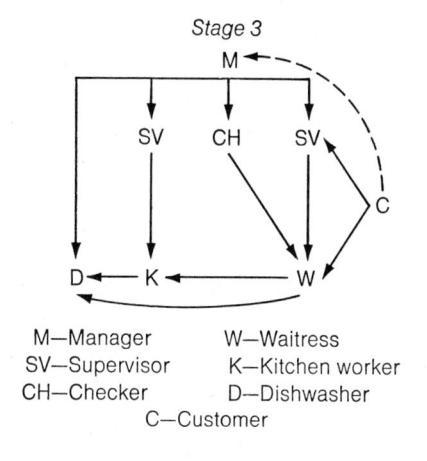

Stage 3

M—Manager
SV—Supervisor
CH—Checker
W—Waitress
K—Kitchen worker
D—Dishwasher
C—Customer

In time the owner-manager finds that he can accommodate a larger number of customers if he takes one more step in the division of labor. Up to now the cooks have been serving the food to the waitresses. When these functions are divided, both cooking and serving can proceed more efficiently. Therefore, he sets up a service pantry apart from the kitchen. The cooks now concentrate on cooking, the runners carry food from kitchen to pantry and carry orders from pantry to kitchen, and the pantry girls serve the waitresses over the counter. This adds two more groups (pantry girls and runners) to be supervised, and, to cope with this and the larger scale of operation, the owner adds another level of supervision, so that there are two supervisors between himself and the workers. Somewhere along the line of development, perhaps, he begins serving drinks and adds bartenders to his organization.

FIGURE 5-4. Restaurant organizational structure: stage 4

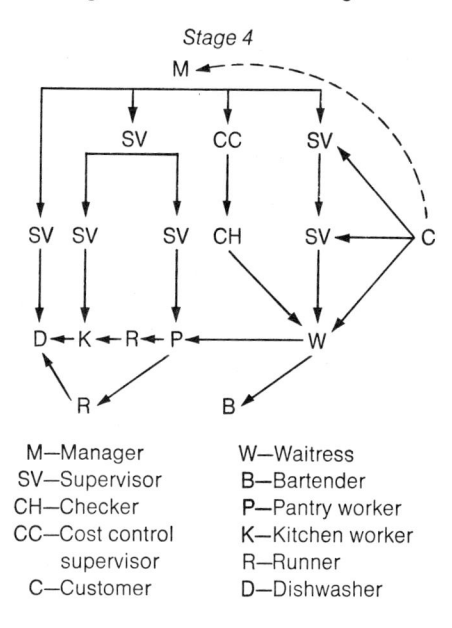

Stage 4

M—Manager
SV—Supervisor
CH—Checker
CC—Cost control supervisor
C—Customer
W—Waitress
B—Bartender
P—Pantry worker
K—Kitchen worker
R—Runner
D—Dishwasher

Stage 5 need not be diagrammed here, for it does not necessarily involve any structural changes in the individual unit. Here several units are tied together into a chain, and one or more levels of authority are set up in a main office above the individual unit structures.[4]

This expansion process magnifies old problems and gives rise to new ones. They may be considered under three headings: administration, the customer relationship, and the flow of work. Whenever we lengthen the hierarchy, adding new levels of authority to separate top executive from workers, the problem of administration becomes more complex. However, this is true for any organization, and therefore these problems of hierarchy need not be given special attention in an article on restaurants.

The particular problem of the large restaurant is to tie together its line of authority with the relations that arise along the flow of work. In the first instance, this involves the customer relationship, for here is where the flow of work begins. The handling of the customer relationship is crucial for the adjustment of the restaurant personnel, and a large part of that problem can be stated in strictly quantitative interaction terms: Who originates action for whom and how often? In a large and

---

[4]The structural changes arising with union organization are beyond the scope of this article. They are discussed in the book, *Human Relations in the Restaurant Industry*, in the chapter, "The Role of Union Organization."

busy restaurant, a waitress may take orders from fifty to one hundred customers a day (and perhaps several times for each meal) in addition to the orders (much less frequent) she receives from her supervisor. When we add to this the problem of adjusting to service pantry workers, bartenders, and perhaps checkers, we can readily see the possibilities of emotional tension—and, in our study, we did see a number of girls break down and cry under the strain.

Our findings suggested that emotional tension could be related directly to this quantitative interaction picture. The skillful waitress who maintained her emotional equilibrium did not simply respond to the initiative of customers. In various obvious and subtle ways, she took the play away from customers, got them responding to her, and fitted them into the pattern of her work. She was also more aggressive than the emotionally insecure in originating action for other waitresses, service pantry people, and supervisor.

While in the rush hour the waitress works under a good deal of tension at best, the supervisor can either add to or relieve it. Here again we can speak in quantitative terms. In one restaurant we observed a change in dining-room management when a supervisor who was skillful in originating action for customers (thus taking pressure off waitresses) and who responded frequently to the initiation of waitresses was replaced by a supervisor who had less skill in controlling customers and who originated for the girls much more frequently and seldom responded to them. (Of the new supervisor, the waitresses would say, "She's always finding something to criticize," "She's never around when we need her," "She's always telling you she doesn't care what you have to say," etc.) This change was followed by evidences of increased nervous tension, especially among the less experienced waitresses, and finally by a series of waitress resignations.

Here we see that the customer-waitress, waitress-supervisor, waitress–service-pantry-worker relationships are interdependent parts of a social system. Changes in one part of the system will necessarily lead to changes in other parts. Furthermore, if the people involved in the system are to maintain their emotional balance, there must be some sort of compensatory activity to meet large interactional changes. For example, when waitresses are subject to a large increase in the originations of customers (at the peak of rush hours), the supervisor allows them to originate action for her with increasing frequency and diminishes the frequency with which she gives them orders. This is, in fact, the sort of behavior we have observed among supervisors who enjoy the closest cooperation with waitresses, as reported by the waitresses.

The customer relationship is, of course, only one point along the flow of work which brings orders from dining room to kitchen and food from kitchen to dining room. In a large restaurant operating on several floors, this is a long chain which may break down at any point, thus leading to emotional explosions in all quarters. The orders may go from waitress to pantry girl and then, as the pantry girl runs low in supplies, from pantry girl to pantry supplyman, from pantry supplyman to kitchen supplyman, and from kitchen supplyman to cook. And the food comes back along the same route in the opposite direction. Where drinks are served, the bar must be tied in with this flow of work, but there the chain is short and the problem less complex.

We have here a social system whose parts are interdependent in a highly sensitive manner. Thus the emotional tension experienced by waitresses is readily transmitted, link by link, all the way to the kitchen.

I have already noted how a skillful dining room supervisor may help to relieve the tension on the entire system at its point of origin. Here we may consider other factors which affect the relations among employees along the flow of work: status, sex relations, and layout and equipment.

I would propose the hypothesis that relations among individuals along the flow of work will run more smoothly when those of higher status are in a position to originate for those of lower status in the organization and, conversely, that frictions will be observed more often when lower-status individuals seek to originate for those of higher status. (This is, of course, by no means a complete explanation of the friction or adjustment we observe.)

While more data are needed on this point, we made certain observations which tend to bear out the hypothesis. For example, in one kitchen we observed supplymen seeking to originate action (in getting food supplies) for cooks who were older, of greater seniority, more highly skilled, and much higher paid. This relationship was one of the sore points of the organization. Still, we discovered that there had been one supplyman who got along well with the cooks. When we got his story, we found that he had related himself to the cooks quite differently from the other supplymen. He sought to avoid calling orders to the cooks and instead just asked them to call him when a certain item was ready. In this way, he allowed them to increase the frequency of their origination for him, and according to all accounts, he got better cooperation and service from the cooks than any other supplyman.

Much the same point is involved in the relations between the sexes. In our society most men grow up to be comfortable in a relationship in which they originate for women and to be uneasy, if not more seriously disturbed, when the originations go in the other direction. It is therefore a matter of some consequence how the sexes are distributed along the flow of work. On this question we gave particular attention to the dining room–service-pantry and dining room–bar relationships.

In the dining room–pantry situation there are four possible types of relationship by sex: waiter-counterman, waiter–pantry girl, waitress–pantry girl, and waitress-counterman. We were not able to give much attention to the first two types, but we did make intensive studies of two restaurants illustrating the third and fourth types. Ideally, for scientific purposes, we would want to hold everything else constant except for these sex differences. We had no such laboratory, but the two restaurants were nevertheless closely comparable. They were both large, busy establishments, operating on several floors, and serving the same price range of food in the same section of the city.

Perhaps the chief differences were found in the dining room–pantry relationship itself. In restuaruant A, waitresses gave their orders orally to the pantry girls. On the main serving floor of restaurant B, waitresses wrote out slips which they placed on spindles on top of a warming compartment separating them from the countermen. The men picked off the order slips, filled them, and put the plates in the compartment where the waitresses picked them up. In most cases there was no direct face-to-face interaction between waitresses and countermen, and, indeed, the warming compartment was so high that only the taller waitresses could see over its top.

These differences were not unrelated to the problems of sex in the flow of work. One of the countermen in restaurant B told us that, in all his years' experience, he had never before worked in such a wonderful place. Most workers who express such sentiments talk about their relations with their superiors or with fellow employees on the same job or, perhaps, about wages, but this man had nothing to say about any of those subjects. He would discuss only the barrier that protected him from the waitresses. He described earlier experiences in other restaurants where there had been no such barrier and let us know that to be left out in the open where all the girls call their orders in was an ordeal to which no man should be subjected. In such places, he said, there was constant wrangling.

This seems to check with experience in the industry. While we observed frictions arising between waitresses and pantry girls, such a relationship can at least be maintained with relative stability. On the other hand, it is difficult to prevent blowups between countermen and waitresses when the girls call their orders in. Most restaurants consciously or unconsciously interpose certain barriers to cut down waitress origination of action for countermen. It may be a warming compartment, as in this case, or as we observed in another restaurant, there was a man pantry supervisor who collected the order slips from the waitresses as they came in and passed them out to the countermen. There are a variety of ways of meeting the problem, but they all seem to involve this principle of social insulation.

The rule that all orders must be written also serves to cut down on interaction between waitresses and countermen, but this in itself is not always enough to eliminate friction. Where there is no physical barrier, there can be trouble unless the men who are on the receiving end of the orders work out their own system of getting out from under. Such systems we observed at one bar and at one of the serving counters in restaurant B. The counter, in this case, was only waist high. While the girls wrote out their orders, they were also able to try to spur the men on orally, and there was much pulling and hauling on this point both at the bar and at the pantry counter.

The men who did not get along in this relationship played a waiting game. That is, when the girls seemed to be putting on special pressure for speed, they would very obviously slow down or else even turn away from the bar or counter and not go back to work until the offending waitresses just left their order slips and stepped away themselves. Thus they originated action for the waitresses. While this defensive maneuver provided the men with some emotional satisfaction, it slowed down the service, increased the frustrations of the waitresses, and thus built up tensions, to be released in larger explosions later.

One bartender and one counterman not only enjoyed their work but were considered by waitresses to be highly efficient and pleasant to deal with. Both of them had independently worked out the same system of handling the job when the rush hour got under way. Instead of handling each order slip in turn as it was handed to them (thus responding to each individual waitress), they would collect several slips that came in at about the same time, lay them out on the counter before them, and fill the orders in whatever order seemed most efficient. For example, the bartender would go through the slips to see how many "Martinis," "Old Fashions," and so on were required. Then he would make up all the "Martinis" at once before he went on to the next drink.

When the work was done this way, the girl first in was not necessarily first out with her tray, but the system was so efficient that it speeded up the work on the average, and the girls were content to profit this way in the long run. The men described the system to us simply in terms of efficiency; but note that, in organizing their jobs, they had changed quantitatively the relations they had with the waitresses. Instead of responding to each waitress, they were originating action for the girls (filling their orders as the men saw fit and sending them out when the men were ready).

Along with our consideration of layout and equipment in the flow of work, we should give attention to the communication system. Where the restaurant operates on one floor, the relations at each step in the flow can be worked out on a face-to-face basis. There may be friction, but there is also the possibility of working out many problems on a friendly, informal basis.

When a restaurant operates on two or more floors, as many large ones do, face-to-face interaction must be supplemented by mechanical means of communication. We saw three such mechanical means substituted for direct interaction, and each one had its difficulties.

People can try to coordinate their activities through the house telephone. Without facial expressions and gestures, there is a real loss of understanding, for we do not generally respond solely to people's voices. Still, this might serve reasonably well, if the connection between kitchen and pantry could be kept constantly open. At least in the one restaurant where we gave this subject special attention, that solution was out of the question, as one call from kitchen to pantry tied up the whole house phone system and nobody could call the manager, the cashier, or anybody else on this system as long as another call was being made. Consequently, the telephone could be used only to supplement other mechanical aids (in this case, the telautograph).

The public address system has the advantage over the telephone in that it can be used all the time, but it has the great disadvantage of being a very noisy instrument. Busy kitchens and service pantries are noisy places at best, so that the addition of a public address system might be most unwelcome. We do not yet know enough of the effect of noise upon the human nervous system to evaluate the instrument from this point of view, but we should recognize the obvious fact that surrounding noise affects the ability of people to communicate with each other and becomes therefore a problem in human relations.

The telautograph makes no noise and can be used at all times, yet it has its own disadvantages. Here we have an instrument in the service pantry and one in the kitchen. As the pantry supplyman writes his order, it appears simultaneously on the kitchen telautograph. The kitchen's replies are transmitted upstairs in the same way. The machine records faithfully, but it does not solve the problem of meaning in interaction. We may pass over the problem of illegibility of handwriting, although we have seen that cause serious difficulties. The more interesting problem is this: How urgent is an order?

When the rush hour comes along, with customers pushing waitresses, waitresses pushing pantry girls, and pantry girls pushing supplymen, the supplyman is on the end of the line so far as face-to-face interaction is concerned, and he is likely to get nervous and excited. He may then put in a larger order than he will actually use or write "Rush" above many of his orders. If he overorders, the leftovers come back to the kitchen at the end of the meal, and the kitchen supplymen and cooks learn, thus, that the pantry supplyman did not really know how much he needed. They take this into account in interpreting his future orders. And, when everything is marked "Rush," the kitchen supplymen cannot tell the difference between the urgent and not so urgent ones. Thus the word becomes meaningless, and communication deteriorates. Stuck in this impasse, the pantry supplyman may abandon his machine and dash down to the kitchen to try to snatch the order himself. The kitchen people will block this move whenever they can, so, more often, the pantry supplyman appeals to his supervisor. In the heat of the rush hour, we have seen pantry supervisors running up and down stairs, trying to get orders, trying to find out what is holding up things in the kitchen. Since they have supervisor status, the kitchen workers do not resist them openly, but the invasion of an upstairs supervisor tends to disrupt relations in the kitchen. It adds to the pressures there, for it comes as an emergency that lets everybody know that the organization is not functioning smoothly.

It is not the function of this article to work out possible solutions to this problem of communication. I am concerned here with pointing out a significant new area for sociological investigation: the effects on human relations of various mechanical systems of communication. It is difficult enough to coordinate an organization in which the key people in the supervisory hierarchy are in direct face-to-face relations. It is a much more difficult problem (and one as yet little understood) when the coordination must be achieved in large measure through mechanical communication systems.

Implications for Theory and Methodology

In presenting our observations on the restaurant industry, I have discussed formal structure, quantitative measures of interaction, symbols in relations to interaction, attitudes and interaction, and layout and equipment (including mechanical systems of communication). Data of these categories must be fitted together. The uses of each type of data may be summarized here.

Formal Structure

We have ample data to show that the formal structure (the official allocation of positions) does not *determine* the pattern of human relations in an organization. Nevertheless, it does set certain limits upon the shape of that pattern. Thus, to analyze the human problems of a restaurant, it is necessary to outline its structure in terms of length of hierarchy, divisions into departments, and flow of work (as done in the five stages above).

Quantitative Measures of Interaction

Within the limits set by the formal structure, the relations among members of the organization may fall into a variety of patterns, each of which is subject to change.

The pattern we observe we call the *social system.* A social system is made up of *interdependent* parts. The parts are the *relations* of individuals in their various positions to each other. This is simply a first description of a social system, but there are important theoretical and practical conclusions which flow from it.

The relations of individuals to one another are subject to *measurement,* sufficient to allow them to be compared and classified. We can, for example, count the number of times that a waitress originates action for her customers compared with the number of times they originate it for her in a given period and observe how often she originates action for her supervisor and how often the supervisor does so for her, and so on, through the other relations in the system. So far, mathematically precise measurements of interaction have only been made in laboratory situations involving interviewer and interviewee.[5] Nevertheless, in the present state of our knowledge, we can get, through interviewing and observation, quantitative data which, though only approximate, are sufficiently accurate to allow us to predict the course of developments or explain how certain problems have arisen and point the way to their possible solution.

As the terms are used here, *interaction, origination,* and *response* are abstractions without content. That is, they are indices which have no reference to either the symbols used or the subjective reactions felt

---

[5] Eliot D. Chapple, with the collaboration of Conrad M. Arensberg, "Measuring Human Relations: An Introduction to the Study of the Interaction of Individuals," *Genetic Psychology Monographs,* no. 22, (1940); Eliot D. Chapple and Carleton S. Coon, *Principles of Anthropology* (New York: Henry Holt, 1941), esp. first four chapters; Eliot D. Chapple and Erich Lindemann, "Clinical Implications of Measurement of Interaction Rates in Psychiatric Interviews," *Applied Anthropology,* 1, (January–March 1942): 1–12.

by the interacting individuals. Such measures do not, of course, tell us all it is useful to know of human relations. Indeed, many students will think it absurd to believe that any useful data can come from abstractions which leave out the "content" of human relations. To them I can only say that science is, in part, a process of abstraction, which always seems to take us away from the "real world." The value of such abstractions can be determined only by testing them in research to see whether they enable us better to control and predict social events.

Since the social system is made up of *interdependent relations*, it follows that a change in one part of the system necessarily has repercussions in other parts of the system. For example, a change in origin-response ratio between waitresses and supervisor necessarily affects the waitress-customer and waitress-service-pantry-girl relations, and changes in those parts lead to other changes in the system. Therefore, in order to study the social system or to deal with it effectively, it is necessary to discover the *pattern* of relations existing at a given time and to observe changes within that pattern. The nature of the interdependence of the parts of the system can be discovered only through observing how a change in Part A is followed by change in Part B, is followed by change in Part C, etc. Therefore, social systems must be studied *through time*. A static picture of the social structure of an organization is of little value. Science requires that we develop methods of study and tools of analysis to deal with constantly changing relations.

Symbols in Relation to Interaction

We cannot be content simply with quantitative descriptions of interaction. We need to know why *A* responds to *B* in one situation and not in another, or why *A* responds to *B* and not to *C*. In part, this is a matter of habituation, for we respond to the people we are accustomed to responding to and in the sorts of situations to which we are accustomed. But we must go beyond that to explain the development of new patterns and changes in old patterns of interaction.

We observe that individuals respond to certain symbols in interaction. I have discussed here status and sex as symbols affecting interaction (the problems of the originating from below of action for high status individuals or by woman for man).

I have noted some problems in language symbols in the discussion of mechanical means of communication. That leaves the whole field of symbols in face-to-face interaction untouched, so that it represents only the barest beginning of an attempted formulation of the relations between symbols of communication and interaction.

Especially in economic institutions, it is important to examine the bearing of *economic symbols*[6] on interaction, but this is a large subject and can only be mentioned here.

As we analyze social systems, symbols should always be seen in terms of their effects upon interaction. They are *incentives* or *inhibitors* to interaction with specific people in certain social situations. Thus, to put it in practical terms, the manager of an organization will find it useful to know both the pattern of interaction which will bring about harmonious relations and also how to use symbols so as to achieve that pattern.

Attitudes and Interaction

Changes in relations of individuals to one another are accompanied by changes in their *attitudes* toward one another and toward their organizations. In recent years we have developed excellent methods for attitude measurement, but the measurement in itself never tells us how the attitudes came about. The whole experience of our research program leads us to believe that the dynamics of attitude formation and change can best be worked out as we correlate attitudes with human relations in the organizations we study.

Layout and Equipment

Here the sociologist is not directly concerned with the problems of the mechanical or industrial engineer. He does not undertake to say which machine or which arrangement of work space and machines will be most productively efficient. However, he cannot help but observe that, for example, the height of the barrier between waitresses and countermen or the nature of the mechanical communication system have important effects upon human relations. Only as these effects are observed do the physical conditions come in for sociological analysis. (Of course, human relations have a bearing upon efficiency, but the sociologist, if he tackles the problem of efficiency, but the sociologist, if he tackles the problem of efficiency, uses types of data and schemes of analysis quite different from those used by the engineer.)

A few years ago there was a great debate raging: statistics versus the case study. That debate is no longer waged publicly, but it still troubles many of us. On the one hand, we see that an individual case study, skillfully analyzed, yields interesting insights—but not scientific knowledge. On the other hand, we find that nearly all statistical work in sociol-

---

[6]See Whyte's "Economics and Human Relations in Industry" to be published in *Industrial and Labor Relations Review*.

ogy has dealt with the characteristics of aggregates: How much of a given phenomenon is to be found in a given population? Such an approach does not tell us anything about the relations among the individuals making up that population. And yet, if we are to believe the textbooks, the relations among individuals, the *group* life they lead, are the very heart of sociology.

So let us have more individual case studies, but let us also place the individual in the social systems in which he participates and note how his attitudes and goals change with changes in the relations he experiences. And let us have more quantitative work, but let us at least bring it to bear upon the heart of sociology, measuring the relations among individuals in their organizations.

6
Organizing Everyday Life

Most Americans live in urban cultural settings. Standing in line, or *queuing,* is a ubiquitous feature of this setting. Although usually thought of as a transitory phenomenon, a mere prelude to some main event, queuing involves a form of social organization in and of itself. Leon Mann describes kinds of lines and the typical behavior of persons waiting in line. He offers a characterization of the queuer and suggests interpretations for all these observations on lines. His article illustrates the use of a guiding concept to sensitize description. His observations center around a few questions concerning the operation of the human mind in this highly specialized setting.

Learning to Live With Lines
Leon Mann

Chances are that today you spent a few frustrating minutes standing in line to get a seat in a cafeteria, to buy a train ticket, or to get tickets for a popular movie. If you did not actually stand while waiting for service, you probably were in your car waiting to get through the tollbooths, off the freeway, and into the crowded parking lot near your university. Perhaps you queued to make a telephone call or waited in line at the checkout counter of the library. With the growth of large cities and the growing demand for all kinds of services, queues have become commonplace, unavoidable, and for some, a way of life. For some years mathe-

From *Urbanman: The Psychology of Urban Survival,* ed. John Helmer and Neil A. Eddington (New York: Free Press, 1973). Reprinted by permission.

maticians in the field of queuing theory have been describing queues in terms of their causes, the special form they take, and the interesting way they build up and shrink (see Liebowitz 1968). Operations researchers concerned more with the problem of shortening queues have tried to control them with an eye to improving economy and efficiency of service. And social scientists, always interested in the way in which man adapts to his changing environment, have begun to investigate how city dwellers learn to live with them (Mann 1969, 1970).

Four Kinds of Queues

The common or garden variety of queue, *a single line with a single server*, can be found in almost every cafeteria, greasy spoon, and airport. Its strength lies in the sense of camaraderie which sometimes develops between adjacent queuers as they complain about the slow service. For the cafeteria owner, its advantage lies in the customer with the big eyes and the "smorgasbord" appetite. Restauranteurs believe the big lineup will eventually disappear; the hungry customer will punch a series of buttons, the orders will be dispensed automatically and will be ready and waiting by the time he manages to find his wallet. It is possible, of course, to have queues for which there is no actual service. For example, in waiting lines for washrooms and water fountains, "self-service" is the rule.

A variation on the single-line–single-server theme is to be found in large supermarkets, airport checkin counters, and small-town banks, where a *series of lines* are routed to a number of different servers. This system can produce a great deal of frustration. The real loser is the unwary customer who has yet to recognize the slow tellers in the bank and the tortoises at the checkins and checkouts. People in other lines come and go while the checker searches for his supply of nickels, or tries to figure out where he left his pencil. This system is at its worst when the person up front produces a piggy bank full of pennies or the lady at the head of the line suddenly drops a dozen eggs on the check out conveyor belt. Then there is nothing you can do except fume while people in other lines smirk at your misfortune. But there is some advantage in a system which includes a diversified series of lines. It permits the setting up of one or two express lines which provide quick service to customers who are fortunate enough to have only a few items to check out.

The frustrations of the multiple-line–multiple-server system can be combated by the more efficient *one-line–multiple-server* system. This system already exists in barbershops with four chairs, British banks, and their larger Manhattan counterparts. There is a single "feeder" line which branches at the service counter to each of four or five clerks. As each clerk finishes serving a customer he cries "next please!" and the next one in the "feeder" line steps up to take his turn. The basic system is sometimes elaborated by installation of a "Take-A-Check" or a "Take-A-Tab" number dispenser. On arriving at the store the customer takes a number, takes a seat, and waits patiently until his number is called. The system works well in the Eastern Airlines office in San Francisco, but poorly at the photography supplies counter of the Harvard Co-op (it seems that Co-op clerks abhor numbers). The system can also be a little tough on the worst barber in the barbershop; if his hoarse cry of "next please!" evokes no visible response from customers waiting for a hair cut, his future in the shop is very uncertain.

Exotic *station-to-station* lines, sometimes called "interconnected" queues, are to be found in most hospitals and some Moscow stores. The customer moves from one line to the next in an ever mounting crescendo of impatience and frustration. For example, a shopper for pickled herring in *Gastronom*, the Moscow food store, must work her way through a queue to the counter where they sell herring. A clerk tells her the price, and she walks across the store to the appropriate cashier's window, tells the cashier she wants herring, pays for it, and receives a receipt slip. Then she must go back to the counter, receipt in hand, all set to pick up the wrapped herring, praying that they have not sold out.

Patients at Manhattan's Metropolitan Hospital are constantly exposed to the rigors of station-to-station queueing. This is what happened to Mason Roberts when he appeared at the Metropolitan's outpatient clinic one afternoon in March 1969 and complained of stomach pains (*New York Times* March 26, 1969). First, he lined up at the central registration window to get forms for the window-6 line, which permitted him to join the chest X-ray line, which set up a wait for the doctor. Somewhere along the line he also queued to pay his bill and to make another appointment. The six different lines took over an hour; the visit with the doctor—who told Roberts he was eating too many spicy foods—took exactly nine seconds. Roberts's experience is fairly typical of what happens in most large city hospitals. Much worse queues can be found both inside and outside the welfare centers of large cities. On a normal day a welfare applicant or recipient can expect to wait in a series of lines for at least two hours before getting to see a caseworker at Manhattan's Gramercy Welfare Center (*New York Times* April 25, 1970).

New York, City of Queues

Beyond a shadow of doubt, New York is the uncrowned queuing capital of the U.S. Over the years there have been some memorable lines on Broadway, outside the Met Opera and the Metropolitan Museum, at Madison Square Garden, and outside Yankee Stadium.

New Yorkers turn out in force when there is an astronaut to be greeted or a hero to be farewelled. During the twenty-four hours when the body of Senator Robert Kennedy lay in St. Patrick's Cathedral (June 1968), thousands of New Yorkers in lines over one mile long waited patiently to file past the casket. The average wait in line was seven hours, but many who could stay only the one hour of their lunch break, and knew they had no chance of viewing the casket, stood in line as a mark of respect for the slain leader.

On February 7, 1963, despite rain, slush, and bone-chilling cold, a crowd of 23,872 New Yorkers queued up at the Metropolitan Museum of Art to get a glimpse of the Mona Lisa. The lines that day stretched over three city blocks. During its three and one-half week sojourn at the Metropolitan, half a million people passed in front of the Mona Lisa. When *I Am Curious (Yellow)* opened at the Rendezvous theater on West Fifty-seventh Street on March 10, 1969, it quickly drew large crowds and long queues; people were queuing six deep for one and a half blocks for the evening sessions, and lines for the 10:00 A.M. session were forming at 7:00 in the morning. Waiting lines for Broadway hit shows are often themselves smash hits. *South Pacific, My Fair Lady,* and *Hello Dolly* drew remarkably long lines during their record runs. When the box office for the musical *Coco* opened on November 3, 1969, the line stretched along Fifty-first Street, turned the corner onto Broadway, headed uptown, and finally came to an end half way up Fifty-second Street.

It would appear that theater owners have caught onto the idea that a long line of customers in front of their movie house can be good for business. In *Esquire* magazine (December, 1969), movie critic Jacob Brackman observed that many Manhattan movie houses, especially the ones screening "art" movies, were deliberately creating lines on the sidewalk out front, although half the seats inside were still empty. In this age of popular causes, a long visible line of eager customers is undeniable evidence of success and provides a free advertisement to any passerby. Even if the movie line is somewhat out in the suburbs, well-removed from the public eye, a shrewd distributor can bring it to the public's attention. The ad for the movie *Monterey Pop,* when it was running on Long Island, featured a large, compact photograph of three bulging lines of teenagers standing outside the theater.

How does the interminable wait to get inside affect the long-suffering moviegoer? Here, too, the theater owners have modern psychology on their side. Several years ago Leon Festinger (1957), a Stanford social psychologist, carried out a series of studies to test his theory of cognitive dissonance. Festinger and his colleagues found that people who become entangled in a dull, boring task, and for no good reason, tend to reduce their feelings of dysphoria (called "cognitive dissonance") by rationalizing that the task was really quite interesting. This can be applied to the customer who has waited for two hours in a long, cold movie line only to find himself viewing a dull, boring movie. Unless he decides to ask for his money back, the best way to throw off a painful bout of cognitive dissonance is to start believing that the movie really was rich in hidden meanings and stunning in its visual effects. If the customer can enlist some social support for his marathon wait by convincing friends and neighbors about the greatness of the movie, cognitive dissonance can be reduced even further.

Not everyone is sensitive to cognitive dissonance, and those who are do not always attempt to reduce it in a way which drums up business for the theater. Even then, a long wait on the sidewalk need not be harmful for business. For some customers, the relief of getting out of the cold and finding a seat is well worth the price of a ticket.

The Optimistic Queuer

Why do people stand in line when their chances of getting to see a hit play or movie range from poor to hopeless? This puzzle is of more than academic interest, for it involves a strange quirk of human behavior. When *My Fair Lady* opened at the Mark Hellinger Theater in 1956, a line would appear nightly outside the theater to wait for the box office to open at 10:00 in the morning. Then thirty standing-room tickets for that night's performance would go on sale. But invariably at dawn, four hours before the opening of the ticket box, there would be many more people in line than tickets available. For some peculiar reason the hopeful failed to appreciate that their chances were really hopeless.

Together with Keith Taylor, a psychologist at the University of Melbourne, I decided to investigate why latecomers in long queues are optimistic about their chances of success (Mann and Taylor 1969).

Our first study involved twenty-two queues of football fans outside the Melbourne Football Stadium, in August 1966. Going on the official notices about the number of tickets on sale, only the first 140 in each queue were likely to get tickets. But, in some of the lines, there were well over 200 people. We decided to interview every tenth person and ask each one to estimate how many people stood ahead of him in line. People in the very first part of the line, as we expected, estimated the length of the queue and their chances of success quite accurately. Then, after the thirtieth person in line, there was a consistent tendency to *over* estimate the number in front, and this occurred all the way up to person 130, almost exactly the point at which the supply of tickets was likely to run out. After the "critical point" the mood of the queuers began to change; people consistently *under* estimated the size of the crowd in front. In other words, they started getting optimistic precisely at the point where they should have given up and gone home. The latecomers' unwarranted optimism seemed to us like a desperate subconscious maneuver to justify standing in line, a case of unintentionally deluding oneself that the line is shorter than it really is. We called this interpretation of the latecomers' optimism the wish fulfillment hypothesis.

We decided to investigate whether this same phenomenon could be found in very long and very short lines. Observations of a single queue at the Collingwood Football Ground several weeks later showed that the point at which the supply of tickets was likely to run out—position 500—again marked the point at which unjustified optimism began. Next we interviewed 66 small boys in line for free Batman shirts, outside a movie house in downtown Melbourne. To attract a large juvenile audience the management had announced that twenty-five Batman shirts would be given away to the first 25 queuers at the morning matinee. Once again, queuers after the critical point tended to underestimate their position in line.

An alternate explanation for this unbridled optimism is the self-selection interpretation. It holds that a difference might exist between the kinds of people who are found in queues before and after the critical point. Early-comers are by nature cautious and pessimistic, while latecomers are adventurous and optimistic. A frivolous variant of the self-selection hypothesis is that the people who join a line after a critical point must be either myopic or psychotic, since normal people give up and go home.

For our final foray into the psychology of latecomers, we arranged to take over a high school for a morning and form the 521 students into two parallel lines. This feat was managed with the cooperation of the principal and staff of Wattle Park High School, Victoria, Australia. Both lines were told that the experiment was a study of attitudes toward queuing, but our hidden purpose was much more devious. We wanted to create an "experimental" line, in which all of the members knew that a valued commodity (chocolate bars) would be distributed to the first half of the line, and a "control" line, in which the members had no idea that chocolate, indeed any commodity, would be made available. We reasoned that if the wish-fulfillment hypothesis is the correct explanation for the latecomers' optimism, then any tendency to give optimistic estimates should be confined almost entirely to the experimental line, and only after the critical point. While there was a tendency for "latecomers" in the chocolate line to underestimate numbers in front, our findings were not nearly so impressive as in the earlier studies.

But we were not inclined to feel pessimistic about this turn of events. We concluded that latecomers in the chocolate line do not experience much pressure to justify standing in line since, in the first place, they were coerced into this hopeless cause by a pair of psychologists. Moreover, in comparison to football tickets and Batman T-shirts, a ten-cent chocolate bar is not quite the stuff delusional fantasies are made of. . . . When the study was over, we fully debriefed the school about the real purpose of our experiment, and for good measure treated every student to a well-earned chocolate bar.

Serving Time in Queues

"First-come first-served." the basic principle of queuing, is an example of what George Homans (1961), a Harvard sociologist, calls the rule of distributive justice. If a person is willing to invest large amounts of time and suffering in an activity, people who believe there should be an appropriate fit between effort and reward will respect his right to priority. In most queues there is a direct correspondence between inputs (time spent waiting) and outcomes (preferential service). The rule of distributive justice is modified in marathon queues, however, because the queuers need to absent themselves from the line from time to time. Continuous residence in a long, overnight line would impose terrible hardship on the queuers, and so they come to an informal understanding about the minimum inputs of time they must spend to validate occupancy of a position. From our observations of football queues in Melbourne and from anecdotal evidence, it is clear that rules regarding the serving of time constitute the core of queue culture.

Every August in Melbourne, thousands of football fans form mammoth lines outside the Melbourne Stadium to buy tickets for the equivalent of the "World Series" of Australian-rules football. Over the past few years, the social psychology students of the University of Melbourne have descended on the lines to make observations and ask questions.

From our interviews and observations we have learned that although arrangements made to control behavior in the queue are informal, they are clearly identifiable. Brief "time-outs," or leaves of absence from the queue, are accomplished by two universally recognized procedures. One technique is the "shift" system, in which the person joins the queue as part of a small group and takes his turn in spending one hour "on" to every three hours "off." The second technique is designed specially for people who come alone and who for various reasons need to leave the line briefly. They "stake a claim" by leaving some item of personal property such as a labeled box, folding chair, or sleeping bag. The rule in leaving position markers is that one must not be absent for longer than periods of two to three hours. If the norm is broken, the person cannot gain reentry into the queue, and many return to find their property smashed or thrown aside. This actually happened in August 1966, when irate latecomers noticed that many people in the middle of the queue had not made an appearance for most of the day and spontaneously seized their boxes and burnt them.

In some marathon queues, "time-outs" are regulated by an ingenious roll-call system. The weekly line for tickets at the Metropolitan Opera House in New York is notable for this kind of arrangement. According to a story in the *New Yorker* (January 14, 1967), the lines begin to form the day before the box office opens. The first person in line is the unofficial "keeper of the list," who registers applicants in order of arrival and assigns numbers. Ordinarily, queuers are required to report for "roll call" every two hours throughout the day and night, although the keeper of the list can and does vary this requirement. Otherwise they are free to wander about or go home. Anyone who misses a roll call has his name struck off the list and must start again from the end of the line. Although the Metropolitan security men keep an eye on the proceedings, it is the "keeper of the list" who keeps order, calls off names, pushes people into place, and hands out numbered tags which are recognized at the ticket office. Nobody seems to know how one gets to be appointed "keeper of the list," or if they know, they are not saying. Apparently the system works well, because most people know the rules and there are very few attempts to jump the queue.

For the 1968 season the Metropolitan people decided to do away with the overnight part of the queue (as a precaution against the possibility of nocturnal violence and robbery), and the system was modified to cut the amount of time actually spent in line while an increase was made in the frequency of the roll calls. The new system, as described by one of my students (a devoted opera buff), consisted of a series of weekend queue reunions. "People check in on Friday night and their names are taken and they are given numbers. They come back on Saturday and check in again with the head of the line. On Sunday the people meet in a park across the street from Lincoln Center at about 7:00 A.M. and check in again. At 8:00 they cross the street to the Met and wait there until 9:00, when the Met hands out its own tags. Then everyone breaks for breakfast and comes back sometime before 11:00 to wait for the box office to open." In 1969, much to the sorrow of opera buffs and queue addicts, there was no Metropolitan Opera season and no opera queues.

The Metropolitan Opera line is a good example of the principle of keeping the queue "honest" by ensuring that only the dedicated, determined few who are prepared to sacrifice sleep and comfort qualify for the privilege of buying tickets. The imposition of hardship ensures that the casual passerby or the less devoted opera fan cannot claim priority on the basis of order of arrival alone, and so cannot gain an advantage over the genuine opera buff. The "roll-call" system illustrates the basic principle that a place in line must be "earned," and to earn it inputs of time and effort are necessary.

Japanese queues for the purchase of home sites provide another example of the roll-call system at work. In Tokyo, where home sites are in chronic short supply, mammoth lines form outside real-estate-company offices whenever it is announced that a parcel of land is about to go on sale. These lines, numbering hundreds of people, will sometimes last for more than two weeks. The *Melbourne Age* (November 11, 1969) has described how the Japanese organize a roll-call system. Soon after they arrive, the queuers elect a committee from among their numbers. This committee acts as a kind of Queue Self-Government Association which compiles a list of people in order of their arrival and fixes the number of roll calls to be held each day. The president of the Queue Association calls the roll—sometimes three times, occasionally seven times, a day. Anyone who misses the roll call loses his place. Similar arrangements for regulating time spent in and out of line are to be found in marathon queues in many large cities.

Prequeues

But mammoth queues which last for a week or two tend to be frowned upon by city authorities. Such queues tend to clutter sidewalks, pose a health hazard, and sometimes require continual surveillance by police and officials to prevent outbreaks of violence.

In the Melbourne football queues of 1965, thousands of people waited for tickets, some of them for over a week, in mud and drizzling rain. Queuers erected a shanty town of tents and caravans, and conditions rapidly became squalid and unhygienic. The following year, to prevent a recurrence of the shantytown, the mayor of Melbourne banned queues outside the stadium until twenty hours before ticket sales started. But football fans, anxious to be sure of getting tickets, spontaneously formed an unofficial prequeue several hundred yards away from the stadium many hours before the official line was allowed to start. When the barricades were lowered by officials and queuing began, people folded their camp chairs and, keeping the line intact, filed in perfect order to the ticket windows to commence the official twenty-hour wait. The formation of a prequeue meant that people did not have to converge on the ticket boxes all at the same time, thus preventing chaos and the possibility of violence.

In Havana lines at the post office, outside ice-cream parlors, and in front of restaurants are commonplace. Sometimes the police will not allow a line to form too much in advance in order to keep the sidewalks clear. The Cubans meet this challenge by forming a prequeue. They station themselves across the street or down the block from the ice cream parlor and check as they arrive as to who preceded them. When formal lining up becomes permitted, the underground line emerges and takes up its official wait.

Prequeues represent an ingenious solution to the problem of how to maintain order when a large throng gathers before the official starting time.

Queue Jumping

One of the biggest headaches associated with life in a queue is safeguarding it against the activities of would-be queue jumpers.

Before we discuss how people actually deal with queue jumpers, try answering this question, an item from the Allport Test of Ascendance-Submission:

> Someone tries to push ahead of you in line. You have been waiting for some time, and can't wait much longer. Suppose the intruder is the same sex as yourself; do you usually:
>
> remonstrate with the intruder...?
> "look daggers" at the intruder or make clearly audible comments to your neighbor...?
> decide not to wait and go away...?
> do nothing...?

The word "remonstrate" sounds a little archaic these days, but in 1928, when Gordon Allport devised the Ascendance-Submission test, it was a perfectly fashionable word. Scores on the A-S scale enabled Allport to decide whether a person was ascendant or submissive, whether he would try to control or dominate a situation, or prefer to yield the right of way.

Several years ago the Ascendance-Submission test was given to 60 Harvard men and a similar number of male students at the University of Melbourne, Australia. Responses to the item about the queue jumper make for some interesting comparisons.

> Forty-two percent of Harvards and 55 percent of Melburnians said they would "remonstrate"
> Thirty-two percent of Harvards and 27 percent of Melburnians said they would "look daggers"
> Two percent of Harvards and 1 percent of Melburnians said they would be inclined to "go away"
> Three percent of both Harvards and Melburnians said they would probably "do nothing"

It is apparent that the Harvard and the Melbourne response is rather passive. What emerges from responses to the test items is evidence perhaps that many young people prefer Gandhian nonviolence over physical aggression as a modus vivendi in waiting lines.

Interviews we have carried out with students from colleges in the Boston area tend to support this preference for nonviolence in dealing with queue jumpers. In November 1969, we spent a morning at Boston Garden surveying the line for tickets to a Rolling Stones concert. There were about 600 long-haired, bearded, and beaded college students waiting for tickets to go on sale at 10:00 A.M. One of the questions we asked was, "What would you do if someone tried to push in front of you?" The answers that morning spoke mainly of peace. "If they want it that bad, let them get in front of me." But some of the queuers seemed ambivalent in their attitudes. One Tufts student, trying to be magnanimous, asserted, "I would tell him to leave, and make it sound serious enough so he wouldn't want to stand around . . . but if he didn't leave, I'd let him stay, because then he'd be spiting himself. But knowing myself, I might just push him out."

Generations of psychologists have long agonized over the apparent discrepancy between people's statements of what they think they will do in a situation and what they actually do. Nowhere is this discrepancy more apparent than in the football waiting line. When quizzed about their preferred ways of handling queue jumpers, football fans, unlike college students, almost always vow they would resort to physical violence to throw out the intruder. But when the queue jumper actually makes his move, it is painfully obvious that the offended victim is more inclined to do nothing.

Why do queuers fail to act together to kick out the queue jumper? The answer to this knotty question lies partially in the varying interests and characteristics of people in different parts of the queue. Naturally, people at the front don't care much about the people who push in behind them, unless queue jumping is so widespread that the entire line becomes vulnerable. For others there is the thought that the intruder might be so desperate that a struggle might bring about injury and damage. There is the fear, too, that if everyone resorts to physical violence, the illusion that the queue is for the most part well controlled and orderly is quickly shattered; once this happens, there is a danger of complete disintegration.

But, if queuers are reluctant to use physical force to discourage intruders, they have other techniques available for guarding their positions. A barricade of strategically placed barriers, camp cots, and boxes can be effective protection. Keeping close interpersonal distance helps keep people warm and also serves to maintain the "territory" against would-be infiltrators. At times of maximum danger, and in the few moments before the ticket box opens, there is always a visible bunching together, or shrinkage, in the length of a line—literally a closing of the ranks. At the head of the line, suspicious-looking outsiders are intimidated by loud catcalls and jeering. Ordinarily this works best during daylight; the sight and sound of fifty jeering people usually inhibits even the boldest queue jumper. But in the dark, when the queue relaxes its vigilance, social pressure tends to be less effective.

It seems puzzling, but it is a fact, that the favorite hunting ground for the queue jumper lies somewhere near the tail of the queue. If someone is going to risk pushing in, why not try at the front, where the rewards are greater and the wait is shorter? Here we must bear in mind that the people at the front almost always belong to a strong, well-knit clique and are ready for police action, either because they came together at the outset, or because they have had time to establish a strong sense of community. The latecomers at the end, alienated and disorganized, are far less able to defend themselves against predators. Then again, the queue jumper risks a lot less toward the end of the line, as fewer people are put out by the violation.

Another reason for the high incidence of queue crashing toward the back is the difficulty the latecomers have in spotting an illegal act of entry from the somewhat more acceptable act of place keeping. It is always hard to decide whether a person who marches confidently into a line is attempting to crash the queue, or is merely joining his group. Thus, latecomers are usually reluctant to challenge anyone who walks into a line unless a furtive manner and a pair of shifty eyes mark the person as a nervous, inexperienced queue jumper. Then the queue rarely acts together to expel the violator, but the onus for kicking him out falls squarely on the shoulders of the person who "let him in"; those further back may jeer, catcall, and whistle, but the immediate victim is expected to get rid of the crasher. The reasoning seems to be that the victim was careless in guarding his territory, so it is up to him to handle the situation quietly and efficiently.

Queue Businesses

Whenever demand exceeds supply, it is almost inevitable that businesses associated with ticket speculation will crop up and flourish both inside and outside the queue.

Two major kinds of professional activity can be observed in queues for hard-to-get tickets. Big-time operators are superefficient entrepreneurs who hire dozens of people to buy up tickets for the black market. This kind of business has been going on for a long time. When Charles Dickens toured America in 1842 to read from his works, enterprising speculators made a fortune scalping tickets to an insatiable public. Speculators engaged teams of up to fifty people to take places in the two-dollar-ticket queue; then having bought up the choice tickets, resold them for as much as twenty-six dollars each. Small-time operators, the amateur scalpers, are often university students who resell their two or three tickets to the highest bidder before a football game. A wealthy patron who neglects to buy his seat through regular channels sometimes commissions a small-time operator to stand in line for tickets. Speculation in the physical position itself, rather than in tickets, has been known to occur in waiting lines for Broadway hit shows. For example, in the overnight lines for *My Fair Lady* in 1956, some people made a business of getting in line early in order to sell their advanced positions to latecomers for as much as twenty dollars.

In mammoth football queues, another kind of business, queue counting, tends to flourish. Concerned at the number of tickets left, some people want to know where they stand in line. Queue counters are boys who run up and down the length of the line at regular intervals; for a fee (usually ten cents) they give customers up-to-date information on the numbers ahead and behind, as well as topical news and gossip.

As far as we know, there are no records of professional place-keepers, people who *mind* places in queues for a fee, but the existence of such a business would not be surprising in the least.

Queues International

How widespread is queue culture, and how typical are the kinds of behavior observed in New York opera lines, Tokyo real-estate lines, and Melbourne football queues? Although lines for sporting events tend to be unique in their atmosphere and makeup, queues for all kinds of services in practically every country have a great deal in common. In most queues, there is a concern with the problem of safeguarding order, a desire to keep the queue "honest," and the emergence of ingenious systems to balance hardship and "time-out." The anthropologist E. T. Hall (1959), in *The Silent Language*, has suggested that a cultural value of egalitarianism is responsible for the manner in which queues and queuing are treated with deference in Western society. In his book, *The Human Dimension*, Hall (1964) asserts that respect for queues can also be attributed to a cultural value of orderliness. Presumably the English are high on both egalitarianism and orderliness, because in England democratic queuing is a way of life.

A friend living in England told me she was once waiting for a London bus at a rarely used stop. Since there was only one other person waiting, an elderly lady, she felt no need to bother about a line. Much to my friend's surprise, the matron began to mutter darkly and, unable to contain herself any longer, snapped out, "Can't you read the sign? You're supposed to get into a queue!"

Queuing is a traditional part of the Soviet way of life. Commenting on Soviet lines, fifty years after the Revolution, I. Korzhinevsky, head of the consumption department at the Ukranian Institute of Trade Research, was moved to observe: "We have simply resigned ourselves to the existence of lines." When he visited Russia in the summer of 1954, Henri Cartier-Bresson, the French photographer, was enchanted by the ubiquitous Moscow lines. His camera recorded lines in front of fruit stores, bookshops, groceries, and butcher shops. He was impressed with the orderliness of the long lines outside Lenin's mausoleum and the patience of shoppers in GUM, the large department store. If Cartier-Bresson were to revisit Moscow today, he would probably find that very little has changed. Moscow, like New York, is still a city of queues.

Of course every large city, and a few not so large ones, is plagued by queues, but it is interesting to note what people are queuing for, since this tells us something about their everyday needs and how cities are failing to cope with them. Outside Havana's ice-cream parlors, called *coppelias*, Cubans stand in line for two hours for a dish of six-flavor ice cream, while in Mexico City, committees wait patiently in line to catch a *pesero*, a shared, fixed-route taxicab. In Tokyo, people wait in lines outside real-estate development offices for as long as two weeks hoping to buy a block of land for a home site. Queues of shoppers form at dawn in Rangoon, Burma, to buy rice, bread, and soap at the "People's Store." And somewhere in Nigeria, long lines of Biafrans wait patiently for a turn to wash their clothes at a primitive outdoor laundry.

Queuing is a truly international phenomenon, and, in most countries, a culture of the waiting line has developed to regulate order and to control such matters as time-outs and place keeping.

Learning To Love Queues

One of the most disconcerting findings in our research on football queues is that people are beginning to accept them, almost as a kind of cherished tradition or ritual. During the regular football season, although it is possible to get choice seats two hours before the start of most Saturday games, long queues form outside stadiums on Friday afternoons. The new attitude is exemplified by a woman who was heard to say, outside the Melbourne stadium, "People are always knocking queues—what I would like to know is what people like myself would do without them?" In 1966, on a mild afternoon before the World Series football tickets went on sale, we interviewed 122 queuers and discovered that 47 percent were happy with the queue system. In 1967, after a dreadfully cold, wet night, we interviewed the all-nighters and found that even then 26 percent reported satisfaction.

Perhaps these statistics should not be regarded as surprising since life in a mammoth queue can be in many ways quite pleasant and relaxing, even though time consuming. The enterprising queuers of Melbourne have learned to cope with the harsh environment outside their stadium by tying tarpaulins to the side of barricades, sleeping on stretchers, and consuming large quantities of liquor. In August 1966, when we went down to Collingwood, a working-class suburb of Melbourne, to interview the football queuers, we were impressed with the successful adjustment they had made to queue living. The first three families in line, numbering approximately thirty men, women, and children, pitched a tent on the sidewalk fronting the ticket box and settled down to a six-day wait around a blazing campfire. Some enthusiasts moved out of their homes and took up formal residence in the queue. Five days before tickets went on sale the general secretary of Collingwood Football Club, Gordon Carlyon, received a letter addressed to "Mr. Alfred McDougall, c/o Queue outside Collingwood Football Ground, Collingwood, 3066." The *Melbourne*

Herald reported that Mr. Carlyon threaded his way through beds and tents on the sidewalk outside the stadium to deliver the letter.

It would appear, then, that urban man, with his remarkable capacity to put up with continual delays and irritations, is not only learning to adapt to queues but is actually beginning to value them as social occasions. The social value of queues is borne out by George Nash, a sociologist at Columbia University, who has carried out surveys of people in movie lines on New York's East Side. He has found that 73 percent of those who wait in movie lines are under thirty and that these young people, rather than complaining about the waste of time (the wait to get in is frequently between one and two hours), regard it as a very rewarding experience. The *New York Times* (April 25, 1970), in reporting Nash's findings, made the following observations:

> Noticing—and getting noticed—is what makes waiting to see a popular "in" movie not just another deadening urban plague to be endured but instead a tolerable and, for many, even pleasurable pastime in itself. The longer the line, the younger, more modish it is likely to be, and the more bemused—and thus not bored—by itself. Almost invariably, the predominant conversational gambit has to do with similar evenings at the movies: not remembered great films, but remembered great lines.

In our survey of ticket lines for the Rolling Stones concert at Boston Garden, we obtained further evidence of the social function of queues. When we arrived at the Garden to conduct our interviews, there were approximately 600 college students communing together on blankets and sleeping bags. The sweet smell of marijuana hung in the air. During the night, many of the kids had met up with old friends or made new ones. To one of our questions, "How do you feel about having to wait in line?" a Radcliffe girl answered, "I'm really excited. It's a kind of social event." A Boston University student told us, "It's a groovy way to meet people." These were fairly typical responses. The evidence suggests that queues for concerts, movies, and sporting events have emerged as occasions for socializing and as opportunities for sociability.

Getting Rid Of Queues

But queues at airports, and in banks, hospitals, and stores are rarely treated as an occasion for meeting people and conducting sociability. The emotional cost of waiting in such lines is formidable (consider the frustrations, fights, and aggravation generated by a long, tiring wait). And their economic cost is incalculable (consider the waste in man-hours and loss of goodwill for the store).

With the proliferation of queues and queuing, it has become increasingly important to formulate measures to reduce the number and length of lines, to reduce the cost in boredom and misery, and to eliminate, wherever possible, their attendant friction and hostility. What can be done about reducing the number and length of lines?

The application of the computer to ticket selling is one possible solution. Only recently, two companies, *Ticketron* and *Computicket*, began to offer instant ticketing to scores of sporting and theatrical events. The system is engagingly simple. The buyer goes to a ticket sales outlet in a department store, railroad station, or supermarket, and tells the clerk the events he wants to see and when. The clerk pushes buttons on a computer console and quizzes a regional memory bank about the best seats available at the preferred price. From its bank of data, the computer provides an instant reading of the best seats at each price level. If the customer decides to buy, the clerk pushes another button and the computer instantaneously delivers a printed ticket for the show.

With the advent of the jumbo 747 jets, computers are being used to speed up airline reservation systems. At the Eastern Airlines terminal in New York, passengers check in baggage and receive their seat numbers in a single quick transaction, without having to wait in long lines during the loading of the aircraft. But even though it is not always economical to install a computer ticketing system, it is still possible to introduce more efficient methods of organization to curtail needless waiting.

We all have experienced interminable delays caused by organizational negligence and inefficiency. My pet story stems from a visit to Mexico in the summer of 1969. We wanted to take a bus from Mexico City to Taxco, a journey of 130 miles. Although there were only twenty people ahead of us in line, it was over ninety minutes before we were served. The clerk required five minutes to locate the bus logbook, write the destination, date, time of departure, and seat number of each ticket, enter the traveler's name and address in another book, and finally exchange the ticket for money. Since the bus company refused to make return reservations in advance, we had to go through the same ordeal the next day in Taxco. In case the manager of the bus company is reading this, here is some (unsolicited) advice. Introduce prestamped tickets (it will reduce service time by one-half); hire a second clerk to help out at peak hours (i.e., always); have the two clerks work from a single common queue (both will be occupied constantly, and no customer will complain about belonging to a slower line); and finally, put on more buses.

What about friction and fighting in lines caused by queue jumping, disputes about rightful position, and so on? A line which is vaguely defined or poorly regulated is extremely stressful for its members. In such lines the responsibility for safeguarding his place falls entirely on the person. He must remain constantly vigilant and therefore cannot relax for a moment. If a dispute arises, and it is inevitable that one will, he must choose to settle it by force, which is unpleasant, or back down, which is humiliating.

Often these problems arise because the seller neglects to decide where and how people should queue, and there are no police or other officials on the scene to adjudicate. Understandably, the seller is reluctant to intercede in disputes about priority of service. But such disputes need not arise if there is a recognized system for registering order of arrival, such as a Take-A-Check or Take-A-Tab dispenser. A number system of this kind helps reduce tension in the queue, because if a dispute erupts, the victimized person can appeal directly to the authority of the number. Number dispensers are not always feasible, but even then, the strategic erection of barriers to force customers into a single line on arrival (as in the rambling, serpentine lines at Disneyland) can help prevent bitterness and bloodshed. Of course, no method of protecting the line is foolproof. The only way to discourage queue jumping (short of making it a capital offense) is to improve speed and certainty of service.

Finally, what can be done to reduce the boredom, tension, and weariness associated with waiting in lines? A look at recent world's fairs is instructive. Queues were a common sight during New York's World Fair of 1964, but fair officials solved the problem outside Michelangelo's *Pieta* by putting visitors on three tiers of conveyor belts and drawing them slowly past the sculpture. Expo '67, the world's fair in Montreal, came up with some novel ideas. Twenty-four computerized electronic signboards flashed facts about the most crowded exhibits and restaurants, and urged fairgoers to visit the less-crowded sites. A typical message read: "Lots of room and no waiting at the Cuban pavilion; why not go there now?" Inevitably there were long delays outside the most popular pavilions (at Labyrinth, the wait was sometimes as long as eight hours, rarely less than three hours). To cope with boredom and irritation, strolling troubadors, jazz combos, clowns, and even ice skaters on a movable rink were dispatched to entertain the longest queues. Then someone decided it would be better to draw crowds away from the congested areas, not to them, and so the entertainers were directed to perform outside the less-popular exhibits.

That is all very well for world's fairs, but what about the typical large city and its labyrinth of waiting lines? We can see it even now. Strolling troubadours, jazz combos, and clowns entertaining the folks waiting to be seen in hospitals, unemployment agencies, and welfare centers. Meantime, joining an urban queue can be a long, boring, and frustrating experience unless, of course, the queue happens to be for football or cinema tickets.

References

Festinger, L. 1957. *A Theory of Cognitive Dissonance.* New York: Harper and Row.
Hall, E. T. 1959. *The Silent Language.* New York: Doubleday.
———. 1964. *The Hidden Dimension.* New York: Doubleday.
Homans, G. C. 1961. *Social Behavior: Its Elementary Forms.* New York: Harcourt.
Liebowitz, M. A. 1968. "Queues." *Scientific American* 219:96–103.
Mann, L. 1969. "Queue Culture: The Waiting Line as a Social System." *American Journal of Sociology* 75:340–54.
———. 1970. "The Social Psychology of Waiting Lines." *American Scientist* 58:390–98.
Mann, L., and K. F. Taylor. 1969. "Queue Counting: The Effect of Motives upon Estimates of Numbers in Waiting Lines." *Journal of Personality and Social Psychology* 12:95–103.

PART THREE
Socialization

We have said that the culture is dynamic, that the society represents varied enactments of the culture. Social phenomena are changeable, essentially unstable, fragile, and often ambiguous. Thus the way in which the culture and its applications are passed on from generation to generation is crucial to the maintenance of order and regularity or even to radical change. The patterns of learning, the processes of acquiring, and the subsequent enactments of that learning are referred to as the *socialization process*.

The socialization process is like the genetic system of the society. It carries on the past and links it to the future. But this process is not unbroken, linear, or for that matter, even particularly orderly. One generation must find out from the preceding one; the older generation must insure that at least minimal aspects of its understanding are passed on intact to the younger one. We are not talking about formal teaching, instruction, or tutoring, although these often make up a part of the process. Rather, we are talking about all forms of social learning, direct and indirect, formal and informal, tacit and explicit. The transmission of a culture is a problem of everyday life. Generations never succeed fully in socializing their offspring in exactly the same way that they were socialized. The human condition has too much flexibility for that, too much instability in both the objective and subjective worlds.

Human beings must become social to survive. The ways in which they accomplish this task are as fascinating and varied as they are regular and predictable. Within a single culture there are general, very broad, themes and values that crisscross every person's socialization experiences; other themes and values are restricted to particular life situations. Growing up female entails certain values of submissiveness that appear to apply to the experiences of all females in varying degrees. Males, on the other hand, generally learn aggressiveness. Simply growing up in American society will mean the acquisition of a sense of competition, an idea of ownership, and a value of individualism. Yet the expression of these core values will vary, and their precise application will change from one life situation to another. From the suburban home to the street-corner gang, there is learning; culture is transmitted, society is constructed. Within all of these circumstances one can discover social and cultural values and their enactment.

The articles in this section look at socialization from several points of view. The first selection gives a first-hand account of the effects of socialization by describing children's understandings of the world around them. The remaining articles deal with adult socialization. One describes entrances into adulthood, another, occupational socialization, and the last, acquisition of multiple self-identities.

7
The Everyday World of Childhood

We often discuss socialization as a learning process that changes children into socially competent adults. Rarely do we have the opportunity to see the results of that process at various stages of acquisition. Although adults and children often share the same physical world, they certainly do not share the same world views. Children have begun a lifelong process of learning, and understanding how they interpret their world can give us insights into the basic values passed on from generation to generation. The authors of this article conducted interviews with children to discover what they thought about the lifestyles and values in their Mexican-American section of a southwestern city. By looking at everyday life through the eyes of children, we gain a glimpse of the world in which they will soon live as adults.

Child's-Eye Views of Life in an Urban Barrio
Mary Ellen Goodman and Alma Beman

Introduction

In this paper we summarize what we have learned, from the children themselves, about the lifestyles and values of school-age children in a Mexican-American "pocket of poverty."

The data presented here are a small part of the findings from a

---

From *Spanish-Speaking People in the United States*, Proceedings of the 1968 Annual Spring Meeting of the American Ethnological Society, pp. 84–103. Reprinted by permission of the University of Washington Press.

three-year study of Houstonians of Mexican ancestry.[1] A report on the full study—an urban ethnography—is now in preparation.

In metropolitan Houston some 7.5 percent of the population—more than one hundred thousand people—are Mexican Americans. These people are widely dispersed through the city and greatly varied with respect to acculturation, education, and economic status. There are, however, sections of the city in which the residents are solidly Mexican-American, largely of very low income and education, and minimally to moderately acculturated.

We selected one such enclave for intensive study. "El Barrio," as we call it, is a kind of "urban village" (Gans 1962) encircled by highways, railroad tracks, and a string of warehouse and industrial structures. It lies about a mile from downtown Houston, but it is socially much further removed. Some forty families, plus partial families and detached individuals, make up the Barrio population.

Barrio household heads and their spouses are mainly (about 70 percent) Texas-born. A relatively small proportion (23 percent) are Mexican-born, and only a few persons were born in states other than Texas. Nearly all the Barrio adults are Spanish speaking, but they use a patois nearly unintelligible to people who speak standard Spanish. In their vernacular, English words are liberally intermixed with local slang, with grammatically distorted and poorly enunciated Spanish.

From the viewpoint of the middle-class Houstonian, El Barrio is a slum. Its turn-of-the-century buildings are unkempt, its streets narrow and rutted, its sidewalks broken and discontinuous. Home ownership is rare, and some of the large old homes are now rooming houses. The heart of the Barrio is an intersection around which are clustered a small grocery, four modest cafes, and a taxi dance lounge. On one edge of the "village" there is a small Roman Catholic church with an adjacent playing field for softball and basketball.[2]

Barrio lifestyles are more varied than an outsider might suppose. There are "routine-seekers" as well as "action-seekers" (Gans 1962),

---

[1] This study was begun in September, 1965 and was continued through summer, 1968.
The study is under the general direction of Mary Ellen Goodman. José de la Isla has served as coordinator and as principal field-worker.
We join in thanking the Texas Department of Mental Health and Mental Retardation for a grant in support of the early phases of the research, and the Center for Research in Social Change and Economic Development, Rice University, for continuing support. This center-sponsored research was funded by the Advanced Research Projects Agency under ARPA Order No. 738 and monitored by the Office of Naval Research, Group Psychology Branch, under Contract Number N00014-67-A-0145-0001, NR 177-909.
We express also our deep appreciation to the sixteen persons—graduate students, undergraduates, and secretarial assistants—who have aided in important ways in the work of the project.

[2] This statement refers to the "ethnographic present." The church is not in use now.

stable families as well as street-corner boys and men, winos, taxi dancers, and others whose lifeways are out of key with family routines and responsibilities. Outside the Barrio, its best known features are its more lurid ones.

> The ───── Lounge attracts men and women from outside the neighborhood, although some taxi dancers and Lounge customers have lived in El Barrio. People now resident in the neighborhood often refer to the ───── Lounge as a place of trouble from which a person would be wise to stay away.
> ... Violence at the Lounge ... is not rare. Fights, stabbings, shootings, and murders have occurred. ...
> Mexican-American men from [other] ... parts of the city seek out Barrio friends at night. These men and their friends usually drink at one of the several bars or cafes. They, like their friends are laboring men. ... (de la Isla 1968, pp. 11–12).

Child's-Eye View

We studied the Barrio in three different ways: (1) participant observation (including a five-month residence maintained by José de la Isla); (2) neighborhood census through a lengthy systematic interview with the head of each independent living unit; and (3) lengthy interviews with each Barrio child in grades one through six. In this paper we review only the child interview data.

Before we proceed to those data, however, we must emphasize a methodological point of major importance.

Our point is that children are an excellent and underutilized source of ethnographic information, that

> what we can learn from child informants is unique and indeed indispensable to a comprehensive new view of [a] society and culture.
> ... That part of culture which is known to the child [must] ... have a peculiar significance, since what is learned early is likely to be fundamental, pervasive, and persistent in the culture (Goodman 1960).

In studies utilizing children as informants (e.g., Leighton and Kluckhohn 1947; Nadel 1937; Dennis 1940; Goodman 1957, 1962, 1964) the focus is not on the mechanics of enculturation or upon how grown-ups view and deal with children. Rather, the focus is such that the investigator, in effect, stands beside the child and looks out with him upon the social scene. The child's-eye views we report here are to be understood in these terms.

For this study we designed and pretested a rather lengthy interview schedule. It contains 123 questions, largely open-ended. The interviews required a minimum of half an hour, often as much as an hour. However, we found the child informants highly cooperative. Nearly always the children seemed surprised and even proud that their opinions were sought. It was a novel experience, and they enjoyed talking.

We have interviewed lower-class Negro and Anglo children as well as the Barrio children. A full and comparative report will be made in a later paper. Here we focus on the Mexican-American children.

The Barrio interviewers are undergraduate and graduate men students who are equally at ease in Texan Spanish and in English.[3] They found ample use for both languages. Two of the children used Spanish throughout the interview, and all of them used at least a sprinkling of Spanish terms. Spanish was used especially in references to kin and to food.

The interview content ranges through factual items such as a list of family members and accounts of the child's everyday home and school routines. We also asked for judgments about good and bad people, good and bad "things to do," "best" and "worst" memories, and plans for the future. We included a few questions designed to sample the child's knowledge about the larger society (e.g., "What town do you live in?" "What state?" "Who is President of the United States?"). These questions were placed near the end of the interview lest the stigma of "test" inhibit communication (see the appended interview schedule).

An interviewer who worked with the children, and later with the Barrio adults as well, commented on the lack of stereotype in the children's responses. Their spontaneity and candor was indeed remarkable. The protocols contain a wealth of detail which we have preserved to a large extent in the process of coding the responses. We do not burden this report with an account of our coding, tabulating, and analytical procedures. It should be understood, however, that what we report in qualitative terms is not impressionistic; it is based on careful coding and tabu-

---

[3] The Barrio interviewers are Ruben Gonzalez and Roberto Guerra. The interviews were conducted during the spring and summer of 1967.

lation of responses in significant categories (e.g., child's-eye views of the physical world, of the social world, and of the values realm).[4]

Background for the Child's-Eye View

In the Barrio we interviewed thirty-four school-age children living in sixteen households. There are seventeen boys and seventeen girls, well distributed across the age range seven to thirteen.[5] The modal household has in it six children. There are a few families of eight or nine children, and a few of two or three.

The households to which the informants belong are simple nuclear families in only seven of the sixteen cases. In nine households there are grandparents or other relatives in addition to, or (in two cases) in place of, parents.

The parents of our children are poorly educated, and their earning power is low. Formal schooling ranges from none to eleven years, with four to six years the level most frequently attained. Fathers are unskilled laborers in construction work or employed as janitors, service station attendants, and the like. The most skilled and best paid is a "plastic molder" who earns eighty-nine dollars a week. This father supports a wife and eight children, ages three to twelve years. Two other fathers, each having eight children of approximately the same age range, support their families on seventy-five and fifty-five dollars a week, respectively. Four mothers and one grandmother are reported (by the children) to work outside the home.

Most of the families claim membership in the Barrio's small Catholic church. When asked "What do you do on Sunday?" two-thirds of the children tell us they go to church. A nine-year-old and a twelve-year-old serve as altar boys.

[4]Our reference to differences between groups (Barrio, Anglo, and Negro) are based on statistical significances. Where use of Chi might be feasible, a rough approximation of differences required [translated to percentages] was arrived at using Zubin's nomograph, as appears in Oppenheim. Note also that a given difference (say, fifteen percentage points) may be significant at the extremes, where one of the percentages approaches zero or one hundred, but not in the middle ranges (Oppenheim 1966, p. 288). We present sample values in the midrange, the largest differences required should two groups only be compared.

Significance Level	$N_1 = 34, N_2 = 43$	$N_1 = 17, N_2 = 17$	$N_1 = 20, N_2 = 23$
10%	58% and 42%	64% and 37%	63% and 38%
5%	62% and 40%	67% and 34%	65% and 36%
1%	65% and 35%	72% and 29%	69% and 31%

[5]It was our intention to interview all Barrio children of first through sixth grades. We are short of that goal, but we have interviewed 75 percent of the school age children.

Given names provide a small clue to family levels of acculturation. Of our child informants two-thirds bear "Anglo" names or at least use Anglicized names (e.g., Juan Enrique is known as "Henry").

However, the prevalence of *compadre/comadre* relationships is but one of many evidences of the retention of Mexican traditions. Nearly all the parental generation claims one, two, three, or four such relationships with people in the neighborhood or in other sections of the city.

There are no schools inside the Barrio. Our interviewees, between them, attend three different elementary schools, located six to nine blocks from their homes. All the children, except two who travel by bus to quite distant special schools, walk to and from these three elementary schools. Their routes take them across railroad tracks and streets bearing heavy traffic. Most of them carry their lunches and do not return home until mid- to late afternoon.

Home Relationships and Routines

In the child's-eye view, the central feature is home and the people at home. Around this focus there are the wider worlds of neighborhood and school. What lies beyond is likely to be fuzzy and vague, even the older children. The Barrio does not figure as a unit in the views of the children, although their elders regard it as a neighborhood and recognize its physical boundaries.

In the child's world of people there are household members, friends, and close neighbors, all ranged in an orderly classification and clearly differentiated. These "significant others" the child places in his personal world—his social space. We infer that the placing depends mainly on his assessments in three dimensions: respect, authority, and affectionate warmth.

The respect dimension is closely linked with age. In general, the older the person, the more respect is due him. Grandparents are in no way deprecated by any of the children, and there are numerous comments suggesting deference. One must not "talk bad" to grandmother. In one household "Abuelita" (little Grandmother) has her own bedroom, even though the rest of the family must sleep together in one other room. Many children say they love their grandparents, and they make such comments before they even mention resident parents.

Grandparents appear to be highly influential, as distinguished from being powerful. The children express appreciation; e.g., because grandparents teach "what is right and not right," because "they are good with me and drag me out of bed," and because they are "fun." Many grandmothers and grandfathers work; this too is admirable. A solicitous attitude is sometimes expressed; e.g., it is a good thing "to save [pick] up my toys so Grandmother does not trip over them."

On the authority dimension, the father takes precedence. He is seen as a somewhat distant authority but not easily forgotten. Nevertheless, the boys seem rather to slight him. Few say they go to him with questions, either for information or for permission to do something. Only four boys want to be like father when they grow up. Two think father is great, but none plans on having a job like father's in later life. That there is a certain remoteness between boy and father may be due mainly to father's frequent absences because of work or for other reasons. He usually leaves home before the children are up and around. Yet our informants were sure to tell us whether he had supper with them, and they report that his homecoming usually determines suppertime.

The girls' attitudes toward parents are quite different. They speak much more often of "mother and father" as an entity. They feel that their parents are equally available to answer questions. Four girls say they ask only father if they need answers. None interpreted this as seeking permission to do something. Girls can describe father's work better than the boys can.

Boys and girls agree on two roles for the male head of the household. A man goes out to work to earn money for the family, and he is the high court of discipline. The men of the family, either father or grandfather, handle crises and major indiscretions—putting a stop to rock fights, for example.

Mothers and grandmothers fill many domestic roles in the child's world. They prepare the breakfast, the "carried" lunch, after-school snacks, and the supper—likely to be beans, tortillas, and rice. They do the dishes, sweeping and mopping, bedmaking and "making everything clean for us," with help from the girls, and occasionally from boys. Mother sets hours to get up, to come in from play, and to go to bed. She scolds, she sometimes slaps or spanks for disobeying small rules, and she stops sibling squabbles. Even in the few families where mother goes out to work, the children feel that her prime activity is at home.

In spite of the continuous and repetitive nature of mother's tasks, she is not thought of as a drudge. "She's good and looks pretty," "She is always helping us and is a lot of fun." Toward their mothers and mother surrogates the children express a feeling of warmth and closeness, a strong bond of affection.

The strength of intrafamily affection declared by Barrio children is conspicuous by contrast with responses of the Negro and Anglo children we interviewed. We asked of all the children, "Who do you love?" No Barrio child included any but relatives in his roster of persons loved, not even a nonrelated peer or a close neighbor. Friends figure importantly for Anglo children and for Negro boys.[6] We might dismiss these findings as indicating mainly a distinctive Barrio definition of the word "love," except that they are wholly congruent with the overall pattern of home-centeredness so evident in the Barrio protocols.

The older brothers, sisters, cousins, uncles, and aunts who are out of school are regarded in a variety of ways. They are accorded mixtures of respect and affection, and they have some authority. The jobs they hold can be described explicitly, often more so than father's: "he [big brother] works in a furniture factory," "she [older cousin] baby-sits for a secretary," "she [young aunt] types, copies whatever they tell her." Several girls hope to be like these slightly older relatives. The not-quite-adult members of the family are looked upon as legitimate disciplinarians, particularly in settling quarrels between children.

Brothers and sisters in their own age range the children praise and censure in about equal proportions. They play together, and they fight together. Sisters have a way of calling names, and being hated for it. One Barrio child calls her brother "stupid Negro," a label intended and understood as particularly insulting. The children tend to be highly critical of their age mates but not of young people significantly older than themselves.

The youngest members of the family are mother's responsibility, though many of the girls feel they have an active share in caring for preschoolers. They give the little ones wagon rides, teach them to play "catch," or just make them laugh. The girls do not seem to feel that this is a burden. They think that even two-year-olds should know how to play, talk, walk, write, "color," and "be good." Only two children mentioned unpleasant things two-year-olds may do: they know how "to bite" and "to fight."

Since most job-holding family members leave home before the children's breakfast, and the school children are gone until afternoon, it

[6]Question number 113: Who do you love? (percent of children giving response)

	Barrio		Anglo		Negro	
	M	F	M	F	M	F
Relatives, only	88	88	44	20	53	94
Nonrelatives and relatives	—	—	56	80	35	6
No One	6	—	—	—	12	—
No Reply	6	12	—	—	—	—
	100	100	100	100	100	100

In the responses to this and to other questions as well, we have the interesting finding that a certain class of answers given by children of one group was absent in another.

is not until evening that the family has a chance to be together. Supper is a family affair; father's return from work sets its time, even though many children are indoors earlier, particularly in winter. The norm is that everybody eats together. The houses of El Barrio are small, the families large, yet we heard one, and only one, comment about lack of space: "It gets kinda crowded sometimes."

Weekend routines, like the rest of life, are home centered. They differ from school-week routines mainly in allowing more time for play, television, and household chores. In three families the children are sometimes taken to visit relatives in other parts of the city. Most of them go to church on Sunday mornings.

Television viewing is a favorite pastime at almost any hour day or evening. Barrio people are most likely to watch in the evening, around suppertime and after, when custom dictates "resting and letting the food go down." For children the popular viewing times are, in order: early evening of any weekday, Saturday morning when cartoons come one after the other, afternoons after school, and anytime on Sunday. Only one family does without a set, a deprivation sorely felt by the girls of the household. More than half the children stay up beyond nine o'clock to watch late TV shows. In the close quarters of the house, one might surmise that the set is a dominant feature. It may be impracticable to restrict viewing hours. In fact, bedtime often seems to be set in terms of programs to be seen. A few boys and girls spoke of doing homework or chores before watching, but they were rare. One young lady says she watches all the time except, perhaps, when she is mopping in the kitchen and cannot see the set.

The boys prefer programs of high adventure and fighting. Girls have no taste for this sort of thing; they prefer comedies, especially those dealing with family situations. We have some evidence that the children learn from TV about certain social types and are inspired to emulate them. Models and ballerinas offer a glittering occupational goal to some of the girls. The boys admire the policemen, firemen, astronauts and "Green Berets."

A few succinct statements taken from our protocols will suggest salient features of relationships within the El Barrio home:

1. My aunt protects me from my brother and sister, mother takes me shopping, and father gives money (girl, age ten).

2. Q. When you do something bad, who yells at you?
A. Almost everybody, because I am the littlest one (boy, age ten).

3. When I ask my grandmother a question, she says to ask my father and my father tells my big sister to go help me (boy, age nine).

110   The Everyday World of Childhood

The boundary between the inner core of home and the periphery of neighborhood is blurred. In part this is because many of the neighbors are also relatives. Eddie lives with his grandparents, uncles and aunts, just a block away from his mother, stepfather, and their children. Some neighbors of long standing have won the kind of respect and appreciation ordinarily felt for relatives. There is Mrs. Guzman, who is regarded as a great person because she has helped other families in times of trouble. There is a "storekeeper lady" who has given fruit to the children. Small incidents accumulate, the children discuss them among themselves, and form their own consensus about El Barrio society.

The story of Eddie's escapade, pieced together from interviews with several children, serves as a prototype of how the children share in neighborhood gossip. Eddie had saved up enough money to go to the movies. He persuaded his friend to go with him, at night, without telling any adult about it. He later told us it was a very bad thing to do—to worry his grandparents, aunts, and uncles. His partner in crime was punished, and Eddie "got in big trouble." Eddie's stepbrother heard all about the "big trouble" and felt that Eddie was a very bad person to stay out so late. The stepsister says it is a bad thing when someone stays out late and worries everybody. Going to the movies at night became a cause célèbre.

The boys are impressed by certain rules, and they explained their importance to us. Rock fights are forbidden; about this Barrio adults present to the children a united front. They were united too when they called a halt to playing in the ditch where men were building a road. Intersibling quarrels are strongly, but not severely, discouraged in Barrio homes. We asked: "When you fight with your brother(s) or sister(s), what does your mother do?" The Mexican children, boys especially, report mainly that they are spanked or "hit," but not whipped. Anglo children claim they are likely to be whipped or scolded. The reports of the Negro children of both sexes emphasize whipping. Of the three groups it is the Negroes who are most likely to be encouraged to "fight back."

The Barrio

Other gossip current at the time of interviewing involved the arrival of a few Negroes in the Barrio. Attitudes were mixed. Members of a Negro family had been seen fighting in the street. This the children found shocking. Fights should be contained within one's own house. If children fight,

"We tell their parents, and they take them in and spank them."

The Barrio is a rather closed society and difficult for any newcomer, even Mexican Americans, to penetrate. Two sisters, ages eight and ten, recently had moved from their parent's hometown some seventy miles away. The girls are keenly aware of being outsiders. They constantly hark back fondly to life in their small native town. Jo Ann sighed, "I don't know where anyone lives here."

Although there are in the Barrio many transients and unattached inhabitants, the children made no comments about them to us. The small grocery store, a favorite stopping place in the morning, was often mentioned but there was no mention of the Barrio's taxi dance hall, or of the bars. The boys play soccer or baseball in the park sometimes. A pair of older girls, close chums, may walk around the park. However, most of the children who play in the afternoons jump rope, play tag or "catch" around their own houses. "Indoors by dark, or when father comes home from work," is the rule.

In their movements through the neighborhood, the children must certainly observe outsiders and people they have been warned against, e.g., winos, prostitutes, and action-seekers of other sorts. But the action-seekers seem to be remote to the young, whose focus of attention is on children's pursuits. The firm demarcation between El Barrio "insiders" and "outsiders," no doubt, also works to put the latter on the periphery of attention. The fact that transients are for the most part men may be significant, because the young of the more stable families live mainly in a world of women. It seems likely that the boys we interviewed, the older ones particularly, are well aware of street-corner men and other action-seekers. It is reasonable to suppose that some of the boys admire these types. Their complete silence in the matter suggests a careful avoidance. It may be that they have learned already a male code of silence about men's pursuits outside the home.

There are "buffers" between the stable families and the action-seekers, but they cannot be depended upon fully to isolate children from the action-seeker society and mores. As the children of the less cohesive family units grow older, and are less subject to family rules, some will probably join the action-seekers. Two cases are illustrative of the many variables at work.

Eddie, who sneaked off to the movies, is in a difficult position. He is like the children in one other household in that he is cared for solely by his grandparents, but he is unique in having younger stepsiblings living nearby. The tightly knit inner circle of El Barrio, with its shared fund of gossip, tends to accentuate the peculiarities of Eddie's position. Even if he is never the instigator of another cause célèbre, the "villagers" are not likely to forget that or any later indiscretions. On the other hand,

Eddie has much "going for him." He is responsive and intelligent. He feels a great deal of respect, affection, and appreciation for his grandparents. He is twelve years old now, an altar boy at church. He wants to be like an astronaut, but he expects only to finish high school and then work as a fireman. If he were without notable personal resources, we would be uncertain whether he might in three or four years identify with the action-seekers and take up their lifestyle. In view of his assets, that seems unlikely.

The Coulombo girls are not as fortunate as Eddie. Aged eight and nine years, they have two younger sisters and three younger brothers, bearing two other last names. Theirs is probably the poorest home in the neighborhood and the only one lacking a recognized male household head. Mother works in a laundry during the day. The interviewer notes that one of the girls "was shy and reserved and sometimes barely audible," the other "loud and inattentive . . . sometimes her answers didn't make sense. Giggled a lot for no reason at all." Both girls are still in first grade. Having neither cohesive family nor strong personal attributes, it is quite likely that as they grow up these girls will gravitate toward the action-seekers and perpetuate their mother's lifestyle.

El Barrio action-seekers are for the most part detached individuals, men and women who have no children, or none of school age living in the Barrio. Among action-seekers there are a few young toughs, street-corner boys, whose wives live in the households maintained by the man's parents. Some have very young children. But the seamy side of Barrio life—the side sustained by resident action-seekers and by action-seeking transients and visitors to El Barrio—is practiced by few of the adults who live in the households of our child informants. At home they are exposed mainly to a routine-seeking life style.

Outside the Barrio

The children's only regularly recurring departure from the neighborhood is their trek to school each day. The detached observer may note the hazards of the trip (e.g., traffic, railroad crossings), but the children find this a time "to play *con los muchachitos*" (with the boys and girls), to have little adventures, and for such minor entertainments as "throwing mud at ants." In the morning there may be a stop at the store to buy something to add to lunch, and here they may meet their friends. The trucks and cars going by are fun to watch, and if the first graders cannot be trusted to stop and wait for traffic, older brothers and sisters are charged with looking after them. The only danger the children see is the chance of being late if a long train should block the railroad tracks that must be crossed.

From the child's point of view school is divided into two parts, work and play. Very few of our informants are enthusiastic about the work, but if they must rank subjects (as we asked them to do), the boys favor arithmetic, the girls favor spelling and reading. There seems to be no relationship between subject preference and whether a child is up to grade level for his age.

Evaluations of the teacher's efforts are largely in terms of the "work" part of school. "My teacher is good, because she teaches us how to read in arithmetic," or "she lets us talk softly after we have finished our work." One teacher is a favorite because she lets the children stop at her home for help after school. Teachers' disciplinary measures—yelling, spankings, and whippings—are reported by more than half our informants.

The play portion of school hours—the recess, lunch hour, and just "fooling with friends"—is not considered part of a learning experience because it is not work. It is the best part of school though. Few denied that.

The schools the children attend are integrated, and in describing their classmates, many spontaneously mention ethnicity. Only two state a preference for Latins, however, and three think the "other kind" (i.e., Negroes) is better.

The children—three-fourths of them—know that their parents and siblings care about their work and progress at school. It is the mother especially who expresses interest, but only a third of the children report comment as specific as "You ought to learn more." It is likely that few parents are able to give much help with homework. This we infer from the low average level of their education and from remarks such as "My mother tells me if she knows," "My teacher tells me to look into a book and find the answer," and "If it's not for school, mother will help me."

In the world of school, the Barrio children are often at a disadvantage. Many of them go to summer school in hope of catching up. Some have at school a friend who is not of the Barrio; e.g., "My best friend is John. I never go [to his house]. I just see him at school." The physical distance between school and home—some six to nine blocks—is much less than the social and cultural distance.

Throughout the interviews, the *muchachitos* show us that, from their vantage point, what is beyond El Barrio is far indeed. Small excursions loom large in their recollections; a class excursion, a fishing trip with grandfather, a trip downtown with mother—these are important and big events. Only one child has been to Mexico, or anywhere else at all remote. In the close-at-hand world of the Barrio, the children center their activities, their interests, and find their heroes and models. Members of their own households are most numerous among the people they admire. Only a local garage mechanic, one teacher, and a few television characters figure as admired but nonhousehold people.

Values

The children's views on what is good or bad, their likes and dislikes, the people they admire or dislike, and their hopes and wishes for the future—these provide our major clues to their values. We are of course aware that they no doubt spoke to us largely in terms of ideal patterns, and that ideal patterns may diverge considerably from behavioral patterns. But the ideal patterns offered us by the Negro and Anglo children are quite different from those of the Barrio, and it is reasonable to suppose that their behavioral patterns differ too. Ideal pattern statements are prime indicators of the standards to which a people aspire and teach their children to accept as proper standards. Without such standard-setting and such teaching, children are unlikely even to pay lip service to values which run counter to ego impulses, immediate gratifications, and the gross acquisitiveness which seems to appear in the cultures of all urban industrial societies. Among Barrio children, though not among Negro and Anglo children, the ideal patterns run strongly counter to these orientations.

The Barrio children value their parents and other kin, of all ages. No one and nothing takes precedence over kin in their value hierarchy. In this the Mexican Americans are unlike the Anglo and Negro children, who are much more oriented toward age-mates and friends.

For Barrio children the "good thing to do" is also the pleasurable thing. In this linkage they are not unlike the Anglo and Negro youngsters. But in the Barrio protocols, there appears another value linked with the good and the pleasurable—an "others-orientation," reminiscent of what has been reported for Japanese children (Goodman 1957). This others-orientation is a matter of concern for, and sensitivity to, the feelings and wishes of people who are important to ego. It is evident in such comments, from the Mexican children, as these: it is good "to play *nice* with my sisters and brothers," "to play ball with the boys when *they* want to," to do well at school (responding to parents' wishes), to be obedient, and to help around the house. In this frame of reference, the "bad-to-do" things are largely the reverse side of the same values coin but with stress on the badness of disobedience and of "talking back" to elders.

Work is valued. The El Barrio girls, more than the boys, have opportunities to work. More girls have earned money for their work. Both girls and boys accept work as they accept play; it is an expected, a taken-for-granted, part of life. It is good to work, bad if father does not have a job. One should not avoid work. We asked: "At your house, who works and what do they do?" Unlike the Anglo and Negro children, the Mexican children answered including those who help at home, as well as the wage earners: e.g., "My father fixes refrigerators. My sister takes care of the [younger] boys when I'm not here," (girl, ten years old).

The Mexican children perhaps value work less for itself than as participation and contribution. In an industrial world's definition, work is closely allied with the acquisition of things and status. But for most of these children, whether they are describing careers or tasks at home, the stress is not on the activity itself nor on the personal achievement. It is, rather, on the contribution made. In the family everybody works in his own way; this is a part of living, like enjoying family meals, watching a television show, or playing with other family members. "Helping," being part of a larger endeavor, fitting into the life at hand, this is the way they have learned to view the chores they perform—the sweeping, mopping, dishwashing, gardening, and taking out of trash.

Power, wealth, high prestige—these are either little valued or little thought about, one way or another. So we judge from the modest aspirations stated by the Mexican children. The future vocations they talk about represent few leaps from the humble roles their parents play. Television has given scope to a certain amount of fancy, but most of the children think of their futures in terms of the roles they have experienced directly—e.g., policeman, fireman, mother, secretary, teacher. It appears that in thinking of the future there is a pervading caution. For girls, however, even planning to go to work represents a certain amount of daring, because it is a departure from the roles of most mothers and most other adult women the girls know.

The same caution, the reaching for goals within easy reach, is reflected in responses when we asked: "If you could make three wishes and get what you wished for, what would you wish?" Only one child wished for money. The greatest number of wishes were for small things—a doll, coloring books, a new pair of shoes, perhaps a guitar. The second largest body of wishes were either abstract—to be happy, to be smart, not to be afraid, or wishes for someone else—an education for my brother, for mother to be a teacher. In view of the modest circumstances of El Barrio, it is perhaps not surprising that the tangible things the children wish for are on a modest scale. But Negro and Anglo children in equally low economic situations tend to reach for the moon. Possessions, power, and wealth are not wholly disdained by Barrio children; e.g., "I wish for my father to have a Cadillac." But such expressions are rare. Moreover, it should be noted that this wish is for the *father*, although we invited the child to state his wishes for himself.

Summary and Conclusions

We know something of the child's-eye view and of its wealth of detail, unimpaired by retrospection. In conclusion we shall consider the Barrio children as we know them and their present situation in relation to the larger context of the city and their prospects in that larger society.

El Barrio is a shrinking "village," physically and socially. There was once a public school in the neighborhood. It has been torn down. The Catholic church has closed since the completion of our work with the children; services are held now in a new building north of the tracks. Over the last three years a number of Barrio houses have been vacated and demolished to make space for a new highway. The very magnitude of surrounding city growth accentuates neighborhood attrition.

The changes are unwelcome to Barrio people, both adults and children. The appearance of a few Negroes causes particularly lively comment and some expressions of shock, resentment, or animosity. As yet, the Barrio children do not speak of leaving the neighborhood. They view the changes as wrong, rather than find fault with the home environment.

In appraising external, non-Mexican influences, we conclude that the children give equal weight to school and television. To be good in school is important, and it takes thought and effort. The goals attainable through schooling are distant and nebulous, whereas those made vivid on television can be tied in to everyday experiences. The Mexican children aspire mainly to simple and locally familiar work roles and pay little attention to the glamor roles and the riches they see on televisions.

The remarkable solidarity of the majority of El Barrio homes goes far to explain the happy tranquility which colors the Barrio child's-eye view. Training in helping, in discipline, and in respect for others all occur early. Most children have numerous relatives who take active interest in them. It is a situation conducive to security, ego satisfaction, and a firm sense of identity.

There are, of course, some breaks in family cohesion. Low economic status has much to do with this; there are underemployed or nonworking fathers in all three of our groups of children in low-income areas. The Mexican ideal of the powerful male would seem to make economic impotence or severe limitations especially threatening. These fathers can hardly swell with pride in their performance as providers nor can they command respect from their children on this basis. However, most Barrio fathers do command respect, and most Barrio households in which there are school-age children do have fathers, legally and functionally.

On average the children aspire to jobs somewhat better than those their adult relatives now have, and they seem aware that job holding means responsibilities. They have no soaring expectations, but rather, a quiet hope, and a tendency to observe and evaluate their situation and their life chances rather realistically. That quiet hope of the children has its parallel among the grown-ups. In the larger study, of which this child study is a part, our research group has learned that the mood of the Mexican-American community in Houston tends to be expansive and optimistic. Anglo prejudice is lessening, the Spanish language is more accepted, things Mexican are gaining in popularity. The rapid industrial development of Mexico has no doubt helped to enhance the image of the nation and its customs, and of Mexican Americans as well. Certainly the Mexican Americans now take a considerable pride in their ethnic heritage.

It is our impression that the lifestyles and values of the Barrio children are on the whole conducive to modest success in the contemporary urban society. It seems likely that their life chances are on average significantly better in this respect than those of the Negro children we interviewed, and perhaps almost as good as those of our Anglo informants. Barrio children in stable families—and they are a large majority of the children we interviewed—are growing up without great ambition but with self-respect and with "character." A recent editorial in *El Sol,* the principal newspaper published by and for Mexican Americans in Houston, states clearly a sense of responsibility for self which we find well developed among stable families in the Barrio and among their children. Referring to the federally-supported anti-poverty programs, *El Sol* said:

> The government can give us opportunity within certain limits, but in the end it is the individual that will determine if he succeeds or fails. One thing Washington cannot give is character (Guerra and Goodman 1968).

References

DeLaIsla III, José. 1968. "Aspects of Social Organization of a Mexican-American Urban Barrio." Unpublished paper. Rice University Center for the Study of Social Change and Economic Development.

Dennis, Wayne. 1940. *The Hopi Child.* New York: Appleton-Century.

Gans, Herbert J. 1962. *The Urban Villagers.* New York: Free Press.

Goodman, Mary Ellen. 1957. "Values, Attitudes, and Social Concepts of Japanese and American Children." *American Anthropologist* 59:979–99.

———. 1960. "Children as Informants: The Child's-Eye-View of Society and Culture." *The American Catholic Sociological Review* 21:136–45.

———. 1962. "Culture and Conceptualization: A Study of Japanese and American Children." *Ethnology* 1:374–86.

———. 1964. *Race Awareness in Young Children.* New York: Collier Books.

Guerra, Roberto and Mary Ellen Goodman. 1968. "A Content Assessment of *El Sol,* A Community Newspaper." Unpublished paper. Rice University Center for the Study of Social Change and Economic Development.

Leighton, Dorothea and Clyde Kluckhohn. 1947. *Children of the People.* Cambridge, Mass.: Harvard University Press.

Nadel, S. F. 1937. "A Field Experiment in Racial Psychology." *British Journal of Psychology* 28:195–211.

Oppenheim, A. N. 1966. *Questionnaire Design and Attitude Measurement.* New York: Basic Books.

FIGURE 7.1 Schedule Child Interview

1. Interviewer _____ Date_____ Where interviewed ___
2. Name_____ 4. Sex_____
3. Address_____ 5. Age _____
   _____ 6. Grade_____

Persons in Household

7. Father _____
8. Mother _____
9. Brothers_____ _____ Age _
10. Sisters_____ _____ Age __
11. Others in household, and relationship, if possible.
_____

12. What time do you get up?_____
13. Who gets you up?_____
14. Do you ever get up without anybody waking you up? Yes___ No___
15. Does somebody tell you what clothes to wear to school?
                                                    Yes___ No___
16. Do you have breakfast before you go to school? Yes ___ No ___
17. Who fixes your breakfast? _____

18. What did you have for breakfast this morning?_____
19. Do you eat breakfast with somebody? Yes____ No ____
20. If "yes," who eats breakfast with you?_____
21. How do you get to school? Walk____ School Bus____ Regular Bus____
    Some other way?_____
22. How much time does it take you to go to school in the morning?_____
23. Do you stop on the way to school? Yes____ No____
24. If "yes," why do you stop?_____
25. What is the name of your school?_____
26. What kind of person is your teacher?_____
27. What kinds of kids are at your school?_____
28. Which kinds of kids are best?_____
29. What are some good things your teacher does?_____
30. What are some bad things your teacher does?_____
31. What is your best subject at school?_____
32. Where do you eat lunch?_____
33. If at school, how do you get your lunch?_____

8
Entering Adulthood

Parties and other forms of relaxation can be significant locations for learning roles and social identities. While having fun, the participants at a party also learn the appropriate forms of behavior, attitudes, and values for their age-group. At the same time they are preparing for the assumption of adult roles and modes of actions. The origin of attitudes like chauvinism and sexism as well as the essential character of a group identity can sometimes be traced to such relaxation rituals. By describing the details of the dance party, the author of this article shows its significance as a socialization mechanism. Insights into the "soulful" character of the party show us how such "get togethers" can have a profound influence on the lives of black, urban-ghetto youths. By probing into the minute aspects of this socialization scene, we can uncover basic processes that operate in the systematic changing of social identities.

The Dance Party as a Socialization Mechanism for Black Urban Preadolescents and Adolescents

R. Milton Clark

Introduction

For years, the study of black people in urban America has been an agenda item for social psychologists, sociologists, anthropologists, and others.[1]

[1] Whether we are talking about the "golden age" of sociological studies on blacks (1899–1945), especially 1930-40, the studies coming out of the "Chicago School," or the period from World War II to the present time, the fact is that black culture, as a topic, has received some treatment in the literature. Indeed, a few scholars have complained that whites and blacks are "preoccupied" with research studies on black people. I refer the reader to Hare 1969.

From *Sociology and Social Research* 55:145-54. Reprinted by permission.

A number of studies have attempted to depict the life of black men and women in the urban ghetto. Ethnographic studies of recent years (to name a very few) have included such books as Rainwater's (1970) *Soul,* an edited compilation of ethonographic studies, Keil's (1966) *Urban Blues,* Liebow's (1969) *Tally's Corner,* Hannerz's (1969) *Soulside,* and Suttles' (1968) *The Social Order of the Slum.* Others of not-so-recent vintage are *Black Metropolis* by Cayton and Drake (1945) and *Blackways of Kent* by Hylan Lewis (1955). In each of these books, the authors purport to look at the culture of blacks in America, but none takes any real in-depth look at the phenomenon of the black dance party vis-à-vis black culture. Indeed, investigation into the ritual of the black party has been infinitesimal.

In view of the prevailing quandary about black culture ("What is soul? What is black culture?"), it is truly surprising that so few sociologists and anthropologists have chosen to look at those subtle aspects of culture which might very well constitute the core of that bogeyman referred to as "soul." Clearly, it is not a ridiculous notion that these dance parties, these cultural celebrations, have some impact on black teenage youth. Nevertheless, in general social scientists have tended to treat this particular phenomenon as if it were superfluous if, indeed, it was treated at all. This is curious behavior on the part of scholars of culture in light of the fact that ceremonies and rituals are often the events most closely examined when one is attempting some analysis of the "soul" of a group of people. Interestingly enough, a cursory analysis of so-called artistic literature brings forcefully home the fact that many black novelists and "creative writers" do a much more exhaustive job of describing the ceremonies, the rituals, the "night life," or social side of black people as an integral part of the totality which has become known as "the black experience."[2]

At least four reasons can be cited to explain why there has been so little written on the socialization of today's urban black youth into adult society by way of the black dance party. First, in conducting research, the investigatory processes will necessarily lead to some parts of a culture being explored in greater depth than others. Of course, the logical extension of this is that some things may not be explored at all. A second reason for the lack of research on the black party is the social science tendency to emphasize the "pathological" aspects of black culture. Another reason for the scarce research on the black party may involve the difficulties of researching it. It may be rather difficult, for example, for a white researcher to act as a participant-observer and "blend in" at the type of black adolescent dance party described here.

[2]See for example Blingsley, Andrew, "Black Families and White Social Science" in Ladner 1973, pp. 448–49. Also, Hannerz 1966, pp. 11–17.

The fourth reason is that the urban black teen dance party is a relatively new occurrence. It was not in evidence on any large scale until the late 1940s and early 1950s.[3]

One of the very few scholars to recognize and investigate the black teen dance party while doing research on black culture was Dr. Joyce Ladner, a black woman. Her book *Tomorrow's Tomorrow* (1971) examines the life of the urban black female teenager while taking a look at the process by which she develops into a black woman. She states: (1971, pp. xxiv–v):

> I attempted to establish a strong rapport with all of them by spending a considerable amount of time in their homes with them and their families, at church, parties, dances, in the homes of their friends, shopping, at my apartment, and in a variety of other situations.

It may be conjectured that because she examined the behavior of the girls at dance parties, Dr. Ladner's analysis of the culture of these youth shows a much fuller insight than it otherwise might have done.[4] The purpose of this research is to examine the dance party and determine if it acts on urban black youth (1) as a socialization mechanism, (2) as a cultural ceremony, (3) as an agent of cultural transmission, and (4) as a source for black cultural growth.

The Dance Party in Perspective

The life cycle of each person is marked by a number of identity changes. As one grows older his or her fellows insist that the person assume new and varied responsibilities. Goodenough (1961, p. 87) has commented on this process:

> As (a person) attempts to play new roles, his self-image and public image both undergo modification. In every society, moreover, there are established procedures for motivating and facilitating these identity changes.

These identity changes have to be internalized by the individual if that person is to mature in the society in which he or she lives. There is at least one body of theory which has suggested that certain "transition rites" can be found in every culture, and these rites "represent solutions which people have found for dealing with the problems accompanying

---

[3]These dates were approximated by the fathers, mothers, and grandmothers I interviewed who ranged in age from twenty-nine to sixty. Most had migrated from the south and all felt that the dance party was an *urban* phenomenon.

[4]Some forms of black adolescent ritualistic behavior have, however, received attention in the literature. One example in this category is that of "the dozens." For a description of this ritual see Cobbs and Grier 1971, Dollard 1939, Seals 1969.

identity change" (Goodenough 1961, p. 88). Arnold Van Gennep (1969) talked of the *rites de passage*. He maintained that ceremonies always accompany the "life crises" of an individual. In a "life crisis," the individual goes through a transition which is marked by some sort of ceremony. Life crises include such universal events as birth, puberty, marriage, and death. There are also various other situations in which changes in behavior or group identification occur.

Structurally, Van Gennep (1969) outlined the ceremony to include three phases. The initial phase, termed *separation,* has to do with the severing of connections with a current way of life. The *transition* phase of the process is a connecting stage in which a person is neither in one group nor the other but, rather, is in "liminal" condition. The *incorporation* stage allows the individual to return to his old group (which is now a "new" group) with altered behavior. Armed with a plethora of field notes and the theory of Van Gennep, it became clear to me that the dance party could be appropriately viewed and discussed as a ritualistic ceremony, which aids individuals who are "in transition from one status or category to another." Five major aspects of the dance party, the cultural ceremony, which deserve discussion here are: (1) party variations, (2) party logistics, (3) dancing, (4) music, and (5) male-female interaction.

Methodology

An attempt has been made simply to describe and analyze what was said and done in the milieu examined. Though some of the behaviors described do not exist solely among black urban youth, the black dance party is a unique enough phenomenon to warrant study as an event distinct from any other. Throughout, the most illuminating interpretations of party dynamics were offered by the respondents during interviews.

The data were collected in the South and West sections of Chicago, Illinois, during the period from January 1972 to February 1973. Participant observation techniques and interviews were used as I visited a total of twenty-seven dance parties at a rate of roughly two per month and at separate times taped open-ended interviews with thirty-three people: eight adolescent males, seven adolescent females, four fathers, eleven mothers, and three grandmothers. The youths, all of whom said they had experienced the black dance party, ranged in age from eleven to twenty, and they all were from low-income black families. The interviews averaged one hour in length, and I visited each dance party generally between three and three and a half hours. Usually field notes were recorded at the party, but when this was not possible, field notes were made as soon as possible after leaving the dance party environment.

To gain sustained entry into the dance party itself, I combined a number of methods: (1) A female adolescent was used as an "informant." She helped me to gain entry into young adolescent house parties and, generally, to give information on the whereabouts of other dance parties being held. (2) Although I am a relatively young black researcher, I still found it necessary to alter my physical appearance:

> Tonight (Friday evening) I picked Stephanie (my informant) up at 8:00 P.M. I was dressed as she had suggested. I was clean shaven. I had on tight-fitting bell bottom pants, a "body shirt" which was slightly open at the top in the front, a pair of brown-suede boots, and I was wearing a large "Shaft" hat which was tilted to one side. Stephanie suggested that I take my glasses off because they made me look "too intellectual."

(3) I accomplished acceptance and familiarization at the dance parties by occasionally drinking from a wine bottle with males outside the party door while casually conversing with both males and females in the party. (4) I talked little but when I did, black English was purposely used as I wished to avoid language I felt would alienate the youth.

In my opinion, though there are certainly some differences and variations in local customs, dance styles, etc., the findings of this research may generally be considered applicable cross-regionally.

Dance Party Dynamics

Variations. There are a number of names which are used as synonyms for the dance party. One of the most common expressions is "house party." This expression refers to the fact that the party is given at somebody's home. Other names which are sometimes used are "get-together," "set," "jam," or "gig." Each of these terms, however, has certain minor but distinct connotations of its own. A "get-together" refers to a dance party in which a small group of mutual friends has come together. It is a bit more exclusionary than a "set" in terms of who comes. A "set" is a dance party designed to be casual and open but not overly crowded. The participants at a "set" do not necessarily have to be mutual friends. A "jam" is thought to be a lively, fast, "jumping" affair. A "gig" is a regional term used in some parts of the West and Midwest which means essentially the same thing as a "jam." Actually, all these names refer to happenings which are, in the final analysis, very similar.

Dance parties are sometimes described in terms of the amount of interaction that takes place. One young woman, Janet, who is sixteen years old and has frequented many house parties, describes the interaction variations one may encounter.

> There are all types of parties. Let's see, where can I start . . . first, there's the depressing party. That's when you go to somebody's house and it's no more than a hole in the wall and you find a whole lot of funky dudes tryin' to get in a rap. You can tell that everybody [males] there is just interested in one thang—gettin' over (having sex) . . . There's the strange party or what I call the "one couch against the other couch" type. Everybody there is scared of everybody else . . . In the boring party, nobody can and the dudes don't know how to rap. I just went to one like that last night. It was a dud . . . You know, there's the orgy-type of party but I've never seen that type but I hear white people are into that . . . I guess the best kind of party is the boss sets when everybody mingles and meets people and is gettin' down on the dance floor. I can really have a good time. Thats the kind of party I really dig.

Most of Janet's interactional styles take place at house parties. House parties are the most common parties among young blacks. The parents usually want to "keep an eye" on their youngsters (especially their girls) and want to be relatively sure of adult supervision. Parents can be fairly sure of this if the party is being sponsored in someone's home. Also, the house party is acknowledged as the type of "set" most frequented by the very young and the very old. Names given to the youngsters are "teenyboppers" and "shorties."

Variations of the house party are some of the dances sponsored by teen centers and "social clubs." The house party can be distinguished from the school dance or "dance hall" type of affair by the sheer differences in numbers. Fewer people come to a house party. It is smaller and more intimate. The house party takes place in a relatively small area, usually not larger than a fifteen-foot-by-fifteen-foot living room or basement, while on the other hand, the school dance is given in a gym or some other very large area.

Party Logistics

The party is primarily a weekend phenomenon, although a few parties are sometimes offered in the middle of the week. The weekend, especially Friday and Saturday, affords a person a greater amount of free time, and he usually "don't have to get up early" the next morning. Exact time and place for the parties are usually transmitted by word of mouth. On any given occasion males and/or females may participate in communicating the whereabouts of a party. There is nothing extremely elaborate about this process. It is done very casually.

> As they are standing around the basketball court, Lil Willie asks Mandrake where "the party" will be held tonight. Mandrake says

that there are two which he knows about. "One is up in the Darrow Homes (low-income housing projects) and there's another one 'out south'" [referring to lower-middle-class black section of town]. Mandrake continues, "If I can get my brother's ride, we can slide by both of 'em, man." "Yeah," Lil Willie responds, "that will sho' nuff be hip."

The young females are equally involved in this communication process. The process is initiated by whoever is sponsoring the party. Both males and females may sponsor a party. In terms of the processes involved, the party may look like this:

> Fourteen-year-old Sandra is "giving" (sponsoring) a party in her home in one hour. Sandra lives in "the projects." She is busy marking the records so that she won't get the ones she borrowed mixed up with her own. Music is already playing as they prepare for the party which is supposed to start around 8:00 P.M. Lucy, one of several girls already there to help prepare, says, "I bet the people don't even start coming till around 9:00." Sandra's fifteen-year-old brother Gerald is moving each piece of the furniture either flush against the wall or out of the living room area completely. He is attempting to develop a large dance area in the middle of the living-room floor. Gerald explains that the folding chairs shouldn't be in the living room because "They're not comin' here to sit down in the first place." Sandra's mother is next door playing cards with the adult neighbors. She comes over approximately every half hour to "check on things." At 8:10 P.M. a couple of girls arrive alone. Sandra tells them to "go and lay your coats on my bed." The girls talk about a black movie called "Cotton Comes to Harlem" and about different young men while they wait for the males to show up. Shirley's inquiry into the whereabouts of "the dudes" brings a knowing response of "Oh girl, you know they don't start coming till around 9." By 8:30, there are about ten females present. The only two males who are there have come with their girl friends. The girls have broken off into small groups. Some are dancing among themselves, others are making light conversation, and some others are in the bathroom "primping" their hair. At approximately 8:45, a group of four or five fellows arrives. As soon as they are in the door, the lights are dimmed to a soft, red hue. The party has officially begun. After this, more males and females arrive, although there is no sequential order. Outside the house, on the sidewalk, a group of the young males, who will eventually come into the party, pass around a bottle of "Ripple" wine. Some take a swallow from the bottle. Others decline.

It is common knowledge that, in general, the males will show up at the parties later than the females. Part of the reason for this is that it is the convention. Males like to see themselves as being more independent than the females. This causes no real problem as the females have grown accustomed to it.

There is some consumption of liquor by a few of the males, usually just before entering the party. Marijuana usage is rare. It is seen more commonly among the older teens. Sherman is a fifteen-year-old high-school student. He admits to becoming "high" before every party he attends. He believes it helps him.

> Yeh man, it's like when I'm high I can deal with the broads better. I started going with my main lady when I was high. I know I can rap my ass off when I'm feeling nice.

When both males and females are at the party, the ritualistic action begins. Each sex begins to attempt to impress the other. Seldom does anyone come alone. Usually three of four mutual friends will enter together. The groups may be all male, all female, or a mixture. There are normally between fifteen and fifty-five people at these parties with the average at about thirty people.

Dancing

Dancing is the principal activity. The types of dancing at these parties reflect two interrelated and important phenomena. First, the dances tend to reflect and satisfy a newly formed adolescent *need* to be close to members of the opposite sex. The "slow dances" especially serve this function by allowing close contact in this socially acceptable environment. Involved in this process, secondly, is the need for these blacks (who by the age of twelve are becoming more aware of the realities of racism) to cling to each other, lean on each other, and depend on each other. Facilitating this need is an institution called "the Grind" or "Slow Drag" which allows very close male/female physical contact. This dance consists of both people holding each other closely while rhythmically, slowly, rubbing their bodies against one another in what can be described as very sensual movement. As one black female stated:

> This an expression of love and love is the condition of human beings being human.

A couple of the males intimated that they had even experienced an involuntary orgasm while doing "the Grind" on the dance floor.

Young blacks learn to dance by watching older blacks, parents, relatives, and friends. The relaxed, but emotional, dance styles of many blacks has been referred to as "soulful" by those outside the culture as well as by other blacks. People often remark that when dancing, blacks don't seem to be faking or forcing anything. They don't have to wear the masks often shown in the presence of whites. Clark and Rush (1971, p.33) have discussed the implications of black dances:

> Dancing helps in part to satisfy that curiosity we feel about the other person. It is a chance to hold hands, to touch, and to move together in an enjoyable unison. For blacks it makes talk unnecessary. One complaint blacks have made about white parties is that whites frequently want to talk while dancing thereby interrupting the absorption and involvement in the physical movement.

Clark and Rush also talk about the white attitude of an "obvious" superior dance ability among blacks. They quote from an "infamous piece" called "My Negro Problem and Yours" where the author, a white man, states:

> I have come to value physical grace very highly and I am now capable of aching with all my being when I notice a Negro couple on the dance floor. They are on the kinds of terms with their own bodies that I should like to be on with mine, and for that precious quality they seem blessed to me. (1971, p.33)

This type of attitude is often seen as "sickening" to blacks. They sometimes feel that whites view them as oddities and they resent it. Young blacks have a difficult time understanding inquiries into "soul" dancing. Jenny, a black girl who goes to a racially mixed school, relates an experience she has had:

> When I'm in the lunchroom, sometimes the girls will bring the conversation around to how blacks dance. I try to be nice but they be askin' all kinds of *stupid* questions. Hecks, all you gotta do is to be yourself! Just move naturally, I tell 'em.

That quality of being "yourself" can be defined as a person having less inhibition about relating on a personal, informal level with other human beings.

In certain dances definite encouragement, group identification, and unity is seen developing among the participants. Males and females in close proximity slap hands and smile at each other. The words "we" and "us" are used. If the music stops, someone may start a chant of "*We* don't need no music," which is taken up by the crowd. The effect is one of a unit and an entity. One name given to this dance is "the soul train line." As individual males and females "come down the line," one hears shouts of "Go ahead on girl," "Right-on," "Do your thang." Both males and females are actively involved in this process. Even though the participants may not know each other, there is a tacit approval of each other because no one feels threatened. There is a spirit of "soul," solidarity, and togetherness at this point.

Music

The "soul" of the party is often helped along by the "soul" music. The music is a very important element of the black party. It sets the tone with a "gutsy soul" quality. Many people describe "black music" as being "more funky." Lonnie is sixteen years old and is in the school band. He comments on the strength of the music.

> I can't see how anybody can listen to James Brown or Wilson Pickett and not at least start pattin' their feet, you know what I mean? The music itself almost pulls you up out of your seat. When James Brown says "Everybody over there, get on up, Everybody over here, get on up," you KNOW he means you and then when his heavy music starts it's almost like somebody sayin' "It's celebration time."

Again, what may be really being described here is the freeness of oneself, that nebulous, intangible, spiritual-emotional feeling which may only be experienced by somebody who has lived under certain conditions in a certain kind of environment (Watkins 1971). These youngsters see what their mothers and fathers have to go through. They develop an acute sensitivity to the oppression under which they must live, though it is often difficult for them to verbalize this oppression.[5] Some simply may say:

> We know what it's like to have the blues because we live them.

Quincy Jones (1972) is a black composer who has suggested the great significance of black music:

> Each musical heritage has so much to do with the sociological thing, the same way it is with black music. I used to sit at the Sophia Mosque, in Turkey, and I couldn't leave, it was just a strange marble place, you know, and in the middle of the night you'd hear these cats with the Arabic chants, with the quarter-tones, and it was the soul of the country, you could just feel the whole thing.

Black music is part of the black experience. The black experience motivates black music and therefore the two cannot be separated.

Male and Female

The conversation at the party is centered around the theme of getting to know people. Although it sometimes happens, seldom will one find

---

[5] The element of oppression, it seems, helps to mold the "souls of black folks." To fully understand it, one must live it. As Fats Waller reputedly told the society matron when she asked him what "swing" was: "If you gotta ask, then you'll never know." See Norman Mailer's (1957) discussion in his essay *The White Negro*.

the teens at a party discussing matters of "importance." The most important matter at a party has to do with the possibility of meeting others. It is interesting to note that often both males and females are initially shy toward one another. Because of a developed lack of trust among urban dwellers, genuine spontaneity initially is not automatic. Parents increasingly warn their children about conversing with strangers. As a consequence, even peer relationships become less spontaneous. The youngsters usually have to "get warmed up" toward each other before the genuine spontaneity will begin. Also, any observable inhibiting force, such as a "strict" parent or a questionable white person, may cause the party dynamics to be suppressed.

As a general rule, male/female interaction will occur rather quickly. The less emotion a male shows, the more "cool" he is supposed to be. For a male to show emotion may mean doom for the male/female relationship because male sensitivity and kindness may often be construed as a weakness by females. This truism may be the result of the influence of the sexism existing in larger American society. Emotion is often seen as a weak, basic, unsophisticated behavior by the sexist (and racist) elements in our society.

Usually, if a male is interested in one of the females, he will try to make conversation with her *after* he has first danced with her. It is at this point that the fellow with a greater verbal dexterity is more likely to woo the girl he wants. He knows how to "rap" to the girl. The female reaction to being wooed? As one young woman told her companion:

> Flattery will get you everywhere.

Rapping may be one-line sentences designed to flatter the girl:

> Hey, baby what's your name?
> My, my, my, I wonder where you've been all my life.

Or more elaborate advances:

> Which one of these dudes is your boyfriend? The reason I asked is cause you look too good to be here alone.
> Hey sweetheart, you sho' look good to me; If God had made anything more beautiful than you, He would have kept it for hisself.

Males who cannot "rap," in general, do not win the affection of as many females as do the bona fide rappers. Nonrappers simply do not make as many contacts as the others.

The youngsters receive socialization into what behaviors are expected and accepted for males and for females. It is here that the female learns that the male must be the aggressor. It is the male who has to make up his mind to ask for a dance. It is the male who usually must initiate any intimate conversation. When a couple is dancing, the male is the "leader" and the female is a "follower." A female learns very early that "this is the way it's spozed to be." The female is even given positive reinforcement by being congratulated and complimented when she has done an excellent job of "following" the male when dancing.

> Lloyd stops dancing in the middle of the record. He tells his dance partner, Bernice, "Now look here, both of us cain't lead this here thang; if you want to play the part of the man, just let me know. Otherwise, just lighten up and follow me."

Also a female is not expected to ask a male to dance. To do so is to risk being termed "fast" or "desperate" or "hard up." The female does have the option to refuse to dance, however, and in this way "get back" at a male she may dislike.

> Mary is extremely overweight and has short hair. She has been standing in the corner most of this evening. Occasionally she will reach in her pocket and pull out a pack of Kool Cigarettes [a very popular brand among black smokers]. She smokes. A very popular hit record is playing. Bernard sees that all the other girls are already dancing so he noncommitally asks Mary to dance. She refuses. Bernard seems surprised at this. Another fellow asks Mary to dance. She obliges. Bernard is upset.

The standard of beauty is an important variable to be examined. The negative characteristics of Mary were her weight and her hair length. Hair length, in terms of long or short, is not criticized as much as body width. Long hair, however, whether straightened or in the Afro style, tends to be valued over shorter hair.

Another ploy used by females (though sometimes unsuccessfully) indirectly to attract a particular male is to make themselves "available." This can be accomplished by having a female friend introduce her or by "just happening" to find herself near the particular male just as a record is beginning. If he wants to dance, she's "available." At all times she is expected to let the male be the aggressor. In this setting she must play the submissive role, although she may or may not, in fact, be a submissive person.

Applying It to the Model

Now let us apply all of this to Van Gennep's model of *rites de passage*. We know that each individual undergoes identity changes throughout his life. These identity changes are accomplished by identifiable transition rites or *rites de passage*. In the black adolescent dance party we can view the phase of *separation* as being that time when the youth loses the desire to do only those same-sex things which eleven and twelve year olds are "supposed" to do. The young preadolescent wants to do what the "big kids" can do. The child is attempting to broaden his experiential base. This phase evolves into the transitional stage where the youth begins to go to dance parties and acts and reacts to the many things there to which he or she is exposed. Repeated exposure to the dance-party atmosphere leads to the *incorporation* stage, when the individual has learned certain behaviors which will help him or her to cope with an adult life as a black person while simultaneously suggesting certain in-group and out-group behaviors for dealing with a racist society.[6]

Discussion

After the socialization is completed, the dance party will have *helped* to satisfy the individual's "need to belong." He may evolve ready to say, "Black is beautiful." She is more likely to say, "I am proud to be black, whiteman!" By dressing in stylish, flashy clothes they say, "I am important." By dancing in certain distinct ways they say, "I am Somebody." As Goodenough (1961, p. 98) has noted:

> The ultimate requisite of identity change is a consolidated sense of self as the new kind of person one hoped to become. Contributing to this are such things as acts of commitment and positive recognition by others, matters we have already discussed. In addition to these things, a person must have some experience which dramatizes his new self to himself, such as success in an undertaking in which he could not have thought of himself as successful at all. "Look at what I can do!" is the child's way of expressing it. And having had such an experience, people seek to repeat it.

These *rites de passage* affect young blacks at the puberty stage before the youngster reaches the adolescent–young-adult stage.[7] The dance party ceremony affects blacks as young as eleven or twelve years old. At this young, impressionable age the party can be nothing less than

---

[6]Van Gennep warns us that each ceremony must be viewed in relation to the other ceremonies; that is, we must take into account the "ceremonial whole" existent in the social order. In the black ghetto, for example, other microcosmic "pieces" of the ceremonial whole (aside from the family) are organized sport teams, gangs, and social clubs. Each of these forces makes a contribution in the entire process of the formation of a person's total *rites de passage*. As with any other single source of influence, it is not a simple task to measure the extent to which the socialization affects any given person. Though it is clear that the dance party has some impact on individuals, the exact (or even approximate) degree of influence will require further research in this area.

[7]Most young black teenagers will have experienced a party by the time they are thirteen or fourteen. This initial contact with the new party environment begins the socialization process that the individual experiences.

a very potent socializing force for these youth. Kimball (1965, p. 177) has observed the influence of ceremonies affecting the very young in a society:

> From a societal point of view the most significant *rite de passage* is initiation into tribal membership and adulthood at puberty. The ceremony marking this event may be quite brief, but it may also extend over a lengthy time period depending upon the nature of the instruction which must be given. Even among those groups which do not have formal observance of physiological puberty as the point in time for initiation, there are other occasions, or educational devices, which serve the same purposes and which incorporate the basic ritual and instructional aspects. The important point is that each society does have ways to *claim* the young.

The black teen dance party should be seen as one of the "educational devices" which helps cover these "instructional aspects."

Conclusion

An attempt has been made to show that as a socialization mechanism, as a cultural ceremony, as an agent of cultural transmission, and as an arena for black cultural growth, the dance party is uniquely equipped to serve its black population. It offers an introduction to black unity and an introduction to ways of acting as an adult. Just as marriage and funeral ceremonies often show ritualistic family solidarity, the dance party ceremony shows elements of a ritualistic black family solidarity. There is a "coming together" of people who have something in common. The black unity, the spirit of community, is expressed at the party primarily in the dancing and in the "soul music." Through conversations and interaction with peers and adults—who happen to be the most important socializing influence among adolescents—the youngster learns standards of beauty, "appropriate" emotions for different situations and racial attitudes.[8] It is clear also that certain patterns of interaction with members of the opposite sex can be seen developing in the social interaction between black teens at these house parties. Elements of chauvinism and sexism, for example, are seen very readily. Finally, the dance party is a socially accepted vehicle for adolescent female/male interaction until they "outgrow" or "graduate" to lounges, bars, clubs, or other adult social activities.

[8]Significantly, too, urban blacks today have had less contact with the white world than any previous generation. Consequently, there is a greater polarization and a greater cultural particularism.

References

Clark, C., and S. Rush. 1971. *How to Get Along with Black People: A Handbook for White Folks.* New York: Third Press-Joseph Okpaku.

Cobbs, P., and W. Grier. 1971. *The Jesus Bag.* New York: McGraw-Hill.

Dollard, J. 1939. "The Dozens: Dialectic of Insult" *American Imago* (January): 3–25.

Drake, S., and H. Cayton. 1945. *Black Metropolis.* New York: Harcourt, Brace.

Goodenough, W. 1961. "Education and Identity." In *Anthropology and Education.* Philadelphia: University of Pennsylvania Press.

Hannerz, U. 1969. *Soulside.* New York: Columbia University Press.

Jones, Q. 1972. "Quincy Jones Sees the Whole Thread." *Rolling Stone* 104 (March 16): 22.

Keil, C. 1966. *Urban Blues.* Chicago: University of Chicago Press.

Kimball, S. 1965. "The Transmission of Culture" *Educational Horizons* 43: 161–86.

Ladner, J. 1971. *Tomorrow's Tomorrow: The Black Woman.* New York: Doubleday.

Ladner, J., ed. 1973. *The Death of White Sociology.* New York: Vintage Books.

Lewis, H. 1955. *Blackways of Kent.* Chapel Hill: University of North Carolina Press.

Liebow, E. 1969. *Tally's Corner.* Boston: Little, Brown.

Mailer, N. 1957. *The White Negro.* San Francisco, Calif.: City Lights Books.

Rainwater, L., ed. 1970. *Soul.* Trans-Action: Aldine Publishing Company.

Seals, H. 1969. *You Ain't Thuh Man Yuh Mamma Wuz.* Chicago—: Independently Published Article.

Suttles, G. 1968. *The Social Order of the Slum.* Chicago: University of Chicago Press.

Van Gennep, A. 1969. *The Rites of Passage.* Chicago: University of Chicago Press.

Watkins, M. 1971. "The Lyrics of James Brown: Ain't It Funky Now, or Money Won't Change Your Licking Stick." In *Amistad 2,* ed. J. Williams and C. Harris. New York: Random House.

9

Learning an Occupation

Socialization refers to a learning process that continues throughout life. It involves the acquisition of action patterns and meanings appropriate to varied social contexts. In childhood we usually learn more general and unspecialized patterns, while in adulthood the patterns narrow around significant events and persons. The child acquires generalized ways of thinking and behaving for the society; the adult must learn specific roles. But since adults often presume that they already know how to behave and think, learning new roles and activities sometimes becomes problematic. The most significant socialization experiences for adults probably occur in conjunction with an occupation. In this article Arthur Neiderhoffer, once a policeman himself, describes the process of learning that takes place throughout the career of a policeman.

On the Job

Arthur Neiderhoffer

The Rookie at the Precinct

The recruit reports to his precinct with some anxiety but, in general, ready to practice what has been preached to him at the academy. According to the general code of deportment, which covers the behavior of the newcomer, he is expected to be a good listener, quiet, unassuming, and deferential without being obsequious toward his superior officers. Despite a good deal of hazing as part of the breaking-in period, the recruit usually adapts to these standards without difficulty.

From Arthur Neiderhoffer, *Behind the Shield* (New York: Doubleday, 1967). Reprinted by permission.

For a month or so, he receives lenience and sympathy for routine mistakes. After that he is on trial and carefully watched to see how he measures up to the challenge of police patrol. His reputation is made in the next few weeks and will shadow him for the rest of his police career: no matter where or when he is transferred, a phone call will precede his arrival, reporting the evaluation that was made of his handling of his first few important cases.

On these cases the new patrolman must resolve the dilemma of choosing between the professional ideal of police work he has learned at the academy and the pragmatic precinct approach. In the academy, where professionalism is accented, the orientation is toward that of the social sciences and opposed to the "lock-them-up" philosophy. But in the precinct a patrolman is measured by his arrest record. Thus the new man is needled when he shows signs of diffidence in arresting or asserting his authority. Over and over again well-meaning old-timers reiterate, "You gotta be tough, kid, or you'll never last." Fifteen years ago Westley observed this phenomenon in the police force he studied and explained the basic rationalization behind the slogan:

> Expecting the excuse, the argument, the evasion, the officer tries to get tough first, to treat them tough, to make them respect the law, a particular judgment of the law. . . .This is the origin of the get tough, make them respect you thesis which predominates throughout police work.[1]

It is disconcerting to find that a similar solution to the practitioner-client problem is widely accepted in other service professions, which have none of the authoritarian flavor of the police force. In probation and parole work, Lloyd Ohlin found that:

> The (social) worker experiences widespread pressure by the police and other official functionaries to define his role as that of the enforcement officer who should use control measures to restrict the client's freedom and coercion to punish him for wrongdoing. When he attempts to resist these pressures, he finds probation and parole interpreted as leniency and himself identified as a "sob sister."[2]

According to Howard S. Becker's analysis of the teacher-pupil relationship, some teachers adopt the same attitude toward their charges:

> You can't ever let them get the upper hand on you or you're through. So I start out tough. . . .You've got to start tough then you can

---

[1] William A. Westley, "The Police: A Sociological Study of Law, Custom and Morality," (Unpublished doctoral dissertation, University of Chicago, 1951) p. 112.
[2] Ohlin, op. cit., p. 221.

ease up as you go along. If you start out easy-going, when you try to get tough, they'll just look at you and laugh.[3]

That a "get-tough" ideology dominates many workers in the major institutions devoted to the education, control, and welfare of the public is of prime importance to sociologists. Why should the field practitioner, in actual contact with the clientele he is supposed to serve, develop a philosophy so contrary to the creed of altruism and service that his profession exalts? Apparently, practical experience leads to the acceptance of a Hobbesian model of the social system.

In the case of the young policeman, the choice between professionalism and pragmatism is apt to depend largely on the circumstances of the case. It is, for example, no great feat for a policeman working in an upper-class neighborhood to protect the rights of his white clientele. It is much more difficult in a lower-class community. In a slum area the professional ethic loses most of the time; the civil rights of lower-class individuals do not count as much as the necessity to accomplish a staggering amount of police work as expeditiously as possible. Shifting from idealism to pragmatism, the newcomer to a lower-class precinct house enters a new reference group whose members are a little contemptuous of all the academy represents.

Learning the Ropes: Language

The identification with this new group is revealed in many facets of behavior and personality. Speech patterns increasingly reflect the loss of influence of academy training, which demanded a decent level of grammar and vocabulary. Police terminology, which substitutes broad stereotypes for precise distinctions, becomes a linguistic crutch. The colloquialism "desperate" means anything bad, unpleasant, or derogatory. "Radical" is used to label anyone who is not reactionary, or at least conservative, even those policemen who are articulate in protesting about long-accepted conditions in the department. A "detail" is a special job or assignment—usually a desirable one. "Rabbi" means a person with influence in the department. Although Jewish policemen suspect the dark origins of this neologism, they cannot help being amused when they overhear conversations like the following:

"Say, did you hear that O'Grady finally got that detail to the detective division?"
"No. But I knew that he had a contract in. Who was his rabbi?"
"His rabbi? Why his uncle, the priest, of course."

[3]Howard S. Becker, "Social Class Variations in the Teacher-Pupil Relationship," *Journal of Educational Sociology* 25 (1951–1952): 459.

The word "contract" is very important in the police world. It can mean any obligation, debt, errand, request, agreement, or arrangement.[4]

A whole class of colorful idioms is derived from parts of the body. "Hairy" stands for smart, shrewd, and conniving. "On the arm" and "egghead" are fairly well known in common parlance. A courageous policeman who stands up for his rights is complimented with the description, "he has a lot of balls."[5]

In the precinct even the well-educated officers adopt this slovenly jargon, sometimes consciously, to merge their identities with those of the "common men" on the force. They purposely say mischiev-*i*-ous and mispronounce other common words in order to belong and conform.[6] The police role and its special argot cannot, however, be donned for eight hours a day without making serious inroads: when the time comes for the intellectual to slough off his occupational speech patterns, he is often unsuccessful, to his great embarrassment.

Although official police policy strongly condemns any reciprocity between policemen and criminal elements, it nonetheless exists and is mirrored in a shared vocabulary. This social interaction is unwittingly recognized as unavoidable by the authoritative *FBI Law Enforcement Bulletin.* The editors, listing a glossary of several hundred words and phrases commonly used by the underworld, are forced to justify the fact that at least one-half of the list is included in the police lexicon:

> Just as the newspaperman, the short-order cook, or the baseball player has a specialized manner of expressing himself, so has the juvenile gang member, the criminal and, by necessity, the police officer. . . .
>
> The words on pages 24, 25 are included in the jargon of the violator as well as that of the law enforcement officer, since it is difficult to separate one from the other. The policeman, finding it necessary to be cognizant of the criminal's lingo, frequently absorbs it as part of his own speech and uses the terms and phrases in his general

---

[4]There are varying degrees of obligation in each contract. When it is performed, a reciprocal obligation arises to fulfill a contract in return. Sometimes, in the performance of a contract, several intermediaries are approached in order to attain the final result. Each of these middlemen becomes enmeshed in this contractual web. Thus, it forms an unofficial system of rights and obligations that often controls interpersonal relations more stringently than do bureaucratic protocol and hierarchy.

[5]For a parallel study of the use of "body" terms in the jargon of an all-male society, see Henry Elkin, "Aggressive and Erotic Tendencies in Army Life," *American Journal of Sociology* 51 (1945–46): 411–12.

[6]In "The Intellectuals and the Language of Minorities," *American Journal of Sociology* 64 (1958–59): 25–35, Melvin Seeman has shown that where intellectuals are minorities, they often employ defensive tactics of this type.

police activities, as well as contributing to it many colorful forms of expression of his own.[7]

Ritual

Along with a new vocabulary, the new patrolman also picks up a series of rituals, several of them vital to the world of the policeman. One—the "coffee-and" ritual which began each tour of duty—operated with unforgettable potency during the time I was on the beat. Each day en route to his post, the patrolman stopped almost compulsively at his favorite luncheonette or cafeteria for coffee and cake. Even when a tough "shoofly"[8] was reported in the vicinity, a "real" cop felt obliged to risk the chance of receiving a complaint to stop for his coffee. Since the ritual was followed even on sweltering summer days, it could not be related to his desire to warm up. It had nothing to do with hunger because in most cases the men came to work just after a heavy meal. It was not a "break" to relieve fatigue; the tour was just starting. In some manner the coffee seemed to allay the vestige of anxiety every thinking policeman carries with him on his tour of patrol. Life and death are so closely bound up with police work that the ceremonious interruption, like a religious duty, may have constituted a libation to the gods.

Foot Patrol

The basic job of the police force is patrol, where most recruits start. The patrolman pounding his beat is the proletarian of the department, and, like proletarians in most countries, accorded a very low status. His position has been realistically described in the *Police Management Review*, issued by the Planning Bureau of the New York City Police Department:

> Yet, more than anyone else in the Department, the foot patrolman is prone to boredom and inertia. Young and initially enthusiastic men are often bored at a time when a proportion of the Force is overworked.[9]
>
> The working hours of the foot patrolman, the recurrent bad publicity, the indifferent attitudes of the public, the fact that promotion and earnings are almost completely divorced from the performance of his duties, all constitute an imposing array of antimotivating factors.[10]

---

[7]"Juvenile Gangs and Underworld Have Own Lingo," *FBI Law Enforcement Bulletin* 30 (January 1961): 22–23.

[8]A "shoofly" is a supervisor of patrol who purposely dresses in civilian clothes rather than in proper uniform in order to avoid being spotted by the men on patrol.

[9]Lieutenant Matthew J. Neary, "Motivating the Foot Patrolman," *Police Management Review* (November 1963): 5.

[10]Neary, "Motivating the Foot Patrolman," p. 7.

The patrolman can find little satisfaction in his work when something goes wrong on his post; although the investigation starts at the very top, inevitably the "buck" is passed down until the final responsibility and blame come to rest upon him. When, however, praise is lavished, some superior officer or member of the force in a special assignment appears from nowhere to accept the accolade. Moreover, the patrolman, although he does a little of everything, is being increasingly restricted to trivialities because police work is constantly developing specialties that only trained experts can handle. Just when the work becomes most interesting, a specialist is assigned to replace the lowly "man on the post."

In the exciting cases, such as homicides or serious felonies, the patrolman on post must notify the station house as soon as he discovers the incident. Within minutes, a superior officer from the Detective Division assumes command. From then on the patrolman is a supernumerary. Detectives swarm over the scene searching for clues, interviewing witnesses and suspects, handling specific parts of the investigation. The Photo Unit arrives to take pictures. The Mobile Laboratory rolls up, and scientific instruments are trundled into the crime area. The patrolman, shunted to one side, is sometimes allowed to guard the scene, by which time he may be wondering just how necessary he really is. It may, however, be worth noting that even the detective who supplants the patrolman will have only a moment of glory if he solves the case. The computer has invaded the world of the police. Soon, the record of his achievement will be a few holes punched in an IBM card stockpiled in some basement storeroom. Alienation may not be as universal a condition in contemporary society as some social critics allege, but a computerized milieu fosters foreboding uneasiness.

The foot patrolman with heavy responsibility but no prestige either on or off the job becomes first bitter, then apathetic. Many times I have asked a young patrolman how many years he has had on the job. A common response is, "I have seventeen years, four months, two weeks, and three days to go until retirement." Small wonder that the score of foot patrolmen on the cynicism questionnaire was significantly higher than the mean score of the total sample.

Keeping the Law

Another potent source of cynicism is the new policeman's realization that it is literally impossible to enforce every law "on the book"—the jails would be too small to hold the prisoners—and that one of the important arts he must master is the sense of when to take action and, perhaps more important, when not to. An officer who brings too many trivial cases into the station house is considered incompetent, but an officer who brings in too few is considered a shirker.

The conventional wisdom of the job sets the standard. The old sages of the station house dispense didactic tales to which new members of the force listen avidly, thereby learning that typical incidents to be settled on the street or occasionally even dodged are the annoying drunk, the case of disorderly conduct involving adolescents who congregate on street corners, and quarrels between: husband and wife, taxi driver and his fare, neighbor and neighbor, store owner and customer, and landlord and tenants.

When an officer clearly observes a serious violation of law, his discretion is limited; he must arrest. But the average crime is not committed in full view of the policeman. He must conduct a preliminary investigation which places him in the middle of a labyrinth, following conflicting reports of witnesses into blind alleys. Each suspect denies any connection with the crime. Perpetrators claim to be victims. From time to time progress is barred by a wall of silence. Shall he make an arrest or not? Which of the suspects should he arrest? Just when he needs them most, the usual guideposts are silent. His wisest procedure is to trust no one. Cynicism improves his technique as an investigator.[11]

It is the individual policeman's responsibility to decide if and how the law should be applied, and he searches for the proper combination of cues on which to base his decision. These are derived from the typical sociological variables: class, education, clarity of role prescriptions, reference groups, self-conception, and visibility. Because the application of the law depends to a large degree on the definition of the situation and the decision reached by the patrolman, he in effect makes the law; it is his decision that establishes the boundary between legal and illegal.

Always searching for this tenuous and blurred dividing line in the behavior of others, the policeman frequently loses the ability to distinguish between law and license in himself. As the result of United States Supreme Court decisions, kaleidoscopic changes in the practical application of the law have confused the average patrolman until he is often uncertain of the proper course of action. His ignorance dims the luster of the law because the policeman learns to manipulate law in the name of expediency, and this loss of respect, in turn, breeds more cynicism.

In the administration of justice, the poor, the minorities, and the deviants need all the protection possible. They suffer most when the police fail to take proper action. In busy precincts covering sections inhabited by Negroes or Puerto Ricans, this sphere of inaction is large.

[11]Despite his typical mistrust, the average policeman fancies himself a keen psychologist, who can by intuition, and/or experience, sense when a person being interrogated is lying or telling the truth.

Incidents that would cause commotion and consternation in quiet precincts seem so common in ghetto neighborhoods that they are often not reported. The police rationalize this avoidance of duty with theories that the victim would refuse to prosecute because violence has become the accepted way of life for his community, and that any other course would result in a great loss of time in court, which would reduce the efficiency of other police functions. These decisions are rarely subjected to review, a particularly disturbing situation to men who are interested in creating a better system of justice.[12]

> Police decisions not to invoke the criminal process largely determine the outer limits of law enforcement. By such decisions, the police define the ambit of discretion throughout the process of other decision-makers—prosecutor, grand and petit jury, judge, probation officer, correction authority, and parole and pardon boards. These police decisions, unlike their decisions to invoke the law, are of extremely low visibility and consequently are seldom the subject of review. Yet an opportunity for review and appraisal of nonenforcement decisions is essential to the functioning of the rule of law in our system of criminal justice.[13]

When the professionals attack this nonenforcement of the law, the articulate defender of the status quo has a powerful riposte: he can plead that the social sciences so profusely quoted by the profession also teach the lesson of cultural relativity. This doctrine encourages an observer from one culture to respect the integrity of another, although its standards of behavior may be different from his own. The implication is that the policeman has some justification for accepting a minority group's way of life on its own terms and, thus, for acting the way he does. There is no easy answer to this paradox.

A harsher indictment of the police officer's neglect or refusal to enforce the law has been pronounced by Martin Luther King who held that nonfeasance amounts to malfeasance:

> The most grievous charge against municipal police is not brutality, although it exists. Permissive crime in ghettos is the nightmare of the slum family. Permissive crime is the name for the organized crime that flourishes in the ghetto—designed, directed, and cultivated by white national crime syndicates operating numbers, narcotics, and prostitution rackets freely in the protected sanctuaries of the ghettos.

---

[12]Joseph Goldstein, "Police Discretion Not to Invoke the Criminal Process: Low Visibility Decisions in the Administration of Justice," *The Yale Law Journal* 69 (1960): 574–75. See also Herman Goldstein, "Police Discretion: The Ideal Versus the Real," *Public Administration Review* 23 (September 1963): 140–48; and Wayne R. LaFave, *Arrest: The Decision to Take a Suspect into Custody* (Boston: Little, Brown 1965).

[13]Joseph Goldstein, "Police Discretion," p. 543.

Because no one, including the police, cares particularly about ghetto crime, it pervades every area of life.[14]

The Summons

Even the routine, apparently trivial duties that the young policeman must learn to handle may easily escalate into a near riot unless he controls them properly. Take, for example, the serving of a summons on a peddler. The public observing this event is apt to react with hostility toward the policeman. The officer himself may feel a little guilty.

This appears to be a universal dilemma for policemen. Anatole France has written a short story, "Crainquebille,"[15] which depicts the repercussions in the life of a French vegetable seller when Constable 64 arrests him for peddling. When the policeman orders Crainquebille to move on, the vendor mutters something under his breath which sounds to the policeman like "*Mort aux Vaches*," in those days, a vile insult that meant literally "Death to the Cows," but was interpreted as "Down with the Cops."[16]

During World War II, a New York City policeman had an equally harrowing experience with a peddler, selling pretzels, who set up her daily shop in front of a well-known department store. One of the patrolman's important duties was to keep the post clear of peddlers, by no means an easy assignment on a busy shopping day. Although Molly, as we shall call her, was small and elderly, she had the strength and speed of an athlete. She dexterously threaded her way through the crowds, unseen by the police until she set down her basket at a suitable spot. No matter how many times she was chased away, she always reappeared.

One day the patrolman became so exasperated that he decided to serve her with a summons. At the sight of his summons book, Molly began to scream, "Murderer! He's killing me! Why doesn't he catch criminals instead of ruining a poor woman who is trying to make an honest living? Nazi!" With this she threw herself down on the ground and rolled around in a fit of fury or despair, never stopping the stream of epithets. The policeman (who was Jewish himself) was thoroughly embarrassed by the obvious rancor of the crowd of hundreds gathered to watch the show. Arrest seemed the only answer, and in desperation he asked a bystander to call the precinct for a patrol wagon.

---

[14]Martin Luther King, "Beyond the Los Angeles Riots: Next Stop: The North," *Saturday Review* 48 (November 13,1965): 34.

[15]Anatole France, "Crainquebille," in *Golden Tales of Anatole France* (New York: Dodd Mead, 1926), pp. 215–57.

[16]It is interesting to note that in France the police were called "cows" in the vernacular, but to Americans the police are "bulls."

After a struggle, he placed Molly and her heavy pretzel basket into the wagon, climbed in himself, and signaled the driver to proceed. Suddenly he noticed a transformation in the prisoner. The histrionics had stopped. As they slowly pulled away from the scene, Molly peered intently through the rear grating, a quiet smile of triumph on her face. The officer glanced out. From the subway kiosk Molly's husband, Abie, was emerging, loaded down with an overflowing basket of pretzels, certain of a couple of uninterrupted hours of brisk sales. It was impossible to escape the suspicion of prearrangement.

Police management hotly denies the existence of a summons quota. Men at the patrol level are not so sure about this. In November 1960, there was a well-publicized altercation between then New York Police Commissioner Kennedy and Patrolman John J. Cassese, the president of the Patrolmen's Benevolent Association. Patrolman Cassese bought advertising space in the New York City press in which he alleged that there was definitely a quota system and that he could prove it.[17] Thereupon the delegates to the PBA were given questionnaires demanding whether or not they knew of any summons quota system. According to the *Herald Tribune*, delegates who answered negatively admitted later that they had lied[18] to keep from having to reveal the names of the superior officers responsible for ordering the quota system. The so-called rat rule requires a member of the force having knowledge of a violation of departmental regulations to report it to a superior officer, but these policemen preferred to perjure themselves rather than be known as informers.[19]

Graft

Every policeman patrolling the streets sooner or later faces the temptation of a "payoff." As in most other large organizations, there are the few who have their price, but their betrayal of the public trust has unjustifiably tarnished the whole department. The image of the crooked cop projected in literature has fortified this misconception. In *The Iceman Cometh*, Eugene O'Neill described ex-Lieutenant Pat McGloin as "the biggest drunken grafter that ever disgraced the police force." McGloin's former position lures him, and his one hope is to be reinstated because "there's

---

[17]It is of interest that Commissioner Kennedy on December 9, 1959, sent a teletype message to all commands explaining why there could not be a quota: "Inasmuch as there is no quota on persons killed and injured, there cannot be and there is no quota on enforcement." See New York *Herald Tribune*, November 29, 1960, p. 15.

[18]New York *Herald Tribune*, November 29, 1960, p. 15.

[19]A statement concerning the existence of a summons quota was included in the cynicism questionnaire. Well over half the patrolmen, and more than 40 percent of the superior officers apparently do believe that a summons quota exists.

fine pickings these days."[20] Actual policemen seem to accept graft for other reasons than avarice. Often the first transgression is inadvertent. Or they may be gradually indoctrinated by older policemen. Step by step they progress from a small peccadillo to outright shakedown and felony.

A Denver policeman involved in the police burglary scandal of 1961 recalls his downfall.

> So the rookie . . . is turned over to a more experienced man for breaking-in. . . .
> He knows he is being watched. . . . He is eager to be accepted.
> He does what he can to show he has guts. He backs up his partner in any way he can. . . .
> It may happen like this: the older man stops at a bar, comes out with some packages of cigarettes. He does this several times. He explains that this is part of the job. . . .
> So he, the rookie, goes into a Skid Row bar and stands uncomfortably at the end, waiting for the bartender to acknowledge his presence and disdainfully toss him two packages of butts.
> The feeling of pride slips away, and a hint of shame takes hold.
> One thing leads to another for the rookies. After six months they have become conditioned to accept free meals, a few packs of cigarettes, turkeys at Thanksgiving and liquor at Christmas from the respectable people in their districts. . . . .[21]

Lincoln Steffens, one of the great muckrakers, studied police corruption in New York and other cities at the end of the nineteenth century.[22] His report of the Schmittberger saga is documented by the records of the Lexow Commission. The blemished hero of the story is a baker named Schmittberger, who became a member of the New York City Police Department and was assigned to the Tenderloin district. He was so honest, and so dumb, that when someone came up to him one day and put ten dollars in his hand while he was on patrol, he immediately turned it over to his captain. The captain was so impressed by this honesty that he rewarded Schmittberger in the most fitting way possible—by making him his graft collection man. Schmittberger showed great talent for his new job. Finally, he turned state's evidence during the Lexow investigation and thus retained his job. Theodore Roosevelt, the new police

[20]Eugene O'Neill, *The Iceman Cometh* (New York: Random House, 1946), pp. 55, 57.
[21]Mort Stern, "What Makes a Policeman Go Wrong?" *Journal of Criminal Law, Criminology and Police Science* 53 (March 1962): 98–99.
[22]Lincoln Steffens, *The Shame of the Cities* (New York: McClure Phillips, 1904); Lincoln Steffens, *The Autobiography of Lincoln Steffens* (New York: Harcourt, Brace, 1931). For one of the latest of the many books on the subject of police corruption, see Ralph L. Smith, *The Tarnished Badge* (New York: Thomas Y. Crowell, 1965).

commissioner, was eager to eliminate vice in the city and corruption in the department. Steffens advised him to rely upon Schmittberger as the spearhead of the campaign. Schmittberger, the most assiduous collector of graft under the former regime, responded by devoting his tremendous energy and experience to the problem of arresting or outlawing gamblers and prostitutes.

Schmittberger's initial encounter with graft was not unique. The pattern has repeated itself through the years. A similar case from the 1940s involved a young policeman who held a college degree. The commanding officer of the precinct, favorably impressed by the patrolman's obvious attempt to do a good job, called him into his office to discuss the problem of organized gambling in the precinct and shortly after assigned him to a special park post to arrest, if possible, the suspected bookmakers who were supposed to operate in the area.

The park was as famous as Hyde Park in London. Radicals and political dissenters of every persuasion made it their headquarters. On the crosswalks, rival speakers harangued listeners and thundered against each other, the system, and the "lackeys of the ruling class." Our college-trained patrolman grew so familiar with the appellation that he did not even flinch at it, but thought it odd that they were berating him for protecting their right to fulminate against the power elite. He was in his element. College had prepared him for such an assignment.

Among the various groups—some arguing vociferously, others deeply immersed in the latest *Daily Worker*—the officer walked his post with a smug sense of accomplishment. What other officer could mediate so well among Stalinists, Trotskyites, Lovestone-ites, nazis, and fascists? Whether it was dialectic materialism, united front, permanent revolution, or any of the other current political clichés, our hero could handle himself well.

He became a species of referee to whom disputants would appeal for redress. A supporter of the fascists would accost him and whisper to him that a dangerous "red" with a knife had threatened to stab him. A Trotskyite might slip him a note containing allegations against a nazi. He did a wonderful job of controlling the political tempers and wars in the park. But he never noticed any sign of bookmaking or gambling.

This went on for several months. One winter night about 6:00 P.M. almost everyone had deserted the park because it was raining heavily. One persistent group however, was still busily engaged in a discussion of some abstruse point in the *Worker*. The patrolman approached them and, wanting to get them out of the park so he could "grab a fast cup of coffee," called out roughly, "Why don't you go home? Here you are trying to settle the world's problems, and you don't even know enough to get out of the rain." The apparent leader of the group said, "Officer,

I'll speak to you later." The officer, anticipating the usual accusations against rival groups in the park, responded, "Don't bother speaking to me at all. Just pack up and get out of here." Then he turned and walked away.

He heard someone follow him from the group and felt a wad of paper thrust stealthily into his hand. Certain that it was another "piece of vital information" he looked at it contemptuously. He was shocked to see that this time there were two bills in his palm.

When he saw his side partner, Big Fred, he eagerly told the story. Big Fred looked at him queerly and said, "That was Izzy, the bookie. Do you mean to tell me you've been working in the park this whole time and don't know Izzy?" At that moment the rookie saw how far he had to travel before he became a real "cop." The bookie and his horseplayers had been busy all those weeks discussing not the Third International at Moscow but the Third Invitational at Hialeah. Behind every *Daily Worker* had been a copy of the *Daily Racing Form*.

The strange thing is that a policeman can take the payoff and still consider himself an honest or innocent man. The Denver policeman reacted to graft by saying

> that this is okay, that all the men accept these things, that this is a far cry from stealing and they can still be good policemen.[23]

Lincoln Steffens gives a more involved explanation to the same effect:

> The collections, he, Schmittberger, was to make for his captain were the regular monthly payments by gamblers, prostitutes, saloons—all law-breakers—for the privilege of breaking the law, rightly called police protection. . . .
>
> The big business was the regular graft that Schmittberger handled for years, all in the day's work, without losing either his honesty or, it seemed to me, all his innocence. I often afterward reviewed this part of his experience; it bore upon my old interest in moral and ethical psychology. My note was that the process of corruption had begun so quietly with the first tip and proceeded so gradually in an environment where it was all a matter of course, that this man never realized what he was doing till the Lexow Committee's exposure.[24]

Knowing that the penal law and the police regulations clearly prohibit such malfeasance, how is it possible for an experienced policeman to accept money and at the same time maintain that he is innocent of any wrongdoing? Such psychological prestidigitation can be accomplished only by artful casuistry based on cynicism. The policeman rationalizes

---

[23] Mort Stern, "What Makes a Policeman Go Wrong," p. 99.
[24] Lincoln Steffens, *The Autobiography of Lincoln Steffens*, pp. 272–73.

with twisted logic: "I am not hurting anyone. Everyone is doing the same thing. Most people are much worse. The public thinks a policeman is dishonest whether he is or not. Therefore, I am not doing anything wrong by taking graft."

The Arrest

The function of the police department that justifies the claim of professional status is crime prevention. This special function is measured, validly or not, by the "good pinch." Not only the public, but also the police themselves accept this standard; as a result, they glorify the felony arrest.

> The apprehension of the felon then represents for these men a source of prestige in the police department . . . and in the community.[25]

Yet according to the research division of the International Association of Chiefs of Police, "the percentage of the police effort devoted to the traditional criminal law matters probably does not exceed ten percent."[26] Police forces have been overwhelmed with onerous administrative and regulative duties which keep them from devoting their major attention to preventing crime. Moreover, the advocates of professionalism, by stressing the qualities of police integrity rather than mere performance, have given a curious twist to the act of arrest. It is well known that gambling syndicates are the commonest source of police corruption. Thus the professionals on the force hail the arrest of a known gambler or bookie as a great feat and often allow it to assume more significance than an arrest for a serious felony. The patrolman, not sharing the professionals' artificial viewpoint on this subject, never considers the bookie as a criminal in the same class with a rapist or a mugger and explains the peculiar reversal of values in which a "bookie's" arrest is a cause for more celebration than a felony arrest is by ascribing either stupidity or hypocrisy to the "big brass."

One overpowering reason for cynicism among patrolmen is that it stimulates an outstanding arrest record. The very cynical officer rejects the possibility of decent impulses in others. By undertaking many investigations and never letting up in his relentless justification of this morbid

---

[25] Westley, "The Police," p. 225.
[26] Richard A. Myren and Lynn D. Swanson, *Police Contacts with Juveniles: Perspectives, Guidelines, and Review Draft*, June 1961 (Washington, D.C.: Children's Bureau, United States Department of Health, Education, and Welfare, 1961), pp. 1-4. In an empirical study of the Syracuse Police Department, 801 incoming telephone calls were analyzed over a period of eighty-two hours in the summer of 1961. Only 20 percent of the calls were related to crime or violence. See Elaine Cumming, Ian M. Cumming, and Laura Edell, "Policeman as Philosopher, Guide and Friend," *Social Problems* 12 (Winter 1965): p. 279.

distrust, he is following the advice laid down by the experts. For example, in the obituary of James Leggett, former chief of detectives of the New York City Police Department, the *New York Times* reported that Leggett frequently urged his subordinates to probe, probe, probe until they came up with the answers.

> You have to be nosey, use your eyes and your ears, and continually ask questions. . . .
> Keep saying to yourself, over and over, "What's the answer?" Take nothing for granted. . . .[27]

A high arrest record reinforces the cynicism that inspired it in the first place, while often establishing a policeman's reputation for initiative and efficiency. His superiors recommend him for assignment to the detective division. This route to promotion appeals to many young policemen who have little hope of passing a written competitive test for promotion and impels many of them to adopt cynicism as a rational and functional way to advancement.

The Five-Year Man

By the time a patrolman has had five years on the force, he has usually started casting about for a "good detail" in order to escape from foot patrol duty. Upon hearing rumors of impending transfers, patrolmen seek to arrange "contracts with rabbis." The lower ranks tend to believe that special assignments depend on "whom you know," and not on merit.[28]

In most cases, detective work is the detail preferred above all others. However, most policemen will accept any detail "as long as I get 'out of the bag' (uniform)." Defining this as simply the desire for upward mobility would be shortsighted. The implications go much deeper to reveal the policemen's urge to escape from foot patrol duty in uniform, not only because of its low status, but also because a large proportion of the men become "fed up" with this basic job of all police systems. Their service motivation has become extinguished; they want to remove the uniform that publicly identifies them as policemen.

This desire impels many officers to prepare for the second ladder of upward mobility, the civil service promotion test. Day after day the patrolman studying for the sergeant's examination plods his way to the

---

[27] *New York Times*, January 17, 1962, p. 33.
[28] In the study of cynicism, 40 percent of the patrolmen shared this view, in the face of strong protestations to the contrary by top officials of the department.

"cram" school, sometimes to two or three schools on consecutive days. There are men who have been attending such classes for twenty years and are still optimistic.

All too quickly, the policeman moves along his career line. Until his twelfth year there is the possibility of leaving police work for a more attractive and remunerative position. After this, he realizes that in only eight more years he will be entitled to a pension, and his desire to leave quickly diminishes.

The Jewish Patrolman

The Great Depression was mainly responsible for the entry of a number of Jews into the classically Irish police force.[29] In those days Jews faced prejudice. The prevailing attitudes toward them were of thinly disguised contempt and disbelief that they would make good cops. Jewish policemen were forced to prove themselves worthy.

One Jewish patrolman finally convinced the oppositon. He won so many awards for his police work that his nickname became "Medals." But his finest hour came when the other policemen and his personal friends outside the force started calling him "Reilly." There were not many Jewish "Reillys" at the beginning.

Jewish policemen faced more than prejudice. A high percentage of these newcomers were college men. They naturally became the target for the antiintellectualism that policemen shared with many other Americans. A Jewish policeman with a college degree soon realized that for him the police world was out of joint. His handling of police situations often seemed feasible by college standards but frequently was impractical according to the standards of traditional police practice. With middle-class antecedents and his Jewish heritage, he almost inevitably attempted to solve problems verbally rather than by force.

There are several recurrent, unpleasant situations that confront the Jewish policeman. Often the non–Jewish policeman tries to be friendly by hailing him with *"Mach a leben?"* To the non–Jew this remark is equivalent to saying, "How are things?" To the Jew it not only is bad grammar but also covertly insinuates that Jews are mainly interested in making money. It is also difficult for the Jewish policeman to deal with an anti-Semitic civilian. The problem is complicated by the fact that anti–Semites are reputedly sensitive to Jewishness and able to recognize a Jew quickly but are fooled by the police uniform which they

---

[29]Nathan Glazer and Daniel P. Moynihan, *Beyond the Melting Pot* (Cambridge, Mass.: MIT Press and Harvard University Press, 1964), p. 261.

associate with the Irish, or at least, non–Jewish policemen. Repeatedly an anti–Semite will sidle up to the Jewish policeman and "out of a clear sky" start blaming the evils of the world on the Jews. Only a little less irritating to his pride as a policeman is the reaction of the Jewish occupants of a car that he has stopped for a traffic violation. The officer will hear them say in Yiddish, "Give him a few dollars to forget the ticket, and let's get out of here."

Today relative deprivation describes the state of Jewish patrolmen. A generation ago, Jewish policemen, compared with members of different faiths, or ethnic groups, had real grievances; they were discriminated against and treated as inferiors. Deprivation was not at at all relative but absolute. Except in isolated instances this is no longer true. If the Jewish policeman experiences frustration today, it is probably due to his commitment to the traditional Jewish *Weltanschauung* from which he is not completely emancipated. This tradition is typified by the advice their leaders gave Jewish immigrants near the end of the nineteenth century:

> Select a goal and pursue it with all your might. No matter what happens to you, hold on. You will experience a bad time but sooner or later you will achieve your goal. . . . A bit of advice for you: Do not take a moment's rest. Run, do, work, and keep your own good in mind. . . . A final virtue is needed in America—called cheek. . . . Do not say, I cannot; I do not know.[30]

Jewish mothers-in-law have learned subtle techniques to disguise their disappointment at having gained a policeman son-in-law when they lost their daughter in marriage. For example, one mother-in-law bravely surmounted her loss of status by introducing her policeman son-in-law as a college graduate with two degrees. Others try to conceal the police blemish by describing the policeman relative as "in youth work" or, if he is lucky enough to be attached to the Police Academy, as "a teacher."

Jewish parents look forward to the wonderful day when they can proudly introduce their offspring with the ritual words, "My son, the doctor." It cannot give them the same degree of satisfaction to present, "My son, the cop." They suspect their friends of translating the words "My son, the cop" into an altogether different phrase "My cop-son." It is one of those ironical coincidences that in the Yiddish colloquial speech the term of mild contempt commonly used to signify "a person who will never amount to anything" is pronounced phonetically "cop son."

While contemporary Jews have no high regard for police work as

---

[30]Moses Rischin, *The Promised City: New York's Jews 1870–1914* (Cambridge, Mass.: Harvard University Press, 1962), p. 75.

an occupation, older Jewish people remember the old-country ghettos, and the respect they were forced to display to policemen. On the other hand, since several European nations barred Jews from the police force, "émigré" Jews are often secretly proud that in America a Jew can become an influential official with the power of life and death over others. This ambivalence is mirrored in the attitude of Jewish policemen who sometimes feel like failures but are often inwardly proud that they have succeeded in an occupation that once had this particular significance for their forebears.

The Detective

Crime novels often portray police department detectives as stupid, sadistic, lecherous, and altogether second-rate when compared with the "private eye"—that omniscient and ithyphallic standard-bearer of all that is noble. Erle Stanley Gardner, who mass-produces "whodunits" and qualifies as an expert on this phase of American culture, has some interesting and relevant opinions:

> And as far as detective fiction is concerned, the "dumb" cop is a fixture because the public demands him! In fact, it is as necessary to have a "dumb" cop in a detective story as it is to have a clever detective.
>
> For some years now, I have been interested in better law enforcement and my conscience got to bothering me about the manner in which Perry Mason pulled an intellectual razzle-dazzle on the dumb cops I had created in my books. Therefore, I decided to write a book in which I would show the police in their true colors and in which Mason would race neck and neck to a solution with the character who had previously taken the part of the dumb cop. The result was that the publisher was literally deluged with letters of protest from book dealers and public alike.[31]

Contrary to the fantasies of the paperback thrillers, the public actually accords great respect and prestige to the detective, far more than it grants to the uniformed beat patrolman. A detective's clothes, mannerisms, easy familiarity with superior officers, and snobbish aloofness from uniformed patrolmen are all part of his impressive front, helping him to dramatize his status and work performance. Within the police hierarchy, the detective also enjoys an exalted status. Almost every cop dreams of the day when he will "make the bureau" and become a "big dick." Commissioners

---

[31]Erle Stanley Gardner, "The Need for New Concepts in the Administration of Criminal Justice," *Journal of Criminal Law, Criminology and Police Science* 50 (May–June 1959):22.

grant assignment to the detective bureau as a reward for exceptional performance. All members of the force know the benefits of detective work. Most imagine many more than exist, but there are three immediately apparent advantages: higher salary, more interesting work, and "getting out of the bag."

> Nearly every patrolman who comes into the department dreams of one day "making the bureau." He glories in thoughts of working in street clothes, sometimes in the most deceptive disguises, tracking down a dangerous gunman, searching for a clue at the scene of a homicide, lifting a fingerprint from a bloodied axe handle. . . .[32]

Candidates for detective units are usually given some preparatory training at the police academy. Their anticipatory socialization immediately displays itself. Their clothes take on an "Ivy" look: jackets, hats, carefully knotted ties, and trench coats replace the sweaters, lumberjackets, and hunters' caps worn by the less fortunate patrolmen.

Detectives are the upper class of police society and haughtily guard their special status and privileges. Their quarters are separate from those of the uniformed force. Within this private domain, democratic camaraderie eliminates the social distance that ordinarily divides the various ranks of a burcaucratic hierarchy. A lower-ranking detective may call a detective "captain" by his first name without causing any surprise; he may walk arm-in-arm with a detective inspector (a very high superior officer) while discussing an important case.

Some cynics explain this nonchalant disregard of organizational protocol as the result of nepotism in department appointments. They claim that since almost every detective must have an important "rabbi" to get in the division, no clever operator would risk antagonizing some unknown and powerful sponsor by being rude to his protégé, and thus adopts a friendly and democratic policy toward subordinates.

Because of the higher status of detectives within the department, a new policeman tends to assume that they are superior to uniformed men in intelligence or motivation. A strong minority on the force asserts, on the contrary, that a detective's value and future success depend on the private sources of information at his disposal, and his willingness to do the necessary legwork. They support this opinion by citing the many brilliant detectives in police history who could never have passed an IQ test, could hardly write an intelligible report, and whose techniques of investigation constantly violated every recommended principle of scientific detection.

[32] *Spring 3100* 30 (July–August 1959): 15.

Unexpected corroboration for this minority belief comes from a fabled detective whose heyday was forty years ago. As head of New York City's famed Italian Squad, which successfully battled the Mafia, Lieutenant Fiaschetti spoke with authority about the requirements for success as a detective and evaluated the story book detective-intellectual rather pungently:

> It makes me tired to read how those bulls in books solve mysteries with their deductions. In the honest-to-God story of how the detective gets his man, stool pigeon's the word.[33]

It is also true that ambitious detectives strive to build up a private circle of informers which automatically connects them to the criminal underworld.

This interaction between detective and criminal is by no means confined to the American police force. In London, Scotland Yard sometimes depends on streetwalkers for tips. The effectiveness of this liaison was demonstrated after prostitutes were forbidden to solicit on the streets. As one Scotland Yard detective complained:

> One quite eccentric result of the street clearing was shown almost immediately by a series of successful jewel robberies at night in London which caught the police unprepared. "It's the fault of that Act," said one of the detectives to the press. "The girls used to notice when anything funny was up—they hadn't much else to do walking about—and they'd tip us off." Nowadays, the police depend on the ordinary marks, and have to do without streetgirl volunteers. It wasn't a very wide or reliable source of information; but it was something.[34]

The freedom of the detective division to form and utilize contacts with the criminal world underlines the peculiarly open structure of this segment of the police force. With its easygoing approach to interpersonal relations, its lack of concern for the formal regulations that hamstring the rest of the department, and its informal discipline, the division forms what might be called a mock bureaucracy.[35] It is of special significance that this high-status unit, to which every member of the lower echelon

---

[33]Michael Fiaschetti, *You Gotta Be Rough* (New York: Doubleday Doran, 1930), p. 27.

[34]Raymond Postgate, "London: Goodbye to Hullo, Darling," *Holiday Magazine* 28 (November 1960): 50.

[35]In *Patterns of Industrial Bureaucracy* (Glencoe: Free Press, 1954), Alvin Gouldner describes three theoretical types of bureaucracy: the punishment-centered, the representative, and the mock. All three types can be found among police departments. The traditional police force with its authoritarian structure corresponds to the punishment-centered bureaucracy. The professional force stresses a persuasive, more democratic kind of discipline and can be equated to the representative type. The detective division, of course, fits nicely into the description of the mock bureaucracy.

aspires, performs best when disregarding formal regulations and official procedures. Adopting detectives as models, other members of the force do not remain as fervently dedicated to these official rules and procedures as they might if they lacked this example.

The Superior Officer

Superior officers of the old regime were autocrats. Patrolmen responded fearfully to their wrath and would not have risked approaching them casually. Supervisors were quick to register complaints, generally about subordinates who failed to acknowledge a superior's innate charisma.

In contemporary police culture, democratization and demilitarization have replaced the formerly rigid code for several reasons. In the first place, there is no police counterpart of West Point at which the superior officer may be trained (although the National Academy of the Federal Bureau of Investigation gradually has attained an equivalence). In America police superiors rise from the ranks and have no aura of glamor, upper-class background, or unique endowments with which to impress the rank and file. A superior's reputation precedes him; he cannot expect to be treated with rigid deference.

The influx of college men into police work during and after the Great Depression upset the established pattern of upward mobility within the ranks. Educated policemen were able to shorten by half the time required for promotion to sergeant. After World War II, many men transferred from the armed forces to the police. Fed up with ostentatious rituals, combat veterans coined barbed epithets for those who insisted on exaggerated compliance with protocol and consequently helped to democratize patterns of interaction in the police system. Professionalization also accelerated this process. Policemen, regarding themselves as experts and leaders, became involved in role conflicts. Trying to impress the public with his leadership, the policeman only perfunctorily salutes or otherwise recognizes differences in rank and thus compromises his professional self-conception and the demands of protocol.

The current loosening of rigid discipline is so evident that police administrators are beginning to classify the sergeant as a foreman in industry who has allied himself with labor rather than with management. Some police experts, unwilling or unable to accept the sergeant's reduced prestige, consider it a damaging blow to the force and to the community. In the following comments, Paul Weston, a high-ranking police officer before he became a college professor of Police Administration, expresses the sentiments of the old regime:

A slow eating or wearing away of the responsibility and authority of a patrol sergeant has been taking place. If it is not halted, this deterioration will undermine the entire hierarchy of any police unit, contribute to the waste of human resources, and interfere with attempts to gain objectives which will provide a community with a climate of law and order.[36]

While top-level management and even friendly sergeants may be somewhat responsible for this transformation, Weston feels that the true miscreants are industrial sociologists and psychologists, who

preach the creed that a happy worker is an efficient and productive worker. "Fear," they said, "should never rule."

Requests and suggestions, instead of orders, would keep the workers happy.

These experts in human relations in industry say that supervision should not be brutal and reign through fear, and that supervisors must like people, help them, and constantly strive to get along with them. While it is true that brutality has no place in supervision, it is possible that fear can have its constructive aspects.

Every police department has one or more "tough" sergeants, men who appear to dislike people, offer little apparent help, and seem to have little or no interest in getting along with them. This type of supervisor commands respect despite the environment of fear he creates, and though he sets high standards of performance, he is usually as demanding of himself as he is of his subordinates. Men may not like him, but they like working for him, and he develops subordinates as he spurs them to peak performance.[37]

---

[36] Paul Weston, "The Role of the Patrol Sergeant," *Law and Order* 7 (September 1959): 31.

[37] Weston, "The Patrol Sergeant," p. 31. The reduction of the social distance between superiors and subordinates has not yet reduced the policeman's traditional distrust of the disciplinary system. There were three items in the cynicism study that pertained to this topic. In item 1, only two of the sample of eighty-four patrolmen agreed that the average police superior is very interested in the welfare of his subordinates. More than one-half of the eighty-four thought that superiors were mostly concerned with their own problems.

In statement 2, three-quarters of the patrolman sample chose the C alternative to the effect that the average departmental complaint is the result of the pressure on superior officers from higher authority to give out complaints. It is notable that more than 50 percent of the superior officers also accept this completion as the most nearly correct.

The answers to the third question on this point (item 9) indicated a general loss of faith in the disciplinary system. More than 50 percent of the patrolmen circled choice C, which stated that when a patrolman appears at the Police Department Trial Room, he will probably be found guilty even when he has a good defense.

If these responses are an indication of the general attitude of members of the force toward their superior officers and the disciplinary system, what is the effect on morale? Either morale is low, or the interesting possibility is present that there may be high morale even when members of an organization are deeply dissatisfied.

The Administrators

The higher echelons of large police forces assume a chauvinistic posture in order to defend their organization. They decry the lack of respect for law and order and the difficulties created by the courts that seem to the police to be overprotective of criminals. At the same time police administrators are quick to take offense when criticized.

To maintain, at all costs, the virtue of their force, the administrators must sometimes do an abrupt about-face. For example, their most popular proof of police efficiency is an impressive statistical report. But if other statistics indicate a reduction in efficiency, they must somehow cushion the impact of figures. A good illustration of such a reversal occurred when the FBI published data for the first nine months of 1965, showing a 6.5 pecent rise for New York City crime over the comparable period of 1964. The New York *Times* reported that "a spokesman for the Police Department here declined to concede that this proved an unusually high incidence of crime here"[38] and quoted a deputy commissioner:

> [The statistics] were only three-quarters of the picture and reflect a crime bulge from the summer months.
>
> [The statistics] might show a drop at the end of the year and that could create a whole new average. Until you get the whole picture of the full year, you have only statistics.[39]

When statistics imply discredit, adminstrators either attack their source or devalue the statistics per se. In this case, since it is next to impossible for any police department to discredit the FBI, the statistics become the target. Police officials are not so lenient with critics of law enforcement.

> When the Federal Narcotics Bureau was condemned for its treatment of suspects, the Bureau's answer was (according to Benjamin DeMott) a propaganda line hinting that "Any man who interests himself in the problem of 'unknown criminals' must have unsavory reasons for doing so."[40]

When civil-rights groups criticized the FBI for its ambivalence in circumventing Mississippi segregationists, J. Edgar Hoover countered that Martin Luther King, Jr., was "the most notorious liar in the country."[41] Former New York City Police Commissioner Michael Murphy followed the same pattern in defending the action of his department in the civil rights disorders during the summer of 1964. Describing

---

[38] *New Yew York Times*, December 1, 1965, p. 95.
[39] *New York Times*, December 1, 1965, p. 15.
[40] "The Great Narcotics Muddle," *Harper's* 214 (March 1962): 50.
[41] *New York Times*, November 20, 1964, p. 1.

the frustration of the police who were "puzzled, bitter, and deeply resentful," he moved to the attack, asserting

> that the public image of law enforcement—particularly as it involved the police—was unfairly "distorted and smeared today as never before in our history."
>
> He said part of the picture was caused by "certain groups determined to weaken the democratic process."[42]

Probably the zenith of this administrative tropism was exemplified by Commissioner Vincent Broderick, the successor to Commissioner Murphy. Suffused by this extraordinary spirit of bureaucratic loyalty, he fought Mayor Lindsay himself, at the eventual cost of his job. The expected twist became apparent when the commissioner elected publicly to interpret the mayor's call for a Civilian Review Board as an unwarranted political interference with the internal workings of the department rather than to accept it as an idealistic innovation to honor a campaign pledge to promote better relations between the police and the city's minority groups.[43]

Police officials in this country envy the sacrosanct status enjoyed by Scotland Yard and the bobbies. But even these latter institutions seem to be losing their power to induce faith and silence criticism. In recent years Scotland Yard has had to cope with an England that can no longer be characterized as a nation of quiet, law-abiding citizens. The crime rate is rapidly increasing; the clearance rate is decreasing; sensational train robberies surpass TV thrillers; armed criminals kill policemen; race riots and teenage-gang rumbles signal social distress. Fleets of motorcycles roar through once peaceful communities. Traffic volume overwhelms the narrow streets of historic towns, and the police have antagonized the motoring public by traffic summons campaigns. Scandals have rocked the government.

These indications of disquiet are underlined by British press reports of bribery, brutality, forced confessions, racial discrimination, and illegally planted evidence. It is becoming difficult to attract capable recruits. When British police administrators submit annual reports, they are forced to defend certain obvious inadequacies. The British Police Superintendents' Association recently complained in a memorandum to the home secretary that

> Britain's Bobbies are being pilloried, bullied, restricted, and increasingly unjustifiably criticized by members of the public in all walks

---

[42] *New York Times*, August 23, 1964, p. 48.

[43] It is notable that former Police Commissioners Francis Adams and Michael Murphy support Commissioner Broderick in his stand. *New York Times*, February 10, 1966, p. 1.

of life, . . . traditional British respect for the law [is] dwindling, and . . . the police [can] not cope with a growing criminal element under present conditions.[44]

It is somewhat ironic, but nonetheless a testimonial to the efficiency and prestige of our own great police forces, that Roy Jenkins, the British home secretary, charged with responsibility for his country's police establishment, came to New York and Chicago on a police fact-finding mission.[45] It will certainly prove interesting to New York City police officials that there were more than nine thousand complaints lodged against Britain's police in 1965 and that as a result the influential *Economist* has proposed the formation of a civilian-dominated review board "on New York City's model."[46]

The Old-timer

Walking the streets, climbing stairs, lifting stretchers, and searching basements for armed criminals, the beat patrolman leads an active life that keeps him physically fit. It is a wrench the first time a rookie or youngster on his post calls him "Pop." Yet with fifteen years of service behind him, he is fast entering the circle of old-timers. In many of the personal interviews with policemen of this group, the men demonstrated a peculiar soul-searching type of introspection. Looking back over the years, they experienced a revulsion in reviewing all the distasteful acts of omission and commission in which they had participated.

They gradually assume the elder-stateman role and transmit the wisdom of the job to the new men. Seniority entitles them to the easier assignments, which allow them time to regale the younger men with endless reminiscences of the good old days when a cop could really be a cop. When arguments occur, the split reveals a conflict of generations, each group paying allegiance to a different value system.

They recall with nostalgia their early years on the job and often wonder at their former brashness. More and more their conversation becomes larded with the typical refrain of the aging: "When I was a rookie, things were different." Until this stage, the majority of the men talk confidently of retiring as soon as possible. However, at the approach of the twenty year retirement limit, old-timers often begin to waver. What can the ordinary veteran policeman offer a prospective employer?

---

[44]*New York Times*, October 26, 1965, p. 13.
[45]*New York Times*, October 1, 1966, p. 16.
[46]*The Economist*, August 20, 1966, p. 711.

His main talent, if he has one, is that of a low-level practitioner of applied psychology or sociology.

The typical position available to a former policeman is that of bank guard, night watchman, mail room clerk, or messenger. This demoralizing situation impels the policeman to stay with the force,[47] where he can be somewhat satisfied in knowing that he earns a salary many professional men would envy.

Even when they retire, most policemen preserve some connection with the force. Many former officers keep their revolvers, for which they must now obtain a permit. The retired patrolman's organization issues shields somewhat like those worn by active members of the force. Frequently, the retired men find new employment in security jobs requiring general police skills.

Significantly, disllusioned and threatened by his exposure to the job-hunter's world, the old-timer renews his commitment to the police occupation he probably deprecated as a recruit. Cynicism patterns over twenty years reflect this change among veterans approaching the twenty-year milestone. Their degree of cynicism is consistently lower than that of men with less time on the job.

[47]Appointments to the force are reported in the department's Annual Reports. Retirements can be found in the magazine *Spring 3100*. With the aid of these sources I traced a cohort of 1,674 policemen from appointment to the time of eligibility for retirement, covering a twenty-four-year period from 1941 until 1965. Counting all retirements except those for medical reasons, I found that more than 50 percent of the cohort was still on the job at the beginning of 1965 when the cohort's average service was twenty-two and one-half years.

10
Acquiring New Identities

Lifelong socialization involves acquiring many different identities. Our social selves are complex, composed of components that seem unrelated. The physician, calm and deliberate during an examination, becomes an excited and impulsive fan at the Sunday-afternoon football game. Sociologists include as part of the process of socialization the continuous modification, deletion, and addition of components of the social self. Even the most stable, sedentary, and regularly behaving people experience changes in their self-identities throughout life. At times these changes are deep rooted and influence the character of the entire self. Other changes are superficial and do not have such a profound impact. The following selection describes a trend of changes in the self from surface to deep levels. It illustrates how an ordinary activity can be defined as a major ingredient in one's life and hence as a definitive attribute of the social self.

The Short and the Long of It: Legitimizing Motives for Running

Jeffrey E. Nash

The snow has been melting for several days. The temperature is twenty-six degrees. Along the windy streets, heavy traffic has left large, ankle-deep puddles of muddy ice water. At this time of year in this city, people stay inside or bundle up on their way from a building to their cars. The children, who in warmer times would play in their yards and up and down the sidewalks, are nowhere to be seen. Yet one solitary figure,

This article was written especially for this volume.

clad in sweat clothes, hooded in a ski cap, socks pulled over his hands, and wearing Tiger Cortez shoes, runs down the street and dodges cars and mud puddles as he looks for solid footing. He is getting in his miles for the week. This creature is the distance runner and can be found in any large city, at any season of the year, around the parks, and on the back roads, doing his thing—running.

Running, of course, is a natural means of locomotion for the human being. No doubt, all persons who have normal physical development run at one time or another in their lives. In the city we may run down the hall when late for an appointment or chase after a bus or a stray pet. However, running is not an activity we seek out. If circumstances make it unavoidable, we may run a short distance. The runner's activity differs from ordinary, rushed locomotion. He is not running to a place in order to simply get there. He is not hurrying to keep a schedule or to make an appointment, but he may hurry to beat yesterday's time. He is not running as a part of his routine life as a businessman, father, teacher, milkman, or carpenter. He is running for the sake of running. He has carved out of his ordinary everyday life a niche for running, and that niche may become the most significant activity of his life. Running has become an expression of his inward identity; his purpose is to run. He thinks of himself as "a runner." He may have a training schedule, and he carefully traces his development. When asked, he can tell you how far he ran last week and how much time he requires to run various distances.

Although we can describe the runner as athletic, he is not an athlete in the ordinary sense of that word. He does not train under a coach and is not a member of some team. He is probably too old for that. His times are too slow, and he never really thinks of himself as a serious competitor for local, regional, or world records. He probably has some occupational identity, such as a professional, a businessman, or a salesman. Running, nevertheless, is a major component of his social being.

Our puddle-dodger admits that he is probably a little crazy. He remembers a time when he would never venture out in such weather. He used to jog around the local high-school track on the weekends and feel proud of his one- and two-mile treks. Now he runs ten to fifteen miles a day and refers to others still on the track as "fair-weather joggers" and "springtime trotters" and as people who "should really be careful not to hurt themselves." They are the kind who give running a "bad image."

There is a transformation that takes place when a person changes from a casual, part-time jogger to a full-time, all-year-round distance runner. This transformation is reflected in the reasons that people give for running. I call the transformation "the process of legitimizing motives." It is one thing to put on your old work pants and a pair of paint-spotted tennis shoes in order to jog around the outdoor track a few times or to visit a gym and take a few laps around the indoor track. However, it is quite another thing to daily seek out routes of five-, ten-, fifteen-, and even twenty-mile runs that take you from one park to another through neighborhoods strewn with kids' tricycles and toys and along streets where dogs nip at your heels. The runner must also meet the challenges of menacing weather and the ever-present automobile. Long-distance running requires more than strenuous effort; it means a change in identity from a person exercising to a person running. This identity change and the conditions that produce it make up the central theme of this paper.[1]

To illustrate the process of acquiring a runner's identity, I suggest different types of people who go out of their way, break their daily business and family routines in order to run. Those who run fall into three types: (1) the jogger, (2) the regular runner, and (3) the distance runner. They vary on a continuum from minimal commitment to the identity of running to running as an integral part of their social selves.

Joggers have the least commitment to running. They are casual in their attitude toward the activity and make little or no special effort to rearrange and accommodate their lives to running. They are motivated by reasons served by running but not intrinsic to it. They seek some result from running: they see it as a means to an end.

Regular runners are more convinced of the intrinsic worth of the act than are joggers. Regulars often emerge from joggers who have continued running even though they have accomplished their original objectives. As a type, they have the following attributes: they regularize the activity; they accommodate their daily routines to running rather than running the reverse to daily routines and they begin to assert an identity associated with running.

Distance runners are the epitome of all runners. They manifest the greatest degree of commitment to the act itself. They stress what they take to be the intrinsic worth of the act. Their self-identity is expressed

---

[1]Data for this paper was gathered through participant observation. Observations were made in two midwestern cities over a two-year period. All quoted materials are reconstructions of conversations with runners and are not necessarily verbatim. The perspective of the paper is primarily masculine. Although there are increasing numbers of female joggers and runners, such activities are still predominantly male. All of my informants for this paper were male, and hence, that point of view is preserved throughout. However, there is some information that indicates that similar transformations from jogging to running occur for women. For example, one female runner reports:
>Although my pace would certainly be considered . . . jogging if the same pace was used by more experienced and better runners, I am running . . . call me an inexperienced, noncompetitive, slow runner, but don't call me a jogger. (Sidney Landau, "What Do You Call People?" *Runner's World Magazine* [January 1975] : 28–31).

Also in a recent *Ms.* magazine, a runner writes in a literary fashion of her commitment to running, not jogging. She describes her pain and pleasure during her six-mile run (Patricia Breen-Bond, "Running in the Rain," *Ms.* [January 1975]: 14, 16).

through the act of running. Outward signs, such as special equipment, clothing, and shoes, show this inward state. They have special magazines to learn about running events and news, and they have special training habits, diets, and affiliations with other runners.

Casual Running: The Jogger

Joggers treat running casually, as something they do for exercise. They have varying motives for running, or jogging, as they prefer to call it. They say that what they do is not really running. They move at a pace slightly slower than a trot and slightly faster than a walk. Of course, the actual speed of travel differs according to length of legs, body type, and so on. The important consideration for differentiating between running and jogging is commitment rather than speed or pace. Joggers say that they are not so much concerned with running per se as with exercise or something to be gained *from* running. They do not necessarily try to increase their speed or distance, and they have no desire to compete with other joggers. Instead, in response to the question, Why do you run?, they give such reasons as "to feel better," "to increase stamina so that I work better and longer," "a good way to keep fit," "I like the way I feel when I'm finished," and "it makes me look better in my clothes." These motives can be organized into four themes: (1) self-preservation, (2) higher-order values, (3) body image and weight control, and (4) a sense of competition.

Self-preservation motives refer to reasons that reflect the runner's conception of kinds of activities that are "good for me." That is, all three types of runners have some idea about the physical condition of their bodies. They believe that increased exercise will improve blood circulation and strengthen their heart, thereby decreasing the chances of heart attack or stroke. On occasion an honest jogger will even attest to improved sexual performance as a function of jogging. Many of the reasons reported for jogging have to do with relating exercise to the quality and longevity of everyday life.

> I never realized how out of shape I was 'til I started jogging. I've been jogging two years now, two miles every other day. It hurt a little at first, and sometimes I found it hard to force myself over to the track or down to the park. But afterwards, I always felt so much better. I'm sure I've added years to my life.

Higher-order reasons for jogging come from a different concern. Instead of referring to physical existence, these reasons usually pertain to "spiritual values." They may find support in the Biblical belief that the body is the temple of God and the correlative tenet that it should be kept fit. Or more commonly among the joggers I have known, there is a kind of body worship. They believe that to keep the body fit, to eliminate a slovenly appearance, increases the power and quality of one's mental life. Therefore, jogging through the litter along the side of the road or passing others on the sidewalk or track can produce a transcendental mental state, a sense of freedom from the mundane, a feeling of getting above it all.

> I like to jog near school yards. There's always a lot of paper and junk around on the ground, and when I run over it, it gives me a feeling of beating all the filth of the city. I sometimes say to myself, while airplanes fly low over my head, I'm not really a part of this madness. They will never get me. When I think this way, I can usually go a little farther.

Another higher-order, or transcendental, value is the self-actualizing value. In this instance the jogger believes that an important part of knowing himself is a physical awareness of the self. This motive for running is often captured in phrases like "being in touch with oneself," "really knowing what you can do," and "seeing what you are really made of." Jogging from this motive produces a feeling of accomplishment.

> It gives me a good feeling to know I can run. When I first started, I was twenty-four years old and couldn't make a quarter mile without feeling like I was about to die. A friend of mind had been exercising some and asked me to join him on a Saturday afternoon. That was when I knew how bad a shape I was in. I was ashamed that I couldn't make it around that track without huffing and puffing. Now I can do two miles without any strain. It gives me a feeling of accomplishment, of pride in myself that comes from knowing I improved. The improvement is real; I can feel and experience it.

Perhaps the most common reason among joggers for running is weight control. They believe that running is a highly effective exercise for losing weight and maintaining a trim and fashionable body profile. Although some attest to weight gains from jogging programs, the overwhelming sentiment among joggers is that they will lose weight only if they can exercise enough. They jog in order to achieve this goal. Whether they actually do lose weight is irrelevant. What matters is the mythology of the jogger.

> When I first started to jog, I weighed over 200 pounds. After two years of two miles a day, I'm down to 185. I feel great and look great. I can wear clothes that I never dared to wear before. My wife is always complaining about being overweight, I just say,

"start jogging with me." A few times she tried, but she doesn't like to sweat and breathe that hard.

In American society competition is perhaps one of the most basic values. We teach our children the value of competition when they are still quite young. It should come as no surprise that a version of this value appears as a motive for running. Running is fundamentally a solitary event.[2] There are running clubs and organizations that I will discuss later; however, most people who run to sustain a regular exercise program do so alone. They think to themselves while they run. It is very difficult to maintain conversation while running, even if you do attend the track with another jogger. Most runners of all types disapprove of conversations except on short training runs, warm-ups, or on special occasions, such as introducing a new person to the practice. All of this implies that a person must learn to push himself, to endure pain, or to motivate himself to keep up an activity he would not otherwise engage in. Hence, the individual competes with himself, satisfying the competitive drive by beating his past performance. To accomplish this feeling, several devices are used by the jogger.

Jogging is characteristically done over a designated area, such as an indoor or outdoor track, a path in the park, or a route around city blocks. Since these running areas typically are circular, the problem of counting to keep a record of distance emerges. On a quarter-mile layout, for distances longer than one mile, counting becomes an important part of competing with oneself. There are several methods used for this counting. In "finger counting," the jogger extends fingers in direct ratio to the number of laps run; e.g., one finger for one lap, two fingers for two laps, and so on. This method, of course, is good for only ten laps.

---

[2]Alfred Schutz discusses motivation according to the levels of social reality in his *The Phenomenology of the Social World* (Evanston, Ill.: Northwestern University Press, 1967), p. 28ff. He begins by identifying the level of the solitary actor, the person alone with his own thoughts. Motives are complexes of meanings which seem to the actor himself adequate grounds for conduct (See also C. Wright Mills, "Situated Actions and Vocabulary of Motives," *American Sociological Review* 5 [October 1940]: 904–13; and Marnin Scott and Sanford Lyman, "Accounts," *American Sociological Review* 33 [February 1967]:46–62). Hence, a person runs in order to achieve certain results or simply to run and has run because of the grounds which he takes as adequate for the action. This paper is written mostly from the perspective of the solitary actor, from the knower's vantage point. However, as is well known, Schutz considered the problem of intersubjectivity, or how we know of the other's state of mind, of critical importance for analysis. In my analysis of the identity shift from jogging to distance running, I am taking into account the presence of the other only indirectly, i.e., through the mind of the knower (see Andrew Weighert, "Alfred Schutz on a Theory of Motivation," *Pacific Sociological Review* 18 [January 1975]: 83–102).

On indoor tracks, which are usually an eighth of a mile, sixteen laps equal two miles. So persons devise various ways of coping, such as "mile-interval-forward-backward counting," that is, counting forward to eight then backward to 8, then forward again with reminders of the numbers of miles—8/1, 8/2 . . . 8/n. Another variation of this method consists of counting forward then reversing running direction at mile or two mile intervals and starting the count over. Such a method is best employed on less frequently used tracks. However, I have observed persistent direction changers on crowded tracks who resort to passing tactics —you take the high road, I'll take the low; you go inside and I'll go outside—in order to avoid running in the same direction.

Some exotic counting techniques include dropping a personal item at mile intervals, then starting the count from 1. For example, count four laps on a quarter-mile track, then drop a glove to mark the first mile; repeat the counting for four more laps then drop the other glove; repeat four more, then drop your sweat shirt. The use of articles of clothing has obvious disadvantages for the long-distance runner both in terms of warmth during the winter months and modesty in the summer season. Other runners will carry an item such as a car key or house key in one hand and switch hands at intervals which they deem significant of marking—one-half, one, or two miles. Perhaps the most unusual counting device I have discovered is the use of finger counting methods from the language of the deaf. The deaf-language counting system is done on one hand and corresponds to verbal counting. Thus, one can count up indefinitely on one hand. When your hand is in the position signifying the number six, it is a simple matter to move to number seven and on up into the teens without the problem of remembering the intervals. Of course, you must master this counting competency before it can be used to demark distances in running.

Mechanical distance counters are widely used. These devices are usually hooked to one's waist or held in the hand. They work by recording the bounces resulting from the running movement and relieves the jogger of the necessity of mentally keeping track of distance. Although the machines are not always accurate, some joggers prefer to use them so that they can think of things other than running while going round and round. Casual runners are typically distance-conscious. They run for the distance, not the time. Although often aware of the time a particular distance requires for them, they do not stop when they have completed a prescribed time. Rather, they go one mile, two miles, or even up to five miles, according to their schedules or the way they feel while running.

Another common way of counting is to attend to both time and distance to accumulate aerobic points. Persons who engage in this activity are typically devotees of Dr. Cooper's exercise plan.[3] Either they can be found in places or clubs especially designed for business executives where exercising can be done in privacy and under medical supervision, or they are less well financially endowed persons who can afford the price of the paperback and who follow this plan for a better and longer life. Such joggers often have schedules or score sheets at home on which they accumulate daily points for various exercises and for walking or jogging over prescribed distances in specified time intervals. For example, two miles in twenty minutes scores six points out of a prescribed twenty points per week. The object is to build up to numbers of points that Dr. Cooper believes indicative of the right amount of exercise and, consequently, of being in good shape for persons of a particular age and sex grouping. His book serves as a standard for running style and attitude. If one wishes to run for health, what better course than to refer to the medical profession itself and all for the price of the paperback?

Of course, mistakes occur in any counting scheme. For instance, a person may count forward in mile intervals and forget the number of the lap just completed. He may forget to change direction at the correct interval or drop the counter or have the personal items stolen or lost in the wind. There are two possible courses of action in such an event: run an extra lap, just in case, or proceed with the next number in sequence. The first adaptation ensures that the distances are conservatively experienced, while the second leaves the jogger with the nagging doubt that he really did not run that far. Although there are, without question, many personality correlates with these tendencies to over- and under enumerate distance, I propose that the handling of this type of mistake can serve as a clue to occurring shifts from the jogger's casual commitment to the more serious types of running. The underenumerator is on the way to identifying in a personal way with the act of running, while the overenumerator does not see such trivial errors as reflective of his selfhood.

---

[3]Kenneth H. Cooper is the recognized authority on this approach to exercising through running. He has published many books on the subject, among them are: Kenneth H. Cooper, *The New Aerobics* (New York: Bantam, 1970); and Mildred Cooper and Kenneth H. Cooper, *Aerobics for Women* (New York: Bantam, 1972). For a report in a sports magazine, Kenny Moore interviewed the people at the aerobics center in Texas (see Kenny Moore, "A Run for Their Money," *Sports Illustrated* [November 1974]:74–75). He discovered that the philosophy there is that people must be made to feel that they are paying for some expert or special service not readily available to the general public and that the clientele must be handled with care to keep up their motivation to exercise. One staffer related, "My job is to keep people motivated and motivation is skin deep and soluble in alcohol." Of course, this is in sharp contrast to the self-motivation of the distance runner.

All of the devices for counting are typical of casual runners. They serve as ways to mark progress and to give the relatively short-distance runner a sense of competing with and outdoing himself. Also, the fact that such counting is necessary indicates that the act of running occurs in a location taken for granted as a place for runnng. At such places, nonexercising persons cannot see the jogger or consider his behavior appropriate for that kind of location. In these places one does not have to assume the identity of a runner. Instead, he is just another person exercising or jogging.

Casual runners avoid public identification with the act of running. They run in the privacy of a gym or on the track of a local high school or college. They visit these places in early-morning hours when, as they say, they will not interfere with others. More accurately, they are concerned about being seen by others. If they run at gyms or during popular times at the tracks, they run with others who are, also, merely exercising. An extreme example of a casual jogger comes to mind. A high-level administrator of a local college found it increasingly inconvenient to visit the gym for jogging, both because of the time required and because of the inevitability of meeting his lower-status colleagues. It is difficult to maintain one's aloof demeanor garbed in sweat clothes and panting uncontrollably. So embarrassing did this administrator find the public display of his jogging, yet so important did he regard the activity for his health, that he took to "running in place" in the privacy of his home. He would regularly jog in one spot for upwards of thirty minutes. He continued this practice until his ankles became so badly swollen that he sought a physician's care. The doctor, upon examining the problem, quickly remarked, "Been running in place, huh?"

Beginning to Run: The Regular Runner

Although many persons remain joggers indefinitely, some begin to take running seriously. Usually they share the motives for exercising exposed by the jogger. They run for their health, to feel good, for spiritual reasons, and for self-actualization. However, they differ from the jogger primarily in the accent they place on these motives. As they routinize their running, as they become frequent visitors to the track, and as they become recognized by others as a regular, they start placing less emphasis on the reasons for which they engage in this extraordinary activity and more on the routine or taken-for-granted character of the practice. They begin to assume the established nature of their action. They take for granted that they run every day, every other day, or five to six times a week. Their daily life is slowly modified to include running as a regular activity. The jogger will miss exercise or skip his morning jog when events which he deems important interfere. The regular runner is beginning to see running as so important that it must become a permanent part of his life.

> When I first started running, I ran whenever I could. My job keeps me pretty busy, lunch appointments, some night work at home and, sure, the traveling. I would go for weeks without jogging. Sometimes I'd feel guilty about that, so I'd jog more than usual on the weekends. That really started to hurt me. So after a time I began to see that I either was going to run all the time or not at all. That's when I started taking my running shoes with me on trips. That's when I cancelled my lunch appointments on Monday and Wednesdays. I've been jogging regularly for a year now.

The regular is beginning to consider running an integral part of his life. The challenge of getting in one's miles, regardless of anything else, becomes important, and there is an awareness that such activity is difficult, if not impossible, to conceal. The track or gym becomes a place where the regular claims a kind of membership. When a neighborhood athletic field is the location for running, there are invariably others present: in the fall, the high-school or college football team; in the spring, the track team. Regular appearances may earn the runner the right to be present when others who do not have such an identity are forbidden. He is garbed appropriately and looks the part. Athletic officials (track and football coaches) rebuke and sometimes expel other students who stroll across the track, children who play on the football field, or adults who merely stand within the boundary of the athletic area. At the least they view such intruders with suspicion. The adult standing around will be questioned, "What are you doing here?" or, more politely, "May I help you? Are you looking for someone?" while a regular of the same age and the same sex either will not be questioned (everybody knows that he is a regular runner) or will be openly welcomed. For instance, the regular may be invited to run warm-up laps with the team or even to pace the distance for a few laps. The regular is accommodated. Such adaptations require both that the others at the track identify the person as a runner and that the runner likewise accepts such a typification. Casual and infrequent jogging does not require such a commitment.

The routinization of running has other consequences as well. Frequent running means that some clothes become known as running clothes to the regular runner. Sweat shirt, sweat pants, and most significantly, running shoes become familiar and function as emblems of the act of running. The casual jogger can wear "any old thing," work clothes, tennis shoes, or even Hush Puppies. However, when a person runs daily, he cannot afford such a nonchalant attitude toward apparel. There are several factors contributing to increased seriousness about dress. Frequent running will "spoil" clothes with sweat, grime, etc., and running in whatever one has at hand can greatly increase the laundry task. Also, longer distances mean greater wear on the feet, and improperly fitted shoes soon produce painful sores. Small details of footwear emerge as significant concerns. The extended rubber ridge on tennis shoes can cut the inside of the opposite ankle if one's running gait is particularly narrow. The reinforcement lapping upwards from the sole of the shoe can rub blisters on the tops of the toes, and cardboard braces inside the heel of the shoe can cause painful and even bloody sores on the heel. Then there is that subjective feel of the clothes. When running is habitual, the runner selects a favorite garb, one for cold weather, one for wet, for hot, and so on. Sometimes these clothes become like a private uniform, "my running clothes." For the jogger these clothes may vary with individual predilections, even though the overall appearance unmistakably communicates "I am a runner." The beginning runner may not include some of the paraphernalia of the more serious runner; the sweatband for the forehead, or the warm-up suit, the track shorts, and the right brand-name shoes. (These items will be discussed as a part of the self-identity of the serious runner.) However, he is approximating the look of one who is serious. He does have running shoes, although they will typically be less expensive and "heavier" than the serious runner's. He will don sweat clothes rather than merely run in blue jeans or old work pants, and in cold weather he wears old gloves rather than the more status signifying sweat socks over the hands. Nevertheless, regular runners have all the distinctive marks of becoming serious about running.

Since regulars typically frequent local running haunts, they become acquainted with others whose running schedules coincide or overlap with their own. Although little conversation takes place between regulars either while running (breathing will not allow) or before or after the run (time will not allow), there are passing ritual exchanges: "good day for running" (can have two meanings: (1) beautiful weather, (2) only runners would be out on a day like today), or "How many miles did you get today?" These rituals serve to indicate that others share motives about the importance of this activity. During zero weather when the snow is blowing, during spring rains, or on hundred-degree days, the presence of others on the track or path can be quite reassuring, and running in inclement weather can serve as a conspicuous display of the seriousness of one's intent. Conversational exchanges are often not necessary on such days; mere presence conveys like-mindedness on the necessity of running and of its serious nature.

Discovering runners in other areas of one's life also occurs at the early stages of serious running. Tom, in the religion department of the same college campus, discovers that Harry also jogs a little, and when they meet in the halls, they stop to discuss progress (miles per week, etc.) and individual running habits. They often exchange information on places to run and where to purchase equipment and sporting goods required. Dick, who works in the accounting department of the 4G Company, was talking about his running to Jim, who said that he heard that Mike up in sales is running a tremendous number of miles every day. Such information exchanges function to shift the reasons a person has for running away from the highly individualized motives of self-preservation, higher-order values and the like toward the motives of challenge-running and comparisons. That is, Tom compares with Harry and Dick through discussion with Mike. The mentality shifts from "I" do this because . . . to "we" do this together. This is a transformation of motives from psychological to sociological. Now I can think about this activity as something other people do, and if I can discover someone who runs farther, faster, and in more inclement weather than I do, my own action seems less strange, less extraordinary.

Another consequence of routine running is the problem of confounded lap counting. The casual jogger and the beginner runner are both conscious of distances. I listed some of the methods casual joggers employ to count laps. Increased seriousness about running invariably means more frequent running and longer running. The nascent runner, then, is faced with the problem of keeping track for longer and longer distances. A five-mile run on a quarter-mile track means twenty laps, a seven-mile run, twenty-eight, and so on. For a time, such higher mathematics is tolerated for the assurance of knowing accurately that one has run five miles. However, the exhilaration of these accomplishments soon changes into the boring task of counting very slowly to oneself. When thoughts drift to problems of the business world or to what's for supper or to the cold beer at the end of the run, it is easy to lose count ("Oh, shit! Was that fifteen or sixteen?").

One common solution to confounded counting is to run for time. A regular runner will quickly learn how much time he requires to run one mile, two miles, and so on. For example, "I try to pace myself to seven minute miles." Thus, this runner can avoid the problem of confounded counting by timing himself ("I run for fifteen minutes; I do thirty minutes, etc.), then simply translating these times into miles by dividing the time into mile equivalents: twenty minutes equals about three miles, thirty minutes about four, and so on. In this way, when others inquire how far you ordinarily run, you can reply with confidence, "I run five miles a day." You know that you actually run forty minutes around and around the oval track.

Only a little imagination is required to understand that such track habits can become mentally tedious. They also harbor hidden psychic dangers. The runner will begin to wonder if he is developing a counter-clockwise lean, or if his "outside" leg is becoming stronger than his "inside" or if it is "fair to stay on the inside lane (the shortest distance around the track) or if he should vary to the outside lanes. To compensate for such sources of worry, runners can be observed changing direction, running in a zigzag fashion, switching lanes, and varying pace.

The Distance Runner: A Self-Identity

Although some persons remain joggers and runners indefinitely, there is pressure resulting from peer-group membership, others typifying your action as running, and the problems of boredom and confounded counting to become a distance runner. The following events, although not necessarily in any order, mark the emergence of self-identity as a distance runner: (1) leaving the track, (2) joining a club or association, (3) preparing for competition, (4) competing, and (5) consciousness of diet.

Leaving the track marks the emergence of a runner's identity since that act necessitates several serious commitments on the part of the person. First, leaving the track requires the selection of a new route. Others who have already taken the plunge may suggest routes. Tom learns from Harry that from the college, down Tarven street, around the lowland's park, and back to the college is five miles, knowledge that only runners, and perhaps paperboys, would have. Harry, a distance runner, gives Tom five other routes from his house of varying lengths and terrain. For instance, there is the five-mile hilly route; a ten-mile road route, five miles mostly dirt footing; and ten miles of road, dirt, and track.

Of course, the distance runner soon begins to mark off his own routes, sometimes making a special trip in his car to "measure off" routes and their distances. Quickly, these routes become favorites and develop reputations and character for the runner. Some are used for various training purposes. Difficult runs prepare for races; easier ones can be used for "off days," "after the race," or during the "off-season" ("off-season" is a matter of when the individual decides to train since there are sponsored races all year round; however, a greater selection of races is offered during the spring and summer months, so most runners train less rigorously in winter). Also, routes become identified with the weather. The lowland's park track drains best during a rain; the river route is good footing and scenic in the summer months but should be avoided in winter since snow accumulations make running impossible. The five-mile run up to the bridge has less car traffic, fewer dogs and kids, and so on.

The act of leaving a place designated as a running area means that the runner must now display his identity. He is on territories not specifically identified for exercise. He uses streets, sidewalks, parks, and golf courses for his own private intentions. He imposes his definition of the "use-purpose" of the terrain. He must be willing to run past women with arms loaded with grocery bags, dodge bicycles, dart through or around persons walking slowly on the sidewalk or standing and conversing at a street corner. Sometimes the definition of the sidewalk as a place to run is difficult to sustain:

> One time I was running on the sidewalk when I met a couple strolling toward me. There was a wall on one side and small patch of grass on the other. They saw me but refused to move over. I passed them on the grass, brushing shoulders with the girl. I had slowed my pace and we barely touched but the guy got "pissed off." He started yelling at me that sidewalks are not for running. I didn't stop. He didn't follow.

Often there are accommodations worked out between distance runners and others on the sidewalks about the proper use of this space. Distance runners rarely cut through face-to-face conversations. Whenever possible, they will move so as not to disrupt whatever activity is taking place. Such bypassing, or "running past," appears expected of one who engages in unusual uses of the sidewalk. Occasionally, one will encounter a helpful fellow traveler:

> I'd been running about four miles when I passed some kids on bicycles. They were headed at me and I heard one holler "stay right." The kid who hollered looked older than the other one, looked maybe like a sister.

No doubt the most dangerous obstacle of off-track running in the city is the automobile. The distance runner must negotiate city streets, intersections, and traffic lights. Runners are very conscious of these dangers. During a road race through the city several years ago, a runner was struck by a truck. He was not badly injured, but such close calls serve as a reminder of the deadly threat. A paragraph in the local paper, page three, reads:

> Mr.———was struck and killed by a car at 6:30 A.M. Tuesday while jogging along Lewis Avenue. The road was icy and Mr.———apparently slipped and fell into the path of the approaching auto.

Most serious runners of any experience at all are aware of the war with the car and choose routes that have little "traffic hassle." Or they may run during the light traffic hours, early morning or early afternoon before the 5:00 P.M. home-bound traffic. The jogger may also run in the early morning hours, but he does so to avoid being seen; the runners do so to avoid being hit. Joggers rarely mention the threat of the car when questioned about the hassles of running, whereas runners will often place this concern at the top of the list. In spite of the threat of traffic, more than half of the runners I know prefer the afternoon hours for running instead of the early morning hours. They don brightly colored shirts or even place luminous, Litefoot reflective strips on the heels of their shoes so that they may be spotted by approaching motorists. Nevertheless, they may develop a cavalier attitude toward traffic. Pacing or acquiring a sense of how fast or slow a certain distance can be traveled is important to runners. Thus, they view stopping for traffic as a hindrance and often cross on red lights when they judge that they can "make it." They will "pace and time" traffic so that they will run immediately behind cars passing in one direction and pause momentarily in the middle of a four-lane street so that they can cut between cars traveling in the opposite direction. They will run in the street to find good footing, they will share the street with the cars, the runner using a small, imaginary path next to the curb, the car using the marked lane. Runners develop techniques for coping with this sharing of the street:

> I always watch the front wheels of approaching cars. If I see it move at all, I quickly jump up on the curb, even if this means hitting the mud.

or:

> I keep my eye on the driver. I can usually see the driver well. I've learned to anticipate movement of the steering wheel. Also, I watch for the kind of driver and the kind of car. If it's a big car, like a Caddy or a Merc I'm ready to hit the dirt. Smaller cars give me more room, and I've noticed a curious thing; smaller cars seem to move over slightly where bigger cars don't. Also teenagers frighten me, they drive very fast even on the back streets. Old people are a hazard too. They seem to see me, but instead of moving over or just going straight they seem to veer toward me. I can see people, and they don't seem to know that. Anyway it's easy to tell what they have in mind.

Whether such runners really can "tell what drivers have in mind" and how many runners actually are injured by the automobile are questions I cannot definitively answer.[4] However, it is true that runners must cope

---

[4]The problem is widespread enough in the opinion of some to merit the attention of insurance companies. See Michael E. Tymn, "Insurance for Road Runners," *Runner's World Magazine* (January 1975):34–35.

with traffic. They must either develop strategies for running with cars or seek less heavily traveled areas of the city for running. The longer the distance traveled over city terrain, the more likely the runner will cross purposes with the car. Such activity necessitates a strong will and resolute intention. The distance runner cannot be self-conscious about his appearance to others. He must assert himself and his intent. His appearance must read "I am a runner; I need this space to accomplish my goal."

Other hassles of off-track running are taunts by children, usually teenagers. A runner passes a group of kids on the corner; they yell "run, one, two, three, run!" or "sweat man, sweat," "you are too slow," "goin's tough, let's see how tough you are," or perhaps the most debilitating, "look at that old man go." Runners generally do not respond to such taunts. They simply continue to run. Taunters will rarely follow for more than a block or two. More persistent bothers, however, are the dogs. For some unexplained reason, dogs seem to enjoy chasing runners. They seem to relish barking and nipping at heels. Distance runners soon learn where such dogs reside, avoid those areas, or discover that the dogs are harmless, can be spooked away by stopping and yelling at them, or that the dogs are penned up or on a leash. Some runners report frightening encounters with large dogs:

> One day last winter I was running down the sidewalk. The snow was still about a foot deep, I didn't see the German shepherd resting on the step of that house. Just when I was about to pass the walk up to the house, he came running out, right in front of me. He had that low, deep-in-the-throat growl. I thought I'd had it. Scared me pretty good. Luckily he just growled a bit and went back up on the step. I never run down that street without looking for him now.

Again, to brave such perils on a daily basis, to endure indignities usually reserved for mailmen, paperboys, and delivery people, a person must have acquired a way of thinking about running as a positive activity, as an assertion of "the way I am or what I enjoy doing." Many distance runners express this sentiment as "running is my hobby." When a person starts thinking about running in such a fashion, he is ready to seek out support for this thinking. There are people all over the city who run. He may discover that people who think like he does have a home. They have an organization.

Over the past ten years almost every major city in the country has become the home of a running club. These clubs are variously named, Windy City's Runners, Northern Distance Runners Association, and so on. These voluntary associations differ from the AAU clubs, although they may require an AAU affiliation for membership. The AAU clubs are made up of serious competitors. These people are usually ex-varsity athletes who wish to continue their competition; some even have Olympic aspirations. The clubs I am referring to are composed primarily of hobby runners and function to organize opportunities for these people to get together for races. The clubs also function to provide a center for the communication of race information, advertisements for special running equipment, and most importantly, to legitimize running as a hobby.

The overwhelming proportion of the members of such associations are men and women who run avocationally. They come from various walks of life, although most are professionals, semiprofessionals, or of white-collar occupational backgrounds. A complete profile of the membership of these clubs is a subject for another report. It is sufficient for my purposes here simply to note the existence of such clubs. A runner can join such a club and know that others are engaging in the same activities, braving the same hazards, and experiencing the same pain and exhilaration of running. Just going through the act of joining a club, filling out papers, and paying dues, gives an aura of legitimacy to the extraordinary act of running. That there are others of like-mindedness and that these others meet regularly to hold races open to even the slowest and least competitive increases what some sociologists call "consciousness of kind."

Now one can tell oneself and others, if they ask, "I am preparing for the race next week" or "I am in training for the St. Mike's Day Race." One can increase distances, run longer times and faster times with the knowledge that there is a race to aim for, a formal reason for running. Of course, many of the motives outlined earlier are still operative: I run to stay alive, to become a whole person, and so forth. But now there are more immediate and more tangible goals. There are shorter four-, five-, and six-mile races, and there are the longer marathons. A distance runner can select from races to set his own training and prepare for the race that he judges fits his schedule and aspirations.

The decision to race represents a significant event in the acquisition of a runner's identity. Jogging and regular running involve a form of self-competition. When one decides to race, a new consciousness emerges. The jogger simply does what feels right, pushes a little and betters yesterday's time, runs a little longer, and so on. Now he must make his performance comparable to that of others. Before the decision to race, the jogger may compare his performance to others in an implicit and indirect matter. After the decision, he makes his comparisons explicitly.

> When I jogged, I took pride in the knowledge that most people can't even run a quarter mile. I felt good knowing I could beat most people. After I decided to race, everything changed. Now I was against others better than I am or at least as good. I was really getting serious about training then.

Preparation for racing is at first specific to a race. A four-mile race, the shortest distance run on most race calenders, is usually the first race for most runners. Training, then, takes the form of working up to a number of miles per week, twenty, thirty, or forty and then running the four miles for time. There are many variations in training schedules, and runners will often compete week after week in races while aiming for one important race. They say they are "training through," i.e., running the race not to win nor achieve their best times but to prepare for a race they deem more significant. Of course, some people will compete without proper training, much to the regret of genuine runners, since the chances of injuries are much greater and dilettantes in the field often cause problems for faster competitors who must negotiate their way through crowds at the start of the race. Sometimes this problem is anticipated by classifying runners and stacking the start with the runners in front and the joggers behind.

For the trained as well as the untrained, concern about appearance emerges. The jogger is not very concerned about appearance since his identity is not at stake. Serious joggers or runners, the stage preceding distance running, are beginning to look like runners. However, when the decision to race is made, when the entry blank has been signed and the fee is paid, it is time to think about the actual race, and invariably an aspect of this thought assumes the form, "What will I wear?"

> I used to never worry about what I wore. In warm months I jogged in cut-offs, old T-shirt, and tennis shoes. In the winter I was still jogging so I decided to buy some sweat pants, and by then I had some good shoes (heavy but leather with a running sole). But then the St. Mike's Day race rolled around and I committed myself to running. I told everybody at school I intended to run, and I didn't want to make up excuses. I started wondering how I would look. I asked around and discovered "any old thing will do." Not so. When I arrived at the race, I saw some guys who looked like they were runners. They had on shorts even though it was cold that day. They had warm-up suits, not sweat pants, and their shoes were very light, some foreign brand. Oh sure, there were some overweight guys there with tennis shoes on. I was glad I fell somewhere between the fancy guys and the fat guys.

After the completion of a few successful races (this means finishing the race somewhere near the top of your racing category if the race was arranged in that manner or just finishing with the pack with a respectable time), the runner's identity will be more and more reflected in his dress. Finally, the distance runner will be outfitted in a suit from the sporting-goods store, not from the discount store. The "grubbies" will have been replaced with the warm-up suit, the tennis shoes with the running shoes, the tennis shorts with track shorts, and finally, on the chest of the runner will be a shirt from a previous race, the name of his club on the tank-top runner's shirt. The runner will have completed his metamorphosis from the sloppy jogger to the outfitted distance runner.

The next step is continuous competition and getting to know other distance runners. Race schedules span the entire calendar year and competition can be maintained year round. Running in the "deep freeze four," a four-mile race in December, is a mark of genuine commitment. Such winter races in the northern climate are referred to by runners as instances of the "crazies." However, runners are already "crazy" from the perspective of nonrunners or even joggers. To go out and run long distances for no apparent specific purpose, surely, is a form of being crazy. However, I have already indicated "crazies" are legitimized by acquiring an identity as a runner. Among runners, excessively long distances, running the marathon race, cold-weather running are "crazies" of a different sort. They refer to things that runners either are willing to try themselves or admire in others who try.

What happens to distance runners can be captured in "the Olympics phenomenon": you run for a while; your times go down; you cover longer distances; and you begin to think of the best in the field, and they and their performances become the standard against which you run. Although you know that you may never be a "class runner," while you run, during the periods of extreme exhaustion and exertion, you imagine the "big time," and that motivates you to go a little farther and a little faster. This mentality allows you to endure more pain and develop that intangible quality known as "guts."

It is this mentality that separates "real" distance men from casual joggers. During a north-country blizzard, when the winds were gusting to fifty-five miles per hour and the temperature was near ten below, the runners were out on their favorite "bad" weather routes around snow-packed parks and frozen lakes. One person commented later, "You can tell who the real runners are in weather like this. I sure enjoyed that." And, of course, the supreme test is the marathon (26.2-mile races). Not all runners compete in the marathon, but they often have that as an implicit standard, a goal in the back of their minds which someday will be attempted. A fifty-one-year-old professor at a West Coast university responds to the question "what makes you run?"

> A deep-seated frustration, something like a nonconsummated love affair. I started running when I was sixteen, in Europe, but the war put a stop to it. If I had had a chance to develop, perhaps to compete in the 1944 Olympics, that would have been that. But there were

no Olympics in 1944, and I was left with this longing. Here I am, a man in his fifties, who conceals a teenager's dream in his heart.[5]

Most distance runners I talked to and observed had some athletic experience in their background, although not necessarily track. All, however, seem to be "jocks" at heart. They expressed sympathy with and have admiration for Alphonse Juilland's description of his marathon trial:

> With two interminable miles to go, . . . a friend of mine came by in his car to encourage me. He opened his mouth, took a look at me, and closed it. In his face, I saw my agony. He was thinking, This guy is going to die.
>
> I had reached a point of absolute collapse and was telling myself that there was nothing I could do about it, no way I could stay on my feet for another minute. Then, for some reason, Sartre's story, *The Wall* crossed my mind. It saved me.
>
> Sartre's idea is that man is absolutely free. People say, "What do you mean he's free? Is the victim of torture free not to break?" Sartre's story replies to this kind of question. What he means by absolute freedom is not that man can do anything which crosses his mind, but that he always has a choice, regardless of circumstances. What choice has the man under torture to avoid breaking down? Well, at least he can choose the moment of his breakdown. There is no point, even in the most brutal torture, when the victim can't tell himself, "I can take it for another five seconds." And then, perhaps for another five. There is no objective breaking point. The man under torture chooses when to break down.
>
> When this story came to my mind, I was about to lie down in the middle of the street and start crying. But then I told myself, "Look, you can take a little more, you can drag yourself for another 200 yards. You'll cry at the next traffic light." And then the next and the next.
>
> I kept postponing my collapse. And when I did collapse, it was across the finish line. My friend caught me and congratulated me, perhaps for still being alive. He took my shoes off, and then my stockings, and all my toes were bleeding. I looked at them and said, "What a nice dramatic touch." I dragged myself to a telephone booth and called my wife long distance. All I could mumble was, "Never again. Never again."[6]

The distance runner's life is organized around the act of running. To illustrate this point, I will discuss briefly the changes in diet that occur as one moves from jogging to running. The jogger is often on a beer-and-beef diet. He runs to go home and refresh himself with a

---

[5]"World's Fastest Intellectual," *Sport* (October 1974):8.
[6]"World's Fastest Intellectual," pp. 8, 12.

cold beer. He works up an appetite or jogs to work off his last meal. His eating habits are typical of whatever social milieu he represents and are undistinguishable from those of the people around him. For most this means meat and potatoes, hamburgers, french fries, etc. Occasionally, you will overhear a jogger jokingly remark, "I better cut down on this. I'm in training." But serious modifications in diet emerge only after a runner's identity is assumed.

The distance runner eats to improve his running physique. Health foods are popular, and exotic concoctions are often part of the daily intake of food. These may range from ordinary food supplements, such as Tiger's Milk, to specially devised energy drinks. For example, many distance runners I know drink Gookinaid, also called E.R.G., Electrolyte Replacement with Glucose, a mixture designed by a distance-running chemist. There are also the homemade thirst killers, such as the pineapple-apple-orange juice mixture with wheat germ added. Distance runners are almost always knowledgeable about vitamins, minerals, and the basic food supplements that they believe replace vital bodily fluids lost during running. One sixty-two-year-old runner reports, "I've always been a food nut." He continues, "I eat to stay healthy so I can run. The real fun of running comes from being fit for competition. It [competition] is what makes exercise fun; you don't have to win, but you want to know you did your best."

There are many more aspects to the world of running than I have mentioned here. My purpose, however, has been to describe the emergence of a runner's identity, to show how a "crazy," indeed, a totally superfluous activity in the modern world can become a legitimate course of action and a way in which an individual may define his accomplishments as worthwhile, significant, and distinguishable from the quotidian behavior of those around him.

PART FOUR
Differentiation and Stratification

Our social experiences, the social world into which we were born and how we live, are marked by a pattern of organization best described by the word *inequality*. Some of the differences in the things that people have and the way that they think about themselves are invidious. One man inherits his father's fortune; another is born into a migrant family that follows the agricultural harvest. Other differences are simply matters of the way in which tasks are organized. In an operating room, the work is divided among the nurses, doctors, and attendants. Sociologists refer to the first system of inequalities as *stratification* and the latter as *differentiation*. Obviously, the more complex and varied the work in a society becomes, the greater the differences among the tasks assigned to members of the society. However, these differences are rarely left as mere tasks to be done. Instead, each task is judged as different from others in its importance and deserving of different rewards. Thus within this society there are patterns of status, prestige, and esteem.

In American society, as in most societies, there are clearly recognizable differences in the quality of life associated with doing particular kinds of work. Doctors have higher status than nurses, tenants higher than janitors, and so on. These differences in styles of life require particular mentalities for their display and maintenance. As we have learned to anticipate by now, the way a person knows about and interprets the physical and social world depends, in large part, upon the position that person occupies in life. The apartment house is a place for janitors to work, and it represents a better job than most for the janitor. To the tenant, it is a place where a recalcitrant and often bossy servant must be coerced and cajoled into "doing his job."

Systems of inequality are widespread within our society. We are often confused about how these operate. Who has what status and why? Clear and precise description of these systems is prerequisite to understanding them. Through meticulous examination of the operating room, we see how complex work tasks are organized and differentiated. Then, we discover that small, seemingly insignificant acts, such as sending Christmas cards, can involve the display of invidious differences. When janitor meets tenants, we learn that money alone is insufficient to establish status. Finally, we uncover the bias that the legal system has against poor people who have "failed" according to the prevailing standards of decency and worth.

11
Division of Labor

Social activities differentiate into patterns. The more difficult the task, the more specialized the work and, usually, the greater the complexity of the social organization. The coordination of many interrelated tasks into a smoothly functioning unit requires clearly defined patterns of authority. It means that people need to know the role expectations and patterned relationships among these roles. Observation of these differentiated activities are sometimes made easier by thinking in terms of analogies. In this article Robert Wilson suggests that we think of the operating room as a form of drama. Players in the cast perform according to a script; they succeed or fail to meet the expectations and requirements of their fellow players; they supply a character to their roles. The overall effect of these enactments is excitement and intense involvement. From a sociological perspective such a scene provides an excellent illustration of a highly differentiated form of social interaction.

Teamwork in the Operating Room
Robert N. Wilson

Introduction

Like all dramas, a surgical operation has certain important plots and subplots, a cast of characters, and a spatial setting. In narrative form, surgery at a large general hospital often occurs in a sequence such as the following:

>From *Human Organization* 12 (Winter 1954):9–14. Reprinted by permission. The material on which this article is based was gathered when Dr. Wilson was a research associate (1951-54) at the New York State School of Industrial and Labor Relations, Cornell University, engaged in a field study of several hospitals. The study was part of a larger project sponsored by the American Hospital Association. The research was under the general direction of Temple Burling, M.D. Miss Edith M. Lentz was the field work supervisor and senior research associate. The Carnegie Corporation of New York has provided the major support for this study.

"At seven o'clock in the morning, nurses have arrived on the surgical floor. They find maids finishing the cleaning of the operating suites and corridors. Notices of scheduled operations for the day are posted in prominent places, listing the patient's name, type of case, operating surgeon, and appropriate operating room. Orderlies and nurses' aides are wheeling small tables into the rooms, with sterile equipment laid out ready for use. The charge nurse assigns to their respective cases the scrub nurses (who will actually assist the surgeon) and the circulating nurses (who will perform general tasks around the operating room such as fetching water and counting sponges).

"As the hour of surgery, eight o'clock, approaches, the scrub nurses are washing hands and arms in the small scrub rooms next to the operating rooms; when they are thoroughly washed, according to specific procedures and an allotted time, they slip into sterile gowns and gloves. Their scrubbing must precede that of the doctors, since the nurses will be expected to assist the latter in their scrubbing and gowning. The first patients are in the corridor or preparation room where they have been wheeled by an orderly, and they are already in a semiconscious state from drugs of a sedative type.

"With the arrival of M.D.'s on the scene, the tempo of preparation increases. Nurses are now untying the sterile bundles and spreading instruments out for instant use. Usually, orderlies and the charge nurse are checking lights, suction hoses, etc. The anesthetist is setting up his tanks and dials at the head of the operating table. Interns and their more advanced colleagues, the surgical residents, are ordinarily scrubbing before the operating surgeon appears. Much joking and chatter occurs between these younger doctors and the nurses. When the operating surgeon, an older and more dignified M.D., starts to scrub, the tone of levity may decrease markedly. His appearance signals an even more alert and faster level of preparation on the part of other members of the operating team. The nurses assist the doctors in dressing for surgery; they hold gowns ready for the doctors to step into when scrubbed, and when the gowns are on they tie them securely. They hold rubber gloves up so that the doctors can put them on more easily. At this stage, before the incision has even been made, the motif of watchful cooperation has been established between nurses and doctors in the process of gowning.

"Now the patient has been wheeled into the room, and the anesthetist is busily caring for him, making him comfortable, and applying anesthetic. (The anesthetist is the patient's direct 'companion' in this venture, the person who reassuringly sedates him and establishes a close personal connection.) In a difficult case, the surgeon has perhaps previously consulted a colleague about the technique he plans to use and what conditions he expects to find. As the moment of cutting draws nearer, however, he is 'on his own' as the captain of the team; his lonely responsibility is mitigated by the presence of younger doctors and nurses, but he must be the key decision-maker.

"At the signal from the anesthetist that the patient has reached a proper depth of unconsciousness, the surgeon makes his first incision. (The patient has already been draped and painted by the cooperation of house staff and nurses, under the surgeon's direction.) Immediately, by spoken word or conventional hand signals, the surgeon calls on the nurse for sponges and instruments; the young doctors assisting at the operation are brought into play to hold retractors and clamps which staunch the flow of blood and keep visibility good in the operative field. At each stage in events, the surgeon consults the anesthetist to keep check on the patient's condition. Some portions of the operation may actually be performed by the surgeon's assistants, although he is always in close supervision and handles the critical moves himself. It is a mark of status to be allowed to work in the operative field, and actual surgery is done only by well-trained resident doctors. Nevertheless, the familiarity gained by simply holding the wound open for the surgeon is a vital part of the young intern's experience.

"There are two parallel status lines at work in the room. The surgeon passes on commands to the senior resident, who in turn passes them to junior residents and interns. The scrub nurse likewise initiates action for the circulating nurse and any students present. These chains of authority are crisscrossed by orders form the surgeon to the scrub nurse and from any doctor to any of the nurses; however, action is seldom, if ever, initiated in reverse: nurses do not issue orders to any doctors, and the lower echelons rarely direct the activities of the higher.

"The operating surgeon, after finishing his major task, consults the anesthetist again with respect to the patient's general condition and the length of time required to close the wound. As the closing process begins, there is a visible relaxation of tension and vigilance; joking becomes more frequent, and the pace of work more leisurely. Before a stitch can be taken, however, the nurses must count the sponges used in the operation, as a safeguard against leaving foreign objects in the patient's body. Here, at least, the nurses do initiate action, for the surgeon waits for their assurance that the sponge count is correct.

"During the sewing-up phase, the junior members of the surgical team usually take a more prominent role than they have in earlier stages. Often the chief surgeon will remove his gloves and stand around chatting or even leave the room entirely. The resident is left in charge, and he and the interns proceed to apply the finishing touches. After the sutures are all in place, the anesthetist takes charge of dressing the patient and moving him from the table to a cart which will return him to his bed.

In this he is assisted by nurses and usually an orderly; sometimes the junior doctors will help out, but the chief surgeon is not engaged in this phase.

"At length the patient, anesthetist, and doctors leave the room. The nurses are last to leave, as they were first to arrive. They pick up the doctors' discarded gowns and gloves and prepare the room for the next case. The whole process, requiring from thirty minutes to six or more hours, has included a large cast of characters exhibiting much communication. Yet they are so familiar with their jobs that the number of spoken words may have been slight."

A marvelous example of teamwork has taken place. Although innumerable orders have been given, most of them have flowed from the dictates of the patient's presence and condition. In a very real sense, few of the directives issued during surgery are arbitrary decisions on the surgeon's part. Rather, in the last analysis, the patient's needs have been the controlling element in the entire situation. Thus, the person who seems to have been least capable of exerting authority—the prone, unconscious "object"—has in fact assumed the star role and has exercised the preponderant influence on the course of the drama.

In the days before modern techniques of asepsis had been developed but after the idea of cleanliness had begun to be accepted in medicine, it was the custom to spray the operating area with an antiseptic solution. A certain noted surgeon, therefore, used to pause before the operation and intone, "Brethren, let us spray." Somehow this irreverent remark typifies an important aspect of life in the surgery: where the job to be done is intrinsically abnormal and fraught with anxieties, the atmosphere is deliberately made as mundane and casual as possible. In this most serious of situations, efforts are directed toward pulling the psychological climate into "normalcy." Like the small boy whistling past the graveyard, the inhabitants of the room make things prosaic; further, there is reason to think that energies must be mobilized for the work itself, not allowed to drain off in unproductive fear and trembling. While operating rooms are not truly places of levity, and *Ars Chirurgica* advises the surgeon to be "fearful in dangerous things," the pattern of joking and small talk is perhaps the most striking feature of surgery to the outsider. There is drama, but only a fraction of total operating time looks anything like the Hollywood stereotype of tight-lipped tenseness and mute solemnity. The self-consciousness which one would expect to characterize a person invading another's body and literally "holding a life in his hands" is for the most part dispelled by technical considerations; a job must be done, a careful exacting task, and this is the focus of energy and intellect. Operating rooms, then, are workmanlike. The first impression dispels any thought of "constant crisis."

Every operating room is:

1. like *all* other operating rooms
2. like *some* other operating rooms
3. like *no* other operating rooms

This logical scheme was originally applied to the field of personality, but it fits the operating room equally well. In fact, it might well be said that the surgery *has* a personality of its own, a distinctive blend of characteristics setting it apart from the rest of the hospital. It is perhaps a misnomer to speak of "the" operating room; rather, there are probably many types which may be classifed in several ways.

Every Operating Room Is Like *All* Other Operating Rooms

What do all operating rooms share as identifying marks? At least the following features are proposed:

Drama, Excitement, Intensity: An Air of Importance

Surgery is so obviously worthwhile and effective that it may be trite to comment on its importance. Yet there are many other aspects of medicine, and many aspects of every job, which lack the immediacy and lauded purpose of surgery. In the operating room, there can be no doubt that what is being done is dangerous and vital. Because we all share a belief in the importance of the body, because it is a basic part of the human being's security, and drastic manipulation (such as cutting) is cause for excitement. Further, the power to enter and change the body[1] signifies an immense responsibility on the surgeon's part and insures that the atmosphere shall include a sense of awe. And there is an element of drama, despite the stricture that it does not resemble the movie version. Each operation is a problem, a challenge, whose course can be plotted but not thoroughly predicted. One piano chord in the

---

[1] It has been remarked by many observers that in some sense the body on the table is no longer a human being in his fullest significance. The "person" becomes an "object," so that a complete emotional response to him (it) is no longer necessary or possible. As the chief surgeon once remarked to an observer seated in the gallery of the operating room: "This is a man; just wait, we'll put him back together and you'll see." T. S. Eliot, in *The Cocktail Party*, (New York: Harcourt, Brace and World, 1950, p.30) has also commented on the patient as object: . . .

old-fashioned cinema announced that "something is going to happen." Just so, in an operating room everyone knows that "something is going to happen."

As one graduate nurse expressed it:

> Down here you have the patient at the most critical time of his life and you know by the time he leaves the operating room what his chances are. You feel as if you are really important in his life. You're only with him a little while but still it's the crucial time so far as he is concerned.

We have stressed the mundane aspects of operating room life and pointed out the joking air which often precedes and follows the surgery. One can hear much talk of fishing trips, much mutual kidding, etc. All these contribute to a reduction of tension. But the tension exists; everything is not sweetness and light. A recurrent index of tension is the tendency to quick flare-ups of "temperament," of irritated and antagonistic remarks. Some impression of this index is gained from a record of part of an operation by an observer seated in the gallery.

> At this point, we have an interesting piece of interaction between the scrub nurse and Dr. *M*. The nurse hands him one swab, retaining another in her hand. He takes the swab as she hands it to him, and throws it angrily on the floor on the other side of the operating table. He asks, "Is this phenol?" (referring to the swab left in her other hand). The nurse replies (pointing disgustedly to the floor) "That one was phenol. This one is alcohol." Dr. *M*.: When I called for phenol twenty minutes ago, I *meant* phenol. I've got to swab that whole end off. Now get me some phenol." The nurse then fills a small cup with phenol and hands it the Dr. *M*. with a swab. This procedure he accepts.

> Dr. *M*. is now under great tension. It shows. His remarks become more brusque, irritated, profane. When the nurses have trouble getting a hose fixed up, he says, "Let's get going here. Dammit, it takes twenty minutes to do a thing and there is one way to do it right." The nurses begin to count sponges in a fairly loud voice. *M*. shouts to them, "Stop counting sponges! Don't do *anything* until I stop this bleeder." A moment later he shouts at *Y* (the assistant resident), "Pull back those fingers. Jesus, let's see this thing."

Emphasis on Teamwork and Cooperation

It might be said that every operation is a *co*-operation. In surgery, no one can "go it alone"; each person is dependent on many others, and the patient is of course dependent on all members of the team. So necessary is teamwork, in the nature of the job, that even individuals who are personally antagonistic often act in concert during the course of surgery. (In this, the operating team is like a jazz band or baseball club. Legend has it that the members of the famous double-play combination of Tinkers to Evers to Chance did not speak off the field for many years.) The individuals composing an operating team are so close-knit and understand the task at hand so thoroughly that verbal signals are often unneccessary. A language of gesture has developed whose meanings are crystal clear to persons following the operation intently. Perhaps the outstanding examples of intuitive cooperation occur in these pairs of team members:

> surgeon-nurse
> surgeon-anesthetist
> surgeon-assistant surgeon

To the nurse, the intimate comprehension of the surgeon's technique and his recognition of her competence may become a prime reward of her job. The desirability of a close harmony is recognized as is illustrated by the comments of an operating nurse and a surgeon respectively:

> Morale is high in the operating room because there is a team spirit. The finest point in the nurse's life comes when she is finally taken in and fully accepted as a member of the team. On a certain day, everything changes. There is almost a clean break with the past; ... the surgeon will recognize you and call you by name. A kind of emotional block is broken, and you know you are accepted. Any nurse feels very wonderful about this. The main reward for doing operating-room nursing lies in a special relationship with the surgeon.

> Both instruments and nurses have to be worked with for a couple of years before you know them. If she (nodding at nurse) stayed with the same guy for two years she would do everything before he even asked for it.[2]—A senior resident.

It is obvious that the surgeon and anesthetist must work together. The degree of anesthesia to be given a patient depends on the type of operation and the various stages in its progress. Conversely, the surgeon must be kept informed of changes in his patient's condition. One interview note states:

> We then got into a discussion of how the anesthetist works. Dr. D. described as perhaps the most important point a close cooperation with the operating surgeon. He said it is desirable that the anesthetist know the surgeon well, know his technique, and be able to cooperate with him almost automatically.

---

[2]It should be noted that this comment, while perhaps not "typical," illustrates more than a simple stress on intimacy and experience. It expresses also the prestige difference between the two main hospital roles, with the surgeon implicitly derogating the nurse role by comparing her with an "instrument" or tool of the doctor.

Technical Criteria and "The Religion of Competence"

All operating rooms place great stress on efficiency and expertness. In part, this is due to the complicated nature of surgical work—the fact that it rests on an exacting knowledge of multiple factors. The irascible surgeon who is highly skilled, and thereby gains respect, is a familiar figure. Unpleasant personal characteristics may often be overlooked if competence is high enough. The judgment of colleagues and nurses soon enough labels any doctor according to the degree of mastery he is observed to exercise, and the palm goes to the expert.

In part, too, the importance of cleanliness contributes to a desire for efficiency. The rituals connected with sterility promote a precise mode of behavior which infuses the nonsterile portions of technique. Surgical work is, by definition, careful.

The surgical job itself is such a demanding one in terms of exactitude that it draws all related jobs into the orbit of mechanical perfection. Because surgery must be orderly, the tasks which facilitate it are also orderly. "A neat job," then, can describe everything from a virtuoso performance by a heart surgeon to the measured folding of towels by a nurse's aide.

In the surgery, all tasks are "obvious" and can be quickly judged by ideal criteria; nowhere is the American talent for the admiration of "know-how" more clearly expressed. It is plain that the emphasis on technique and precision is necessary to high-level effort in surgery. Yet we may also mention the possibility that some portion of this emphasis serves a subsidiary function: it keeps the hands and mind busy on detail in a setting where excess imagination or sensitivity might interfere with the psychological boldness required. Inspection, not introspection, is the imperative of operating room activity.

The Surgeon's Authority

> The surgeon is like the captain of a ship. He is ultimately responsible for everything that happens in the operating room.—Chief of surgery.

Huge responsibilities demand huge grants of power, for responsibility and power must be some way commensurate. The surgeon's authority is unquestioned, it would seem, because of three interrelated factors. First, there is the right relation between authority and responsibility; a person held to account for something must, fairly, be in a position to affect the process by which the thing comes about. Second, the surgeon stands at the very top of a skilled hierarchy. He is not a replaceable part, and ideally, he knows more about the job at hand than anyone else in the room. Therefore, it is natural that he would be vested with the authority to direct the work on grounds of competence. Third, there is an aura of magic and reverence surrounding the figure of the surgeon; this aura has its roots in the ancient connection of priest and healer. When the three factors are combined, one sees a potent basis of authority. Although the authority is mitigated in several ways, it is a "constant" characteristic of the surgery. Relaxation of power may occur when long acquaintance and close work relations, especially those between doctor and nurse, have vitiated the third factor, the priestly aura, or "charisma." Implicit or explicit resistance (or rarely, transgression) to authority often stems from a surgeon's failure to fulfill wholly the standards of competence, so that respect is weakened. At any rate, the overpowering nature of the surgeon's position is almost certain to produce an undercurrent of resentment among lower-status members of the work team. This is illustrated in the exasperated aphorism of an operating-room nurse: "Nurses spend half their lives waiting on doctors, and the other half waiting *for* them."

Physical and Psychological Isolation from the Rest of the Hospital

For reasons of sterility and general work flow considerations, the operating suite is always separated from the hospital as a whole. It has its own floor, or part of a floor, and is for most purposes a "closed system." Although patients must be brought to surgery and taken back to their beds when the operation is over, this task is performed by orderlies, and other hospital personnel rarely visit the surgery. Of course, casual visiting is prohibited, since nonessential onlookers would tend to disrupt the precision of work and might increase the danger of infection.[3]

The isolation of the operating room means that, in the eyes of other employees, this area is strange and forbidding. All nonsurgical people are in a fundamental sense on the "outside" and may be curious about what occurs in the sanctum. They have, further, a definite attitude of awe and admiration for the activities that go on there and the "initiates."

Conversely, the surgical staff, from doctors to maids, develop a strong feeling of camaraderie. They recognize their status and role as a special group. Their world is the surgery, not the hospital. This implies great warmth and cohesion, as well as agreement on a variety of values. They must and do learn to live together as an elite corps.

[3]The separate, confined spatial arrangement of the surgery may, in some cases, contribute to the surgeon's feeling of tension. He, the captain, is alone with the heavy responsibility of a difficult job. In one hospital, perhaps inadvertently, the physical arrangement was such that fellow surgeons might drop by the open door to the scrub room for a casual chat and for consultation. The door leading to the hospital corridor remained closed, but the scrub room entrance, always open, provided easy access for interested colleagues. Numerous observations demonstrated convincingly that certain elements of support were derived from this "open-door" situation.

Every Operating Room is Like *Some* Other Operating Rooms

There seems to be a number of *types* of operating room, which share certain secondary characteristics. These qualities are like an overlay, supplementing and modifying but not drastically changing the conditions noted above. They include:

The Extent of Teaching Carried On

On this factor, operating rooms may vary from those that include no personnel in training to those that involve students, nurses, interns, and residents. Obviously, in the teaching situation, part of everyone's energy must go into the initiation process. The presence of students keeps people on their toes, keeps an air of questioning and striving alive, which infuses the surgery. Out-dated and incompetent elements, be they surgeons, nurses, or surgical techniques, have little chance of survival.

Methods and attitudes undergo constant changes, as the operating room keeps pace with the advance of medical science. And the surgery is "conscious" of its work, measuring and evaluating it in the light of high criteria of excellence. The stress on *competence* is heightened because every case is in one sense a model for the learners.

Division of labor is pushed further in teaching hospitals. For one thing, more hands are available; for another, there is a constant effort to split off suitable practice tasks which can give a student experience and afford him a gradual introduction into the core of the operation. Both nurses and doctors in training follow a series of stages whereby they approach ever more closely the condition of standard excellence. Nurses move from circulating duties to scrub nurse, from easy to hard cases. Interns and residents progress from holding retractors and stitching incisions to the actual work of the operating surgeon. The accentuated division of labor means that coordination of all the parts is more difficult to achieve, and, therefore planning is essential. Since a very large number of people are involved, interpersonal relations take on added significance; morale and skill must be high to insure smooth functioning.

Differences in prestige are multiplied in the teaching situation. The ladder of status has many extra rungs, within both medical and nursing staffs. Thus we find not only the invariant distinction between surgeon and nurse, but finer distinctions between scrub nurse and circulating nurse, between chief surgeon, assistant surgeon, resident, and intern. These gradations have the advantage of inducting "raw" individuals through manageable stages, so that they are not thrust from student to full professional in a single immense jump. However, they also tend to increase social distance and multiply the opportunities for friction. An amusing account of status-laden behavior, as told by two operating-room nurses, will illustrate the theme:

> They asked the question, "Who is the first person to leave the operating room after an operation?" And immediately answered it with, "The surgeon, of course." They said first the surgeon steps back from the table, takes off his gown and gloves, throws them in a heap on the floor and walks out of the room. Then the lesser fry close up the incision and then they leave, also stripping off their gowns and gloves and dropping them in a heap any place on the floor. They described how even the young resident will rip off a towel from the operating table, perhaps with several instruments on it, and just throw it to the floor while preparing the patient to go back downstairs, and then the resident will wait for the nurse to untie his gown and stalk away. After everyone has gone the nurse or nurses and the anesthetist are left to clear up the place and to get the patient back downstairs. Miss *R.* exclaimed, "After the great big doctors are all finished, who do you think moves the patient back on to the stretcher to take him downstairs? The nurse, of course." At this point Miss *M.* interjected, "Yes, that is what happens. They just walk out after shouting at you for two solid hours."

The fact of teaching means that each stage in surgery itself will be carefully scrutinized and explained. Although not all surgeons converse during the course of an operation, it is usual for the surgeon, his assistant, and/or the senior resident to carry on a running commentary, describing the significance of the work at hand. In recent years there has been a shift away from didactic teaching in medicine—one demonstrator or lecturer confronting a mass of students. The stress now falls on clinical teaching which introduces material to the student through his active participation in a case. Thus, the learners at an operation will be scrubbed up and actually assisting, rather than watching from the gallery. (Few operating rooms are now being constructed with amphitheaters, as a result of this trend.)

Problems are introduced by the teaching emphasis, many of them concerning the amount of participation allowed to the student. In surgery, only one man can operate; in the teaching of medicine, multiple diagnoses of the same individual may be made for practice purposes. There is a story of a young intern which points up the dilemma. After a particularly impressive piece of surgery, the doctors retired to the surgeons' lounge just off the operating room. The chief, who had performed the operation, began discussing it with his team. At length, turning to a very young intern whose duty at the operation had been to hold the distal end of the retractor, the great man asked, "And what did you learn from this operation, my boy?" The intern replied, "I think I have definitely established, sir, that the assistant resident has a terrible case of dandruff." Yet a chief of neurological surgery has commented that in his own experience the gradual progression up the ladder of responsibility was an excellent introduction to his specialty. He noted especially the fact that the slow rise to a central position in the operating team insured that he would not feel too much pressure when he, at length, held full authority, that he would not feel "on the spot" in his first cases as operating surgeon.

Nonteaching hospitals lack the special difficulties involved in this sort of on-the-job education. On the other hand, they also lack the detailed explanations to members of the team and the general air of competence and easy expertness which the presence of distinguished chiefs instills.

It might also be pointed out that nonteaching hospitals have no scapegoats as ready at hand as students. A latent function of student nurses and interns would seem to be found in their position as legitimate targets for the impatience and anxieties of graduate nurses or surgeons. Without disrupting the rapport of key team members, it is possible to vent anger at the circulating nurse who trips over her own feet or the intern who is woolgathering when he should be watching the operation.

The Difficulty of the Case in Progress

The relative seriousness of an operation determines many features of an operating room. For instance, in general terms, more difficult cases imply the involvement of more personnel, greater lengths of time, greater numbers of instruments, etc. In these important ways, a chest operation in Hospital X will be more nearly like a chest operation in Hospital Y than like a hemorrhoidectomy in Hospital X. While it is true that no two pieces of surgery are ever *exactly* alike, the major varieties show definite similarities.

In a fairly easy case, the atmosphere of the room tends to be rather relaxed, and the requirements of strict attentiveness and speed on the part of all concened are less rigorous. The tension which introduces friction into casual interactions is largely absent. However, in avoiding the extremes of pressure, the operating team misses the excitement and feeling of importance that accompany a major challenge to skill. Thus there may be complaints that the work is dull or routine, that the challenge is not great enough to hold one's interest at a high, sustained level.

Because fewer people work on a minor operation, the need for precise coordination is also less pronounced. In the teaching hospital, these cases are often used as opportunities for the young student to begin testing his own skills. A surgical resident may be given a vein ligation as his first solo flight, or a student nurse may serve as scrub nurse on the same type of operation. It is not true that these cases are taken "casually," but they do include a greater margin for error and seldom require split-second timing.

Since minor cases are usually short, the factor of fatigue is also less critical. In a long, exacting surgical effort, physical exhaustion may cause outbursts of temper; mistakes may be less well tolerated toward the close of a lengthy job. Often a long case will involve shifts of personnel, especially nurses, thus adding to the need for tight coordination. The more difficult work, sometimes requiring six or even eight consecutive hours, points up the need for physical endurance in surgical personnel. A noted surgeon once remarked the possession of "good legs" as one of the qualities of a competent surgeon, since long hours of standing are so often necessary.

These two characteristics—the extent of teaching and the nature of the operation—may be viewed as scales having various values. Any operation will fall at a certain point on each scale and share the qualities of that point with other operating rooms to form a "type." Thus we might speak of "major surgery in a teaching hospital," or "minor surgery in a small, nonteaching hospital," and find many elements in common within the designated category. There are undoubtedly other characteristics which contribute to a classification of operating rooms (for instance, whether the surgical staff is "open" or "closed"), but these seem to be the most critical.

Every Operating Room Is Like *No* Other Operating Room

Three elements appear to account for the *unique* quality of each operating room—and, for the matter, of each single operation. They are:

1. the personality of the surgeon
2. the personality of the nurse
2. the creative course of surgery itself

Certain facets of the surgeon's and nurse's personalities have already been discussed, those features which seem to be invariant. Such, for example, are the factors associated with tension and fatigue (stereotypes of the "irritable" surgeon or the "snippy" nurse) or connected with formal lines of status and authority (the "authoritarian" surgeon, or "subservient" nurse). But over and above these behaviors which seemed to be determined by "the situation" is a host of actions, attitudes, and traits which make each individual, in surgery or anywhere, unique.

An interview with a clinical instructor, a graduate nurse, provided an interesting illustration of the variations introduced by the surgeon's particular tastes in the matter of talking and joking during an operation:

> "The operating room," said Miss *D.*, "takes its tone from the personality and attitude of the surgeon. It is not a joking place if the surgeon does not make jokes, and not a talking place if the surgeon does not like to talk while operating." She described several different staff members and their variations in operating-room leadership and atmosphere. She said that Dr. *T's* operating room was always very friendly and filled with witty exchanges, while Dr. *H.'s,* although friendly, was strictly business. One distinguished surgeon allows no talking whatever in his room, while another is so jovial that he always remarks during an operation that he considers himself very lucky to have been given the very best nurses available for *his* operation.

Nurses, too, may be impersonal or warmly involved, although they do usually follow the surgeon's lead. When a nurse and surgeon are extremely well-acquainted and have between them the bond of countless shared experiences, their mutual personality adjustment may greatly enhance the technical efficiency of the team.

Surgery takes a different course each time it is performed. This is natural, since the bodies of patients are by no means uniform. But the truly individual character of some few operations stems from the creative element in new types of surgery. Perhaps a maneuver is being performed for the first time; perhaps the operation is exploratory and uncovers an unexpected cancer; perhaps a dramatic turn of events provokes an unanticipated crisis. In any event, something has been added to routine, and the operating room acquires a distinctive aura of excitement and discovery. In surgery, as in any other creative activity, there is room for novel aspects which thwart the attempt at rigid classification. Part of the peculiar charm and attraction of the operating room lies in this creative facet, the fact that routine may always be upset. If there were no possibility for innovation and inspiration, if surgery were really "routine," it is unlikely that it would attract the caliber of persons who *are* attracted to an operating-room team.

12
Little Ways to Show Big Differences

The differences among people and the value placed on these differences pervade every aspect of life. Although we may not pause to think about it, even the most mundane of our activities feels the influence of social status and prestige. The yearly task of sending Christmas cards takes up the time and energy of many people in our society. From a sociological perspective, this task also takes on the characteristics of class and status. In this article Sheila Johnson organizes her experiences and those of her friends around the proposition that people who send and receive Christmas cards can "be explained in terms of certain social characteristics, especially their social status and mobility aspirations."

Sociology of Christmas Cards
Sheila K. Johnson

Anyone who has ever composed a Christmas card list has pondered the inclusion and exclusion of names on the basis of a variety of fairly explicit considerations. Shall I send so-and-so a card this year, since he didn't send me one last year? Or, I *must* send so-and-so a card this year, even though he probably won't send me one, because I want to be remembered by him. Like the decisions we make about whom to vote for, we like to think of these choices as purely individual, rational matters. Nevertheless, sociologists have demonstrated that, regardless of how and why we choose a candidate, voting behavior can be analyzed as a function

From *Transaction* 8 (January 1971): 27–29. Reprinted by permission.

of one's socioeconomic status, mobility aspirations, ethnicity, and religious affiliations. Similarly, it seems likely that the patterns in which people send and receive Christmas cards can also be explained in terms of certain social characteristics, especially their social status and mobility aspirations.

This proposition first occurred to me several years ago as I was opening some Christmas cards and noticed that there was a strange disjunction between the cards we were receiving and the ones we had sent out. About half of the cards we received were from people to whom we had also sent cards, but the other half came from people to whom we had not sent cards and to whom we had had no intention of sending cards, and we ourselves had sent half of our cards to people from whom we had not expected to receive (and did not receive) a card in return. When I studied the names that fell into each of these three categories, it dawned on me that the people with whom we had exchanged cards reciprocally were either relatives or people with whom we were on equal social footing—professional friends of my husband or personal friends in different, but nevertheless comparable, occupations. The cards we had sent but to which we had received no reply, I discovered, went invariably to individuals whom *we* wanted to cultivate—people with regard to whom we were, in sociological terms, "upwardly mobile," such as professional acquaintances who might someday prove useful or important or social acquaintances whom we wished we knew better. By the same token, the cards we received and to which we did not reply came from individuals who wanted to cultivate us—some of my husband's graduate students and office employees, the liquor store, the hairdresser, and foreign scholars who obviously expected to visit the United States at some time in the future.

In order to test out my theory, I telephoned several friends shortly after Christmas and asked them to sort the cards they had received into two piles—reciprocals and those to whom they had not sent cards—and also to count up the number of cards they had sent "upward." (Some of the incensed replies to this request would indicate that the nature of Christmas-card sending is a very touchy subject indeed.) Those of my friends who continued to speak to me and who complied with my request corroborated my theory. Several couples in their late thirties or early forties who, although in different professions, were rather similar to ourselves in their mobility aspirations and in the number of people they knew who were upwardly mobile with regard to them found that their Christmas cards could be grouped into equal thirds (one-third sent and not received, one-third sent and received, and one-third received but not sent). However, a young graduate student reported that about 70 percent of his cards were reciprocal, with 30 percent sent upward and none received from people who were trying to curry favor with him. This is clearly the pattern for those with their foot on the bottom rung of the status ladder. At the other end, several retired people reported that 90 percent of their cards were reciprocal, with only 5 percent sent upward and 5 percent received from people who still regarded them as important. A man who had retired but taken a second job, however, reported that 70 percent of his cards were reciprocal but that 10 percent had been sent upward and 20 percent had come from people trying to cultivate him.

While the percentages of cards an individual sends and receives tell us a good deal about his mobility aspirations, the fact that he sends Christmas cards at all places him rather firmly in the middle class. Members of the upper class—particularly a closed upper class to which one gains admission by birth rather than through the acquisition of wealth—have no need to send cards upward, and sending cards to other members of the upper class is a formality that many are dispensing with. In England, for example, it is increasingly common for upper-class families to place an ad in the personal columns of the *London Times* stating that Lord and Lady So-and-So send warm greetings to all their friends for Christmas and the New Year as they will not be sending cards. (Several years ago an upper-class English wit poked fun at these ads by placing one asking *his* friends to send him Christmas cards as he would not be able to read the *Times* columns during December.) In the United States, because the upper class is more fluid than in England and because the country is simply too large for all one's upper class friends to read the same daily newspaper, the custom of sending cards among upper-class individuals has not died out. One would predict, however, that most of the private card sending of the upper class is reciprocal and that only its business Christmas cards are sent upward, since there is always room for upward mobility in the business world.

Lower-class and working-class individuals also send few or no Christmas cards but for entirely different reasons. Sociologists have demonstrated that lower- and working-class individuals tend to rely upon tightly knit family networks and neighbors for their friendships and that they are less geographically mobile than the middle class. Thus a skilled union man will probably have a large number of relatives living in the same town or same general area as he does, and he will be on friendly terms with many of his neighbors. There is no need to send these people Christmas cards, however, since he sees them nearly every day. He may be upwardly mobile in terms of his job, but this is handled by the union, and a Christmas card to the front office is not likely to do the trick. Only if he is upwardly mobile to the extent of trying to leave his stratum and become a white-collar worker may he take to sending Christmas cards to people who can help him. In that case he may adopt other middle-class behavior patterns, such as joining various clubs and lodges, in which he will make a broader range of friends to whom he will also want to send cards at Christmas.

Senders and Recipients

It is the middle class—particularly the upper middle class, consisting of high managerial and professional people—who are the Christmas card senders par excellence. These are the people who are both geographically and socially mobile—growing up in one place, going to college somewhere else and them moving about as success in one's firm or profession seems to dictate. Kinship ties tend to be far-flung and tenuous, since it would not be advantageous to be tied down to a given area by one's aging parents or embarrassed by the sudden appearance of a lower-class cousin. Friendships are formed among social equals—at school, at work, in professional or social organizations—but these, too, change as one moves up the ladder of success or to a different section of the country. Such are the ideal conditions for the exchange of Christmas cards. Friends and relatives are scattered widely, but one wants to keep "in touch," and there are vast sources of upward mobility to be tapped.

I realize that some people will object strenuously to this analysis of their Christmas card sending and receiving. While I was attempting to collect data on the subject, several of my friends declined to cooperate on the grounds that they did not fit into the pattern I had just described to them. "Really," one of them said self-righteously, "I keep an up-to-date Christmas list, and the only people I send cards to are people who send me cards. There is no upward sending or downward receiving in our family: it's strictly reciprocal." This is pure propaganda, nurtured by the myth of absolute social equality that exists in this country. Everyone can think of some acquaintances to whom he simply *has* to send cards, regardless of whether he gets one in return. The obligatory nature of the act is the real tip-off to the social pressures at work. As for people who receive cards they were not expecting—that is, cards being sent upwards to them—and who then shamefacedly rush out on Christmas Eve to mail the forgotten sender one of theirs, they are simply insecure in their status position. Imagine the president of Chase Manhattan Bank receiving a Christmas card from the janitor and saying remorsefully, "Oh, my God, and I didn't send *him* one." Yet thousands of people do roughly the same thing when they receive a card from someone who looks up to them. What should they do instead? The answer is nothing, except sit back and enjoy it. Of course, if the upward sender shows other indications of increased social status, it might be wise to send him a Christmas card next year, but that would depend on circumstances ranging far beyond the scope of this article.

In a recent film, "Diary of a Mad Housewife," the husband is shown counting the family's Christmas cards and remarking to his wife "One-hundred-and-fifty-three. That's fine. Three more weeks to go until Christmas and we've already reached the half-way mark . . . We sent out 300." He then goes on to instruct his wife to note carefully who has sent cards to them, since there's "no point" in sending cards the following year to people who have not sent them one this year. Here the authors of the film have missed a bet, however, since the husband is depicted as a social climber of the first order who would clearly insist on sending Christmas cards to certain "important" people—the same people whom he invites to his abysmal party and tries to cultivate in other ways.

In addition to scrutinizing the number of Christmas cards people send and receive for signs of social status and mobility aspirations, one can also tell a good deal about the personality of the sender by the kind of card he chooses. There may still be a few rare individuals who choose every Christmas card individually to suit the *recipient* but for the most part those days went out with the advent of boxed cards. Somewhat more common is the tendency for people with two radically different constituencies—for example, businessmen who keep their business and private acquaintances well compartmentalized—to choose two diferent sets of cards. However, in such cases it is not at all clear whether the two sets of cards are chosen to suit the different sets of recipients or to reflect the different personality that the businessman wishes to convey to each group—sober and elegant cards for his business acquaintances and mod, swingerish cards for his personal friends. In general one may assume that cards reflect the sender rather than the receiver, and that a Madison Avenue executive would no more receive a museum card from his Aunt Emma in Vermont than he would send her a Hallmark Santa Claus with a rhymed poem inside.

How can one classify some of the cards that people consciously or subconsciously select to convey not only their Christmas wishes but also their personality? Among university types, whom I know best, there seem to be several distinct patterns. Well established WASP professors tend to send museum cards or rather small studio cards of abstract design. Usually, the more powerful the professor, the smaller the card. (This appears to be a snobbish, willful inversion of the usual business pattern: the more important the executives, the bigger and more lavish the card.

An academic friend argues that there are exceptions to this rule and cites Professor Henry Kissinger, from whom last year he received an absolutely gigantic Christmas card portraying both sides of the globe. I would maintain, however, that this Christmas card merely illustrates Professor Kissinger's defection from the academic ranks and his adoption of the big-business ethos of the Nixon administration.) Jewish and youngish, slightly left-of-center professors tend to send UNICEF cards, often choosing a design that reflects their area of academic interest—India specialists send the Indian-designed card, Africa specialists send the African-designed card, and so forth. A similar tendency may be observed among government officials.

From professors who have (or think they have) artistic wives we get hand-screened, hand-blocked, or otherwise handcrafted Christmas cards. From professors who have just had their first child we get (you guessed it) baby photographs, and from professors who are doing research abroad we often get photos of their children in native dress. From professors abroad sans children or from those who've been there before we get interesting Chinese, Japanese, or Thai renderings of the nativity. (The most fascinating Thai card we ever received, from a high-ranking Thai army officer, was a photograph of the gentleman himself posed proudly beside his new Jaguar XKE. *Joyeux Noel* indeed!)

People with strong political convictions tend to remind us of these at Christmas time. Thus we get our share of CORE and CND cards. From less political but equally morally outraged friends we get a strange assortment of messages: cards that say on them "printed by spastics" or "designed by the deaf" and cards depicting felled redwood trees or oil-stained beaches. From our wealthier, nonacademic friends we get cards supporting the Symphony Association and the Junior League.

In addition to all of these types of cards, we get, every year, a couple of photographs of houses. These are never from the academic world—although some professors I know live in very nice houses—because the houses displayed on Christmas cards have a special status significance. Most of the houses that I have seen on Christmas cards belonged to friends who had just retired to Florida or Hawaii, or they were the dream-come-true of people who had finally bought that acre in the country. Whatever the occasion, the house depicted is usually the visible sign of a major change in social status, and it is certainly no accident that the president's Christmas card almost always features the White House.

Finally, and perhaps hardest of all to pin down sociologically, there is the catgegory of Christmas card known as the mimeographed Christmas letter. I would like to hold a contest sometime for the most fatuous Christmas letter, but I'm afraid I'd be deluged with entries. It is hard to attribute the Christmas letter to a particular type of person or a particular station in life, because almost everyone who has ever had an eventful year, taken an exciting trip, or accomplished a great deal has felt the urge to compose one. I have received them from internationally famous professors who were attempting to describe their world travels, from graduate students describing their Ph.D. research in the field, and from relatives recounting the latest family gossip. Perhaps mimeographed Christmas letters should be used as a vanity indicator, since they expose those among us who yielded to, rather than resisted, the pervasive temptation to blow one's own horn.

A Matter of Tone

The chief defect of the Christmas letter is its tone—that peculiar half-personal, half-distant note that makes most of them sound as if they were addressed to mentally defective thirteen-year-olds. This tone is the inevitable result of trying to address a single letter to a score or more of different friends. As any letter writer knows, one usually manipulates the tones of a letter to convey a certain personal image to a specific correspondent. If it is often difficult to send the same *card* to business as well as personal acquaintances because of the image to be conveyed to each group, how much more difficult to compose a letter that will ring true to a variety of recipients.

Not only is the tone of Christmas letters muddled by the lack of a clearly defined recipient, but it also often lacks the unifying voice of a single sender. Most Christmas cards can convey the status and life style of a couple or a family as readily as they can those of an individual. But this is because cards deal in visual symbols whereas letters traffic in words. It is always hard to believe that a mimeographed letter from "Betty and Bob" is really a joint verbal product, and so one looks for telltale "I's" and "he's" or "she's" to pin down the author. In a genuine Christmas letter, however, such slips never occur, and one is left to figure out for himself who is being the more sanctimonious from sentences that announce: "While Bob worked like a demon interviewing local politicians and village chiefs, Betty spent her time learning how to cook native dishes and teaching English to some of the wives and children." (For the full effect, one must try substituting "I" for each of the proper nouns in turn.)

There are doubtless still other sociological and psychological facets to the sending and receiving of Christmas cards. However, having said all of this, I would not want readers to conclude that I am trying to denigrate Christmas cards or that I personally am above sending them. Far from it. Having already passed through my family photograph, foreign, and UNICEF phases, I may even succumb to sending a Christmas letter one of these years. My card this year was a small, high-status museum number, depicting a medieval knight being hoisted on his own petard. The motto on his banner reads: *Honi soit qui mal y pense.* I think it suits me rather well.

13
When High Meets Low

Our interactions with other people depend, in part, on how we catgegorize those people and ourselves. The kind of work we perform provides us with one means for thinking about ourselves and others because these occupations are ranked in terms of status and income. Whenever a relationship occurs between two persons of unequal status in which their respective incomes do not reflect the same inequality, we have a strategic event for uncovering the meanings they attribute to interaction. In this article Ray Gold relates aspects of such status dilemmas by discussing the results of interviews he conducted with janitors. He questioned them about their relations with the tenants of their buildings. He identifies several patterns of interactions and focuses on the way the janitors interpret these encounters and resolve the dilemmas.

Janitors Versus Tenants: A Status Income Dilemma
Ray Gold

There is some kind of status relationship between the worker and the person served in almost any occupation where the two meet and interact. For example, when the salesperson and the customer meet, each brings to bear on the other valuations by which the other's status category can be tentatively ascertained. This tentative status designation enables each to make a rough judgment as to how to act toward the other person

From *American Journal of Sociology* 57(1952):486–93. Reprinted by permission.

and as to how he thinks the other person will act toward him. If their association is resumed, their initial judgments strongly influence the character of their subsequent interactions. If they are separated by wide barriers of social distance, they may carry on an almost formal salesperson-customer relationship for years. Or their respective status judgments may be such that the status barriers are gradually penetrated. In any case, the status relationship between them is always present, unless it is resolved into an absolute equalitarian relationship. Likewise, in the case of the physician and his patients, the plumber and his customers, the minister and his parishioners, and in others, there is a status relationship of which both parties are more or less aware and which influences the pattern of their interactions. Such being the case, the nature and form of these status relationships can and should be studied wherever they occur.

The present example, which concerns the apartment-building janitor and his tenants, is a case study in such status relationships. The form these relationships have taken is that of a marked dilemma of status and income.

Status and Income

The status-income dilemma may be expected to occur in two situations. One is that in which an individual earns too little to pay for the goods and services generally associated with his other social characteristics. The other is that in which he earns enough to pay for goods and services generally associated not with *his* other social characteristics but with those of members of higher social classes. When an individual in the first dilemma meets and interacts almost daily on a rather personal level with one in the second as, respectively, in the case of the tenant[1] and the apartment-building janitor, they develop an association whose form and content are of sociological interest.

The data in this article are based entirely upon interviews with janitors.[2] What results is a penetrating view of the janitor's conceptions

---

[1] The term "tenant" herein refers to the housewife, as the janitor seldom comes in contact with the man of the house.

[2] Thirty-seven janitors were interviewed by the author during the fall of 1949 and winter of 1949–50. The interviews were open-ended, averaging about two and one-half hours in length. A verbatim record of the interview proceedings was kept. A complete report and discussion of interfindings is in Ray Gold, "The Chicago Flat Janitor" (M.A. Thesis, University of Chicago, 1950).

of tenants and of his interpretations of their conceptions of him. Thus, we obtain an intimate understanding of the janitor's view of how he and tenants spar to resolve their respective dilemmas. Although many of the tenants may not be so sensitive as the janitor to this contest, it is safe to assume that, through his untiring efforts to play the game with his rules, the tenants are aware that he is agitating to change their traditional patterns of interaction.

In the early part of this century, before janitors in Chicago were unionized, they catered to virtually every whim of their employers and tenants in order to establish job security. Since they have become unionized, their duties have been greatly delimited, their wages increased, and their privileges extended to include a rent-free basement apartment in one of the larger buildings which they service. At present, they are required to fire the furnace to provide heat and hot water for the tenants, to remove the tenants' garbage regularly, to make minor emergency repairs, and to keep the building and grounds clean.

Having a history, the janitor also has a reputation. The tenant-public seems to look upon him as an ignorant, lazy, and dirty occupational misfit. There has developed a general belief that, if a man cannot do anything else successfully, he can always become a janitor. This stereotype has been perpetuated by the public because of a number of beliefs, principally the following: (1) many janitors are foreign-born and therefore strange and suspicious; (2) the janitor is always seen wearing dirty clothes, so the tenants seem to feel that he habitually disregards cleanliness; (3) the janitor lives in the basement, which symbolizes his low status; and (4) the janitor removes the tenants' garbage, a duty which subserves him to them. It is because the public has singled out these features in their view of the janitor that his ascribed status has been lowly. In the public's view it seems that the janitor merely is a very low-class person doing menial work for the tenants.

It is true that the performance of janitorial duties requires neither lengthy training nor a high order of mechanical or technical skills. However, the nature of the janitor's situation has led him to play roles and incorporate self-conceptions which frequently overshadow those which others expect of a combination caretaker and handy man. Because he does not work under direct supervision and can plan his work to suit himself, he feels that he is his own boss: he, alone, is in charge of the building and responsible for the safety of the tenants. After becoming proficient at making repairs for tenants, he magnifies his handyman role into that of a master mechanic. Combining these two roles, he then sees himself as an entrepreneur who runs a cash business of attending to the tenants' service needs.

These roles, together with others which stem from the work situation, contradict the public's stereotyped view of the janitor. Being sensitive to these social conceptions, the janitor strives to gain the tenants' acceptance as a person who has risen above the disreputable fellow these conceptions describe. Toward this end he not only plays the role of a respectable, dignified human being but of one who has a very substantial income (about $385 per month in Chicago). In this setting it is evident that the janitor's social relationships with the tenants are of crucial importance to him. These relationships are pervaded by his persistent disowning of his unhappy occupational heritage and the justification of his claim to middle-class status.

So important are social relationships with the tenants that the janitor defines success in terms of them. As many janitors have pointed out:

> The most important thing about a janitor's work is that you have to know how to deal with people. Then, when you show the tenants that you have a clean character and are respectable, you can train them to be good tenants, that's what's really important in being a success.

Because the janitor attempts to realize his self when interacting with his tenants, his efforts to train them are actually channeled toward the establishment of relationships which support, rather than oppose, his self-conceptions. The "good" tenants support his self-conceptions; the "bad" tenants oppose them.

It will be well now to examine the nature of these social relationships to determine how they give rise to the personal and social dilemmas which comprise the central theme of this discussion.

The janitor believes that, in general, tenants hold him in low esteem. Even the most friendly tenants maintain some social distance between the janitor and themselves. Tenants, generally, overlook his qualifications as an individual and see him only as a member of a low-status group. In their view he is merely an occupational type.[3] The most militant proponents of this view are the "bad" tenants.

There are two characteristics of a special group of "bad" tenants which are apposite to this presentation. These characteristics, jealousy and resentment, are descriptive of only those tenants who are embittered by the janitor's economic prowess. They are people whose incomes are usually below, but sometimes slightly above, the janitor's income. The janitor often refers to these tenants as "four-flushers." They live on the

---

[3]R. E. Park "Suggestions for the Investigation of Human Behavior in the Urban Environment," in *The City,* ed. R. E. Park (Chicago: University of Chicago Press, 1926): "Why is it that to the average American all Chinese like all Negroes look alike? It is because the individual man is concealed behind the racial type. The individual is there to be sure, but we do not meet him."

brink of bankruptcy, and he knows it.[4] Status symbols are very important to them. Unlike the janitor, they apparently strain their budgets to improve the appearance of their persons and their apartments. When they see the janitor's new car or television aerial, their idea of high-status symbols, it is almost more than they can bear. It violates their sense of social justice. In consequence of his high income, the janitor can acquire things which these tenants may interpret as a threat to the established social order.

The janitor's new car, parked conspicuously in front of the building, serves constantly to remind tenants of his pecuniary power. It draws the most criticism from the jealous tenants. Commenting on the tensions thereby engendered, Janitor No. 35 remarked:

> There is a certain amount of jealousy when janitors try to better themselves. A whole lot are jealous because the janitor makes more than they do. But they don't consider the time a janitor puts in. When I got my Dodge two years ago somebody said, "Huh, look at that fellow. He must be making the money or he wouldn't be buying a new car." I know one party, they think a janitor should be in working clothes all the time. Just because a janitor likes to go out in an auto and they don't have any, there is that feeling between janitor and the tenant, that's for sure.

Some of these four-flushers do own an automobile. But if the janitor's car is bigger and newer than theirs, they are extremely mortified. Janitor No. 33 experienced the wrath of such people:

> About a third of the tenants are very pleasant about it when they see my car, but the rest say, "Holy cripe, the janitor got a new car!" The same majority is the ones you are in trouble with all the time. They say, "How is the 'nigger' with the big car? Meaning I am a "nigger" because I got a Buick and my car is bigger than theirs.

The janitor finds that the jealous tenants are impossible to accommodate. They do not want to be accommodated by him. "No matter what you do," protested Janitor No. 14, "they squawk." Their animosity seems to know no bounds. They deliberately attempt to create trouble for the janitor by complaining about him to his employer.

Besides complaining about him, these tenants reveal their resentment of the janitor's mobility efforts by making nasty remarks to him. This

---

[4] In the boiler room the janitor sorts out the noncombustible garbage from the combustible garbage, the former to be removed by a scavenger and the latter to be burned by him in the furnace. In the course of these sorting and burning operations he wittingly or unwittingly comes across letters and other things which serve to identify the different bundles or other forms of garbage accumulation. Thus, each of the tenants is readily identified by her garbage. What the garbage reveals about the tenant over a period of time enables the janitor to make intimate judgments about her.

was shown very clearly in a conversation with Janitor No. 12 and his wife:

> JANITOR: When we got our 10 percent raise a short time ago, the tenants didn't like it. You see how nice this [first-floor] apartment looks. Well, there ain't another apartment in the building that's decorated as nice as this. I had all those cabinets in the kitchen tore out and got new ones put in. That brick glass and ventilator in the transom opening—I had it done. Tenants didn't like to see me do all that. They resent it.
>
> INTERVIEWER: How do they show their resentment?
>
> WIFE: Mostly by making snotty remarks. One woman told us that we shouldn't live in such a nice apartment on the first floor, that we should live in a hole [basement apartment] like other janitors. Then they are sarcastic in a lot of other ways. They just don't like to see us have a nice apartment and a new car. I guess they'd rather see us live like rats.

The basement apartment is symbolic of the janitor's subservient status. If he can arrange with his employer to obtain a first-floor apartment, there is nothing that the jealous tenants can do to stop him. They can only try to make life miserable for him.

Jealous tenants disdainfully address him as "Janitor," rather than using his given name. It is bad enough, from his standpoint, that all other tenants address him by his given name, thereby indicating his historically servile status. But these resentful tenants go further. They call him by his occupational name. Symbolically, their use of this "dirty" name means that they want their relationship with him to be as impersonal as possible. They want the janitor to be aware of the great social distance which he would dare to bridge. Janitor No. 4 commented on this form of address:

> JANITOR: The bad ones squawk as long as they live. No matter what you do they squawk. They're the ones that don't call you by your name. They're a lower class of people, but they try to make you feel even lower than them.
>
> INTERVIEWER: Why do they call you "Janitor"?
>
> JANITOR: It's either out of stupidity or to make you think you are a slave to them—an underdog. Janitors get the same crap all over the city, I know.

These four-flushers who address him as "Janitor" are unalterably opposed to his efforts to better himself. The longer they live in the building, the worse their relationships with him become. This point was brought out by Janitor No. 4:

> Boy, I'll tell you about one thing that happened to me last Christmas morning. This woman rings my bell when I'm out and gives an enve-

lope to my wife to give to me. I passed by the back windows here a little while later and looked in like I always do to wave at the kid, and my wife called me in because she thought there must be a present in the envelope. So I went in and opened it up and there was a note inside that said, "I'll be home today so please keep the heat up." I was so mad I coulda booted her ass right over the fence if she was there. That's how the tenants get when they been living here too long. Most of them think they own the building, and you should do just what they want.

As Janitor No. 4 insisted, the four-flushers' unthinking demands for personal service, their utter disregard for the janitor's integrity and authority, and their possessiveness toward the building increase with their length of residence. The building becomes more and more like "home" to them the longer they live there. "They can't afford to have a home and servants of their own," observed Janitor No. 18, "so they try to treat the janitor as their servant." They like to think of him as a mobile part of the building, always at their beck and call. Still, the deep-seated animosities between these tenants and the janitor preclude any mutually satisfactory adjustment of their respective roles. Through the years they continue to be jealous and resentful of him. Meanwhile, he continues to resent their uncooperativeness and disrespect. The building becomes as much "home" to him as it does to them. But there is something about "home" that can never be remedied. From the standpoint of these four-flushers, that something is the janitor. From the janitor's point of view, that something is the four-flushers.

Turning now from janitors whose tenants have incomes that are marginal to theirs to janitors whose tenants are plainly well-to-do, it is evident that there is a remarkable contrast in janitor-tenant relationships. The following conversation with Janitor No. 26 will serve as an introduction to this contrast:

> INTERVIEWER: Some fellows have told me that many of their tenants resent their getting a new car or a television set. Have you ever come up against that?
>
> JANITOR: That class of people don't live here, of course. The class of people you're talking about are making two hundred a month, don't have a car, and are lucky they're living. Yeah, I've met up with them. . . . People here aren't jealous if you got a new car. People here feel you have to have a car, like bread and butter.

Tenants whose incomes are clearly higher than the janitor's have no cause to be jealous of him. They do not compete with him for symbols of pecuniary power. There is more prestige attached to having an engineer in the building than to having a janitor, so they call him "the engineer." These people obviously do not have the status-income problems of the four-flushers who comtemptuously address him as "Janitor." Clearly, then, tenants who are well-to-do have no need to make demands. As Janitor No. 17, many of whose tenants have incomes marginal to his, so penetratingly observed:

> The people that don't have anything put up the biggest front and squawk a lot. The people who got it don't need any attention. I'd rather work for rich tenants. The ones we got here are middle ones. Those tenants that sing don't have a right to. . . . Some few tenants just got here from the Negro district. They were stuck there until they could find a place to move to. Man, they're real glad to be here. They don't give me no trouble at all.

Demonstrating remarkable insight, Janitor No. 17 pointed out that the "rich" tenants do not feel that they need attention from the janitor, that the "refugee" (like the poor) tenants feel that they are in no position to make demands, and that the four-flushers or "middle" (probably lower-middle) tenants are the most troublesome.

When a janitor works for many years in a building occupied by well-to-do tenants, it is not unusual that a genuinely warm relationship develops between him and these tenants. They probably come to see him as an old family employee, while he believes that he has been accepted for himself. As Janitor No. 26 asserted, "They feel they're no better than me—I'm no better than them, and they always invite me in for coffee or something like that." There is no problem in sharing identification of "home." The building is undisputedly "home" to both the janitor and the "rich" tenants, because they most probably view their relationship with him as a status accommodation, which he interprets as an equalitarian relationship.

In the next section the status-income dilemma is illustrated in terms of the janitor's professional behavior and outlook, which are in marked contrast with the tenants' lack of respect for him.

Professional Behavior and Professional Attitudes

It is likely that in every low-status occupation, where the worker associates with the customer, the workers meet with certain customer-oriented situations in which they typically behave in accordance with standards that people have traditionally called "professional." These low-status workers certainly do not label themselves "professionals," nor do others so label them. Yet, there is ample evidence that some of their behavior is ethically comparable to the behavior exhibited by members of the so-called "professions." R. E. Park, some twenty-six years ago, made similar observations of the tendency of even the lowest status occupations to become quasiprofessions in some respects:

> In the city every vocation, even that of a beggar, tends to assume the character of a profession and the discipline which success in any vocation imposes, together with the associations that it enforces, emphasizes this tendency—the tendency, namely, not merely to specialize, but to rationalize one's occupation and to develop a specific and conscious technique for carrying it on.[5]

While it is true that the janitor's self-conceptions are instrumental in forming the superstructure of his professional behavior, the foundation of such conduct is formed primarily out of situational requisites. This being the case, his status-income dilemma is intensified because he is frequently called upon to act in a professional manner toward the disrespectful tenants. Thus, whether mainly out of choice (expression of self-conceptions) or out of necessity (fulfillment of situational requisites), the relationship between janitor and tenant sometimes assumes the character of that between professional and client.

The nature of the janitor's work leads him to find out a great deal about the pesonal lives of his tenants. He meets with many situations which force him to decide how much and to whom he should tell what he knows about them. Generally, he exercises scrupulous care in the handling of this intimate knowledge, as he considers himself to be entrusted with it in confidence.

The janitor gets some of his information from sources other than the tenants themselves. When he acts as an informant (e.g., for insurance checkers), he finds out a great deal about their personal affairs. One tenant tells him about another. The garbage reveals much about them. From these sources he acquires information of a very confidential nature.

The janitor also gets information directly from the tenants. They confide in him not only about illnesses but also about personal problems. As Janitor No. 20 remarked, "Some of them stop you and think they have to tell you if they got a toothache."

How the janitor dispenses his intimate knowledge about tenants was related by Janitor No. 32:

> If tenants want to know what's going on, they come to me about it. You hear and see a lot of things in your time. There are even times when you are requested to keep quiet. And there are times when you have to answer—for FBI and insurance inspectors. You can't tell them everything, either, you know. See and not see; hear and not hear—that's the best policy.

[5] R. E. Park, "Behind Our Masks," *Survey Graphic* 56 (May 1926):136.

Like the bartender and the barber, whose ascribed occupational status beclouds the fact that they frequently share their customers' personal secrets, the janitor is placed in problematical situations requiring some kind of ethical rules. When it is understood that occupational problems which accrue from the same kinds of situations are basically the same without respect to status, then the similar receipt of confidences by the janitor, the lawyer, or the bartender becomes clear. These workers are, in this instance, in the kind of situation which requires them to protect the customer's personal secrets. Whether the disposition of these secrets involves as little as remaining silent or as much as stretching the truth, the workers protect their relationship with the customer by protecting his confidences. Likewise, in other given kinds of work situations which require the solution of ethical problems, the worker-customer relationship becomes overly complicated unless the worker makes and observes appropriate rules. Such ethical rules are not simply a matter of honorable self-conceptions or formalized professional codes. They are fundamentally a matter of situational requirements, irrespective of personal and occupational status.

Another area in which professional behavior is found concerns the janitor's relationships with overamorous tenants. Janitor No. 12 described what he considers to be the proper procedure for easing gracefully out of such a delicate predicament:

> Another thing about janitors—lots of women try to get you up in apartment just "to talk" or for some phony excuse. When you walk in they are on couch, ask you to sit down, and that means only one thing. When that happens to me and I begin to sweat, I know I better leave. Thing is not to refuse them so they get embarrassed, so I act dumb. I excuse myself and say I forgot about water running some place which I must shut off right away. It's hard to do, but it's best.

One can easily imagine hearing the bishop advise the young minister or the elderly doctor instruct the young doctor in a similar vein. The minister and the doctor must be prepared to meet such situations in a like fashion. The janitor instructs tenants to call him for repairs only during daylight hours, except for what he considers to be genuine emergencies. In the same way, the physician teaches his patients to call him only during office hours, except for a bona fide emergency. Some janitors recognize the similarity to doctors' problems. As Janitor No. 19 observed:

> Did you ever stop to think that we have a lot in common with doctors? I used to meet them in the halls at all hours of the night. We'd kid each other about making emergency calls at all hours of the night and never getting through with work.

Not only the janitor and the physician but others who deal routinely with customers' emergencies have problems of the same kind.

Yet another cluster of work situations wherein the janitor exhibits professional behavior concerns those occasions when he is called upon to do mechanical work for the tenants. The most clear-cut evidence of professional behavior in this area was submitted by Janitor No. 11.

> Some of the repair work the tenant is responsible for and I'm supposed to charge for it. Well, if I replace some glass that costs me three and a half dollars, I may charge the tenant a half dollar or two dollars more for my labor, depending on how much she can afford. If it's a little thing and the tenant isn't well off, I won't charge her anything for it if she's supposed to pay.

The janitor's practice of charging for repairs on the basis of the customer's ability to pay is a high standard of service—quite in the tradition of the medical profession—and he knows it.

The Dilemma

The janitor's professional behavior, together with his substantial income, contradicts what he believes are his tenants' conceptions of him. His struggle to gain their respect is a struggle for status. His high standards of conduct constitute a way of favorably influencing their estimation of his worth. Still, he finds that tenants regard him as hardly more than *a janitor.* He strongly resents their failure properly to recognize him, particularly in the case of the four-flushers. As Janitor No. 18 bitterly remarked:

> They're the kind that are very important. They think you're a fireman—should drop everything and run to them. They adopt a superior attitude: "I'm the tenant and you're the janitor." Like the East and the West in that saying. Confidentially, a lot of us janitors could buy out most tenants. They put on airs and try to be bossy.

The janitor has a higher income than many of the tenants; yet, the latter "adopt a superior attitude." So he does considerable soul-searching to seek a satisfactory explanation of his relatively low status. The conversation which we had with Janitor No. 28 is in point:

> INTERVIEWER: What things are janitors touchy about?
> JANITOR: A lot of tenants figure he's just a goddamn janitor, a servant. Here [with "rich" tenants] it's not so bad. You say something to them and they [the "bad" tenants] say, "Hell, you're nothing

but a janitor." Or when you're talking to even a working man and you tell him you're a janitor, he smiles—you know, people think there's nothing lower than a janitor. You get that feeling that they're looking down on you, because you're working for them. I know I feel that way sometimes. During the depression I was making better than most, so what the hell. It's good earned money.

INTERVIEWER: Well, why do you say you get that feeling that they are looking down on you? Why do you feel so sensitive?

JANITOR: In different places you hear people talk janitor this and janitor that, and they say they'd never be a goddamn janitor. So you think people here must say and think the same, but not to you. It makes you feel funny sometimes.

It is noteworthy that Janitor No. 28 does not reject his idea of the tenants' definition of a janitor. For that matter, virtually no other janitor does so either. To explain this, it is necessary to understand how the janitor relates himself to other janitors in terms of the occupational title.

The individual janitor strongly identifies himself with the name "janitor," despite his belief that tenants look down on janitors. Their view does not annoy him very much because he, too, looks down on *other* janitors. He feels that he is different from and better than other janitors. So, when tenants (nonjanitors) speak disparagingly of janitors, he does not resent it because of the group solidarity in the occupation, for, in reality, there is little such solidarity. Rather he resents it because his self-conceptions are so involved in the name "janitor" and because the tenants fail to recognize his individual worth. Thus, when a janitor (No. 8) proudly states, "Tenants never treated *me* like a janitor," there is no doubt that he agrees with their definition of janitors but that he, by virtue of being singularly superior to other janitors, has been treated in accordance with his conception of himself.

This attitude of "different and better" may be characteristic of the members of any occupation (or other group) whose public reputation is one of censorious stereotypes. This attitude implies that the individual member agrees that most of his colleagues do have the characteristics attributed to them by the public. The interesting question is: Why does the member agree with the public? The study of janitors suggests that the answer is likely to be in terms of (1) the nature of the member's association with his colleagues (he probably knows only a few of the "better" ones) and (2) the status relationship between the member and the portion of the public he associates with in his work.

Although the individual janitor capably defends himself from the public's conceptions of janitors, he still must perform tasks which preclude advance to a higher occupational, hence social, status. The janitorial reputation refers to the members' personal characteristics and work habits. Closely related to, but distinguishable from these alleged personal traits are readily verified features of janitoring which involve dirty work (e.g., shoveling coal and removing garbage). Work is dirty when society defines it as such, that is, when society defines it as being necessary but undesirable or even repugnant. Middle-class people seem consciously to avoid such tasks. They apparently realize that the kind of work one does is often more important than one's income when it comes to getting established as a member of the middle class. Yet, in a materialistic society, certain costly things, like a new automobile and a television set, become symbolic of high status, even to them. This accounts for the dilemma of the four-flushers.

But what about members of occupations which require the performance of dirty tasks? It seems that, like members of the janitorial occupation, they have the financial but lack the occupational qualifications for acceptance by the middle class. Speaking on this dilemma, Janitor No. 35 argued:

> A lot think they're better than the janitor because he has to take down their trash. Still the janitor makes more money. I believe the janitor *should* be making a lot more money than white-collar workers. After all, a janitor has a whole lot of responsibility and long hours.

Janitor No. 35, in summarizing the status-income dilemma, is painfully aware that tenants look down on the janitor. Their trash, the garbage, is undoubtedly the biggest single element in the janitor's continued low status. The removal of garbage is dirty work, incompatible with middle-class status. It causes the janitor to subserve the tenants, all of his individual attributes notwithstanding. The garbage symbolizes the dilemmas of the janitor-tenant relationship.

Conclusion

This account of the status-income dilemma suggests that, since high-prestige and high-income occupations are frequently distinguishable from one another, the *kind* of work a person does is a crucially qualifying factor in so far as his status possibilities are concerned. Viewed another way, the trend toward professionalization of occupations becomes an effort either to bring status recognition into line with high income or to bring income into line with high-status recognition. The janitor-tenant relationship has been graphically presented to call attention to a dilemma which is so prevalent that it is apt to be overlooked.

14
The Law and the Poor

A judicial system administering justice and enforcing the law without regard for social background may have built-in discriminatory practices. Frequently, those in control of the system are unaware of these implications. However, experiencing the "wrong end" of the system may give rise to adaptive strategies. The poor and habitual public drunk acquires elaborate ways of "beating the drunk charge." James Spradley identifies these strategies, describes their effectiveness, and shows how they relate to some of the core values of American society.

Beating the Drunk Charge
James P. Spradley

It could be Miami, New York, Chicago, Minneapolis, Denver, Los Angeles, Seattle, or any other American city. The criminal court may be in the basement of a massive public building constructed at the turn of the century, or high above the city in a modern skyscraper. The judges who hear the never-ending list of cases may be veterans of the bench or men whose memories of law school are fresh and clear. But one scene does not change. Each weekday morning, a group of unshaven men file into court with crestfallen faces, wrinkled clothing, and bloodshot eyes. They stand before the prosecuting attorney and hear him say, "You have been charged with public drunkenness, how do you plead?"

From *Conformity and Conflict*, ed. James P. Spradley and David W. McCurdy (Boston: Little, Brown, 1971). Reprinted by permission.

The most staggering problem of law and order in America today is public drunkenness. In 1968 the FBI reported that one and a half million arrests for this crime made up nearly one-third of all arrests. This means that every twenty seconds another person is arrested and charged with being drunk in public. During 1967, in Seattle, Washington, 51 percent of all arrests and 65 percent of all cases that appeared in the criminal court were for intoxication. In that same year, the chief of police stated, "As a public official I have no choice. Whether alcoholism is a disease or not would not affect my official position. Drunkenness is a crime. So we must enforce the law by arresting people. We know in the police department that probably right at this moment there are more than two hundred men in the city jail serving sentences for drunkenness who have never posed any threat to the community in any fashion at all."

Who are these men that are repeatedly arrested for drunkenness? Who are the ones who spend much of their lives in jail for their public behavior? The first task in this study was to discover how these men identified themselves. This was necessary because the police, courts, social scientists, and most citizens see them as criminals, homeless men, derelicts, and bums who have lost the ability to organize their behavior in the pursuit of goals. The word these men used to identify their subcultural membership was the word *tramp*. There are several different kinds of tramps recognized by informants; for example, a "mission stiff" is a tramp who frequents the skid-road missions, while a "rubber tramp" travels about in his own car. This category system constitutes one of the major social identity domains in the subculture.

Tramps have other ways to conceptualize their identity when they "make the bucket," or are incarcerated. As an inmate in jail, one is either a *drunk,* a *trusty,* a *lockup,* a *kickout,* or a *rabbit.* In the particular jail studied, there are over sixty different kinds of trusties. This fact led some tramps to believe they were arrested to provide cheap labor for the police department. In their capacity as trusties, nearly 125 men provide janitorial service for the city hall, outlying police precincts, and the jail. They assist in the preparation of food, maintain the firing range, care for police vehicles, and do numerous other tasks. Most men soon learn that doing time on a drunk charge is not a desirable occupation; so they use many strategies to escape the confines of the jail or to reduce the length of their sentence. When a man is arrested, he is placed in the drunk tank where he awaits his arraignment in court. Those sentenced to do time will spend it in close association with other tramps. If a man is not experienced in the ways of this culture, he will learn them while he is in jail, for it is a veritable storehouse of invaluable information for those who are repeatedly arrested for public intoxication. He will learn to think of himself as a tramp and to survive on the street by employing more than a dozen "ways of making it." More important, as he discovers that the jailhouse has a revolving door for drunks, he will do his best to "beat the drunk charge." The casual observer in court may find the arraignment and sentencing of drunk cases to be a cut-and-dried process. From the perspective of these men, however, it is more like a game of skill and chance being played by the tramp and law-enforcement agencies. In this article we shall examine the rules of this game, the strategies employed by tramps, and the underlying American cultural values that make it intelligible to the outsider.

Plans for Beating the Drunk Charge

Every culture contains one type of shared knowledge called *plans*. These are related to the achievement of goals. A plan is a set of rules that specifies a goal, conditions under which the goal will be chosen, techniques for the attainment of the goal, and conditions under which a particular technique will be used to attain the goal. The methods of ethnoscience are designed to map culturally shared systems of knowledge and were used in this study to discover the plans tramps employ in their relationship to law-enforcement agencies.

The Goal: Maximize Freedom—Minimize Incarceration.

There are many goals which tramps pursue. Most aims are referred to in a specific manner, such as "making a flop," "making a jug," "getting a dime," or "bailing out." Freedom is a general objective that includes such specific goals as rabbiting from jail, concealing one's identity, making a payoff to a bull, leaving town, avoiding the police, and beating a drunk charge. Men do not always select one of these goals in order to maximize freedom—they sometimes even choose paths leading to *incarceration*. In a sample of a hundred men, 10 percent reported they had gone to jail and asked to be locked up in order to stop drinking. At other times a tramp will go to jail on his own to request a place to sleep or something to eat. Such cases are rare, and most tramps abhor imprisonment because they have learned a lifestyle of mobility, and the restrictions in the bucket lead to intense frustration. A testimonial to the fact that men do not seek imprisonment, as some outsiders believe, is the large number of strategies this culture has for avoiding incarceration. Almost every experience in the tramp world is defined, in part, by noting the degree of risk it entails for being jailed.

Techniques for the attainment of the goal. Because of the public nature of their lifestyle, sooner or later most of these men end up in jail. Their specific objective at that time is to "beat the drunk charge." If successful, this could mean freedom in a few hours or at least a sentence of shorter duration than they would otherwise have received. The techniques for reaching this goal were discovered during interviews in which informants were asked: "Are there different ways to beat a drunk charge?" They responded with many specific instances in which they had taken action to beat the charge. These were classified as follows:

1. Bail out.
2. Bond out.
3. Request a continuance.
4. Have a good record.
5. Use an alias.
6. Plead guilty.
7. Hire a defense attorney.
8. Plead not guilty.
9. Submit a writ of habeas corpus.
10. Make a statement:
    a. Talk of family ties.
    b. Talk of present job.
    c. Talk of intent to work.
    d. Tell of extenuating circumstances.
    e. Offer to leave town.
11. Request the treatment center (alcoholic).

Each of these techniques labels a *category* of many different acts that are considered equivalent. For example, a man may bail out by using money he had with him when arrested, by borrowing from another man in jail, by contacting an employer who loans or gives him the money, and so on. There are several ways to "have a good record": a man must stay out of jail for at least six months for his record to begin to affect the length of his jail sentence. In order to do this a man may travel, quit drinking, stay off skid road, or go to an alcoholism treatment center for a long stay. Each kind of statement includes specific instances, varying from one man to another and from one time to the next. The category system is extremely important to tramps. Once they have learned these techniques, they practice them until their skill increases. Judges may consider an old-time tramp as a "con artist," but in this culture he is a man with expertise in carrying out these culturally shared techniques.

Conditions influencing selection. When a man is arrested he must process a great deal of information before he makes a decision to employ one or more of these techniques. He must assess his own resources, the probabilities of success, the risk of doing more time, etc. He needs to know the sentencing practices of the judge, the population of the jail, and the weather conditions. The most important factors that influence his decision are shown in Table 14-1.

American Cultural Values

Every society is based upon shared values—conceptions of the desirable in human experience. They are the basis for rewards and punishments. It is not surprising to most Americans that our culture, like most others, has rules about the undesirability of certain behavior *in public*. We have outlawed nudity, begging, drinking, elimination of wastes, and intoxication in public places. We are offended by many other acts—if they occur in public. Tramps are booked for public intoxication, but they are often arrested because they urinate, sleep, or drink in some public place. Poverty has made it impossible for them to conceal their behavior behind the walls of a home. The extent of these restrictions upon *public* acts are in contrast to many non-Western societies where there is a wider range of acceptable public behavior. Because public drunkenness, which covers a multitude of other public sins, involves more arrests each year than any other crime, we may conclude that *privacy* is an important value in our culture.

TABLE 14-1. Conditions influencing selection of a way to beat a drunk charge

Strategy	Risk of outcome?	Risk offending bulls?	Risk getting more time?	Risk doing dead time?	Money needed?
Bail out	No	No	No	No	$20
Bond out	No	No	No	No	$20+
Request a continuance	Yes	Yes	No	Yes	Yes
Have a good record	No	No	No	No	No
Use an alias	Yes	Yes	Yes	No	No
Plead guilty	Yes	No	No	No	No
Hire a defense attorney	Yes	Yes	No	Yes	Yes
Plead not guilty	Yes	Yes	Yes	Yes	No
Submit a writ of habeas corpus	Yes	Yes	Yes	Yes	No
Make a statement	Yes	No	Yes	No	No
Request a treatment center	Yes	Yes	Yes	Yes	No

Above the judge's bench in the criminal court where this study took place, there is a large wooden plaque inscribed "Equal Justice for All

Under the Law." Given the laws prohibiting public behavior of various kinds, we might still expect that the punishment for violation would be distributed *equally*. Thus, if two men with the same criminal record are found guilty of the same crime, they should receive the same punishment. If two men are found drunk in public for the first time, it would be unfair to fine one a few dollars and require the other to pay several hundred dollars. Upon examining the penalties given for public drunkenness, we discover a rather startling fact: *the less a man conforms to other American values, the more severe his punishment*—not because he violates other laws, but because he does not conform to the values of *materialism, moralism,* and *work*. These values are the basis for a set of implicit "punishment rules." Although they are unwritten, those who administer justice in our society have learned to punish the drunk offender on the basis of these rules.

Rule 1: *When guilty of public drunkenness, a man deserves greater punishment if he is poor.* In every society, when individuals violate legal norms they are punished. Physical torture, public humiliation, incarceration, and banishment from the society are some of the forms this punishment takes. It is not surprising that in our society, with its emphasis upon the value of material goods, violators are punished by making them give up some form of property. An individual may be fined after he has been convicted of public drunkenness. Most offenders pay money in the form of a "bail" prior to conviction. A few hours after being arrested, most men are able to be released from jail in a sober condition. They are still innocent before the law, and an arraignment is scheduled at which time they may plead guilty or not guilty. If they enter the latter plea, they must appear in court at another time for a trial. In order to insure that a man returns for his arraignment he is asked to deposit bail money with the court, which will be returned to him when he is sentenced or acquitted. In most courts a man may choose to ignore the arraignment and thereby "forfeit" his bail. It is still within the power of the court to issue a warrant for his arrest in this case and compel him to appear in court, but this is seldom done. Instead, much like bail for a traffic violation, forfeiture of the drunk bail is considered as a just recompense to society for appearing drunk in public.

When arrested, tramps are eager to post bail since it means an immediate release from jail. They do not need to wait for the arraignment, which may not occur for several days. The bail is twenty dollars and is almost always forfeited. This system of punishment treats offenders equally—*unless a man does not have twenty dollars.*

Those who are caught in the grip of poverty are usually convicted, and their punishment is "doing time" instead of "paying money." In America the rich have money, the poor have time. It might be possible to punish men equitably using these two different commodities, but such is not the case. If a man is poor he must be unwilling to expend his energies in the pursuit of materialism and therefore his punishment should be more severe than that given to those with money. How does this occur? Each time a man is arrested, his bail is always twenty dollars, but if he is indigent, his sentences become longer with each conviction. A man can be arrested hundreds of times and bail out for only twenty dollars, but not if he is poor. Consider the case of one man who was arrested in Seattle over one hundred times during a twenty-one-year period. On many arrests he bailed out, but for about seventy convictions he was sentenced to jail, and gradually his sentences grew to the maximum of six months for a single arrest. During this period he was sentenced to nearly fourteen years in jail—a punishment he could have avoided for only a hundred dollars for each of those years. This man was given a life sentence on the installment plan, not for being drunk but for being poor. There are many cases where a rich man and a poor man are arrested and booked for drunkenness on the same night. The rich man is released in a few hours because he had twenty dollars. The poor man is released in a few months because he did not have twenty dollars. One way then to beat a drunk charge is to bail out. If you do not have money, it is still possible to use this strategy by bonding out or asking for a continuance. A bond requires some collateral or assurance that the twenty dollars *plus* a fee to the bondsman will be paid. A continuance enables you to wait a few more days before being sentenced, and during that time, it may be possible to get money from a friend or an employer. Whether he can use these ways to beat a drunk charge or not, the tramp who is repeatedly arrested soon learns he is being punished because he does not conform to the value of materialism.

Rule 2: *When guilty of public drunkenness, a man deserves greater punishment if he has a bad reputation.* Most cultures have a moralistic quality that often leads to stereotyping and generalizing about the quality of a man's character. In our society once a person has been convicted of a crime, he is viewed by others with suspicion. He may never violate legal norms again, but for all practical purposes he is morally reprehensible. Since judges increase the length of a man's sentence with each arrest, he must engage in behavior designed to give him a "good record" if he is to beat the drunk charge. One way to do this is by traveling. For example, if a man stayed out of jail in Seattle for six months, subsequent convictions would begin again with short sentences; thus, when arrested several times, he often decided it would be better if he went to another town. When his arrest record began to grow in this new place, he would move on; after a period of time he would return to Seattle. Men learn to calculate the number of "days hanging" for each city where they are arrested, and their mobility is determined by the magnitude of the next sentence. Some men use an alias when arrested in an attempt to obscure the fact that they have a long record. If this ploy is successful, a man who, because of his record, deserves a sentence of six months, may only be given two or three days. Another way to beat a drunk charge is to volunteer to go to an alcoholism treatment center. A man may not believe that he is an alcoholic or even that he has a "drinking problem," but if he will agree with society's judgment—that his long record of arrests shows he is morally debased—and ask to be helped, his incarceration will be reduced. But not all men are candidates for treatment. Those with the worst records are rejected and must do their time in jail. A man with a bad reputation thus will be given a more severe punishment for the same crime than one with a good reputation.

Rule 3: *When guilty of public drunkenness, a man deserves greater punishment if he does not have a steady job.* American culture places great value on work as an end in itself. Resistance to hippies and welfare programs alike is based, in part, on the value of work. Tramps know that judges punish more severely those who do not have steady employment. If a man cannot beat a drunk charge in some other way, he will make a statement telling the judge that he will find a job, return to a former job, or provide evidence that he is currently employed in a respectable occupation. Tramps often earn a living by "junking" to find things to sell, "spot jobbing," or "panhandling" (begging on the street)—but all these "occupations" are not admired in our society and cannot be used as evidence that one is conforming to the value of work. When a man appears in court with evidence that he is working, the judge will often suspend or shorten his sentence.

Tramps who have been unable to beat the drunk charge before being sentenced may capitalize on this value in another way. One man reported that he had written a letter to himself while in jail. The letter appeared to have been written by an employer in another city offering the man a steady job. The inmate asked another man who was being released from jail to carry the letter to that city and mail it from there. When it arrived, he used it to convince the judge that he should receive an early release in order to accept steady employment. Another inmate, when released from jail, went personally to the judge and pretended to be a contractor; he told him that a man who had worked for him was in jail and he would employ him if he were released. The judge complied with the request, and the two tramps left town together—proud of their achievement, surer than ever that one of the best ways to beat a drunk charge was to understand the value of work in American culture.

The values our culture places upon privacy, materialism, moralism, and work are not the only ones affecting the lives of tramps. These are men who live in a society that holds no place for them. Their lifestyle is offensive to most Americans, and for this reason they are arrested, jailed, and punished by standards that do not apply to the rest of society. In response to these practices, they have learned a culture with well-developed plans for survival. They have adopted a nomadic style of life—moving from one urban center to another to maximize their freedom. In spite of their efforts, sooner or later, most tramps find themselves arrested, and it is then that the techniques for beating a drunk charge will be found most useful.

PART FIVE
Sex Roles

Sex differences are among the most basic social and physical distinctions in any society. Ordinarily, these differences are simply taken for granted by the members of the society. People know what type of activity, what attitudes, and what behavior are appropriate for each sex. Universally, the patterned differences involve inequities giving males more power and authority than females. Males, in general, have higher status than females, and the latter may actually be relegated to second-class citizenry. As in American society, numerous devices may serve as subtle reminders to women of their position, and particular mechanisms whose sole reason for being is to keep women in their place. These often operate from invidious bases and continue to function even in an unfavorable climate.

Rapid social change, technological development, and the reduction in importance of childbearing and child-rearing activities have increased our consciousness of the disparity of status and reward. The taken-for-granted nature of sex-related activities is being questioned. Women now enter previously all-male occupations. They are policewomen on the beat, jockeys at the race track, and business executives at the office. Men assume greater proportions of the child-care activities in society. They do the housework, shop at the supermarket, and prepare the family's meals.

Recently, sociologists have focused on sex roles as a major ingredient in the contemporary societal scene. Extensive changes have led to confusion, conflict, and negotiation in the entire area of the relationship between the sexes. Descriptions of these encounters are useful in understanding how our society is redefining sex-related activities and for anticipating the new forms that will emerge in relationships between male and female. The new forms, without question, will retain elements of the past. They will, also, contain novel arrangements. The following articles relate the general patterns, describe encounters, sketch the rules of the sex-role games, and provide the reader with basic information about how members of this society decide what constitutes sex-relevant activities and attitudes.

15
Woman's Work in a Man's World

Social scientists have long identified work, attitudes, and behavioral characteristics by sex. American society, like most others, has divided tasks on the basis of gender. Males perform active, assertive tasks, females passive and supportive kinds of work. Although such traditional divisions of labor are changing, the patterns are deeply ingrained in our consciousnesses. They continue to make up the way most of us, male and female alike, think about our daily activities. In this selection James Spradley and Brenda Mann give an account of the attitudes and meanings associated with sex roles in a college bar. They specify some of the rules for male-female interaction that are used more generally in our society.

Division of Labor

James P. Spradley and Brenda J. Mann

The continued existence of any society depends on the performance of certain necessary tasks. Individual members need food, water, and protection from the elements. The goods and services necessary to life must be distributed. Ongoing social life requires some means to recruit new members as older ones leave or die off. Children must be taught the knowledge and skills of adult life if they are to participate as full

From James P. Spradley and Brenda J. Mann *Cocktail Waitress: Woman's Work in a Man's World*, (New York: John Wiley and Sons, 1975). Reprinted by permission.

members. Some form of social control is needed to protect people from the destructive elements in human behavior. Cooperative activities of all kinds require a system of communication. These and other prerequisites constitute the *functional requirements* of human societies.

Brady's bar is, in a sense, like a small society, and it also requires the performance of certain necessary tasks. Because it is part of a larger, complex society, the number of functional requirements for this bar's existence is relatively small. Nevertheless, doors must be locked and unlocked, electricity turned on, beer and liquor purchased and stocked in the cooler, and bills must be paid. If no one ever washed the glasses or emptied ash trays at Brady's, it would take only a few days before the bar as it now exists would cease to function. Unless fights were stopped and destructive drunk persons forced to leave, innocent bystanders would be injured, and the news would spread that Brady's Bar was a dangerous place. Unless someone recruited new cocktail waitresses and bartenders when old ones quit, the number of customers would dwindle, and the bar would close or undergo a radical change in character. Like human societies in general, if this institution is to function, it requires some way to insure that necessary activities are performed.

But even in the smallest society it is impossible for everyone to work at all the things that need to be done. For this reason every culture contains rules for allocating jobs; every society has a division of labor. In a Bushmen band in South Africa, for example, men track down wild animals to provide meat for the people while women dig roots and gather berries to add to the common food supply. Among the Kurelu of New Guinea, men protect the borders of the tribal territories from attack and participate in offensive warfare. The women, on the other hand, have their assigned tasks such as gathering salt by soaking banana leaves in a salt spring, drying the leaves, and then burning them to retrieve the salt. In some societies, young girls are assigned the task of caring for small children, boys take the herds of goats or cattle for pasture and water, old men stay home to protect women and children, and young men do the heavy work of house-building. Every culture, then, has a division of labor, and we were not surprised to find this a feature of bar culture. Indeed, if the fifteen or twenty people who work at Brady's Bar all came to work on the same night and tried to carry out the same activities at the same time, chaos would reign. If all the employees took orders from customers, if all crowded together behind the bar at the same time to mix drinks, and if, each evening, everyone tried to do everything, the confusion and disorder would eventually destroy the bar. Like a small tribal band, the people who work at Brady's share a set of rules for allocating jobs and dividing up necessary tasks.

Female and Male Roles

The most frequent method for creating a division of labor employs male and female differences. This principle, a sexual division of labor, is prominent at Brady's. The men who work in the bar mix drinks, serve the customers seated around the long horseshoe bar, control the money, and manage business transactions with the outside world. The women, on the other hand, focus their activities on serving the customers who sit at tables.

One of our first goals was to discover the nature and meaning of these female role assignments. Our primary question was, "What does a person have to know in order to do what a cocktail waitress does?" The answer initially appeared rather simple—she has to find out what customers want to drink, tell the bartender, carry drinks back to the table, collect the payments, and later clear away empty glasses. As outside observers, it would have been easy to identify these actions and interpret them from our perspective as researchers. In fact, we constantly faced the temptation to recast the cultural world of Brady's Bar in our own terms, a tendency increased by familiarity with the language and other external features of this culture. Had we gone to a remote, non–Western society with an unintelligible language, strange foods, exotic rituals, and a radically different lifestyle, the striking contrasts would have been instructive. In such a setting we would have been compelled to seek the categories and interpretations of the participants. But we believe that ethnography in our own society also required an approach to get at the native's point of view.

We balanced observations of behavior by listening to cocktail waitresses talk about their work. They offered their interpretations of actions, events, and situations, instructing us in the specialized knowledge they had learned. We sought to discover the terms they used to identify customers, drinks, places, and their own behavior. Just as people in every society classify the significant features of their experience such as kinsmen, animals, hunting equipment, and edible plants, for example, the people at Brady's Bar categorize what is significant to them. Our informants identified a long list of things they "had to do" each night. Each had acquired the cultural rules for such behavior when they started working, and most would sooner or later pass them on to newcomers. These actions were divided into a small number of general categories labeled as *setting up, waiting on tables, keeping busy, giving last call,* and so on. Each of these categories included a great many smaller activities. For example, waiting on tables included such things as *remembering drinks, giving orders, rearranging drinks,* and *making change.* The named activities of cocktail waitresses make up a folk taxonomy, and the major terms in this taxonomy are shown in Figure 15-1.

Sex and Symbol

Before we examine in more detail the activities of waitresses, we need to ask about the significance of dividing the work at Brady's Bar into women's work and men's work. Why does this culture assign tasks on the basis of sex at all? It is apparent that jobs could be assigned on some other basis. Most of the females quickly learn how to mix drinks and even do so on occasion. They carry heavy cases of beer from the cooler, a job men could do as well. Waitresses, on the other hand, could easily wash the glasses, a task assigned to men. The bartenders know how to make change, add up the prices of drinks, wipe off tables, and take orders from customers; yet these are waitress tasks. It almost seemed that this bar had created a division of *geography* rather than a division of *labor.* With few exceptions, what the females did in one part of the bar, males did in another—taking orders, serving drinks, wiping off table surfaces, receiving tips, cleaning ash trays, visiting with customers. Yet from the perspective of our informants, the rigid distinction between what men and women do has great importance. No one at Brady's thinks to suggest that a male could be hired to work as a cocktail waiter or a female as bartender; if they did, the vocal outcry of protest would probably come from men and women alike.

But while there is a clear distinction between the tasks assigned to male and female, at many points their separate tasks require mutual dependency. Denise or Holly cannot serve customers unless the bartenders prepare the drinks, even though such as assignment of tasks is arbitrary. Mark, Steve, or George, on the other hand, cannot get monetary payments from the customers or retrieve dirty glasses without the aid of the girls. Over and over again the organization of work at Brady's creates a special kind of interaction ritual between male and female. Consider the following example.

It is 12:40 A.M., and Sandy knows that in twenty minutes the bar will close. She would like to tell the six guys at the corner table that the time has come to order their last drinks for the evening because it is near closing. Last call generally occurs around 12:45, and if she doesn't give last call soon, it will be impossible to get them to leave before 1:30 A.M., since they will take that long to finish their drinks. But the appointed time comes and goes. Although it would be a simple

FIGURE 15-1. Cocktail waitress activities

"Things a Waitress Does"	Coming to work	
	Hanging around	
	Getting ready	Setting up tray
		Punching in
		Taking menu down
	Keeping busy	
	Waiting on tables	Taking orders
		Giving orders
		Serving orders
	Taking a break	
	Giving extra service	
	Rechecking tables	
	Carding	
	Running errands	
	Picking up tips	
	Giving last call	
	Clearing tables	
	Turning in money	
	Punching out	

Note: This taxonomy is incomplete in at least two ways. First, there are other activities or duties of the waitress that could be included at the first level of contrast but have been omitted, such as "greeting the bartender," and "visiting with the waitress." This taxonomy provides the most important general categories in the lexicon of waitresses. Second, many more specific actions could be included for each term. Even a simple act like "picking up tips" involves many smaller actions. Some writers restrict the term "taxonomy" to a set of terms related by strict inclusion where each term is "a kind of" the cover term. This taxonomy is based on the semantic relationship of "X is a thing Y has to do." It could be restated as "X is a kind of activity that Y does," but such a formulation is awkward and not precisely the one expressed by informants.

matter for her to tell the table, "Last call, would you like anything else to drink?" and in fact, she wanted to announce it fifteen minutes ago, she cannot take this simple step on her own initiative. At 12:55 Jim, the bartender working the lower section of the bar, tells her "Give last call." Finally, she can make this announcement to the customers seated in her section. Because he delayed his permission, however, it will be closing time when Sandy delivers the last round of beers to the six guys from St. John's and much later before she can retrieve the empty bottles. The cultural rules at Brady's Bar require that a male must tell the waitress when it is time for last call, and they require that a female must serve the last round to the tables. Over and over again we discovered such arbitrary rules interlocking male and female performances.

As the structure of this sexual division of labor became clear—its arbitrary nature, the spatial aspects of work, the mutual dependency—we saw a deeper meaning to the way work was divided up. An important latent function of this structure is that *routine tasks become symbols of sexuality*. The values that underlie femininity and masculinity are restated continuously each night merely by the act of working. As a symbol of one's sex, work is transformed into a ritual activity that announces to the audience of customers the significant differences our culture attaches to sexual gender.

Beneath the patterns of interaction between men and women in our society lie the hidden rules for male-female relationships. Traditional roles that rigidly assign activities to men and women are especially significant for revealing these underlying cultural rules and the tacit definitions of masculinity and femininity. As we discuss the work of cocktail waitresses, we want to examine more than merely what these girls are expected to do each night. We hope to show how many of the assumptions and rules of the male-female relationship are implicit in their activities. We begin with the informal period before actual work begins and follow the waitresses through an evening until they "hang around" again after closing.

Hanging Around

An 8:00 A.M. class, an exam in her 10:00 A.M. class, and a student government meeting that lasted all afternoon—it has been an incredibly rough day for Denise. At 5:30 P.M. she went to the food service for dinner, but the long lines and a whiff of the worst of the school's rotating menu changed her mind. She headed back to the dorm to get ready for work.

Better to have a sandwich down at Brady's than to face that scene at the food service tonight. Besides, it was snowing heavily outside, and she would start out early anyway. It would be nice to get away from the dorm, the giggling girls, ringing phones, bright lights—the institutional atmosphere—and sit quietly at Brady's before starting to work. Like all the waitresses, it wouldn't be the only time she went to work early just to hang around. And while it isn't "required" like some other activities, the waitress who never comes early to hang around soon gains a reputation of being aloof or cold.

Denise made it to Brady's a little after six. When she walked in, the bar was empty except for Ted, the day bartender, and Mark and Sandy. They all exchanged greetings as Denise made her way back to the kitchen. Sally, the day waitress, was in cleaning up and Denise said, "Hi," put her purse under the counter and walked back out to sit at the bar.

"Do you have a check for me, Ted?" Ted pulled out the drawer under the cash register and looked through a pile of envelopes. "What'd you say your name was, kid?"

"Ted! After all I've meant to you! You don't remember my name?"

"A pretty face is a pretty face. You've seen one, you've seen 'em all, honey."

"Just give me my check, smartie." And turning to Mark, Denise added, "When are you going to get some decent bartenders around here?"

"When we get some decent waitresses."

Denise stomped off in a pretend huff and went into the kitchen to make herself a sandwich. She wrote up the check for the inventory, placed it on the nail, and went out to sit at the bar again. Sandy and Mark were discussing the highlights of a near-fight that took place in the bar the night before. Ted was standing behind the bar sipping his usual anisette and charge and Mark, who would soon take over, was on his second scotch and water.

"Could I please have a vodka tonic, Ted?" Denise asked, giving him her sweetest smile. She knew what the answer would be, but it never hurt to try. Sometimes you can catch the bartender in a benevolent mood.

"Look, you know you can't have a drink. You start work in a little while and you might fall on that pretty face of yours. Do you want a Coke?"

"Okay. But how about some quarters for the juke box?" Ted handed her four quarters, she picked out her favorites and then went back to eating her sandwich and sipping her Coke. She sat there, listening to her music, and watching Ted clean up the bar—restocking the beer and washing the dozens of dirty glasses that had accumulated during the lunch-hour rush.

Two employees are sitting at the bar, hanging around before work; one has the right to drink anything, the other does not. The reason for this restriction? Being a female. This particular rule may be unique to Brady's Bar, but we found this simple pattern of interaction repeated itself again and again in other situations. These specific cases merely reflect an important rule in our culture that governs much of male-female interaction, what we call *the handicap rule*. At every turn, we discovered evidence that the cultural rules at Brady's Bar place certain handicaps on all those players who were born female. The specific content of these handicaps changed from situation to situation, from one encounter to the next, but the fundamental rule remained, often outside the awareness of the players. Still, everyone acted in terms of this principle. If a waitress tried to set aside a particular handicap, such as "no liquor before work," others quickly reminded her to play according to the rules. And she usually acquiesced, giving silent assent to the legitimacy of this rule. Before we examine some of the more specific handicaps, we need to see the nature of this basic cultural rule that operates in male-female encounters.

Games are played according to certain fundamental ground rules. For example, an *equal application rule* holds for most games in our culture: "everybody in the game must play by the same rules." It doesn't matter if you are short or tall, you must tag each base as you make your way around the baseball diamond. Male or female, every player is restricted from introducing extra cards from another deck in a game of bridge. Old or young, rich or poor, all golf players are required to hit the ball rather than throw it with their hands. In some cases, players often make an explicit decision to substitute a *handicap rule* for the principle of equal application. This practice originated several hundred years ago when some horse racers faced a serious problem. A particular horse had won so many races that most other horse owners refused to race against this superb animal. In the face of waning attendance and dying interest, race officials decided to use different rules for this swift horse—they required that it must begin the race several moments after the others were underway. They called this practice a *handicap*. Since that time, the equal application rule came to be suspended in many games from chess to golf, requiring that some participants with special skill or ability would have to play by different rules.

A handicap is any arbitrary rule that places some players at a disadvantage. It does this by imposing an impediment, an embarrassment, a disability, or other restrictions on some participants in the game, but not others. It means the rules are not applied equally. But the inequality is determined by the nature of each specific game and a player's strength, speed, or competence. Never is the handicap rule based on some arbitrary criteria like sex, color of hair, date of your mother's birthday. Furthermore, in most games the handicap rule is used in an open, explicit manner; all the players *know* the nature of the handicap involved. Hidden advantages or disadvantages are not handicaps at all—we call that cheating. If some players secretly attempt to play by different rules, the others will immediately cry, "Foul!"

Let's go back to the social encounters between male and female workers at Brady's Bar. Here, the arbitrary handicap rules imposed on females are often hidden or at least justified as instinctual, God-given traits: "Women can't hold their liquor," "Women are too emotional." As in the wider culture, females are repeatedly required to play with an arbitrarily imposed handicap. It is as if all the players in the game made a tacit agreement that women must play by different rules than men. Even a suggestion to make these rules the same arouses male anger, and all the waitresses soon find this out as the following examples makes clear. One night Denise was hanging around before work, and Ted asked her to watch the bar for a few minutes. Dave, one of the bartenders for the evening, came in and sat down. "Hey, bartender!" he called to Denise as he playfully banged his fist down on the bar. "I'll have a bourbon sour." Feeling especially powerful behind the bar, Denise replied, "Oh, I'm sorry, Dave, but you're working tonight. No drink for you. How about a nice big Coke?" The tone of her voice indicated to Dave that she was teasing, and Dave's response was also outwardly light: "Be a good bartender now and give me my drink!" And, of course, she complied. But Denise could tell she had said the wrong thing. She had unmasked the handicap rule by her actions, momentarily exposing its arbitrariness. Later that night, after the bar closed and all the employees gathered at the bar for a drink, Dave served the others, ignoring Denise's request for a gin and tonic. Denise was then forced into the position of having to beg Dave before he would serve her a drink—a kind of ritual reminder that she is not to question the implicit handicap rule.

Drinking at Brady's is the central symbol of membership in this small society, and when someone is excluded from this kind of ritual participation, they become, even if momentarily, marginal participants. Handicap rules for women in our culture often function in this way; they function to insure that males stay at the center of social significance and that women remain "in their place" at the periphery. Every now and then, however, a bartender will temporarily suspend the handicap rule about waitresses drinking before work and serve them a drink. Such an act is seen by both male and female as a gracious and friendly gesture, but it does create a sense of indebtedness on the part of the waitress. On these occasions the bartender will mix a drink and set it down in front of the waitress, surprising her. She is then expected to be pleased and happy about this exception to the rule, and she thanks the bartender profusely. However, the bartender has not asked her if she would care for a drink or what her preference might be. He simply fixes her the usual and gives it to her, expecting her to be pleased by the gesture. And so the handicap rule, whether enforced or suspended, symbolizes the control exercised by males and the subordinate role of females.

Getting Ready and Sitting Around

At 7:00 P.M. Denise started inching herself off the barstool and onto her feet for work. There were still no customers, and once she took care of a few details, she could sit down again. She went to the kitchen and Sally was still cleaning up the daytime mess. She was fiddling around with the remains from lunch—gulping a lukewarm bowl of mulligan stew that she hadn't had time to eat until now. In between spoonfuls, she sipped at the scotch and water Ted always made for her after work, smoked her cigarette, and intermittently stuffed food back into the refrigerator. Denise knew Sally would be hurt if she didn't make some polite conversation, so she inquired how the day had gone. "Oh, honey. It *was* miserable! Didn't get a chance to stop running all day long." She grimaced and pointed to her feet that were encased in gold wedgies. "Must have been a record day for Brady's." She dismissed the subject with a wave of her hand and went back to her tasks.

A mirror hangs over the small sink in the kitchen, but Denise knows that with Sally there she had better not comb her hair. She decides to forget it for now, turns the blower on high, punches in, and checks outside the kitchen door to see if the menu for day customers is still hanging up. Sally usually forgets to take it down as she has tonight. Denise brought it into the kitchen, "Anything I can do to help, Sally?" Good girls always asked Sally that.

"Check those tables, will you, honey" was what she always replied. So, she checks the tables, wiping some of them off, relighting the candles, emptying the dirty ashtrays, and bringing the tips she finds to Sally. "You keep them, honey." But, somehow, Sally always ends up with them. She checks with Sally once more and then goes back out to the bar. It looks like a quiet empty room this early in the evening, and most girls find that time drags slowly from now until more customers begin to arrive.

Denise takes one of the trays from the bar. On it she places a small pile of cocktail napkins, several books of matches, two ashtrays stacked one on top of the other (the top one for change, the bottom one for tips), and then she sneaks around the bar to steal a pen from the bartender. Sally comes out of the kitchen with her coat and purse and puts ten dollars on the tray for Denise, her working money for the night. Ted finishes mixing himself another of his special drinks, asks Sally if she wants another, and then comes out from behind the bar to sit down.

The five of them sat there for a few minutes, sipping their drinks and puffing on cigarettes. The conversation was easy and relaxed.

"Mr. Gulick was in today, Mark," said Ted. "He wanted to know if you wanted more glasses. I told him to come back tomorrow."

"Fine. Did Skeeter come in?"

"Yep. He was telling me about his hot date last night. He picked up some broad from the Redwood Club and I guess they really had a wild time. Ended up passed out somewhere on Sixth." said Ted.

"Skeeter's going to really get himself in trouble one of these days," added Sally. The conversation continued for about twenty minutes. Ted finished off his drink and turned to Sally, "Ready to go?" Ted always gave Sally a ride home. They put their coats on, finished the last of their drinks and cigarettes, and walked out the door. Sandy also left, saying she had to study tonight.

Denise and Mark sat there alone, but it wasn't more than five minutes before they heard the outer door open. They both turned and waited to see who was coming. It was Mike and Stubbs, two Cougar football players from the university who are regular customers at Brady's.

"Hey, Mike, Stubbs. How are you?" Mark stood up and playfully punched Mike on the shoulder, and he returned the greeting. Both of the guys nodded and smiled at Denise. Mark turned to Denise and said, "Hey, Denise. Be a good girl and get behind the bar for me." The way he said it, she felt he was both giving her permission and giving her an order, but this was an opportunity that no waitress passed up. She crawled under the gate that closes at the end of the bar and turned to Mike and Stubbs for their order. "Schlitz for both of them," said Mark. Denise opened one cooler after another until she found the one containing the Schlitz, found the opener attached to the side of the cooler, opened them, and placed them on the bar in front of Mike and Stubbs. She looked around for the beer glasses, and by the time she had placed a napkin with a glass on it in front of each of them, they were halfway finished with their bottles. The minutes dragged slowly by as the men talked, but Denise busied herself exploring behind the bar: opening coolers to find out where the different kinds of beer were, checking the ice supply, examining the different bottles of liquor. Another customer came and looked surprised to see her there but ordered a bourbon sour as if nothing was out of order.

"Bartender. Oh, bartender. Can I have another beer?" That was Stubbs, calling attention to this reversal of roles. Mike joined in, "Me too. Isn't that a funny looking bartender? Mark sure has changed. That's a nice dress you have on, Markie." Denise smiles and concentrates on opening two more beers. She places them in front of the two guys, "Here you are." She took one of the dollar bills from the counter and rang it up on the cash register. Same old jokes every time a girl gets behind the bar—she had seen it happen to others and knew what to expect. She always felt somewhat uncomfortable back there but it was fun, the opportunity to mix drinks. Like the other girls, she watches the bartenders make drinks all night, every night, and so she knows almost as well as they do how to make a vodka gimlet, a tequila sunrise, an old-fashioned, or anything else. While it never lasted very long, it was fun to work behind the bar, a special treat. All of the girls respond eagerly when Mark or one of the other bartenders sets aside the rules governing female behavior that normally keep them out of that area.

What we have witnessed here is a kind of role change, what we call the *cross-over phenomenon.* Situations in which men and women temporarily reverse their roles are not uncommon in our society. Whenever male and female activities are linked together, opportunities for individuals to cross over present themselves. Mr. Jones, for example, normally drives when his wife is in the car, but he lets her drive this morning so he can read some papers for an early meeting at the office. On other mornings he pulls up to his office building, and she slides over to take his place behind the wheel and drive home. Mrs. Jones normally bathes their two children after dinner each night, but on Tuesdays her husband takes over and performs this task so she can attend the university. The cross-over phenomenon probably occurs in all cultures of the world. The cultural rules for crossing over and doing tasks assigned to the opposite sex could easily be *symmetrical.* That is, on occasion men do women's work and vice versa. In the process there is an open appreciation for this exchange of responsibilities that are usually divided. But the rules that regulate the cross-over phenomenon in Brady's Bar are not the same for each sex. They are *asymmetrical,* functioning in such a way as to put women at a disadvantage in the game of social interaction.

Although Denise and Sandy and the other waitresses get behind the bar occasionally and they are always eager to do so, bartenders *never* cross over to perform some of the female tasks in the bar. If Rob and Denise were sitting at the bar and a group of customers came in and sat at a table, Denise could never turn and say, "Rob, will you take care of those customers for me?" Even if she were busy taking his place behind the bar and customers entered, no bartender would voluntarily get up to wait on the tables for the cocktail waitress. Denise would simply come from behind the bar, wait on the table, go back behind the bar and fix the drinks herself, and then serve them. This is expected of her. Furthermore, none of the waitresses would think of asking the men to clean the tables or to wait on their customers. They have learned the rules well. Both men and women seem to act as if the tasks assigned to women at Brady's might have a polluting affect on men, contaminating their ritual purity. The reverse is not true. A man loses if he does women's work and participates in the cross-over phenomenon, and so he avoids it or refuses to switch. A women gains and is usually eager to cross over.

An interesting dimension of this cross-over phenomenon relates to the way it requires the female to express gratitude. When a man crosses over to assist a woman, she should thank him, expressing gratitude to him for his assistance. If one of the male employees ever stepped in to assist a busy waitress, it would be seen as an act of chivalry and the girl in question would openly express her gratitude. But when a woman crosses over to assist a man, engaging in some typical male activity, such as tending bar, *she must still express gratitude,* for he has allowed her to partake of a more valuable social world. It is doubtful that a husband would thank his wife for driving the car when they are traveling together. After all, in our cultural idiom he has "let her drive." His wife, on the other hand, would express gratefulness if he cooked dinner or did the dishes for her. When a waitress at Brady's is allowed to tend bar, she feels that a privilege has been extended to her. Not only does she operate with a handicap, but she almost always sees these particular rules as legitimate.

Denise glances at the Hamm's Beer clock hanging over the jukebox. She is surprised to see that it is already 8:30. Time passes quickly for the girls when they get behind the bar to work. Sue, the second waitress for this evening, will be in soon, and although Denise hasn't worked that hard yet, she will be able to take a break, to sit at the bar and have a cigarette and a Coke.

Keeping Busy

Sue comes in at 8:45, and right behind her is Dave, the second bartender for the evening. Everyone at the bar turns to greet them. Dave, looking a little hung over, goes straight to the bathroom. Sue heads for the kitchen, quickly deposits her coat and purse, punches in, and joins the others at the bar.

"I didn't know *you* were working tonight!" says Mark. "Where's Joyce!"

"She called and said she wasn't feeling well and asked me to sub for her. That's two nights she owes me now. But aren't you glad to see me? I only said 'yes' to Joyce because I knew *you* were working, Markie." Mark can't let Sue's remark pass.

"Oh, yah?" he replies. "Well, if I had known I was going to have to work with you two miniboobs tonight, *I* would have gotten a sub!" Dave emerges from the back and goes behind the bar to mix himself a drink.

"You don't look so hot," observes Denise. Dave just looks at her and grunts and continues to mix his drink.

"Poor baby," says Sue. "He didn't leave here until five o'clock this morning." Dave stayed at Brady's last night to drink and play cards with some of the other bartenders, a frequent activity for the male employees.

Sue got up and set up her tray. She and Denise conferred for a moment, and it was decided that Sue would work the upper section tonight since she was tired and it really wasn't her night to work. Sue asked Dave to hand her the burglar alarm from the bar, and she slipped it into her skirt pocket. The girl who works the upper section has to carry the alarm, which is the size of a transistor radio. Brady's has been robbed a couple of times, and so now if someone tries to hold up Brady's, the waitress simply pushes the silent button on the alarm, and the police are notified that they are needed. Occasionally, one of the girls sets the alarm off by mistake. This happened to Holly one evening, and when she realized that she had inadvertently pushed the button while leaning across a table to serve some customers, she told Dave immediately. He called the police, but they were already on the way. He charged out the door and came face to face with three policemen, their guns trained on the entrance to Brady's.

It is after nine by now, and the girls have taken their places to work. Dave is behind the bar, but he is visiting with Mark who is still sitting with Mike and Stubbs. Mark and Dave will trade off working the bar during the evening while it is slow. Mark will work half an hour and then Dave will work half an hour while Mark takes a break, and so forth. Using this method, each gets more break time than they normally would working the bar together. Both will work behind the bar together only if it becomes extremely busy. But Sue and Denise, the two waitresses, are not allowed to work out this kind of schedule between themselves. Both must work, and each is allowed one fifteen-minute break during the evening. Joyce and Sharon tried altering this routine one night. "One girl can handle both sections just as easily as the bartenders can work the whole bar, unless it gets really busy," they explained to Mark when he caught them trying this arrangement. But Mark wouldn't have it. He claimed it looks sloppy to have his girls sitting on the job. And so we see the handicap rule applied to more and more situations.

In the bar, as in the wider society, men's work is considered more valuable than women's work. In part, this accounts for the necessity for women to keep busy, to give the appearance of always working. In situations where men and women work together, the same activity may be labeled *nonwork* if it is done by women, but some special form of *work* if it is done by men. For example, in an office setting, a group of women congregated around a coffee machine are merely gossiping and are quickly urged to get back to *work*. It makes no difference that they were discussing the economic situation, politics, or office business. But a group of men in the same setting, perhaps even discussing last night's football game, *must* be talking over important business matters.

Denise has just waited on a table, and after she serves them, she stops to chat with a regular customer who is sitting next to the table. While she's talking, Dave calls her from across the bar so she quickly excuses herself and goes to see what he wants. "I need some stuff from the cooler. Get me some Heineken lights and a bottle of juice. Okay? That's a sweet girl." He turns back to his discussion with a friend sitting across the bar while Denise heads back through the kitchen to the cooler. "Why can't Dave get this stuff himself anyway?" she grumbles to herself. "He's always sending us back to carry this stuff. It should be his job, not the waitresses'." Denise thought about the time she had brought this up one night after work and had gotten nowhere. "Bartenders are never idle," she was told. "When they aren't mixing drinks and serving the bar, they are P.R.'ing and that is good for the bar." "So," thought Denise, "They call standing around talking to friends, P.R.'ing, but if we do it, they call it loafing." Although she may be able to visit a little later in the evening, even then, because of this handicap rule, she will have to do it so as to avoid the accusation that she is merely wasting time, loafing around.

There are some acceptable ways, however, for waitresses to help pass the time and keep busy. Most of these involves games with the bartenders. Things were still slow around 9:45 one night when Dave caught Sue reaching over the bar for some olives. She was hungry and bored, but Dave decided that she couldn't have any more olives. He let her have all the lime twists, orange slices, and cherries she wanted, but not olives. Every time Sue tried to reach over and grab a few olives, he attacked her with the little plastic swords used to spear fruit for cocktails. Then he picked up the container of olives and carried it with him to insure the safety of his cache. He would turn and smile at Sue from the other side of the bar, hold up the bowl of olives for her to see, and occasionally pop one into his own mouth. And Sue would cross her arms, pout, and beg Dave for some olives, "Please?" Both of them knew that she didn't really want the olives all that badly, but it was something for them to do. Other games involve making faces on the bar with the fruit used in cocktails and a variety of verbal games.

Because bartenders are in charge of the work situation, they control the assignment of tasks. While their own duties are clearly outlined, the tasks assigned to the waitress are ambiguous. That is, she may be asked to do almost any task that needs to be done around Brady's. For this reason it might be said that "a woman's work is never done." While bartenders are allowed the luxury of taking time to "P.R.," to divide their work schedule for long breaks, and to assign tasks to the waitresses, the females are not granted so much leeway. Again, the division of labor is asymmetrical. Waitresses have to keep busy.

Taking Orders

The major portion of a waitress's job is the task of waiting on tables. The girls divide this activity into a sequence of three consecutive events: (1) taking the order from the customers at the table, (2) giving that order to the bartender at the bar, and (3) serving the order to the customer (see Figure 15-1). Each event is a complex unit unto itself, and together they form a sequence of activities that the waitress performs dozens of times in one evening.

Waitresses at Brady's take waiting on tables very seriously although it would not appear so to watch the girls at work. As Holly said, "I have to be the little, jolly, flirtatious girl and run around and smile and take everything very lightly. All the time, underneath, I'm serious." The girls must concentrate on kinds of drinks, prices of drinks, matching drinks with customers, making change, balancing the tray, and avoiding dangerous obstacles like stray feet and elbows, and just plain maneuvering around furniture and people in the dark, crowded room. "But on the outside," stresses Holly, "you're supposed to be like it's nothing. Something really easy to do. I guess it does get easier. But it's never *easy.*" Taking orders is the first step in waiting on tables.

By about 10:00 P.M. Brady's begins to fill up rapidly. Sue has been working both sections while Denise takes her break, but she hasn't had to hurry because only a few customers are seated at the tables. Both girls are on their feet now, each looking after her section.

Three customers walk in, two men and a girl, and sit in Sue's section. Almost mechanically, Sue picks up some napkins, walks over to the table, smiles and places a napkin in front of each person. "Hello," she says and then waits. She has worked at Brady's for several months now and knows it's unnecessary to say more. Not feeling especially jovial tonight, she just smiles, turns to the girl first, and waits. "I'll have a Bacardi," says the girl. The men both want beers; Special Exports. Sue nods her head to signal that she understands and walks away from the table to the bar.

Getting this information from the customer, however, is not always this easy. For example, one night three girls came and sat in Stephanie's section. She went through the ritual of placing the napkins down in front of each girl and then waited for them to order. She looks at the girls expectantly but they sit and say nothing. "Are you ready to order or should I come back?" Stephanie asks. "Oh, no. We'll order now." The girls begin to confer among themselves as to what they want to drink, stopping occasionally to ask questions.

"How much is a Harvey Wallbanger?"

"Do you have green chartreuse?"

"What kinds of drinks don't taste like alcohol?"

Stephanie answers their questions, thankful that she knows the answers. When she first started at Brady's, customers' questions, even simple ones like "What's in a Tom Collins?" would send her running back to the bar for the answer. She didn't know anything about bar stock, prices, or what went into the various drinks. Finally, the girls are ready to order: a Harvey Wallbanger, a Smith and Currants, and a Singapore Sling.

New girls find that the ability to take orders from customers and to interpret their orders correctly requires a vast amount of knowledge concerning the prices of drinks, the content of drinks, and also the ability to translate a customer's words into the correct drink at the bar.

Sue's first night on the job involved what was at that time an ordeal for her. She went to the table and the man said, "I'll have a tequila and lime." She went to the bar, gave the order to George, who was tending. He poured a shot of tequila into a glass and added lime juice and ice. But shen she returned to the table with the drink, the customer looked at the drink and said, "I want a *shot* of tequila with a *twist* of lime and some salt." She returned the drink to the bar and explained her mistake. The bartender was a little upset, but he fixed her another drink. That same night another customer ordered a "Red Beer." Sue had no idea what that was and neither did the bartender. Another trip to the table, a conference with the customer, and a trip back to the bar: "That girl wants a beer mixed with tomato juice. She calls it a *red beer.*" George looked at her like she was crazy. Sue shrugged her shoulders as if to say, "Well, I didn't order it." George refused to mix the two together and, instead, gave Sue a can of tomato juice, a glass, and a bottle of beer with the instructions, "Tell her to mix it herself."

Another problem for the waitress is the customer who doesn't know the language of the bar and cannot name the drink desired. Holly dislikes two girls who often sit in her section. "They are really dumb," she says. "Every time they come in, it's 'I'll have a vodka and orange.' Why can't they just say 'Screwdriver'?" she always wonders. Some customers come in and order "rum and Coke with a twist of lime." Holly delivered this order to the bartender numerous times before Dave curtly informed that "rum and Coke with a twist of lime is a 'Cubálibre'."

Waitresses need to know about the different contents and styles of drinks in order to correctly take order. For example, a customer may say "I'll have a martini up." A new girl may only hear the word, "martini" and would probably not be listening for any further instructions. Even if she did hear the orders, she would not understand what is meant by the adjective "up." So, instead of bring the customer a martini in a stem glass without ice, she brings him a regular martini with ice and will immediately have to make another trip to the bar, explaining her mistake and thus slip further behind in keeping up with her tables. A customer may mutter "*frozen* daiquiri" and blame the waitress when she returns with a plain daiquiri. The noise of laughter or the juke box may transform banana daiquiri or daiquiri cocktail into simply, "daiquiri." The customer complains, the bartender is angry at time lost making difficult and expensive drinks, and the waitress is caught between them, now stigmatized by the label "dumb waitress."

Taking orders also requires an ability to remember details and all the girls express amazement at the way their memories improved. New girls find they have to write down anything over two drinks, but the ability to remember large orders increases with experience. Those who've been working at Brady's for at least a month take the majority of orders in their heads. When Sharon began working, she took her tray along each time she went to take an order, madly scribbling the names of two or three drinks on a cocktail napkin so that she could remember the order. Before long, she could proudly tell you what each person in her section was drinking—sometimes the whole bar if she has been working it by herself.

A large table presents a challenge, and the girls make games out of remembering all the drinks. One night ten people sat together at a table in Joyce's section. She took their order and as soon as she got back to the bar, she wrote it down so she wouln't forget it in case they wanted to order another round of drinks: two frozen daiquiris, a banana daiquiri, a Bacardi, a Manhattan, an Old-Fashioned, a vodka gimlet, a Tom Collins, a Singapore Sling and a Wallbanger. After serving the first set of drinks, Joyce went back to the bar and memorized what she had written on the napkin, then threw it away. From time to time she went over the list in her head, trying to keep it in her mind. But when she took the order for the second time, everyone decided to change their drinks and order something else!

The girls have several memory strategies, but they also know that some circumstances might arise to make them useless. When you are keeping seven drinks in mind on your way to the bar and a customer stops you, puts his arm around your waist, asks if you are free after work, waits for your explanation, and finally releases you to go about your job, it is difficult to remember any order. The best strategy is to associate drinks with seating arrangements at the table. As the bartender fixes each drink it can be arranged on the tray in a way that reflects the place each person has at the table. A waitress will stand at one place near the table, and her hand will be placed at a similar position under the tray. A left-handed waitress might then remove drinks from her tray in a clockwise manner, going around the table in the same direction; a right-handed girl goes in the reverse direction. But in either case she can easily remember who gets which drink.

As the evening progresses, more and more customer demands occur, often creating *rushes,* periods of time when everyone seems to need her attention. Then, arranging drinks according to seating arrangement will not work because the girls have to take orders for several tables at the same time. Furthermore, some large orders for a single table cannot be properly balanced on a tray and also reflect the order in which people are seated. The waitress will then group similar drinks together: bourbons, gins, scotches, and fancy drinks. Then she silently repeats over and over again which drinks belong to whom and hopes it is correct. Often, the noise in Brady's Bar and the unwillingness of customers to assist her make it impossible when she returns to a table to find out who had which drinks. A good waitress who works regularly finds an uncanny ability developing to remember an incredible number of details about an order and serve many tables at once without forgetting or mixing orders.

Every waitress can also take orders without any form of verbal communication with the customer and even without going over to his table. A frequent customer will get the waitress's attention across the room as he enters or simply raises two fingers indicating "two of the usual." Or, if he is a regular customer, he will get the waitress's attention and just nod his head or point to himself. Sandy once turned this process into a private joke on one of her regular customers. Bill was seated across the room, and he held up two fingers, and Sandy knew he wanted two more Buds at his table. But she just smiled and in response, casually raised her hand, and made a peace sign. "He got upset because he thought I didn't understand, but I got the beer, took it over to him, and he didn't say anything because he probably didn't want to show that he thought I had misunderstood him. But I was giving him the peace sign."

Customers do not always cooperate to the best of their ability with the waitress who is trying to take their order. And so the girls find that in taking orders, they often must deal with difficult customers, customers who sometimes have other things on their minds than just giving the waitress their order.

Sue had one of those kinds of customers one evening. A couple came in and sat in the back of her section, at one of the small tables. The man had his arm around his date and they were cuddling. Sue walked up to the table and asked them what they would like to order. He says, "Whiskey and water," and his date orders "Calvert's and water, weak." Later that evening, Sue goes up to see if they want another round and the guy's date has taken off for the bathroom. He wants to talk to Sue. "You look awfully familiar, where do you hang out?" Sue tells him she is sure they haven't met before. He grabs her by the arm and pulls her closer to the table. "What nights do you work? I'd like to come over and see you." Pointing to the chair where his date had been sitting Sue said, "I don't think *she* would like it." He said, "What?" "I *said,* I don't think she will like that," repeating herself in a louder voice just as the girl walked up behind her. "Like what?" the girl asked. Sue took off and let him do the explaining.

Meanwhile, Denise had her hands full with taking the orders in her own section. She walked up to a newly arrived table of six guys, smiled, and asked them if they would like to order. One of them yelled, "Let's hear it for the waitress," and the table burst into applause. Denise waits for the noise to die down so that she can take the order, and then goes on her way.

Her next table is a group of regulars who are begging her for free drinks. "We're all out of money. Couldn't we have one on the house? We come here all the time, and Brady's should owe it to us by now." Denise, as well as the other girls, dislike customers' requests for free drinks; only the bartender has the right to dispense drinks on the house. The usual response from the girls and the one Denise gives this group is, "It's not my house. You'll have to ask the bartender." She was still hassling this issue with them when a customer at the next table, said, "You! You! I want some service."

"I'm sorry," said Denise, "I didn't know you wanted some service."

"I'm sure you didn't."

Denise gave him a dirty look and retorted, "I really didn't." She wasn't going to let him get away with that. She took his order, a beer, and brought it back to him immediately. "Just to make him feel rotten," she said, "I was super nice to him." So with a big smile Denise asks, "Would you like anything else?"

The pace is really picking up now. It's 11:30. Denise glances at the clock above the juke box and sighs. At least two more hours to go and it's just beginning to really get busy. She doesn't know if her feet will hold up that long. The tables are almost all occupied, and the bar and the aisles have been full of people since 10:00 P.M. At 10, the customers were easy to move, but now, well on their way to inebriation and somewhat testy, they are difficult to maneuver around. Eight Cougar football players enter, and Denise hopes they will not choose her section. They don't. Instead, they head for Sue's where they take the only table left and proceed to recruit chairs from various areas of the bar.

After seating themselves, they inquire about Sue's name and proceed to make frequent use of it. "Sue. I need a Screwdriver over here." "Soohoo. Will you get me another beer?" "We need two more Buds over here, Sue. Would you please?" "Sue. Would you come here a minute? What are you doing tonight after work?" "Where do you go to school?" And one gallant gentleman: "If any of these guys give you any shit, Sue, you just tell me and I'll handle it." They settle down, prepared to spend the evening. When she gets a moment, Sue glances down at Denise and catches her eye, an instant message of sympathy hidden to everyone else. Sue nods her head at the clock, and Denise shakes her head in agreement: "It's a long time until closing."

Giving Orders

In our society it is a cultural rule that males do the central, important tasks in the division of labor while females do the supporting tasks. A male surgeon performs a delicate operation while his nurse stands ready to hand him the instruments he needs; Perry Mason goes into court to plead a case, and Della Street carries his files; businessmen make important decisions and their secretaries record them on paper. In Brady's the working relationship between bartenders and waitresses reflects this basic arrangement. This is particularly evident in the way each waitress gives orders to the bartender.

Earlier in the evening, Stephanie took the order from the three girls who wanted a Harvey Wallbanger, a Smith and Currants, and a Singapore Sling, a simple order. Carrying this message to the bartender was an easy task. When Stephanie arrives at the bar, George is mixing a stinger for a customer there. While she waits for him to finish, she totals in her head the prices of the drinks: "Wallbanger, $1.25; Smith and Currants, 90¢; and Singapore, $1.25. That's $3.40." As soon as George finishes, she gets his attention by leaning on the bar and catching his eye as he turns. "George, I need a Harvey, a Smith and Currants, and a Singapore Sling. Please." In one continuous movement, George grabs some glasses, dips them into the ice, and then sets them on the edge of the bar, filling each one with an appropriate shot of liquor. As he adds the mix, Stephanie inserts straws into the drinks and stirs the mixture. She also adds fruit and nuts to some of the drinks. George shoves the completed drinks across the counter and holds out his hand for the money. Stephanie gives him a five dollar bill saying, "That's $3.40." George rings it up on the cash register, drops the change into her hand, and Stephanie thanks him. He nods back and goes over to talk with his friends at the bar. Stephanie sorts her change, arranges the drinks on her tray so they are evenly balanced, and heads for the table.

Although George and Stephanie work together to fulfill this necessary task, waitresses feel that the division of labor is far from equal. George performs the major task of mixing the drinks and ringing up the total for the order on the cash register. And Stephanie must do all she can to make this easy for George: translating the customer's order into language the bartender can immediately recognize; adding straws and fruit to the drinks; stirring the drinks as the mix is added to the alcohol; totaling the order for him; handing him the correct amount of money for the order; and finally, placing the drinks on the tray. While it would be possible for George to help Stephanie by performing some of these tasks himself, he does not. New girls often wait for the bartender to do things like place drinks on the tray or add up the prices, but they rapidly learn that it is their duty to make things as easy as they can for the bartender. "When I first started," says Joyce, "I gave the bartender the order and just stood there." But Joyce soon noticed the other girls helping by adding the nuts and straws to the drinks. A couple of times, Dave asked Joyce to do those things for him, and it wasn't long before Joyce just started doing all those things automatically.

The three most difficult things for a waitress to learn to do are totaling the price of an order, learning to recognize drinks, and arranging the order for the bartender. New girls are expected to rapidly learn the prices of drinks but are not given a list of prices to examine. Instead, the girls learn by asking the bartender and other waitresses. Bartenders are extremely impatient, however, with waitresses who do not know the prices and who are slow in adding up an order. One night when Holly hadn't been working very long, she gave Mark a long order, and while he was preparing it, she busily scribbled away on a napkin trying to add up the prices before he had the drinks ready. But the drinks were on the tray and his hand was extended before she could come up with the answer. He stood there waiting, but finally lost his patience, grabbed some bills from Holly's tray, and totaled the order on the register. He threw the change on her tray, "Learn those prices," he told her, never questioning the fact that he had access to the register for totaling the cost while she had to calculate in her head. "It got me so upset and I was so uptight about doing the job right and proving that I wasn't a dummy that for the longest time, I would stand to the side of the bar and add up my drinks on a napkin even before I would approach the bar to give the tender my order." This strategy slowed Holly down a little, making her work under more pressure from the customers in her section, but enabled her to save face in front of the bartender.

A second difficult task for the girls is learning to recognize drinks as the bartender places them on the bar. An unwritten rule says she must not bother the bartender by asking, so if she doesn't learn this skill quickly, she runs the risk of upsetting customers who receive a wrong drink. A waitress may give the bartender an order for a scotch and soda, a scotch and water, a brandy and water, and a Seven-Seven. To the untrained eye and especially in the darkness of the bar, all these drinks look alike. But a waitress soon learns to distinguish one drink from another; soda is cloudy, water is flat, Seven-Up is bubbly. The girls use other cues, too, such as observing the container from which a drink is poured and smelling drinks to check the contents. Once in a while, however, waitresses get distracted in the process of watching their order being prepared and lose track of which drink is which. They must then ask the bartender who names each drink and, with evident irritation, shoves it across the counter. When waitresses ask Dave this question, he often sticks his finger in the drink, tastes it, and then tells the girls which is which.

A third skill the girls must develop in order to be a good waitress and make work easier for bartenders involves rearranging orders. She must translate the customer's order into a convenient language and a proper sequence for the bartender. Once the order is taken from the table, it may undergo a couple of alterations. Names of drinks, for example, are often shortened or changed altogether. A customer may order "Special Export Beer" or a "vodka and orange" but the waitress tells the bartender: "I need an Export and a screwdriver." Also, drinks must be arranged so that the bartender does not have to run back and forth behind the bar just to fill one order, and so that he can better remember what the waitress asks him to prepare. For a waitress to do this, she must have a knowledge of the setup behind the bar, how drinks are made, and what goes into them. For example, if Sue gets an order from a table for a Budweiser, a Schlitz, a vodka gimlet, a brandy-water, and a Harvey Wallbanger, she has two requirements. First, she needs to remember drinks in this order so she can match drink and customer when she returns with a full tray. Second, she must rearrange them for the bartender so he can prepare them in a sequence that simplifies his work. She would hold the original sequence in mind and also mentally rearrange this order and tell Dave: "I need a brandy-water and brandy seven, a vodka gimlet, a Harvey Wallbanger, a Bud, and a Schlitz." Performing this task for the bartender does complicate the job for the waitress and places an added burden on her memory. The bartender, on the other hand, could take the drinks in any order and simply prepare them in the easiest order for him, but he never does this except with a new waitress.

All the waitresses eventually acquire these skills and become quite proficient at processing all this information rapidly and in the midst of confusion. Given the volume of business at Brady's, it seldom happens that the waitress has total silence and uninterrupted time to manage all this information. Tonight, for example, Sue stands at the bar, waiting for George to see her and come over to take the order. It's late, the bar is packed with more than a hundred customers, and the juke box is blaring. She has a large order, and while she waits she concentrates on it so she won't forget before George finds time to help her. It takes a few minutes for George to stop talking to one of the customers and in the meantime, a guy standing next to the bar hands her a dollar and asks her to see if she can get him a beer. Another customer grabs her from behind and wants some matches, and the people sitting in the middle table in her section begin waving frantically at her and calling, "Miss. Miss." They want to order another round of drinks at their table. Sue is beginning to feel a little frantic, but she remains calm on the outside. George is ignoring her and taking his time getting over to her station. She calls his name once. He turns around and gives her a look that means, "Just a minute!" She knows if she has forgotten the order or cannot give it instantly when George appears at her station, he will be annoyed and probably start drumming his fingers on the bar and say loudly, "Is it a secret or can I know too?" or "Spit it out, dumbhead."

George arrives, but before she can even start to give the order he says, "I need some ice from the kitchen. I'm getting low, can you bring me some quick?" His needs must always be first and though Sue wants to say, "You can just fill this order first and get your own damn ice!" she dutifully heads through the crowd for the kitchen, hoping no one will try to stop her and ask for another round, or yell, "Where is my order?" In the kitchen she curses out loud, gets the ice, and then it is a long series of "Scuse me! Scuse me!" as she works her way back to the bar all the time trying to remember the order and be ready to "spit it out" when the bartender is ready.

Back at the bar she hoists the ice up for George to take and waits for him to dump it into the ice container. He looks up, and she says, "I need two Hamm's, a Grain Belt, a vodka tonic, screwdriver, brandy-Seven, and a blackberry brandy and Seven." He quickly sets the beer and the vodka tonic on the bar, but in fixing the screwdriver he also drops the heavy orange juice container. "Fuck," he says as he grabs the container with both hands. Finally, Sue heads back to her tables, and she knows they will be upset that service here is so slow. She always feels caught between the demands of the customers and those of the bartenders. And always she feels trampled on and wishes that just once she could be the one to give the orders.

But if in the midst of pressure a girl manages well, she will often hear the bartender say, "You're a damn good waitress," or she may find out that one or another bartenders like to work with her because of her efficiency. More often, however, even though each girl strives to please the bartender, she will be told, "You bitches have no brains. It's a good thing you go to college because you wouldn't make it in the real world."

Serving Orders

It's now midnight. Sue glances at the clock again and sighs; it seems like hours but only twenty minutes have dragged by. The place is packed and blaring with noise, and she is busy, but time isn't going anywhere tonight. George hands her the change from her order, and she turns, balancing her tray, and begins pushing her way through the aisles. "Scuse me. Scuse me." Slowly, she makes her way to the tables and stops at the first one. Instead of four people, extra chairs have been pulled up and one customer is doubling up on a lap so that seven people have managed to crowd around it. She can't get close enough to the table to place each drink of front of each customer so she begins handing them out to the closest individual with instructions to pass it on. But no one seems to mind. "That's $5.50." One of the guys hands her a ten. She makes change and goes to the next table. She has one drink left to serve and places it squarely on the napkin in front of the girl seated at the table, a blackberry brandy and Seven. The girl turns and says, "Put it on the tab."

"I'm sorry, but I can't do that without the bartender's permission. May I have your name?" The girl mumbles something that is inaudible with all the noise. "Could you repeat that, please? I couldn't hear."

"Runklebury," the girl shouts in an annoyed tone of voice. Sue goes back to the bar and asks Mark if a girl named "Runklebury" can start a tab. Mark says, "No, I never heard of her." So Sue has to make another trip back to the table to inform the girl that she has to pay for her drink now. The girl takes a dollar out of her purse and throws it at Sue. Sue leaves her change on the table and moves on, thinking to herself, "Some people."

Meanwhile, Stephanie is having her own set of hassles in the upper section. The section is stuffed, and as Stephanie approaches a table carrying a tray with two Buds and a couple of beer glasses, she trips and spills a bottle of beer into the customer's lap. As she told Sue after work, "It was so funny. He picked up the money from my tray and wiped himself with it! He wasn't mad, but I felt terrible!"

Every girl at one time or another spills a drink or two on someone, and Stephanie was lucky to encouter a good-natured customer. Sharon wasn't feeling well one night and she tripped over a man's foot, spilled her tray, broke several glasses, and dumped two old-fashioneds on one man. "I thought I was going to cry," said Sharon. "I wasn't feeling well, and I did apologize, but the customer was so nasty. He insisted that not only should I buy them an entire round of drinks, but I should pay for his cleaning bill too! And he only had on jeans and an old sweater." But she told John about it, and John gave her a new round of drinks and told her to forget it.

Stephanie finished cleaning up the mess she had made when she spilled the beer and took a large order to the big table. There were three young couples and an older woman at this table. She passed out the drinks and took the ten dollar bill one of the men offered her. As she started to make change, the older woman grabbed her by the wrist, "Didn't I tell you to let me pay for this round?" The woman had indeed requested this when Stephanie took the order, but the man had offered the money first, and the girls turn almost automatically to the male for payment in such cases. "You know what," the lady continued with a nasty look on her face, "you are really stupid." Stephanie apologized and replied, "Yes, but this young man is so eager to treat you to a drink," and then took off. She told Mark about the incident, and Mark asked her to point them out. "Don't pay any attention to her," he said, "you're a good waitress." It wasn't much, but small compliments like this one are repeated to other waitresses and become a source of strength on busy nights.

The girls run into other problems when serving drinks too, and although some of them are not their fault, they must often take the blame. Bartenders occasionally confuse orders and give waitresses the wrong drink. Instead of a whiskey-Seven, a waitress may end up with a brandy-Seven. When this occurs, the waitress must take the blame for the mistake. The customer complains directly to her, not to the bartender, and often makes the assumption that the waitress is "stupid" or she would have brought the correct drink. The girls have strategies that help them save face in such situations. New girls can always say, "Oh, I'm sorry. I haven't worked here very long." Others will say, "It was so busy up at the bar, I must have confused your drink. I'm sorry." Occasionally, however, a waitress will simply tell the customer:"I'm sorry. The bartender must have mixed up the order." When a drink is exceptionally good, however, customers rarely say to the waitress, "That's a good drink. Thank you." or "You really serve good drinks here." Instead, they say, "Tell the bartender he makes a good drink." Despite the fact that the drink on the table in front of the customer is the result of a cooperative effort, success is credited to the bartender, failure to the waitress.

One part of serving orders involves collecting money. Waitresses like it when a table will pay for their drinks in "rounds." That is, one individual will pay for the entire table, and they will take turns each time a set of drinks are served. Stephanie walks up to a table of four girls and places their drinks on the table. "That's $3.45," she tells them. "How much is mine?"

"And mine?"

"We want to pay separately." So Stephanie goes around the table: "95¢, 75¢, 50¢ and $1.25." In response she receives a ten dollar bill, a five dollar bill, a one, and a check for twenty dollars. She doesn't carry enough money with her to make change for all of them so she must make a special trip back to the bar to cash the check and to get the correct change.

It's 12:25 and things have slowed down a bit. The customers are satisfied for the moment with their drinks, but the girls are busy providing extra services for some of the customers and visiting with a few of their favorite ones. Sue is busy being somebody's "lucky charm." Jeff and Mike, two of the regulars, are flipping to see who has to chug a shot of tequila. Jeff insists he always wins if Sue calls for him, and she is busy doing just that.

Stephanie is making the rounds, emptying ash trays, picking up empty bottles and dirty glasses, and making sure no one is sitting there dry. She makes a run to the cigarette machine for one man, and he tips her a quarter for the trouble. One very drunk customer handed her two dollars and told her to take a Harvey Wallbanger to his friend across the bar and tell him "to get fucked." She took the money and delivered both the drink and the message. The guy told her to keep the change and that meant a 75¢ tip for her. Tips are scarce in Brady's because the girls serve mainly a college crowd. A good night brings in five dollars, and Sharon says she thinks ten dollars is the most any girl has made. This is a meager amount given the volume of customers the girls serve in one evening.

One table stops Sue to ask her what goes into a Tom Collins. She tells them and remains to chat a few minutes, talking about the various kinds of drinks and their preposterous names: Sloe Screws, Wallbangers, Salty Dogs, Zombies, and Peashooters. Things are very slow in the upper section, but Stephanie catches Sue on the run. "Anything I can do to help?

"Would you clean off that table in the middle?" Denise asks as she darts by. Stephanie goes over to the empty table and removes the dirty glasses and trash, empties the ash tray and wipes the table. She picks up the quarter lying on the table and when she can catch Sue, she gives it to her. It is Sue's tip. Then Stephanie heads back to her own section.

Last Call

Sometime after midnight, things begin to slow down quite a bit and, around 12:30 or so, the waitresses usually have little to do. The girls can begin to catch their breath. Some of the more successful hustlers leave with a girl on their arm. The less fortunate remain for a consolation drink.

Anywhere from 12:45 to 12:55, the bartenders will give Sue and Stephanie permission to give "last call." When this happens, they begin circling their tables, stopping at each one and smiling and saying, "Last call, would you like to order anything else?" And if the customer wants anything more to drink tonight, he has to order it now. It is illegal for Brady's to sell drinks after 1:00.

Tonight, Mark waits until 12:50 before he gives the word to the girls. As last call is given, the bartender slowly raises the lights, exposing tired waitresses, bleary-eyed customers, girls with smudged mascara, dirty glasses and empty beer bottles, and a littered carpet. As the lights go all the way on and George switches the juke box off, a few groans are heard around the bar as people adjust to the brightness.

Sue and Stephanie momentarily forget their customers after having served them their last drinks as they put in their order for their own first drink of the evening, hurry to collect the candles and ash trays from tables, and cart them off to the kitchen. The wax must be drained from all the candles, and they are shelved. The ash trays must be set to soak in sudsy water overnight. The girls attack empty tables, clearing them of debris, glasses, and bottles, and wiping them off. A few have splotches of wax spilled on them, and they must scrape it off the surface. The girls are eager to get everyone to leave so they can clean their tables, punch out, and sit at the bar for a quiet drink after work and relax.

Some of the customers are belligerent, however, and don't want to leave, a chronic problem with strategies for dealing with it. Stephanie begins by removing the table from the customer, piece by piece: his ash tray comes out from under a burning cigarette, a partially consumed beer bottle is whisked away. The latter is usually a feint tactic, however. Stephanie knows the customer isn't through with it, she merely wants to emphasize the fact that they should drink a little faster if they don't want to lose the drink altogether.

Those customers who resist such tactics are subject to more direct attack. Sharon, for example, stands next to the table with her sponge in one hand, the other hand on her hip and stares at the customer. She may even add a gentle verbal hint such as: "Let's move it." or "It's time to go home now." Sometimes an appeal to the customer's better nature is made: "I've had a hard night and I want to go home. Could you please hurry it a bit?"

Meanwhile, Mark does what he can about the situation. He periodically booms out, "Okay, folks. Let's move it. We're closed now." John Brady has a routine he does over the loudspeaker:

> Attention, everyone. Brady's Bar has enjoyed serving you this evening, and we hope you have been satisfied with our little place. Now, on behalf of the management we would like to request that you "GET THE HELL OUT OF HERE!"

Everyone had left Stephanie's section but three rather obnoxious men. They had come in at 12:55, ordered beers, and had just begun to drink them. She finished cleaning off her last table, and they came up and sat down in her section. "Gimme an ash tray," one of them told her. She said, "It's almost time to go home. Would you mind sitting at the bar? I've just cleaned this section." "Don't give me any lip. Bring us an ash tray." So she brought them an ash tray, and the guy said, "I want some music. You. Tell the bartender to turn it up." She said, "You'll have to ask the bartender."

"No. *You* ask him to turn it up. You're the one who works here." So Stephanie went over and told Mark the situation, and Mark sent her back with the message that the bar was closed. This angered them, and they shouted over to Mark, "Bartender. What kind of a joint are you running here? Put some music on, you bastard." Mark yelled back, "Shove it, will ya? We're closed." At 1:30 Stephanie tried to remove the bottles from the table and again, "Hey, now. You're getting a bit uppity. Leave that bottle alone." Finally, and to Stephanie's relief, they got up and left.

Sue saw one of her customers get up and walk out the door with two full beer bottles under his coat. She told the bouncer, and the bouncer ran out the door after him, returning a few minutes later with the bottles.

After Closing

At 1:45 A.M. the last customer is shown out the door. Dave, the bouncer this evening, locks the door behind them. Stephanie and Sue check their tables to make sure everything is clean, then punch out and sit down at the bar, sticky from the spilled drinks, stale beer, and cigarette ashes. Both girls hand Mark their ten dollars and Sue turns in the burglar alarm. Mark puts a handful of quarters on the bar for one of the girls to put in the juke box, and instructs them, "Play 223, 245, and 152." He then lowers the lights while George begins making a round of drinks for those who've remained. There's a knock on the outside door and Dave goes over and yells, "Who is it?" The muffled reply is, "Jim." So Dave unlocks the door, and in walks Jim and Sandy. With the exception of Joyce, Steve, and Sharon, all of Brady's night employees are present. Some came in earlier in the evening, despite the fact they weren't scheduled to work, just to drink, and have remained past closing. Larry is there too. And so is Steve's wife. After closing, the drinks are on the house. The bartenders and waitresses who've worked that night always stay for at least one drink, and on weekend nights, almost all the employees show up for the informally scheduled "party."

George checks around the bar to make sure everyone is set with his favorite drink and then turns to emptying the cases of beer that Dave carried out earlier, placing the bottles in the cooler so they will be cold and ready to serve by the time the bar opens again. "Hey, Sue," laughs

Mark, "Your favorite customer came in tonight and he was telling me all about you. You know, the guy with the skunks in his face?" Sue knew who he meant, an ugly but sweet customer who came into Brady's quite regularly. "He was telling me how much he loved you. He said what a nice waitress you are!"

"Well, Mark. Wait until I tell you about the girl who was in tonight asking about *you*!" retorted Sue. George interrupted the banter to ask if anyone cared for another drink. Most said, "Yes," and those who insisted they didn't want another drink found one placed in front of them anyway. The joking continued; the evening was rehashed in detail with special emphasis and attention give to mistakes and mishaps made by specific employees.

At 2:30, and after several more drinks, the Brady family begins to break up. Often, the whole group would drink until three or so and then leave together for the nearest all-night restaurant for breakfast. On the weekends, it is rare if everyone makes it home before 4:00 A.M. But tonight, the guys have planned a card game, and things break up earlier than usual. The men begin moving tables together and setting the scene for an all-night poker game: fresh drinks, potato chips from the kitchen, ash trays, and cards. Loosened neckties are removed altogether and shirt sleeves rolled up. The girls decide to leave and have breakfast on their own this morning. They put on their coats, finish what they can of their drinks, and say "Goodnight."

As Sue and Stephanie start for the door, Mark comes over, puts an arm around each one and says, "You did a great job tonight, girls. It was a rough night, but you were great." He unlocks the door for them and as they leave, he gives Sue, who is the last one out of the door, a friendly pat on the rump. Mark's way of saying, "Thanks."

16
The Female Gender

Socialization into any culture involves differential learning. The most basic differences are those associated with the sexes. Males and females learn that there are male and female ways of thinking, talking, acting, and aspiring. Such socialization may take place on two levels. One is the explicit level in which adults and peer group members actively and consciously tutor beliefs and action. The other level is tacit and is composed of subtle cues and often constant reminders of appropriateness. This tacit level is not necessarily the consequence of conscious efforts. Rather, it results from implications and limited or structured options in modes of interpreting the world that are learned by both sexes. Alan Graebner here identifies some of the tacit assumptions about the nature of being female in American society. He shows how these operate in producing Nancy, a "female human being." He also shows how this understanding of being female is often thought of as the natural condition of the female, both by those socialized and the socializers alike.

Growing Up Female

Alan Graebner

In every society culture is transmitted at two levels: explicit and tacit. Parents and other adults instruct the young by explicit reminders, explanations, warnings, and advice. They also teach, however, without conscious, verbal instructions. This tacit transmission coveys ways of behaving, thinking, and perceiving that are unconscious and taken for granted.

Explicit and tacit transmission often take place simultaneously, but

From *The Nacirema*, ed. James P. Spradley and Michael A. Rynkiewich (Boston: Little, Brown, 1975). Reprinted by permission. This article is based on Chapter 2 in the author's previous work, *After Eve, The New Feminism* (Minneapolis: Augsburg, 1972).

tacit enculturation usually occurs without the learners' recognition of what is going on. In fact, the teacher, too, is often unaware of what is happening. The tone of voice, subtle body movements, facial expression, spatial arrangements of objects and people, unspoken (often unexamined) expectations, the things left unsaid—these are some of the ways in which the tacit dimension of culture is conveyed. The transmission of the tacit culture is subtle, but its content is basic. These two facts mean that many people do not think of the results as "culture" at all but tend to believe that the tacit dimension is something inherent in human nature.

This whole process can be clearly seen in the way definitions of male and female are learned. Certainly there is an explicit level of transmission. But most of the definition is conveyed on the tacit level, and done in such an unspoken but pervasive way that neither teachers nor learners are aware of it but instead do not look on the definitions of male and female as culture at all, but as part of human nature.

To examine this process I shall focus on the way our middle-class American society defines women and transmits this definition to the young. So that we can observe closely, we should concentrate on the life of one particular woman; although this means we may not discuss some variations, the basic process is generally representative. Let us take a case study of a woman we might name Nancy.

An American Girl

Nancy was her parents' first child. Her father then was beginning what was to become a successful accounting firm. Her mother was, in her own description, "just a housewife." When Nancy's father told his friends the baby had arrived, they congratulated him and then asked whether it was a boy or a girl. When he said, "a girl," they usually laughed and told him not to be disappointed; the *next* one would be a boy. His wife told him the same thing. They were right, too, for Nancy was only a year old when she had a baby brother, David. Their father complained contentedly of the expense of buying blue baby things instead of wearing out Nancy's pink paraphernalia.

The two children were so close in age they were good playmates. However, as they grew older, they received toys that were increasingly different. At Christmas and birthdays, David received cap pistols and erector sets and finally, an electric train. For Nancy it was play kitchen utensils, dolls, and finally, a large dollhouse. She was not unhappy about getting a doll instead of an erector set, because she quickly learned that there were boys' toys and girls' toys. She noticed how one boy in her second-grade class was teased when he unguardedly admitted he liked dolls. And when she once began to play with her brother's train set, he and his friends told her very self-righteously trains were not for girls.

Nancy's grandparents visited frequently, something Nancy liked very much, for her grandfather always told them stories and teased the two children. "What are you going to be when you grow up?" he would ask David, and they would all laugh as Dave went from fireman to race-car driver to doctor. Then would come the question for Nancy: "Whom are you going to marry when you grow up?" Again they would all laugh when her grandfather teased her about the little boy next door.

Nancy and her brother liked to imitate their parents by "helping" in household tasks. Of course at first they were only a bother, but in time Nancy's mother would call her for help in the kitchen and in cleaning, while David assisted his father with carpentry or repairs. As each got better at these tasks, it made more sense to expect their participation in such jobs.

In school Nancy was a bright child who loved to read. Although there were nearly always more male than female characters in her books, somehow even mother bears wore aprons and kept house. Nancy's books gave her many ideas for games she organized with neighbor children. One of the boys would play the man who was a doctor or a businessman or a banker while Nancy was a nurse, secretary, teller, or someone who stayed home to cook and sew and clean.

Much of the time, however, Nancy ran around in the neighborhood, climbing trees, wading in ditches, and if the boys would let her, playing football or double-touch tag with them. Several times she overheard her mother and grandmother discussing her exploits, worrying that she was becoming a tomboy. And gradually she learned that a lady could never be a tomboy. Since she wanted very much to be grown-up—they had all the privileges, like staying up late—she tried to be a little more restrained and to act like a lady. Acting like a lady, she discerned, meant she could not use physical force or be too strong, but should rely on various psychological ploys to get what and where she wanted.

Being a lady came a bit easier in junior high and in high school. Nancy's mother did not encourage early dating, but her girl friends spent a great deal of time talking about boys. They knew it was important for a girl to attract boys, because that was what determined her success. Television shows, movies, popular songs, and the magazines said so.

Even their parents and ministers told the girls essentially the same thing when they warned that a promiscuous girl would suffer; she would lose her popularity with boys. If Nancy and her friends missed the point after all of this, they could still pick it up from the mental images that went with the terms for unmarried adults. Single men they knew as bachelors, and most bachelors were "eligible." Single women they heard called old maids, and no one spoke of an "eligible" old maid.

Nancy and her girl friends also knew that physical appearance was important to attract boys. All the girl and woman models in magazines, televsion, and billboard advertisements had one common asset: their looks. Nancy and her friends took this for granted; they were accustomed to such images, and they used these standards to judge themselves and other girls. They understoood that boys did too, for the boys had also grown up seeing women this way.

Nearly everyone Nancy knew seemed to think girls did not have much aptitude for certain ways of thinking. She heard a lot of joking references to girls and mathematics, for instance. Nancy did not do badly in the math courses she took, but none of her girl friends were taking more math, so she stopped too. She did not take any physics in high school, either. She heard that the physics course included a lot of time with mechanical things, and she knew boys were a lot better at that than girls; her brother and father were always tinkering with things while she helped her mother in the kitchen. Besides, she was not taking the math courses that would help in physics. Of course that meant when she was with a group of friends and the boys began arguing about something mechanical like a car, she did not have much idea of what they were talking about. But she could tell them right out she was dumb; boys knew that girls were not very good at machinery. Anyway, she learned it made boys feel good to explain to her.

In her junior and senior years, her high-school counselors began having conferences with each student, suggesting what could be done after graduation. Nancy's grades were good and everyone took it for granted that she would go to college. All her close friends were going. Besides, as one counselor said, she would need college to get some kind of job "just in case." She knew what that meant, of course: just in case she did not get married or was widowed early. Something to "fall back on," her father said.

Nancy was not very sure what she wanted to do, so she and her counselor talked over a number of possibilities. Her test scores were high, and she liked books; so the counselor suggested she think about being a teacher (perhaps high-school English) or a librarian. But Nancy was undecided. Her best friend wanted to work with people and was talking about nursing or social work. The boys Nancy dated, who got about the same grades she did, spoke of being lawyers and doctors and architects. Nancy was pleased and rather proud of herself to be dating boys like that. She knew her mother was, too. The idea of becoming a lawyer never occurred to her, and no one ever suggested it. She did not even know any women lawyers; neither did her father. There was one woman doctor in town, but she was a specialist whom few girls ever visited. All the other physicians were men, just as in the doctor programs on television.

Nancy had still not made up her mind when she went off to college. A year later her brother was in college too. Their slowness in choosing majors worried their father. He wanted his son to take over his company, and although Dave was hesitant, he never considered asking Nancy—and Nancy did not think of the idea, either. During Dave's sophomore year he had long talks with his father, trying to decide on a career. Nancy was a junior by this time, but she overheard her father tell David, "Now, your sister, that's different, because she's a woman and is going to get married and settle down with children. But how are you going to amount to anything unless you have a good job?"

In her senior year Nancy and Michael, a boy she had been dating, became serious about each other and soon announced their engagement. By then Nancy was an English major. One of her professors had been talking to her about graduate school, but since she was engaged she decided she had better be practical and take the necessary courses to teach high school so she would be able to have an income as soon as she graduated. Her fiancé was an engineer who was going on to business school, and they both expected Nancy to support them until he finished.

And that is about the way things turned out. They were married just after graduation. That fall Michael began his graduate work while Nancy found a teaching job in a nearby high school. She found she was much better at teaching than she had anticipated. The principal of her school was exceptionally cooperative, and she was able to try out some of her own rather unorthodox and innovative ideas. They worked so well she thought of carrying them further. However, when Michael finished school his best job offer was on the West Coast, so as a matter of course they moved, although Nancy could not find a job at all comparable to the one she had left.

Nancy did not mind too much because they planned to start a family anyway. In a few years she and Michael had a boy and a girl. The family kept Nancy busy all day long and part of the night besides. The women's magazines she bought by subscription or at the supermarket always described changes around the house that Nancy felt she should try, though they took a great deal of time because they kept raising her standards. Michael was quite successful in his job, and they were able to live in a very pleasant suburb with lots of open land for the children to play in. Nancy thought occasionally about returning to teaching or of going back to school at a nearby university but gave up the ideas after she saw a friend try. Finding a full-time baby-sitter was nearly impossible in their suburb. The friend's husband often grumbled that the house and meals were not the same as when his wife was home all day, so she had to get up early to do all the housework before she left, and that made her and the children irritable for lack of sleep. Then one of the neighbors hinted that they must be in a real financial squeeze for her to endure such problems. That made her husband even unhappier, and Nancy's friend finally quit. Nancy decided the lesion was clear, at least until the children were a good deal older.

By her early thirties Nancy joked on her birthdays about not revealing her age. But she realized with some contentment that she had already achieved most of her dreams. As she chauffeured the children and their dog around to shopping, dentist appointments, cub-scout and brownie meetings, and music lessons, the group made an appealing picture. In fact, Michael, who left the office early one day and saw them as they arrived home, told Nancy they looked like an automobile ad in a woman's magazine: a pretty, well-dressed mother with two attractive children and a bouncing dog in a late model station wagon, living in a comfortable suburb. Michael was very proud of them and happy with himself that he had been successful enough to give his family a good life, even though it meant he was not at home as much as he should have been. And Nancy was rather pleased too—all this and a loving husband. As she reminded herself when she occasionally got restless, what more could a woman want?

Human Female or Female Human?

What had happened to Nancy? It may be said that a great many pleasant things had happened to her. She had grown up in a closely knit, loving family, something she valued so highly she wanted to replicate it as an adult. She had found someone whom she could trust as an intimate companion, and who reciprocated that trust. She was able to accept and enjoy sex as a great gift. And she knew the fascinating and sometimes awesome experience of parenthood.

But that was not all that had happened to Nancy. As a child she had learned that girls are judged by a standard different from that for boys and had begun measuring her conduct by that standard. She recognized that when measured by the boys' criteria, girls do not do well. Nancy's formal education, it is true, had been much like her brother's, but there was one key difference. As Bruno Bettelheim puts it, "boys have no doubt that their school is intended, at least, to help make them a *success* in their mature life. . . . But the girl is made to feel that she must undergo precisely the same training only becuase she may need it if she is a *failure.*" Nancy's sensitivity about her age was part of all this, for it reflected her knowledge that in our society the major female asset is physical attractiveness, a quality that unlike male assets, such as ambition and power, depreciates with age. Nancy's concern for husband and children were also a part of this; she had learned to define her life in terms of others' lives, especially those of her family.

Much of Nancy's life had become the way it was because of cultural definitions. This is common in every culture, but in American society, at least, the enculturation is different according to sex. If the child is a boy, the "programming" is a comparatively open-ended shaping to foster choices of life patterns out of a large variety of human activity. If the child is a girl, the programming is a rigorous delimitation to female activities: sexual partner, wife, mother. As a final blow, this programming has more than its share of ironic contradictions. For example, girls, who all their lives are taught that the normal goal is to marry, are forbidden to initiate explicit proceedings to gain that end. They may use subtle, manipulative strategies but do not openly ask for dates and propose marriage; boys do.

Another way of putting this is that much of Nancy's life had been controlled because of her being defined in our culture as a human female, though it defined her father and her brother and her husband as male humans. The culture defined her first of all as a female, while it defined the men first of all as human. Her sex was the prime condition in her role. Their humanness was the prime condition in their roles. At this point enculturation became objectification. Nancy was treated as an object, not as a full human being.

This was concealed, because Nancy was a "success" according to the standards of middle-class American culture, standards she had accepted as they were presented to her. But was she really given so few opportunities to choose something else? After all, no one told her *explicitly* she could not be an attorney or airline pilot or engineer. But to put things that way is to ignore the existence of tacit enculturation. When the whole weight of the culture's tacit dimension was opposed to women attorneys, no one had to tell Nancy she could not be one for her to bypass that possibility. Nancy's parents, friends, teachers and husband— in sum her whole world—identified her primarily by her sex. It is hardly surprising she responded by identifying herself the same way. Nor is it surprising that no one—her family, her associates, Nancy herself—was aware of the subtle process. They were not unintelligent; they were aware of some of the culture's more obvious pressures. They would have been quick to see the process of making objects of women in the pages of something like *Playboy* magazine. They understood that the women there are automatically identified as sexual beings. But the tacit dimension can be much deeper and Nancy's parents did not recognize it at work when women were automatically identified primarily as wives and mothers in the pages of the *Ladies Home Journal* or even in their own home. Unlike many fathers, who according to surveys are quite antagonistic to the idea of carreers for their daughters, Nancy's father had been, he thought, "neutral." He *had* been neutral on the level of explicit transmission of culture. But on the level of tacit transmission, neutrality is practically impossible. Neutrality does not offset unstated cultural assumptions and so really turns out to be advocacy of the status quo supported by tacit enculturation.

White Americans have begun to realize this in the area of race relations. When children see television shows in which black actors appear only as dometic servants or comics; when they read textbooks in which black people are hardly ever mentioned; when they see advertisements that picture only pretty white girls; when they hear jokes that refer to blacks by uncomplimentary names and depend for humor on negative racial stereotypes—when children experience all this, they are the objects of tacit enculturation, and no one has to tell them outright that in America black people are set apart from whites and are not worth as much.

Much of the same process holds true for boys and girls. They grow up watching women on television whose main problems are how to get their wash whiter and floors shinier and to make themselves more beautiful and to smell better and to attract or retain a husband. Children read textbooks that hardly ever mention women and, when they do, emphasize women in a domestic capacity; after all, Betsy Ross is famous for her sewing. Children see ads that use women for specific physical traits and hear endless jokes about the ineptitude and failings of women. The lessons are unconsciously picked up boys, and they shape boys' attitudes toward girls.

Former Senator Charles Goodell tells the story of the congressman visiting a third-grade classroom who was asked by a girl if he thought some day there could be a woman president. He replied affirmatively, pointing out there are more women than men and if they got together they could elect a woman president. And then came a little male voice from the back of the room: "Now what did you have to go and tell them that for?" On a school playground during recess, a teacher watched a group of third-grade boys eagerly milling about in concentration on an active game of kickball. One of their group ran across the field with the pack, but clear of it, shouting over and over in a shrill, worried, little voice, "but that's a girls' game; that's a girls' game." He was the voice of future attitudes for the group.

Girls in our culture also learn these lessons and at an early age. For example, one mother who was admitted to medical school found her four-year-old daughter heartbroken by the news, for she thought it meant her mother would have to turn into a man and not be a mother any more. When asked if they "could be" governor of the state or a judge, California junior-high girls were much less likely than boys to answer yes (17 percent of the girls, 44 percent of the boys on the governor; 26 percent, 49 percent regarding the judge). In other words, the result of female enculturation is a human being who from an early age is likely to be self-deprecating and fearful in areas other than home and family. This in turn means that these traits are likely to proceed essentially unmodified for yet another generation without either mother or child realizing that they are teacher and student.

Perhaps becuase it usually occurs outside of our awareness, the tacit enculturation we have surveyed in Nancy's case (and we studied only its more "obvious" manifestations) is impressively tenacious. How tenacious can be shown in a number of ways. One illustration is that cultural definitions about women become so taken for granted that people confuse them with biological definitions and can assume a woman is a female before she is a human being. Another example is the way cultural definitions of women and their roles lag behind changes in their activities. For instance, women are defined—and treated—as if they were full-time mothers who stayed at home, as most women formerly did. Yet because of smaller families and greater longevity, the greatest number of years in a woman's life are likely to be after the last child is in school. Furthermore, most women today work outside the home. But, so far, these facts have had little impact on the definitions of women being transmitted to the young.

Finally, the strength of these definitions may be measured when they are directly challenged. When a Maryland school board recently considered a proposal for coeducational tennis, opponents produced the argument that "a high school boy beaten at a game of tennis by a girl his own age would feel castrated." The adolescent boy, said the opponents, learns to accept defeat from a male peer. "But if he should take a real walloping from a girl his age, why then, we very often see a true withdrawal from sports altogether. . . ." Here is unconscious recognition that what is involved is tacit transmittal of culture. A boy defeated by a girl would feel like withdrawing only if convinced that a girl is by definition inferior. But since personal experience obviously did not teach him that, then it must have been inculcated by a variety of other means. Further, there is obviously a double standard at work: a concentration on the damage of defeat to the boy rather than on the benefits of victory to the girl. The unquestioning way male mental health gains priority over female mental health rests on a firm base of cultural differentiation between men and women, to the disadvantage of women.

One drawback to a case study is that it may not cover all possibilities. In this instance, Nancy was a "success." So there is no opportunity to survey the range of penalties middle-class society imposes on "failures" in order to enforce the whole pattern of limits on women. If these limits were conveyed entirely at the explicit level of cultural transmission, it might be easier to recognize and thus to change this patten. Obviously, they are not transmitted explicitly, and this enormously complicates the dynamics of culture change.

This has immediate application when traditional cultural definitions of women are challenged by feminists. Because tacit rather than explicit enculturation is chiefly involved, we may expect a feminist campaign to be a difficult one. We can predict that some of the most ardent antifeminists will be women. At the same time, it is reasonable to expect a large number of rather sudden conversions as women, vaguely uneasy about their position, see for the first time the process of tacit enculturation as it has been imposed on them and learn to recognize more and more of its manifestations. Because we are dealing with a tacit level, we ought to expect that a change of laws—an equal rights amendment or abortion reform, for example—will in itself not be a full solution, though it will be part of the solution. And finally it is likely, because of the subtlety of the forces involved, that thoroughgoing change in cultural definitions of women will, even in the best circumstances, take several generations to accomplish.

17

Sex Roles in Everyday Life

Rituals are principal elements of any cultural scene. They provide routine solutions to the problems of everyday life. Without them every potential action would have to be negotiated, and a novel solution acceptable to everyone involved would have to be reached. Routines and rituals are, thus, necessary for social order. However, the culture out of which the rituals have emerged changes. Even those aspects of the culture thought of as relatively stable often change. For example, sex roles and values are currently changing. Laurel Walum here describes some of the adaptations to these changing meanings of sex roles. She shows how the door ceremony is like a window that reveals the underlying values in our society and how those values are in a state of transition. The description presents several types of door-opening encounters and includes a description of the cultural context of the ceremony. She also suggests some future directions for the appearance of new ceremonies.

The Changing Door Ceremony: Notes on the Operation of Sex Roles

Laurel Richardson Walum

A young woman and a young man, total strangers to each other, simultaneously reach the closed classroom door. She steps slightly aside, stops, and waits. He positions himself, twists the handle, pulls open the door, and holds it while she enters. Once she is safely across the threshold, he enters behind her. An everyday, commonplace social ceremony has been performed. It is not accidental that their performance in this cere-

From *Urban Life and Culture* 2(1974):506–515. Reprinted by permission.

monial ritual of "door opening" has gone so smoothly, although they have never rehearsed it with each other. Nor is it by chance that such trivial, commonplace ceremonies between the sexes occur day after day.

Of the multitude of such ceremonial occasions between the sexes in middle-class society—occasions wherein the interplay of cultural values and self-image are displayed—the "Door Ceremony" is probably the most common. We are confronted constantly with doors: car doors, house doors, bathroom doors, revolving doors, electric-eye doors. Ad infinitum are the physical structures which must somehow be penetrated if we are to complete our daily round of activites. And nearly as often as we confront the door, we are in a social situation in which a ceremonial ritual concerning it may occur. The pervasiveness of the occasion is difficult to deny. The relevance of the ceremony for the maintenance of cultural values and self-esteem, its true *nontriviality,* was initially suggested to me by entries in student journals—the jounals having been written for a Sociology of Women course. It was subsequently underscored by a series of norm-violation experiments performed by undergraduates and by my own observation. I draw my illustration and develop my analysis from these data sources.

I am concerned with four major questions: (1) How does this ceremony function to bind the society together? (2) What cultural values are being enacted? (3) What consequences has the women's movement had on the ceremony? and finally, speculatively, (4) What might the future hold?

Goffman has paid special attention to these ceremonial occasions. In our everyday associations we abide by rules of conduct, a kind of guidebook which is followed "not because it is pleasant, cheap, or effective, but because it is suitable and just" (1967, p. 48). These rules establish both our obligations—the way we are morally constrained to act and our expectations—the way others are morally required to act towards us. Commitment to the rule becomes a commitment to a given self-image. Ceremonial rules guide

> conduct in matters felt to have secondary importance—officially anyway—as a conventionalized means of communication by which the individual expresses his character or conveys his appreciation of other participants in the situation [Goffman 1967, p. 54].

These rules are incorporated in what we call "etiquette." To be properly mannered we convey an appropriate demeanor, expressed through our dress, deportment, bearing, and an appropriate deference, or appreciation and confirmation of an actor's relationship to a recipient.

The rules of conduct bind actors and recipients in appropriate interaction, encourage their interaction, and serve in a daily pedestrian way to hold together the social order. The very dailiness of the ceremonies, the lack of substantive investment, permits the constant reaffirmation of the kinds of persons we think we are and the kinds of rules we deem appropriate. The ceremony, then, affirms the nature of the social order, the morality of it, as well as the properness of the self who is engaged in the action. As Goffman succinctly states, "The gestures which we sometimes call empty are perhaps, in fact, the fullest things of all" (1967, p. 91).

Binding the Society

The door ceremony exemplifies the etiquette developed to "bind" the sexes together. The daily drama of Betty Coed and Joe College at the Classroom Door, which began this analysis, is descriptive of the usual ritual. Joe College, under the ceremonial rules of conduct, is *obliged* to open the door for Betty Coed, and Betty Coed *expects* to be the recipient of his courtesy. In the ritual, both of them have confirmed their images of themselves as respectively, male and female. As one "Joe College" wrote in his course journal:

> I have dated several girls including my fiancée who want to be treated like a lady. My courtesy like opening the car door makes them feel more feminine and they enjoy this. I enjoy also being a gentleman and making them feel this way. Personally, I prefer a girl who is feminine over a more rugged-looking and -acting girl.

And as a Betty Coed declared:

> Tonight I had a date with a gentleman. When I opened the door to let myself in, he closed it and opened it again. To tell the truth it made me feel good. He said he enjoyed doing these little things for me because he derived a feeling of protectiveness. I was reassured. I didn't want him to think I was crude. It's nice to *feel* like a woman.

The activity as traditionally structured, then, affirms the generalized notion of "masculinity" and "femininity." But what are the components, the elements, of the personal self-image enacted in the door ceremony that lead the male to perceive himself as "masculine" and the female to see herself as "feminine?"

To be masculine, first and foremost, means to have authority, to be in charge, in control. And in our culture, in most encounters, the person with higher authority holds the door. The doctor ushers in his patient; the mother, her children; the Dean, his faculty; and the young and able facilitate the old and infirm. Note that the phrase "the gatekeepers of knowledge" symbolically acknowledges the role of authority vested in those responsible for the door.

Second, and pervasively, to be "masculine" means to be "active"; to be "feminine" means to be "passive." This distinction pervades the entire ceremony. The male is the active party in the encounter; the female waits passively for the door to open and for the door to close. The passivity is closely linked to another prescribed feminine trait, namely "dependence." By waiting for the service to be performed, the woman communicates that she *needs* someone to help her through her daily round of activities. The male, in turn, communicates his independence by actively meeting the challenge of the door and overcoming it. Other male virtues of physical strength, mechanical ability, worldliness, self-confidence, and efficacy are called into play in the ceremony. If Joe College goes through his routine without mishap, he has engaged all these traits culturally associated with masculinity, and of course, he does *feel* masculine. And Betty Coed, by acting out her expectations, has drawn upon the perceptions of femininity recognized by the culture: frailty, weakness, ineptitude, and protectibility. She *feels* womanly.

Affirmation of Cultural Values

The door ceremony, then, reaffirms for both sexes their sense of gender-identity, of being a "masculine" or "feminine" person. It is not accidentally structured. In a very profound way, the simple ceremony daily makes a reality of the moral perspective of their culture: the *ideology of patriarchy*. These virtues of "masculinity" are precisely those which are the dominant values of the culture: aggression, efficacy, authority, prowess, and independence. And these virtues are assigned to the dominant group: the males (cf. Millet 1970, pp. 23–58). Opening a door for a woman, presumably only a simple, common courtesy, is also a *political* act, an act which affirms a patriarchal ideology. The male who wrote the following recognized not the irony of his words.

> Some women feel that if you open a door for them it is a sign of male chauvinism. In other words, you can't be nice to a female without showing your true colors.

His words, however, are perhaps less naive than this more commonly heard statement:

> I'm all for Woman's Lib. I think women should get equal pay for equal work. But women should keep their femininity. I like being treated like a lady.

One might suggest that these people are missing the relevance of minor courtesies perpetuating the ideology of patriarchy. Analytically, in terms of our understanding of the relationship between the cultural values and everyday ceremonies, women can't have it both ways.

Effects of the Woman's Movement

As more and more women and men "recognize" the meaning that common courtesies have for the perpetuation of the patriarchal ideology, increasing numbers of what Goffman refers to as deference-confrontations occur. The world which has been taken for granted, the rules of conduct once abided by, are called into question. Ceremonial rituals, once performed with propriety, become imbued with substantive meaning and are perceived by some as insulting, assaulting, and degrading. As a consequence, the once routine—matter-of-fact—door-opening ceremony becomes situationally problematic to increasing numbers of people. What are some of the responses to the altered consciousness? What stances do persons take to make sense out of their changed ceremonial world? I offer a kind of typology of such stances based on empirical observations and student reports. I do not claim that it is an exhaustive theoretical accounting, but, rather, only an analytical categorization of known patterns.

The Confused

Many persons confronted for the first time with a ceremonial profanation are uncertain what to do about it. They have practiced the standard behaviors and do not know how to respond when one of the actors is out of "character." A woman reports the following:

> I approached a door ahead of a fellow and then with common courtesy, I held it open for him to go through. He bumped right into me even though he could see me. He looked awfully puzzled and it took him forever to get through.

The "confused" man could indeed see her, but he could not perceive what was "happening" and was unable to make sense out of it. He acted along his normal path—destined for collision. Confusion is even more explicit in another reported episode:

> I came to a door at the same time as this guy. He reached to open it for me but then I started to open it myself and he just let me do it. *It was like neither of us knew what to do.*

The confused, embarrassed, and awkward literally don't know yet how to make sense out of the situation.

The Tester

The tester, unlike the confused, *recognizes* that the routine rules of conduct in any given encounter are violatable and yet wants to maintain proper demeanor as well as proper deference. For example, a woman reports that "A man opening a door holds it open for me, asking, 'Are you a liberated woman? If not, I'll hold this door open for you.' " Or, take, the following overheard conversation:

> Female: Well, aren't you going to open the door for me?
> Male: I didn't know that girls still liked for boys to do that.
> Female: I'm not in Woman's Lib.

Often, the tester has other motives in mind, such as wanting to act properly in order to "score." This excerpt from a male student's journal is illustrative:

> It's almost like discovering a third sex to deal with liberated women. In the past I would make advances to my date almost as a matter of course. Now, I must "discover" if my date is sexually traditional or not before I decide on the conduct of our date. I can't just open door and light cigarettes and expect to score. In fact, if I do treat those so-called liberated women like chattels, we never make it.

This male has found, then, that the whole course of his sexual life can hinge on the perception of appropriate deference.

The Humanitarian

The humanitarian, like the tester, recognizes that the situation is changing but has drawn upon other cultural values to explain and guide behavior, particularly the values of "sensitivity" and of "considerateness" of all people. For example, one male states,

> A male shouldn't *circle* the car to open the door for a woman. I believe each sex should treat the other with mutual courtesy. If a woman reaches the car first, there is nothing wrong with her opening it.

Or, as another male student writes,

> I had a 15-second encounter with a pro-libber which has left a bad taste in my mouth all day. She had a large stack of papers and I pushed open and held the door for her. I would have done this for a woman or a man. Instead of thank you I got the coldest, bitterest, most glaring stare that went right through me. I resent being seen as a Pig when I was being courteous to her as a *person*.

There are women humanitarians, also, who open doors for men in similar straits. As one reports,

> I entered the elevator ahead of a football player who lives in my building who had an armful of groceries. I quickly held the door back so he could get on. He was so embarrassed he couldn't even say thank you.

The Defender

The defender recognizes there is change afoot in the land but wants no part of it. For example, one woman relates:

> I opened a door to enter a building and a boy walked in ahead of me. It was just like he expected me to open the door for him. My first reaction was frowning and thinking some people have a lot of nerve. I believe in manners that did not enter the mind of the boy. I wondered if most boys now take it for granted that girls are woman's liberationists and will want to hold the door open for boys.

And a male student observes:

> It happens many times in this University that the female *purposefully* beats the male to the door and opens it herself. To the male, this is a discourtesy and an example of bad manners. To him it appears that the female is a hard and calloused woman who has never been taught proper manners. They are trying to assert their person over their sex.

Another male student concluded a multiparagraph moral indictment of "lady door-openers" with this clincher: "It's fine that women are liberating themselves, but I wouldn't want to marry one." The vehemence of defenders occasionally creates poignant episodes, as evidenced by this journal entry:

> "I don't care how uncomfortable you are. You are not going until you act like my wife should," my husband stormed. I conceded. I let him open the car door. I had to give in. I don't have a driving license.

The Rebel

The rebel recognizes that the rules of conduct are changing and is anxious to speed the change on its way. Rebels are oftentimes involved in badly demeanored profanations and report pleasure in their sacrilege. One woman states:

> I had a date with this same fellow [previously referred to as a gentleman] and this time I *deliberately* opened the door. He looked distressed. So I rubbed it in and told him I was capable of opening the door myself. I never wanted to go out with him in the first place. Ha!

Another woman student reports:

> So this Dude says to me, "Hey, let me help you with the door." And I say, "You ain't got nothin' to help me with."

Males appear also in the rebel ranks. Says one,

> I don't open doors for women. I'm glad not to. I don't want to serve them just because they're women. If they had their heads screwed on right they wouldn't trade doing laundry for me lighting their cigarettes.

What the Future Holds

As is obvious from the illustrations, these five types are in frequent interaction with each other, making the ceremonial occasion increasingly complex and nonroutine. Where do we go from here? Can we expect to get through these doors? Durkheim and Goffman argue that the social order is dependent on the routine daily acting-out of the morality of people who are simultaneously being bound together and providing living testimony of the cultural values. If altered consciousness continues and courtesies are rebuked, then ceremonial profanations will increase in frequency. The increase in violations of rules of conduct leads to increasing normlessness—anomie. The anomic period provides a time for the emergence of new *substantive* rules of conduct. A potential substantive change, then, might be forthcoming. If patriarchal values, which now govern the ceremonial conduct between the sexes, cannot be routinely enacted, these values cannot persist. Looking to changing values in other realms, and speaking optimistically, we might even be able to foresee ceremonial occasions dominated by a humanitarian perspective. If so, we might all get through our daily rounds with increased efficacy and joy.

References

Goffman, E. 1967. "The Nature of Deference and Demeanor," in *Interaction Ritual: Essays on Face-to-Face Behavior.* Garden City, N.Y.: Doubleday Anchor, pp. 47–96.

Millett, K. 1970. *Sexual Politics.* Garden City, N.Y.: Doubleday.

18
Sex Role Games

Many occupational role relationships occur between individuals of different status. The foreman outranks the worker; the vice-president has higher status than the secretary. Often this inequality is reflected in subtle games of communication. All parties to the game must learn and follow the rules to maintain the status quo and accomplish necessary communication. But it is no accident that differential status in occupational roles frequently involve male-female relationships. The bartender-waitress, boss-secretary, doctor-nurse, as well as many other relationships merely express more deeply held values in our society about men and women. In this article Leonard Stein describes the game that transpires between doctors and nurses. The nurse must be indirect and differential in conveying advice, while the physician must be supportive of and receptive to the advice.

The Doctor-Nurse Game

Leonard I. Stein

The relationship between the doctor and the nurse is a very special one. There are few professions where the degree of mutual respect and cooperation between co-workers is as intense as that between the doctor and nurse. Superficially, the stereotype of this relationship has been dramatized in many novels and television serials. When, however, it is observed carefully in an interactional framework, the relationship takes on a new dimension and has a special quality which fits a game model. The underly-

From *Archives of General Psychiatry* 16 (1967): 699–703. Reprinted by permission.

ing attitudes which demand that this game be played are unfortunate. These attitudes create serious obstacles in the path of meaningful communications between physicians and nonmedical professional groups.

The physician traditionally and appropriately has total responsibility for making the decisions regarding the management of his patients' treatment. To guide his decisions he considers data gleaned from several sources. He acquires a complete medical history, performs a thorough physical examination, interprets laboratory findings, and at times, obtains recommendations from physician-consultants. Another important factor in his decision making is the recommendations he receives from the nurse. The interaction between doctor and nurse through which these recommendations are communicated and received is unique and interesting.

The Game

One rarely hears a nurse say, "Doctor, I would recommend that you order a retention enema for Mrs. Brown." A physician, upon hearing a recommendation of that nature, would gape in amazement at the effrontery of the nurse. The nurse, upon hearing the statement, would look over her shoulder to see who said it, hardly believing the words actually came from her own mouth. Nevertheless, if one observes closely, nurses make recommendations of more import every hour and physicians willingly and respectfully consider them. If the nurse is to make a suggestion without appearing insolent and the doctor is to seriously consider that suggestion, their interaction must not violate the rules of the game.

Object of the game

The object of the game is as follows: the nurse is to be bold, have initiative, and be responsible for making significant recommendations, while at the same time she must appear passive. This must be done in such a manner so as to make her recommendations appear to be initiated by the physician.

Both participants must be acutely sensitive to each other's nonverbal and cryptic verbal communications. A slight lowering of the head, a minor shifting of position in the chair, or a seemingly nonrelevant comment concerning an event which occurred eight months ago must be interpreted as a powerful message. The game requires the nimbleness of a high wire acrobat, and if either participant slips, the game can be shattered; the penalties for frequent failure are apt to be severe.

Rules of the Game

The cardinal rule of the game is that open disagreement between the players must be avoided at all costs. Thus, the nurse must communicate her recommendations without appearing to be making a recommendation statement. The physician, in requesting a recommendation from a nurse, must do so without appearing to be asking for it. Utilization of this technique keeps anyone from committing themselves to a position before a sub-rosa agreement on that position has already been established. In that way open disagreement is avoided. The greater the significance of the recommendation, the more subtly the game must be played.

To convey a subtle example of the game with all its nuances would require the talents of a literary artist. Lacking these talents, let me give you the following example, which is unsubtle but happens frequently. The medical resident on hospital call is awakened by telephone at 1:00 A.M., because a patient on a ward, not his own, has not been able to fall asleep. Dr. Jones answers the telephone and the dialogue goes like this:

> This is Dr. Jones.
> (An open and direct communication.)
> Dr. Jones, this is Miss Smith on 2W—Mrs. Brown, who learned today of her father's death, is unable to fall asleep.
> (This message has two levels. Openly, it describes a set of circumstances: a woman who is unable to sleep and who that morning received word of her father's death. Less openly, but just as directly, it is a diagnostic and recommendation statement; i.e., Mrs. Brown is unable to sleep because of her grief, and she should be given a sedative. Dr. Jones, accepting the diagnostic statement and replying to the recommendation statement, answers.)
> What sleeping medication has been helpful to Mrs. Brown in the past?
> (Dr. Jones, not knowing the patient, is asking for a recommendation from the nurse, who does know the patient, about what sleeping medication should be prescribed. Note, however, his question does not appear to be asking her for a recommendation. Miss Smith replies.)
> Pentobarbital mg 100 was quite effective night before last.
> (A disguised recommendation statement. Dr. Jones replies with a note of authority in his voice.)
> Pentobarbital mg 100 before bedtime as needed for sleep; got it?
> (Miss Smith ends the conversation with the tone of a grateful supplicant.)
> Yes, I have, and thank you very much doctor.

The above is an example of a successfully played doctor-nurse game. The nurse made appropriate recommendations which were accepted by the physician and were helpful to the patient. The game was successful because the cardinal rule was not violated. The nurse was able to make her recommendation without appearing to, and the physician was able to ask for recommendations without conspicuously asking for them.

The Scoring System

Inherent in any game are penalties and rewards for the players. In game theory, the doctor-nurse game fits the non-zero-sum-game model. It is not like chess, where the players compete with each other and whatever one player loses the other wins. Rather, it is the kind of game in which the rewards and punishments are shared by both players. If they play the game successfully they both win rewards, and if they are unskilled and the game is played badly, they both suffer the penalty.

The most obvious reward from the well-played game is a doctor-nurse team that operates efficiently. The physician is able to utilize the nurse as a valuable consultant, and the nurse gains self-esteem and professional satisfaction from her job. The less obvious rewards are no less important. A successful game creates a doctor-nurse alliance; through this alliance the physician gains the respect and admiration of the nursing service. He can be confident that his nursing staff will smooth the path for getting his work done. His charts will be organized and waiting for him when he arrives, the ruffled feathers of patients and relatives will have been smoothed down, his pet routines will be happily followed, and he will be helped in a thousand and one other ways.

The doctor-nurse alliance sheds its light on the nurse as well. She gains a reputation for being a "damn good nurse." She is respected by everyone and appropriately enjoys her position. When physicians discuss the nursing staff it would not be unusual for her name to be mentioned with respect and admiration. Their esteem for a good nurse is no less than their esteem for a good doctor.

The penalties for a game failure, on the other hand, can be severe. The physician who is an unskilled gamesman and fails to recognize the nurses' subtle recommendation messages is tolerated as a "clod." If, however, he interprets these messages as insolence and strongly indicates he does not wish to tolerate suggestions from nurses, he creates a rocky path for his travels. The old truism "If the nurse is your ally you've got it made, and if she has it in for you, be prepared for misery" takes on life-sized proportions. He receives three times as many phone calls after midnight as his colleagues. Nurses will not accept his telephone orders, because "telephone orders are against the rules." Somehow, this rule gets suspended for the skilled players. Soon he becomes like Joe Bfstplk in the "Li'l Abner" comic strip. No matter where he goes, a black cloud constantly hovers over his head.

The unskilled gamesman-nurse also pays heavily. The nurse who does not view her role as that of consultant, and therefore does not attempt to communicate recommendations, is perceived as a dullard and is mercifully allowed to fade into the woodwork.

The nurse who does see herself as a consultant but refuses to follow the rules of the game in making her recommendations has hell to pay. The outspoken nurse is labeled a "bitch" by the surgeon. The psychiatrist describes her as unconsciously suffering from penis envy, and her behavior is the acting out of her hostility towards men. Loosely translated, the psychiatrist is saying she is a bitch. The employment of the unbright, outspoken nurse is soon terminated. The outspoken, bright nurse whose recommendations are worthwhile remains employed. She is, however, constantly reminded in a hundred ways that she is not loved.

Genesis of the Game

To understand how the game evolved, we must comprehend the nature of the doctors' and nurses' training which shaped the attitudes necessary for the game.

Medical Student Training

The medical student in his freshman year studies as if possessed. In the anatomy class he learns every groove and prominence on the bones of the skeleton as if life depended on it. As a matter of fact, he literally believes just that. He not infrequently says, "I've got to learn it exactly; a life may depend on me knowing that." A consequence of this attitude, which is carefully nurtured throughout medical school, is the development of a phobia: the overdetermined fear of making a mistake. The development of this fear is quite understandable. The burden the physician must carry is at times almost unbearable. He feels responsible in a very personal way for the lives of his patients. When a man dies leaving young children and a widow, the doctor carries some of her grief and despair inside himself; and when a child dies, some of him dies too. He sees himself as a warrior against death and disease. When he loses a battle, through no fault of his own, he nevertheless feels pangs of guilt, and he relentlessly searches himself to see if there might have been a way to alter the outcome. For the physician a mistake leading to a serious consequence is intolerable, and any mistake reminds him of his vulnerability. There is little wonder that he becomes phobic. The classical way in which phobias are managed is to avoid the source of the fear. Since it is impossible to avoid making some mistakes in an active practice of medicine, a substitute defensive maneuver is employed. The physician develops the belief that he is omnipotent and omniscient and therefore incapable of making mistakes. This belief allows the phobic physician to actively engage in his practice rather than avoid it. The fear of committing an error in a critical field like medicine is unavoidable and appropriately realistic. The physician, however, must learn to live with the fear rather than handle it defensively through a posture of omnipotence. This defense markedly interferes with his interpersonal professional relationships.

Physicians, of course, deny feelings of omnipotence. The evidence, however, renders their denials to whispers in the wind. The slightest mistake inflicts a large narcissistic wound. Depending on his underlying personality structure, the physician may be obsessed for days about it, quickly rationalize it away, or deny it. The guilt produced is unusually exaggerated, and the incident is handled defensively. The ways in which physicians enhance and support each other's defenses when an error is made could be the topic of another paper. The feeling of omnipotence becomes generalized to other areas of his life. A report of the Federal Aviation Agency (FAA), as quoted in *Time* (August 5, 1966), states that in 1964 and 1965, physicians had a fatal-accident rate four times as high as the average for all other private pilots. Major causes of the high death rate were risk-taking attitudes and judgments. Almost all of the accidents occurred on pleasure trips and were therefore not necessary risks to get to a patient needing emergency care. The trouble, suggested an FAA official, is that too many doctors fly with "the feeling that they are omnipotent." Thus, the extremes to which the physician may go in preserving his self-concept of omnipotence may threaten his own life. This overdetermined preservation of omnipotence is indicative of its brittleness and its underlying foundation of fear of failure.

The physician finds himself trapped in a paradox. He fervently wants to give his patient the best possible medical care, and being open to the nurses' recommendations helps him accomplish this. On the other hand, accepting advice from nonphysicians is highly threatening to his omnipotence. The solution for the paradox is to receive sub-rosa recommendations and make them appear to be initiated by himself. In short, he must learn to play the doctor-nurse game.

Some physicians never learn to play the game. Most learn in their internship, and a perceptive few learn during their clerkships in medical school. Medical students frequently complain that the nursing staff treats them as if they had just completed a junior Red Cross first-aid class instead of two years of intensive medical training. Interviewing nurses in a training hospital sheds considerable light on this phenomenon. In their words they said:

> A few students just seem to be with it, they are able to understand what you are trying to tell them and they are a pleasure to work with; most, however, pretend to know everything and refuse to listen to anything we have to say and I guess we do give them a rough time.

In essence, they are saying that those students who quickly learn the game are rewarded, and those that do not are punished.

Most physicians learn to play the game after they have weathered a few experiences like the one described below. On the first day of his internship, the physician and nurse were making rounds. They stopped at the bed of a fifty-two-year-old woman who, after complimenting the young doctor on his appearance, complained to him of her problem with constipation. After several minutes of listening to her detailed description of peculiar diets, family home remedies, and special exercises that have helped her constipation in the past, the nurse politely interrupted the patient. She told her the doctor would take care of the problem and that he had to move on because there were other patients waiting to see him. The young doctor gave the nurse a stern look, turned toward the patient, and kindly told her he would order an enema for her that very afternoon. As they left the bedside, the nurse told him the patient has had a normal bowel movement every day for the past week and that in the twenty-three days the patient has been in the hospital she has never once passed up an opportunity to complain of her constipation. She quickly added that *if* the doctor wanted to order an enema, the patient would certainly receive one. After hearing this report the intern's mouth fell open, and the wheels began turning in his head. He remembered the nurse's comment to the patient that "the doctor had to move on," and it occurred to him that perhaps she was really giving him a message. This experience and a few more like it, and the young doctor learns to listen for the subtle recommendations the nurses make.

Nursing Student Training

Unlike the medical student who usually learns to play the game after he finishes medical school, the nursing student begins to learn it early in her training. Throughout her education she is trained to play the doctor-nurse game.

Student nurses are taught how to relate to physicians. They are told he has infinitely more knowledge than they, and thus he should be shown the utmost respect. In addition, it was not many years ago when nurses were instructed to stand whenever a physician entered a room. When he would come in for a conference, the nurse was expected to offer him her chair, and when both entered a room the nurse would open the door for him and allow him to enter first. Although these practices are no longer rigidly adhered to, the premise upon which they were based is still promulgated. One nurse described that premise as, "He's God almighty and your job is to wait on him."

To inculcate subservience and inhibit deviancy, nursing schools, for the most part, are tightly run, disciplined institutions. Certainly, there is great variation among nursing schools, and there is little question that the trend is toward giving students more autonomy. However, in too many schools this trend has not gone far enough, and the climate remains restrictive. The student's schedule is firmly controlled, and there is very little free time. Classroom hours, study hours, mealtime, and bedtime with lights out are rigidly enforced. In some schools meaningless chores are assigned, such as cleaning bedsprings with cotton applicators. The relationship between student and instructor continues this military flavor. Often their relationship is more like that between recruit and drill sergeant than between student and teacher. Open dialogue is inhibited by attitudes of strict black and white with few, if any, shades of gray. Straying from the rigidly outlined path is sure to result in disciplinary action.

The inevitable result of these practices is to instill in the student nurse a fear of independent action. This inhibition of independent action is most marked when relating to physicians. One of the students' greatest fears is making a blunder while assisting a physician and being publicly ridiculed by him. This is really more a reflection of the nature of their training than the prevalence of abusive physicians. The fear of being humiliated for a blunder while assisting in a procedure is generalized to the fear of humiliation for making any independent act in relating to a physician, especially the act of making a direct recommendation. Every nurse interviewed felt that making a suggestion to a physician was equivalent to insulting and belittling him. It was tantamount to questioning his medical knowledge and insinuating he did not know his business. In light of her image of the physician as an omniscient and punitive figure, the questioning of his knowledge would be unthinkable.

The student, however, is also given messages quite contrary to the ones described above. She is continually told that she is an invaluable aid to the physician in the treatment of the patient. She is told that she must help him in every way possible and that she is imbued with a strong sense of responsibility for the care of her patient. Thus she, like the physician, is caught in a paradox. The first set of messages implies that the physician is omniscient and that any recommendation she might make would be insulting to him and leave her open to ridicule. The second set of messages implies that she is an important asset to him, has much to contribute, and is duty-bound to make those contributions. Thus, when her good sense tells her a recommendation would be helpful to him, she is not allowed to communicate it directly, nor is she allowed not to communicate it. The way out of the bind is to use the doctor-nurse game and communicate the recommendation without appearing to do so.

Forces Preserving the Game

Upon observing the indirect interactional system which is the heart of the doctor-nurse game, one must ask the question, "Why does this inefficient mode of communication continue to exist?" The forces mitigating against change are powerful.

Rewards and Punishments

The doctor-nurse game has a powerful, innate self-perpetuating force—its system of rewards and punishments. One potent method of shaping behavior is to reward one set of behavioral patterns and to punish patterns which deviate from it. As described earlier, the rewards given for a well-played game and the punishments meted out to unskilled players are impressive. This system alone would be sufficient to keep the game flourishing. The game, however, has additional forces.

The Strength of the Set

It is well recognized that sets are hard to break. A powerful attitudinal set is the nurse's perception that making a suggestion to a physician is equivalent to insulting and belittling him. An example of where attempts are regularly made to break this set is seen on psychiatric treatment wards, operating on a therapeutic community model. This model requires open and direct communication between members of the team. Psychiatrists working in these settings expend a great deal of energy in urging for and rewarding openness before direct patterns of communication become established. The rigidity of the resistance to break this set is impressive. If the physician himself is a prisoner of a set and therefore does not actively try to destroy it, change is near impossible.

The Need for Leadership

Lack of leadership and structure in any organization produces anxiety in its members. As the importance of the organization's mission increases, the demand by its members for leadership commensurately increases. In our culture human life is near the top of our hierarchy of values, and organizations which deal with human lives, such as law and medicine, are very rigidly structured. Certainly, some of this is necessary for the systematic management of the task. The excessive degree of rigidity, however, is demanded by its members for their own psychic comfort rather than for its utility in efficiently carrying out its mission. The game lends support to this thesis. Indirect communication is an inefficient mode of transmitting information. However, it effectively supports and protects a rigid organizational structure with the physician in clear authority. Maintaining an omnipotent leader provides the other members with a great sense of security.

Sexual Roles

Another influence perpetuating the doctor-nurse game is the sexual identity of the players. Doctors are predominately men, and nurses are almost exclusively women. There are elements of the game which reinforce the stereotyped roles of male dominance and female passivity Some nursing instructors explicitly tell their students that their femininity is an important asset to be used when relating to physicians.

The Community

The doctor and nurse have a shared history and thus have been able to work out their game so that it operates more efficiently than one would expect in an indirect system. Major difficulty arises, however, when the physician works closely with other disciplines which are not normally considered part of the medical sphere. With expanding medical horizons encompassing cooperation with sociologists, engineers, anthropologists, computer analysts, etc., continued expectation of a doctor-nurselike interaction by the physician is disastrous. The sociologist, for example, is not willing to play that kind of game. When his direct communications are rebuffed, the relationship breaks down.

    The major disadvantage of a doctor-nurselike game is its inhibitory effect on open dialogue which is stifling and anti-intellectual. The game is basically a transactional neurosis, and both professions would enhance themselves by taking steps to change the attitudes which breed the game. . . .

PART SIX
The Family

Institutions are standardized and taken for granted. They are composed of mutual expectations, action patterns, and ways to interpret meaning and actions that are presumed to be widely and evenly distributed over the society. We do not have to invent an institution to cope with every problem of our social existence. We inherit standard procedures, orderly and regular "normal forms" of action and thought.

Without doubt, the family is one of the most important of these normal forms. In the family the social world is first introduced to the new, potential member of society. The family plays a strong role in the socialization of the child, and in many ways, the forms, trends, and tendencies of the family's way of doing things reflect the basic values of the society.

Our ideas about basic, or first, things, such as attitudes toward our bodies toward sex, toward the possession of the valued material things of the society, in short, the very organization of our everyday lives, are often profoundly influenced by the family. This influence may be reflected in areas not ordinarily thought of as familylike in nature. What we learn as the "institutional" way may become a part of the way we generally construct our social worlds and interpret those of others.

Describing the family as an institution is like telling in detail the standard features of the setting in which the first act of the drama of life will be played out. Seeing how the players relate to one another, knowing the assumptions of their background knowledge, which both impose limits and define plausible courses of action, can aid us in our journey through the American society. Our focus is on the typical, even if we find it in the most atypical of places.

The first selection in this section portrays the family as a dramatic happening, introducing us to the actors and their roles to illustrate the structure of the American family. Understanding how spouses are selected tells us more than how people decide upon marriage partners. It reveals the values and status arrangements for the society in general. The final two articles illustrate the subtle effects of the family on nonfamily life. The first describes how total institutional confinement assumes familylike characteristics and the second, how modern singles live in groups that fulfill some of the needs met by more traditional family structures.

19
Society as Drama

Sometimes the use of analogy can reveal overlooked features of a social phenomenon. By thinking about family life as if it were a drama, we can see interrelationships among the players, expectations that the players have for each other, and the character of the roles they play. There are principal actors and supporting actors. There is a script for the behavior of each participant. Each player has a front-stage appearance. Annabella Motz describes the family as drama. She develops insights into the "staged" nature of family life and points to some consequences of typecasting and negative reviews of performances.

The Family as a Company of Players
Annabella B. Motz

All the world's a stage, and we are all players.

Erving Goffman in his *The Presentation of Self in Everyday Life* views our everyday world as having both front stage and back. Like professionals, we try to give a careful and superior performance out front. Backstage we unzip, take off our masks, complain of the strain, think back over the last act, and prepare anxiously for the next.

Sometimes the "onstage" performances are solos; sometimes we act in teams or groups. The roles maybe carefully planned, rehearsed, and executed or they may be spontaneous or improvised. The presentation can be a hit or it can flop badly.

From *Transaction* 2 (March-April 1965): 27–30. Reprinted with permission.

Picture a theater starring the family. The "stars" are the husband, wife, and children. But the cast includes a wide range of persons in the community—fellow workers, friends, neighbors, deliverymen, shopkeepers, doctors, and everyone who passes by. Usually, husband and wife are the leads, and the appeal, impact, and significance of their performances vary with the amount of time on stage, and times of day and week, the circumstances of each presentation, and the moods of the audience.

Backstage for the family members is generally to be found in their homes, as suggested by the expression "a man's home is his castle." The front stage is where they act out their dramatic parts in schools, stores, places of employment, on the street, in the homes of other persons, or as when entertaining guests, back in their own homes.

My aim is to analyze the performances of family members before the community audience—their *front stage* appearances. The behavior conforms to the rules and regulations that society places upon its members; perhaps the analysis of the family life drama will provide insights into the bases of the problems for which an increasing number of middle-class persons are seeking professional help.

Many years ago, Thorstein Veblen noted that although industrialization made it possible for the American worker to live better than at any previous time in history, it made him feel so insignificant that he sought ways to call attention to himself. In *The Theory of the Leisure Class,* Veblen showed that all strata of society practiced "conspicuous consumption"—the ability to use one's income for nonessential goods and services in ways readily visible to others. A man's abilities were equated with his monetary worth and the obvious command he had in the marketplace to purchase commodities beyond bare necessities. Thus, a family that lives more comfortably than most must be a "success."

While conspicuous consumption was becoming an essential element of front-stage performance, the ideal of the American as a completely rational person—governed and governing by reason rather than emotion—was being projected around the world. The writings of the first four decades of this century stress over and over again the importance of the individual and individual opinion. (The growth of unionism, the Social Security program, public opinion polling, and federal aid to education are few examples of the trend toward positive valuation of each human being—not to mention the impact of Freud and Dewey and their stress on individual worth.) The desirability of rule by majority and democratic debate and voting as the best means of reaching group decisions—all these glorified rationality.

As population, cities, and industry grew, so also did anonymity and complexity, and rationality in organizations (more propely known as bureaucratization) had to keep pace. The individual was exposed to more and more people he knew less and less. The face-to-face relationships of small towns and workshops declined. Job requirements, duties and loyalties, hiring and firing, had to "go by the book." Max Weber has described the bureaucratic organization: each job is explicitly defined, the rights of entry and exit from the organization can be found in the industry's manual, and the rights and duties of the worker and of the organization toward the worker are rationally defined; above all, the worker acts as a rational being on the job—he is never subject to emotional urges.

With the beams and bricks of "front" and rationality the middle-class theater is built; with matching props the stage is set.

There are two basic scenes. One revolves about family and close personal relationships. It takes place in a well-furnished house—very comfortable, very stylish, but not "vulgar." The actors are calm, controlled, reasonable.

The other scene typically takes place in a bureaucratic anteroom cluttered with physical props and with people treated like physical props. The actors do not want the audience to believe that they *are* props—so they attract attention to themselves and dramatize their individuality and worth by spending and buying far more than they need.

What does this mean in the daily life of the family stars?

Take first the leading lady, wife, and mother. She follows Veblen and dramatizes her husband's success by impressing any chance onlookers with her efficient house management. How does one run a house efficiently? All must be reasoned order. The wife-housekeeper plans what has to be done and does it simply and quickly. Kitchen, closets, and laundry display department store wares as attractively as the stores themselves. The house is always presentable, and so is she. Despite her obviously great labors, she does not seem to get flustered, overfatigued, or too emotional. (What would her neighbors or even a passing door-to-door salesman think if they heard her screaming at the children?) With minimal household help she must appear the gracious hostess, fresh and serene—behind her a dirty kitchen magically cleaned, a meal effortlessly prepared, and husband and children well behaved and helpful.

Outside the home, too, she is composed and rational. She does not show resentment toward Johnny's teacher, who may irritate her or give Johnny poor marks. She does not yawn during interminable and dull PTA programs (what would they think of her and her family?). At citizen meetings she is the embodiment of civic-minded, responsible, property-ownership (even if the mortgage company actually owns the property). Her supermarket cart reflects her taste, affluence, efficiency, and concern. At church she exhibits no unchurchly feelings. She prays that her actions and facial expression will not give away the fact that her mind has wandered from the sermon; she hopes that as she greets people, whether interested in them or not, she will be able to say the "right" thing. Her clothes and car are extremely important props—the right make, style, finish; and they project her front-stage character, giving the kind of impression she thinks she and the other members of the family want her to give.

Enter Father Center Stage

The male lead is husband, father, and mån-of-affairs. He acts in ways that, he hopes, will help his status and that of his family. At all times he must seem to be in relaxed control of difficult situations. This often takes some doing. For instance, he must be both unequal and equal to associates; that is, he is of course a good fellow and very democratic, but the way he greets and handles his superiors at work is distinctly, if subtly, different from the way he speaks to and handles inferiors. A superior who arrives unexpectedly must find him dynamically at work, worth every cent and more of his income; an inferior must also find him busy, demonstratng how worthy he is of superior status and respect. He must always be in control. Even when supposedly relaxing, swapping dirty jokes with his colleagues, he must be careful to avoid any that offend their biases. He has to get along; bigots, too, may be able to do him good or harm.

Sometimes he cannot give his real feelings release until he gets behind the wheel—and the savage jockeying which takes place during the evening rush may reflect this simultaneous discharge by many drivers.

The scene shifts back to the home. The other stars greet him—enter loving wife and children. He may not yet be ready or able to reestablish complete emotional control—after all, a man's home is his backstage—and the interplay of the subplots begins. If his wife goes on with her role, she will be the dutiful spouse, listening sympathetically, keeping the children and her temper quiet. If she should want to cut loose at the same time, collision will probably still be avoided because both have been trained to restrain themselves and present the right front as parents to their children—if not to each other.

Leisure is not rest. At home father acts out his community role of responsible family head. The backyard is kept up as a "private" garden, the garage as a showroom for tools on display. He must exhibit interest—but not too much enthusiasm—in a number of activities, some ostensibly recreational, retaining a nice balance between appearing a dutiful husband and a henpecked one. Reason must rule emotion.

The children of old vaudevillians literally were born and reared in the theater—were nursed between acts by mothers in spangles, trained as toddlers to respond to footlights as other children might to sunlight. The young in the middle-class family drama also learn to recognize cues and to perform.

Since "front" determines the direction and content of the drama, they are supposed to be little ladies and gentlemen. Proper performances from such tyros require much backstage rehearsal. Unfortunately, the middle-class backstage is progressively disappearing, and so the children, too, must be prepared to respond appropriately to the unexpected—whether an unwanted salesman at the door who must be discreetly lied to about mother's whereabouts or a wanted friend who must not be offended. They are taught rationality and democracy in family councils—where they are also taught what behavior is expected of them. Reason is rife; even when they get out of hand, the parents "reason" with them. As Dorothy Barclay says when discussing household chores and the child, "Appealing to a sense of family loyalty and pride in maturity is the tack most parents take first in trying to overcome youngsters' objections (to household chores). Offering rewards comes second, arguing and insisting third."

"Grown-up" and "good" children do family chores. They want the house to look "nice"; they don't tell family secrets when visitors are present, and even rush to close closet and bedroom doors when the doorbell rings unexpectedly.

The child, of course, carries the family play into school, describing it in "show-and-tell" performances and in his deportment and dress. Part of the role of responsible parenthood includes participation in PTA and teacher conferences, with the child an important player, even if offstage.

To the child, in fact, much of the main dynamic of the play takes place in the dim realm of offstage (not always the same as backstage)—his parents' sex activities, their real income and financial problems, and many other things, some of them strange and frightening, that "children are not old enough to understand."

They early learn the fundamental lesson of front stage: be prepared; know your lines. Who knows whether the neighbors' windows are open! The parent who answers a crying child with, "Calm down now, let's sit down and talk this over," is rehearsing him in stage presence, and in his character as middle-class child and eventually middle-class adult.

Often the family acts as a team. The act may be rehearsed, but it must appear spontaneous. Watch them file in and out of church on

Sunday mornings. Even after more than an hour of sitting, the children seem fresh and starched. They do not laugh or shout as on the playground. The parents seem calm, in complete control. Conversations and postures are confined to those appropriate for a place of worship.

Audience reaction is essential to a play. At church others may say, "What nice children you have!" or "We look forward to seeing you next Sunday." Taken at face value, these are sounds of audience approval and applause; the performers may bask in them. Silence or equivocal remarks may imply disapproval and cause anxiety. What did they really mean? What did we do wrong? Sometimes reaction is delayed, and the family will be uncertain of their impression. In any case, future performances will be affected.

Acting a role, keeping up a front, letting the impressions and expectations of other people influence our behavior does result in a great deal of good. Organized society is possible only when there is some conformity to roles and rules. Also, a person concerned with the impression others have of him feels that he is significant to them and they to him. When he polishes his car because a dirty one would embarrass him, when his wife straightens her makeup before answering the door, both exhibit a sense of their importance and personal dignity in human affairs. Those who must, or want to, serve as models or exemplars must be especially careful of speech and performance—they are always onstage. When people keep up appearances, they are identifying themselves with a group and its standards. They need it; presumably, it needs them.

Moreover, acting what seems a narrow role may actually broaden experience and open doors. To tend a lawn, or join a PTA, social club, or art group—"to keep up appearances"—may result in real knowledge and understanding about horticulture, education, or civic responsibility.

For the community, front produces the positive assets of social cohesion. Well-kept lawns, homes, cars, clean children and adults have definite aesthetic, financial, and sanitary value. People relate to one another, develop common experiences. People who faithfully play their parts exhibit personal and civic responsibility. The rules make life predictable and safe, confine ad-libs within acceptable limits, control violence and emotional tangents, and allow the show to go on and the day's work to be done. Thus, the challenging game of maintaining front relates unique personalities to one another and unites them in activity and into a nation.

So much for the good which preoccupation with front and staging accomplishes; what of the bad?

First, the inhibition of the free play of emotion must lead to frustration. Human energies need outlets. If onstage acting does not allow for release of tension, then the escape should take place backstage. But what if there is virtually no backstage? Perhaps then the releases will be found in the case histories of psychiatrists and other counselors. Communication between husband and wife may break down because of the contrast between the onstage image each has of the other as a perfect mate and the unmasked actuality backstage. Perhaps when masks crumble and crack, when people can no longer stand the strain of the front, then what we call nervous breakdown occurs.

Growing Up with Bad Reviews

And how does the preoccupation with front affect the growth and development of the child? How can a child absorb and pattern himself after models which are essentially unreal? A mother may "control" her emotions when a child spills milk on her freshly scrubbed floor and "reason" with him about it, she may still retain control when he leaves the refrigerator open after repeated warnings, but then some minor thing such as loud laughter over the funnies may suddenly blow off the lid, and she will "let him have it, but good!" What can he learn from such treatment? To respect his mother's hard work at keeping the house clean? To close the refrigerator door? Not to laugh loudly when reading the comics? That mother is a crab? Or, she's always got it in for him? Whatever he has learned, it is doubtful it was what his mother wanted! Whatever it was it will probably not clarify his understanding of such family values as pride in work, reward for effort, consideration of other people, or how to meet problems. Too, since the family's status is vitally linked with the maintenance of fronts, any deviance by the child, unless promptly rectified, threatens family standing in the community. This places a tremendous burden on a child actor.

Moreover, a concentration on front rather than content must result in a leveling and deadening of values and feelings. If a man buys a particular hat primarily because of what others may think, then its intrinsic value as a hat—in fact, even his own judgment and feelings about it—become secondary. Whether the judgment of those whose approval he covets is good or bad is unimportant—just so they approve. Applause has taken the place of value.

A PTA lecture on "The Future of America" will call for the same attentive front from him as a scientist's speech on the "Effects of Nuclear Warfare on Human Survival." Reading a newspaper on a crowded bus, his expression undergoes little change whether he is reading about nuclear tests, advice to the lovelorn, or Elizabeth Taylor's marital problems. To his employer he presents essentially the same bland nonargumentative, courteous front whether he has just been refused a much-deserved pay raise or told to estimate the cost of light bulbs. He seems impartial, objective, rational—and by so doing he also seems to deny that there is any difference to him between the pay raise and the light bulbs, as well as to deny his feelings.

The Price of Admission

What price does the community pay for its role as audience?

The individual human talents and energies are alienated from assuming responsibility for the well-being and survival of the group. The exaggerated self-consciousness of individuals results in diluted and superficial concern with the community at a time when deep involvement, new visions, and real leadership are needed. Can the world afford to have overzealous actors who work so hard on their lines that they forget what the play is all about?

It is probable that this picture will become more general in the near future and involve more and more people—assuming that the aging of the population continues, that the cold war doesn't become hot and continues to need constant checks on loyalty and patriotism, that automation increases man's leisure at the same time as it keeps up or increases the production of consumer goods, and that improved advertising techniques make every home a miniature department store. The resulting conformity, loyalty, and patriotism may foster social solidarity. It may also cause alienation, immaturity, confusion, and much insecurity when new situations, for which old fronts are no longer appropriate, suddenly occur. Unless people start today to separate the important from the tinsel and to assume responsibility for community matters that are vital, individual actors will feel even more isolated and the society may drift ever further from the philosophy that values every person.

Tomorrow's communities will need to provide new backstages, as the home, work place, and recreation center become more and more visible. Psychiatrists, counselors, confessors, and other professional listeners must provide outlets for actors who are exhausted and want to share their backstage thoughts. With increased leisure, businessmen will probably find it profitable to provide backstage settings in the form of resorts, rest homes, or retreats.

The state of the world is such today that unless the family and the community work together to evaluate and value the significant and direct their energies accordingly, the theater with its actors, front stage, backstage, and audience may end in farce and tragedy.

20

Selecting Spouses

The institution of the family is interrelated with other aspects of society, such as the class structure. We can see the precise nature of this relationship by examining the rules that govern the selection of potential mates. In this article John Scott focuses on the college sorority, its effect on marriage-partner selection, and the effect of these selections on the existing class structure. In this work we can see how threads in the fabric of society often overlap and perform the same function.

Sororities and the Husband Game
John Finley Scott

> Marriages, like births, deaths, or initiations at puberty, are rearrangements of structure that are constantly recurring in any society; they are moments of the continuing social process regulated by custom; there are institutionalized ways of dealing with such events.—A. R. Radcliffe-Brown, *African Systems of Kinship and Marriage.*

In many simple societies, the "institutionalized ways" of controlling marriage run to diverse schemes and devices. Often they include special living quarters designed to make it easy for marriageable girls to attract a husband: the Bontok people of the Philippines keep their girls in a special house, called the *olag,* where lovers call, sex play is free, and marriage is supposed to result. The Ekoi of Nigeria, who like their women

From *Transaction* (September–October 1965). Reprinted by permission.

fat, send them away to be specially fattened for marriage. Other peoples, such as the Yao of central Africa and the aborigines of the Canary Islands, send their daughters away to "convents" where old women teach them the special skills and mysteries that a young wife needs to know.

Accounts of such practices have long been a standard topic of anthropology lectures in universities, for their exotic appeal keeps the students, large numbers of whom are sorority girls, interested and alert. The control of marriage in simple societies strikes these girls as quite different from the freedom that they believe prevails in America. This is ironic, for the American college sorority is a pretty good counterpart in complex societies of the fatting houses and convents of the primitives.

Whatever system they use, parents in all societies have more in mind than just getting their daughters married; they want them married to the *right* man. The criteria for defining the right man vary tremendously, but virtually all parents view some potential mates with approval, some with disapproval, and some with downright horror. Many ethnic groups, including many in America, are *endogamous*, that is, they desire marriage of their young only to those within the group. In *shtetl* society, the Jewish villages of eastern Europe, marriages were arranged by a *shatchen*, a matchmaker, who paired off the girls and boys with due regard to the status, family connections, wealth, and personal attractions of the participants. But this society was strictly endogamous—only marriage within the group was allowed. Another rule of endogamy relates to social rank or class, for most parents are anxious that their children marry at least at the same level as themselves. Often they hope the children, and especially the daughters, will marry at a higher level. Parents of the *shtetl*, for example, valued *hypergamy*—the marriage of daughters to a man of higher status—and a father who could afford it would offer substantial sums to acquire a scholarly husband (the most highly prized kind) for his daughter.

The marriage problem, from the point of view of parents and of various ethnic groups and social classes, is always one of making sure that girls are available for marriage with the right man while at the same time guarding against marriage with the wrong man.

The University Convent

The American middle class has a particular place where it sends its daughters so they will be easily accessible to the boys—the college campus. Even for the families who worry about the bad habits a nice girl can pick up at college, it has become so much a symbol of middle-class status that the risk must be taken; the girl must be sent. American middle-class society has created an institution on the campus that, like the fatting house, makes the girls more attractive; like the Canary Island convent, teaches skills that middle-class wives need to know; like the *shtetl*, provides matchmakers; and without going so far as to buy husbands of high rank, manages to dissuade the girl from making alliances with lower-class boys. That institution is the college sorority.

A sorority is a private association which provides separate dormitory facilities with a distinctive Greek-letter name for selected female college students. Membership is by invitation only and requires recommendation by former members. Sororities are not simply the feminine counterparts of college fraternities. They differ from fraternities because marriage is a more important determinant of social position for women than for men in American society and because standards of conduct associated with marriage correspondingly bear stronger sanctions for women than for men. Sororities have much more "alumnae" involvement than fraternities, and fraternities adapt to local conditions and different living arrangements better than sororities. The college-age sorority "actives" decide only the minor details involved in recruitment, membership, and activities; parent-age alumnae control the important choices. The prototypical sorority is not the servant of youthful interests; on the contrary, it is an organized agency for controlling those interests. Through the sorority, the elders of family, class, ethnic, and religious communities can continue to exert remote control over the marital arrangements of their young girls.

The need for remote control arises from the nature of the educational system in an industrial society. In simple societies, where children are taught the culture at home, the family controls the socialization of children almost completely. In more complex societies, education becomes the province of special agents and competes with the family. The conflict between the family and outside agencies increases as children move through the educational system and is sharpest when the children reach college age. College curricula are even more challenging to family value systems than high-school courses, and children frequently go away to college, out of reach of direct family influence. Sometimes a family can find a college that does not challenge family values in any way: devout Catholic parents can send their daughters to Catholic colleges; parents who want to be sure that daughter meets only "Ivy League" men can send her to one of the "Seven Sisters"—the women's equivalent of the Ivy League, made up of Radcliffe, Barnard, Smith, Vassar, Wellesley, Mt. Holyoke, and Bryn Mawr—if she can get in.

The solution of controlled admissions is applicable only to a small proportion of college-age girls, however. There are nowhere near the number of separate, sectarian colleges in the country that would be needed to segregate all the college-age girls safely, each with her own kind. Private colleges catering mostly to a specific class can still preserve a girl from meeting her social or economic inferiors, but the fees at such places are steep. It costs more to maintain a girl in the Vassar dormitories than to pay her sorority bills at a land-grant school. And even if her family is willing to pay the fees, the academic pace at the elite schools is much too fast for most girls. Most college girls attend large, tax-supported universities where the tuition is relatively low and where admissions policies let in students from many strata and diverse ethnic backgrounds. It is on the campuses of the free, open, and competitive state universities of the country that the sorority system flourishes.

When a family lets its daughter loose on a large campus with a heterogenous population, there are opportunities to be met and dangers to guard against. The great opportunity is to meet a good man to marry, at the age when the girls are most attractive and the men most amenable. For the girls, the pressure of time is urgent; though they are often told otherwise, their attractions are in fact primarily physical, and they fade with time. One need only compare the relative handicaps in the marital sweepstakes of a thirty-eight-year-old single male lawyer and a single female teacher of the same age to realize the urgency of the quest.

The great danger of the public campus is that young girls, however properly reared, are likely to fall in love, and—in our middle-class society at least—love leads to marriage. Love is a potentially random factor, with no regard for class boundaries. There seems to be no good way of preventing young girls from falling in love. The only practical way to control love is to control the type of men the girl is likely to encounter; she cannot fall dangerously in love with a man she has never met. Since kinship groups are unable to keep "undesirable" boys off the public campus entirely, they have to settle for control of counter-institutions within the university. An effective counter-institution will protect a girl from the corroding influences of the university environment.

There are roughly three basic functions which a sorority can perform in the interest of kinship groups:

It can ward off the wrong kind of men.
It can facilitate moving-up for middle-status girls.
It can solve the "Brahmin problem"—the difficulty of proper marriage that afflicts high-status girls.

Kinship groups define the "wrong kind of man" in a variety of ways. Those who use an ethnic definition support sororities that draw an ethnic membership line; the best examples are the Jewish sororities, because among all the ethnic groups with endogamous standards (in America at any rate), only the Jews so far have sent large numbers of daughters away to college. But endogamy along class lines is even more pervasive. It is the most basic mission of the sorority to prevent a girl from marrying out of her group (exogamy) or beneath her class (hypogamy). As one of the founders of a national sorority artlessly put it in an essay titled "The Mission of the Sorority":

> There is a danger, and a very grave danger, that four years' residence in a dormitory will tend to destroy right ideals of home life and substitute in their stead a belief in the freedom that comes from community living . . . culture, broad, liberalizing, humanizing culture, we cannot get too much of, unless while acquiring it we are weaned from home and friends, from ties of blood and kindred.

A sorority discourages this dangerous weaning process by introducing the sisters only to selected boys; each sorority, for example, has dating relations with one or more fraternities, matched rather nicely to the sorority on the basis of ethnicity and/or class. (A particular sorority, for example, will have dating arrangements not with all the fraternities on campus but only with those whose brothers are a class-match for their sisters.) The sorority's frantically busy schedule of parties, teas, meetings, skits, and exchanges keep the sisters so occupied that they have neither time nor opportunity to meet men outside the channels the sorority provides.

Marrying Up

The second sorority function, that of facilitating hypergamy, is probably even more of an attraction to parents than the simpler preservation of endogamy. American society is not so much oriented to the preservation of the status quo as to the pursuit of upward mobility.

In industrial societies children are taught that if they study hard they can get the kind of job that entitles them to a place in the higher ranks. This incentive actually is appropriate only for boys, but the emphasis on using the most efficient available means to enter the higher levels will not be lost on the girls. And the most efficient means for a girl—marriage—is particularly attractive because it requires so much less effort than the mobility through hard work that is open to boys. To the extent that we do socialize the sexes in different ways, we are more likely to train daughters in the ways of attracting men than to motivate them to do hard, competitive work. The difference in motivation holds even if the girls have the intelligence and talent required for status climbing on their own. For lower-class girls on the make, membership in a sorority can greatly improve the chances of meeting (and subsequently marrying) higher-status boys.

Now we come to the third function of the sorority—solving the Brahmin problem. The fact that hypergamy is encouraged in our society creates difficulties for girls whose parents are already in the upper strata. In a hypergamous system, high-status *men* have a strong advantage; they can offer their status to a prospective bride as part of the marriage bargain, and the advantages of high status are often sufficient to offset many personal drawbacks. But a *woman's* high status has very little exchange value because she does not confer it on her husband.

This difficulty of high status women in a hypergamous society we may call the Brahmin problem. Girls of Brahmin caste in India and southern white women of good family have the problem in common. In order to avoid the horrors of hypogamy, high-status women must compete for high-status men against women from all classes. Furthermore, high-status women are handicapped in their battle by a certain type of vanity engendered by their class. They expect their wooers to court them in the style to which their fathers have accustomed them; this usually involves more formal dating, gift-giving, escorting, taxiing, etc., than many college swains can afford. If upper-stratum men are allowed to find out that the favors of lower-class women are available for a much smaller investment of time, money, and emotion, they may well refuse to court upper-status girls.

In theory, there are all kinds of ways for upper-stratum families to deal with surplus daughters. They can strangle them at birth (female infanticide); they can marry several to each available male (polygyny); they can offer money to any suitable male willing to take one off their hands (dowries, groom-service fees). All these solutions have in fact been used in one society or another, but for various reasons none is acceptable in our society. Spinsterhood still works, but marriage is so popular and so well-rewarded that everybody hopes to avoid staying single.

The industrial solution to the Brahmin problem is to corner the market or, more specifically, to shunt the eligible bachelors into a special marriage-market where the upper-stratum women are in complete control of the bride-supply. The best place to set up this protected marriage-market is where many suitable men can be found at the age when they are most willing to marry—in short, the college campus. The kind of male collegians who can be shunted more readily into the specialized marriage-market that sororities run are those who are somewhat uncertain of their own status and who aspire to move into higher strata. These boys are anxious to bolster a shaky self-image by dating obviously high-class sorority girls. The fraternities are full of them.

How does a sorority go about fulfilling its three functions? The first item of business is making sure that the girls join. This is not as simple as it seems, because the values that sororities maintain are more important to the older generation than to the college-age girls. Although the sorority image is one of membership denied to the "wrong kind" of girls, it is also true that sororities have quite a problem recruiting the "right kind." Some are pressured into pledging by their parents. Many are recruited straight out of high school, before they know much about what really goes on at college. High-school recruiters present sorority life to potential rushees as one of unending gaiety; life outside the sorority is painted as bleak and dateless.

A membership composed of the "right kind" of girls is produced by the requirement that each pledge must have the recommendation of, in most cases, two or more alumnae of the sorority. Membership is often passed on from mother to daughter—this is the "legacy," whom sorority actives have to invite whether they like her or not. The sort of head-strong, innovative, or "sassy" girl who is likely to organize a campaign inside the sorority against prevailing standards is unlikely to receive alumnae recommendations. This is why sorority girls are so complacent about alumnae dominance, and why professors find them so bland and uninteresting as students. Alumnae dominance extends beyond recruitment, into the daily life of the house. Rules, regulations, and policy explanations come to the house from the national association. National headquarters is given to explaining unpopular policy by an available stratagem; a favorite device (not limited to the sorority) is to interpret all nonconformity as sexual, so that the girl who rebels against wearing girdle, high heels, and stockings to dinner two or three times a week stands implicitly accused of promiscuity. This sort of argument, based on the shrewdness of many generations, shames into conformity many a girl who otherwise might rebel against the code imposed by her elders. The actives in positions of control (house manager, pledge trainer, or captain) are themselves closely supervised by alumnae. Once the right girls are initiated, the organization has mechanisms that make it very difficult for a girl to withdraw. Withdrawal can mean difficulty in finding alternative living quarters, loss of prepaid room and board fees, and stigmatization.

Sororities keep their members, and particularly their flighty pledges, in line primarily by filling up all their time with house activities. Pledges are required to study at the house, and they build the big papier-mâché floats (in collaboration with selected fraternity boys) that are a traditional display of "Greek Row" for the homecoming game. Time is encompassed completely; activities are planned long in advance, and there is almost no energy or time available for meeting inappropriate men.

The girls are taught—if they do not already know—the behavior appropriate to the upper strata. They learn how to dress with expensive restraint, how to make appropriate conversation, how to drink like a lady. There is some variety here among sororities of different rank; members of sororities at the bottom of the social ladder prove their gentility by rigid conformity in dress and manner to the stereotype of the sorority girl, while members of top houses feel socially secure even when casually dressed. If you are born rich, you can afford to wear Levi's and sweatshirts.

Preliminary Events

The sorority facilitates dating mainly by exchanging parties, picnics, and other frolics with the fraternities in its set. But to augment this the "fixer-uppers" (the American counterpart of the *shatchen*) arrange dates with selected boys; their efforts raise the sorority dating rate above the independent level by removing most of the inconvenience and anxiety from the contracting of dates.

Dating, in itself, is not sufficient to accomplish the sorority's purposes. Dating must lead to pinning, pinning to engagement, engagement to marriage. In sorority culture, all dating is viewed as a movement toward marriage. Casual, spontaneous dating is frowned upon; formal courtship is still encouraged. Sorority ritual reinforces the progression from dating to marriage. At the vital point in the process, where dating must be turned into engagement, the sorority shores up the structure by the pinning ritual, performed after dinner in the presence of all the sorority sisters (who are required to stay for the ceremony) and attended, in its classic form, by a choir of fraternity boys singing outside. The commitment is so public that it is difficult for either partner to withdraw. Since engagement is already heavily reinforced outside the sorority, pinning ceremonies are more elaborate than engagements.

The social columns of college newspapers faithfully record the successes of the sorority system as it stands today. Sorority girls get engaged faster than "independents," and they appear to be marrying more highly ranked men. But what predictions can we make about the system's future?

All social institutions change from time to time, in response to changing conditions. In the mountain villages of the Philippines, the steady attacks of school and mission on the immorality of the *olag* have almost demolished it. Sororities, too, are affected by changes in the surrounding environment. Originally they were places where the few female college students took refuge from the jeers and catcalls of men who thought that nice girls didn't belong on campus. They assumed their present, endogomy-conserving form with the flourishing of the great land-grant universities in the first half of this century.

On the Brink

The question about the future of the sorority system is whether it can adapt to the most recent changes in the forms of higher education. At present, neither fraternities nor sororities are in the pink of health. On some campuses there are chapter houses which have been reduced to taking nonaffiliated boarders to pay the costs of running the property. New sorority chapters are formed, for the most part, on new or low-prestige campuses (where status-anxiety is rife); at schools of high prestige fewer girls rush each year and the weaker houses are disbanding.

University administrations are no longer as hospitable to the Greeks as they once were. Most are building extensive dormitories that compete effectively with the housing offered by sororities; many have adopted regulations intended to minimize the influence of the Greeks on campus activities. The campus environment is changing rapidly: academic standards are rising, admission is increasingly competitive, and both male and female students are more interested in academic achievement; the proportion of graduate students seriously training for a profession is increasing; campus culture is often so pluralist that the Greek claim to monopolize social activity is unconvincing.

The sorority as it currently stands is ill-adapted to cope with the new surroundings. Sorority houses were built to provide a setting for lawn parties, dances, and dress-up occasions, and not to facilitate study; crowding and noise are severe, and most forms of privacy do not exist. The sorority songs that have to be gone through at rushing and chapter meetings today all seem to have been written in 1915 and are mortifying to sing today. The arcane rituals, so fascinating to high-school girls, grow tedious and sophomoric to college seniors.

But the worst blow of all to the sorority system comes from the effect of increased academic pressure on the dating habits of college men. A student competing for grades in a professional school, or even in a difficult undergraduate major, simply has not the time (as he might have had in, say, 1925) to get involved in the sorority forms of courtship.

Since these days almost all the "right kind" of men *are* involved in demanding training, the traditions of the sorority are becoming actually inimical to hypergamous marriage. Increasingly, then, sororities do not solve the Brahmin problem but make it worse.

One can imagine a sorority designed to facilitate marriage to men who have no time for elaborate courtship. In such a sorority, the girls—to start with small matters—would improve their telephone arrangements, for the fraternity boy in quest of a date today must call several times to get through the busy signals, interminable paging, and lost messages to the girl he wants. They might arrange a private line with prompt answering and faithfully recorded messages, with an unlisted number given only to busy male students with a promising future. They would even accept dates for the same night as the invitation, rather than, as at present, necessarily five to ten days in advance, for the only thing a first-year law student can schedule that far ahead nowadays is his studies. Emphasis on fraternity boys would have to go, for living in a fraternity and pursuing a promising (and therefore competitive) major field of study are rapidly becoming mutually exclusive. The big formal dances would go (the fraternity boys dislike them now); the football floats would go; the pushcart races would go. The girls would reach the hearts of their men not through helping them wash their sports cars but through typing their term papers.

But it is inconceivable that the proud traditions of the sororities that compose the National Panhellenic Council could èver be bent to fit the new design. Their structure is too fixed to fit the changing college, and their function is rapidly being lost. The sorority cannot sustain itself on students alone. When parents learn that membership does not benefit their daughters, the sorority as we know it will pass into history.

21
"Normal" Family Forms

Within any society there are commonsense understandings about appropriate and proper family relations. These understandings determine the forms within which specific instances of family life are molded. Thus, we use our understandings of what is typical to decide when to interpret an individual relationship as familylike in character. To illustrate the strength and flexibility of these forms, we can examine their application under extreme conditions. Barbara Carter's article on "Reform-School Families" reports one such extreme condition, the forced absence of heterosexual contacts. Under this condition, the typical understanding of what constitutes family life still operates. The girls she describes "go with one another," experience love and romance, and have families. Although the players have changed, the typecasting is the same, and the story is about family life.

Reform-School Families
Barbara Carter

Inmate culture in a girls' reform school is best understood as a complex of meanings through which the girls maintain continuity between their lives inside and outside of the institution and as social forms established to mitigate and manage the pains of confinement and problems of intimate group living. The informal world of reform-school girls is one of make-believe families, homosexual courting relations, and adolescent peer-

From *Society Magazine* 11 (November–December 1973): 36–43. Reprinted by permission.

group culture. It is the world of the adolescent girl on the outside, imported into the institution, and appropriately modified to fit the formally structured world of the institution.

Love and Romance: Going with Girls

Adolescent concern with boy-girl love relationships is no less intense for girls in the institution than it is for adolescents in the world outside of the institution. But for these girls, many of whom have gotten into trouble because of their associations with boys, there are no boys around with whom to explore courtship, romance, and love. To fill the painful void created by the total absence of boys, the girls turn inward to each other and create their own world of love relationships.

"Going with girls" is a relationship which attempts to capture the characteristics and qualities of the traditional adolescent boy-girl relationship. Girls in the institution go with girls for much the same socioemotional reasons that boys and girls in the society at large go with each other: they seek recognition, companionship, and emotional involvement.

Courtship in the reform school allows a girl to acknowledge a romantic and symbolically heterosexual attachment to another girl. While in part a state of mind and a world of fantasy, this acknowledgement is objectively concretized, like its outside counterpart, by pleas for and declarations of love, flirting, and jealousy; by the exchange of letters and verbal messages; and, generally, by seeking out a present or prospective courting partner in a variety of informal settings. These courting relationships, like boy-girl relationships in the external world, provide the substance for everyday social conversations.

Smiles, stares, glances, pushes, pats, and name-calling take on important and exaggerated meaning for the conversational and romantic lives of the training-school girls. Physical contact per se is a relatively minor component of the courting relationships and is most often manifested in hand-holding, touching, and to a lesser extent, by kissing. For most girls more extensive physical contact appears to be both undesirable and/or unattainable. The vast majority of the courting relationships are emotional and symbolically sexual rather than physical.

Generally, informal group pressure encourages but does not demand that one go with girls. The decision to do so is entirely voluntary. The threat of force, or its actual use, is neither a socially accepted nor practiced way of inducing girls to participate in the courtship system.

Despite the absence of overt coercion and in the presence of formal restrictions against it, somewhere around 70 percent of the girls participate in the courtship system. This estimate is based on my own counting and familiarity with the declarations and activities of the girls. Girls participating in courting activities estimate that close to 90 percent of all girls go with girls. The specific estimates of the noncourting girls cluster around 50 percent. The few staff estimates elicited tended to be considerably lower and most often characterized as "not many." It is clear that estimates about the extent of participation in the courting system are influenced by one's relationship to that system.

Courtship Roles

"Butch" and "femme" are the two pivotal roles in the courtship system. Auxiliary roles are the "stone butch," the "half-ass butch," the "jive butch," and the "stone femme."

The butch is that position in the courtship system assigned to the girl who assumes the masculine role in the courting relationship. An important part of being a "good butch" is learning to look the part. In a setting where real sex differences are nonexistent, nuances of dress, hair style, carriage, and posture take on great social significance.

In summary, then, to be a butch simply means to "act the part of a boy." However, a butch may still show interest in some traditionally feminine activities like knitting, crocheting, and sewing. Also she may, like the other girls, decorate her room with dolls, stuffed animals, and bric-a-brac. The butch is permitted to play a role without assuming an identity which implies a "real" or permanent commitment. She is permitted to maintain an image of herself as female. It is this permissiveness which gives rise to the distinction between the butch and the stone butch. The butch plays a role while the stone butch purports to have accepted an identity.

A girl may be a butch for the duration of her stay in the institution, or she may be a butch one day and a femme the next—a butch in one relationship and a femme in a concurrent relationship. Most of the terms used by girls in describing roles in the courtship system are terms taken from black culture. That this is so reflects the dominance of the soul orientation in reform school life. For example, the label "half-ass butch" is applied to the girl who calls herself a butch but generally fails to play the part. The black societal counterpart is "half-ass nigger."

The term "jive butch" is most frequently used to describe the butch who courts many girls at once without being "serious" about any. Its equivalent on the outside is the playboy. To call a butch "jive" is at once to offer a compliment and a criticism; to be jive means that one is popular, but to openly exploit that popularity is bad. The black societal counterpart is "jive nigger."

The female counterpart of the butch is the femme. Within the reform school culture, the femme affects in an exaggerated fashion behavioral patterns culturally associated with femininity. Most girls perceive this as just acting "natural." A femme is expected to take pride in her personal appearance and to wear jewelry, makeup, and lipstick to make her attractive to butches. The femme is expected to be submissive or, as the girls say, "to do what the butch tell her." She is expected to "obey" her butch.

At any given moment in the courting system, femmes probably outnumber butches by at least two to one. This uneven distribution, of course, contributes to the internal dynamics of "going with girls" by further allowing butches—as scarce commodities—to assume a role of dominance by defining the terms of the courting relationship. The *single* most important factor determining this distribution is race. Within the context of the institution, race becomes a highly visible constant for imagined sex differentiation. Blacks, grossly disproportionate to their numbers in the institution, become butches, and whites, equally disproportionately, become femmes. The most common and desirable arrangement is a relationship consisting of a black butch and a white femme.

Whether black girls become butches because they have been socialized to be more aggressive than white girls, or are more aggressive because they have become butches, is unclear. I am inclined to believe that the two are mutually reinforcing: the black girls are in fact "tougher" than the white girls, but their toughness is made acceptable and manageable to white girls by having the blacks become the symbolic masculine figures in a social context which is microcosmic of a society that assigns toughness and power to males and not females.

A second argument is that the purpose of creating symbolic males in an all-female population is to permit the vast majority of girls to continue to maintain their preinstitution identities as "feminine people." One might then argue that due to past and present position in society, black girls are more willing to temporarily give up their female roles for certain high-status rewards.

The Dynamics of Courtship

Courting relationships in the reform school, like teenage courtships on the outside, are highly charged emotionally and often short-lived. Girls frequently estimate that during the course of nine to twelve months in the institution, the typical girl may go with anywhere from five to ten girls, with five or six girls being the most common estimate given.

Despite, and maybe because of, the relatively short duration of most courtships, going with girls is one of the most alive, emotionally intense and conversationally consuming experiences of the girls. These relationships are the source of considerable anxiety for many girls. Girls talk about, dress for, "showoff" for, and look forward to seeing each other, even momentarily and at a distance. Girls are excited and joyous when things go well and sometimes angry or sad when things go badly.

Daily courtship relations revolve around the exchange of written and verbal messages; the sharing of "goodies" and the exchange of small gifts; the arranging and engaging in momentary and public rendezvous; hand-holding, smiles, glances, kisses, petty jealousies and continually recapturing these moments in conversations with friends.

The single most prominent feature of going with girls is the regular exchange of "pen notes." These illegal written communications are saved, hidden, and treasured by the girls who receive them. The themes of loneliness, frustration and a need for love are common to most of the letters.

A code for various phrases is used. Presented below are some of the most common phrases.

1 4 3	I love you
2 1 6	As a sister
2 2 6	As my mother
2 2 3	As my man
2 4 3	Go fuck off
2 2 4	Go to hell
2 2 5	As my woman *or* It is quits
2 1 8	As a daughter
1 3 3	I dig you
3 2 4	Pen me back *or* Pay me back
6 3 7	Always and forever
2 6 8	We belong together
2 1 7	As a brother
4 4 6	True love always
4 2 3	Kiss my ass
4 2 4	Take me back

The codes reflect the sense of a need for secrecy, but also seem to create some emotional distance. For example, in face-to-face encounters, girls are far more likely to say, "1 4 3" than "I love you."

A common pattern observable at recreational activities is the informal sorting of femmes and butches into separate groupings. These groupings are often seen as some combination of the sorting of symbolic males and females to discuss their respective partners and activities and as an informal grouping of blacks (butches) and whites (femmes). In first discussing this phenomenon with the observer, one femme vividly recalled how she had been told to leave an informal grouping of butches, some of whom were her close friends, because the conversation was to be about things which she, as a femme, should not hear. With respect to the second basis for groupings (race), the observer notes that a considerable portion of conversation content for butches centers around the recounting of preinstitution experiences, events and places known to the blacks coming from common urban area ghettos.

The dynamics of the courtship system can be elaborated further by describing the everyday language of courtship. Girls talk about "digging" girls, and this is their way of saying that one girl is attracted to another and would like to enter into or continue a courting relationship. Talk about who is "digging" whom is very common. A girl may communicate this particular attraction for another girl by penning a note or more informally, by a variety of nonverbal gestures such as stares, smiles, winks, pushing, or hitting. Presented below is one girl's description of how the observer could identify when one girl is "digging" another. "If that name keeps popping up. They keep bringing it up and you get suspicious. That's what Lee did with Helen. We were talking about cars and she said, 'Don't Helen look cute today.'" To accuse a partner of "digging" another girl is to charge her with unfaithfulness. Such accusations of jealousy are common and lively features of the courtship drama. These accusations, often true, lead to many breakups. While butches and femmes probably make an equal number of accusations, butches are more likely to take the initiative in ending relationships. This is so because femmes are more numerous than butches, and consequently, it is easier for butches to find new partners than for femmes to do so. Then, too, femmes are less likely to end relationships when partners are suspected of being unfaithful, because there is a general consensus that butches, like males, are to some extent "jive." That is, butches, like men, are expected to be playboys.

Girls also talk about "rapping." Girls "rap" to each other, but especially butches to femmes. Rapping is variously described as, "You make a girl think you like her," "You talk bull," or "Play up to her." "Rapping" is the act of artistically persuading one to believe the impossible or improbable. Historically, it is similar to the art of making the master believe that he is loved by his slave.

"Slobbing" is the local and graphic vernacular for "French" kissing.

FIGURE 21.1

Love Is Here and Now You're Gone, I'm Your Puppet, Hello Stranger, Respect, Ain't No Mountain High Enough, Reach Out

Time—To pen you
Place—My lonely room
Thought—Of you
Reason—I love you
Desire—To be with you
Hope—We meet on the outs
Wish—You were here now!
Want—You and your loving
Need—You and your loving
Care—For you
Hurt—By love
Love—You
Hate—I hate——(I hope she drops dead)
Happy—Not now
Sad—Yes
Mood—Confused
Songs—I Do Love You, Stand by Me, Since I Lost My Baby

Say Love,

Time plus pleasure permits me to write you these few sweet lines. Hon I hope I did not upset you but I just had to tell you. And if I did not tell you when I did decide to tell you which I probably would you would have either been angry or hurt because I didn't tell you before. Paula I do love you and I mean it but hon I don't know how to prove it to you but believe me I'll do anything to prove it to you. Hon, I want you to go to board and go home why should you suffer because of me oh sure you'll say you're not suffering but I'll know and deep down you will too. And if you go home and behave I'll probably be able to see you in June or even on my Xmas weekend and remember one thing even if we don't meet on the outs or for that matter ever see each other again remember there will always be someone else that you will love and be happier with than me.

You may not think that now but when you do meet that someone you'll look back and say Pony really knew what she was talking about and then after a while you'll forget me and then it will be hard for you to think that we were more than friends but I hope that doesn't happen to us but if it does, well that's life and boy life sure is hard. Isn't it?

Well I got to go see you tomorrow sometime I hope

1 4 3
6 3 7
Little Miss Supreme

P.S. But promise me never again as long as you live to touch that Dope! and I mean it hear?

Well good night and

1 4 3
6 3 7*

*This love note is typical of those which the girls regularly write to each other. 1 4 3 means "I love you" and 6 3 7 means "always and forever."

Though frequently described as a "natural" feature of courting relationships, this activity seems to occur as frequently, if not more so, between noncourting partners as it does between courting partners. "Slobbing" is perceived as one of the "big" things that girls can engage in. It certainly carries a greater penalty from the school's administration than writing pen notes. Physical contact for most courting partners seldom goes beyond "slobbing." Most girls say that this limitation is imposed by the girls themselves, but a small number do see it as an expedient reflecting the absence of opportunities for more extensive contacts. The actual amount of "slobbing" occurring in the institution is open to debate. Some girls estimate that it is a frequent activity and say that about three-quarters of courting partners slob each other; others place the figure higher, and some estimate that it is an activity in which as few as one-third of the courting girls are engaged.

While the dominant relationship in the romance complex is the courting relationship, marriage relationships are also acknowledged. Except for the name, and a ceremony which accompanies it, it is usually impossible to distinguish between courting and marriage. Girls, however, say that marriage relationships, like those relationships in the external world, imply a degree of permanence, stability, faithfulness and commitment not necessarily implied by a courting relationship.

Most courting girls do not get "married." "Marriage" relationships last no longer than the more common courting relationships, and girls may get married one day and divorced several days later. Many girls involved in courting simply refuse to get married on the grounds that it, unlike courting, is "too unrealistic."

One girl summed up the meaning of marriage by saying, "It means that they like each other a whole lot more than kids just going together. They have to stay together or get a divorce. The girl takes the last name of the butch."

Marriages, like most other activities, take place during recreational periods in the presence of other girls. Like marriages on the outside, they are performed by preachers. Any butch may become a preacher simply by performing a marriage. (There are few female preachers in the outside world and none in the institution.) The marriage ceremony varies both with the style of the preacher, the setting, the risk of discovery, and the amount of time available for performing the ceremony. It may be as simple or as embellished as the preacher desires but always consists of the lines "Do you *(pen name)* take *(pen name)* to be your lawfully wedded butch/femme." Each marriage must be witnessed by at least two people, but more are usually present, often standing as camouflage or lookouts.

Divorces most often seem to occur because partners lose interest in each other, though it is reported that some girls simply get divorced before they leave the institution, maybe to denote a real end to a symbolic existence. Below is a brief description of how one girl described her divorce and the circumstances surrounding it:

> She quit me for no reason at all. I wasn't going with anybody. At first I thought she was jealous or something, but she wasn't. She just said that she wanted to go with Thelma. [Have you had other breakups like this?] No we haven't. We quit each other before but usually we were back together in five minutes. . . . Yet we got a divorce. A preacher divorced us. [Did you have to stand together?] No. It was a one-way divorce. I didn't want to get it. She told me that she wanted a divorce and I said no. I thought she would just forget all about it but she didn't. Then the girl who divorced us told me that we were divorced. [What did you do when told about the divorce?] I turned in her dirtiest pen note. She lost her weekend and everything. But I don't care. I'm glad. She hurt me.

New girls learn the language and etiquette of courting by talking with, listening to, and observing their peers as they act out the daily courtship drama. These girls learn that it is a voluntary activity which "gives you something to do" and which "helps to pass the time." But, too, they learn of the verbal ambivalence of even those girls who participate in the system: that going with girls is "fun" and "exciting" but also "wrong," "crazy," "sick" and "stupid" and that one can get in trouble for it. They learn that the staff officially and usually informally disapproves of it and that one can really get in trouble for a "dirty pen note" if it is discovered. They learn that some matrons who are otherwise accepting get really upset when they hear girls talking about going with girls and that a few staff members also see it as a "game" and will laugh or smile when they overhear girls talking about it. Mostly they learn that it's best to try to keep going with girls a secret.

Most girls stop going with girls when they leave the institution, for they know that "it's only something you do up here," and "once you leave you forget all about this place." After all, almost everybody prefers life on the outs to life inside and boys to girls.

Having a Family

In recreating life on the outside, the girls do not stop at boy-girl relations. Just as they miss having boyfriends, they long for their mothers, fathers, sisters, and brothers. The following is a typical letter written by one of the girls to her family at home.

> Dear Ma and Dad
> I hope this letter finds you in the best of health.
> Ma and Dad I lonely and blue and I need you very much. more than I did before. because I know How much you & the kids mean to me now. I never knew how much yous mean tell now. So I am asking for yours and Dad forgives. Please! take me back I need you and I need your love.
> I know you say she only fooling around so she can come home. but am not I mean every word I am saying to you. Ma please take me in your arms and love me like you do the other kids. Please! Rock me and hold me in your arms Ma. Someone said to me (You can have a lot of fathers but you can only have one mother. Cause she the one who brought you in this world. I believe that if only you would let me love you and you love me. Ma please understand what I am trying to say. Well thats all for now. Please forgive me.
> I already forgave you and ready to try again.
>   Love & Kisses & Hugs
>   Dena

Dena writes from the heart and paints a plea for love, acceptance, and affection. Her letter, unfortunately, is typical of many I read during my fieldwork at the Girls' Reform School.

Dena, like many girls at the school, is estranged from her family and feels an intense loneliness for them. Families, both loved and hated, are everyday topics of conversation for the girls, their visits anticipated and letters anxiously awaited.

Girls in the institution talk about and long for their families. Yet there is little that one can do about families on the outside except write to them, wait for their visits, hope for an infrequent weekend, send apologies and ask for forgiveness and acceptance. Perhaps this is the reason that girls create their own make-believe familial relationships within the institution.

Girls use kin terminology to describe a variety of close relationships between them and other girls in the institution and speak of having "sisters," "brothers," "mothers," "fathers" and "daughters." Kin relationships generally lack the tone of emotional excitement so characteristic of the courting relationships, and the vast majority of girls acknowledge not just one but several make-believe relatives on the grounds. This commonly ranges from a low of two or three relatives to a high of fourteen or fifteen. Girls most typically have about four to seven family relations. Having family relations distinguishes courting from noncourting friends and thus reduces feelings of jealousy, suspicion and distrust among courting partners involved in multiple relationships.

I have found it convenient to divide kin relationships into two broad categories: macro- and microfamily groupings. Girls speak of the macro-groupings as "grounds families," meaning that these families are institution-wide. The most popular of these large groupings at the time of my research were the Robinsons and the LaMonts. Girls simply identified themselves as belonging to one of the "grounds families" and often took the family name as their pen note surnames. Belonging to a large family grouping seemed to convey some positive status on girls. The major function of these groupings presently seems to be to provide a sense of social rather than emotional integration.

When asked about the history of the two dominant macrofamilies the responses ranged from "don't know" to constructions of a recent past. Many times I was told that the Robinson family, the larger of the two families, was started up in the fall of 1966 by two girls who were "married" to each other. Others reported that the Robinson and LaMont surnames have been used by the girls for many years. Thus the girls have attempted to create a past and legitimate the families and interrelationships.

One becomes a member of a family grouping simply by being asked or so identified by someone who is already a member. Getting out of a family is as simple as getting into it. A girl simply declares that she no longer wants to be in that family.

From the perspective of the girls the large grounds family groupings are seemingly less important on the level of day-to-day interaction than are the smaller, comparatively more closely knit nuclear and sibling groups into which the girls also organize themselves.

A sizable number of girls are mothers or daughters, and an even larger number of girls acknowledge sister or brother relationships. (Interestingly, there are no "sons." A girl assuming a butch role in a courting relationship will usually become a brother to another girl or even a daughter. In most cases it seems that a girl identifying herself as a butch will not have a parent unless she has alternated between the roles of butch and femme.) It is not uncommon that a girl will be a mother or father in one relationship, a sister or brother in another, and a daughter in still another.

In general, girls who acknowledge kin relations regularly write pen notes to each other, send verbal messages, share with each other and exchange small gifts. These girls seek out each other and talk together at recreational activities, hold hands, exchange affectionate hugs and kisses and often move in the same circle of friends. In terms of observable content, these relationships are practically indistinguishable from courting relationships. Importantly, however, these relationships lack the talked-about glamour and excitement of the courting relations. Of course, in the outside world, adolescent girls take families for granted and talk, instead, about boyfriends.

A sister or brother, most commonly a sister, is frequently the first kin relation to be acknowledged by a girl on the grounds and this tie is frequently established within a week or two of a girl's arrival at the institution. Some girls establish these ties within a few days after their arrival, but others do not choose or are not chosen until much later. One girl, for example, reported that she was at the institution for five months before she acknowledged a kin relation. At the time of our conversation, she acknowledged five sisters, several brothers, an aunt and uncle (both unusual since the term "aunt" is usually reserved for matrons) and a host of "good friends" described as "not worthy" of being called sisters and brothers. Another girl, however, reported that on her first day at the institution she received six pen notes with several of them containing requests for a sister relationship. At present this girl is in the Robinson grounds family and acknowledges a mother, two daughters, four sisters and two brothers.

Mother-daughter relations are less common than sibling associations, and the girls seemed at a loss to describe the parent-child relationship. In explaining why she had chosen a particular girl as her daughter, one girl said it was "because I like her. She's little. I don't know, I like little people. If they're smaller than me they can be my daughter." Mothers are nearly always older than their daughters. Girls typically describe those who become mothers as "more mature girls."

Mothers give advice, provide a sense of security, and help meet material needs. Parents assume some responsibility for socializing their children into the informal culture of the institution. When asked to describe the relationships which commonly exist between parent and child on the grounds, the girls almost always say that the parent tells the child what to do, how to behave and how to avoid trouble. One, in fact, frequently hears parents, as well as girlfriends and relatives, telling the girls to "be good" or "You'd better make A-Party" (for girls who have adhered to all school rules for the week) or to obey the matrons.

Family members on the grounds, like the idealized concept of families on the outside, "like" and "care" for each other. The girls themselves see the parental role as being one which provides the child with a sense of emotional security, social direction, and physical protection. The parent fulfills the desire to nurture; the child has her need to be nurtured fulfilled. These are intensely personal needs which cannot be fulfilled by the formal structure of an institution.

The child-parent relationships are effective channels for socializing recruits into life on the grounds; it is an informal but powerful channel of social control. The girls want to protect their social system and to maintain a comfortable social order where staff discipline is minimal. To the extent that parents (and other kin and friend relations) express concern about the behavior of their children by telling them to "be good" or "make A-Party," and children obey these commands, the child-parent unit becomes an important informal source of support for the formal structure's emphasis on discipline and order. To the extent that the entire enterprise is successful, parents become informal social control agents of the formal institutional structure.

Families—parents, daughters, sisters, and brothers—are important to adolescents both inside and outside the institution. For these adolescent girls on the inside, plagued by real family conflicts and often social and emotional estrangement and certainly physical separation, make-believe families function to fill a void not otherwise filled by the institution. There is some interaction between girls and matrons characteristic of child-parent interaction, and though girls may develop special attachments for certain matrons, these attachments clearly do not erase the need for make-believe families. In the final analysis, say the girls, even most of the "nice" matrons are people who just *work* at the institution. Furthermore, not even the matrons themselves feel equipped to provide the twenty-five girls in their cottages with the "love and affection" they are perceived as needing.

These reform-school girls have attempted, consciously and subconsciously, to affect their restricted environment, finding ways to compensate not only for their incarceration but also for deprivation in their lives outside of the institution. Make-believe boyfriends, girlfriends, and families provide, at least temporarily, the romantic, sibling and parental relationships that these girls crave.

22
Domesticated Singles

The institution of the family is venerable. Part of the reason for its durability is that it has been able to meet the needs of society. These needs are not static; they often change in dramatic ways when changes occur in other segments of society. The move from productive to consumptive economic forms has been accommodated, in part, by a change from the traditional position-oriented family to the more personal, psychologically oriented modern family. In its extreme form, the move culminates in the single adult. Even though this change is radical, many of the same needs for cooperation, emotional support, and emergency care are still experienced. Mimi Rodin gives an interesting account of how these essentially familylike functions are served by informal relationships among singles living in the modern apartment building.

Tuesdays and Saturdays: A Preliminary Study of the Domestic Patterns of Young Urban Singles
Mimi Rodin

Introduction

The purpose of this study is to provide a description of the social and domestic organization of young, never-married, urban, American apartment dwellers, whose lifestyles have never been studied by anthropologists or sociologists.

From Urban Anthropology 2 (1973):93–112. Reprinted by permission. The first draft of this paper, under the title of "The One-Person Household," was submitted to David W. Plath for a graduate seminar at the University of Illinois given in the fall semester at 1971. A subsequent draft under the same title was presented at the Central States Anthropological Society meetings in the symposium on Adult Socialization chaired by Plath on April 27, 1972.

Approximately one-third of American adults between the ages of twenty-one and thirty are single. The majority of these singles live in areas classified by the census as urban (United States Bureau of the Census 1972, p. 2). If we include divorced persons in the same age group, nearly one-third of these urban singles live alone (United States Bureau of the Census 1970, p. 1–54).

The census of 1890 reported similar proportions of single adults in the age group twenty-one to thirty. Although the majority of singles in 1890 lived in urban areas, only an insignificant proportion of them lived alone (United States Bureau of the Census 1895, p. clxx).[1]

In his study of urban families in Chicago in 1880, Sennet (1970, p. 82) remarked on the development of small, but identifiable, districts of singles. His breakdowns of census figures for 1880 show that the singles of a century ago were comparable to today's singles with regard to age, sex, and ethnicity. However, his figures include a higher proportion of lower-class workers than those of 1970. This is probably related to the changing educational and occupational composition of American society as a whole.

[1] Nearly one-third of American men between the ages of twenty-one and thirty are single. Although numerically there are more single men than women in this age group, a higher proportion of American women are single (United States Bureau of the Census 1972, p. 2). The majority of these singles live in areas classified by the census as urban.

The census of 1890 reported nearly identical proportions of single adults between the ages of twenty-one and thirty. The higher proportion of singles, however, were men. Again, the majority of singles lived in urban areas (United States Bureau of the Census 1890, p. clxx).

The census heading "single-member household" includes household types of varying etiology, the never-married, the divorced, and the widowed of all ages. Ten percent of American adults live alone. The predominant types of single-member households cluster at opposite ends of the age scale. The two most common are widows and widowers over sixty-five and singles and divorced persons under thirty-five. Including the divorced, one-third of unmarried young American adults live alone, and more women in this category live alone than men (United States Bureau of the Census 1970, pp. 1–54).

This is quite different from the conditions reported in the census of 1890, when an insignificant percentage of young singles lived alone. In 1890, the major eastern cities were experiencing a severe housing shortage. As many as eight families, or more than twenty persons, were commonly reported as occupying the same dwelling unit (United States Bureau of the Census 1895, p. clxxix). Working singles continued to live with their parents until, or even after, marriage or boarded with surrogate parents in rooming houses and private homes.

Working from census data for Chicago of the 1890s, Sennet (1970, p. 82) found small but identifiable districts of singles growing up in the transitional areas between respectable lower-middle-class residential districts and the warehouse fringe that encircled the central downtown area. These districts were composed of shoddily constructed, run-down apartment buildings and blue-collar boardinghouses for the shopgirls and day laborers who had left the farms and small towns of America and Europe for the industrial cities.

Singles today, at least in Chicago, appear to occupy the same ecological niche within the city. They cluster in the older districts near the city center and in bands along the major routes of access to the central city, sandwiched between the affluent strip of lakefront high-rises and the inner-city slums, but they do so as autonomous adults.

The "swinging single" of popular mythology is evidently not an entirely recent innovation. Perhaps it is only the glamorized stereotype of singles as the ideal of the ethic of liberated individualism marketed through the popular media that is completely new. At least, the single's lifestyle is very different now than it was at the turn of the century. The maiden aunts and school teachers, Sister Carries, shop girls, blue-collar nomads, boarding-house boys, and notorious divorcées are nowhere to be found in the bachelor pads, four-plus-ones, and "kitsch-y" singles bars today.

Most sociological considerations of American kinship, marriage and residence have focused on the statistically most common form, the neolocal, nuclear family (see for example Blood and Wolfe 1960). Anthropologically oriented studies have emphasized class-specific and ethnic-specific household and family types in order to discover the organizational principles which underlie the varying forms such units display (see, for example, Farber 1971, Gonzalez 1970, Lewis 1965). In order to account for their data, they have dismantled the conceptual triad of kinship, marriage, and residence. Following Goodenough's (1970, p. 9) criticism of traditional anthropological description and theory in this field, I will emphasize the kinds of human social problems involved, and the social transactions which are intended to solve them.

The entry of women into the urban labor market and their liberation from strictly domestic labor are closely related to the demand for skilled labor, the need for increased income to meet desired standards of living, and the availability of goods, services, and housing. The facts that women today have achieved the legal adulthood denied women of the 1880s and that economic independence can be achieved by men and women at earlier ages than a century ago are certainly causal factors in the emergence of large numbers of singles in American urban centers.

The discussion of singles that follows will, I hope, indicate some parameters along which further research on American and more generally, urban, family, and domestic structures might proceed. The following findings will be discussed:

1. The maintenance of a household among middle-class Americans is generally assumed to take the form of a division of labor between husbands and wives. Tasks are conceptually divided into sexually appropriate repertoires. Husbands provide the income or subsistence for the household and care for the exterior of the home. Wives do housekeeping, cooking, and child care. Single persons must devise strategies to adapt this "traditional" (and I use this word with a great deal of reservation) division of labor to their own situations.

2. The model of a division of labor between husbands and wives undergoes an interesting transformation as it is adapted by singles. The

relevant categories are collapsed in that an employed single of either sex is, by definition, supporting a household. Singles prefer apartment accommodations in order to eliminate the remaining "traditionally" male tasks.

3. The women's repertoire undergoes a less complete transformation. In households single women perform a relatively complete list of "traditionally" female work. To a lesser degree, men assume a truncated version of it.

4. The sexual basis of the division of domestic labor is blurred but not erased. It reemerges in the domestic patterns of unmarried couples when we see that women extend their domestic services to more than one household. A corollary pattern also emerges, as couples who wish to share domestic work divide the "traditionally" female work between them.

5. There exists among young unmarried adults a nexus of social relationships which is domestic and conjugal in nature. Goods and domestic and sexual services are exchanged.

6. Men are the active agents in extending social networks, but women crystalize modes of intense reciprocity. In such couples, women focus their performance of domestic activities on their own and one man's residence, and by doing so assert their claim of exclusive sexual access to him.

7. There is a superficial similarity between single and married domestic patterns, indicating that there is a range of culturally acceptable domestic patterns. An individual's choice of domestic arrangement is related to economic means and notions of stages in a life cycle: the young single, living alone, has achieved autonomous adulthood but is holding in abeyance the confining jural responsibilities of marriage and of parenthood.

Methodology

The original group of informants included eight singles, four men and four women. They were white, between the ages of twenty-three and twenty-eight, all with at least some college education. All were employed full-time in a small Midwestern city. A list of occupations included a nurse, a clerical worker, and six semiprofessionals from a local newspaper.

The eight original informants were selected for several specific reasons. First, because of their educational backgrounds and professional experience, they were especially keen and accurate observers of their own and others' actions. They all trained themselves to recall details of conversations, names, dates, and times. All of the informants were at least peripherally known to each other. Although it may have biased the study somewhat to select six persons from the same office, I felt that this selection offered an opportunity to see to what extent the place of work shaped personal networks. Finally, because personal accounts overlapped in many areas, each of them was to some extent verifiable by comparison with the others.

The decisions to accept employment in the town by all but one woman were made on the basis of already existing local networks. All either grew up in or near (within a hundred miles of) the city and had relatives or high-school friends in the community and/or attended college in the city.

Since the completion of the study, two of the informants accepted positions in other cities and have moved away. One has become engaged, and two others are seeking employment in larger cities.

Other sources of data include informal interviews with single people who live alone but who were not included in the original sample and casual conversations with singles in Chicago about themselves and other singles they know. Information of this type is included only as it is supported by data derived from the diaries and interviews.

My conclusions are undoubtedly influenced by the composition and small size of my group of informants and need to be corroborated by a larger study. Specific aspects of the patterns to be discussed were found to differ in regular ways for lifestyles of older singles and divorced or widowed singles who were interviewed.

In order to describe and analyze single persons' households, I was interested in two classes of data: data concerning the private worlds of people who live alone and data on their public worlds. By public worlds, I am referring to the networks of social relationships that link them. Each of these classes of data pose a somewhat distinct methodological problem. The latter is open to direct questioning and participant-observation. The former would be violated by the presence of an observer and might entail undue invasion of privacy.

To get at categories of private activity that are representative of the way people organize their activities while alone, I asked some informants to keep a diary of their activities over the period of one normal week. In a brief handout, I explained in colloquial terms the notions of "behavior-specimen" and "episode" as developed by Barker and

Wright (Barker 1963).[2] By having informants observe and record their own activities, the integrity of their environments were preserved, and the natural units recorded were cognitively salient. This technique was only partially successful.

The success of the method described was borne out by the diaries that were completed. The records were complete and ordered enough that missing information was readily recalled in later interviews. The diaries were thus valuable mnemonic devices. However, only a few of the original group of informants were able or willing to keep such a rigorous record. In this regard, the method was only of selective value to the study. None of the men completed their diaries. Three of the women did, though one was not available for further interviewing. All informants were quite willing to talk informally.

In the discussion that follows, I shall make an analytical distinction between the private organization of time, space, and property of singles' households, and their networks of social relationships. The last section of the discussion, which focuses on the division of household labor and quasi-conjugal households, will demonstrate how the internal and external order of singles' lives are brought together.

---

[2]Roger Barker and Herbert Wright (Barker 1963) attempted to get away from the inherent bias of laboratory environments by developing a methodology of naturalistic accounts of children's behavior. Their basic source of data was the behavior specimen—an accurate transcript of everything a child did or said in the context of his every day environments. An essential hypothesis validating their method is that a natural stream of behavior would exhibit an orderly hierarchy of behaviors. They took the behavior episode as their fundamental unit. An episode is composed of one or more behaviors with the following definitive characteristics: constancy in the direction of behavior, occurrence within the normal behavior perspective, the whole having more potency than its parts. That is, an episode is goal oriented; for example, climbing a tree has as its goal reaching a certain point in the tree. An episode is bounded in time and space. Excluding careers, such as succeeding in business, it must be short enough to be readily observed by the investigator but within the awareness of the actor. The third defining characteristic implies that a change in goal, when stacking bricks becomes building a house, signals the beginning of a new episode (161–62). For the purpose of this study, respondents were asked to record all episodic behaviors, when, where, and the duration of their occurrence. I felt that any behavior insignificant enough not to be labeled by the actors, were not significant enough to be accorded further interest. The respondents produced episodes such as washing the dishes, writing a letter, getting ready for work in the morning, walking the dog, and mixing a drink.

Social and Domestic Networks[3]

Turning first to social and domestic networks, informants who indicated a repetitive pattern of visiting and telephoning in their diary entries were asked to list "who they know" and then to limit the lists of people whom they would normally telephone, visit, or ask favors of with the expectation of reciprocity. This arbitrary limitation produced a uniform patterning of networks for all informants.

Four categories of persons emerged: (1) relatives and old friends;[4] (2) college friends; (3) acquaintances through voluntary associations such as political parties, athletic teams, and drama groups; and (4) people from the place of work.

Each category may be labeled a sector of an ego's personal network. There was some overlap between personnel from family and college sectors, college and voluntary association sectors, and voluntary association and place of work sectors. There were no overlapping personnel between family and place of work sectors, family and voluntary association sectors, or college and place of work sectors.

People who work together daily share common experiences and perspectives. They meet for lunch, a drink after work, office parties,

---

[3] In an earlier draft of this paper, I borrowed Bott's (1957) typology of networks characterizing some categories of an individual's personal (or ego-focused) network as loose or tight-knit and using the concept of connectedness to get at social networks (or nonego-focused networks). I also applied Mayer's (1966, pp. 97–98) concept of the quasi-group or action-set to further characterize the latter. After a discussion with Lawrence Crissman (personal communication and 1969), I revised my terminology. He correctly pointed out that the terminologies above did little to elucidate the important aspects of networks, the dynamics of social roles, the distinctions between social groups and corporations, aggregates and categories. In fact the terminology was only confusing the description. Therefore, I have followed his suggestions and used little specific terminology, relying only on commonly used descriptive terms. As I am using it, the word "network" means "people one knows." An aggregate of people who include each other in their personal networks are merely sectors of the total social network, which ultimately includes the entire society. The categories of people one knows are sectors of a personal network. Stack (1972) has found the notion of "domestic networks" extremely useful in characterizing economic exchanges and transactions in parenthood among poor, urban Blacks, where more traditional concepts in this field, such as the "Matrofocal family," failed to explain their adaptive strategies.

[4] My use of the designation "relatives" reflects respondents' use of the term. On further questioning it was found that the category "relatives" as well as the labeling of named individuals as a relative, corresponds to Schneider's functional definition of term: "a person related by blood or marriage" (1968, p.21). Old friends, people the respondent grew up with, and parents' old friends are often subsumed under the same category. Such people are often fictive kin, especially if they are of the parental generation to the respondent. Contact with them in the home town is often maintained through kin ties ("Mom wrote to tell me about J's baby").

and gossip sessions. Dating couples appear to arise most frequently from this sector and from the voluntary association sector. Singles said that they preferred to work in places with a large number of other singles and that one motivation for joining voluntary associations was to meet singles of the opposite sex.

Several informants were asked to list who had been present at parties they had attended within the last six months and whom they would feel free to take along to parties given by various members of each sector of their networks. They noted that their acquaintances also kept sectors of their networks discrete. When asked to make up guest lists for parties at their homes, they observed the discreteness of each sector.

Within the period of the study, informants staged (or attempted to stage) gatherings for sectors of their personal networks. Sectors of personal networks can thus become groups for the purposes of recreation and reaffirming of old relationships.

Gatherings are often occasioned by culturally determined holiday seasons. Over the last Christmas–New Year holiday, one person organized a reunion of his high-school graduating class. Another attempted to organize a week-end reunion of several college friends, now married, in their old college town. Both reunions failed. A third donated his apartment for a highly successful office Christmas party.

Two examples illustrate the consequences of violating the discreteness of sectors of one's networks. One woman stated that whenever she had invited her boyfriend, whom she had met at work, to gatherings of her college friends, he sulked in a corner. Another told of inviting friends from work and friends from a voluntary association to a party. The party broke up into two groups along the lines of prior acquaintance, and she spent the evening moving back and forth between them.

Membership in any of the above categories differentially calls into play informal social pressures to communicate with others. As greater social and geographical distances arise between members, due to marriage and job changes, the pressures on people to reaffirm these relationships decreases. This is especially true of some relatives, old friends and college friends. Ultimately, the relationships are terminated or reduced to networks of letters, occasional telephone calls, or symbolic exchanges of Christmas cards.

As was noted above, six of my informants shared the same occupation and place of work. In a closer examination of the personal networks of each of these people, it was found that the place of work was the basis of the formation of a primary set of acquaintances. Informants labeled this sector of each of their networks "the gang" or "the group." This network, or category, exhibited several features which I tentatively suggest as characteristic of the single's lifestyle. It may, however, be an artifact of my sampling and ought to be checked against a larger sample.

Members of "the gang" were predominantly single, and predominantly male, although the office employed about equal numbers of men and women. Several women carried the burden of entertaining. When informants were asked who had been present at parties, they noted that several people had dropped out of the party circuit after marriage. These married individuals no longer gave parties for "the gang," although they occasionally invited individuals from it home to dinner. Subsequently, two informants observed that acquaintances from their college and voluntary association sectors also became socially detached from them after marriage.

I have labeled this phenomenon the "dropping out through marriage phenomenon." It effectively functions to keep social networks distinct on the basis of marital status. It is interpreted as a sign of marital problems for a married man to appear on the single's party circuit.

Perhaps the least easily explainable feature of singles' networks is the predominantly male composition, although it appears to be related to the "dropping out through marriage phenomenon." When women were asked to account for how they met people, they included in their list of acquaintances that the connecting individuals were usually men. I was not able to confirm this for men, but the following generalizations appear to be true. Single men meet single women at work and through other men in their job and voluntary association networks. Women meet men through the same sectors of their networks, which are predominantly male by actual count. Same-sex acquaintances are recruited the same way. This would appear to indicate that men have more acquaintances than women and that men are the active links through which both men and women extend their networks.

The discussion suggests a process by which singles prune their networks of past associations based on kinship and childhood, propelling themselves into a world rooted firmly in the present. After marriage, former singles drift away from their single acquaintances. The remaining singles operate, as they grow older, in a world that is progressively more oriented around their place of work and more masculine in composition.

The masculine composition of singles' networks is explainable if we refer to the census figures from 1895. Single men in the age group in question outnumber single women. In the personal networks I studied, the men were usually several years older than the women with whom they associated. This is consistent with census data that shows that the median age at marriage for men is slightly higher than for women. Only a small percentage of adults over the age of thirty-four have never married. Functionally this means that men are marrying women who are several years their juniors. There are indications then that singles' networks function to bring potentially marriageable people into contact with each other.

The place of work as a progressively more important factor in the formation of singles' networks is also understandable by reference to the residence histories and mobility patterns of singles. As young adults advance in their careers, they are drawn upward through the hierarchy of central places, so that the most career oriented of them cluster at the top in the large metropolitan centers. Singles who recognize this pattern also migrate to the large cities in search of the more stimulating company they expect to find there. As distance, time, and lifestyles separate a single from his social and geographical origins, the most immediate source of acquaintances becomes the place of work, at least until secondary sources of relationships are developed.

The more active role men play in introducing new members to existing networks of singles can be seen in light of a cultural bias towards male dominance. It could also be a case of seniority rule or a simple case of majority rule.

We have examined some of the ways networks of singles are formed and some of the ways in which they function. Certainly, a good proportion of relationships between singles are shallow and purely social in nature, but there is another aspect of these networks that is rarely seen from the outside. There is a measure of solidarity among singles in the way that they look after their own.

This other side is essentially domestic and mutually supportive in nature. Singles move often. During the period of the study, I documented four moving parties demonstrating how sectors of personal networks can become cooperative labor groups. "Saturday at my place. Free beer for anyone who helps load the van. Bring a muscle-bound friend." There are apartment-painting parties, "booze and brushes provided by the management." Another singles-set mailed out engraved invitations to "a gala fete in honour of D.D., on his natal date." Friends look in on each other when they are ill. They stay up all night with emotionally distressed friends and call sick at work while bringing a friend down from a bad drug experience.

The following example illustrates the extent to which singles' networks provide support for their members:

> Nan moved to Chicago, found an apartment on the near-north side and a job at the firm. She met Sara at work and they found they both lived in the same apartment building. Every now and then they had dinner together at home or went out. A couple of times a week they went singly or together to Mother's. Mother's is a bar, one of about two dozen such establishments located within three blocks

of each other on North Lincoln Avenue. Like the others, it caters to singles. Nan says: "I don't like bars, but I like Mother's. If you've gotta get out, there's always someone there you know. And if some guy starts hassling you, Andy throws them out." Andy is the bartender and part-owner of Mother's. He is a former roomate of Sara's boyfriend. Meredith was one of Sara's friends from Mother's. She was out of work for two months until Sara and Nan found an opening for her at the firm. During those two months she crashed with Sara. Andy gave Meredith a free steak sandwich and fries every night at Mother's until her first paycheck. "He says it's good for business." After that, Nan loaned Meredith her car to go apartment hunting.

Organization of Time, Space, and Property

Perhaps the most unique aspect of the singles' lifestyle lies in the amount of time that can be spent alone at home. This is generally the hours after work and days off. It was found that the amount of time spent alone was related to the sex of the informant. Men spent very little time alone. It was also found that for men and women, the maintenance of a single-person household actually increased the potential amount of company they could have.

> I used to share a place over on Front St. with Tina. The games she used to play with her boyfriend just about drove me out of my tree. I'd be walking around with nothing on, and he would pop out from under the sink or something. I was broken up with Mike then and I could afford it, so why not? Besides, I kind of thought we'd get back together after a while, and that way we'd have more privacy. (Anne, age twenty-five)

> I'm a slob, nobody could stand to live with me. Besides, I'd wanna sleep and that's when Gary would come in with some drunk eighteen-year-old chick and I'd have to leave. Besides, I only go home to sleep anyway. Whaddaya mean do I wanna get married? (Jack, age twenty-eight)

At some time after leaving the parental home, most informants had lived with others either in college dormitories or two-and-three-person apartments. Several spontaneously volunteered that sharing a place was restrictive because bathroom habits, receiving guests, and telephone access had to be negotiated with roommates. Most said they would share again but only if they had to save money, found a completely compatible roommate, or a "really spectacular place."

Several types of activity were specifically reserved for time alone, including sleeping, bathing, writing letters, daydreaming, and reading. Housekeeping and hobbies were always done alone. Several practiced musical instruments. One woman hooked rugs. One man, a semiprofessional musician, used his time alone to arrange and compose music. Another man spent several years remodeling his attic apartment and refinishing antiques. All stated that the presence of family would limit the amount of time they had to follow creative outside interests or restrict the specific time periods when they could do so.

It is interesting that none of the informants' timetables placed such activities as housekeeping, eating, or sleeping in the same time periods for any two consecutive days, except as noted below in the discussion of quasi-conjugal households. Some activities were used specifically to fill up time. Women mentioned watching television, unnecessary housekeeping, and cooking. Men mentioned only watching television.

The diaries indicated that people who live alone actually spend very little time alone. Time alone was always punctuated by telephone calls from others who lived alone. Informants said that if they felt lonely or were suffering from "cabin fever" that they phoned friends to talk or to arrange to meet them. Women met other women for a drink, shopping, or a movie. Men went to bars, played pool or golf, visited female friends, or found card games. If none of these activities were possible, all resorted to television or going to sleep. Most of the time that singles spent alone at home was accompanied by noisemaking devices such as radio, stereo, or television.

There was a noticeable tendency for men to spend less time alone at home or even at home than women. Men were less likely to answer the telephone than women when they were alone. This is apparently related to several of the findings previously discussed under social networks. Men are the active links in arranging social meetings. It appears that women will remain alone rather than violate that norm. It has also been suggested that women simply have a greater tolerance for solitude, which may or may not be biologically based, but it is not my purpose here to discuss such notions. It is clear, however, that single men and women do structure their solitude in ways that are generally characteristic of their sex, as it is socially defined.

"Cabin fever" was mentioned only by women and was brought on not so much by being alone as by self-imposed solitary confinement during periods of nervousness, depression, or embarrassment. Such feelings were termed "the blue funk." Women were also more likely than men to mediate solitude with nonhuman companionship (such as pets) or by using the telephone.

Singles' time is relatively loosely scheduled, and this characteristic is carried over into the way they organize their living space. American houses are designed to provide for the privacy of their residents by partitioning of internal space by function. Living rooms and dining rooms are public and social gathering places. Bedrooms and bathrooms are private.

Although singles differ from members of family households in their organization of property and time, their usage of space maintains many of the same features. They have few possessions, but, as one woman observed, these possessions spread out to fill the available space, besides, "Why buy it? I'd only have to move it." After a moment's reflection, she observed that her activities also spread out to fill the available space.

All of the singles lived in at least two- or three-room apartments. Several had four or more rooms. Though they felt free about states of undress and rarely closed doors, even to the bathroom, they observed a discreteness of function for the areas of their apartments.

There was an air of impermanence to their apartments, a lack of investment in time or money. Furniture was sparse, provided by the landlord, obviously secondhand or collapsible. Steamer trunks were left packed. Luggage was shoved in a corner, not stowed out of sight in a closet. Laundry in its wrapping paper lay on, not in, chests of drawers. Dishes, silverware, and linens were rarely of matched sets. A few maintained office addresses or post office boxes in lieu of home mail delivery.

This pattern is rather different from that of older singles who were less eager or likely to marry or remarry. Their residence histories indicated that they moved less often. The older singles to whom I talked placed their first purchases of furniture soon after their decisions to remain single, at least for the time being. Older singles (over thirty) had acquired matched sets of linens, dishes and silverware, draperies, carpets, life insurance and annuity policies, and home mortgages.

This is especially instructive if we notice that in American society a permanent home, furniture, and matching housewares are expectably acquired by newlyweds. These things are a material representation of the stability of married life. The distinction seems to be the difference between "my place" of the young single, who regards himself as going through a stage of independence before settling into marriage, and "my home" of the older single whose complete residence expresses his personal completeness.

The Domestic Division of Labor

We have looked at some of the reasons why singles choose to live alone and how they organize their homes. The discussion of singles' social networks has given some insight into the nature of their social relationships and how these relationships are formed. Turning to the problems singles encounter in maintaining their homes, we will see how the public and private worlds of singles are drawn together.

Blood and Wolfe's (1960, ch. 2 and 3) study of American marriages used the neolocal, nuclear family as their basic unit of comparison. The power to make decisions for the household and its members, with regard to choice of residence, jobs, major purchases, and the division of household labor, was found to be influenced by husbands' and wives' concepts of appropriate sex-role performances. Household tasks were conceptually divided into "men's work" and "women's work." The balance of power between husbands and wives was found to be further modified by the competence of each partner in meeting the requirements of sex-roles.

Blood and Wolfe found that there was a fairly strict division of labor by sex. Cooking, laundry, ironing, child care, and housecleaning, including vacuuming, floor scrubbing, dusting, and straightening up, were considered to be "traditionally" women's work. Men "traditionally" supported the household, cared for the exterior of the house and grounds, and sometimes repaired major appliances. Husbands and wives shared dishwashing, bookkeeping, and grocery shopping.

A single person, living alone, is the functional analogue of a nuclear family. Singles are autonomous decision-making units. They are solely responsible for supporting and maintaining their households. The unique character of singles' lifestyles emerges when we look at the strategies they devise to schedule and accomplish household work, or how they recruit others to share in the responsibilities of their households.

Single persons' households are interesting with regard to the ways that the "traditional" domestic division of labor is modified.

All of my informants lived in apartments, partially because of availability and expense, partially for convenience. Care of the exterior and grounds of the building, maintenance and repairs were the responsibility of the landlord. This exhausts the list of "traditionally" male domestic tasks.

Women's diaries included accounts of housekeeping chores. Although there was no orderly scheduling of chores, women mentioned that in the course of a normal week they vacuumed, scrubbed floors, dusted, straightened up, washed dishes, and did laundry and ironing. Usually these entries were prefaced by a statement such as "This place is a sty," or "I ran out of clean silverware." In interviews, men mentioned only straightening up and washing dishes. All but one of the men sent his laundry out.

Women shopped for groceries fairly regularly, about once every week or ten days, with short trips daily or less often for single items.

They purchased some convenience foods but also staples and perishables. Men shopped in total less frequently and purchased only a few items at a time. They bought few perishables or staples and proportionally higher amounts of convenience foods, usually enough only for one meal at a time.

Grocery shopping is related to meal habits. Women took most of their meals alone at home, watching television. They minimized cooking several ways. They made sandwiches or used prepared foods. More often, they cook for several days at a time. None of the women found cooking to be intrinsically interesting, but it was "something to do." Women took some care in maintaining a balanced diet.

This is quite different from the patterns of single men. Men said that they usually ate at restaurants and bars, got carryout food or accepted invitations to dinner from married friends and women. If they found themselves home alone during dinner hours, they snacked on canned and packaged convenience foods or skipped meals entirely. Men said that they did not cook because cooking is "too much trouble" and it "messes up the kitchen."

In summary, single women perform a relatively complete "traditional" repertoire of household labor, but single men perform only a very truncated list of housekeeping tasks. The "traditional" male repertoire of household duties is largely obviated by definition. We discover one of the definitive patterns of the singles' lifestyle, the quasi-conjugal household, when we find that within the general exchange of labor and emotional support, characteristic of singles' networks, some women extend a full range of housekeeping service to independent men in their personal networks.

Quasi-Conjugal Households

Earlier in the discussion, it was shown that singles can mobilize sectors of their social networks as cooperative labor groups to assist for special purposes, such as moving and house-painting. Individuals exchange domestic services as well. Such a reciprocal relationship can become routinized between a single man and a single woman, while each continues to maintain a separate residence. I have termed this a quasi-conjugal household.

All eight of the original group of informants are currently, or have recently been, members of one or more quasi-conjugal households. Some of the households were regarded as preliminary to living together in a marriagelike joint household, either as a preface to marriage or not. Other households were regarded as satisfactory without the likelihood of eventual marriage.

Although all of the singles in the original sample expressed the desire to marry "sometime" in the future, they had many reservations about immediate marriage, even with the people they planned to marry "eventually." The following passage is quite typical in giving reasons for not marrying, and for maintaining separate residences.

> Right after college I got very uptight about not being married. But then I decided I had my own life to lead. No, I'm not in any rush to get married. Children seem like an awfully heavy responsibility. After that (getting together again after breaking up) Mike decided we should live together. He said it would be cheaper since we did everything together anyway. But I decided not to because if we broke up then I would be the one to move out and there wouldn't be anywhere to go home to. It's security. (Anne, age twenty-five)

The division of labor in quasi-conjugal households is nearly identical to that described by Blood and Wolfe for nuclear families. Women provided shopping, cooking, and housekeeping services for their boyfriends. Men sometimes assisted them in this, and usually offered to share expenses for the running of both households. This kind of division of labor developed after the establishment of a sexual relationship in all cases.

One woman said that she regularly kept house for her boyfriend but never initiated such activities until he asked her to or offered some sort of trade in the form of a "heavy date." She said that once he had offered cash payment for a particularly thorough job, which she accepted rather than be "pushy." She felt that if she kept house for free, that the man might "take her for granted" or suspect that she was escalating the relationship to marriage. By not permitting him to reciprocate immediately, she felt she would have endangered the relationship.

Some tasks are highly indicative markers of the degree of commitment by partners to a relationship. Men and women agreed that washing dishes was not a loaded service. But one man added, "You've got to watch out when they start wanting to do your laundry." Sometimes women will attempt to force reciprocation on men who are not willing.

> I'd just like to find a nice girl to call up and go out for a beer. Just to have fun. But the first thing they do when you bring them home, like the first thing they do when they come in, is start picking up your socks. (Hal, age twenty-six)

The degree of commitment to a quasi-conjugal household and the relationship it symbolizes is measurable along two axes: the number and kind of domestic services traded and shared and the degree of routinization and coordination of scheduling between members. Scheduling increases with the intensity of the relationship. Activities, especially meals, become increasingly routinized into predictable time slots, unlike the timetables we saw for unattached singles.

In more fragile relationships, the exchange of services is carefully negotiated and casually scheduled. Several stable couples in the sample, both during and prior to the study, reciprocated services easily and spent three or more evenings a week together. Because they spent so much time in each others' apartments, they frequently kept toothbrushes, changes of clothing, and other personal items in both apartments, thus symbolically staking out a joint territory.

In each of the quasi-conjugal households I found, there seemed to be no routinized pattern of sleeping arrangements. The sexual business of the household was conducted about equally under both roofs. Singles felt that if they stayed away from their own apartments too regularly that their independence would be challenged. Men especially felt that women should not spend "too much" time in their apartments.

Schneider (1968, p. 116) says that in American culture, kinship is traced through the children of the married couples. He states that marriage is no more than legitimate sexual relations. He does not take into account the legal standing of such relations and especially the prescriptions in law pertaining to the maintenance of a joint-residence by married couples. In some states joint-residence acquires jural standing in definitions of common-law marriages and provisions for the legitimation of the children of couples who have not legally married.

The conjugal nature of quasi-conjugal households derives from the fact that the sexual aspect of the relationship is routinely conducted within the homes of its members. Sexual encounters of brief duration, such as "one-night stands" or encounters situated in borrowed apartments, hotels, and motels, are not accorded the same aura of legitimacy.

It is important to recognize that quasi-conjugal relationships are further routinized to the degree that partners reciprocate domestic services. The relationship has no jural content, however. There are no enforceable sanctions for failure to reciprocate. The relationhip is based rather on mutual expectations. When expectations on the part of either or both parties no longer coincide and negotiation fails to restore agreement on the content of the relationship, the quasi-conjugal household is dissolved.

> Anne told me that Laura's boyfriend, Jack, was a real SOB because he had started seeing Carol even though Laura continued to do his laundry, as she had for nearly six months. Anne said that Laura was being a real idiot for letting Jack "use" her that way. But Laura kept on doing Jack's wash. Later Jack defended his actions to Don, who worked in the same office as Jack, Laura and Anne. Jack said

that he had no intention of marrying her. But despite his protests, Laura insisted on helping him.

As single men and women form intense, personal relationships, women extend their housekeeping to more than one residence. To a much lesser degree, men extend domestic services to women. Since most of these services are given by women and taken by men, we may say that a woman establishes sexual rights in a man to the degree to which she keeps his house. A single man validates her claim to the extent that he permits and publicly encourages her in this.

Sexual relationships between single men and women are mediated through this exchange of domestic services. Either party can symbolically assert the right to other sexual partners by refusing to accept or to perform domestic services. The giving and taking of some services are more obligating than others.

Not every quasi-conjugal household leads to marriage, but an individual's willingness to escalate its conjugal nature indicates a willingness to marry. By following the career of a quasi-conjugal household, and by seeing whether reciprocity is increasing or decreasing, it is possible to tell whether it is a transitional stage to living together or marriage. A quasi-conjugal household can also be a steady and ambiguous state in which each member remains self-sufficient and nominally head of his or her own household.

Summary

This study is not intended to account for all possible singles' lifestyles. Thus, such subjects as "the singles' bar complex" and the "swinging-singles" lifestyle have not been considered here. Instead, I have focused on a limited sample of semiprofessional singles in a small midwestern city, where the possibility of developing the kind of lifestyle that is alleged to be characteristic of big-city singles' life is less likely to develop because of the lack of the appropriate facilities (such as singles bars) and conditions (such as the anonymity of urban housing and settings). For these reasons it would be inappropriate to draw broad general conclusions from this research. Thus, the following statements are offered more as tentative hypotheses for further testing than as conclusions.

Urban singles operate as autonomous individuals in a social milieu devoid of kin or conjugal ties. Few of their interpersonal relationships are invested with jural rights and duties. That is to say, their personal relationships are not formed or sanctioned in terms of extrapersonal rules or norms other than those applicable throughout the society. Concomitantly, singles are free of enforceable obligations to others. Their freedom from such restriction is expressed in their high degree of job and residence mobility. Thus, the majority of personal relationships among singles lack the time depth and the complexity of overlapping identities that are characteristic of married people.

Young urban singles, however, develop strategies for building a modicum of stability and predictable reciprocity into their relationships. Through processes of social selection, singles form personal relationships primarily with other singles. The resulting personal networks provide the basis for various kinds of cooperative and supportive activities and exchanges. The shared knowledge that they all lack other sorts of support groups draws them together.

Although men and women conducted distinctly different types of households, the social networks of these singles functioned to distribute the sum of the women's housekeeping skills and activities among the available single men. Men and women pair off in quasi-conjugal relationships that share many features with conjugal pairings while preserving the essential autonomy of the individuals.

As the personal relationship between a man and a woman approaches the conjugal form and becomes more or less stable, the man begins to perform the traditionally male tasks involved in maintaining both of their residences, thus approximating the form of the conjugal family in terms of the division of labor. An alternate pattern may also develop as the man assumes or shares some of the traditionally female tasks, such as shopping or laundry, creating a division of domestic labor in which men and women are structurally and functionally equivalent.

References

Barker, Roger G., ed. 1963. *The Stream of Behavior.* New York: Appleton-Century-Crofts.

Blood, Robert O., Jr. and Donald M. Wolfe. 1960. *Husbands and Wives: The Dynamics of Married Living.* New York: Free Press.

Bott, Elizabeth. 1957. *Family and Social Network.* London: Tavistock Publications.

Crissman, Lawrence. 1969. "On Networks." *Cornell Journal of Social Relations* 4(1):72–80.

Farber, Bernard. 1971. *Kinship and Class.* New York: Basic Books.

Gonzalez, Nancie. 1970. "Toward a Definiton of Matrifocality." In *Afro-American Anthropology: Contemporary Perspectives*, ed. Norman Whitten and John Szwed. New York: Free Press, pp. 231–44.

Goodenough, Ward H. 1970. *Description and Comparison in Cultural Anthropology.* Chicago: Aldine Publishing Company.

Lewis, Oscar. 1965. *La Vida: A Puerto-Rican Family in the Culture of Poverty—San Juan and New York.* New York: Random House.

Mayer, Adrian C. 1966. "The Significance of Quasi-groups in the Study of Complex Societies." In *The Social Anthropology of Complex Societies,* ed. Michael Banton. Association of Social Anthropologists Monograph, no. 4. London: Tavistock, pp. 97–122.

Schneider, David M. 1968. *American Kinship: A Cultural Account.* Englewood Cliffs, N.J.: Prentice-Hall,

Sennet, Richard. 1970. *Family Against the City: Middle-Class Homes of Industrial Chicago, 1872–1890.* Cambridge, Mass.: Harvard University Press.

Stack, Carol B. 1972. *Everything That Goes Round Comes Round: Kindred and Exchange Networks in a Black Community.* Ph.D. dissertation, University of Illinois.

United States Bureau of the Census. 1895. *Report on the Population of the United States at the Eleventh Census, 1890. Part 1.* Washington, D.C.: U.S. Government Printing Office.

——. 1970. *U.S. Census of Housing, series HC(1)-A1.* Washington, D.C.: U.S. Government Printing Office.

——.1972. *Current Population Reports,* Series P-20:223, 225. Washington, D.C.: U.S. Government Printing Office.

PART SEVEN
Education

Educational institutions are composed of formally organized, independently existing systems of training and teaching. The most common manifestation of this institution is the classroom. The classroom is used to instruct virtually every art and science known to any member of society. Subjects from demolition to Descartes are taught in this standard setting. As the society places more value on skills and their use, we see the application of education increasing. In ever-widening circles, these institutions exert control over people and are, in turn, affected by the individuals they serve.

Almost simultaneously a child confronts both the family and education as institutions. In modern society the length of time a person spends, in one way or another, with educational organizations has dramatically increased. From the day-care center and preschool classes to continuing education and retraining programs for adults, we all feel the impact of the schoolroom. We act out our lives in the context of teachers, textbooks, audiovisual equipment, and the "authorities" of the school. To most, the schoolroom is "second nature." We know it well, and are affected by it.

As a context for socialization, the educational scene transmits the basic values of the society. It serves as a reflection of the needs and organizational character of the society to which it belongs. It occupies the time of children who have nothing to do or no real purpose in the societal scheme of things. It trains them in the formal skills and knowledge required in adulthood. Yet it is also a place where informal incidental learning takes place, where friends are made, relationships are consummated, and most importantly, where the social competencies necessary to accomplish these feats are acquired. It is a setting for rehearsing the goals, conflicts, and aspirations that will be used in future roles. In a genuine sense, educational institutions are microcosms of the general society.

Although these ubiquitous institutions are much discussed, theorized about, lauded, and criticized, little actual description of the classroom and its related settings has been reported. We have gathered materials that related the nature of the school as an action setting, tell what really goes on inside those four walls, and even sometimes describe what goes on inside the minds of that peculiar species, the student.

Everyday Life in the Classroom

We have repeatedly emphasized the interrelated nature of the institutions of the society. A function once performed by one institution may be taken over by another. The institution of education in the modern society assumes more and more responsibility for the total socialization of the individual. Harry Gracey discusses the function of kindergarten as a training ground for the everyday battles of our society. He takes us through the minute-by-minute routine of this classroom scene and relates the underlying rationale and effects of the practices on the future members of the adult world.

Learning the Student Role: Kindergarten as Academic Boot Camp

Harry L. Gracey

Introduction

Education must be considered one of the major institutions of social life today. Along with the family and organized religion, however, it is a "secondary institution," one in which people are prepared for life in society as it is presently organized. The main dimensions of modern life, that is, the nature of society as a whole, is determined principally by the "primary institutions," which today are the economy, the political

From *Readings in Introductory Sociology,* ed. Dennis Wrong and Harry L. Gracey (New York: MacMillan, 1972). Reprinted by permission. This article is based on research conducted with the Bank Street College of Eduction under NIMH Grant No. 9135. The study is more fully reported in Harry L. Gracey, *The Civil Structure and Ideology of an Elementary School,* Chicago, University of Chicago Press, 1972.

system, and the military establishment. Education has been defined by sociologists, classical and contemporary, as an institution which serves society by socializing people into it through a formalized, standardized procedure. At the beginning of this century, Emile Durkheim told student teachers at the University of Paris that education "consists of a methodical socialization of the younger generation." He went on to add:

> It is the influence exercised by adult generations on those that are not ready for social life. Its object is to arouse and to develop in the child a certain number of physical, intellectual, and moral states that are demanded of him by the special milieu for which he is specifically destined. . . . To the egotistic and asocial being that has just been born, [society] must, as rapidly as possible, add another, capable of leading a moral and social life. Such is the work of education.[1]

The educational process, Durkheim said, "is above all the means by which society perpetually recreates the conditions of its very existence."[2] The contemporary educational sociologist, Wilbur Brookover, offers a similar formulation in his recent textbook definition of education:

> Actually, therefore, in the broadest sense education is synonymous with socialization. It includes any social behavior that assists in the induction of the child into membership in the society or any behavior by which the society perpetuates itself through the next generation.[3]

The educational institution is, then, one of the ways in which society is perpetuated through the systematic socialization of the young, while the nature of the society which is being perpetuated—its organization and operation, its values, beliefs, and ways of living—are determined by the primary institutions. The educational system, like other secondary institutions, *serves* the society which is *created* by the operation of the economy, the political system, and the military establishment.

Schools, the social organizations of the educational institution, are today for the most part large bureaucracies run by specially trained and certified people. There are few places left in modern societies where formal teaching and learning is carried on in small, isolated groups, like the rural, one-room schoolhouses of the last century. Schools are large, formal organizations which tend to be parts of larger organizations, local community school districts. These school districts are bureaucratically organized, and their operations are supervised by state and local governments. In this context, as Brookover says:

---

[1] Emile Durkheim, *Sociology and Education* (New York: Free Press, 1956), pp. 71–72.
[2] Durkheim, *Sociology and Education*, p. 123.
[3] Wilbur Brookover, *The Sociology of Education* (New York: American Book Company, 1957), p. 4.

the term education is used . . . to refer to a system of schools, in which specifically designated persons are expected to teach children and youth certain types of acceptable behavior. The school system becomes a . . . unit in the total social structure and is recognized by the members of the society as a separate social institution. Within this structure a portion of the total socialization process occurs.[4]

Education is the part of the socialization process which takes place in the schools, and these are, more and more today, bureaucracies within bureaucracies.

Kindergarten is generally conceived by educators as a year of preparation for school. It is thought of as a year in which small children, five or six years old, are prepared socially and emotionally for the academic learning which will take place over the next twelve years. It is expected that a foundation of behavior and attitudes will be laid in kindergarten on which the children can acquire the skills and knowledge they will be taught in the grades. A booklet prepared for parents by the staff of a suburban New York school system says that the kindergarten experience will stimulate the child's desire to learn and cultivate the skills he will need for learning in the rest of his school carrer. It claims that the child will find opportunities for physical growth, for satisfying his "need for self-expression," acquire some knowledge, and provide opportunities for creative activity. It concludes, "The most important benefit that your five-year-old will receive from kindergarten is the opportunity to live and grow happily and purposefully with others in a small society." The kindergarten teachers in one of the elementary schools in this community, one we shall call the Wilbur Wright School, said their goals were to see that the children "grew" in all ways: physically, of course, emotionally, socially, and academically. They said they wanted children to like school as a result of their kindergarten experiences and that they wanted them to learn to get along with others.

None of these goals, however, is unique to kindergarten; each of them is held to some extent by teachers in the other six grades at the Wright School. And growth would occur, but differently, even if the child did not attend school. The children already know how to get along with others in their families and their play groups. The unique job of the kindergarten in the educational division of labor seems rather to be teaching children the student role. The student role is the repertoire of behavior and attitudes regarded by educators as appropriate to children in school. Observation in the kindergartens of the Wilbur Wright School revealed a great variety of activities through which children are shown and then drilled in the behavior and attitudes defined as appropriate for

[4]Brookover, *Sociology of Education*, p. 6.

school and thereby induced to learn the role of student. Observations of the kindergartens and interviews with the teachers both pointed to the teaching and learning of classroom routines as the main element of the student role. The teachers expended most of their efforts, for the first half of the year at least, in training the children to follow the routines which teachers created. The children were, in a very real sense, *drilled* in tasks and activities created by the teachers for their own purposes and beginning and ending quite arbitrarily (from the child's point of view) at the command of the teacher. One teacher remarked that she hated September, because during the first month "everything has to be done rigidly, and repeatedly, until they know exactly what they're supposed to do." However, "by January," she said, "they know exactly what to do [during the day] and I don't have to be after them all the time." Classroom routines were introduced gradually from the beginning of the year in all the kindergartens, and children were drilled in them as long as was necessary to achieve regular compliance. By the end of the school year, the successful kindergarten teacher has a well-organized group of children. They follow classroom routines automatically, having learned all the command signals and the expected responses to them. They have, in our terms, learned the student role. The following observation shows one such classroom operating at optimum organization on an afternoon late in May. It is the class of an experienced and respected kindergarten teacher.

An Afternoon in Kindergarten

At about 12:20 in the afternoon on a day in the last week of May, Edith Kerr leaves the teachers' room where she has been having lunch and walks to her classroom at the far end of the primary wing of Wright School. A group of five- and six-year-olds peer at her through the glass doors leading from the hall cloakroom to the play area outside. Entering her room, she straightens some material in the "book corner" of the room, arranges music on the piano, takes colored paper from her closet, and places it on one of the shelves under the window. Her room is divided into a number of activity areas through the arrangement of furniture and play equipment. Two easels and a paint table near the door create a kind of passageway inside the room. A wedge-shaped area just inside the front door is made into a teacher's area by the placing of "her" things there: her desk, file, and piano. To the left is the book corner, marked off from the rest of the room by a puppet stage and a movable chalkboard. In it are a display rack of picture books, a record player, and a stack of children's records. To the right of the entrance are the sink and cleanup area. Four large round tables with six chairs at each for the children are placed near the walls about halfway down the length of the room, two on each side, leaving a large open area in the center for group games, block building, and toy-truck driving. Windows stretch down the length of both walls, starting about three feet from the floor and extending almost to the high ceilings. Under the windows are long shelves on which are kept all the toys, games, blocks, paper, paints, and other equipment of the kindergarten. The left rear corner of the room is a play store with shelves, merchandise, and cash register; the right rear corner is a play kitchen with stove, sink, ironing board, and bassinette with baby dolls in it. This area is partly shielded from the rest of the room by a large standing display rack for posters and children's artwork. A sandbox is found against the back wall between these two areas. The room is light, brightly colored, and filled with things adults feel five- and six-year-olds will find interesting and pleasing.

At 12:25 Edith opens the outside door and admits the waiting children. They hang their sweaters on hooks outside the door and then go to the center of the room and arrange themselves in a semicircle on the floor, facing the teacher's chair which she has placed in the center of the floor. Edith follows them in and sits in her chair checking attendance while waiting for the bell to ring. When she has finished attendance, which she takes by sight, she asks the children what the date is, what day and month it is, how many children are enrolled in the class, how many are present, and how many are absent.

The bell rings at 12:30 and the teacher puts away her attendance book. She introduces a visitor, who is sitting against the right wall taking notes, as someone who wants to learn about schools and children. She then goes to the back of the room and takes down a large chart labeled "Helping Hands." Bringing it to the center of the room, she tells the children it is time to change jobs. Each child is assigned some task on the chart by placing his name, lettered on a paper "hand," next to a picture signifying the task—e.g., a broom, a blackboard, a milk bottle, a flag, and a Bible. She asks the children who wants each of the jobs and rearranges their "hands" accordingly. Returning to her chair, Edith announces, "One person should tell us what happened to Mark." A girl raises her hand and when called on says, "Mark fell and hit his head and had to go to the hospital." The teacher adds that Mark's mother had written saying he was in the hospital.

During this time the children have been interacting among themselves, in their semicircle. Children have whispered to their neighbors, poked on another, made general comments to the group, waved to friends on the other side of the circle. None of this has been disruptive, and the teacher has ignored it for the most part. The children seem to know just how much of each kind of interaction is permitted—they may greet in a soft voice someone who sits next to them, for example, but may not shout greetings to a friend who sits across the circle, so they confine themselves to waving and remain well within understood limits.

At 12:35 two children arrive. Edith asks them why they are late and then sends them to join the circle on the floor. The other children vie with each other to tell the newcomers what happened to Mark. When this leads to a general disorder Edith asks, "Who has serious time?" The children become quiet, and a girl raises her hand. Edith nods and the child gets a Bible and hands it to Edith. She reads the Twenty-third Psalm while the children sit quietly. Edith helps the child in charge begin reciting the Lord's Prayer, while the other children follow along for the first unit of sounds and then trail off as Edith finishes for them. Everyone stands and faces the American flag hung to the right of the door. Edith leads the pledge to the flag, with the children again following the familiar sounds as far as they remember them. Edith then asks the girl in charge what song she wants and the child replies, "My Country." Edith goes to the piano and plays "America," singing as the children follow her words.

Edith returns to her chair in the center of the room, and the children sit again in the semicircle on the floor. It is 12:40 when she tells the children, "Let's have boys' sharing time first." She calls the name of the first boy sitting on the end of the circle, and he comes up to her with a toy helicopter. He turns and holds it up for the other children to see. He says, "It's a helicopter." Edith asks, "What is it used for?" and he replies, "For the army. Carry men. For the war." Other children join in, "For shooting submarines." "To bring back men from space when they are in the ocean." Edith sends the boy back to the circle and asks the next boy if he has something. He replies "No" and she passes on to the next. He says "Yes" and brings a bird's nest to her. He holds it for the class to see, and the teacher ask, "What kind of bird made the nest?" The boy replies, "My friend says a rain bird made it." Edith asks what the nest is made of and different children reply, "mud," "leaves," and "sticks." There is also a bit of moss woven into the nest and Edith tries to describe it to the children. They, however are more interested in seeing if anything is inside it, and Edith lets the boy carry it around the semicircle showing the children its insides. Edith tells the children of some baby robins in a nest in her yard, and some of the children tell about baby birds they have seen. Some children are asking about a small object in the nest which they say looks like an egg, but all have seen the nest now, and Edith calls on the next boy. A number of children say, "I know what Michael has, but I'm not telling." Michael brings a book to the teacher and then goes back to his place in the circle of children. Edith reads the last page of the book to the class. Some children tell of books which they have at home. Edith calls the next boy, and three children call out, "I know what David has." "He always has the same thing." "It's a bang-bang." David goes to his table and gets a box which he brings to Edith. He opens it and shows the teacher a scale-model of an old-fashioned dueling pistol. When David does not turn around to the class, Edith tells him, "Show it to the children," and he does. One child says, "Mr. Johnson [the principal] said no guns." Edith replies, "Yes, how many of you know that?" Most of the children in the circle raise their hands. She continues, "That you aren't supposed to bring guns to school?" She calls the next boy on the circle and he brings two large toy soldiers to her which the children enthusiatically identify as being from "Babes in Toyland." The next boy brings an American flag to Edith and shows it to the class. She asks him what the stars and stripes stand for and admonishes him to treat it carefully. "Why should you treat it carefully?" she asks the boy. "Because it's our flag," he replies. She congratulates him, saying, "That's right."

"Show and Tell" lasted twenty minutes, and during the last ten, one girl in particular announced that she knew what each child called upon had to show. Edith asked her to be quiet each time she spoke out, but she was not content, continuing to offer her comment at each "show." Four children from other classes had come into the room to bring something from another teacher or to ask for something from Edith. Those with requests were asked to return later if the item wasn't readily available.

Edith now asks if any of the children told their mothers about their trip to the local zoo the previous day. Many children raise their hands. As Edith calls on them, they tell what they liked in the zoo. Some children cannot wait to be called on, and they call out things to the teacher who asks them to be quiet. After a few of the animals are mentioned, one child says, "I liked the spooky house," and the others chime in to agree with him, some pantomiming fear and horror. Edith is puzzled, and asks what this was. When half the children try to tell her at once, she raises her hand for quiet, then calls on individual children. One says, "The house with nobody in it"; another, "The dark little house." Edith asks where it was in the zoo, but the children cannot describe its location in any way which she can understand. Edith makes some jokes, but they involve adult abstractions which the children cannot grasp. The children have become quite noisy now, speaking out to make both relevant and irrelevant comments, and three little girls have become particularly assertive.

Edith gets up from her seat at 1:10 and goes to the book corner, where she puts a record on the player. As it begins a story about the trip to the zoo, she returns to the circle and asks the children to go sit at the tables. She divides them among the tables in such a way as to indicate that they don't have regular seats. When the children are all seated at the four tables, five or six to a table, the teacher asks, "Who wants to be the first one?" One of the noisy girls comes to the center of the room. The voice on the record is giving directions for imitating an ostrich and the girl follows them, walking around the center of the room holding her ankles with her hands. Edith replays the record, and all the children, table by table, imitate ostriches down the center of the room and back. Edith removes her shoes and shows that she can be an ostrich, too. This is apparently a familiar game, for a number of children are calling out, "Can we have the crab?" Edith asks one of the children to do a crab "so we can all remember how" and then plays the part of the record with music for imitating crabs by. The children from the first table line up across the room, hands and feet on the floor and face pointing toward the ceiling. After they have "walked" down the room and back in this posture, they sit at their table and the children of the next table play "crab." The children love this; they run from their tables, dance about on the floor waiting for their turns and are generally exuberant. Children ask for the "inch worm," and the game is played again with the children squirming down the floor. As a conclusion Edith shows them a new animal imitation, the "lame dog." The children all hobble down the floor on three "legs," table by table, to the accompaniment of the record.

At 1:30 Edith has the children line up in the center of the room; she says, "Table one, line up in front of me," and children ask, "What are we going to do?" Then she moves a few steps to the side and says, "Table two over here, line up next to table one," and more children ask, "What for?" She does this for table three and table four and each time the children ask, "Why, what are we going to do?" When the children are lined up in four lines of five each, spaced so that they are not touching one another, Edith puts on a new record and leads the class in calisthenics, to the accompaniment of the record. The children just jump around every which way in their places instead of doing the exercises, and by the time the record is finished, Edith, the only one following it, seems exhausted. She is apparently adopting the president's new "Physical Fitness" program in her classroom.

At 1:35 Edith pulls her chair to the easels and calls the children to sit on the floor in front of her, table by table. When they are all seated she asks, "What are you going to do for worktime today?" Different children raise their hands and tell Edith what they are going to draw. Most are going to make pictures of animals they saw in the zoo.

Edith asks if they want to make pictures to send to Mark in the hospital, and the children agree to this. Edith gives drawing paper to the children, calling them to her one by one. After getting a piece of paper, the children go to the crayon box on the right-hand shelves, select a number of colors, and go to the tables, where they begin drawing. Edith is again trying to quiet the perpetually talking girls. She keeps two of them standing by her so they won't disrupt the others. She asks them, "Why do you feel you have to talk all the time?" and then scolds them for not listening to her. Then she sends them to their tables to draw.

Most of the children are drawing at their tables, sitting or kneeling in their chairs. They are all working very industriously and, engrossed in their work, very quietly. Three girls have chosen to paint at the easels, and having donned their smocks, they are busily mixing colors and intently applying them to their pictures. If the children at the tables are primitives and neorealists in their animal depictions, these girls at the easels are the class abstract-expressionists, with their broad-stroked, colorful paintings.

Edith asks of the children generally, "What color should I make the cover of Mark's book?" Brown and green are suggested by some children "because Mark likes them." The other children are puzzled as to just what is going on and ask, "What book?" or "What does she mean?" Edith explains what she thought was clear to them already, that they are all going to put their pictures together in a "book" to be sent to Mark. She goes to a small table in the play kitchen corner and tells the children to bring her their pictures when they are finished and she will write their message for Mark on them.

By 1:50 most children have finished their pictures and given them to Edith. She talks with some of them as she ties the bundle of pictures together—answering questions, listening, carrying on conversations. The children are playing in various parts of the room with toys, games and blocks which they have taken off the shelves. They also move from table to table examining each other's pictures, offering compliments and suggestions. Three girls at a table are cutting up colored paper for a collage. Another girl is walking about the room in a pair of high heels with a woman's purse over her arm. Three boys are playing in the center of the room with the large block set, with which they are building walkways and walking on them. Edith is very much concerned about their safety and comes over a number of times to fuss over them. Two or three other boys are pushing trucks around the center of the room, and mild altercations occur when they drive through the block constructions. Some boys and a girl are playing at the toy store, two girls are serving "tea" in the play kitchen and one is washing a doll baby. Two boys have elected to clean the room, and with large sponges they wash the movable blackboard, the puppet stage, and then begin on the tables. They run into resistance from the children who are working with construction toys on the tables and do not want to dismantle their structures. The class is like a room full of bees, each intent on pursuing some activity, occasionally bumping into one another, but just veering off in another direction without serious altercation. At 2:05 the custodian arrives pushing a cart loaded with half-pint milk containers. He places a tray of cartons on the counter next to the sink, then leaves. His coming and going is unnoticed in the room (as, incidentally, is the presence of the observer, who is completely ignored by the children for the entire afternoon).

At 2:15 Edith walks to the entrance of the room, switches off the lights, and sits at the piano and plays. The children begin spontaneously singing the song, which is "Clean up, clean up. Everybody clean up." Edith walks around the room supervising the clean up. Some children put their toys, the blocks, puzzles, games, and so on back on their shelves under the windows. The children making a collage keep right on working. A child from another class comes in to borrow the 45-rpm adaptor for the record player. At more urging from Edith the rest of the children shelve their toys and work. The children are sitting around their tables now, and Edith asks, "What record would you like to hear while you have your milk?" There is some confusion and no general consensus, so Edith drops the subject and begins to call the children, table by table, to come get their milk. "Table one," she says, and the five children come to the sink, wash their hands and dry them, pick up a carton of milk and a straw, and take it back to their table. Two talking girls wander about the room interfering with the children getting their milk and Edith calls out to them to "settle down." As the children sit, many of them call out to Edith the name of the record they want to hear. When all the children are seated at tables with milk, Edith plays one of these records called "Bozo and the Birds" and shows the children pictures in a book which go with the record. The record recites, and the book shows the adventures of the clown, Bozo, as he walks through a woods meeting many different kinds of birds who, of course, display the characteristics of many kinds of people or, more accurately, different stereotypes. As children finish their milk they take blankets or pads from the shelves under the windows and lie on them in the center of the room where Edith sits on her chair showing the pictures. By 2:30 half the class is lying on the floor on their blankets, the record is still playing, and the teacher is turning the pages of the book. The child who came in previously returns the 45-rpm adaptor, and one of the kindergartners tells Edith what the boy's name is and where he lives.

The record ends at 2:40. Edith says, "Children, down on your blankets." All the class is lying on blankets now, Edith refuses to answer the various questions individual children put to her because, she tells them, "it's rest time now." Instead she talks very softly about what they will do tomorrow. They are going to work with clay, she says. The children lie quietly and listen. One of the boys raises his hand and when called on tells Edith, "The animals in the zoo looked so hungry yesterday." Edith asks the children what they think about this and a number try to volunteer opinions, but Edith accepts only those offered in a "rest-time tone," that is, softly and quietly. After a brief discussion of animal feeding, Edith calls the names of the two children on milk detail and has them collect empty milk cartons from the tables and return them to the tray. She asks the two children on cleanup detail to clean up the room. Then she gets up from her chair and goes to the door to turn on the lights. At this signal the children all get up from the floor and return their blankets and pads to the shelf. It is raining (the reason for no outside play this afternoon), and cars driven by mothers clog the school drive and line up along the street. One of the talkative little girls comes over to Edith and pointing out the window says, "Mrs. Kerr, see my mother in the new Cadillac?"

At 2:50 Edith sits at the piano and plays. The children sit on the floor in the center of the room and sing. They have a repertoire of songs about animals, including one in which each child sings a refrain alone. They know these by heart and sing along through the ringing of the 2:55 bell. When the song is finished Edith gets up and coming to the group says, "Okay, rhyming words to get your coats today." The children raise their hands and as Edith calls on them, they tell her two rhyming words, after which they are allowed to go into the hall to get their coats and sweaters. They return to the room with these and sit at their tables. At 2:59 Edith says, "When you have your coats on, you may line up at the door." Half of the children go to the door and stand in a long line. When the three o'clock bell rings, Edith returns to the piano and plays. The children sing a song called "Goodbye," after which Edith sends them out.

Training for Learning and for Life

The day in kindergarten at Wright School illustrates both the content of the student role as it has been learned by these children and the processes by which the teacher has brought about this learning or "taught" them the student role. The children have learned to go through routines and to follow orders with unquestioning obedience, even when these make no sense to them. They have been disciplined to do as they are told by an authoritative person without significant protest. Edith has developed this discipline in the children by creating and enforcing a rigid social structure in the classroom through which she effectively controls the behavior of most of the children for most of the school day. The "living with others in a small society" which the school pamphlet tells parents is the most important thing the children will learn in kindergarten can be seen now in its operational meaning, which is learning to live by the routines imposed by the school. This learning appears to be the principal content of the student role.

Children who submit to school-imposed discipline and come to identify with it, so that being a "good student" comes to be an important part of their developing identities, *become* the good students by the school's definitions. Those who submit to the routines of the school but do not come to identify with them will be adequate students who find the more important part of their identities elsewhere, such as in the play group outside school. Children who refuse to submit to the school routines are rebels, who become known as "bad students" and often "problem children" in the school, for they do not learn the academic curriculum and their behavior is often disruptive in the classroom. Today, schools engage clinical psychologists in part to help teachers deal with such children.

In looking at Edith's kindergarten at Wright School, it is interesting to ask how the children learn this role of student—come to accept school-imposed routines—and what, exactly, it involves in terms of behavior and attitudes. The most prominent features of the classroom are its physical and social structures. The room is carefully furnished and arranged in ways adults feel will interest children. The play store and play kitchen in the back of the room, for example, imply that children are interested in mimicking these activities of the adult world. The only space left for the children to create something of their own is the empty center of the room, and the materials at their disposal are the blocks, whose use causes anxiety on the part of the teacher. The room, being carefully organized physically by the adults, leaves little room for the creation of physical organization on the part of the children.

The social structure created by Edith is a far more powerful and subtle force for fitting the children to the student role. This structure is established by the very rigid and tightly controlled set of rituals and routines through which the children are put during the day. There is first the rigid "locating procedure" in which the children are asked to find themselves in terms of the month, date, day of the week, and the number of the class who are present and absent. This puts them solidly in the real world as defined by adults. The day is then divided into six periods whose activities are for the most part determined by the teacher. In Edith's kindergarten the children went through serious time, which opens the school day, sharing time, play time (which in clear weather would be spent outside), work time, cleanup time, after which they have their milk, and rest time, after which they go home. The teacher has programmed activities for each of these times.

Occasionally the class is allowed limited discretion to choose between proffered activities such as stories or records, but original ideas for activities are never solicited from them. Opportunity for free individual action is open only once in the day, during the part of work time left after the general class assignment has been completed (on the day reported, the class assignment was drawing animal pictures for the absent Mark). Spontaneous interests or observations from the children are never developed by the teacher. It seems that her schedule just does not allow room for developing such unplanned events. During sharing time, for example, the child who brought a bird's nest told Edith, in reply to her question of what kind of bird made it, "My friend says it's a rain bird." Edith does not think to ask about this bird, probably because the answer is "childish," that is, not given in accepted adult categories of birds. The children then express great interest in an object in the nest, but the teacher ignores this interest, probably because the object is uninteresting to her. The soldiers from "Babes in Toyland" strike a responsive note in the children, but this is not used for a discussion of any kind. The soldiers are treated in the same way as objects which bring little interest from the children. Finally, at the end of sharing time, the child world of perception literally erupts in the class with the recollection of "the spooky house" at the zoo. Apparently, this made more of an impression on the children than did any of the animals, but Edith is unable to make any sense of it for herself. The tightly imposed order of the class begins to break down as the children discover a universe of discourse of their own and begin talking excitedly with one another. The teacher is effectively excluded from this child's world of perception, and for a moment she fails to dominate the classroom situation. She reasserts control, however, by taking the children to the next activity she has planned for the day. It seems never to have occurred to Edith that there might be a meaningful learning experience for the children in recreating the "spooky house" in the classroom. It seems fair to say that this would have offered an exercise in spontaneous self-expression and an opportunity for real creativity on the part of the children. Instead, they are taken through a canned animal-imitation procedure, an activity which they apparently enjoy but which is also imposed upon them rather than created by them.

While children's perceptions of the world and opportunities for genuine spontaneity and creativity are being systematically eliminated from the kindergarten, unquestioned obedience to authority and rote learning of meaningless material are being encouraged. When the children are called to line up in the center of the room they ask "Why?" and "What for?" as they are in the very process of complying. They have learned to go smoothly through a programmed day, regardless of whether parts of the program make any sense to them or not. Here the student role involves what might be called "doing what you're told and never mind why." Activities which might "make sense" to the children are effectively ruled out, and they are forced or induced to participate in activities which may be "senseless," such as the calisthenics.

At the same time the children are being taught by rote meaningless sounds in the ritual oaths and songs, such as the Lord's Prayer, the Pledge to the Flag, and "America." As they go through the grades children learn more and more of the sounds of these ritual oaths, but the fact that they have often learned meaningless sounds rather than meaningful statements is shown when they are asked to write these out in the sixth grade; they write them as groups of sounds rather than as a series of words, according to the sixth-grade teachers at Wright School. Probably much learning in the elementary grades is of this character, that is, having no intrinsic meaning to the children but rather being tasks inexplicably required of them by authoritative adults. Listening to sixth-grade children read social-studies reports, for example, in which they have copied material from encyclopedias about a particular country, an observer often gets the feeling that he is watching an activity which has no intrinsic meaning for the child. The child who reads, "Switzerland grows wheat and cows and grass and makes a lot of cheese" knows the dictionary meaning of each of these words but may very well have no conception at all of this "thing" called Switzerland. He is simply carrying out a task assigned by the teacher *because* it is assigned, and this may be its only "meaning" for him.

Another type of learning which takes place in kindergarten is seen in children who take advantage of the "holes" in the adult social structure to create activities of their own, during work time or out-of-doors during play time. Here the children are learning to carve out a small world of their own within the world created by adults. They very quickly learn that if they keep within permissible limits of noise and action, they can play much as they please. Small groups of children formed during the year in Edith's kindergarten who played together at these times, developing semi-independent little groups in which they created their own worlds in the interstices of the adult-imposed physical and social world. These groups remind the sociological observer very much of the so-called informal groups which adults develop in factories and offices of large bureaucracies. Here too, within authoritatively imposed social organizations people find "holes" to create little subworlds which support informal, friendly, nonofficial behavior. Forming and participating in such groups seems to be as much part of the student role as it is of the role of bureaucrat.

The kindergarten has been conceived of here as the year in which children are prepared for their schooling by learning the role of student. In the classrooms of the rest of the school grades the children will be asked to submit to systems and routines imposed by the teachers and the curriculum. The days will be much like those of kindergarten, except that academic subjects will be substituted for the activities of the kindergarten. Once out of the school system, young adults will more than likely find themselves working in large-scale bureaucratic organizations, perhaps on the assembly line in the factory, perhaps in the paper routines of the white collar occupations, where they will be required to submit to rigid routines imposed by "the company" which may make little sense to them. Those who can operate well in this situaton will be successful bureaucratic functionaries. Kindergarten, therefore, can be seen as preparing children not only for participation in the bureaucratic organization of large modern school systems, but also for the large-scale occupational bureaucracies of modern society.

24
Managing Everyday Disruptions

Classrooms require orderly behavior. Potentially disruptive behavior may be handled in a variety of ways depending on the nature of the situation and the values held by those in control. Most patterns of control exhibit some degree of organization; those with distinctive patterns can be identified as strategies. In this selection Carol Dixon describes what she calls a "guided-options management strategy." She documents the children's responses in a Head Start program, how the teachers and aides manage what they defined as disruptive behavior, methods for anticipating it, and how motives were assigned to the children. She argues convincingly that disagreement over values of permissiveness *versus* authoritarianism in educational policy can be clarified by identifying the actual practices of teachers in dealing with children.

Guided Options as a Pattern of Control in a Head Start Program

Carol Dixon

The assembling of children under specialized adult supervision is a ubiquitous feature of American society. And the manner in which such specialized supervision is to be organized is a topic of continuing concern and diatribe. At one extreme are the defenders of conventional and authoritarian organization of these specialized assemblages called classrooms (Bagley 1907, Bettelheim 1969). At the other extreme are

From *Urban Life and Culture* 1(1972):203–216. Reprinted by permission.

proponents of permissiveness and various notions of the "open classroom" (Neill 1960, Kohl 1969, Rasberry and Greenway 1970).

Despite much concern and advocacy, relatively little attention has been directed to how educational assemblages of children are in fact organized. This paper is an account of one pattern of organization and control, as observed in a Head Start preschool.

The observed pattern of organization and control will be called the "guided-options management strategy." If methods of classroom control are seen as a continuum, with the extremes of an authoritarian system on one end and total permissiveness on the other, guided options may be seen as falling somewhere in the middle. The strategy is not one of prohibiting certain actions or of allowing all actions but rather one of suggesting or making available alternatives among which the child can choose as replacements for the unacceptable option.

Setting

The observations reported are drawn from participant observation in a Head Start program in an industrial, West Coast city. The center is located in a black, low-income neighborhood. The children are from three to five years old; there are eight boys and ten girls. All are black except for one boy, who is white.

The head teacher, a young black woman, receives a salary, as does her assistant, a neighborhood mother whose child is in the program. The classroom assistants, who do not come every day and who are not paid, are three neighborhood black women, two white girls, and a white male volunteer who came late in the observation period. A typical session would consist of fourteen children, the head teacher, her assistant, and one or two classroom assistants.

I worked in the program as a classroom assistant three days a week for two months. Notes on events were written up after each session.

Orienting: Suggested Techniques

Volunteers in the program are oriented from their first day with a variety of suggested techniques. The main ones are: (1) diversionary tactics, (2) territorial reassignment, (3) cooperative offers of help, and (4) reminders. All of these are embodied in the initial instruction I received from Rose, the head teacher:

> When a child is doing something you don't want him to do, NEVER say "that's bad" or "you're a bad boy" but instead try to distract him. "Would you like to come help me fix the blocks here" [diversionary tactics] or "would you please go into the other room and see if there are any blocks there?" [territorial reassignment] etc. If he leaves toys out, instead of just ordering him to pick them up, offer to help him. "Should I help you put these away now?" [cooperative offers of help] or if he refuses, say, "here, I'll put these away now and next time it will be your turn." Keep track of who's been playing with what and then at clean-up time you can say, "oh Edward, you forgot to take care of your blocks" [reminders].

These tactics may be accompanied by specific gestures, such as holding out a hand to lead the child to his newly assigned territory, or handing him one of the blocks he forgot to put away.

Children's Responses

As suggested by Rose's "or if he refuses" remark, the child's response to the initial suggestion will influence further interaction and possible techniques. There appear to be five main ways in which a child can respond other than accepting the guided option.

1. He may simply *ignore* the caretaker:

> Aleisha started pulling books out of the bookshelves and complaining, saying she didn't want to hear that old stuff. Mrs. Sloan told her she didn't have to, but asked her what she did when she first got up? Who woke her up or did she get up herself? Aleisha didn't answer but continued to try disrupting the small group by walking around, interrupting, and trying to get a story read instead.

2. On the other hand, he may *force the situation*, possibly by refusing loudly and deliberately, forcing the teacher to take note of his activities. In the incident above, for example, Aleisha was trying to force the caretaker to notice her at the same time that she was ignoring the caretaker's questions. At other times the refusal is verbal:

> As each child came in, I'd ask them if they'd met Dan, he was a new volunteer, tell him their name, then get a name tag and put it on. Sara didn't want one, I tried putting it in a different place. "let's see, would you like it on your pocket? How about the hem

of your dress?" etc., all responded to with "NO." "It's only for today, so that Dan can tell who you are, you've met Dan haven't you, so Dan will know who you are?" "NO." She went into the other room with Rose, after a while I went in there; Sara still didn't want a name tag, Rose went through the explanation again, "now let Carol put the name tag on you, it's for Dan, he's the new volunteer, and it's so he can call you by name, otherwise he'll just have to say 'hey you girl,' instead of your name, you want him to call you Sara, don't you?" "NO."

3. There is also *passive resistance,* used especially in connection with territorial reassignment. The child goes limp, if they want him in the other room, they're going to have to carry him there. Passive resistance can also be used to disrupt orderly activities through sheer delay:

> Going back from the park Vivian had sand in her shoes, so first we kept the group waiting while she poured sand out of one and I tied it for her; then we all started off, got to the grassy corner, and she stopped to do the other one. This time she was going to tie it herself, she knew how, what she did was verrry slowwwly put the laces around her ankle, attempt to tie it in back, meanwhile the group was getting way ahead and I knew they were going to have to wait for us at the corner again.

4. Or the child may move over into *active resistance,* including the use of threats. He may jerk away from the gesture of an offered hand; he may run away; he may kick, squirm, and spit.

> Aleisha at one point was getting pretty lively, asked her if she wanted to come work on a puzzle or something with me; she bared her teeth and said "I'll bite you," pretty serious about it too; can't always use lead-by-the-hand as management strategy.

In this instance, Aleisha effectively countered her caretaker's combination of diversion and territorial reassignment.

5. Another response, often connected with cooperative offers of help, is the *smother-with-affection* resistance that Rose warns against.

> One kid will come and hug you around the neck, and then another will want to, and another and another, and pretty soon they're strangling you—it's not fun, not a game, but strangling.

This smother-with-affection resistance can also be used to disrupt teacher-led activities:

> Rose had them jumping, doing jumping jacks, running in place, sitting down on the floor and touching their toes; . . . when she sat down, one of the girls immediately held onto her arm, so she couldn't do the exercise, she asked the girl to let go because she couldn't do it, another came and clung to her, too; she eventually stood up again.

Handling Disruptive Behavior

Obviously these are just possible responses, not invariant ones. But they do occur, and the teacher is then likely to respond with an additional range of tactics for handling this disruptive behavior. I observed six main tactics directed toward managing disruptive behavior.

1. Sometimes *ignoring* the child works:

> Walking back from the park, Tammy and DeeDee were holding Aleisha's hand, and began to dig their nails into her hand, she started crying, they let go and she clung to my hand crying; this was getting a little awkward, I was holding Vivian's coat and her hand; Audrey was semiwrapped around my leg; and Aleisha on the other hand, and the coat was slipping but I couldn't get free enough to get it more firmly over my arm. . . . Vivian then tried digging her nails into my hand to see if it could hurt, luckily they're short and didn't so I didn't react at all, like I didn't even notice, and she stopped.

Here the smother-with-affection techniques had effectively disabled the caretaker: she "couldn't get free enough" to respond physically to Vivian by pulling her hand away. A verbal request might not have been effective without forcing a scene, perhaps slipping into authoritarian commands and threats. A reasonable alternative, which worked this time, was to ignore the behavior until the child stopped it of her own accord.

2. At other times, however, a caretaker may attempt to handle disruptive behavior by *response-demanding* behavior of her own. For example, when the child ignores the caretaker, she may simply repeat her suggestion until he answers; or she may use a response-demanding question, coupled perhaps with a rhetorical exhortation like "let's get it together."

> As line-up hassles continue, kids keep wandering off, sit down to get sand out of their shoes, go back to turtle-thing, Rose becomes more insistent. "Now we can't spend so much time lining up, if you can't line up we're going to have to spend tomorrow in the building all the time and not come here, do you want that, [name]? . . Do you hear me, [name]? . . . Do you understand me, [name]?

Rose's questions were directed to specific children, and she waited for each to answer before going on to the next child.

3. At other times it may be enough to simply suggest a *new diversion:*

> Meanwhile James F. was careening around on the floor with a big wooden truck, trying to run into things, sort of sullen expression on his face, mostly trying for attention: first I asked him to please take the truck onto the carpet so it wouldn't make so much noise, he very carefully didn't hear. Then I asked him if he would like

to come to our tea party, and he nodded yes and came over and sat down on one of the chairs by me.

4. Especially when faced with situational forcing or active resistance, the teacher may use the method of *leaving up in the air,* in which she can postpone resolution or send an "over to you" to another caretaker:

> Aleisha also keeps tilting her chair, Rose asks her a couple of times to get it up to the table, then asks, "Carol, will you help Aleisha get her chair up to the table?" so I move it up.

Rose, sitting at the head of the table, was too far away from Aleisha to do more than ask her to move her chair. Rather than demanding a response when her requests were ignored, she turned the situation over to the teacher sitting right beside Aleisha, using approximately the wording of a cooperative offer of help. The second teacher was then able to "help" Aleisha without encountering resistance.

This technique may fail miserably, however, if the caretakers don't get their signals straight:

> The fight started I think when Timothy threw some sand in James C.'s face. . . . Sandi and I could maybe have stopped it better if there'd been another supervisor, because then she could have watched the other eight children as we kept these two apart until they cooled down, but—no other supervisor. And I sort of left it to Sandi, as they were over by her, and she probably sort of left it to me.

5. *Explanation* is another technique which is used frequently. It is sometimes used when a child has rejected the option he was being guided toward, in an attempt to make him decide that he wants that option after all. The earlier example of Sara and the name tag illustrates this use of explanation. It is also used to soften incidents of deprivation:

> Began to be pushing and hitting and shoving on the slide itself, so I took the slide down: "someone is going to get hurt so we aren't going to play with this any more today."

It is often used with repetition, explaining over and over until the child eventually changes his behavior, perhaps out of sheer boredom:

> Asked Wilson if he wanted David to teeter him, Wilson said no, so I explained to David that Wilson didn't want him to do that, that Wilson was doing a trick and that then it was Timothy's turn to play on the slide, he could be after Timothy, along with holding his arm, keeping him away, explaining twice so he started getting bored with the long explanation and wandered off.

6. So far the management techniques described have fit fairly well with the philosophy of soft control present in the guided options-strategy.

Occasionally, however, a more authoritarian tactic is used, that of *seclusion*. It usually occurs when nothing else has worked and when for some reason it seems impossible to leave the situation up in the air. Even when used, it is usually couched in the language of options as a request or suggestion, although in fact the child's options are extremely limited at this point. He can either stop what he is doing or he can wind up in seclusion.

> James F. was creating a disturbance in the other room and Rose brought him into the kitchen to be with her, saying 'if I can't be out there to be with you, then you come into the kitchen so you can be with me, sit right there.'

> Rose ignored them at first; then when [they] got too loud and didn't stop when she asked them to, she mentioned that maybe they could go to the office. They stopped.

Anticipating Disruptive Behavior

The above techniques are all ones designed to deal with problems already present. Other techniques may be used to try to prevent or to head off problems.

1. One such technique is the adult organization of activities to *keep periods short*. The children come about 9:00. About 10:00 there is a snack for anyone who wants one. About 11:00 there is "cleanup time"; then if the weather is good everyone goes to the park. They come back sometime after 11:30, and then it's time for "Sesame Street" for all who want to watch it. Lunchtime is about 12:00; the children leave about 12:30. The periods of group activities, such as singing or exercising, are also kept short, with the teacher changing or terminating activities before the children get too restless:

> Started with "Twinkle, twinkle" and they knew that one fairly well. A few shouters at least make it sound like everyone's singing! Tried one or two others; had trouble with "This little light of mine" since Rose knew a different tune, we ended up singing that one without piano accompaniment; she started to teach them the words to "Freedom's comin'" but then switched to having each kid who wanted to, sing a song for the group (this was good, as attention was beginning to wander—we'd been doing this about fifteen minutes and that's long enough).

2. Besides keeping periods short, the adults *control the introduction of new activities*: they decide which days to try making playdough, operat-

ing the new "language master," or running a big cardboard-box store. On days when the children seem already excited, the store may remain "closed," but lots of puzzles are on the tables, and there are many books to read. The child is guided toward a certain option before it is even presented to him.

> Rose had a cold today, was going to go home after others came to take over . . . we have store closed today (Rose's suggestion) so some chaos averted. . . . Before Rose left, she said that if it was necessary we could use just one room . . . room two since it has quieter activities going on in it.

3. Another technique used in anticipating disruptive behavior is the use of *preemptive praise:*

> Rose asked him to help her out by watching the turtle and not letting the other children touch it since that would be hard on it. He said ok; she added, ostensibly to me but so that David could hear, "he can be the best helper when he wants to be—he's a very good helper."

> When she was getting the kids quiet, Rose would say (of quiet children) stuff like, "ah, he's my brother, that's the way I like to see a brother," etc.

4. *Promises* can also be used as a means of heading off difficulty, but they are not used too often, primarily because the children can exploit them too easily: either through harassment or constant requests or in inducing promises, then playing one caretaker off against another. This may occur especially in connection with the privileged position of "first in line" walking to the park, when too many children have received promises from different teachers that today they can be in front. The teacher's response when a promise like this falls through may be an apology coupled with explanation ("Oh, I'm sorry, I didn't know that Rose had already promised Gilbert that he could be in front"); or a further promise ("well, tomorrow you can be in front").

In an attempt to forestall making promises which may fall through, the teacher may handle requests by ignoring them or by directing the child to another teacher, a version of the leaving-up-in-the-air method mentioned above. If constant requests have led to an implied promise, she may use direct intervention to get the promise honored.

> Wilson asked if he could be in front; meanwhile most of the kids were running over the grass . . . continued to straggle all over, some lying down on the sidewalk until we passed them, etc. Wilson asked again, I said ok, you go up and ask Cheryl to let you be in front, up with whoever was ahead at that point. He went up, came back with his "pout" look, I asked him if he'd asked Cheryl, he said

yes, but she hadn't said anything (probably didn't even hear him or was too busy with others); when we caught up at one corner I asked Cheryl for him, explaining that being in front was a big deal; told Wilson to pick a partner, he went up with Samuel, off we started again.

In this incident the teacher was distracted by other children's activities and would not have been able to enforce any promise; Wilson's request was ignored in the press of other business. When he asked again, she directed him to another teacher who was at the head of the line and therefore in a position to grant his request. When this half-promise ("OK") fell through, she interceded with the other teacher to place Wilson at the head of the line.

Assigning Motives to Disruptive Behavior

A guided-options pattern of control is more than simply a set of tactics in the control of children. It implies, in addition, a special rhetoric of motives assumed to be the only motives that children can have. If, sociologically conceived, motives are transacted imputations of why people act as they do (Mills 1940, Scott and Lyman 1968), there is then the question of what "vocabulary of motives" or "accounts" seems associated with the guided-options management strategy.

In the Head Start setting, practically the only motives ever assigned to disruptive behavior are those of accidents or forgetting:

> At one point I heard Rose answering someone, "he just fell because it was an accident, he wasn't doing anything bad."

Having an accident or forgetting is correctable. The child can be approached with cooperative offers of assistance, reminders, requests, explanations: all sorts of guided options are available to help him out, without resorting to the necessity of labeling him an incorrigible, as one might do in more authoritarian arrangements.

> Also his running; we're going to have to do more than just "James, remember to walk" because it's not taking effect. Rose said we're going to have to try giving him a reminder, a warning, then the third time sit him down in a chair quiet somewhere . . . sit with him, doing a puzzle or something, until he quiets down.

The child is coached to accept this explanation of correctable motives:

> David came running into the room for lunch and was reminded to walk. One of the children said something to the effect that he always

runs, he's bad; and Rose said, "no, he just forgets." David sat down, sort of tilted his head and earnestly agreed, "I just forget, is all" and Rose responded, "Yes, he just forgets, is all."

In fact, the caretaker is somewhat at a loss if the child chooses to reject this coaching and states that he did it on purpose:

> Tammy and DeeDee informed me that they knew how to dig their nails in so it hurt (so you can hardly use the old "it-was-an-accident" routine when they're smugly explaining exactly what they did!) I semi-smoothed it over, "ooh, that can hurt someone though," mostly concentrated on soothing Aleisha.

In this instance, the caretaker's response was primarily that of leaving up in the air, with a twinge of explanation added: she quickly focused on comforting the injured child rather than on exploring the motives of the offenders. Another response might be that of offering options for the future:

> Rose replied, "From now on, James, if you want someone to get off the slide or to let you play with something, you come ask us, don't do it yourself, OK?"

Again, the motive is not emphasized, since it was neither an accident nor a lapse of memory ("I knocked him off the slide"). If it should recur, however, it could then be considered forgetting ("Oh, James, you forgot to come ask us, remember?"), and the motive would then be an acceptable one.

This particular rhetoric of motives appears to have three main consequences. (1) The child is being socialized into an appropriate vocabulary of motives (Mills 1940) to be utilized in his future educational environment, a public school inculcating mostly middle-class values. ("I forgot" is a more acceptable motive than "I didn't want to do your fucking assignment.") (2) This vocabulary of excuses is used in mitigating or relieving responsibility for one's conduct. If an account is a manifestation of the underlying negotiation of identities (Scott and Lyman 1968), then using only a vocabulary of excuses is bestowing an identity of "not responsible" upon the child, including the assets and liabilities of that role in ongoing social interaction. (3) The child is given little opportunity self-consciously to integrate his actions with another's. Pushing because he forgot or had an accident is generally a solitary act; deliberately hitting because he wants something from someone or has been hit himself is a social act.

The possible consequences of allowing the children to claim other motives for disruptive behavior would depend on what vocabulary of motives was substituted, but would probably include the following:

1. Substitution of motives would lead to a significantly different pat-

tern of control. If the new accounts led to negative labeling, a more authoritarian system would be likely to appear as the teachers attempted to cope with "unruly" or "bad" children. If, on the other hand, the variety of accounts were seen as allowing the child to negotiate an identity of "responsible self," more permissive interaction would take place.

2. The new vocabulary of motives might not be as appropriate to the public school, if the "polite excuses" for one's behavior were lacking. The child might be less likely to fit into the social situation of the classroom and might be more likely to be labeled deviant in some way.

> Mrs. Adams, a kindergarten teacher in the public schools, was observing today. . . . James was building something with the domino blocks, evidently as he went by Timothy knocked them over. . . . Mrs. Adams leaned over to me and murmured, "personally, I'd put one like that in an iron cage."

3. In a more permissive system, with its wider range of accounts, the child could have more opportunities to try out a variety of accounts and consequent identities. Through interaction, he could learn to negotiate identities and to test their situational appropriateness by the reactions of others (Strauss 1959).

Conclusions

The study of a Head Start classroom has suggested the existence of a pattern of control here called the guided-options management strategy. No claim is made that this pattern characterizes all Head Start programs or that it is characteristic of preschool settings in general. These are questions to be addressed in their own right.

It seems likely, indeed, that there is a variety in control patterns, all variations falling between the extremes of authoritarianism and permissiveness. If we are to understand the microsociological texture of schooling experiences, a prime task is that of identifying in a close-up fashion the characteristics of these variations. It is through close, empirical accounts that we can, perhaps, debate educational practice in more meaningful ways than simply gross contrasts between authoritarianism and permissiveness.

References

Bagley, W. C. 1907. *Classroom Management: Its Principles and Techniques.* New York: Macmillan.

Bettelheim, B. 1969. "Psychoanalysis and education," *School Review* 77: 73–86.

Kohl, H. 1969. *The Open Classroom: A Practical Guide to a New Way of Teaching.* New York: New York Review.

Mills, C. W. 1940. "Situated actions and vocabularies of motive." *American Sociological Review* 5: 904–913.

Neill, A. S. 1960. *Summerhill: A Radical Approach to Child Rearing.* New York: Hart.

Rasberry, S. and R. Greenway. 1970. *Rasberry: How to Start Your Own School . . . and Make a Book.* Freestone, Calif.: Freestone.

Scott, M. B. and S. M. Lyman. 1968. "Accounts." *American Sociological Review* 33: 46–62.

Strauss, A. L. 1959. *Mirrors and Masks.* New York: Free Press.

25
Schedules for Students

There are many social senses of time. Clock time (seconds, minutes, and hours), no doubt, owes its origin to the necessities of coordinating complex work tasks and large numbers of people. Education, especially higher education, produces different ways of experiencing time. Students are expected to utilize their time in order to accomplish assignments according to their own judgment. Education often involves demands that seem never-ending to the student and roles that may be individually defined within a wide range of acceptability. Such a set of circumstances fosters strategies, coping mechanisms, and most importantly, a sense of time. Bernstein describes the organization of this student sense of time around the theme of the "fritter." Frittering is a way of passing time, a way of marking events significant from the student's point of view. In his excursion into the world of the student, Bernstein identifies four classes of fritters, describes the character of each type, and relates the way each operates.

Getting It Done: Notes on Student Fritters
Stan Bernstein

Social roles vary in the degree to which their constituent tasks are "closed" or "open" in character. At one extreme are roles such as assembly-line workers, where precise definitions communicate when the task starts, one's progress in it, and when it ends. At the other extreme are roles such as student, where the tasks are highly open or never-ending. The role of student, in particular, involves learning to think and learning the "facts" of various fields. The infinite expandability of these

From *Urban Life and Culture* 1 (1972):275–92. Reprinted by permission.

The author acknowledges the invaluable assistance of Mr. Jeff Hart (Boston College) in the development of the idea of fritter. Special thanks are due Ms. Susan Wilcox for assistance.

tasks places no practically determined restrictions on the amount of time occupants can dedicate to the role. Like politicians, housewives, and other entrepreneurs, students' work is never done. Indeed, students are counselled that people only stop learning when they die. Death is not, students lament, in sight, but learning demands are.

This paper seeks to explore how people cope with roles that are open or never-ending in their demands. In particular, it focuses upon how students justify not working under the ever-present pressure to work. Frequently, when there is work to be done, students fritter away time. An analysis of strategies students adopt in accounting for their time not working will be presented. The objective truth or falsity of the strategies is irrelevant to the purpose of this analysis. What is important is their use in coping with open-ended situations.

Neutralization, Accounts, and Fritters

The present effort both follows and departs from prior research. Matza (1964) discusses how an individual in a subculture of delinquents neutralizes his guilt over performing delinquent acts. Relevant here, Matza notes that the delinquent's relation to the norms he violates includes strong elements of normative acceptance. It is not sheer rejection of legal norms but, for most, ambivalence or acceptance with definitions of extenuating circumstances. Students' attitudes toward normatively expected study are also frequently complex and ambivalent. Matza notes that delinquents only occasionally commit delinquent acts. Intermittent violation is also a characteristic of most students' work avoidance.

An important element in Matza's discussion is the fact that neutralization techniques are common in the subculture of delinquency as a way of freeing the individual from moral constraint in violating legal norms. The legal system is the one which labels the acts deviant. The relationship of the definitions of justified action of the delinquent groups to the social control agents' definitions is studied. In individual role management, however, the individual is his own social-control agent. It is not clear whether the neutralizations in Matza's discussion are to be considered as justified accounts to others (especially members of one's own group) or primarily as accounts to self.

A more general presentation of accounts can be found in the excellent treatments by Scott and Lyman (1970, 1968). In introducing their discussion, they present the study of accounts as necessary for an understanding of the maintaining of social order after failure to meet social expectations. How does the individual explain his act to others when he has not met their expectations?

1. How does he excuse his wrong action (escape responsibility) or,
2. how does he justify his behavior (neutralize the pejorative portrayal of the consequences)?

Accounts repair the breaks in satisfying the expectations of others. Scott and Lyman's presentation is complex. Group differences in acceptable accounts, the style of accounts, audience selection for accounts, and many other questions are sensitively handled. The relation of accounts given to others and accounts offered to self in role management is, however, not discussed. Accounts are considered part of a sociology of talk. An account is "a statement made by a social actor to explain unanticipated or untoward behavior—whether the behavior is his own or that of others, and whether the proximate cause for the statement arises from the actor himself or someone else" (Scott and Lyman 1968, p. 46). To their discussion, I here add that the recipient of the account may be the actor himself. Further, an explanation may succeed as an account only for the actor.

This analysis treats a student population. It is this population that the author knows best from years of active participation as an undergraduate and graduate student and as a teacher of undergraduates in two college settings. The central notion is that of fritter devices, or strategies. A fritter is "a justification a student gives to himself for not doing student work in response to felt pressures to work." While the success of a fritter in neutralizing work pressure or guilt is increased by its receiving social support, this consideration is not part of the definition.

The dynamic nature of fritters makes categorizing them difficult. In actual practice, combinations or complex sequences are likely as the student continually reconstitutes his work-avoiding as new kinds of justified activity. For ease of presentation, they may be divided into four classes: (1) person-based, (2) social-relations-based, (3) valuative-based, and (4) task-based.

Person-Based Fritters

Person-based fritters involve definitions of biological need and personal history.

Biological Necessity

Even a student is human. Being human involves, among other things, the satisfaction of biological needs. These practical necessities are just that—necessities. Therefore, they are foolproof justifications for not working. When, for example, nature calls, what is a person to do but respond to his mother's entreaty? Similarly, hunger can serve as a justification for work avoidance. Not only can an argument be made for biological necessity, but the student can also argue that hunger impairs studying ability. This argument need not be limited, of course, by actual hunger. The great business done by vending machines in dormitories and the concentration of all-night eating places in areas of high student residence attest to the utility of this justification. Some popular student foods (pizza in particular) are not eaten alone. Time must be spent gathering other people. And once you have them, you can do more with them than eat.

Cleanliness is yet another excellent justification. Anything next to godliness surely takes precedence over work. Washing and showering can serve another function. An entire battery of work-avoidance tactics can be justified by their necessity in keeping the student awake. These activities include preparing and drinking cups of coffee, cold showers, long walks in cold weather, running a half-mile, standing on one's head for a few minutes, listening to Sousa marches, Chopin preludes, or acid rock, and eating rich food. A variety of drugs are now routinely used to fight fatigue. The effects of these are frequently not restricted to fatigue reduction. Subtle and not very subtle alterations of consciousness are common. Attending to these changes can become more interesting than studying. Should these activities fail, or even should they succeed, another way of handling "fatigue" is the I'll-get-up-very-early-tomorrow-morning-when-I'll-be-able-to-work-better fritter. Students have to keep healthy, too. Many regimens, physical and medical, may be required. At some times, it may be crucial that the student get "adequate rest."

Rest on Your Laurels

Focusing on personal history leads to the nostalgia or rest-on-your-laurels fritter. Using this strategy involves employing past accomplishments as justification for present work avoidance. This can take the form of delaying work, since previous history shows (or can be interpreted to suggest) it well within one's capability and therefore not a matter of pressing concern. Or when the present activity proves frustrating to the point of work avoidance, the individual may bolster his esteem by "celebrating" previous successes. A variant on this theme is especially handy for avoiding work when a number of different tasks must be done. Upon completion of one of them, the student may use a you-owe-it-to-yourself justification for work avoidance, the avoidance period being defined as self-payment for a job well done.

An owe-it-to-yourself break may also be seen as necessary to let the worker change psychological set or recover from fatigue. More work is more fatiguing than almost any nonwork activity. It is easier to change set to most nonwork acts than to most other work.

Social-Relations-Based Fritters

Fritters based upon social relations directly employ other people in the action of avoiding work. The impact of employing other people, however, is not so much in having an audience before which one gives accounts as simply in having an audience. There are three main patterns of social-relations fritters.

Group Discussion

The group-discussion fritter is also called the commiseration fritter. Commiserating may be done in a large group or in pairs, either in person or over the telephone. It involves "getting together" and consoling one another on the unreasonability or irrationality of the assignment. Complaining about the assigned work is an excellent fritter technique. It justifies work avoidance by directly protesting against the work itself. The more intelligent or discriminating the complaints, the clearer it is that the work task is within the student's later capability. Critical ability may be developed in avoiding studying as well as in doing studying. Sometimes discussions of this sort get around to a comparison of actual work done, leading to the social-comparison fritter.

Social Comparison

Students sometimes compare their progress with one another. When a student discovers he is ahead of others in his work, he can then feel justified in freeing time for work avoidance. This fritter has two aspects. First, there is the time spent gathering comparisons of others. This may involve personal contact or telephoning. Or the comparison-others may not be real-others working on the same task. Instead, high relative standing earlier in the course may be extrapolated to the present. Because of information from the past, the student may believe he is at present ahead of others. When this is coupled with the perception that relative position is the criterion of final evaluation, it becomes possible, for example, for "curve-breaking" midterm students to free time from final studies and projects. Second, there is the effect of the comparison. The choice of comparison others is a strategic choice. For a student to feel justified in his current work avoidance, he must compare his work with someone who is less advanced than he. (Choice of other will vary depending on whether the student wishes to take a break from work or gain incentive to continue it.) The two dangers of this technique for the student are: first, he may choose someone who is, in fact, more advanced in the work; and, second, he may fritter away the time needed for students to catch up and pass him. This second possibility exists because, in seeking a justification for work avoidance, students frequently stop at discovering they are ahead, do not collect information on the rate of progress of others, and thus easily misestimate the time it takes others to close the gap. This problem is less threatening and the fritter more successful if the time before the deadline is small. One possible result of such a technique is to make distributions of student performance more closely approximate the normal curve than would otherwise be the case.

Group Work

The decision to study in a group has a number of work-avoidance functions. On the one hand, it immediately makes possible commiseration and social-comparison fritters. Study groups from the same course can, of course, commiserate easily. Students studying together but for different courses are able to have even longer commiseration sessions. Each can complain about his course without redundancy and without risk of contradiction or challenge. Social-comparison fritters are also possible both as a group enterprise in relation to a group-defined standard of adequate knowledge for the course and as a sort of distributive justice notion for comparison between courses with groups of students studying for different courses. A group norm of "reasonable work for any course" can then develop independent of the actual demands of the actual courses being studied.

Getting a number of people together functions, on the other hand, to increase enormously the range of alternatives to studying. These activities can be justified using any number of the techniques elsewhere mentioned. Work avoidance maneuvers with group approval are especially difficult to ignore. There is a "risky shift" in the direction of longer fritters, too. This is because, once you have stopped working, it is difficult to know when to suggest to your partners that you should get back to work. It may be hard to stop frittering without being impolite or pressuring. Responsibility for directing attention back to work becomes diffused through the group.

Valuative-Based Fritters

While the above-mentioned fritter techniques are common and successful, they do not have the guilt-binding power of valuative fritters. One way work can be avoided especially, but not exclusively, in the early college years is using time to discuss values. Political, moral, and aesthetic topics are common in these conversations. Finding out who you are, "getting your shit together," and so on are important tasks. Mundane work considerations do not look very important measured against this large activity. Valuative fritters based on already-held values place work and work avoidance within a larger framework of values and choices. It is here that considerations of nonstudent activities enter with greatest effect. Three primary types of valuative fritters may be described and ordered in terms of increasing generality and abstraction.

Higher Good

In the higher-good work-avoidance strategy, the student ranks being a student as less important to him in his scheme of values than other interests and aspects of his identity. Here friendship, love, cultural values (e.g., charity, service), political interests, physical fitness (the sound-mind-in-a-sound-body fritter), and much else can be justified as more worthy of attention for the moment than the study tasks at hand. These other values, of course, vary in strength and, therefore, in their guilt-free binding power in role management. For this reason, the strength of each of the alternative values is enhanced immeasurably if it can be asserted that the opportunity for acting on that value is soon to be gone. Stated another way, *rare events,* or at least infrequent events, have a special ability to bind time from studying, even if the value of the act would otherwise be questionable in relation to the pressure to study. Makes-Jack-a-dull-boy valuative fritters, involving, say, a movie, will be more potent the last day the picture is playing than the first day of an extended run, concerts involving great and infrequently heard performers are able to appease guilt from role violation, and eclipses of the moon draw crowds of guilt-free students as an audience.

Experience Broadens

The experience-broadens fritter is less specific in the sense of presenting a less clear-cut value conflict. It has, nonetheless, the attraction of serving as a ready back-up to the post-facto unjustified valuative fritter (say, the movie was lousy, the instruments out of tune, the friend crabby, the eclipse cloud-ridden, or what have you). In such an event, or generally in any event, it can be argued somehow that experience qua experience broadens the person, makes him more complete, or wiser, or what have you. This can bind successfully enormous amounts of time on a scale much larger than the mere work requirements for a specific course. Even career decisions (or decision evasions) can be justified under the experience-broadens rubric. The crucial difference from the higher-good fritter is that any experience will do.

Existential

The most general of valuative fritters is the existential, or the what-the-hell-sort-of-difference-will-it-make fritter. In this strategy, the decision to work or not work is cast as having no lasting practical or existential effect on the course of one's life (or sometimes, other's, as in the would-be author's no-one-will-be-reading-novels-in-ten-years-anyway fritter). Scholastic failures of prominently successful individuals may be remembered. Einstein's failure of a high-school math course can offer solace to the fritterer. If one's activities are ultimately of no consequence anyway, the immediate consequences of work avoidance are not even worthy of consideration. Extreme application of this principle can lead to failure in the student role, in which event one's very studenthood may be justified as an experience-broadens fritter from what one should really be doing.

Task-Based Fritters

Fritters discussed to this point are based upon the student's history, biology, social relations, and values. We come finally to the task itself. Task-based fritters focus upon the direct handling of study time and the allocation of work resources. Specifically, there appear to be four main clusters of task-based fritters: time-related, preparation-related, creativity-related, and task-involved.

Time-Related Fritters

The Time-Symmetry Fritter. Many students appear to find it easier to start studying on the hour, half hour, or, at the very least, quarter hour than at any other minute. This may be due to the ease these times make for scheduling fritters discussed below. These times are more generally important in plans and schedules between individuals. A common social use of time shapes action. (On a larger scale, weekends, holidays, or Mondays assume special status in the week.) It is, further, "easier" to compute total study time and pages per hour if you start at some such prominent time division. One of the advantages of this technique is that, with a little effort, a large amount of time can be frittered if the activity one chose to do until, say, the quarter-hour starting time, can be extended just a few minutes beyond this starting point. The student is then, by the same logic, justified in waiting until the next prominent time division. Depending on the individual and on the amount of time already spent in time-symmetry fritters, the student can choose to wait for the next hour, half hour, or quarter hour. As good a fritter technique as this is, there is a problem in its use. Each time it is used in succession, the student feels less justified in invoking the time-symmetry fritter. This is sometimes manifested by the setting of the starting time at progressively shorter prominent intervals: e.g., at 7:00, 8:00, 8:30, and then 8:45. In any event, at some point, this technique loses its efficacy. Fortunately, there is a larger-scale, more successful technique which can then be used.

The Great-Divide Fritter. At some point, say, in an evening to be devoted to work, it becomes too late to get serious work done (or finish the task, the scheduled amount, or what have you). At this point the student feels perfectly free to give up for the rest of the night all pretense to studying. It is simply too late to get enough work done to make any work worthwhile. Some other activity is then chosen to occupy the remaining time, but without any need for a higher-good valuative justification. Thus, a particular student might not consider it worthwhile to start studying after 9:00 at night. The time-symmetry fritter brought the student up to 8:45, a biological-imperative fritter or a phone-call-for-a-commiseration fritter might be sufficient to add enough time to set up a great-divide fritter.

Scheduling Fritters. Students justify spending enormous amounts of time making up work schedules. These can be done for the day, evening, week, or whatever the relevant work session to be planned. Plans can be made not just for the coming work, but also for coming work breaks. Fritters of the future become bound into a longer series of work intentions and are in that way neutralized. Of course, scheduling may be resorted to whenever the actual progress of the work falls far enough off schedule to warrant the writing of a new one. Schedule-related fritters, then, become a consideration whenever something goes wrong or could go wrong with the schedule. Indeed, the more detailed the schedule, the greater the chance of derailment.

There are two salient forms of scheduling fritters. First, there are anticipated-interruption fritters. If one knows in advance that at a certain point in the work period, studying will be interrupted by some other activity, there is set up a situation in which frittering the time until after the interruption is justified. This can be considered the application of a great-divide fritter on a smaller scale. Second, there are disruption-of-sequence fritters. These occur whenever the student, for some reason, performs a task out of order from the planned sequence. If this involves successful completion of the different task, conditions are set up for an owe-it-to-yourself fritter as well as a new scheduling fritter. The disruption of sequence can also justify waiting for a new, prominent starting point, like a new day, before actually working.

Deadline-Change Fritters. On occasion a teacher will change the date that some work is due either for the whole class or, by special arrangement, for single students. When this happens, the student feels free to use a postponed-deadline fritter. Since study time is reckoned backward from a deadline date rather than forward to new work opportunities, when the deadline is postponed, time is freed to avoid working. If, for example, a paper due Friday is postponed for one week on Wednesday, the student can wait for the following Wednesday before working again.

Preparation-Related Fritters

Preparation fritters involve all activities immediately attendant to preparing to study: getting books, paper, pens, cleaning the desk, and what have you. These are easily justified activities, preparatory as they are to work. These immediate preparations are easily escalated. Thus, a student decides that, in the interest of greater efficiency, he should clean his desk top (no matter what the actual nature of his work habits—tidy or abominable). Having done this, a crucial point is reached. He can now actually start to work. Instead, he says while-I'm-at-it and proceeds to clean out the whole desk or rearrange all his books or even move on to cleaning the whole room or apartment. This technique is especially interesting, developing as it does from the preparation fritter, in that it quickly ignores the originally work-related starting point. A good job is worth doing well, as long as it isn't the good job you have to do.

Preparation can be difficult (or made difficult), and work can be delayed. In the spread-resources, or shuttle, fritter the student does not bring, or chooses work for which he cannot bring, all the needed materials to one place for work. Travelling between work sites becomes necessary. What started as the path to work intersects with other paths (perhaps to other places).

Creativity-Related Fritters

Once all the material preparations have been completed there are two other factors left to be prepared—the student and, say, the paper. Let us consider these in reverse order. Preparation of the paper itself will offer many opportunities for work avoidance.

(1) For the-first-step-is-the-hardest. This can mean working for a long time on an outline or, commonly, working hard at getting exactly the proper first sentence or first paragraph. The opening of a paper is felt in an important way to constrain the range of alternatives, stylistic and organizational, for the rest of the work. It becomes, therefore, of utmost importance that the opening be precisely correct—no matter how much time it takes.

(2) In addition, the student must be ready to work. Every creative endeavor, however, has an incubation period, and every endeavor, creative or not, requires motivation. Both needs can require time, justified time. It is best to wait until you are bursting with ideas or are sufficiently motivated, even if the motivation is guilt due to unsuccessful previous application of fritter techniques. This is therefore the let-it-brew-for-a-while fritter (closely related to this is the I'll-lie-down-and-think-about-it fritter; the possible danger in this tactic is, of course, very clear: listing all things people are designed to do horizontally, studying is one of the lowest on the list).

(3) Related to these is the I'm-sure-there-is-something-else fritter. No matter how much advanced preparation there has already been, the conscientious student is justified in allowing some free time to think of something else which should be included (say, in a paper, or when considering how to psych out the teacher's exam questions). This is especially useful when, for example, a paper is on a topic requiring an interdisciplinary approach or a number of different viewpoints for elucidation. The "something else" can then be in an area only vaguely related to the original topic. This justification can thus successfully be used to allow additional time for readings and thinking more and more peripheral to the original topic—i.e., to the work itself. When the task is taking a test, students can spend a great deal of time trying to psych out the teacher. Information on prior exams and teachers' specialization or personal quirks may be important in deciding what significant knowledge is.

Task-Involved Fritters

Finally, the student, to remain in concept and in fact a student, must occasionally actually work. Once work is started, however, there are still some devices which can be used to slow it or end it quickly without endangering one's view of self as student.

(1) One important consideration, especially to someone who has been using scheduling fritters, is a reliable measure of how quickly the work is going. Time is thus justifiably spent computing pages, hours, words per minute, or what have you. This is the what's-my-rate fritter.

(2) Every work goal can be divided into subgoals whose individual accomplishments are significant since each contributes to the final completion. This is the principle behind the logical-stopping-point fritter. Small owe-it-to-yourself fritters are justified by the completion of the subgoals. As the time-symmetry fritter has prominent dividing points for the time continuum, so the logical-stopping-point fritter divides up the work task itself. Thus, for example, one may set up subgoals such that one is justified in taking a break after completing only a single chapter in an assigned book. This technique, however, like the time-symmetry fritter, is conducive to fractionalization. The subgoal can shift from finish the chapter to finish the topic of discussion or, more extremely, the page or the paragraph.

(3) Sometimes the student has more than one project to work on at once. The jack-of-all-trades fritter is a way of avoiding working too hard on any one subject by shifting from task to task before the work gets too taxing in any one of them.

(4) The hard-working student occasionally reaches a difficult place in his work. Work may slow down in the face of difficulty and require intense concentration. Overinvolvement, overconcern, and improper distance from the work may create problems. The student can then choose from a wide variety of more proper, and comfortable, distances from the work.

(5) As a result of using other fritter strategies, the working student may find the work cannot be done as determined in the remaining time before its deadline. It is possible to do an incredible-shrinking-work fritter. This allows a "settling process" to take place in which the wheat is separated from the what becomes chaff.

Recovery Fritters

Sometimes the student does not complete the task when it is due. If he can get an open-ended extension, he is free to postpone additional work for a long time. This is the effect of the you-can't-pick-up-spilled-milk fritter.

Fritters and Guilt

This presentation has been silent as to why fritters are successful in getting their work (avoiding work) done. It is clear how the time is frittered away, but it is not yet very clear how the student staves off guilt. Some suggestions of the mechanisms follow.

Many fritters deny that work performances are not being done as they should. A large number of fritters, especially task-related ones, disguise themselves as ways to get the task done. They either facilitate work (e.g., preparation), promise to improve it (e.g., related areas), or look like work (e.g., jack-of-all-trades). Biological necessity is sometimes seen as needed to get the task done, though occasionally this is a justification in its own right. Alternately, fritters can deny that there should be any pressure felt for not working. On one hand, the past shows no danger (prior capability, successful past work avoidance); on the other, there are no real consequences of not working (a form of what-the-hell sort. . . .).

Other fritters turn the fritterer's attention to other values above the successful study. These put the student role in larger perspective (alternate values) or put work in limits of "propriety" (appeals to fairness, "reasonable work" definitions).

Some fritters place special conditions on the way that work is done. Certain times to start (time symmetry), times to make progress (great divide, anticipated interruption), and times and places to stop (logical stopping point) are used to structure work sessions.

Finally, fritters can neutralize work pressure by subtle (or not so subtle) changes in how the definition of work is made. Is work "really" make work (one form of what-the-hell . . .), doing better than others (social comparison), for posterity or your proctor (involved in psych out fritters), work you do or work due (postponed deadline), a magnum opus or just some work (incredible shrinking work)?

Concluding Remarks

Elements of the above presentation of fritter strategies lend themself readily to further research. Different fritters are used for different kinds of work. They are offerable as accounts to different others. Different others are needed to invoke particular fritters. Different fritters are used at different points in the phases of a work act. Different fritters are more subjectively available in different places, as, for example, the number of work cues varies by setting, requiring different fritter strategies. A student's cleaning the entire library before settling down to work would be rare. Some fritters are used without social support; others are not. Different materials are needed to use different fritters. Different fritters are used by students at different stages in their academic careers. Conditions which facilitate the adopting of different particular strategies must be elaborated. There is no evidence available yet on whether there are different subcultures of fritter or if these justifications are common currency among students in general. Because they are accounts to self which are only sometimes offered to others, students are often surprised when discussion reveals how widespread is their use.

There are features of the student role which facilitate the use of these strategies. Students are granted great liberty in the planning of their use of time. Student time is more often "individual time" than "social time." Time demands are stricter in high schools than in colleges. Required class time and daily evaluated assignments are less characteristic of the college years. The schools frequently cite the increased maturity of the students as the reason for the greater liberty permitted. However, time use in statuses occupied by even more mature adults are frequently more regulated by institutions. Perhaps most important, the student is in a transitional role. The schools and the population as a whole are not favorably disposed to lifetime students. It is an early stage in commitment to professional careers and a late stage in formal education for yet other careers. Widespread use of fritter techniques can ease the difficulties of early commitment for the former and aid the termination of formal education for the latter.

References

Matza, D. 1964. *Delinquency and Drift.* New York: John Wiley.
Scott, M. and S. Lyman. 1970 "Accounts, deviance and social order." In *Deviance and Respectability,* ed. J. D. Douglas. New York: Basic Books, pp. 89-119.
⎯⎯⎯ 1968. "Accounts." *American Sociological Review.* 33, 1: 46–62.

26

Negotiated Interaction in the Classroom

Interaction in the classroom derives partially from the accepted definition of the situation. Both teacher and student expect, and are expected to do and think, certain things. However, the reality of social life rarely conforms to the prefabricated understandings that the interactants bring with them to the scene. Instead, what transpires often has the character of joint decisions that are *after the fact,* invented, partially remembered, and worked out on the basis of immediate, face-to-face occurrences.

We are so accustomed to these occurrences that we may fail to grasp the degree to which they actually compose the nature of social interaction in the classroom. An outside observer can point out part of this to us, but there is no substitution for participation in the lived-through interaction. Anedith Nash reports a sociologically unique classroom setting, one where she, as a sign-language interpreter, stood between the teacher and the student. She was in a position to appreciate both the predetermined understandings that students and teachers brought with them to the classroom and the negotiated results of their coming together.

Observations in a Bilingual Classroom: The Role of the Interpreter

Anedith Nash

John looks up from his desk at the woman seated on a stool directly in front of him. He looks at the clock, looks back at her, and signs, "Bored me, hurry time!" The woman laughs silently and signs in reply, "Ten minutes more." It is a private conversation although there are about thirty other people in the room, students and an instructor. No one else understands the exchange. It has become such a feature of the daily

This article was written especially for this volume.

routine that no one appears to take notice. The student is deaf. The woman is his interpreter. Between the deaf student and his hearing classmates, instructors, and friends stands the interpreter. Between the interpreter and the private knowledge stocks of the deaf stands the deaf student. It is a truly unique relationship. In this one-classroom scene there are two simultaneous linguistic worlds. The first is the world of standard spoken English. The second is the silent language of signs.

In many parts of the country, at all levels of the educational system, standard spoken English has lost its place as the sole medium of classroom communication.[1] Black English, Spanish, Navaho, and other native languages have become recognized for their value in the learning process. In some cases, when bilingual teachers cannot be found, a new role has emerged—the educational interpreter. This person provides a bridge between the different linguistic worlds that meet in a single classroom. Nowhere is the interpreter more necessary than in the bilingual class, where hearing and deaf must communicate. The goal of this paper is to describe the role of the interpreter for deaf students. I want to focus on the expectations that both students and teachers have for such interpreters and how these expectations affect the role of interpreter in the classroom.

Interpreters in the Classroom

Until recently, American Sign Language (Ameslan), the native language of most deaf Americans, has been poorly understood, and in educational settings the use of signs was systematically suppressed.[2] In public and private classrooms for the deaf, young children were frequently punished for using their hands to communicate. Teachers believed that signs thwarted the primary goals of speaking and lip reading English. Adolescents could only sign in special schools for the deaf after they demonstrated "failure" to learn through the medium of spoken English.

In the past ten years there has been emerging in American educational institutions a strong philosophical commitment to "mainstreaming," the concept that all cultural and linguistic differences among students served by a school system should be accommodated within the

---

[1] Courtney B. Cazden, Vera P. John, and Dell Hymes, eds. *Functions of Language in the Classroom* (New York: Teachers College Press, 1972).

[2] For a journal devoted to understanding sign language and related social phenomena see *Sign Language Studies*, nos. 1-6.

main classroom activities. The deaf have been included within this concept along with other "handicapped" people. Since the deaf have historically been trained to perform blue-collar or technical jobs that require little or no use of spoken English, vocational-technical institutions have become the focus of "mainstreaming" for deaf students at the postsecondary level. With the help of federal incentives in the form of grants, these schools have included deaf students within their existing programs. This accommodation entails a recognition of the linguistic dimension of deafness; i.e., the deaf students require some form of visual communication. In order to provide them with visual communication in the classroom, several public vo-tech schools have instituted their own training programs for interpreters. Through these programs, in six weeks or less, hearing people, sometimes other students, are taught sign language and the fundamentals of interpreting for the deaf.

Metropolitan Vocational Technical School (a pseudonym) sits at the bottom of a hill near the industrial section of a large midwestern city. It has several thousand students who come from all over the city each day to crowd into the old brick buildings for their classes. I attended an interpreter training program at this school, which had a new, but comparatively extensive, federally funded postsecondary program for the deaf. After the training, I accepted a job as classroom interpreter at the school. The incidents described here are based on real happenings during the time I worked there, although names and specific details have been altered to some extent to preserve the anonymity of the interactants. This school offered the standard major areas found in most vocational-technical institutions, such as drafting, auto mechanics, electromechanical training, keypunch, office practice, machine-tool processing, nurses aide, restaurant and hotel management, etc. Most of these classes were open to any deaf student after one quarter of "prep" classes and consultation with a staff of advisors/counselors. All the teachers in these major areas were hearing, and none were fluent bilinguals in American Sign Language. A few signed a little; fewer were proficient enough to handle deaf students in a hearing class without an interpreter.

The usual practice at Metropolitan is for an interpreter to be assigned to each class in which deaf students are enrolled. The interpreters are usually trained as I was at the school. They are not guaranteed a job after training, but the school absorbs several, sometimes many, from its own training program. The interpreters seek this training for many different reasons. Almost all have had no previous knowledge of sign language, and the turnover in the job is quite high. Still, in a short time in training and then on the job, many acquire remarkable proficiency in the signs as a second language. Both signed English and American

Sign Language are taught as part of the training.[3] Interpreters are encouraged to sign English in the classroom, but quickly begin to adjust their signs to the native language of the students they work with.

I entered the classroom with the clear understanding that the interpreter functioned to transmit communication between hearing and deaf. I was to be a neutral channel for use by the teacher and the deaf student as they interacted in this educational setting. I was to interpret what the teachers said, whether or not my signs were ignored by the deaf student; I would translate signs into spoken English for the teachers, whether or not they listened. The decisions about the relative importance of these messages were for student and teacher to make; they were certainly beyond the scope of my function. During the training program we had studied the professional interpreters' code of ethics as drawn up by the National Registry of Interpreters for the Deaf (a certifying and support group for interpreters). It states that "The interpreter shall interpret faithfully and to the best of his ability, always conveying the thought, intent and spirit of the speaker. He shall remember the limits of his particular function and not go beyond his responsibility." In our training we were encouraged to follow this code and to be aware of our unique position as professional interpreters. I found, however, that the "limits of my function" and the delineation of my responsibilities were often beyond my control.

As an interpreter I discovered that I was also in a strategic position to be a sociological observer. Classroom activities always involve social interaction between student and teacher, student and student. This interaction is negotiated, whether openly through formal arrangements or silently, without either party aware of their strategic maneuvers, the assumptions they employ, or even of the problematic nature of the negotiation.[4] I was in a position not only to observe the negotiated character of the interaction but indeed at times to mediate or affect it.

Teachers' Expectations for Interpreters

Teachers hold different tacit assumptions about their role and their relationships with students. The interpreter may be seen as an intrusion into

[3] William C. Stokoe, Jr., "Sign Language Diglossia," *Studies in Linguistics* 21 (1970):27-41.
[4] Aaron Cicourel, K. H. Jennings, S. H. M. Jennings, K. C. W. Leiter, Robert MacKay, Hugh Mehan, and D. R. Roth, *Language Use and School Performance* (New York: Academic Press, 1974).

their private domain of teaching or as a valuable assistant. Interpreters quickly become aware of differences among teachers in their attitudes and expectations. From the first day on the job I began to sense some of these assumptions about what for me was a new role.

I walked into Mrs. Miller's typing class for the first time to find her shuffling papers at her desk while students drifted into class. I introduced myself, and she responded by saying, "I'm Janet Miller. I've never had deaf students before so I don't know how to work with an interpreter. What do I do? What do you do?" Although she claimed to be completely naive, in the weeks to come she asserted her function as teacher for both deaf and hearing and developed definite ideas about what an interpreter should do.

Mr. Malone, an English teacher, was not so relaxed and confident. As I first walked into his class on the second day of the term, one of the students finger-spelled his name to me and motioned me to a chair in front of the class. "Fine," he signed. I assumed he was the only deaf student, and in a few minutes, while the students were filling out some first-of-the-term forms, Mr. Malone introduced himself and asked, "Do you know whether Mike can lip read? Do you know anything about his background? Does he have any hearing?" Of course, having just met Mike, I could say almost nothing about his language skills. Through the term Mr. Malone demonstrated reluctance and insecurity about teaching through an interpreter.

Just after Mr. Malone's class, I reported to Mr. Smith's drawing class. He saw the deaf members of his class as *his* students. He was signing hesitantly, mostly finger-spelling, to a student in the front row of tables. "Oh, you must be the interpreter," he said, seeing me walk in (there is a uniform dress prescribed at the school). He introduced himself and said, "Have you met George Anderson? Glad to have you here today. What was your name again? Can I get you a stool?" A few minutes later, when the teacher was busy with other students, George explained that there had been no interpreter yesterday, and that, while Mr. Smith has been trying to learn sign language, he had been frustrated by the effort of his awkward signs and simultaneous speech. Nevertheless, he was obviously a teacher who had overcome insecurity about teaching deaf students. In fact, I later discovered that he was actively involved in developing classroom materials for use with the deaf. Still, simultaneous lecturing and signing is, for the hearing signer, a feat that requires practice and experience. Perhaps in this class my responsibilities would be clear and my function that of interpreter only, with the teacher quite able to communicate with the student on a personal basis.

The Deaf Student as Object

Teachers sometimes expect interpreters to join them in treating deaf students as objects, as less than full-fledged members of the class. For instance, after an exam Mr. Malone announced, "We will now correct our test papers. Pass your paper to a neighbor and exchange. I will read the answers." He walked to Mike's desk, took his test, and handed it to me. The other students around Mike exchanged papers. He sat and watched the grading process. I attempted to sign the answers and at the same time correct Mike's paper. Mr. Malone's action was embarrassing to me and implied some inadequacy on Mike's part to interact in the classroom even with an interpreter. All the deaf student needs is an interpreter. His significant problem as a "minority" person is a language barrier.

Another situation I encountered that drew me into treating the deaf student as an object involved the problem of "talking about" or "discussing" the deaf student with the teacher. Although I had the best intentions of maintaining my function as a neutral communicative channel, I found myself a hearing among hearing, talking *about* the deaf student with his teachers and conveying to him partial or altered versions of the discussion when questioned. For example, one day Mr Malone asked me, "How can Mike have missed pronouns in school? I can't believe they were never taught. He must be lying." Whether or not Mr. Malone would have said this face-to-face with a hearing student I can't judge, but it was clear to me that this was not a communication to relay verbatim to the student. "It's possible," I answered, "but since he was in a hearing school, his lip reading skills may not have been good enough alone for him to catch the discussions in class." Mike, who had been watching, signed to me, "What he say?" I answered, "Surprised him that your school didn't teach pronouns." "True, never learned this before," he confirmed. This exchange appeared innocent enough, but it denied Mike direct access to the teacher's feelings about him, feelings which he might take to be prejudicial to his grade in the class. Perhaps a hearing student would have had the choice of working this out and establishing an altered relationship with his teacher. In this case I had clearly affected the negotiations.

A similar situation occurred in Mrs. Miller's typing class a few days later. She confided to me that the model office class planned for next year could accommodate only a few of the typing majors. "I know that they want to put Carole (a deaf student) in the class, but she has so many absences. Is she really sick that often?" I answered that I knew she had regular examinations related to allergies, although I knew and kept to myself that these were scheduled only monthly. Mrs. Miller then commented that Jane and Susan (also deaf students) would not be accepted because their work did not measure up to the standards set for the program. Of course, the students were not supposed to know this, at least not yet. Carole looked up from her typing and asked me what the teacher was saying. Then they were all watching me—Carole, Jane, and Susan. I answered "She said there will be only one model office class next quarter." All three indicated to me that they were anxiously waiting to find out whether they would be accepted. I was put in the position of having privileged information about their future that I was not expected to reveal to them. I observed eighteen- to twenty-two-year-old students being left out of decisions that were vital to them. My "neutral" role was in this instance defined for me, and I kept the information I had to myself.

Treating students as objects was not always as direct as talking *about* them in their presence. Sometimes it only involved talking to the interpreter instead of the student, expecting the interpreter to then take the message to the student. Direct communication between the teacher and student was thus avoided. Mrs. Miller, who was dealing with deaf students and an interpreter for the first time, was nevertheless very patient and open to suggestions. Her class included about fifteen deaf students and fifteen hearing. About half of the deaf students had some hearing and "good oral skills"; that is, they could lip read about 40 to 60 percent of what was said, fit it into context, and come up with usually close approximations of the communication, and they could talk well enough to be understood by those who became accustomed to their "accent." At first, Mrs. Miller felt some insecurity and talked to me even though the student was present, saying, for example, "Tell Susan to complete Lesson 4. Tell her to practice these exercises and then tell her I will come back and observe her work." This form of communication is confusing to the deaf person trying to lip read since the conversations take the form of talking about a third party. I saw the opportunity to encourage direct communication between teacher and student and explained to Mrs. Miller that Susan had "good oral skills," and that, in fact it was advantageous for many deaf people to be able to watch the lips of the speaker. "Talk to *her.* If she doesn't understand, she will ask me to help. Or she can use both my signs and your lip movements to understand exactly what you are saying." Mrs. Miller caught on almost immediately and was very good at producing clear but natural lip movements that greatly facilitated the girls' understanding. Soon the students with some hearing or good oral skills were communicating directly with her, with the understanding that I was always available to explain if necessary. Mrs. Miller's attitude and her early amicable relationship with me and the deaf students allowed the girls to feel free to use all their skills and gave them confidence in their own work in the class. Even though she knew no signs, Mrs. Miller was able to work out her relationships with the students on a "normal" basis. I signed all lectures and interpreted individual questions and conferences at the students' requests, while those students who could or who wanted to try, practiced direct communication with her at no additional risk to their grades or success in the class.

Becoming a Substitute Teacher

Many hearing teachers, due to their feelings of awkwardness with deaf students, to their lack of interest, or possibly to their decisions about their own responsibilities and duties in teaching, turn over to the interpreter the responsibility for tutoring and/or teaching the deaf students. For example, the student with the pronoun problem continued to fail his English assignments. I asked him, "Do you want me to talk to your teacher again? Or could you get a tutor?" Mike responded, "No time for tutoring. Why can't teacher help me? That's his job." I went to Mr. Malone and said, "Mike needs some help understanding pronouns. Could you give him some explanation?" "The day you were absent," he answered, "Anne [substitute interpreter] explained the lesson to him. That seemed to help, she told me." Feeling a bit put-down, I returned to Mike's desk and told him, "Mr. Malone doesn't have time right now. Could I help?" "That's okay," he signed, "will get lesson from some other deaf. Don't understand why teacher can't explain more." Later, feeling responsible for Mike's predicament, I went to the counselor and asked what to do about the English class. Charles said, "We will pay you to tutor him. Interpreters make the best tutors." Obviously, Mike didn't want tutoring, even if both he and I could have found the time in our already fully scheduled days. He wanted the same help in class that he saw the hearing students receiving daily. Mr. Malone was self-conscious at being interpreted and easily frustrated by the difficulties of explanation and response in translation. Tension inevitably built if Mike didn't understand him the first time.

The fact that we were expected to function not only as tutors but also often as teachers for the deaf students was borne out in the experiences of other interpreters I worked with. One, who had worked at the school two or three years, told me that she finally just took the deaf students from a math class to another room during the class period and prepared and taught the lesson herself with the teacher's blessing. She had no teaching credentials and had to spend a great deal of time outside of school hours preparing for this responsibility. Another interpreter told several of us during a coffee break one day that the typing teacher she worked for expected her to teach the deaf students in the class while he took care of the hearing group.

For whatever reasons, these teachers viewed the interpreter's role as that of teacher/tutor for the deaf students in their classes. Other teachers I encountered would not relinquish their responsibility for teaching either hearing or deaf students. For example, Mr. Smith would almost always come to John's desk after a lecture and ask in signs, "Was this okay today, John? Have any questions?" John would almost always answer, "Fine, I understand. No questions." Even this perfunctory exchange seemed to convey to John the feeling that he could communicate with Mr. Smith and that the teacher and I were not, at least not completely, "managing" his experience in the class. He had the same opportunity to question and learn as the hearing students had. In this case I was able to function as a communication channel for teacher and student without being required to effect or intervene in their relationship.

Some teachers openly acknowledged that the language difference made their responses to the deaf students less "normal" than their accommodations to hearing students. One day, after repeatedly asking several hearing students to stop talking and get to work, Mrs. Miller turned to me and said, "That chatter really irritates me. I know the deaf students are probably doing the same thing, but I can't hear their signs so it doesn't bother me." Later, she caught on that in spite of my efforts to turn a "blind eye" to their conversations and to indicate to the girls that they should be working instead of discussing boyfriends, they were on some days doing no classwork at all. She began to force herself to become sensitive to the hands and often asked me, when she saw them signing, if they "had a problem with their work," how much they had finished, or to interpret to them her disapproval.

Social Control

Frequently, the same teacher who viewed the interpreter's role as more than just a communication channel in academic matters also expected the interpreter to monitor and modify the deaf students' behavior, to act as their keeper. For instance, several times Mrs. Thompson reminded me that the deaf students were repeatedly late to her class. "You tell them," she said, "that I'm going to mark them late and that this class starts at ten minutes after 2:00 P.M." I repeated the message to the students, but I felt that Mrs. Thompson intended for me somehow to enforce it. On another occasion early in the quarter, I reported to the office that the students I had been sent to interpret for didn't need me for the first day of class and that they would not need to attend classes for the rest of the day. A counselor found me and told me to go find the three boys and tell them that "they are supposed to be in class this hour." I told him that I didn't see that as part of my job and that I thought the students would resent my interference. He didn't agree but dropped the matter.

I was often in the position of being asked about students' absences. Sometimes I had no special knowledge and would say so. At other times I was forced to conceal things I knew. When Mrs. Miller asked about Carole's absence one day, I honestly reported that I didn't know but assumed she was sick. "She sure is absent a lot," commented Mrs. Miller. "Maybe you should talk to the counselor about it. On another occasion Carole had told me on Thursday that she would be staying home the next day since it was her birthday. "But don't tell the teacher." On Friday Mrs. Miller again commented about Carole's frequent absences and asked me if she was sick that day. Since I usually coped with such situations by trying to smooth over things and "cover" for the student, I answered, "I heard she was sick. She has allergies, you know." I knew I was allowing Carole to sidestep her responsibility at least to do her own lying. Furthermore, I was making myself vulnerable to eventual loss of credibility with instructors and contributing to mistrust and suspicion of the "secret" language used among those who sign. Other interpreters indicated to me that they chose instead to "side" with the teacher in similar situations. This response has its risks as well. Perhaps it is possible under such circumstances to remain neutral. But the unwary interpreter or one who is tired of "managing" these situations can be trapped into becoming a "keeper."

Intervention

Related to the function of "keeper" is that of "intervening" on the student's behalf, thereby directly affecting interaction between teacher and student. There is some truth to the assumption that a deaf student cannot always adequately represent his case in exact translation. To argue a point for another person requires some use of the intervenor's own persuasive tools. There is, in fact, some acceptance to this assumption by teachers in their dealings with other cultural groups on the grounds that there must be some *over*compensation in cases of deprivation. Interpreters appeared to take several different approaches in coping with the problem of intervention. The more experienced interpreteres tended to be "jaded," skeptical, and paternalistic, following the inclination of many teachers to suspect the worst and grant privileges reluctantly.

Other interpreters, more idealistic, usually new to the job, intervened on the student's behalf, explaining his problems, making reasonable cases for his requests, and defending him in his absence. For example one day Jane signed to me that she wanted to leave during typing class and go to the counselor to talk about her courses for next quarter. She had been fidgeting for an hour, discussing her plans about scheduling with the other deaf students and doing none of her assigned classwork. I relayed her request to Mrs. Miller, who said, "Can't she see him some other time?" "She is so upset about her schedule," I explained, "that she isn't getting anything done in class." "I understand," replied Mrs. Miller. "Okay." I had chosen to convert my knowledge of the situation into persuasive English and had convinced the teacher to allow this privilege. At other times I remained neutral and merely conveyed the teacher's answer. Some interpreters reported that they anticipated teachers' responses to such requests and told the students "no" themselves. Of course, the type of relationships involved, either teacher-interpreter, student-interpreter, or student-teacher, affected interpreters' decisions about intervening. Possibly for this reason, several interpreters indicated to me that they preferred not to have social contact with the students outside the classroom and that they tried to minimize personal interaction regarding non-class-related things.

Student's Expectations for the Interpreter

In the daily routine of the classroom, the interpreter's duties were varied and sporadic, depending upon the type of class, the teachers' experience and expectations for the interpreter, and the needs and expectations of individual students. Some students expected only professional services. They needed the interpreter to translate, to add explanation in Ameslan if necessary, and generally to help them understand variations in classroom routines. However, many of the students also needed help with written English, and often a large part of the interpreter's responsibility was explaining written instructions, tests, workbooks, etc. Other students defined the "duties" of the interpreter in such a way that the interpreter, rather than or in addition to the teacher, could be "blamed" when things went wrong. Since the student has, and should have, the option to ignore interpreting in the classroom, "blaming" often created frustration and confusion about responsibilities for the interpreters. Once again, this supposedly neutral person was drawn into the interaction between teacher and student, becoming an intermediary in the relationship and sometimes a scapegoat for misunderstanding.

Explaining the System

Probably the biggest job I had in the classroom was that of "explaining the system." Once routines were established, the students gained confidence and usually worked more independently, although any deviation from routine could create a kind of "first-day" chaos. The degree of responsibility that fell upon me for this initiation into routines varied with the student's prior experience, level of communication, and previously negotiated arrangements with the teacher. The experienced student, particularly if he had worked with the instructor before, usually incorporated me within the relationship that already existed between him and the teacher. Often he would indicate that he had no need of elaborate explanations at the beginning of the class. For example, on the first full day of class, Mr. Smith announced to the drawing class that their grade would be based on "four exams plus a shop project which you will work on during the last half of the quarter." I signed this message to John. He indicated to me that he already knew the information. "I've been in his classes before. He always grades the same way."

Problems developed when the student thought he understood on the basis of partial explanation but was mistaken. I was sometimes able to foresee the misunderstanding but was reluctant to say to the student that he had made a mistake. One day Mrs. Miller was in the process of explaining some procedures in typing class. Carole signed to me impatiently, "Yes, yes, I know. I had this book in high school. I was already up to Lesson 85." Mrs. Miller was discussing grading procedures specific to this class, but Carole had cut off attention to the explanations as soon as she saw something familiar. She was later frustrated by having to redo work due to her lack of knowledge of these preliminary instructions.

Many students asked questions until they were thoroughly familiar with the routines. Others let explanations pass them until they were directly aware of the need to know. Still others never asked, and their work usually suffered from lack of knowledge of the routines. Of course, I observed this variation among hearing students as well, but as an interpreter I was caught in the middle, a third party to the relationship between the teacher and the deaf student with the option of intervening to try to "protect" the student. Many of them expected this of me.

Once routines were established in the classroom, most students seemed to feel a security about proceeding on their own. Then a change would be introduced. Several weeks into the quarter, Mrs. Miller announced, "Today you will turn in timings only if you make three or less errors and only if your speed represents improvement." Until this day students were required to turn in all timings and had, in fact, had enough trouble just getting the headings right on their papers and figuring words per minute. I signed the communication to the deaf students as Mrs. Miller talked. Ten minutes later, timings were finished, and the students were leaving for lunch. All of the deaf students turned in timings. Only one of them had three or fewer errors *and* better speed than the week before. With absences, lack of attention, and general misunderstanding, this change in routine was not established for about three weeks.

Some interpreters resorted to nagging the students in similar situations; others gave up or refused to condescend to students by closely observing their work. Others, I noticed, took on the phrasing and attitude of disgusted parents when faced with the problems of relaying instructions.

Explaining Written English

Written instructions solve few of the problems of misunderstanding in the classroom. There is a common misconception among hearing people, including some educators of the deaf, that if a deaf person can be taught to read and write English, then language barriers vanish. So, you can't sign. Write the instructions to the deaf student or give him a workbook, dittoed instruction sheet, etc. This belief completely ignores the natural language attributes of Ameslan and has at its root the idea that English is the basis of sign language. A large part of an interpreter's job at Metropolitan was translation of written English into Ameslan. This type of explanation was needed and expected by many of the deaf students. For example, one day in typing class I had spent several minutes trying various ways of explaining an instruction in the typing manual to Carole: "Type the following exercise twice, SS; DS between lines." She couldn't understand and finally turned to Susan, the deaf student sharing her desk, and signed, "Don't understand." Susan signed, picturing the page with her fingers, "2, space, 2, space, 2, space." "Understand, yes," replied Carole. I spent much of my time in that class learning from the students how to convert written English into accurate Ameslan.

Early in the quarter, all the students in Mrs. Miller's typing class were given a pretest to determine prior knowledge of the subject matter and placement in the programmed text. Without exception the deaf students did poorly on the exam even though several had taken typing classes before and two even had office experience. Mrs. Miller and I discussed the test results, and the counselor and I both described to her the problem of translating written English for deaf students. She agreed to retest the students at different times so that I could be available to each one to interpret questions. Both English sentence structure and vocabulary were a problem for the students. Of course, even the lowest level textbooks are usually written in formal rather than conversational English, presenting problems for many hearing students. The deaf are doubly affected, first, by the problem of translation if they have limited use of English and by the problem of formal statement of the information. The second round of testing was more effective for placement of the students. For several, their low scores were solely a matter of misunderstanding word order or nontechnical vocabulary.

Interpreting tests, however, had its problems. Often teachers asked and expected me to explain instructions or the statement of questions to deaf students during an exam. Sometimes it was not possible to do so without in some way "giving away" the answer. For example, one question on the typing placement test asked the student to identify the function of the "margin release" on the typewriter. Jane asked me, "What means 'margin release'?" Was this a problem of translation from English or lack of knowledge of the subject? In the course of explaining to her, I actually gave her the answer.

In a math class I interpreted for, one of the objects of testing was for the students to learn to understand "word problems" and translate them into mathematical operations. David invariably could not make sense of the English statement of the problems. Mr. Logan, the teacher, told me to help him with the words. Even David was aware that this amounted to cheating. I rationalized that his grades were so low, since he didn't understand the mathematics either, that the other students certainly could not resent my signing to him during exams.

The Option to Ignore

We were instructed in our interpreter training sessions that we should interpret whatever was said by the instructor in the classroom, by students in discussion, by administration personnel using the loudspeaker, etc., whether the student watched us or not. Like hearing students who can "tune out" their classes at will, the deaf student shall have the option to ignore. It was tempting for interpreters to stop signing when the students stopped watching. I observed that the more experienced interpreters would not continue to sign without a student's attention, particularly if he habitually ignored. Several said that they would read or talk to other students under these circumstances. One or two even walked out of classes. Other interpreters continued to sign regardless of what the student did. Many students preferred this reponse since they could then always look up and tune-in to check the progress of the lecture at will. In addition, some deaf people apparently have incredible peripheral vision and may, in fact, be getting most of the message when they appear to be doing something else. In drawing class I discovered early in the quarter that John really didn't need the lecture material and worked mostly on his own, doing workbook assignments. Nevertheless, I signed every word that came from the teacher's mouth, partly because I knew Mr. Smith took notice if I stopped. I didn't really know how John felt about it, but I knew that at least I was doing what the teacher expected. Finally, one day John looked up as I was signing the lecture. He signed to me, "Interpreter talks to herself." I laughed but kept up with the teacher's words. "Right. Continue," said John. "You need the practice."

Occasionally, I had to make the decision to call a student's attention to some crucial information, such as a test date, class dismissal, or assignment deadline. Usually, the student appreciated and expected this intervention. However, many resented the efforts of some new interpreters, or occasionally more experienced ones, to force their attention. After missing a drawing class one day, I apologized to John the next day and asked him about the substitute interpreter. He answered, "She was okay. But she kept poking me and telling me to pay attention. Finally, I told her I already knew the lesson and finished my homework."

Setting Up the Interpreter

Some students hold the interpreters responsible for storing information and sorting essential bits of knowledge to feed them later. This sets up a situation for blaming the interpreter if anything goes wrong for the student. I got such comments from students as, "I didn't know we had a test today. You didn't tell me." "I didn't learn about fractions. You didn't explain that." "I took my test home. You didn't tell me we were supposed to leave them in the classroom." "I didn't know timings were one-third of our grade. You didn't explain that well." All of these complaints involved things that I had signed as they were discussed in class. Of course, just because I had conveyed the information, even with the students' attention, didn't necessarily clear the possibility of blame. If I argued that I had in fact told the students these things, I would often get a reply such as "You didn't explain it well," or "you told me the wrong thing," or "you said this assignment was okay." In typing class Carole repeatedly held up her work for me or Mrs. Miller to see and asked, "Is this right?" She usually became angry when the answer was "No." But the anger at that point was not as difficult to handle as allowing her to think that the work was acceptable, then later telling her that the teacher had found something wrong while grading the work. She would then explode with anger, blame me and/or Mrs. Miller and sulk or leave the class. By "setting up" one or both of us in asking for a fast "okay," she provided herself with a scapegoat (or two) for later when grades were assessed.

Conclusion

In this paper I have described the role of an interpreter through my observations of the hearing and deaf together in a bilingual classroom.

I discovered that the two language worlds represented—Ameslan and spoken English—placed me as the interpreter under constant pressure. As the incidents described indicate, my functions and responsibilities were frequently altered by forces outside my control. Initially, I understood my role as that of a neutral channel for communication, but my experience produced different roles for me. Hearing teachers and deaf students alike constantly redefined my role in accordance with their own needs and expectations. Both saw me as an active participant in their interactions, and I had to renegotiate my function on a continuing basis. In the process, I found myself in a strategic position to reaffirm, through my observations, the "worked-out" nature of social interaction.

PART EIGHT
Religion

Religion as an institution traditionally addresses itself to questions of an ultimate nature. It deals with the "truth," "revelation," "faith," and "divine knowledge." It provides answers to questions, such as What is the purpose of living? Why do I suffer? How can I achieve everlasting life? What is God?, and so on. Answers to these questions become standard for periods of time and for certain social groups, depending upon the character of the society in which the groups exist. In folk societies the scope of religious institutions encompasses everything from weather to play. In the technological society the scope may become specific, focusing on the personal and emotional needs of the believers in coping with death and tragedy.

The manifestation of religious beliefs and sentiments in contemporary American society shows great diversity. The Protestant, Catholic, and Jewish faiths have been joined by hundreds of sects and diverse religious movements. Converts to Buddhism, Hinduism, and other Eastern religions actively seek new members in every large city. Conventional expressions of religion such as church membership have dwindled; the Jesus people and movements such as glossalalia (speaking in tongues) have mushroomed. But the diversity of religious institutions and the apparent changes taking place must not blind us to the fundamental fact that religion remains an important aspect of life in modern society.

Religious beliefs and practices also function to provide believers with identities. These identities set them apart from nonbelievers and unite them with others of similar beliefs. An important characteristic of modern society is the sense of isolation that persons experience from one another and from themselves. Our social selves are complex, composed of many varied and often independent components. A woman may act as a mother to her children, work as a surgeon heading a team in the operating room, preside over a business meeting at her local church, and lecture to medical students—all in the same day. Individuals in these various groups probably never meet or interact.

We are taught to be many different people, play many different roles, perform in many different capacities. We must figure out for ourselves who we are, what we are about, what our inner fiber consists of. When a person becomes a believer, when he uses some doctrine of faith as a basis for organizing life, all the pieces fit together more easily. Perhaps it is fitting that in modern society we find a plurality of religious institutions, many religious components, that can serve this unifying function. The conventional church can integrate a person's identity directly into other institutions in the society; e.g., a deacon is a good loan risk. A religious social movement can provide a sense of togetherness, even if only for a short period of time. And at the extreme, the "evil devil-worship" cults can provide self-identity around the negative themes of traditional religion.

The selections in this section describe several religious scenes in our society. Although surveys of religious institutions provide important information, our goal has been to provide a sense of *being there*. The following articles describe meaning and function for several selected forms of the religious institutions in America.

27
Civil Religion

Religious modes of thinking have a way of sanctifying everything to which they are applied. Over a period of time a secular practice or custom, when associated with a sacred act, has taken on many of the characteristics of its religious counterpart. When this phenomenon occurs, some sociologists speak of "civil religion." Although the practice may not be officially a religious holiday or observance, it is essentially religious in institutional flavor. Lloyd Warner's well-known description of the American Memorial Day observance illustrates these points in a fascinating fashion.

An American Sacred Ceremony
W. Lloyd Warner

Memorial Day and Symbolic Behavior

Every year in the springtime, when the flowers are in bloom and the trees and shrubs are most beautiful, citizens of the Union celebrate Memorial Day. Over most of the United States, it is a legal holiday. Being both sacred and secular, it is a holy day as well as a holiday and is accordingly celebrated.

For some it is part of a long holiday of pleasure, extended outings, and great athletic events; for others it is a sacred day when the dead

From W. Lloyd Warner, *American Life: Dream and Reality* (Chicago: University of Chicago Press, 1953). Reprinted by permission.

are mourned and sacred ceremonies are held to express their sorrow; but for most Americans, especially in the smaller cities, it is both sacred and secular. They feel the sacred importance of the day when they or members of their family participate in the ceremonies, but they also enjoy going for an automobile trip or seeing or reading about some important athletic event staged on Memorial Day. This chapter will be devoted to the analysis and interpretation of Memorial Day to learn its meanings as an American sacred ceremony, a rite that evolved in this country and is native to it.

Memorial Day originated in the North shortly after the end of the Civil War as a sacred day to show respect for the Union soldiers who were killed in the war between the states. Only since the last two wars has it become a day for all who died for their country. In the South only now are they beginning to use it to express southern respect and obligation to the nation's soldier dead.

Memorial Day is an important occasion in the American ceremonial calendar and as such is a unit of this larger ceremonial system of symbols. Close examination discloses that it, too, is a symbol system in its own right existing within the complexities of the larger ones.[1]

Symbols include such familiar things as written and spoken words, religious beliefs and practices, including creeds and ceremonies, the several arts, such familiar signs as the cross and the flag, and countless other objects and acts which stand for something more than that which they are. The red, white, and blue cloth and the crossed sticks in themselves and as objects mean very little, but the sacred meanings which they evoke are of such deep significance to some that millions of men have sacrificed their lives for the first as the Stars and Stripes and for the second as the Christian Cross.

The ceremonial calendar of American society, this yearly round of holidays and holy days, partly sacred and partly secular, but more sacred than secular, is a symbol system used by all Americans. Christmas and Thanksgiving, Memorial Day and the Fourth of July, are days in our ceremonial calendar which allow Americans to express common sentiments about themselves and share their feelings with others on set days preestablished by the society for this very purpose. This calendar functions to draw all people together to emphasize their similarities and common heritage; to minimize their differences; and to contribute to their thinking, feeling, and acting alike. All societies, simple or complex,

---

[1]George H. Mead, *Mind, Self, and Society* (Chicago: University of Chicago Press, 1934); Neal E. Miller and John Dollard, *Social Learning and Imitation* (New Haven, Conn.: Yale University Press, 1941); Jean Piaget, *The Language and Thought of the Child* (New York: Harcourt, Brace, 1926); see also C. K. Ogden and I. A. Richards, *The Meaning of Meaning* (New York: Harcourt, Brace, 1927).

possess some form of ceremonial calendar, if it be no more than the seasonal alternation of secular and ceremonial periods, such as that used by the Australian aborigines in their yearly cycle.

The integration and smooth functioning of the social life of a modern community are very difficult because of its complexity. American communities are filled with churches, each claiming great authority and each with its separate sacred symbol system. Many of them are in conflict, and all of them in opposition to one another. Many associations, such as the Masons, the Odd Fellows, and the like, have sacred symbol systems which partly separate them from the whole community. The traditions of foreign-born groups contribute to the diversity of symbolic life. The evidence is clear for the conflict among these systems.

It is the thesis of this chapter that the Memorial Day ceremonies and subsidiary rites (such as those of Armistice Day) of today, yesterday, and tomorrow are rituals of a sacred symbol system which functions periodically to unify the whole community, with its conflicting symbols and its opposing, autonomous churches and associations. It is contended here that in the Memorial Day ceremonies the anxieties which man has about death are confronted with a system of sacred beliefs about death which gives the individuals involved and the collectivity of individuals a feeling of well-being. Further, the feeling of triumph over death by collective action in the Memorial Day parade is made possible by recreating the feeling of well-being and the sense of group strength and individual strength in the group power, which is felt so intensely during the wars when the veterans' associations are created and when the feeling so necessary for the Memorial Day's symbol system is originally experienced.

Memorial Day is a cult of the dead which organizes and integrates the various faiths and national and class groups into a sacred unity. It is a cult of the dead organized around the community cemeteries. Its principal themes are those of the sacrifice of the soldier dead for the living and the obligation of the living to sacrifice their individual purposes for the good of the group, so that they, too, can perform their spiritual obligations.

Memorial Day Ceremonies

We shall first examine the Memorial Day ceremony of an American town for evidence. The sacred symbolic behavior of Memorial Day, in which scores of the town's organizations are involved, is ordinarily divided into four periods. During the year separate rituals are held by many of the associations for their dead, and many of these activities are connected with later Memorial Day events. In the second phase, preparations are made during the last three or four weeks for the ceremony itself, and some of the associations perform public rituals. The third phase consists of the scores of rituals held in all the cemeteries, churches, and halls of the associations. These rituals consist of speeches and highly ceremonialized behavior. They last for two days and are climaxed by the fourth and last phase, in which all the separate celebrants gather in the center of the business district on the afternoon of Memorial Day. The separate organizations, with their members in uniform or with fitting insignia, march through the town, visit the shrines and monuments of the hero dead, and finally, enter the cemetery. Here dozens of ceremonies are held, most of them highly symbolic and formalized. Let us examine the actual ritual behavior in these several phases of the ceremony.

The two or three weeks before the Memorial Day ceremonies are usually filled with elaborate preparations by each participating group. Meetings are held, and patriotic pronouncements are sent to the local paper by the various organizations which announce what part each organization is to play in the ceremony. Some of the associations have Memorial Day processions, memorial services are conducted, the schools have patriotic programs, and the cemeteries are cleaned and repaired. Graves are decorated by families and associations and new gravestones purchased and erected. The merchants put up flags before their establishments and residents place flags above their houses.

All these events are recorded in the local paper, and most of them are discussed by the town. The preparation of public opinion for an awareness of the importance of Memorial Day and the rehearsal of what is expected from each section of the community are done fully and in great detail. The latent sentiments of each individual, each family, each church, school, and association for its own dead are thereby stimulated and related to the sentiments for the dead of the nation.

One of the important events observed in the preparatory phase in the community studied occurred several days before Memorial Day, when the man who had been the war mayor wrote an open letter to the commander of the American Legion. It was published in the local paper. He had a city-wide reputation for patriotism. He was an honorary member of the American Legion. The letter read: "Dear Commander: The approaching Poppy Day [when Legion supporters sold poppies in the town] brings to my mind a visit to the war zone in France on Memorial Day, 1925, reaching Belleau Wood at about 11 o'clock. On this sacred spot we left floral tributes in memory of our town's boys—Jonathan Dexter and John Smith, who here had made the supreme sacrifice, that the principle that 'might makes right' should not prevail."

Three days later the paper in a front-page editorial told its readers: "Next Saturday is the annual Poppy Day of the American Legion. Everybody should wear a poppy on Poppy Day. Think back to those terrible days when the red poppy on Flanders Field symbolized the blood of our boys slaughtered for democracy." The editor here explicitly states the symbolism involved.

Through the early preparatory period of the ceremony, through all its phases, and in every rite, the emphasis in all communities is always on sacrifice—the sacrifice of the lives of the soldiers of the city, willingly given for democracy and for their country. The theme is always that the gift of their lives was voluntary; that it was freely given and therefore above selfishness or thoughts of self-preservation; and finally, that the "sacrifice on the altars of their country" was done for everyone. The red poppy became a separate symbol from McCrae's poem "In Flanders Fields." The poem expressed and symbolized the sentiments experienced by the soldiers and people of the country who went through the first war. The editor makes the poppy refer directly to the "blood of the boys slaughtered." In ritual language he then recites the names of some of the city's "sacrificed dead," and "the altars" (battles) where they were killed. "Remember Dexter and Smith killed at Belleau Wood," he says. "Remember O'Flaherty killed near Château-Thierry, Stulavitz killed in the Bois d'Ormont, Kelley killed at Côte de Chatillon, Jones near the Bois de Montrebeaux, Kilnikap in the St-Mihiel offensive, and the other brave boys who died in camp or on stricken fields. Remember the living boys of the Legion on Saturday."

The names selected by the editor covered most of the ethnic and religious groups of the community. They included Polish, Russian, Irish, French-Canadian, and Yankee names. The use of such names in this context emphasized the fact that the voluntary sacrifice of a citizen's life was equalitarian. They covered the top, middle, and bottom of the several classes. The newspapers throughout the country each year print similar lists, and their editorials stress the equality of sacrifice by all classes and creeds.

The topic for the morning services of the churches on the Sunday before Memorial Day ordinarily is the meaning of Memorial Day to the town and to the people as Christians. All the churches participate. Because of space limitations, we shall quote from only a few sermons from one Memorial Day to show the main themes, but observations of Memorial Day behavior since the Second World War show no difference in the principal themes expressed before and after the war started. Indeed, some of the words are almost interchangeable. The Reverend Hugh McKellar chose as his text, "Be thou faithful until death." He said:

"Memorial Day is a day of sentiment and when it loses that, it loses all its value. We are all conscious of the danger of losing that sentiment.

What we need today is more sacrifice, for there can be no achievement without sacrifice. There are too many out today preaching selfishness. Sacrifice is necessary to a noble living. In the words of our Lord; 'Whosoever shall save his life shall lose it and whosoever shall lose his life in My name shall save it.' It is only those who sacrifice personal gain and will to power and personal ambition who ever accomplish anything for their nation. Those who expect to save the nation will not get wealth and power for themselves.

"Memorial Day is a religious day. It is a day when we get a vision of the unbreakable brotherhood and unity of spirit which exists and still exists, no matter what race or creed or color, in the country where all men have equal rights."

The minister of the Congregational Church spoke with the voice of the Unknown Soldier to emphasize his message of sacrifice:

"If the spirit of that Unknown Soldier should speak, what would be his message? What would be the message of a youth I knew myself who might be one of the unknown dead? I believe he would speak as follows: 'It is well to remember us today, who gave our lives that democracy might live, we know something of sacrifice.'"

The two ministers in different language expressed the same theme of the sacrifice of the individual for national and democratic principles. One introduces divine sanction for this sacrificial belief and thereby succeeds in emphasizing the theme that the loss of an individual's life rewards him with life eternal. The other uses one of our greatest and most sacred symbols of democracy and the only very powerful one that came out of the First World War—the Unknown Soldier. The American Unknown Soldier is Everyman; he is the perfect symbol of equalitarianism.

There were many more Memorial Day sermons, most of which had this same theme. Many of them added the point that the Christian God had given his life for all. That afternoon during the same ceremony the cemeteries, memorial squares named for the town's dead, the lodge halls, and the churches had a large number of rituals. Among them was the "vacant chair." A row of chairs decorated with flags and wreaths, each with the name of a veteran who had died in the last year, was the center of this ceremony held in a church. Most of the institutions were represented in the ritual. We shall give only a small selection from the principal speech:

"Now we come to pay tribute to these men whose chairs are vacant, not because they were eminent men, as many soldiers were not, but the tribute we pay is to their attachment to the great cause. We are living in the most magnificent country on the face of the globe, a country planted and fertilized by a Great Power, a power not political or economic but religious and educational, especially in the North. In the South they had settlers who were there in pursuit of gold, in search of El Dorado, but the North was settled by people seeking religious principles and education."

In a large city park, before a tablet filled with the names of war dead, one of our field workers shortly after the vacant-chair rite heard a speaker in the memorial ritual eulogize the two great symbols of American unity—Washington and Lincoln. The orator said:

"No character except the Carpenter of Nazareth has ever been honored the way Washington and Lincoln have been in New England. Virtue, freedom from sin, and righteousness were qualities possessed by Washington and Lincoln, and in possessing these characteristics both were true Americans, and we would do well to emulate them. Let us first be true Americans. From these our friends beneath the sod we receive their message, 'Carry on.' Though your speaker will die, the fire and spark will carry on. Thou are not conqueror, death, and thy pale flag is not advancing."

In all the other services, the same themes were used in the speeches, most of which were ritualized, oratorical language, or were expressed in the ceremonials themselves. Washington, the father of his country, first in war and peace, had devoted his life not to himself but to his country. Lincoln had given his own life, sacrificed on the altar of his country. Most of the speeches implied or explicitly stated that divine guidance was involved and that these mundane affairs had supernatural implications. They stated that the revered dead had given the last ounce of devotion in following the ideals of Washington and Lincoln and the Unknown Soldier and declared that these same principles must guide us, the living. The beliefs and values of which they spoke referred to a world beyond the natural. Their references were to the supernatural.

On Memorial Day morning the separate rituals, publicly performed, continued. The parade formed in the early afternoon in the business district. Hundreds of people, dressed in their best, gathered to watch the various uniformed groups march in the parade. Crowds collected along the entire route. The cemeteries, carefully prepared for the event, and the graves of kindred covered with flowers and flags and wreaths looked almost gay.

The parade marched through the town to the cemeteries. The various organizations spread throughout the several parts of the graveyards, and rites were performed. In the Greek quarter ceremonies were held; others were performed in the Polish and Russian sections; the Boy Scouts held a memorial rite for their departed; the Sons and Daughters of Union

Veterans went through a ritual, as did the other men's and women's organizations. All this was part of the parade in which everyone from all parts of the community could and did participate.

Near the end of the day all the men's and women's organizations assembled about the roped-off grave of General Fredericks. The Legion band played. A minister uttered a prayer. The ceremonial speaker said:

"We meet to honor those who fought, but in so doing we honor ourselves. From them we learn a lesson of sacrifice and devotions and of accountability to God and honor. We have an inspiration for the future today—our character is strengthened—this day speaks of a better and a greater devotion to our country and to all that our flag represents."

After the several ceremonies in the Elm Hill Cemetery, the parade re-formed and started the march back to town, where it broke up. The firing squad of the American Legion fired three salutes, and a bugler sounded the "Last Post" at the cemetery entrance as they departed. This, they said, was a "general salute for all the dead in the cemetery."

Here we see people who are Protestant, Catholic, Jewish, and Greek Orthodox involved in a common ritual in a graveyard with their common dead. Their sense of separateness was present and expressed in the different ceremonies, but the parade and the unity gained by doing everything at one time emphasized the oneness of the total group. Each ritual also stressed the fact that the war was an experience where everyone sacrificed and some died, not as members of a separate group but as citizens of a whole community.

Memorial Day Ceremonies

Lincoln—an American Collective Representation Made by and for the People

Throughout the Memorial Day ceremony there were continual references to Lincoln and his Gettysburg Address. The symbol of Lincoln obviously was of deep significance in the various rituals and to the participants. He loomed over the memorial rituals like some great demigod over the rites of classical antiquity. What is the meaning of the myth of Lincoln to Americans? Why does his life and death as conceived in the myth of Lincoln play such a prominent part in Memorial Day?

Some of the answers are obvious. He was a great war president. He was the president of the United States and was assassinated during the Civil War. Memorial Day grew out of this war. A number of other facts about his life might be added; but for our present purposes the meaning of Lincoln the myth is more important to understand than the objective facts of his life-career.

Lincoln, product of the American prairies, sacred symbol of idealism in the United States, myth more real than the man himself, symbol and fact, was formed in the flow of events which composed the changing cultures of the Middle West. He is the symbolic culmination of America. To understand him is to know much of what America means.

In 1858, when Lincoln ran against Stephen Douglas for the United States Senate, he was Abraham Lincoln, the successful lawyer, the railroad attorney, who was noted throughout the state of Illinois as a man above common ability and of more than common importance. He was a former congressman. He was earning a substantial income. He had married a daughter of the superior classes from Kentucky. His friends were W. D. Green, the president of a railway, a man of wealth; David Davis, a representative of wealthy eastern investors in western property, who was on his way to becoming a millionaire; Jesse Fell, railway promoter; and other men of prominence and prestige in the state. Lincoln dressed like them; he had unlearned many of the habits acquired in childhood from his lowly placed parents and had learned most of the way of those highly placed men who were now his friends. After the Lincoln-Douglas debates, his place as a man of prestige and power was as high as anyone's in the whole state.

Yet in 1860, when he was nominated on the Republican ticket for the presidency of the United States, he suddenly became "Abe Lincoln, the rail splitter," "the rude man from the prairie and the river-bottoms." To this was soon added "Honest Abe," and finally, in death, "the martyred leader," who gave his life that "a nation dedicated to the proposition that all men are created equal" might long endure.

What can be the meaning of this strange transformation?

When Richard Oglesby arrived in the Republican convention in 1860, he cast about for a slogan that would bring his friend, Lincoln, favorable recognition from the shrewd politicians of New York, Pennsylvania, and Ohio. He heard from Jim Hanks, who had known Lincoln as a boy, that Lincoln had once split fence rails. Dick Oglesby, knowing what appeals are most potent in getting the support of the politicians and in bringing out a favorable vote, dubbed Lincoln "the rail splitter." Fence rails were prominently displayed at the convention, to symbolize Lincoln's lowly beginnings. Politicians, remembering the great popular appeal of "Old Hickory," "Tippecanoe and Tyler too," and "The Log Cabin and Cider Jug" of former elections, realized that this slogan would be enormously effective in a national election. Lincoln, the rail splitter, was reborn in Chicago in 1860; and the Lincoln who had become the successful lawyer, intimate of wealthy men, husband of a well-born wife, and man of status was conveniently forgotten.

Three dominant symbolic themes compose the Lincoln image. The first—the theme of the common man—was fashioned in a form preestablished by the equalitarian ideals of a new democracy; to common men there could be no argument about what kind of man a rail splitter is.

"From log cabin to the White House" succinctly symbolizes the second theme of the trilogy which composes Lincoln, the most powerful of American collective representations. This phrase epitomizes the American success story, the rags-to-riches motif, and the ideals of the ambitious. As the equal of all men, Lincoln was the representative of the common man, as both their spokesman and their kind; and, as the man who had gone "from the log cabin to the White House," he became the superior man, the one who had not inherited but had earned that superior status and thereby proved to everyone that all men could do as he had. Lincoln thereby symbolized the two great collective but opposed ideals of American democracy.

When Lincoln was assassinated, a third powerful theme of our Christian society was added to the symbol being created by Americans to strengthen and adorn the keystone of their national symbol structure. Lincoln's life lay sacrificed on the altar of unity, climaxing a deadly war which proved by its successful termination that the country was one and that all men are created equal. From the day of his death, thousands of sermons and speeches have demonstrated that Lincoln, like Christ, died that all men might live and be as one in the sight of God and man. Christ died that this might be true forever beyond the earth; Lincoln sacrificed his life that this might be true forever on this earth.

When Lincoln died, the imaginations of the people of the eastern seaboard cherished him as the man of the new West and translated him into their hopes for tomorrow, for to them the West was tomorrow. The defeated people of the South, during and after the reconstruction period, fitted him into their dark reveries of what might have been, had this man lived who loved all men. In their bright fantasies, the people of the West, young and believing only in the tomorrow they meant to create, knew Lincoln for what they wanted themselves to be. Lincoln, symbol of equalitarianism, of the social striving of men who live in a social hierarchy, the human leader sacrificed for all men, expresses all the basic values and beliefs of the Middle West and of the United States of America.

Lincoln, the superior man, above all men, yet equal to each, is a mystery beyond the logic of individual calculators. He belongs to the culture and to the social logics of the people for whom contradiction is unimportant and for whom the ultimate tests of truth are in the social structure in which, and for which, they live. Through the passing generations of our Christian culture the Man of the Prairies, formed in the mold of the God-man of Galilee and apotheosized into the man-god of the American people, each year less profane and more sacred, moves securely toward identifications with deity and ultimate godhead. In him Americans realize themselves.

The Effect of War on the Community

A problem of even greater difficulty confronts us on why war provides such an effective context for the creation of powerful national symbols, such as Lincoln, Washington, or Memorial Day. Durkheim gives us an important theoretical lead.[2] He believed that the members of the group felt and became aware of their own group identity when they gathered periodically during times of plenty. For his test case, the Australian aborigines, a hunting and gathering tribe, this was the season when food was plentiful. It was then when social interaction was most intense and the feelings most stimulated.

In modern society interaction, social solidarity, and intensity of feelings ordinarily are greatest in times of war. It would seem likely that such periods might well produce new sacred forms, built, of course, on the foundations of old beliefs. Let us examine the life of American communities in wartime as a possible matrix for such developments.

The most casual survey supplies ample evidence that the effects of war are most varied and diverse as they are reflected in the life of American towns. The immediate effect of war is very great on some towns and very minor on others. During its existence it strengthens the social structure of some and greatly weakens the social systems of others. In some communities it appears to introduce very little that is new, while in others the citizens are compelled by force of circumstances to incorporate whole new experiences into their lives and into the social systems which control them.

In some communities during World War II there was no decided increase or decrease in the population, and war did not change the ordinary occupations of their people. Their citizens made but minor adjustments in their daily lives; no basic changes occurred in their institutions.

---

[2]Emile Durkheim, *Elementary Form of the Religious Life*, trans. J. W. Swain (New York: Macmillan, 1926), and *Division of Labor in Society*, trans. George Simpson (New York: Macmillan, 1933).

For example, there were many small market towns servicing rural areas about them where the round of events substantially repeated what had occurred in all previous years from the time the towns grew to early maturity. A few of their boys were drafted, possibly the market crops were more remunerative, and it may be that the weekly paper had a few more war stories. Changes there were, but they were few and minor in their effect on the basic social system.

At the other extreme, most drastic and spectacular changes occurred in World War II. Small towns that had formerly existed disappeared entirely, and their former localities were occupied by industrial cities born during the war and fathered by it. Sleepy rural villages were supplanted by huge industrial populations recruited from every corner of America. Towns of a few hundred people, traditionally quiet and well composed, suddenly expanded into brawling young cities with no past and no future. Market towns became industrial areas. The wives and mothers in these towns left their homes and joined the newcomers on the assembly line. The old people went into industry to take jobs they had to learn like the youngest boy working beside them. This and that boy and some of their friends left high school because they received tacit encouragement from their elders and the school authorities to go to work to help in the war effort. In some communities, the whole system of control that had formerly prevailed ceased to function or was superseded by outside authority. The influx of population was so great that the schools could teach but a small portion of the children. The police force was inadequate. The usual recreational life disappeared, to be supplanted by the "taxi dance hall," "juke joint," "beer hall," and "gambling dive." Institutions such as the church and lodge almost ceased to function. In some towns one could drive through miles of trailer camps and small houses pressed against one another, all recently assembled, where the inhabitants lived in squalid anonymity with, but not of, the thousands around them. They were an aggregate of individuals concentrated in one area, but they were not a community.

We have described only the two extremes of the immediate influence of war on the community. Soon, however, those communities which had been little affected by the war felt some of its effects, and those which had been disorganized developed habits of life which conformed to the ordinary pattern of American town life. The two extremes soon approached the average.

But wars influence the average town quite differently. Changes take place, the institutional life is modified, new experiences are felt by the people, and the townsmen repeatedly modify their behavior to adapt to new circumstances brought them by new events. These modifications do not cause social breakdown. The contrary is true. The war activities strengthen the integration of many small communities. The people are more systematically organized into groups where everyone is involved and in which there is an intense awareness of oneness. The town's unity and feeling of autonomy are strengthened by competition in war activities with neighboring communities.

It is in time of war that the average American living in small cities and towns gets his deepest satisfactions as a member of his society. Despite the pessimistic events of 1917, the year when the United States entered World War I, the people derived deep satisfaction from it, just as they did from the last war. It is a mistake to believe that the American people, particularly the small-towners, hate war to the extent that they derive no satisfaction from it. Verbally and superficially they disapprove of war, but at best this is only partly revealed in their deeper feelings. In simpler terms, their observed behavior reveals that most of them had more real satisfaction out of World War II, just as they did in the previous one, than they had had in any other period in their lives. The various men's and women's organizations, instead of inventing things to do to keep busy, could choose among activities which they knew were vital and significant to them and to others.

The small-towner then had a sense of significance about himself, about those around him, and about the events which occurred, in a way that he had never felt before. The young man who quit high school during the depression to lounge on the street corner and who was known to be of no consequence to himself or to anyone else in the community became a seasoned veteran, fighting somewhere in the South Pacific—a man obviously with the qualities of a hero (it was believed), willing to give up his life for his country, since he was in its military forces. He and everyone else were playing, and they knew they were playing, a vital and significant role in the present crisis. Everyone was in it. There was a feeling of unconscious well-being, because everyone was doing something to help in the common desperate enterprise in a cooperative rather than in a private spirit. This feeling is often the unconscious equivalent of what people mean when they gather to celebrate and sing "Hail, hail, the gang's all here." It also has something of the deep significance that enters into people's lives only in moments of tragedy.

The strong belief that everyone must sacrifice to win a war greatly strengthens people's sense of their importance. Everyone gives up something for the common good—money, food, tires, scrap, automobiles, or blood for blood banks. All of it is contributed under the basic ideology of common sacrifice for the good of the country. These simple acts of giving by all individuals in the town, by all families, associations, schools, churches, and factories, are given strong additional emotional support by the common knowledge that some of the local young men are representing the town in the military forces of the country. It is known that some of them may be killed while serving their country. They are sacrificing their lives, it is believed, that their country may live. Therefore, all acts of individual giving to help win the war, no matter how small, are made socially significant and add to the strength of the social structure by being treated as sacrifices. The collective effect of these small renunciations, it is believed, is to lessen the number of those who must die on the altars of their country.

Another very strong integrative factor contributed by a war that strengthens the social structure of the small town and city is that petty internal antagonisms are drained out of the group into the common enemy. The local antagonisms which customarily divide and separate people are largely suppressed. The feelings and psychic energies involved, normally expended in local feuds, are vented on the hated symbols of the enemy. Local groups which may have been excluded from participation in community affairs are given an honored place in the war effort, and the symbols of unity are stressed rather than the separating differences. The religious groups and the churches tend to emphasize the oneness of the common war effort rather than allow their differing theologies and competitive financing to keep them in opposing groups. The strongest pressure to compose their differences is placed against management and labor. (The small number of strikes is eloquent proof of the effectiveness of such pressure.) A common hate of a common enemy, when organized in community activities to express this basic emotion, provides the most powerful mechanism to energize the lives of the towns and to strengthen their feelings of unity. Those who believe that a war's hatreds can bring only evil to psychic life might well ponder the therapeutic and satisfying effects on the minds of people who turn their once private hatreds into social ones and join their townsmen and countrymen in the feeling of sharing this basic emotion in common symbols. Enemies as well as friends should be well chosen, for they must serve as objects for the expression of two emotions basic to man and his social system—hatred and love.

The American Legion and other patriotic organizations give form to the effort to capture the feelings of well-being when the society was most integrated and feelings of unity were most intense. The membership comes from every class, creed, and nationality, for the soldiers came from all of them.

Only a very few associations are sufficiently large and democratic in action to include in their membership men or women from all class levels, all religious faiths, and most, if not all, ethnic groups. Their number could be easily counted on the fingers of one hand. Most prominent among them are the patriotic associations, all of them structural developments from wars which involved the United States. The American Legion is a typical example of the patriotic type. Less than 6 percent of several hundred associations which have been studied include members from all social classes. Of the remaining 94 percent, approximately half have representatives from only three classes, or fewer than three, out of the six discussed in Chapter 3. Although the associations which include members from all levels of the community are surprisingly few, those which stress in action as well as in words such other principles of democracy as the equality of races, nationalities, and religions are even fewer. Only 5 percent of the associations are composed of members from the four principal religious faiths in America—Protestant, Catholic, Jewish, and Greek Orthodox—and most of their members come from the lower ranks of the society.

Lincoln and Washington and lesser ritual figures (and ceremonies such as Memorial Day) are the symbolic equivalent of such social institutions as the patriotic societies. They express the same values, satisfy the same social needs, and perform similar functions. All increase the social solidarity of a complex and heterogeneous society.

How Such Ceremonies Function in the Community

Memorial Day and similar ceremonies are one of the several forms of collective representations which Durkheim so brilliantly defined and interpreted in *The Elementary Forms of the Religious Life.* He said: "Religious representations are collective representations which express collective realities." Religious collective representations are symbol systems which are composed of beliefs and rites which relate men to sacred beings. Beliefs are "states of opinion and consist in representations"; rites are "determined modes of action" which are expressions of, and refer to, religious belief. They are *visible* signs (symbols) of the invisible belief. The visible rite of baptism, for example, may express invisible beliefs about cleansing the newborn infant of sin and relating him to the Christian community.

Ceremonies, periodically held, serve to impress on men their social nature and make them aware of something beyond themselves which they feel and believe to be sacred. This intense feeling of belonging to something larger and more powerful than themselves and of having part of this within them as part of them is symbolized by the belief in sacred beings, which is given a visual symbol by use of designs which are the emblems of the sacred entities, e.g., the Cross of the Christian churches.

That which is beyond, yet part of, a person is no more than the awareness on the part of individuals and the collectivity of individuals of their participation in a social group. *The religious symbols as well as the secular ones must express the nature of the social structure of the group of which they are a part and which they represent.* The beliefs in the gods and the symbolic rites which celebrate their divinity are no more than men collectively worshiping their own images—their own, since they were made by themselves and fashioned from their experiences among themselves.[3]

We said earlier that the Memorial Day rites of American towns are sacred collective representations and a modern cult of the dead. They are a cult because they consist of a system of sacred beliefs and dramatic rituals held by a group of people who, when they congregate, represent the whole community. They are sacred because they ritually relate the living to sacred things. They are a cult because the members have not been formally organized into an institutionalized church with a defined theology but depend on informal organization to bring into order their sacred activities. They are called a "cult" here, because this term most accurately places them in a class of social phenomena which can be clearly identified in the sacred behavior of non-European societies.

The cult system of sacred belief puts into the organized form of concepts those sentiments about death which are common to everyone in the community. These sentiments are composed of fears of death, which conflict with the social reassurances that our culture provides us to combat such anxieties. These assurances, usually acquired in childhood and thereby carrying some of the authority of the adults who provided them, are a composite of theology and folk belief. The deep anxieties to which we refer include anticipation of our deaths, of the deaths or possible deaths of loved ones, and less powerfully, of the deaths or possible deaths of those we know and of men in general.

Each man's church provides him and those of his faith with a set of beliefs and a way of acting to face these problems, but his church and those of other men do not equip him with a common set of social beliefs and rituals which permit him to unite with all his fellows to confront this common and most feared of all his enemies. The Memorial Day rite and other subsidiary rituals connected with it form a cult which partially satisfies this need for common action on a common problem. It dramatically expresses the sentiments of unity of all the living among themselves, of all the living to all the dead, and of all the living and

---

[3] A. R. Radcliffe-Brown, *The Andaman Islanders* (Cambridge: Cambridge University Press, 1922); W. Lloyd Warner. *A Black Civilization* (New York: Harper and Brothers, 1937).

dead as a group to the gods. The gods—Catholic, Protestant, and Jewish—lose their sectarian definitions, limitations, and foreignness among themselves and become objects of worship for the whole group and the protectors of everyone.

The unifying and integrating symbols of this cult are the dead. The graves of the dead are the most powerful of the visible emblems which unify all the activities of the separate groups of the community. The cemetery and its graves become the objects of sacred rituals which permit opposing organizations, often in conflict, to subordinate their ordinary opposition and to cooperate in expressing jointly the larger unity of the total community through the use of common rites for their collective dead. The rites show extraordinary respect for all the dead, but they pay particular honor to those who were killed in battle "fighting for their country." The death of a soldier in battle is believed to be a "voluntary sacrifice" by him on the altar of his country. To be understood this belief in the sacrifice of a man's life for his country must be judged first with our general scientific knowledge of the nature of all forms of sacrifice. It must then be subjected to the principles which explain human sacrifice whenever and wherever found. More particularly, this belief must be examined with the realization that those sacrifices occur in a society whose deity was a man who sacrificed his life for all men.

The principle of the gift is involved. In simple terms, when something valuable is given, an equally valuable thing must be returned. The speaker who quoted scripture in his Memorial Day speech, "Whosoever shall save his life shall lose it and whosoever shall lose his life in My name shall save it," almost explicitly stated the feelings and principles involved. Finally, as we interpret it, the belief in "the sacrifice of American citizens killed in battle" is a social logic which states in ultimate terms the subordinate relation of the citizen to his country and its collective moral principles.

This discussion has shown that the Memorial Day ceremony consists of a series of separate rituals performed by autonomous groups which culminate in a procession *of all of them as one group* to the consecrated area set aside by the living for their dead. In such a place the dead are classed as individuals, for their graves are separate; as members of separate social situations, for they are found in family plots and formal ritual respect is paid them by church and association; and as a collectivity, since they are thought of as "our dead" in most of the ceremonies. The fences surrounding the cemetery place all the dead together and separate all the living from them.

The Memorial Day rite is a cult of the dead, but not just of the dead as such, since by symbolically elaborating sacrifice of human life for the country through, or identifying it with, the Christian church's sacred sacrifice of their god, the deaths of such men also become powerful sacred symbols which organize, direct, and constantly revive the collective ideals of the community and the nation.

28
Religion and Self

Religious beliefs sometimes provide a way of organizing the personal and social meanings that people attribute to their lives. One function of religion is to establish a unified identity for the believer. However, these identities are not fixed, and they may undergo radical changes in the course of a person's life. David Gordon discusses two forms of such changes in identities found within the Jesus movement. The first involves the kind of shift in which a person assumes a new identity based on a totally new way of interpreting the nature of the social world. The second involves new identities that are extensions of former ones. By focusing on beliefs and styles, he describes types of universes of discourse and movements among them. The Jesus movement makes available to many people a way of putting together and legitimizing contradictory past experiences and beliefs. For those who believe, the ultimate questions of life have clear answers.

The Jesus People: An Identity Synthesis
David Gordon

The emergence of the Jesus movement has come as a surprise to many. It would appear that many young people have suddenly returned to values against which they had earlier rebelled: a puritanical moral code, literal belief in the Bible, and religious zeal for the God of their fathers. The paradox is heightened by the fact that many Jesus people keep their long hair and hip clothes. This paper will attempt to unravel that paradox

From *Urban Life and Culture* 3 (1974): 159–178. Reprinted by permission. Victor Lidz supervised my masters paper, from which this paper is adapted, and Barry Schwartz provided valuable criticisms of both versions of the paper. I am grateful to both of them for their assistance.

by showing how the activities, beliefs, and membership of the Jesus movement synthesize and reconcile otherwise contradictory aspects of a young person's life. It is my view that the Jesus movement combines elements of the moral code into which these young people were originally socialized as well as elements of the youth culture into which they were later socialized. I will introduce a type of identity change called "consolidation" in an attempt to show how this is accomplished. Religion's major function in this process will be seen as establishing and legitimating a unified identity for the believer.

For the purpose of this paper, I will define Jesus people as those who consider themselves saved Christians and who participate in the activities of the Jesus movement. Although this definition includes all age groups, there are very few adults who participate in movement activities. The Jesus people themselves see only the first half of this definition as necessary,[1] but there are saved Christians who do not participate in these activities and who therefore do not concern us here.[2]

The material for this paper was gathered by participant observation of various Bible studies, rallies, and revivals in the Chicago area over a period of about eight months during 1971 and 1972. Near the end of this period, twelve open-ended, informal interviews were tape-recorded. Most of the biographical material utilized is drawn from those interviews. The bulk of the material presented here was gathered at Billy Williams's God's Outreach, Inc. (a pseudonym, as are all names of the participants). At the time the study was conducted, this was a full-time ministry of eleven young people living together in a large old house in the inner city. They ranged from eighteen to thirty years in age and included several married couples. They conducted Bible studies in the house three nights each week, held revivals, spoke to various groups when requested, and witnessed on the streets.

Activities and Style

The Jesus people in the Chicago area engage in seven major types of activities all of which are used to gain conversions, despite other possible

---

[1] They say that one is a Jesus person if he or she "loves Jesus." This means that one has admitted and repented of his sins and has asked Jesus into his life as his personal savior.

[2] The Jesus people are, for the most part, independent from any organized church, although some attend church services. By the same token most members of organized churches do not participate in Jesus movement activities.

purposes. These are revivals, rallies, Bible studies, street witnessing, speaking engagements, marches, and use of the mass media. These activities are all dominated by the style of contemporary youth culture, including spontaneity, expressiveness, rock music, hip language, and hip clothes. Speaking engagements at churches and schools, distribution of Jesus papers, which are admittedly patterned after underground newspapers, and appearances on radio and television talk-shows are all undertaken to gain maximum public exposure for the movement. The march also serves to attract attention and is held prior to a revival, with the site of the revival as its destination. Street witnessing involves handing a gospel tract to a passerby and telling him that Jesus loves him. If the passerby shows any interest an attempt is made to convert him. Most street witnessing in Chicago is aimed at youth and is thus done in areas where youths tend to congregate.

Although the Jesus people attempt to remain apolitical, occasionally a situation arises which calls for a rally to muster political support. For example in 1971 two members of God's Outreach, Inc. were arrested while witnessing on Rush Street, Chicago's nightclub district. Feeling that their freedom of the streets was being threatened, the group organized a rally to obtain petition signatures.[3] Its format was identical to that of most political rallies, including several speakers, cheers for Jesus, and a rock band. There were also, however, prayers, testimonies of how various people got saved, and religious songs.

Such a combination of "styles" is also evident at revivals, large-scale conversion-oriented affairs. The format is indistinguishable from that of the revivals of such American "greats" as Moody, Sunday, and Finney.[4] Language and sermons, however, are geared to young audiences. At one revival in Chicago, for example, Billy Williams told the story of Shadrach, Meshach, and Abednego. He referred to them as the original Jesus freaks—"a bunch of young, radical kids turned on for Jesus," who went around singing, "Oh How I Love Jesus," and "all that other good stuff." When they refused to bow down to the golden idol and the king threatened them with the fiery furnace, they "pulled

---

[3]While this rally appears to be in violation of the Jesus peoples' norm of submission to authority, one of the leaders explained to me that their freedom of the streets was essential to their work. In addition, he explained, only proper, legal channels were employed in bringing about the political pressure, so that the Jesus people were merely exercising their rights, not defying authority. A similar argument is often made for the acceptability of applying for conscientious objector status with the Selective Service. In important matters such as these, however, the action is taken only if the person feels that it is God's will that he do so.

[4]This format includes preaching, personal testimonies, music, prayer, an invitation to come forward and accept Jesus, and collective singing.

out a big red sticker, stuck it on his nose," and they handed him a Jesus paper. These descriptions all drew laughs from the crowd.

Revivals include Jesus rock—rock music with lyrics praising Jesus—Jesus cheers, and traditional Christian songs. Those who are often featured as model Christians at such gatherings are those who can best legitimate the movement to young people. At the revival mentioned above, for example, the featured speaker was a former black militant.

The Bible study allows for a more intimate gathering of Jesus people. It is the most frequent and perhaps most important activity for the movement in this area. Bible studies are usually held once or twice a week, and each has its regular participants. A typical meeting includes prayers, both silent and spoken, a period during which experiences with Jesus are related, a discussion of a Bible passage or passages, and singing. Following the meeting most people stay to talk informally and refreshments are often served. Bible-study meetings seem to provide group support to members for witnessing to others and for living a Christian life, instruction in exactly what a Christian life involves, and an opportunity for informal recreation.

The visual style of the Jesus movement imitates that of youth culture, but its content often parodies the content of youth culture. The walls of the meeting room at God's Outreach provide a good example. They were adorned with colorful Jesus posters and bumper stickers displaying such sayings as, "Jesus—Like a Bridge Over Troubled Water," "Repent—Boycott Hell," and "Turn On With Jesus," these being parodies of popular music, protest, and drugs, respectively. The primary symbol of the movement, an upraised forefinger, parodies the peace sign, and was represented here in red, white, and blue on a banner in the front of the room.

Beliefs and Norms

The Jesus people believe that the Bible is the literal word of God, that Heaven and Hell exist as real places, that Satan is a real being, that the individual is a worthless sinner, and that the only way to avoid eternal damnation is to admit one is a sinner and to ask Jesus into one's life as one's personal savior. This is called "getting saved," and the two steps involved are called "dying to self" and being "born again." In addition to the admission of sin, "dying to self" involves repenting of these sins and giving up all personal desires in order to follow God's will completely. When a person is "born again," Jesus not only comes into his life but actually enters into the person and works through him. After salvation, a person can drift back into sin, however, and require another salvation-like experience which is called "getting right with God."[5] When a person gets saved, he is immediately freed from sin (no longer has a desire to sin and is forgiven for past sins), immediately begins living a joyful and fulfilling eternal life, and is guaranteed an eternal place with Jesus in Heaven after death.

Finally, the Jesus people believe that the end of the world is coming soon and that this will coincide with Jesus' return to earth. The fulfillment of Biblical prophecy by present world events, especially the founding of Israel, is given as evidence for this assertion.

Probably the most powerful norm for a Jesus person is to follow God's will rather than his own. All important decisions are allegedly made for the believer by God; the mortal must not let his own choices interfere with those which God makes for him.[6] One also follows God's will by being submissive to all suffering, events, and authority. Submission to suffering is seen as a great privilege and as an opportunity to share with Jesus. The source of most suffering is seen as the ridicule of nonbelievers. Being submissive to events and authority involves a fatalism so powerful that all but two of those interviewed said they would kill in Vietnam if they found themselves in that situation, because they were thus "intended" to do so.

The only occasion in which it is permissible to defy authority occurs when obedience would endanger the person's salvation. This situation arises if an authority attempts to force a believer to worship a false god or to defy Jesus in some way. Such a view allows the Jesus people to see themselves as spiritual rebels against most established churches and against the corrupt world, while submitting to all civil and family authority in nonspiritual matters. Thus, Shadrach, Meshach, and Abednego, like the Jesus people, are a bunch of "young radical kids." The leader of a Bible study told me, "Jesus makes you do all sorts of radical things." They are often perceived as radicals by others as well. Many reported resistance from their parents to their membership in such a band of radicals.

---

[5] A further step in getting close to God is getting baptized in the Spirit, often symbolized by a baptism by water. This gives the individual the added power of the Holy Spirit which results in greater strength for witnessing and makes gifts such as speaking in tongues available to him.

[6] The actual process by which a decision is made seems to involve following one's inclinations, the most practical course, the opinions of those around one, or some combination of these three. In describing an important decision one member said, "So there were a lot of things which I thought were of the Lord. I was assured of them by circumstances, the Word in the Bible and assurance within the heart, and testimony from other people. Now that's a lot to put together. And if you all agree man it's got to be the Lord."

In terms of political radicalism, however, the Jesus people are individually rather than structurally oriented, believing that the way to change the world is through individual, subjective change and that social problems are really problems of individual sin. In terms of cultural radicalism, they are reactionaries. Drugs are forbidden, extramarital sex is forbidden, drinking and smoking are forbidden. Often a member will impose a prohibition against secular rock music upon himself to avoid slipping back into a presalvation frame of mind. In addition, women are definitely required to be submissive to men and are cast in traditional female roles.

Despite the prohibitions on certain activities, some norms of personal conduct are similar to those found in contemporary youth culture. Members are encouraged to be expressive and spontaneous regarding their emotions. During a revival one speaker asked, "How many have danced before the Lord lately, amen? Sometimes you get to dancing before the Lord and you just can't stop." During prayer sessions most people moan, speak individual but simultaneous prayers aloud, make exclamations of joy and love, or even cry. In terms of interaction with others, openness and candor are encouraged. Members openly hug each other and call one another "brother" and "sister." Jesus people also stress the brotherhood of all, equality before God (but not before earthly authority), antiintellectualism, and antimaterialism. In addition, as Ellwood (1973, p. 18–23) points out, the Jesus movement, like the counter culture, sees subjectivity as the key to reality, holds a "high" as its goal in life, expresses itself through music, is alienated from mainstream culture including science and technology, is suspicious of history, is nostalgic for an earlier time when life was simpler, and has a tendency to proselytize.

Identity

Gregory Stone has said that identity

> is not a substitute word for "self." Instead when one has identity, he is *situated*—that is, cast in the shape of a social object by the acknowledgment of his participation or membership in social relations. One's identity is established when others *place* him as a social object by assigning him the same words of identity that he appropriates for himself or *announces* . . . [Stone 1962, p.93].

Identity, then, has an internal, subjective component and an external, objective component. When these two components coincide a person's identity is established. Richard Travisano (1970, p. 596) points out that identity is established in the context of a universe of discourse or set of meanings. This universe of discourse is the informing aspect of an individual's life and, in turn, is based upon the source of authority to which he gives allegiance. Religion is one type of universe of discourse important for the grounding of identity.[7]

Orrin Klapp (1969, p. 39) adds a third component to the concept of identity outlined above: the individual's feelings, which are validated when they feel "real" and are shared with others. As Klapp points out, it is possible for a person to define himself as a member of a particular religion, be defined as a member by others, and yet consider himself a fake because he does not feel strongly enough about it. I will adopt this summarized view of identity and refer to this third component as the emotional component.

Two types of identity change are generally recognized. The first involves a radical discontinuity in the person's life such as the adoption of an importantly different religion or political ideology. One assumes an identity within a new universe of discourse, gives allegiance to a new authority, adopts new central meanings which contradict old ones, and reevaluates his old identity as wrong or inferior. Furthermore, emotional upset and rejection by old friends and associates are usual accompaniments.

The second type of identity change does not involve radical discontinuity; it involves, rather, a new stage or extension of the former identity. Being confirmed in church, graduating from high school, or becoming a parent are all examples. Here, a new identity is adopted but within the same universe of discourse. The person gives allegiance to the same authority, retains old meanings, and does not reject or reevaluate his old identity. He usually does not undergo emotional upset or rejection by old friends and associates. I shall call the first type of identity change "conversion" and the second type "identity alteration."[8]

My material from the Jesus movement suggests the existence of yet a third type of identity change, which I will call "identity consolidation." By this, I refer to the adoption of an identity which combines two prior but contradictory identities.[9] Consolidation involves two stages:

---

[7]For a discussion of this point see particularly Berger and Luckman (1967, pp. 99–100), and also Parsons (1958, p. 72) and Bellah (1970, p. 11).

[8]I have thus preserved Travisano's (1970) typology but for reasons of clarity have changed his term "alternation" to "alteration." His typology states that a conversion, "involves the adoption of a pervasive identity which rests on a change (at least in emphasis) from one universe of discourse to another" (Travisano, 1970, p. 601). Alternations "are relatively easily accomplished changes of life which do not involve a radical change in universe of discourse and informing aspect, but which are a part of or grow out of existing programs of behavior" (Travisano, 1970, p. 601).

first, the partial adoption of an identity which rests on a change from one universe of discourse to another (that is, a partial conversion), and second, the adoption of an identity which rests on both of these universes of discourse. The first stage of this transformation is fraught with guilt and emotional upset which, unlike complete conversion, persists long after the transformation is made. The second stage involves a release from this guilt and upset.

Consolidation itself can be either direct or indirect. In direct consolidation the person returns to the universe of discourse from which he began. In my material, for example, this would be a person raised in a Southern Baptist church, who rejected these beliefs for drugs and perhaps eastern religion, and who then became a Jesus person. Since his intervening identity (as a member of youth culture) had an impact on his view of himself, he did not return to the Baptist church, but rather, adopted an identity within the original universe of discourse (fundamentalist Christianity) which contained elements of his intervening identity.

In indirect consolidation the person goes on to a third universe of discourse rather than returning to the one in which he began. An example would be a person raised as a Catholic, who rejected his Catholicism for the youth culture, and later became a Jesus person.

The universes of discourse from which my materials are drawn are illustrated graphically in Figure 28-1.

Cells 1 and 3 together comprise the fundamentalist Christian universe of discourse, including all denominations and sects which subscribe to the set of beliefs discussed above. "Jesus people" is an identity within this universe of discourse, distinguished from other identities within it on the basis of style and activities.[10] This is represented by a dotted rather than a solid line between cells 1 and 3.

---

[9]Other evidence which suggests the process of identity consolidation in the Jesus movement has been presented by Adams and Fox (1972); Enroth, Ericson, and Peters (1972); and Ellwood (1973). In addition, Robbins (1969) and Robbins and Anthony (1972) present evidence which suggests this process in the Meher Baba movement. There have also been accounts suggesting the possibility of this process occurring in nonreligious contexts. For example, Nolan (1973) reports the existence of a pan-sexual movement which combines the identities of male and female. Palson and Palson (1972) report on swinging (wife swapping), which seemingly combines the identities of married and nonmarried. Schwartz, Turner, and Peluso (1973) discuss an identity which they call the "hippie greaser." Finally, Toch (1965: 167) very briefly mentions the possibility of grasping a third ideology in order to bridge the discontinuity between two contending ideologies.

[10]The Jesus people call fundamentalist Christians who object to their dress, their spontaneity, and their informality "the conservatives." One Jesus person told me that he was raised in a "conservative" church and that he was put off by the informal aspects of the movement when he first encountered it. Once he got used to these aspects, he said, he realized that the Jesus movement met his needs better than his conservative church. The point is that once he could tolerate the difference in style, he could switch allegiance with no change in belief. Although there are doctrinal differences of opinion within this universe of discourse, they cut across the churches and the Jesus movement.

FIGURE 28-1. Types of universes of discourse

	BELIEF	
STYLE	Saved	Not Saved
Straight	1 Fundamental Christian	2 Conventional
Hip	3 Jesus People	4 Youth-Drug

Cell 2, Conventional, contains a variety of belief systems, including Judaism, Catholicism, and nonsalvation-oriented Protestantism. Following Will Herberg (1960), I will group these together and assume that they form an American conventional universe of discourse.

Cell 4 contains the youth-drug subculture, which is distinguished from the conventional universe of discourse on the basis of both style and meaning. Since, as it appears from my material, shifts among eastern religions and cults such as witchcraft and astrology are made rather easily, we will combine these also. Perhaps the major distinction to be made within this cell is one between radical-activists and drug-dropouts. Since I have encountered no former radical-activists among the Jesus people, however, they will not concern us here.

The changes in universes of discourse which constitute the various types of identity change presented above can be illustrated by referring to Figure 28-1. Since the focus here is on the Jesus people identity, we will consider only those possibilities which have this identity as an end state.

A conversion is a move from cell 2 to cell 1, Conventional to Fundamental Christian, or to cell 3, Conventional to Jesus People. The following example, like those which follow it, is a summary of a case history constructed from field notes and interview transcripts. Duane is an example of a converter.

> Duane was raised on a farm. His parents did not get along and there was much tension in the family. By age sixteen Duane attempted suicide and became a heavy drinker.
>
> Duane's father had turned against religion when his first wife died. Duane's mother was raised in a liberal Lutheran church and she taught Sunday school in the local Methodist church. Duane attended Sunday school there until he was in the fourth grade. At that time his mother stopped attending and so did he.

> After high school Duane became increasingly unhappy and lonely. He was saved when he opened a devotional which a minister had once given him and read a prayer in it. He went to bed and awoke feeling like a new person.
>
> As a result of this experience he joined a Baptist church. Later, at a Baptist camp, Duane met Billy Williams, who was conducting a rally there. Duane was impressed by Billy and later became a member of God's Outreach.

Duane's conversion, then, took him from cell 2, Conventional, to cell 1, from a weak and nonfundamentalist background into a fundamentalist Baptist church. His later move into the Jesus movement can be considered an alteration.

An alteration is a move from cell 1, Fundamental Christian, to cell 3, Jesus People. An example of an alterator is Keith.

> Keith also grew up in a rural area. His parents and brother and sister were all saved, and the family belonged to a Mennonite church. When he was eight years old, Keith prayed with his parents and was saved. He never strayed from his faith but considers his greatest sin to be his apathy toward it.
>
> After high school Keith entered Moody Bible Institute where he encountered Duane. Duane enlisted him into his street witnessing, and Keith now feels that his faith is renewed and his apathy overcome.

Keith, then, never rejected his beliefs or his identity but adopted a new identity which helped to affirm his beliefs.

A direct consolidation is a move from cell 1, Fundamental Christian, to cell 4, Youth-Drug, to cell 3, Jesus People. An example of a direct consolidator is Celia.

> Celia was raised as a Baptist and was saved during an altar call in church when she was eight years old. When she was twelve her parents were divorced. Celia started gaining weight, went on diet pills, and became addicted. In college she went on to other drugs and became involved with a drug-oriented crowd.
>
> After two arrests on drug charges, Celia encountered two people from God's Outreach and asked Jesus into her life for a second time. She eventually became a member of the God's Outreach staff.

Celia said that her original salvation at age eight was still valid and that she had only temporarily drifted away from God. It is significant that she "returned" to God's Outreach rather than to the Baptist church.

Finally, an indirect consolidation is a move from cell 2, Conventional, to cell 4, Youth-Drug, to cell 3, Jesus People. Jack is an example of an indirect consolidator.

> Jack was raised in a large city as a Catholic but was always dissatisfied with the church for its lack of sincerity about religion. In high school, in order to become popular, he grew long hair and started using drugs. This "worked" and for the first time in his life he felt popular. After high school Jack joined a West Coast commune and started searching for God through drugs. He was saved when the commune was visited by some Jesus people one night when he was high on LSD.

In this case Jack first rejected his Catholicism and conventional life style, then rejected the drug philosophy which had replaced it and finally moved to a third universe of discourse, the Jesus movement.

I suggest that each type of Jesus person has encountered problems validating different components of his identity and that the Jesus movement is particularly suited to solving these problems. My material on converters is too incomplete to attempt any general statements about them, beyond saying that there do not appear to be very many in the movement. However, there is evidence to suggest that alterators were seeking after both social and emotional identity validation. Keith, for example, who is discussed above, attempted to validate his social identity in high school through athletics, drama, and other activities. But it was not until he met Duane, already a Jesus person, that his emotional identity became validated and he moved into the Jesus people identity. The previous lack of emotional identity validation in Keith's life is clearly seen in his assertion that he was,

> ... faking it a lot of times, like going to church you know. I'd go and maybe I'd pretend that I really enjoyed it and everything, but it really wasn't real in my life.

Grant's story is similar. His search for social identity validation is illustrated in the following excerpt from his interview:

> And this had been the big gig in high school and in college, was seeking after popularity, and the best friends, and all this type of thing. And I really one night just saw myself and saw what a bummer it was, and how fakey and phony I'd been in seeking, uh, in just seeking, you know, a big name for myself, and a lot of friends and a lot of recognition.

Grant had never stopped considering himself a Christian but was not enthusiastic about his faith until he met some "turned on Christians," a group of Jesus people. After associating with them for a time, he prayed and was finally filled with the spirit. He said of this experience,

> And so I really just came to the point and I said, I said, I believe there's more. I believe that You want to completely empower me and fill me with the Holy Spirit.

Alterators' lives are characterized by close and harmonious relationships with parents, which perhaps explains their need to validate social and emotional identity components. In so doing, they establish themselves as individuals and establish their feelings toward their faith as their own.

For consolidators, the identity search involves a quest to validate all three components of identity. First, social identity was usually validated by a move into the youth-drug subculture. Jack reported that he was "out of it" in high school and had no girl friends. When he grew his hair long and started using drugs, he became very popular and sometimes dated four girls at once. In high school Celia had been fat, insecure, and without any boyfriends. After she turned to drugs and began dating a rock musician, she believed others saw her as flamboyant. She gained a wide circle of friends and dated many "guys." Renny joined a rock band at age sixteen, became very popular and respected in high school, and after playing professionally for four years, felt he had achieved all his dreams as a rock musician. Despite the outward success of this course of action, however, the youth-drug culture was, for Renny, as for the other consolidators, not inwardly satisfying. For example, Renny said that on his way to success he "missed the total meaning of life."

The search by consolidators for compelling beliefs to validate emotional identity, as well as the search for meaning within which they could place themselves to validate internal identity, are illustrated in a quote by Jerry:

> Most of my life I was searching for something I could grab onto and something I could say was real. And would answer questions I had like what could make me happy and why was I here on the earth, and what was going to happen to me, what would happen when I die, was this all there was? I wanted something real and something that could make me happy. And my friend had been doing dope and he said it helped him out a lot; it gave him the answer.

Celia also speaks of her need for internal validation. She said she went to three psychiatrists, but that they,

> ... just gave me tests, they gave me tranquilizers, they gave me antidepressants, but they never changed me on the inside. You know, not like God.

Drugs not only failed to give consolidators the answers and identity validation they sought, but they and the free sexual participation which went together in the drug culture began to cause them a great deal of guilt. As Jerry said,

> I thought about committing suicide a lot. I tried cutting my wrists a couple of times but didn't have the courage. I was unhappy with

life, and I was havin' a lot of guilt about the things I was doin'. So I just wanted to get away from it. . . . Well it was mainly sex, but the drugs somewhat, too.

Or Jack, in describing his commune,

People were in and out you know with sleeping bags and you never knew, like what do I do tonight. Well this chick's far out why don't I see if she wants to go to bed with me. You know, weird things like this all the time. And it was just ugly.

Thus, although consolidators did not feel that their original religion was compelling, they had internalized its ethical code to the extent that they felt guilt when they openly violated it.

Just like my parents raised me a Christian and it never really left me. Which is really beautiful, like, I was reading in Proverbs today. It says, train a child in the way he should go and he shall never depart from it. It's true. It just stays with you.

The quest for internal and emotional identity validation among both types of consolidators may have to do with their shared loss of a parent and with family problems. Seven of the eight who were interviewed had suffered the loss of a parent through death, divorce, or lack of love. Celia's parents, for example, divorced when she was twelve; another young woman's father died when she was twelve, and Jerry felt neglected by both parents.

By the time the consolidator encountered the Jesus movement, then, two parts of his identity were engaged in two different universes of discourse. He was announced by others as belonging to the youth-drug subculture, but his guilt and dissatisfaction suggested that the original "straight" universe of discourse still held some power over him. This dilemma led to confusion and uncertainty in his own mind about his identity.

Identity Synthesis

Becoming a Jesus person is a particularly compelling solution for a consolidator. As we have seen, the Jesus movement assumed that being burdened with sin and guilt is the natural condition of man. It tells the sinner that Jesus loves him anyway, promises quick removal of guilt for the asking, and promises eternal life, joy, peace, and a host of other benefits. All that God asks in return is absolute obedience. This, too, may be attractive to the consolidator. As Travisano points out, a universe of discourse is based upon some source of authority. Part of the ideology of the youth-drug universe of discourse is a self-conscious denial of any authority outside of the individual. This, perhaps, hinders or blocks any stable solution to identity problems, which require some external source of authority to legitimate them.[11]

In terms of the consolidator's identity problems, here is an attractive solution. His internal identity is taken over by Jesus who possesses perfect love and perfect knowledge. Since his guilt has done some damage to this portion of his identity, it is with some relief that the consolidator admits that his self is worthless and moves it aside to make room for Jesus. In order to protect him from further guilt, a host of absolute restrictions on behavior are constructed: no drugs, secular rock music, drinking, smoking, swearing, or extramarital sex. Interestingly enough, smoking seems to be the most difficult "vice" to give up, perhaps because the subjective identity never had any strong internalized misgivings about this activity nor was it ever exclusively associated with one universe of discourse. Thus, internal identity returns to the conventional universe of discourse in which it began and which it never completely abandoned.

The consolidator's social identity is allowed to remain in the youth culture. He can dress the same, talk the same, identify with youth and radicalism, attend rallies, marches and concerts, and receive encouragement for expressivity and openness in his relationships with others. There are also the common emphases on spontaneity, subjectivity, anti-intellectualism, brotherhood, equality, anti-materialism, and condemnation of status-seeking. Continuity with the drug experience is seen in the emphasis on ecstasy and immediate gratification. The Jesus experience is described as an ecstatic experience and is said to be a "trip," just as the drug experience is often described as religious. These orgiastic elements are now channeled into activities which have a high degree of legitimacy. The presence of alterators (those who have never used drugs or participated in promiscuous sex) within the movement is itself an element of this legitimacy.

The Jesus movement is emotionally compelling for the very reason that it is able to bring about a satisfactory resolution of the consolidator's identity problems by combining elements of two social worlds. It may also be compelling because it solves a problem which may have contributed to the consolidator's identity problems in the first place: abandonment. Being saved means that one has established a permanent relationship with Jesus. As Berger (1969, p. 38) points out, God can become the most reliable significant other. It is emphasized that Christianity is

---

[11]For a discussion of this point in regard to the Meher Baba movement see Robbins and Anthony (1972).

not a religion but, rather, a permanent relationship with Jesus. For those who have suffered losses or unsatisfactory relationships with significant others in the past, this may be very important. One young woman, for example, told me, "You really should get saved. It's really wonderful. It's not a religion, you know. It's a relationship." And Duane once said, "One of the most wonderful things about being saved is that you have a direct relationship with God and don't need anyone else."

The alterator's emotional identity problem is resolved in the Jesus movement mainly by his coming in contact with people who share the same beliefs and for whom these beliefs are compelling. His social-identity problem is resolved by participation in activities which identify him with others of his own generation. And an additional element of this solution is the opportunity for close contact with those who have been in the youth-drug subculture.

Once in the movement the two types of youths become more like each other. Alterators often adopt some of the clothing and grooming styles of the consolidators, while some consolidators "clean up" and dress more conventionally. Alterators sometimes move from existing or projected careers in the ministry to establishing street ministries and informal Bible studies. Consolidators often give up street life for regular jobs and reconciliation with families.

The fact that the Jesus movement provides a religious solution to identity problems is also significant. Religion here serves as an arbitrator between contradictory social roles; it transcends particular social situations and is able to organize them on the basis of a higher meaning (Berger and Luckman, 1967, pp. 98–99). Christianity, in this case, is also able to offer compelling symbols and rituals which express the reconciliation of opposed social roles. Communion, for example, symbolically combines liquid (wine) and solid (bread), as well as sacred (Jesus) and profane (man). Baptism likewise combines liquid (water) and solid (man), as well as spirit (God) and flesh (man). These dichotomies organize the believer's identity into a meaningful and unified whole. Since the individual's identity before conversion is divided, marginal, and uncertain, he feels unclean inside (Douglas 1966). The unification and categorization brought about by the Jesus movement allow him to feel clean again.

> I was changed. I was different. It was like somebody had given me a shower on the inside. I was, felt clean and fresh on the inside. And the whole burden that had been on me was gone. And the first thing that came to my mind was, I asked God for help and it worked! Man I was so happy.

Conclusion

Before conversion, then, both alterators and consolidators find themselves caught between two social worlds. Alterators are moving away from conventionality toward a world which is attractive because of its identification with youth and its enthusiastic belief. Consolidators are moving back toward conventionality and toward a world which they tried to reject but which still has some hold over them. The reasons for the original movement away from conventionality have been widely discussed and are beyond the scope of this paper. Furthermore, I can only suggest why this movement away from conventionality manifests itself in participation in the youth-drug subculture among consolidators and not among alterators. Alterators have experienced no dramatic losses or unsatisfactory relationships with significant others while consolidators do seem to have experienced such losses. Consequently, alterators have not had this vital link with their universe of discourse disturbed and have been secure in, if not always enthusiastic about, their identity. Consolidators, on the other hand, have had their links with their original universe of discourse disturbed and have not been secure in their identity leading to an internal quest through drugs and subjectivity oriented religions as well as to a social quest among their peers. This dual quest fails largely as a result of internalized norms from childhood which were never completely abandoned and because of a lack of authority to legitimate the new universe of discourse.

The Jesus movement reconciles the difficulties in both of the above situations in a single, cognitively and motivationally meaningful universe of discourse. It provides to both alterators and consolidators a conventional view of morality and ethics while also providing the subjective, expressive, and ecstatic qualities of youth culture. This solution is partially legitimated for each type of member by the presence of the other type, by an appeal to traditional rituals and symbols of American revivalistic Christianity, and by an appeal to a source of authority and meaning which transcends, and is therefore capable of reconciling, the two seemingly contradictory social worlds.

References

Adams, R. and R. Fox. 1972. "Mainlining Jesus: The New Trip." *Society* 9(February):56–56.
Bellah, R. 1970. *Beyond Belief.* New York: Harper and Row.

Berger, P. 1969. *The Sacred Canopy.* Garden City, N.Y.: Doubleday Anchor.
Berger, P. and T. Luckmann. 1967. *The Social Construction of Reality.* Garden City, N.Y.: Doubleday Anchor.
Douglas, M. 1966. *Purity and Danger.* Baltimore, Md.: Penguin.
Ellwood, R. S. 1973. *One Way.* Englewood Cliffs, N.J.: Prentice-Hall.
Enroth, R., E. Ericson, and C. B. Peters. 1972. *The Jesus People—Old Time Religion in the Age of Aquarius.* Grand Rapids, Ia.: Eerdmans.
Herberg, W. 1960. *Protestant—Catholic—Jew.* Garden City, N.Y.: Doubleday Anchor.
Klapp, O. 1969. *Collective Search for Identity.* New York: Holt, Rinehart and Winston.
Nolan, J. 1973. "The Third Sex." *Ramparts* 12(December).
Palson, C. and R. Palson. 1972. "Swinging in Wedlock." *Society* 9(February):28–37.
Parsons, T. 1958. "The Pattern of Religious Organization in the United States." *Daedalus* 87(Summer):65–85.
Robbins, T. 1969. "Eastern Mysticism and the Resocialization of Drug Users: The Meher Baba Cult." *Journal for the Scientific Study of Religion* 8(Fall): 308–17.
Robbins, T. and D. Anthony. 1972. "Getting Straight with Meher Baba." *Journal for the Scientific Study of Religion* 11(June):122–40.
Schwartz, G., P. Turner, and E. Peluso. 1973. "Neither Heads nor Freaks: Working Class Drug Subculture." *Urban Life and Culture* 3(October):288–313.
Stone, G. P. 1962. "Appearance and the Self." In *Human Behavior and Social Processes,* ed. A. Rose. Boston: Houghton Mifflin.
Travisano, R. 1970. "Alternation and Conversion as Qualitatively Different Transformations." In *Social Psychology Through Symbolic Interaction,* ed. G. P. Stone and M. Farberman. Waltham, Mass.: Ginn-Blaisdell, pp. 594–606.

29
The Function of Religion

Although the trends in American society are toward the displacement of sacred with secular beliefs, many magical and quasi-religious beliefs remain. The contents and practices of these modern, sacred, world views are combinations of earlier religious systems and the secularism of contemporary society. Presently, in segments of our society, there is a growth in the practice of witchcraft. Moody describes what kind of people use black magic, and he analyzes the role that such beliefs and practices play in the life of the magician. He is able to demonstrate that Satanic priesthood has a sociological basis and often functions in a supportive fashion for the "true" believer.

Urban Witches
Edward J. Moody

Every Friday evening just before midnight, a group of men and women gathers at a home in San Francisco, and there, under the guidance of their high priest, a sorcerer or magus sometimes called the "Black Pope of Satanism," they study and practice the ancient art of black magic. Precisely at midnight they begin to perform Satanic rituals that apparently differ little from those allegedly performed by European Satanists and witches at least as early as the seventh century. By the dim and flickering light of black candles, hooded figures perform their rites upon the tradi-

From *Conformity and Conflict*, ed. James P. Spradley and David W. McCurdy (Boston: Little, Brown 1971). Reprinted by permission.

tional Satanic altar—the naked body of a beautiful young witch—calling forth the mysterious powers of darkness to do their bidding. Beneath the emblem of Baphomet, the horned god, they engage in indulgences of flesh and sense for whose performance their forebears suffered death and torture at the hands of earlier Christian zealots.

Many of these men and women are, by day, respected and responsible citizens. Their nocturnal or covert practice of the black art would, if exposed, make them liable to ridicule, censure, and even punishment. Even though we live in an "enlightened" age, witches are still made a focus of a community's aggression and anxiety. They are denounced from the pulpit, prosecuted to the limit of the law, and subjected to extralegal harassment by the fearful and ignorant.

Why then do the Satanists persist? Why do they take these risks? What benefits do they derive from membership in a Satanic church, what rewards are earned from the practice of witchcraft? What indulgences are enjoyed that they could not as easily find in one of the more socially acceptable arenas of pleasure available in our "permissive" society?

The nearly universal allegation of witchcraft in the various cultures of the world has excited the interest of social scientists for years and the volume of writing on the topic is staggering. Most accounts of witchcraft, however, share the common failing of having been written from the point of view of those who do not themselves practice the black art. Few, if any, modern authors have had contact with witches, black magicians, or sorcerers, relying instead on either the anguished statements of medieval victims of inquisition torture, or other types of secondhand "hearsay" evidence for their data. To further confuse the issue, authoritative and respected ethnologists have reported that black magic and witchcraft constitute an imaginary offense because it is impossible—that because witches cannot do what they are supposed to do, they are nonexistent.

Witches and Magicians

But the witches live. In 1965 while carrying out other research in San Francisco, California, I heard rumors of a Satanic cult which planned to give an All Hallows' Eve blessing to a local chamber of horrors. I made contact with the group through its founder and high priest and thus began over two years of participant-observation as a member of a contemporary black-magic group. As a member of this group, I interacted with my fellow members in both ritual and secular settings.

The following description is based on the data gathered at that time.

The witches and black magicians who were members of the group came from a variety of social class backgrounds. All shades of political opinion were represented from communist to American nazi. Many exhibited behavior identified in American culture as "pathological," such as homosexuality, sadomasochism, and transvestism. Of the many characteristics that emerged from psychological tests, extensive observations, and interviews, the most common trait, exhibited by nearly all Satanic novices, was a high level of general anxiety related to low self-esteem and a feeling of inadequacy. This syndrome appears to be related to intense interpersonal conflicts in the nuclear family during socialization. Eighty-five percent of the group, the administrative and magical hierarchy of the church, reported that their childhood homes were split by alcoholism, divorce, or some other serious problem. Their adult lives were in turn marked by admitted failure in love, business, sexual, or social relationships. Before entering the group each member appeared to have been battered by failure in one or more of the areas mentioned, rejected or isolated by a society frightened by his increasingly bizarre and unpredictable behavior, and forced into a continuing struggle to comprehend or give meaning to his life situation.

Almost all members, prior to joining the group, had made some previous attempt to gain control over the mysterious forces operating around them. In order to give their environment some structure, in order to make it predictable and thus less anxiety-provoking, they dabbled in astrology, the Tarot, spiritualism, or other occult sciences, but continued failure in their everyday lives drove them from the passive and fatalistic stance of the astrologer to consideration of the active and manipulative role of sorcerer or witch. In articles in magazines such as *Astrology* and *Fate,* the potential Satanist comes into direct contact with magic, both white and black. Troubled by lack of power and control, the pre-Satanist is frequently introduced to the concept of magic by advertisements which promise "Occult power . . . now . . . for those who want to make real progress in understanding and working the forces that rule our Physical Cosmos . . . a self-study course in the practice of Magic." Or, Ophiel will teach you how to "become a power in your town, job, club, etc.," how to "create a familiar [a personal magic spirit servant] to help you through life," how to "control and dominate others." "The Secret Way" is offered free of charge, and the Esoteric Society offers to teach one how herbs, roots, oils, and rituals may be used, through "white magic," to obtain love, money, power, or a peaceful home. They will also teach one self-confidence and how to banish "unwanted forces." The reader is invited to join the Brotherhood of the White Temple, Inc.; the Monastery of the Seven Rays (specializing in sexual magic); the Radiant School; and numerous other groups that promise to reveal the secrets of success in business, sex, love, and life—the very secrets the potential or pre-Satanist feels have eluded him. Before joining the group, the pre-Satanist usually begins to perform magic ceremonies and rituals whose descriptions he receives for a fee from one of the various groups noted above, from magical wholesale houses, or from occult-book clubs. These practices reinforce his "magical world view," and at the same time bring him in contact with other practitioners of the magical arts, both white and black.

Although most of the mail-order magic groups profess to practice "white" magic—benevolent magic designed only to benefit those involved and never aggressive or selfish, only altruistic—as opposed to "black," malevolent, or selfish magic, even white-magic rituals require ingredients that are rare enough so they can be bought only at certain specialty stores. These stores, usually known to the public as candle shops although some now call themselves occult art supply houses, provide not only the raw materials—oils, incenses, candles, herbs, parchments, etc.—for the magical workings, but serve as meeting places for those interested in the occult. A request for some specific magic ingredient such as "John the Conqueror oil," "Money-come" powder, "crossing" powder, or black candles usually leads to a conversation about the magical arts and often to introductions to other female witches and male warlocks. The realization that there are others who privately practice magic, white or black, supports the novice magician in his newfound interest in magical manipulation. The presence of other witches and magicians in his vicinity serves as additional proof that the problems he has personally experienced may indeed be caused by witchcraft, for the pre-Satanist has now met, firsthand, witches and warlocks who previously were only shadowy figures, and if there are a few known witches, who knows how many there might be practicing secretly?

Many witches and magicians never go beyond the private practice of white or black magic, or at most engage in a form of magic "recipe" swapping. The individual who does join a formal group practicing magic may become affiliated with such a group in one of several ways. In some cases he has been practicing black magic with scant success. Perhaps he has gone no further than astrology or reading the designs on the ancient Tarot cards, a type of socially acceptable magic which the leader of the Satanic church disparagingly calls "god in sport clothes." But the potential Satanist has come to think of the cosmos as being ordered, and ordered according to magical—that is, imperceptible—principles. He is prompted by his sense of alienation and social inadequacy to try to gain control of the strange forces that he feels influence or control him, and hearing of a Satanic church, he comes to learn magic.

Others join because of anxiety and inadequacy of a slightly different nature. They may be homosexual, nymphomaniac, sadist, or masochist. They usually have some relatively blatant behavioral abnormality which, though they personally may not feel it wrong, is socially maladaptive and therefore disruptive. As in many "primitive" societies, magic and witchcraft provide both the "disturbed" persons and, in some cases, the community at large with a ready and consistent explanation for those "forces" or impulses which they themselves have experienced. Seeking control, or freedom, the social deviants come ultimately to the acknowledged expert in magic of all kinds, the head of the Satanic church, to have their demons exorcised, the spells lifted, and their own powers restored.

Others whose problems are less acute come because they have been brought, in the larger religious context, to think of themselves as "evil." If their struggle against "evil" has been to no avail, many of the individuals in question take this to mean that the power of "evil" is greater than the power of "good"—that "God is dead"—and so on. In their search for a source of strength and security, rather than continue their vain struggle with that "evil" force against which they know themselves to be powerless, they seek instead to identify themselves with evil, to join the "winning" side. They identify with Satan—etymologically the "opposition"—and become "followers of the left-hand path," "walkers in darkness."

Finally, there are, of course, those who come seeking thrills or titillation, lured by rumors of beautiful naked witches, saturnalian orgies, and other strange occurrences. Few of these are admitted into the group.

Black Magic

For the novice, initial contact with the Satanists is reassuring. Those assisting the "Prince of Darkness" who heads the church are usually officers in the church, long-term members who have risen from the rank and file to positions of trust and authority. They are well-dressed, pleasant persons who exude an aura of confidence and adequacy. Rather than having the appearance of wild-eyed fanatics or lunatics, the Satanists look like members of the middle-class but successful middle-class. The Prince of Darkness himself is a powerfully built and striking individual with a shaven head and black, well-trimmed beard. Sitting among the implements of magic, surrounded by books that contain the "secrets of the centuries," he affirms for those present what they already know:

that there is a secret to power and success which can and must be learned, and that secret is black magic.

All magic is black magic according to the Satanists. There is no altruistic or white magic. Each magician intends to benefit from his magical manipulation, even those workings performed at someone else's behest. To claim to be performing magic only for the benefit of others is either hypocrisy—the cardinal sin in Satanic belief—or naiveté, another serious shortcoming. As defined by the Satanists, magic itself is a suprisingly commonsense kind of phenomenon: "the change in situations or events in accordance with one's will, which would, using normally accepted methods, be unchangeable." Magic can be divided into two categories: ritual (ceremonial) and nonritual (manipulative).

Ritual, or "the greater magic," is performed in a specified ritual area and at a specific time. It is an emotional, not an intellectual, act. Although the Satanists spend a great deal of time intellectualizing and rationalizing magic power, they state specifically that "any and all intellectual activity must take place *before* the ceremony, not during it."[1]

The "lesser magic," nonritual (manipulative) magic, is, in contrast, a type of transactional manipulation based upon a heightened awareness of the various processes of behavior operative in interaction with others, a Satanic "games people play." The Satanist in ritual interaction is taught to analyze and utilize the motivations and behavioral Achilles' heels of others for his own purposes. If the person with whom one is interacting has masochistic tendencies, for example, the Satanist is taught to adopt the role of sadist, to "indulge" the other's desires, to be dominant, forceful, and even cruel in interaction with him.

Both the greater and the lesser magic is predicated upon a more general "magical" world view in which all elements of the "natural world" are animate, have unique and distinctive vibrations that influence the way they relate to other natural phenomena. Men, too, have vibrations, the principal difference between men and inanimate objects being that men can alter their pattern of vibrations, sometimes consciously and at will. It is the manipulation and the modification of these vibrations, forces, or powers that is the basis of all magic. There are "natural magicians," untrained and unwitting manipulators of magic power. Some, for example, resonate in harmony with growing things; these are people said to have a "green thumb," gardeners who can make anything grow. Others resonate on the frequency of money and have the "Midas touch" which turns their every endeavor into a profit-making venture. Still others are "love magnets"; they automatically attract others to them, fascinate

---

[1] The official doctrine of several Satanic groups within the continental United States is contained in Anton Szandor LaVey, *Satanic Bible* (New York: Avon Books, 1969), p. 111.

and charm even though they may be physically plain themselves. If one is a "natural magician," he does some of these things unconsciously, intuitively, but because of the intellectual nature of our modern world, most people have lost their sensitivity to these faint vibrations. Such individuals may, if they become witches, magicians, or Satanists, regain contact with that lost world just as tribal shamans are able to regain contact with another older world where men communicated with animals and understood their ways. It is this resensitization to the vibrations of the cosmos that is the essence of magical training. It takes place best in the "intellectual decompression chamber" of magic ritual, for it is basically a "subjective" and "nonscientific" phenomenon.

Those who have become members of the inner circle learn to make use of black magic, both greater and lesser in obtaining goals which are the antithesis of Christian dogma. The seven deadly sins of Christian teaching—greed, pride, envy, anger, gluttony, lust, and sloth—are depicted as Satanic virtues. Envy and greed are, in the Satanic theology, natural in man and the motivating forces behind ambition. Lust is necessary for the preservation of the species and not a Satanic sin. Anger is the force of self-preservation. Instead of denying natural instincts, the Satanist learns to glory in them and turn them into power.

Satanists recognize that the form of their ritual, its meanings, and its functions are largely determined by the wider society and its culture. The novitiate in the Satanic cult is taught, for example, that the meaning of the word "Satan" etymologically is "the opposition" or "he who opposes" and that Satanism itself arose out of opposition to the demeaning and stultifying institutions of Christianity. The cult recognizes that had there been no Christianity there would be no Satanism, at least not in the form it presently takes, and it maintains that much of the Satanic ritual and belief is structured by the form and content of Christian belief and can be understood only in that larger religious context. The Satanists choose black as their color, not white, precisely because white is the symbol of purity and transcendence chosen by Christianity, and black therefore has come to symbolize the profane earthy indulgences central to Satanic theodicy. Satanists say that their gods are those of the earth, not the sky; that their cult is interested in making the sacred profane, in contrast to the Judeo-Christian cults which seek to make the profane sacred. Satanism cannot, in other words, be understood as an isolated phenomenon but must be seen in a larger context.

The Satanic belief system, not surprisingly, is the antithesis of Christianity. Their theory of the universe, their cosmology, is based upon the notion that the desired end state is a return to a pagan awareness of the mystical forces inhabiting the earth, a return to an awareness of their humanity. This is in sharp contrast to the transcendental goals of traditional Christianity. The power associated with the pantheon of gods is also reversed: Satan's power is waxing; God's, if he still lives, waning. The myths of the Satanic church purport to tell the true story of the rise of Christianity and the fall of paganism, and there is a reversal here too. Christ is depicted as an early "con-man" who tricked an anxious and powerless group of individuals into believing a lie. He is typified as "pallid incompetence hanging on a tree."[2] Satanic novices are taught that early church fathers deliberately picked on those aspects of human desire that were most natural and made them sins, in order to use the inevitable transgressions as a means of controlling the populace, promising them salvation in return for obedience. And finally, their substantive belief, the very delimitation of what is sacred and what is profane, is the antithesis of Christian belief. The Satanist is taught to "be natural; to revel in pleasure and in self-gratification. To emphasize indulgence and power in this life."

The opposition of Satanists to Christianity may be seen most clearly in the various rituals of greater magic. Although there are many different types of rituals, all aimed at achieving the virtues that are the inverted sins of the Christian, we shall examine briefly only two of these: blasphemy and the invocation of destruction. By far the most famous of Satanic institutions, the Black Mass and other forms of ritual blasphemy serve a very real and necessary function for the new Satanist. In many cases the exhortations and teachings of his Satanic colleagues are not sufficient to alleviate the sense of guilt and anxiety he feels when engaging in behavior forbidden by Judeo-Christian tradition. The novice may still cower before the charismatic power of Christian symbols; he may still feel guilty, still experience anxiety and fear in their presence. It is here that the blasphemies come into play, and they take many forms depending on the needs of the individuals involved.

A particular blasphemy may involve the most sacred Christian rituals and objects. In the traditional Black Mass, powerful Christian symbols such as the crucifix are handled brutally. Some Black Masses use urine or menstrual flow in place of the traditional wine in an attempt to evoke disgust and aversion to the ritual. If an individual can be conditioned to respond to a given stimulus, such as the communion wafer or wine, with disgust rather than fear, that stimulus's power to cause anxiety is diminished. Sexuality is also used. A young man who feared priests and nuns was deliberately involved in a scene in which two witches dressed as nuns interacted with him sexually; his former neurotic fear was replaced by a mildly erotic curiosity even in the presence of real

[2]LaVey, *Satanic Bible*, p. 31.

nuns. The naked altar—a beautiful young witch—introduces another deliberate note of sexuality into a formerly awe-inspiring scene.

By far the most frequently used blasphemy involves laughter. Awe inspiring or fear-producing institutions are made the object of ridicule. The blasphemous rituals, although still greater magic, are frequently extremely informal. To the outsider they would not seem to have any structure; the behavior being exhibited might appear to be a charade, or a party game. The Satanists decide ahead of time the institution to be ridiculed and frequently it is a Christian ritual. I have seen a group of Satanists do a parody of the Christmas manger scene, or dress in clerical garb while performing a satire of priestly sexual behavior. The target of blasphemy depends upon the needs of the various Satanists. If the group feels it is necessary for the well-being of one member, they will gladly, even gleefully, blaspheme anything from psychiatry to psychedelics.

In the invocation of destruction, black magic reaches its peak. In some cases an individual's sense of inadequacy is experienced as victimization, a sense of powerlessness before the demands of stronger and more ruthless men. The Satanic Bible, in contrast to Christian belief, teaches the fearful novice that "Satan represents vengeance instead of turning the other cheek." In the Third Chapter of the Book of Satan, the reader is exhorted to "hate your enemies with a whole heart, and if a man smite you on one cheek, SMASH him on the other . . . he who turns the other cheek is a cowardly dog."[3]

One of the most frequently used rituals in such a situation is the Conjuration of Destruction, or Curse. Contrary to popular belief, black magicians are not indiscriminately aggressive. An individual must have harmed or hurt a member of the church before he is likely to be cursed. Even then the curse is laid with care, for cursing a more powerful magician may cause one's curse to be turned against oneself. If, in the judgment of the high priest and the congregation, a member has been unjustly used by a non-Satanist, even if the offender is an unaffiliated witch or magician, at the appropriate time in the ritual the member wronged may step forward and, with the aid and support of the entire congregation, ritually curse the transgressor. The name of the intended "sacrifice" is usually written on parchment made of the skin of unborn lamb and burned in the altar flame while the member himself speaks the curse; he may use the standard curse or, if he so desires, prepare a more powerful, individualistic one. In the curse he gives vent to his hostility and commands the legions of hell to torment and sacrifice his victim in a variety of horrible ways. Or, if the Satanist so desires, the high priest

[3]LaVey, *Satanic Bible*, p. 33

will recite the curse for him, the entire group adding their power to the invocation by spirited responses.

The incidence of harmful results from cursing is low in the church of Satan because of two factors: first, one does not curse other members of the church for fear that their superior magic might turn the curse back upon its user; second, victims outside the congregation either do not believe in the power of black magic or do not recognize the esoteric symbols that should indicate to them they are being cursed.

On only one occasion was I able to see the effect of a curse on a "victim." A member attempted to use the church and its members for publicity purposes without their permission. When the leader of the group refused to go along with the scheme, the man quit—an action that would normally have brought no recrimination—and began to slander the church by spreading malicious lies throughout San Francisco social circles. Even though he was warned several times to stop his lies, the man persisted; so the group decided to level the most serious of all curses at him, and a ritual death rune was cast.

Casting a death rune, the most serious form of greater magic, goes considerably beyond the usual curse designed to cause only discomfort or unhappiness but not to kill. The sole purpose of the death rune is to cause the total destruction of the victim. The transgressor's name is written in blood (to the Satanist, blood is power—the very power of life) on special parchment, along with a number of traditional symbols of ceremonial magic. In a single-minded ritual of great intensity and ferocity, the emotional level is raised to a peak at which point the entire congregation joins in ritually destroying the victim of the curse. In the case in question, there was an orgy of aggression. The lamb's-wool figurine representing the victim was stabbed by all members of the congregation, hacked to pieces with a sword, shot with a small calibre pistol, and then burned.

A copy of the death rune was sent to the man in question, and every day therafter an official death certificate was made out in his name and mailed to him. After a period of weeks during which the "victim" maintained to all who would listen that he "did not believe in all that nonsense," he entered the hospital with a bleeding ulcer. Upon recovery he left San Francisco permanently.

In fairness, I must add that the "victim" of the curse had previously had an ulcer, was struggling with a failing business, and seemed hypertense when I knew him. His knowledge of the "curse" may have hastened the culmination of his difficulties. The Satanic church, however, claimed it as a successful working, a victory for black magic, and word of it spread among the adherents of occult subculture, enhancing the reputation of the group.

Conclusion

Contemporary America is presently undergoing a witchcraft revival. On all levels, from teenagers to octogenarians, interest in, or fear of, witchcraft has increased dramatically over the past two years. It is hardly possible to pass a popular magazine rack without seeing an article about the revival of the black arts. Covens and cults multiply, as does the number of exorcisms and reconsecrations. England, France, Germany, and a host of other countries all report a rebirth of the black art. Why? Those who eventually become Satanists are attempting to cope with the everyday problems of life, with the here and now, rather than with some transcendental afterlife. In an increasingly complex world which they do not fully understand, an anxiety-provoking world, they seek out a group dedicated to those mysterious powers that the sufferers have felt moving them. Fearful of what one witch calls "the dark powers we all feel moving deep within us," they come seeking either *release* or *control.* They give various names to the problems they bring, but all, anxious and afraid, come to the Satanic cult seeking help in solving problems beyond their meager abilities. Whatever their problem—bewitchments, business failure, sexual impotence, or demonic possession—the Satanists, in the ways I have mentioned and many more, *can* and *do* help them. Witchcraft, the witches point out, "is the most practical of all beliefs. According to its devotees, its results are obvious and instantaneous. No task is too high or too lowly for the witch." Above all, the beliefs and practices provide the witch and the warlock with a sense of power, a feeling of control, and an explanation for personal failure, inadequacy, and other difficulties.

Moreover, a seeker's acceptance into the Inner Circle provides a major boost for his self-esteem; he has, for the first time, been accepted into a group as an individual despite his problems and abnormalities. Once within the Inner Circle, that support continues. The Satanic group is, according to the cultural standards of his society, amoral, and the Satanist frequently finds himself lauded and rewarded for the very impulses and behavior that once brought shame and doubt.

Each Satanist is taught, and not without reason, that the exposure of his secret identity, of the fact that he is a powerful and adequate black magician, means trouble from a fearful society. Therefore, in keeping with the precepts of lesser magic, he learns to transform himself magically by day (for purposes of manipulation) into a bank clerk, a businessman, or even a college professor. He wears the guise and plays the role expected by society in order to manipulate the situation to his own advantage, to reach his desired goals. Members of society at large, aware only of his "normal" role behavior and unaware of the secret person within, respond to him positively instead of punishing him or isolating him. Then, in the evening, in the sanctity of his home, or when surrounded by his fellow magicians, he reverts to his "true" role, that of Satanic priest, and becomes himself once again. Inadequate and anxious persons, guilty because of socially disapproved impulses, are accepted by the Satanists and taught that the impulses they feel are natural and normal, but must be contained within certain spatial and temporal boundaries—the walls of the ritual chamber, the confines of the Inner Circle.

PART NINE
Economics

Every society has ways to decide what constitutes a valued object. The valued objects can be used directly or indirectly in exchange for desired goods. Although valued items are usually rare or scarce, they may be merely symbolically scarce. At one time our modern currency was considered valuable since it represented the rare commodity of gold. Now the ordinary paper and ink that are used in the manufacture of money are valuable only because they combine according to a formula unknown by most of us but recognized by all. Money is without question the most valuable, extraordinary, item in modern society. Its use is completely context free. It may be used for virtually any purpose the human mind can imagine.

Our society has developed institutions (standardized knowledge and action) around money and its use. We have elaborate banking and monetary-exchange systems. We have invented the spectacular electronic computer to keep up with the higher mathematics of accounting for and multiplying this medium of exchange. All of these ancillary systems require training for personnel and support from the society. As is true with many institutions, there are different levels of competency and performance within the economic section of modern American society. The complexity of economics in modern society is overwhelming. Yet all of us must master at least some aspects of economic institutions in order to function as full-fledged members of our society.

A significant part of acquiring competencies in our society entails learning how to be an economic person. We do not mean the classical tenet of maximizing pleasure and minimizing pain but rather the details of giving a tip, buying a paper, making change, getting a raise, writing a check, and expressing appropriate values in hundreds of other ways. Very early we learn to use money, exchange it for goods and services, expect it for work, and value it. Often our children learn to count by making change, and we motivate them to do household chores with monetary incentives. Only a short time is required for the typical child to learn that money and its proper use will procure desired goods and power.

Abstract economic principles, the laws of supply and demand, theories of incomes and investments—all these are important but outside the experience of most people. A sociological approach to economics involves the lived-through world of everyday affairs, the highly organized affairs of exchange of desired goods and services. The institutions of economics rest upon procedures, learned and enacted, for deciding what is appropriate, admissible economic action. There are degrees of competencies and involvement in these economic matters, to be sure, but every member of the society is touched directly or indirectly by decisions that derive from assumptions and knowledge about what constitutes an economic matter.

The articles included in this section describe the world of microeconomics in everyday life. They show how even short-term jobs and small-time purchases reflect basic values and standard ways of doing things for this society. By focusing on the minute details of the role of the new car salesman or the encyclopedia man or bargaining over the value of a piece of junk, we can uncover exactly what values and courses of action are embodied in the institutions of economics.

30
Selling the The Culture

The decision to purchase a relatively expensive item such as a set of encyclopedias represents the aspirations and lifestyle of the buyer. A person who buys an encyclopedia set may believe that the knowledge he will acquire will open a new way of life for him or his children; he may simply wish to display the books as a symbol of his already-achieved place in the status hierarchy of the society. The salesman must be able to understand the kind of person he is dealing with. He must be able to place the potential buyer into a social category and to impute motives to the buyer in an accurate fashion. Lynn Buller describes how salesmen are trained in this task so that they can pitch their product to fit the kind of person they believe the buyer to be.

The Encyclopedia Game
Lynn M. Buller

Many people want to make a fast buck, and college students are no exception. They aspire to the high standard of living that comes to those with college degrees. Moreover, their few marketable skills and need for seasonal employment may heighten their receptivity to schemes that promise fast money. During the month of May, when college students most tenaciously seek summer jobs, the classified sections of newspapers are filled with provocative want-ads offering quick and easy money in

From *Life Styles in American Society,* ed. Saul Feldman and Gerald Thielbar (Boston: Little, Brown 1972). Reprinted by permission.

the promotional field. Encyclopedia companies advertise positions for "advertising representatives" which promise time for boating and water-skiing, travel within a five-state area, and a salary of $150 or more per week. With this kind of appeal and few available alternatives, it is not difficult to explain why each summer hordes of students across the country turn to selling encyclopedias. It was such an advertisement that resulted in my spending an entire summer participating in what turned out to be a complex manipulative racket and a fascinating subculture.

Recruitment, Indoctrination, Personnel

Upon answering by telephone a provocative advertisement much like the one described above, I was told the employment supervisor was not in but that his "assistant," to whom I was speaking, would help me. He "just happened" to have an appointment available Saturday at one o'clock, and asked if I could come in then for a personal interview. When I asked the nature of the job, he explained that it would take several hours to explain the job and that he had seven other phones to answer. I had already been conned.

On Saturday, there were twenty other people at my "personal interview," and I later discovered the office had only two telephone lines. The absent "employment supervisor" did not exist, which made it possible for any employee answering the phone to set up job interviews.

A man resembling W. C. Fields—fifty-fiveish, complete with dime-store socks and cheap initial cufflinks—whisked into the room, the inevitable cigarette dangling from his busy mouth. He told us we were permitted to leave during the presentation if we objected to any part of the program or felt we wouldn't like the job; all he asked was that we display enough courtesy to stay until one of the three breaks he would give us. First we saw a film featuring a gentleman wearing a maroon smoking jacket seated in his private library, his soft hand resting fondly upon a leather globe. The musty aura of classic education pervaded the room. We were shown scholarship winners from previous summers receiving their thousand-dollar checks, and travelogue stills of the foreign city where all the successful salesmen would vacation late that summer.

Then the salary was explained to us. We were to receive a base salary of $115 for three weeks, which would be increased to $154 the fourth week. For this amount we were required to "place" two sets of encyclopedias each week with families who promised to "value and appreciate" the books, although we were allowed two fruitless weeks without being fired. For each ten sets above our quota of two per week we were to receive a $500 bonus. Fantastic, we thought.

Following the movie and the salary talk, we were given the opportunity to leave, with Oil Can Harry standing in front of the class, daring us to scrape our folding chairs and crawl over six pairs of feet in the quivering silence. His beady eyes accused us, one by one, of disbelief.

No one left, and our mesmerizer demonstrated the material we would be offering in the "promotional combination offer," complete with commitment questions which were directed at us. He was, in fact, trying to convince us to accept the books. We agreed that the material was truly beautiful and would "place" itself. He said all we had to do was show the material to three interested couples each night and one of them would surely accept the books. It sounded like a whiz. Leading us to anticipate giving three demonstrations nightly made us think we'd be chatting with lots of interested, supportive people and knocking on comparatively few doors.

This was far from the truth. (A corporation higher up confirmed later in an interview that prospective employees are purposely led to believe that they will place more sets than it is likely they will.) He didn't tell us that there would be nights when everyone in a salesman's territory with school-age children was attending high-school graduation, or nights when the wind came up and the rain came down hard, and the field manager sat out the storm in a local bar, not deigning to rescue his rain-soaked crew a minute before the appointed hour. Or that we'd be dodging police all summer and, even more difficult, trying to keep frustration and depression, those white-eyed dogs, from constantly nipping at our heels. Although I didn't believe the job would be as easy as it sounded, I liked the idea of being an advertising representative for a large corporation and living in my own apartment for the summer, instead of going back home to fry hamburgers.

After the pitch we were called into the district manager's office in pairs and asked if we wanted the job. I didn't know whether I'd like it or not, but for $154 a week it seemed an irrelevant point. The girl in the office with me, however, insisted that she couldn't assess something until she'd tried it. I never saw her again. I remember the weasel asking me some closing question akin to "Do you take this company as your personal savior and promise to uphold it with your prayers, your presence, your gifts, and your future," and I remember the guilty twinge of my mouth as I answered yes. He looked like a congenital con-man to me, but if he was capable of asking silly questions like that, maybe he was stupider than I thought. There was a chance I could beat him at his own game. I got the job.

Later that week, at the end of the training period (unpaid), we were given a test in which we were asked the names of several corporation higherups, five reasons why we believed in the company, and whether, "given the choice," we would rather be paid the salary or a straight commission of $83 each for the first ten placements, $92 for each order thereafter, and a free set of encyclopedias as soon as we'd sold twenty sets. Though the employees could nominally choose between the pay plans, I knew of no one who was on the salary plan more than two weeks, either because he quit before that time or because he changed pay plans. The test was a means by which the field managers selected their crews. Anyone who had designated the salary plan was not cheerfully chosen by the field managers, for they had no motivational whip to use on the salary boys.

A small but irritating part of our salaries went to pay for the savings banks we gave to our "placement families" in which to daily save their dimes. Another small portion went into a bail fund to aid salesmen run afoul of local Green River ordinances (prohibiting unlicensed solicitors). The field managers (staff sergeants for one to five advertising representatives) were given no car expense, although they did get a substantial override (kickback) on any orders written out of their cars. In fact, everyone up the management line of the sales division received a percentage of the profit. No employees were salaried; consequently, everyone in management rode the salesmen ("advertising representatives") for orders—and rode them all the time. The salesmen paid for their own motel and food expenses while traveling and for demonstration materials and had no money deducted for taxes or Social Security.

After I'd worked with the company some time, I realized that almost anyone was hired. It was also practically impossible to be fired (mainly because for tax purposes we were considered individual contractors). One man, I heard, was welcomed back "like a long-lost brother" after serving five years in the pen for grand larceny. One girl was said to be an ex-call girl; at any rate, she was a cocktail waitress on weekends. Two seminary students were also hired, plus an honors graduate with a fellowship in psychology at a top university.

Salesmen

According to my observations, the typical experienced bookman has been married twice, has three children, and is occupationally unskilled, although his intelligence is well into the second standard deviation. As a youth, he had high aspirations which were deflected by circumstance or frustration; he aspires to professional status. Most often he grew up on a farm; converted to city-dwelling, he regards small-town residents as cornball and sometimes feels revengeful toward farmers. His style is flamboyant and unsophisticated; his sexual attitudes are adolescent.

Even though nearly all the men in my office had frequent extra-, post-, or premarital sexual relations, they talked about their conquests in the same way ninth-graders are said to brag in the locker room. Any virgin was "open game," and other salesmen heard about every aspect of the hunt. Some salesmen always had a girl friend. One female seemed to fulfill their need about as well as another, and they followed a sequential pattern of courtship-monogamy. Other men tried to manipulate several salesgirls at once. One in particular was such a lady-killer that he talked the psychology graduate out of her fellowship so she could follow him to sell books and live with him in Sioux Falls, South Dakota. Meanwhile, he courted the cocktail waitress and, later, spontaneously married her. Several months later his wife departed with his car and color television. Lately, I hear, he's been dodging authorities regarding a charge of statutory rape. This man is twenty-three years old; he was the president of his high school graduating class and has experienced two unsuccessful marriages. He is an extreme case. Another extreme case is a man who carried his pajamas, a clock-radio, and a fifth of whiskey in his briefcase to be prepared for any available sexual conquest.

Not all the men were disloyal to their wives—several were very happily married. But when one considers that all were away from their families at least twelve hours a day, from noon to midnight, and that most of their wives worked from eight to five, it's easily understandable that their marriages were characteristically less than ideal.

Of course, the female employees were hardly prudish. Several of them had strange habits too. One girl hitchhiked home seven miles through a woods each night after work. She'd been "raped" twice since Christmas. Strangely enough, although she claimed to hate men because of their disloyal and lustful natures, she seduced any available male. After she climbed into bed with me one morning, however, we decided she was most likely a lesbian.

It was not unusual for a crew of males and females to share one motel room, either. This probably was quite a wholesome arrangement, considering the potential audience. But it was hardly the thing to write home to mother.

The book business attracts men of similar lifestyle. Most of the salesmen with my company drove big, bright-colored cars with factory air-conditioning: Pontiac convertibles, Chryslers, Buicks. One salesman drove a Jaguar and sold realty on the side. Their clothes were frequently flashy but never cheap. They treated themselves to three-dollar lunches and good clothes because the money came in easily, if they worked. (Not working was referred to as "leaking off.") The fact that they were paid commissions instead of a salary encouraged free spending. Purchases were priced in order-units: a salesman considered that his rent was two orders a month, food another one, a new coat was one order, and a pinky ring cost a half.

Alan Lippett[1] writes that diamond pinky rings signified success among the salesmen with whom he worked. In my company, no one wore pinky rings. My cohorts apparently aspired to conspicuous consumption of higher class indication than did the other company's salesmen. This statement is supported by my observations within Alan's former company, where I noticed that salesmen drove late-model Fords and Chevrolets and Ramblers with home-installed stereo systems, although they, too, frequented the best restaurants and bars. I think they were less likely to know they were selling books, although my company did a pretty good job of keeping the truth from us. Maybe they were just dumber.

In my company, sales representatives and field managers (called "F.M."s) were very chummy. We called each other by first names from the start. We knew each other's past and present states of mind and affairs, as well as the number of orders each had written for the week. The other company's representatives seemed reluctant to divulge the circumstances of their private lives to each other, and offered no references to their business success or unsuccess. There was apparently less sexual fraternization than in my company, too. Of course, I observed them during the winter when there were fewer opportunities for the kind of hanky-panky which went on within my company while we were traveling in the summer.

Motel owners were not always enthusiastic about letting rooms to encyclopedia salesmen, because of their reputation for sneaking off without paying. I never knew salesmen who did this. I did know of a young crew who had a water fight in their cabin one night and sopped the furnishings so thoroughly they couldn't sleep there. They left the motel, after paying, by telling the proprietor that one fellow's father had got his leg caught in a cornpicker and they had to rush to another city to see him. That the informing telephone call would have had to come across the motel switchboard, if the family even knew where their son was staying, must never have occurred to the innkeeper.

One salesman's many subpoenas on charges of damage to motels and hotels became a joke among the salesmen. Whenever this salesman

[1] Alan Lippett, "There's One Born Every Minute," *Seattle Magazine* 5 (June 1968): 25–30.

came off a road trip, his friends would go over to his house to have a few beers, see the subpoenas he'd accumulated, and hear the story behind each one. This particular salesman was a legend in his own time. One night, the story goes, he and a buddy bought a watermelon. Because they didn't have a knife in their hotel room, the big brute smashed the melon down upon the sink to break it open. He also broke the lavatory off the wall and was accordingly sued for several thousand dollars after twelve inches of water filled the whole motel. On a bet, this same fellow cut a square of deer meat from an animal they'd struck with a car and ate it raw, impaled on his jack knife, and chased it down with straight whiskey. He was also known to drink whiskey for breakfast—tumblersful.

Revelations

It took me almost six weeks to figure out that I wasn't really an advertising representative for the company; I was a book peddler. The "Promotional Combination Offer" was a gimmick clean through. Although people allegedly got the books for writing the company a letter of endorsement and paying only for the services which kept the set up-to-date, they actually paid for everything they received. Their letters of endorsement were used only, if ever, to parlay new promotional participants.

It was claimed by the management that the product was far superior to any other encyclopedia. This encyclopedia had "just been completely rewritten and, indeed, was not on regular sale yet." It was new in the sense that a new edition is printed each year, and it was actually true that the set had been completely rewritten, even though the new version had been on regular sale since 1962. The "new-edition" ploy was helpful in several ways. Whenever a prospective buyer voiced a complaint against this brand of encyclopedia, the salesman could answer assuringly, "That was our *old* set." The completely revised edition was also the basis of the promotional pitch. Placement families were supposedly pretesting this new publication which was "not yet on the general market," and writing letters of endorsement to be used to persuade their neighbors to buy the encyclopedias when they were finally released "for general consumption." Actually, the promotional families are the most general market to which the product is released. Families can obtain the books only through direct sales methods. The sales pitches are informally synthesized by innovative salesmen and lower management personnel. Yet somehow, these bubble-gum and bobby-pin methods sell $450 million worth of books each year.[2]

It was claimed that we were giving the people something they really needed, even if they were sometimes too stupid to realize their need. After all, it was not like we were peddling cyanide pellets disguised as diet pills. If purchasers used the books, they were sure to become better people. Representatives might even have looked upon themselves as missionaries bringing enlightenment to the backwoods. Pouring on the book pitch like cod-liver oil, confident that it was all "for their own good," employees could gloat in good conscience all the way to the bank.

Through talking with many people, especially those in small towns, we came to see ourselves as serving another positive social function—that of relieving people's boredom. Several times, I'm sure, people bought books from me because they were hopelessly bored, and I'd come from afar to entertain them for an hour. They were simply grateful.

The salespeople's true purpose was supposedly withheld from new employees; however, the varying levels of operational awareness within the district's personnel made it nearly impossible to keep the pose intact. Because my field manager confirmed that I wasn't giving books away, I was in a good position to watch other employees' reactions to what they thought they were doing for the company.

It is my theory that three classes of people were hired: "fishes," "sneakers," and "con-men." The fishes actually believe they are advertising representatives, and they stay with the company not only for the money, but because they believe in education and in the product. (These people become very defensive of their jobs to outsiders and bristle at the mention of any other encyclopedia.) The sneakers figure the sales pitch isn't all on the up-and-up, but for the money they aren't going to bother with details. If they realized the extent of their deception, the sneakers probably would be forced by their disquieted consciences to quit. They need the rah-rah of product emotionalism to keep their minds from wandering where it might not be economically advisable. The con-men will do anything for the money offered. Even though the con-men don't always know precisely how they are misleading the public, they are fully aware that the public is being misled. Consequently, the fishes and the sneakers are protected from the truth by the con-men, who build up fine rationalizations to keep everyone enthusiastic and productive. Strangely enough, management is not composed primarily of con-men. It is easier for these people, too, to believe they are doing something worthwhile for mankind than to try to live with a conscience of conflict; some have become almost fishlike themselves.

Promotion in the encyclopedia game is quick and not difficult. If

[2]Eric Geller, "Selling Encyclopedias," *New Republic* (August 24, 1968): 10.

a representative has sold ten orders, holds the business attitudes of either the sneaker or the con-man, and owns a car, he'll soon become a field manager. When he's more senior than most employees (which may mean he's been with the company one year) and has won a sales contest or two, he's likely to be offered an office of his own within the district. This offer is largely a doggie bone tossed out to make eager young men come into the office two hours earlier, without salary, to train recruits, or to run from office to office within the district to help train recruits. The most strenuous aspect of the trainer's job is keeping curious neophytes from discovering what they'll really be doing. By and by someone who heads one of the offices will quit or go to another district or be proselytized by another company and the trainer will get an office of his own. Whoopee. He can now be at work by 9:30 every morning (which means at least a twelve-hour day) to interview, hire, train, and pick his own crews, a task which leaves him too tired to go out and write personal orders in the evening. Any money he earns will be in the form of commissions, overrides on the orders written by his crew, or trainer's fees on recruits he's trained, so it is imperative that his crew be in the field every evening, primed to write orders, and that he himself be knocking on numerous doors, lest he go broke on car, lunch, and bar expenses.

District managers, regional managers, and regional vice-presidents are all paid healthy percentages of the volume of business in their jurisdiction. It must be said that they work hard, goading their inferiors to better performance through sales contests, summer vacation contests, and short-term prize agreements. But their wages are almost ridiculously ample. Regional and district managers are paid in five figures; vice presidents get six, plus lots of time to parlay their earnings. Ironically, education is in no way the primary consideration for promotions within the encyclopedia business. Enthusiasm, endurance, and the ability to hold one's own are the main prerequisites of a management job. One regional vice-president was a dentist. He had no business training whatsoever—no knowledge of marketing, business law, or management. He is probably in the position he now holds because he is one of the few people in the business with a college degree, although he wouldn't have been considered for the job if he hadn't been phenomenally successful as a sales representative.

Mooches

In American society there exist people classified by encyclopedia salesmen as "mooches." Mooches can be generally defined as people who like to buy the product; they see the encyclopedia salesman as the bearer of a rare and desirable gift. Mooches are people whose incomes and occupational levels exceed their educational attainments; persons whose income is in the middle-middle range but whose education doesn't exceed high school, or may not even attain that level. Without education, mooches cannot have professional status, although they might make as much money as a professional; consequently, mooches try to assume professionalism by accruing what they think are indications of professional status. A conspicuously displayed set of encyclopedias tells the mooch's friends that he can afford to consume conspicuously, that he values a highly normative product over creature comforts, and that he provides for the long-range benefit of his protectorate. The mooch associates all these characteristics with professional persons. For him, then, encyclopedias function as easily interpreted professional-status indicators.

Mooches are vulnerable in two ways to a book pitch—because books themselves are status symbols, and because books are considered the tools of professionalism (if not for the parents, then for their children). Being uneducated, mooches cannot differentiate between being wise and being knowledgeable. Even if they memorized all twenty-four full-color volumes, they wouldn't have an Oxford education. But such is the dream mooches are made of.

It doesn't take a new salesman long to spot a mooch, because he's constantly schooled by his seniors to look for specific criteria and readily develops the intuitive knack of mooch-hunting. Mooches show status incongruity in all their material possessions, and are more easily described than defined. Tools in a station wagon typify the moochiness of an artisan, who brings home good money but has no professional status because he works with his hands. Brick houses are not moochy, as opposed to clapboard houses with paint peeling from the siding, because brick houses are too substantial. Someone who buys a small, well-built brick house will not easily be sold on the quick idealistic emotionalism of an encyclopedia pitch; he's too careful an investor.

A mooch is someone who: drives a red Mustang and lives in a small yellow frame house with hurricane fencing around it; leaves rained-on kids' books in the front yard; has all the neighborhood kids' trikes in his driveway plus a portable barbecue; buys a huge turquoise contemporary couch and burns a cigarette hole in it; lives in a maroon house in the midst of white houses; furnishes the living room with lots of big, gaudy ashtrays which match the drapes; buys a series of science books for his children but sits on a slip-covered couch; lives in a $15,000 stucco house in the midst of new $40,000 houses; has a swing set; drives a Cougar, Camaro, or other hot, flashy American car (foreign car owners are usually not moochy, being more economical and probably better educated); works as a mechanic and whose wife drives a bus for Head Start; has too much furniture in his living room, especially if it's formica-topped and includes a color TV set and console stereo; hangs plaster birds on his wall or has plastic flowers in the living room; has a shrine in his bedroom (these people will believe anything); or has a new rocking chair or a piano with sheet music standing on it. While novices are expected to knock on every door, experienced salesmen simply drive around "smelling out" mooches.

Selling Techniques

After three days of training and observing experienced salesmen for two evenings, we novices were dropped into the "field" to finagle on our own. Propagandized and at least half-believing, we were ready to sell encyclopedias for profit, for the good of mankind, or for both. We didn't knock on every door, though we were supposed to. The general age and status of people in a neighborhood proved to be the key to potential sales, and we sought this information in order to economize our effort. Spotting a house inhabited by an older couple we'd knock on the door, greet the woman, appearing as friendly and innocuous as possible, and ask, "Say, is it the green house or the pink house next door that has the children in it?" and ramble on bewilderedly. We usually found out not only about the pink house, but about children's ages and husbands' employments all up and down the block. Another information-gathering tactic was to ask for a glass of water, or use of the bathroom. (It is surprising how many people will admit a stranger to their bathrooms; a family that will let you use their bathroom will tell you nearly anything you want to know.) By these means, we could meet potential customers with some preparation, and we learned which families in the neighborhood needed our services.

Many opening lines were used for getting inside the door. The tactic recommended by my company was composed of a friendly hello, an announcement of one's name as though it were well-known and ought to be recognized, and a request for the spouse of the salesperson's gender by saying, "Stopped out to see your wife (husband)." (Since many of the salesmen were pimple-faced eighteen-year-olds, their briefcases dropped conspicuously beside the front stoop, this tactic wasn't always successful.) The salesman explains that he's doing some work in the area and asks if he may step in and ask the people a couple of questions.

Although it is forbidden for him to describe his work by using the words "survey," "market research," "advertising work," "promotional work," "school district," or any phrase which might indicate that the salesman is involved in one of the above types of work, it is intended for people to believe just that.

Once the salesman announces himself to the spouse of similar gender, he maneuvers the couple together and begins to deliver the spiel called "the Qualifier." This five-minute explanation of the promotional program is the most important tool of the trade. During the Qualifier, the salesman either wins or loses the people's interest and confidence, while taxing their emotions and reasoning to the point of submission. He can also assess the couple's interests, means of income, and special vulnerabilities and utilize these assessments during the material demonstration. Most of the assessment is accomplished nonverbally by observing the family's material acquisitions, looking especially for signs of moochiness. Whenever possible, he engages them in seemingly idle chatter.

After the Qualifier, the salesman brings his bottomless bag of educational goodies into the house and asks the couple to sit side by side facing him across the kitchen table or coffee table, where they can see his materials simultaneously. Saleswomen demonstrate the materials on a high table or on the living room floor from a kneeling position, in order to keep all eyes on the printed matter.

First, the size and binding of the set are displayed by means of a "stretcher," which is simply a foldable, two-dimensional replica of the book-backs with spacing between each volume, which makes the stretcher a third longer than the actual set of encyclopedias. The salesperson stresses that the lettering is stamped in "twenty-four-carat gold," sure mooch-bait. Then the couple is shown the Prospectus, a sample volume which contains nearly all the color pictures in the whole set, and generally highlights the encyclopedia. The "Pros" (rhymes with "loss") is broken down into sections which appeal to different age groups, including preschoolers, although the encyclopedia is written on at least junior-high reading level. Testimonials are numerous and flashy. The Pros of another company includes a full-page color picture of Pope Paul VI autographing their encyclopedia. Such audacity could only be tolerated by a true-blue mooch! Sports, hobbies, and practical skills are stressed, besides the academic appeal of this "particularly excellent recording of the sum knowledge of mankind."

During the demonstration of the Prospectus, the innovative salesman utilizes the earlier observations. If before entering the house he noticed a motorboat in the garage, he will show the couple a few boating pictures as he flips through the Pros; if they have an obvious interest in fine dogs, or their child has won a prize at a local science fair, he will pitch his demonstration to that particular interest. People often believe the salesman mentions their particular interest because it is part of his regular preplacement demonstration. This makes them feel their hobby is considered especially worthy of stress by the company, and transferring the impression, they feel important themselves. Of course, the salesman means for the couple to perceive his craftiness in this way. Hopefully it will make them feel so important that they readily believe their letter of endorsement will be an asset to the company and consequently agree to "participate in the program." In other words, buy the books.

After signing the duplicate contract, in which the merchandise is described as a "combination offer" and the promotional program and required letter of endorsement are not mentioned, the couple has bought all twenty-four color volumes of the encyclopedia, ten supplemental yearbooks, one hundred reference service coupons (all of which they most certainly will not use), a dictionary, a bookcase, and ten volumes of children's books, all at regular retail price. Their one-page, handwritten letter of endorsement received within ninety days of delivery will probably never be used. But the salesman's technique was effective, because he kept "talking the letter" and making the people feel they were truly privileged to be one of a few chosen families in the area. The usual parting line was, "Well, John and Mary, it's been fun getting to know you, and I'm very glad to be able to accept you as one of our advertising families here in the area. I'd like to feel free, if I'm in the vicinity again sometime, to stop in for a cup of coffee with you. May I do that?" Of course, the couple assure the salesman that he is always welcome, and the salesman is assured by their submission to his self-invitation that they won't suspiciously cancel the order.

Individual Sales Tactics

Several guises are successful aids to book peddling. Some representatives use a hard-sell approach, misquoting any source which occurs to them to convince the victim-family that their children will be grammar school dropouts if their parents haven't the foresight or love to provide their children with this complete home reference library. One often-used line goes like this: "You know, John and Mary, we all love our children"—this said by eighteen-year-old, single college students—"but there are so few things we can give them. One is our good name, and the other is a good education. If I died tomorrow and could leave my child $100,000, he could spend it and be poor within six months. But if I give him my good name and a better-than-average education, no one can take from him the potential to earn five times the money I could have left him." From there on, if the parents refuse to take the books, the salesman makes them feel they've cheated their child out of half a million bucks. This kind of salesman often has difficulty giving a pitch when an observer (potential salesman) accompanies him because, even though observers are strictly told not to say a word during the pitch, some novices burst out laughing when the diabolical haze becomes thick. The con-man types spontaneously make up religious affiliations, relatives, and common acquaintances to try to win the family's confidence. They are quite successful if they can find enough people to intimidate, so they seek out mooches, potential fascists, and people without enough courage to shove them out the door.

Sometimes the salesmen appear downright threatening. There is no doubt in my mind that encyclopedia contracts have been signed just to get the salesman out of the house and, hopefully, out of town. One bookman of my acquaintance is particularly successful in Montana and North Dakota, where he drives right out into a farmer's field, urges him off his tractor, slaps him on the back, and offers the fellow a beer from the cooler in his trunk, then drives the man back to the farmhouse to talk with the wife about their views of education. This salesman looks like the original Hells' Angel, is usually half-soused, and doesn't brush his teeth for days. When he flails his timberlike arms in the air and yells, "Ah, you're stupid! Your wife's stupid! Ya want the kids ta be stupid? Sign the fucking card," they sign. For some odd reason his orders are verified the next morning, too.

Another approach, often used by students, is the innocent-little-girl approach. This type of saleswoman appears at the door looking like a runaway teenager needing directions or a glass of water and is invited into nearly every home whose door she knocks upon. Once inside, she gives the Qualifier in an explanatory yet wide-eyed way, and if accosted with suspicion, jokes, "You know it can't be a trick—I couldn't sell anything if I tried." She never polishes her pitch but follows a routinized pattern, knocking on every door, looking sweet, showing the material, and collecting a reasonable check at the end of the week.

Wives often regret admitting college coeds into their living rooms to kneel on the floor in front of their husbands. For this reason it is expedient for female employees to wear wedding bands and explain that their husbands are in the business also, or serving in the armed services. Husbands are not usually hard to fool; wives, unthreatened by a young woman they think to be married, are reminded of their own early marriages and are usually quite friendly, asking particulars which give them an excuse to relate their own wedding stories. Sometimes male and female representatives sell books together, posing as man and wife. Frequently this arrangement represents an actual mobile living arrangement and works quite well if both salespeople are good actors and the age gap is not extreme.

An approach which is consistently successful when pitching married college students is the authoritative approach. This stance seems quite professional; it is very low-key, shows almost no enthusiasm for the product and, by so doing, assumes that the students are already aware of its great intrinsic value. College students are considerably more enthusiastic than most older couples about subscribing to the reference service, which purports to write term papers. This factor contributes to a low-key approach. One salesman pitches to no one but married college students and had developed the search for these couples into a technique which the FBI would be well-advised to emulate. He can spot an outside second-story staircase from a half-block away and distinguish at the same distance if it's being rented to college students or pensioners. The authoritative approach complements the advertising representative pose advised by the company. Within the pitch it is emphasized that the representative has been asked to place the set only with families he or she deems worthy—reverse psychology at its money-making best.

Some salesmen stress the personal relationship between themselves and their customers while addressing the couple as they do all customers. This is the promiscuously personal approach. Foreign students have been particularly successful utilizing this technique. They appear friendly, casual, and informative, and people almost invariably invite them in to chat, if not to look at books. One foreign summer representative spent Thanksgiving at the home of a family to whom he'd sold a set of books, and hadn't previously known. They loved him! Several representatives worked on Sundays and holidays, and would walk right into the midst of a family's Fourth of July picnic to sell them the educational deal of a lifetime while patriotism, the Good Life, and the American Way were still primary in their minds.

The representative's manner of dress doesn't seem to affect his selling success, except that his dress should reinforce whatever poses he presents. One company's top salesman often went into the field dressed in shorts and a paint-spattered sweatshirt. He appeared at people's doors looking like the man next door wanting to borrow some paint to finish painting his boat and often sold five sets of books over a weekend.

Although encyclopedias are almost always books of fine quality and an asset to any family receiving them, the shame of most encyclopedia companies is that they do not grant their customers the conscious privilege of buying books when, in fact, they are. They also do not allow their employees the knowledge that they are selling books when, in fact, they are. As long as the industry provides its customers with professional status indicators and its employees with good wages and something to believe in, this colorful subculture will probably thrive among us, remindful evidence that the race goes not to the diligent, but to the crafty. And when it comes to crafty persuasion, encyclopedia salesmen could give the patent medicine hawkers of the Old West a sure run for the money.

31
Sociology for Selling

Every economic transaction has a social base. In addition to the motivations for earning money and accumulating materials, many economic deals involve the self-concepts of all the parties to the transaction. Certain sales, then, are not merely a matter of having the right amount of money and finding the desired goods at the desired price; some sales are complex and well-ordered processes where the outcome is partially effected by the social skills of the participants. In this article Stephen J. Miller describes the social bases for the sale of the new car. He identifies stages in the sales process: the contact, the pitch, and the close. Each stage has its mode of presentation for both the salesman and the potential buyer. There are special kinds of information, strategies, and ways of protecting one's self-concept at each stage. Miller shows the meaning of this transaction from the perspective of the salesman and the buyer, illustrating the social negotiations necessary to make a sale. He convincingly makes the point that the salesman operates under conditions similar to those of workers in the service occupations.

The Social Base of Sales Behavior

Stephen J. Miller

The automobile salesman, contrary to popular opinion, is no longer an economic entrepreneur operating without restraint and engaged solely in the pursuit of personal profit.[1] In the past the automobile sales agency was somewhat of a provisional undertaking in which the salesman-customer relationship was a random, transitory and, in many cases, unrenewable encounter. Today, the increased complexity of the social organization of sales practices has resulted in the development of the manufacturer-authorized agency which depends upon mutually satisfactory relationships with its customers and encourages at least a modicum of continuity of clientele. Consequently, the salesman has evolved from the "wheeler and dealer" of the early postwar period to the agency employee who operates in a more restrained social situation. In addition, increased automobile production and a competitive market have modified the position of the customer, increasing his ability to direct or attempt to direct the conditions and outcome of the sales transaction. The salesman of today, in general, sells under conditions which are similar to those which influence the behavior of members of the service occupations—that is, he is subject to institutional prescription and comes into direct and personal contact with his customer.

The behavior of the salesman in the contemporary sales agency may be analyzed in a number of ways. The economic character of sales endeavors could be compared and contrasted to the service character of other occupations (for example, the physician) which enjoy a more reputable position in the hierarchy of work. However, such an analysis would exaggerate the obvious, though not always legitimate, distinction between service and business behavior—the altruistic motives of the former and the self-interest or profit motives of the latter.[2] A more comprehensive and meaningful approach, allowing for sociological as well as economic bases of sales behavior, would focus on the generality and constancy of sales behavior as affected by the normative patterns of the sales agency. In other

---

From *Social Problems* 12 (1964): 15-24. Reprinted by permission.

[1] A revision of "The New-Car Salesman and the Sales Transaction," a paper read at the annual meeting of the Midwest Sociological Society, 1963. The research on which the paper is based was supported, in part, by Community Studies, Inc., Kansas City, Missouri. The writer is indebted to Robert W. Habenstein for his comments and criticism and to Howard S. Becker and Blanche Geer for their critical reading and suggested modification of the original paper.

[2] For a discussion of such an analytical scheme and its shortcomings, see Talcott Parsons, "The Professions and Social Structure," in *Essays in Sociological Theory* (Glencoe, Ill.: Free Press, 1954), pp. 34–49.

words, the behavior of the salesman would be seen as influenced not only by the profit to be gained but also by his efforts to advance his self-interests by adherence to the prescribed patterns of behavior which have become institutionalized in the agency.[3] The analysis of sales behavior as the result of institutionalized patterns, though legitimate, would be somewhat limited in that it would not adequately take into account the influence of the direct and personal contact which occurs between salesman and customer.

The object of this paper is to analyze sales behavior by focusing on the interaction which occurs between the new-car salesman and customer during the sales transaction: the "contact," marking the beginning; the "pitch," the middle; and the "close," signifying the end of the social encounter. The sales transaction, as interaction, will be treated as a series of events in which each phase arises logically out of and is influenced by the preceding phase. The underlying concern is with the effect of the course of the interaction on sales behavior rather than the influence of the inherent homeostatic tendencies of the agency. The discussion is based on information and materials gathered during a twelve-month period of observation and limited involvement in the social world of salesmen and operations of sales agencies. Most of the data were collected away from agencies, but frequent visits permitted observation of and actual involvement in more than a dozen completed sales transactions and numerous salesman-customer contacts.[4]

The Contact

The initial social contact between the salesman and the customer occurs in one of two ways: (1) a random contact—the customer is interested in

[3]Talcott Parsons, "The Motivation of Economic Activities," *Canadian Journal of Economic and Political Science* 6 (1940): 187–200. The analysis of sales behavior in terms of the thesis of Parsons' essay would be based primarily on the assumption that the salesman behaves the way he does because a pattern of sales behavior has become institutionalized in the sales agency.

[4]Initial information regarding the salesman and agency operations came from contacts and interviews with the sales manager and a number of salesmen employed by one of the major, high-volume, manufacturer-authorized agencies located in Kansas City, Missouri. It was difficult to arrange lengthy visits to other agencies or to engage salesmen in prolonged conversations while on the agency floor. Therefore, interviews were arranged with salesmen who were contacted informally in restaurants, bars and grills, etc., located on the metropolitan "automobile strip." Informal contact and conversation was the most practical method of gathering information and data. In addition, the writer acted as "bird dog" and "leg man" for a number of salesmen at various agencies. The writer, with few exceptions, was accepted as a person interested in automobiles and, though employed, considering a change in work, possibly employment as an automobile salesman.

or has decided to buy a new automobile and presents himself to a salesman on the floor of the agency; (2) a solicited contact—the customer has been recruited by the salesman or referred to him. In the former case, the customer is either a "suspect" (a person who may need or want a new car but cannot afford or is not interested in making an actual purchase) or a "prospect" (a person who has decided to buy but has not decided on which automobile or where to make the purchase). The recruited customer is more often than not a "buyer" (a person who has decided which automobile to purchase and wishes to enter negotiations).

The unrecruited customer, the "drop in," constitutes a "cold call," a customer contact for which the salesman is not completely prepared, and the determining of a proper sales approach is difficult. The majority of "drop ins" are nothing more than "suspects," offering the salesman little anticipation of a potential sale; this partially explains why salesmen prefer to invest as little time as possible in negotiations with unrecruited customers. The "drop in" may also have "shopped the car," gathering information which would "put him one up on the salesman going into the deal," thereby putting the advantage on the side of the customer and reducing the salesman's control of the situation.[5] If personal profit and agency prescription were the primary motivations for sales behavior, the salesman could be expected to enter negotiations with customers regardless of the circumstances of the contact. A logical rationale would be that the more contacts with customers he has, the greater his opportunity for making a sale, gaining a profit, and meeting the expectations of the agency. However, salesmen are reluctant to enter negotiations if there is little anticipation of making a sale in a manner which affords them the greatest control of the negotiations and the outcome of the transaction.[6]

If a "drop in" proves promising, that is, accepts the role of "buyer," the salesman commits himself to the sales transaction. Though the agency expects a consistent degree of commitment, the salesman invests the majority of his time and effort in sales transactions which are the result of

---

[5]Howard S. Becker, in "The Professional Dance Musician and His Audience." *American Journal of Sociology* 57 (September 1951): 136–44, has hypothesized that a desire on the part of the practitioner to control the interaction of the contact is chronic to service relationships. See, also, Eliot Freidson, *Patients' Views of Medical Practice,* (New York: Russell Sage Foundation, 1961), in which the dilemma of the doctor-patient relationship is presented in terms of potential conflict for control between the doctor and patient.

[6]These same factors explain what, at times, may appear to be a complete lack of interest on the part of the salesman in making a sale. The writer has observed salesmen who, with amazing accuracy, "size up" a customer as one who is either attempting to verify the wisdom of a contemplated or completed purchase at another agency, or plans on "keeping the salesman honest" by employing information gathered at another agency. The salesman refuses to engage in conversation with such a customer unless it is to "foul him up" by supplying him with inaccurate or fabricated information. The accuracy of the salesmen's judgments were verified by subsequent conversations with customers so rebuked.

initiated contacts with recruited customers. The "good" salesman is one who not only can make his "pitch" and "close the deal" but can recruit customers as well. As one sales manager expressed it: "The good salesman does anything to get a customer onto the floor."[7] The recruitment of customers is vital to the occupational role of the salesman since it relates directly to his status as a salesman and increases his control of the transaction.

The means by which the salesman recruits his customers includes the usual direct mailings, telephone solicitations, and "would you takes" (throwaways which are placed on parked automobiles implying a favorable deal if the customer would take a certain amount, usually exaggerated, in trade for his present automobile). However, the most rewarding method of recruitment consists primarily in establishing a system of informants, "bird dogs," located at strategic places in the community (gas stations, repair garages, etc.) who introduce or refer "prospects" to the salesman. Such an informant is paid for his services, but the ideal "bird dog" is the satisfied customer who requires no remuneration.

The advantage of the "bird-dog" system is that it assures that the majority of contacts will be with customers who are at least "prospects," thus increasing the chance of becoming involved in a transaction which will result in a sale. The "bird-dog" referral system also facilitates the work of the salesman during the transaction by placing the seller-buyer relationship on a more personal basis and providing the salesman with information which will allow him to control negotiations. In addition, the "bird dog" has increased the chances of a sale by influencing the customer in favor of purchase. By doing some of the selling himself, the "bird dog" has increased the salesman's advantage.

The Pitch

If the customer accepts the role of "buyer," increasing the salesman's anticipation of a favorable outcome, the salesman commits himself to the role of "seller" by "making his pitch." The individual approach of each salesman to his customer has certain unique characteristics, but sales behavior, once both parties accept their respective roles, is literally a performance, the dialogue and action of which reflects a generic character. The importance of the drama of the situation is well known to the salesman,

[7] A reason expressed by a salesman: "Play on your home court"—a basketball expression, implying that the home team has the advantage.

as the following remarks indicate: "What sells a car? To sell a car it all boils down to this: if I can put a better show on than you had where you been, I stand a chance of selling you a car."

The customer is not simply a spectator but plays an important part in determining the nature of the dialogue and the direction of the action: "You can't sell unless you get the customer to tell you about himself . . . you got to listen and get to know the customer before you can make your pitch." The salesman attempts to develop an understanding of the attitudes and feelings of the particular customer—an understanding from which he can evolve hypotheses about customer reaction to the sales "pitch" and which allows him to modify his sales behavior to increase his control of the situation and the chances of a favorable outcome. The attitudes of the customer constitute a stimulus, the understanding of which and adjustment to necessitates role taking. The anticipation and prediction of response to the role being played is a determinant of the course of sales behavior and the nature of the social activity.[8] Role taking is facilitated by the interpretation of symbols and cues presented to the salesman during two essential stages of the sales transaction: (1) the trade-in evaluation, which the salesman attempts to accomplish as early in the transaction as possible ("Let's see what you're driving"), even though the final appraisal of its value is usually done by someone other than the salesman; (2) the demonstration ride; "I ask him how he likes the way it handles, how about the power and a lot of other things . . . by the time we finish the ride, I have a good idea of what he wants in a car."

The automobile presently owned by the customer allows the salesman to "size up the prospect," in terms of generalized customer categories and set the stage for further action; for example, the car which is outfitted with dual exhaust pipes places the customer in the category of "kid" or "rod," while personal items in the car or trunk indicate the interests of the customer ("If he's got a fishing pole in his car, you know he's interested in fishing and you got something to talk about"). The salesman employs the demonstration ride to establish a situation in which the customer will communicate to the salesman what he values in an automobile and why, information which can be used to stress the merits of the automobile being considered and influence a decision.

The salesman, knowing that the customer is organizing his buying behavior to assure a favorable purchase, realizes that if he is to continue anticipating customer response correctly he must know with some degree of accuracy what the customer is thinking at all phases of the transaction.

[8] For its theoretical orientation, the analysis of sales behavior draws heavily on the work of George H. Mead: for example, *Mind, Self, and Society* (Chicago: The University of Chicago Press, 1934).

A number of methods are employed to facilitate accurate role ascription, including eavesdropping on the conversation between the customer and any person or persons who may have accompanied him to the agency, but the major means is inducing the customer to talk as much as possible: "By listening and getting you to talk, he [the salesman] is going to find out what you're thinking about . . . unless he does, he's not going to sell you . . . he's got to know what you'll take." A salesman who is a poor listener (for example, one who has a rapid-fire delivery of the merits of the automobile he is attempting to sell) is considered one who "talks himself out of a sale."

In addition to offering him information upon which to base his "pitch," "making the customer talk" allows the salesman to counter efforts by the customer to control the situation or set the terms of the deal: "You never let the customer tell you what you are going to do." The salesman desires to keep control, in fact, achieve mastery of his relationship with the customer. The operations of the salesman, similar to those of practitioners in all service relationships, are designed to control the interaction to his advantage.[9] The general sales opinion is that the customer is free to refuse the product and terms he is offered, but "when he tells you what he wants, all you have to do is find it." The customer is never given the opportunity to withdraw from involvement in the sales transaction since, by constantly being offered alternatives, he is not forced to make a decision to accept or reject the final terms; his anticipation of a favorable outcome is never diminished. On the other hand, the salesman is free to control his investment and involvement in the transaction in terms of his anticipation of future negotiations and their outcome.

The Close

The salesman brings the customer to the point where he makes the decision to purchase by associating himself with the customer and with the customer's position by taking the customer role and anticipating the reactions to his own sales "pitch." The "close" of the sale, the acceptance of commitment to the terms of the deal by the customer, is accomplished by the salesman communicating to the customer that he has not only negotiated a mutually acceptable outcome to the transaction but that he has gotten the best of the deal: "Before they buy they got to think they beat you and now you're on their side."

[9]Becker, *"The Professional Dance Musician."*

"Changing sides" is a characteristic of the "close." When a possible deal in mutually acceptable terms has been achieved, the salesman implies that the transaction, if completed, will be greatly in favor of the customer ("You're really beating me to death"). The salesman now suggests he will have to and well might act on the customer's behalf to convince the sales manager to accept the deal on the customer's terms ("I know the sales manager is going to jump all over me when I go in there but we've come to an agreement . . . let me go in there and work on him and see if I can get that car at your price"). Here is what actually happens, as described by one sales manager: "He [the salesman] comes to me and says, 'Here you are' . . . I OK the deal . . . he ain't going to come to me with a bad one . . . he waits, sits down, smokes a cigarette, then goes back to the customer." In fact, the salesman may well come to the sales manager "with a bad one," at least not the best possible deal for the agency.[10] The salesman considers his negotiations with the customer more or less sacrosanct and wishes the agency only to make clear the limits of his operation; for example, "We need at least ———" or "Don't sell for less than ———." He considers the manner in which he has written the contract and the terms of it his concern and resists any interference as long as he has not blatantly violated the economic limits set by the agency. The salesman, on his return to the customer, says he encountered difficulty in having the deal accepted ("You sure got me in a lot of trouble") but that he managed to convince the sales manager ("I got him to accept your deal"). By further implication, the salesman manages to communicate to the buyer that he is a unique and shrewd negotiator ("I'm glad I don't get many like you"). There are a number of variations in method, but "closing the sale" depends upon the customer feeling his negotiations have resulted in the outcome he anticipated.

Cooling The Buyer

The sales transaction has been, for the salesman, a process of "selling the prospect" on the automobile by stressing not only its merits but also the advantages of a continuing relationship, in terms of service, with the

---

[10] The agency attempts, in many cases, to control the salesman by paying him a percentage of the difference between the automobile being purchased and the one being traded in rather than a salary or straight commission. The obvious reason is that this increases the chances of the most favorable deal for the agency being written. however, salesmen admit that they have, at times, allowed more than they had to on a trade-in because they "liked the customer" or to "make the sale."

agency. It is only those transactions which are blatantly exploitative or in which the prospect has been obviously victimized that require he be cooled; that is, that the entire transaction be presented to him in such a way that he may accept its outcome without a feeling of personal failure or loss which would end the relationship. The majority of sales transactions that result in purchase require a less intense and continuing process of "cooling" through periodically communicating the wisdom of the purchase to the buyer as long as and in order that he maintain a relationship with the agency. The buyer may feel that there are no appreciable differences between the automobile he has purchased and the others he might have purchased, but he does wish to regard this particular transaction as evidence of his wisdom and judgment. In much the same way as the "mark" in the confidence game, by entering the sales transaction, he has committed himself to a concept of self as a shrewd buyer, a sharp bargainer, a wheeler and dealer, or at least not "an easy mark."[11]

The salesman, having exploited the self-concept of the buyer, realizes that it must be preserved and the buyer must be made to feel that the transaction is satisfactory; that is, the customer must continue to feel he has gotten the best of the deal and perceive himself as shrewd and sharp. Because the value of the buyer as a future prospect ("kept" or steady customer) and "bird dog" depends upon his satisfaction with the transaction, it is to the salesman's advantage to see that the customer's self-conception remains intact, that he continues to be cooled. The salesman states these reasons for the process of "cooling," though not in these terms, and rarely concerns himself with the image of the agency or its possible embarrassment. "What do I care what they [customers] think about them [agency]," said one salesman, "I sold the car and have to get the guy off my back but keep him happy."

Upon completion of the transaction, the salesman realizes that he cannot continue to "cool" the buyer; he must become disengaged from his involvement with the buyer for a number of reasons. Continued involvement requires that he expend his time in behavior which is not appropriate to his role as salesman and, therefore, costly to him in income and status. The more time he must spend "cooling" buyers, the less time he has for the selection and cultivation of "prospects," and involvement in other sales transactions. Involvement with the buyer after the sale may also involve the salesman in the blame for future disappointments which may be encountered with the agency later. By proper disengagement, the salesman is able to keep the good faith of the buyer and maintain his value as a future "prospect," "kept" customer, and/or "bird dog." In his role

[11]Erving Goffman, "On Cooling the Mark Out: Some Aspects of Adaptation to Failure," *Psychiatry* 15 (November 1952): 451–63.

within the agency, by ending his involvement with the buyer, the salesman is free to act as "cooler" to the buyer-as-owner and make an effort to console him if he encounters any difficulty with the agency or finance company after the purchase. Though salesmen resist such a role, they will comply if they feel it will not subvert their relationship with the customer or if any future relationship has become impossible.

The salesman knowing for his own reasons that the customer must be "cooled" but that he cannot continue the "cooling," arranges for a formal and complimentary transition from buyer to owner. The buyer is ushered to the service department where he is literally promoted from the role of buyer to that of owner and presented with the purchased automobile. The salesman foists the customer on the agency, and the service manager now enters into the relationship with the owner. His role is to see that the owner remains reasonably satisfied with the sales transaction (his role as buyer) by handling any complaints which may arise and by reassuring the owner of the wisdom of the purchase. The "cooling" of the buyer becomes a continuing feature of the service manager's role.

The buyer may resist what amounts to a depersonalization of his relationship with the salesman and resent any attempt to shift responsibility for the outcome of the sales transaction from the salesman to the service manager. Realizing the value of a personalistic approach to the buyer, the salesman attempts to create an atmosphere of comradeship, facilitated by a shift in the nature of the relationship from what was basically antagonistic—the objectives of both parties involved in the transaction were originally opposed—to one which is by implication cooperative. Salesman and buyer, at the salesman's suggestion, now enter into what appears to be a conspiracy against the agency and service manager.

Where the automobile has been oversold or the deal misrepresented by the salesman, the buyer may seek out the salesman and demand satisfaction. The salesman as a last resort then calls in the sales manager, who acts as the final "cooler." The principal technique he employs is to offer the buyer his money back, to rescind the sales transaction. Since the acceptance of the offer would suggest that the buyer himself had negotiated a bad deal, subverting his self-conceptions, it is not surprising that even the most outrageously dissatisfied buyer rarely accepts the offer.

Work, Self, and Customer

A majority of automobile salesmen admit that their customers regard them as "con-men," who attempt to "put one over" on the buyer. In informal conversations regarding what makes a "good salesman," salesmen describe their role in much the same way; for example, "Anybody can sell something they [the customers] want, but the real bit is to make them think they need exactly what you got to sell, only more of it." The consensus appears to be that the "good" salesman is highly proficient at manipulating the situation and customer in such fashion as to produce a favorable deal for the salesman. The object of the sales transaction, as an experienced older salesman who was tutoring the writer in the techniques of "making out" expressed it, is to "make them think they are getting something instead of losing anything."

It would be an oversimplification to treat automobile salesmen as if they all operate with the same perspective, but their behavior appears organized around the premise that monetary and social success are the results of opportunistic dealing. Though such an attitude toward the work appears harsh and lacking in moral scruples, the salesman protects himself from feelings of guilt and resolves the problems presented by the exploitative aspects of his role by attributing to his customers the same characteristics which mark his own behavior. He sees them as opportunistic, "out to make or save a buck any way they can." The salesman's perception of the customer is clearly revealed in the following remarks directed to newly employed salesmen by a sales manager. "He [the customer] wants to get the most car for the least money and your job is to get the most money for your car.... If he gets what he wants, you lose." By selectively perceiving and, if necessary, by misinterpreting the behavior of the customer to fit his own pattern of expectations, the salesman is able to rationalize the exploitative and manipulative aspects of his role, making his work acceptable to himself and tolerable to others.

Salesmen insist that the approach to the customer is the most important factor in selling: "The pitch is the whole bit," but when the customer does not buy, thereby effecting unfavorably on the way the salesman "made his pitch," the salesman blames the customer ("He only wanted to come in out of the rain") or the automobile ("You can't move [sell] that dog") but rarely his own "pitch." The salesman has, by entering into negotiations with the customer, made a substantial investment in the sales transaction; an unsuccessful outcome is not only a loss of time but a threat to his self-conception and status as a salesman. In developing an appropriate "pitch," he is testing and revising, in terms of customer response as measured by successful sales transactions, a behavior pattern. The salesman is usually always "on," that is, playing a role.[12] The "pitch" is

---

[12]Sheldon L. Messinger, in his discussion of dramaturgical analysis, explains "to be on" as operating with a self and social perspective that requires a dramatic performance; the world is a theater in which the actor stages his show. Cf. "Life as a Theater: Some Notes on the Dramaturgic Approach to Social Reality," *Sociometry* 25 (March 1962): 98–110.

the salesman's characteristic interpersonal style, his personal formula for adjusting and adapting to the demands of interacting with the customer.

The successful outcome of a sales transaction not only results in a monetary gain for the salesman but, by indicating to him that he found the formula which enables him to "win friends and influence people," adds to his personal feeling of worth and position as a salesman. He has demonstrated that he is highly proficient in manipulating situations and customers to produce an effect which is generally and occupationally desirable. His work satisfaction and occupational prestige are dependent upon successful interaction with the customer. Selling the automobile reflects favorably upon the way the salesman has performed his role and, in turn, adds to his status with his colleagues as a "good" salesman.

Conclusion

One type of economic behavior, sales behavior, has been explored by focusing on the relationship which occurs between the automobile salesman and his customer. The sales transaction, as well as sales tactics and the behavioral implications of the salesman's conception of himself, his work, and his customer, is influenced by the sociological circumstances of the sales encounter, as much by the dynamics of the salesman-customer relationship as by agency prescription and the immediate profit for the salesman.

The automobile sales agency expects the salesman to engage in negotiations with customers which will result in at least the minimum profit acceptable to the agency. The salesman, looking at the sales situation from the agency perspective, negotiates sales which are in keeping with the economic conditions and limits imposed by the agency. However, the perspective of the salesman, like the perspectives of members of other occupations who come into direct contact with a customer, client, or patient, includes strong opinions regarding the way the sales transaction should be conducted. If the customer, wishing to make the most advantageous purchase possible, attempts to direct the circumstances, conditions, and outcome of the sales transaction, a conflict results. The salesman either counters such attempts by employing the appropriate tactics or, in some manner, terminates his involvement with the customer. The conflict and the importance of control are substantiated by the attitudes and opinions of salesmen. The "good" salesman, as conceptualized by salesmen, is one who not only sells but is also adept at manipulating the circumstances of the negotiation so as to assure his control of the sales transaction.

The salesman engaged in the sales transaction is, of course, calculating the potential economic return to himself and the agency. However, in addition to economic gain, the salesman is vulnerable to loss in such noneconomic areas as status, work satisfaction, and a personally acceptable and socially supportable concept of self. He protects himself from actual loss in noneconomic areas by at times refusing immediate or ultimate profit and by resisting agency prescription—for example, not entering into negotiations with a customer who may have information which would be to his advantage during negotiations. The salesman would prefer the loss of a profit, both for himself and the agency, to involvement in a situation which is controlled by the customer. The implications of the data are not that profit and agency prescription have no influence on the operations and actions of the salesman. Rather, the data suggest that, in addition to institutionalized patterns of economic behavior, there exist other socially based supports for sales behavior making that behavior more social and less economic than it is usually considered to be. The social circumstances and conflicts of the salesman-customer relationship, similar to those found in the practitioner-client relationships of service occupations, constitute such a social base for sales behavior.

32

Core Values in Everyday Economics

The myths and ethics of a society often are reflected in the way the people exchange, interpret, and value goods. Hopes, dreams, and heroic themes may be embedded within a single economic transaction. Myths about the marketplace are composed of idealized accounts of actual events, and these myths function to generate a range of behaviors from fast pricing and buying to extended bantering about the value of the particular item. Within the exchanges, however short or protracted, there is always the hope of some valuable find or some unanticipated and beneficial outcome. Robert Maisel examined the flea market as an action scene in which interaction provides participants with a sense of risk and fateful enterprises. Such interaction breaks up drudgery and ordinary character of social life and gives us a stage for observing the enactment of many basic economic values and idealizations of our society.

The Flea Market as an Action Scene

Robert Maisel

Many social critics and sociologists have pointed to the decline of the work ethic in modern industrial society. Both pride in work and the ambition to get ahead by one's own efforts have been adversely affected by the tendencies of large enterprises to monopolize business opportunity, to rationalize production, distribution, and consumption processes, and to discourage craftsmanship in favor of assembly-line techniques.

From *Urban Life and Culture* 2 (1974):488–505. Reprinted by permission. *AUTHOR'S NOTE:* An earlier version of this paper was presented at the Society for the Study of Social Problems meetings, August 24–27, 1973 in New York City.

In the face of these seemingly inexorable forces, which reduce the sphere of initiative and freedom for traditionally skilled or even professional work, the desire for sojourning (Rosengren 1971), for adventure and for "action" (Goffman 1967) seems to be growing rapidly. Sociological studies of leisure have begun to explore the extent to which nonwork activities replace occupation as a source of personal self-expression and fulfillment in industrial society (Burch 1965, de Grazia 1964, Anderson 1961).

In the face of this interest, it is curious to note that the *marketplace* is neglected by the scholarly literature as a popular place for getting into the action. From Adam Smith to Horatio Alger, business enterprise has been lauded as the sphere of rugged individualism and unlimited freedom and opportunity for the "little man." Further, in the marketplace the distinction between work and play is blurred. The businessman, like the burglar, professional gambler, or athlete, works in an atmosphere of risk and consequence usually associated with playful behavior. Thus, one would expect to find students of work and leisure examining the popular and often novel forms of entrepreneurial activity increasingly prevalent in our society.

The flea market is a major site for what anthropologist Sol Tax has called "penny capitalism." Once the exclusive feature of rural hamlets, these markets (variously called penny markets, swap meets, merchandise marts, or fairs) have proliferated on the urban landscape, selling not just produce or cheap used goods, as formerly, but a wide variety of new and used goods—and not all of it cheap. The popularity of these markets cannot easily be gauged by gross dollar volume or vendor profits, for one of the attractions to buyers and sellers alike is the market anonymity and absence of third-party interference. Indeed, the term "thieves' market" may be an apt one, since stolen goods are often disposed of here. One may deduce from the growing popularity of the weekend flea market—as well as from a similar proliferation of specialized, periodically held markets—a flourishing minicapitalism growing in the interstices of our dominant economic institutions.[1]

To study the flea market is to zero in on but one institution which reflects a revival of entrepreneurial impulses at work in our society. We can observe this trend likewise in the ubiquitous garage sale, in collecting "for fun and profit," in the revival of crafts, and at least in college

[1] *The Flea-Market Voice and Collector's Guide* (April–May, 1973) vol. 2, no. 4, provides this listing of flea markets for the San Francisco Bay Area: fifteen weekly flea markets, twenty-six special shows for the month of May alone; (included in this group are ten flea markets, four antique shows, three shows dealing with gems and minerals, three dealing with stamps and coins, two bottle shows, and one market each for guns, toys, American-Indian wares and a Post-Office auction). For the same month, thirty-two craft fairs were scheduled for the northern California area.

communities such as Berkeley, the appearance of hip, young entrepreneurs in great numbers—both as street vendors and as store owners.

Little material comparable to the ethnographic studies of folk and peasant markets has been gathered for our own "folk" markets, as far as I have been able to determine.[2] This study is thus, of necessity, a preliminary account of one such market. I have deliberately chosen to emphasize materials pertinent to the *action* of the market, for these data best indicates what the flea market is all about.

Methodology

The material on flea-market sellers was gathered by interviewing a sample of seventy-eight sellers at the Alameda Penny Market in Alameda, California, in the fall of 1972. These interviews were conducted by members of a course, "The Theory and Practice of Folk Economics," taught jointly by Professor Sherri Cavan and myself.[3] The sample was drawn by arbitrarily assigning rows to each interviewer who then questioned every third person in his or her rows until ten interviews were completed. In the event of a rejection, the interviewer proceeded to question the next vendor. Systematic observations on buying and selling practices at that flea market were carried out during the same time period. In addition, the author has drawn upon his experience, of at least five years of buying and selling at flea markets throughout northern California, as background material for this account. Also, a variety of published materials, including flea-market newspapers as well as newspaper and magazine articles were utilized in gaining some sense of the range, scope, and structure of flea markets.

---

[2] A search of the popular-magazine literature revealed some interest in, but little material on, flea markets. Anthropologists, on the other hand, have produced a rich ethnographic literature on folk and peasant markets, some of which contains elements also found in flea markets. For a general treatment of this literature, see Belshaw (1965). Useful collections of articles may be found in Dalton (1967) and Shanin (1971). The general sociological features of exchange are discussed by Mauss (1954), Sahlins (1965), and Smelser (1959).

[3] I would like to thank Professor Cavan and the members of the class for the work they put into this project and the many helpful comments and suggestions they made during the course of the seminar concerning flea market behavior.

Structural Features

The Alameda Penny Market is a thriving flea market in the San Francisco Bay Area and one of the three largest in Northern California. On a nonrainy weekend, seven thousand to nine thousand customers pay a twenty-cent admission fee to peruse the wares of over four hundred vendors. Located on the site of a drive-in movie theater in the city of Alameda, the Penny Market is readily accessible to the Bay Area population by car, being no more than a one-half hour's drive from San Francisco, Oakland, Berkeley, and a number of other smaller cities. The ubiquitous automobile allows the flea market to draw its customers from an urban area of some two million in population.

The Penny Market is open Saturday and Sunday throughout the year, weather permitting—as it usually does in northern California. Traditionally, Saturday is the less popular day at the market, while Sunday finds every stall or booth reserved in advance and the crowds appropriately large. Due to its growing popularity, the Penny Market management has rationalized its operation and rents booths on both a monthly and a weekly reserve basis, at a cost of $2.50 on Saturdays and $3.50 on Sundays. In spite of some inconveniences to the sellers, this system is successful. At least for Sundays, every booth is "spoken for" in advance, with the exception of a few marginal locations which are filled on a first-come basis on the day of the sale.

The range of goods sold at the Alameda Penny Market is wide. Most fall under the heading of "used goods," or if considered collectible, given the more exalted titles of "antiques" and "memorabilia." Generally, anything small enough to be hauled in by truck, station wagon, or car (and hopefully hauled out by someone else) may be found for sale at one booth or another. In addition to secondhand merchandise, one ordinarily finds craft goods, unprocessed farm produce, and some new goods (music tapes, clothing, decorative wares, imports, and so forth) being sold in various stalls. Occasionally, a snake-oil salesman can be found making his pitch for a magical cleanser or cheap, genuine Swiss watches, but this type of country fair operation is rare.

Sellers generally arrive before 7:00 A.M. to set up their displays before the market is open to the general public. Each seller is responsible for his stall (which is nothing but a bare space in the parking lot), for its appearance, cleanliness, and to a great extent, its policing. The round of buying and selling begins at 7:00 A.M. or even earlier and has died down by 4:00 P.M. or so, at which time most sellers begin to pack up their wares and clean their stalls. By 5:00 P.M. the market is as bare as it was twelve hours earlier. With a minimum of fuss and overall organization, tens of thousands of items have been unloaded, some sold, and the rest repacked for some future destination.

In this bare outline, we find depicted a routine repeated by flea marketers all over the United States. The Alameda Penny Market differs from others in northern California only in its reputation for a better class of used goods and a larger and more sophisticated buying audience, with a goodly mix of counterculture, gay, and ethnic populations. In order to flesh out this bare bones picture of the market day, we need to take a closer look at the operation of vending and what it entails.

In our interviews with vendors, over 50 percent of the respondents reported that they had been selling regularly at flea markets for at least one year. Thus, the market can count on a goodly supply of what I will call professional vendors to provide a steady flow of goods for its buying public. Only a few vendors admitted to being totally new to the flea market. The rest sold occasionally, thus forming a pool or reserve of potential vendors from which the weekly stalls are filled.

Who sells at flea markets? Given the modest or even lowly repute of flea markets, one might expect that most vendors would be drawn from the poor and from those with marginal or dead-end jobs. The information gained from the interviews did not bear this out. Only 22 percent of the vendors mentioned working in blue-collar type jobs, while 30 percent engaged in white-collar and professional work. Suggestive of the wide base for recruitment into flea market vending is the presence of retired people (13 percent), students (3 percent), housewives (4 percent), as well as persons (22 percent) who claimed that the flea market was their sole means of support (though income may also have existed from other sources such as welfare or unemployment benefits). The occupational range disclosed by our survey was surprising, even if one grants the episodic or marginal role played by flea-market vending to ongoing career patterns.

Almost three-quarters of the vendors lived within thirty-minutes driving time from the flea market, thus giving the market a local coloration. (By contrast, once-a-year markets draw vendors from several states, as well as from all over California.) More than half of the vendors report living in nuclear families and often are accompanied to the market by one or another family member.

The impression one gains through interviews and observation is that the vendors represent a fair cross-section of people in the lower- and middling-middle classes who live in the Bay Area. The seeming overrepresentation of counterculture youth (13 percent of the vendors were so identified by their appearance) is not unexpected in this locality.

What attracts sellers to flea markets? The profit motive certainly is central for most people. However, other factors such as access to merchandise, propinquity to the flea market and enjoyment of the entrepreneurial role are frequently voiced by our respondents. Typical of such comments is the following:

> I am retired and make some extra money this way. The flea market is close to my home, gets me out in the sun and gives me a chance to meet some nice people. A relaxing life. . . . [a sixty-year-old man]

Another attraction is voiced by a young, hip jewelry salesman: "It's a good place to meet the chicks. Relaxed, you know." In a more economic vein, many vendors gain access to salable goods through their weekly jobs as haulers and garbage collectors, laundry workers, wholesale outlet workers, and decorators. The flea market provides for them an easy form of supplemental income.

The easy atmosphere (or "good vibes") which many vendors find attractive is due to the lack of "hassle" they encounter. Stall prices are modest, the schedule is convenient for working people, and there is a minimum of bureaucracy or paperwork to be bothered with or threatened by. Vendors are rarely chastised for doing their thing, whether it be nursing babies, smoking grass, setting up miniencampments, drinking beer, or appearing in various sorts of casual dress (and undress). Perhaps flea marketers feel unconscious pride in being participants in a social activity where blacks and "red necks," hippies and squares, homosexuals and straights visibly rub shoulders as they share the common foci and concerns of the market.

FLEA-MARKET ACTION

At the heart of the workings of the Alameda Penny Market is a sense of what Goffman (drawing from hip argot) has called "the action."[4] More than anything else, "action" draws people to the flea market and causes them to return regularly. In one form or another, action occurs in situations where persons pit themselves against one another in the context of exchange, each striving for a satisfactory outcome.

Although much of the following discussion deals with action as experienced by vendors, the same considerations apply to most buyers as well. In fact, the distinction between buyer and seller is somewhat arbitrary since most flea marketers buy from one another, and many buyers either have shops or themselves sell at flea markets from time to time.

---

[4] "By the term *action* I mean activities that are consequential, problematic, and undertaken for what is felt to be their own sake" (Goffman, 1967: 185).

It is therefore more useful when dealing with the topic of "being in the action" to distinguish between those who are knowledgeable about the markets for used goods, whether buyers or sellers, and the naive or inexperienced. Most vendors tend to fall into the first category.

Anticipation of this action builds up prior to market day by vendors searching for salable goods. Vendors report traveling in a wide circuit to find wares—going to garage sales, following up newspaper ads, visiting junkyards and secondhand stores, soliciting the aid of friends, contracting with wholesalers and even picking up items from the local dumps. This widespread sifting through sources for used goods outside the market in preparation for resale supports the vendor's anticipation of profit and thus entails commitment to serious participation in market action. Here, in the words of one vendor (a railway worker by trade) is a description of his weekly search for merchandise:

> After getting off from work at 2:00 P.M. I follow up ads in the local paper or on bulletin boards. I concentrate on jewelry, Sterling silver (which always has a certain value by weight) and used furniture, if I can get it cheap. On Saturday I start early on a round of garage sales. You have to get to the good ones earlier than they say in the ads or you'll miss out on all the good buys. By Sunday I usually have picked up a few good things to add to my stock, and bring them to the flea market, if I don't sell them to stores first.

The first act of market play is that of *pricing* one's wares, of making one's opening bid in the open market. Pricing is both a crucial decision and a difficult one. If one's prices are too high, nothing gets moved; if too low, then substantial profits will be lost. For this reason, much of the conversation at the flea market revolves around market knowledge of objects and their going prices. Veteran flea marketers constantly search for information on this crucial question.

> "How do I price? Well, I ask around, check the market and do research on some of the older things."
>
> "I usually ask about double what I paid for something, which is still below the store prices."
>
> "I try to charge a fair price, but if the item doesn't sell or if I am told the price is too high by a few people, I will lower it."

While the veterans tend to recognize the need for price flexibility and market knowledge, newcomers often vacillate wildly between choosing rigid formulae (for example, "twice what I paid for it") and panicky selling (for example, the first offer, however absurd). Inexperienced buyers, for similar reasons, fear being "tempted" by the flea market or being taken for suckers and may even avert their eyes from the stalls while sauntering around. Price indeterminacy or variability, which the newcomer often finds in conflict with his retail buying habits, is usually considered by the veteran flea marketer to be a challenge to his knowledge, an opportunity for his wit, and a stimulus to his energy. As one habitué of the market puts it, "You pit your wit against the market. It's wide open."

How are values decided and prices determined in the flea market? Most merchandise is seen to fall into one of two categories: an item is either of utility or of "cultural" significance. Objects judged in terms of their practical value—for example, tapes, tools, clothes, most furniture and household items—are often priced with regard to their replacement cost on the retail market, qualified by factors such as age, fashionability, and/or condition. One man sells new dresses at one-half their retail cost. Another prices tools at about 25 percent of retail. If demand is felt to be poor for certain merchandise such as used clothing or toys, vendors will charge anything they can get. Staple, usable wares (kitchen appliances, tools, small machinery) tend to develop a stable, predictable price structure and become specialties of certain vendors. For those in the market for such goods, careful and even expert scrutiny is required of the items "as represented," to make sure that they are "worth the price."

For objects judged to be of cultural significance, the question as to proper value is more difficult to answer. Antiques, collectibles, memorabilia, or "funk" cannot be evaluated in terms of their use value or compared with their new counterparts but must be assessed in terms of highly specialized market knowledge. Further, the swiftly moving currents of fashionable interest in nostalgia reshapes these markets in an almost dizzying way.[5] This area, where some are in the know and others in the dark concerning value, provides the largest opportunity for windfalls or bonanzas at the flea market—for the dramatic act of the "find" or "steal."

Much market attention is directed toward the search for the good buy or the memorable find. One vendor describes his pattern of search thus:

> Before unpacking, I walk around the market looking for a good buy.
> I head for the back stalls where the "one-shotters" tend to locate.
> I try to get to a stall first and poke around.

---

[5] A sense of the strong demand for certain mass produced items of the recent past can be gathered from the pages of *Curios and Collectibles: A Price Guide to the New Antiques*, Ralph de Vincenzo (ed.). A few examples will suffice: Mickey Mouse Electric Casting set, 1936, original price $1.25, now $25; Mickey Mouse deluxe wristwatch, 1936 (Ingersoll), original price $3.95, now $200; Ace Comic Books, number 4, original price $.10, now $20; Batman Comics, number 2, was $.10, now $50; pocket knife made by Case Brothers, Springfield, N.Y., was $1.25, now $150; Weeden Steam Engine, alcohol heat, 1936, was $.85, now $50. The point is, of course, that neither the original purchase price nor one's aesthetic sensibilities are a guide to the "value" of this trivia.

Another reports:

> I ask for a few prices to see if the seller knows what he's doing. If he's an amateur, I try to see what I can get.

Some try to hide the fact of professional expertise:

> If I'm looking for art pottery such as Rookwood or Weller I might say, "Do you have any vases or bowls or anything like that?" I don't want to tip someone off.

Others prefer to make this expertise known:

> I tell them I'm a dealer and what I can pay for the item. It's all very cut and dried and I don't waste any time.

Some potential buyers move fast to cover the market quickly while others prefer to poke patiently through boxes and accumulations. Some engage in bargaining, others move on. Most prefer the opportunities of the early morning buying, but some will try to take advantage of weakening sales resistance as the day draws on. Whatever the strategies, the possibility of making a coup spurs ambition as buyers move from booth to booth.

The most common form of action at the flea market is not the coup or the quick sale but the attempt to make a deal by means of persuasive techniques. One major form of persuasion is expressed in the covert language of facial and bodily gesture. Vendors scan the behavior of those who pass by their stalls for signs of interest in their wares: for momentary pauses in movement, for the studious gaze, the physical inspection of objects and their prices (if posted), for hesitations in moving on. The more aggressive vendor intrudes at the least sign of curiosity and begins to peddle his wares. The more modest, or perhaps more subtle, ones allow the customer to initiate interaction.

This "conversation of gestures" (à la Mead 1934) continues throughout the more overt, articulate phases of bargaining. Verbal statements are modified by means such as shoulder shrugs, facial grimaces, and body stances. Thus, each party has signs available for reading the other's intentions, without these intentions being expressed openly.

This gestural reading is less prevalent in bargaining proper, where overt commitment to discussing price is involved.[6] In bargaining, both parties attempt to seek agreement on a deal by influencing the other's evaluation of an object. In agreeing to this encounter, disagreement over

---

[6] In other words, talk becomes consequential. Goffman remarks, "when a person volunteers a statement or message, however trivial or commonplace, he commits himself and those he addresses and in a sense places everyone present in jeopardy" (Goffman, 1967: 37).

price becomes a contest of will and judgment, a form of structured conflict.

Vendors express mixed feeling about bargaining, although they agree that the public likes to bargain and seeks to do so at every opportunity. This expectation forces vendors to decide on how they will respond to the bargaining overture, with its potentially threatening overtones.

In primitive and folk markets, we often find widespread agreement on rules of etiquette which dictate propriety in bargaining. This agreement reduces personal threat and, hopefully, expedites business. So, for example, it is reported of a Middle Eastern bazaar that

> while praising the seller for his reliability, the buyer, in his turn, insists on being treated as a client. And to reinforce his insistence, he makes reference to the seller's friends and relatives as having recommended his shop. Meanwhile, he tries to establish the final price and the quality of the commodity without offending the seller, for offending the seller terminates bargaining without concluding the sale [Khuri 1968, p. 701].

At the Alameda Penny Market we find no generally shared agreement on bargaining behavior. Some vendors claim never to bargain, either out of policy or for personal reasons. More commonly, vendors will adopt a selective attitude towards dickering with others, avoiding or turning away from persons they find disagreeable, and dealing mainly with people they like or find like-minded. Vendors also like to be flattered and appreciated. One counterculture entrepreneur maintained that he will act out of generosity for the right people. "If they seem to need the stuff I'll give them a lower price or even give the stuff away." Although this attitude is extreme, many vendors admit to giving better deals to persons who approach them in a nice way.

Some vendors perceive threat in the implied social equality of bargaining interaction and thus often experience bargaining as a form of social or personal degradation. Stereotypes abound concerning the social types one should avoid or treat harshly, among them rich ladies, Chinese, Chicanos, gypsies, Jews, and old people. Personal threat is also expressed in the dislike for dealers, cheapskates, and hustlers—"people who want to get something for nothing." These stereotypes reflect, in part, genuine cultural differences in willingness to bargain as well as in unease with prolonged contact with unsympathetic antagonists.

When bargaining is taken in the spirit of play, it becomes fun. Veteran vendors tend to develop the verbal ability, mental agility, and personal cool so useful for holding one's own in bargaining banter. For them, bargaining is part of the action, stimulating sales which otherwise are unlikely. Even if a sale is not made, the boredom of sitting and watching is avoided for the time being. One has been in the action. Here is an instance of banter between two experienced dealers:

> Buyer: How much do you want for that beat-up old commode?
> Vendor: That's a nice one. It's oak, you know, underneath that coat of paint. Easy to fix up. It's only twenty-five dollars.
> Buyer: (grimacing and moving slightly away) Not in that condition! Seven coats of paint and who knows what's underneath. Tell you what. I'll take a chance at ten dollars and take it off your hands. (Takes out some bills.)
> Vendor: Trying to steal it from me? (Scorn on face, but doesn't move away.) You know that it's worth fifty. But it's a slow day so I'll give you a bargain. Take it for twenty.
> Buyer: Make it fifteen dollars and it's a deal. That's all I can spend.
> Vendor: It's yours.

Both parties conclude with the feeling that their points have been made, their wits tested and a good deal made.

At the Alameda Penny Market bargaining tends to be structured as a rather private interaction. This is in line with the marked disinclination for sellers to hawk their wares. In both instances, action tends to be confined to the stall and its immediate area and not to overflow into larger portions of the market. Compare this reticence with the publicity often given such acts at markets elsewhere:

> Haggling is an exercise which attracts bystanders as well as the principal bargainers—the seller and the buyer. Some of these bystanders may be potential or rival customers; others may simply be interested in getting price information . . . and some may be just spectators whiling away time [Uchendu 1967, p. 39].

On the question of inspection of goods:

> A customer's right to "show" her wares to others, to "consult" with friends and relatives on the reasonableness of her offer, is part of the injunction "buyer beware" [Uchendu 1967, p. 41].

If the customer is in a fighting mood, she may appeal to bystanders to witness how unreasonable the seller is in her demands. The seller may, in turn, call upon bystanders "to witness the insult she has been subject to" (Uchendu 1967, p. 40).

Both the inhibitions on bargaining at the flea market and its narrow social focus may be due to the lack of clear rules regarding the proprieties of interaction. Without proper guidelines to deference and demeanor, it is perhaps inevitable that public demonstrations of bargaining prowess tend to be avoided in favor of private negotiations. The great cultural diversity found among flea-market participants would certainly favor inhibitions of this sort since, without a common cultural framework, trust cannot be presupposed and tacitly relied upon in sensitive interactions. Therefore, it is plausible to suggest that even though the flea-market milieu tends to invite negotiations over price, other factors, especially of a sociocultural nature, tend to discourage such encounters.

Myths and the Market

The types of market action described above create participatory zeal. What sustains and strengthens this zeal is what I shall call the mythology of the market: anecdotes concerning market action. These myths or paradigmatic stories are not merely rationalizations of behavior, nor simply empirical generalizations about what actually happens, but function essentially as meaning-creating and meaning-sustaining acts. In participating in the circulation and elaboration of these myths, flea marketers seek to endow their experiences with greater significance.[7]

Myths commonly relate to the following themes: the "rags to riches" or Horatio Alger myth; the instant success of the "killing;" the Edenic vision of sociability; the "character contest."

The Horatio Alger myth, undoubtedly derived from the entrepreneurial dreams of those bogged down in dead-end jobs, expresses the belief that the flea market is a stepping-stone to economic advancement. Hard work, individual initiative, and luck are the ingredients for entrepreneurial success. This "success story" occurs in several variations at the flea market. Some vendors desire to upgrade their stock (for example, from junk to antiques) and thus attract a better, more lucrative trade. Some dream of opening a store with capital derived from their flea-market profits. Still others hope to make contact with a large supply of highly salable goods that can be turned over for enormous profit.

Stories of windfalls or killings are a staple of flea-market gossip. One hears accounts of treasure troves, secret stocks, or markets where bargains abound. Participants share their experiences of finds, with the exaggerations or embellishments of true storytellers. Typical of such stories is the following:

> A whole houseful of Victorian furniture! I tried not to show my feelings, but asked how much she wanted for the old stuff. She asked

[7]For the following discussion of the function of myth I am indebted to Geertz's analysis of the meaning of the Balinese cockfight. See Geertz (1972).

if $500 was too much! You can bet I got that stuff loaded and gone before someone wised her up. I got a warehouse filled with the stuff now—may open up a shop, or sell it at the right price to dealers.

Of course, no one knows when a windfall will next occur to *him*. That it *does* occur is taken as proof that it *can* occur, and therefore, in the logic of myth, that it *will* occur. Thus is the search glorified and motivated.[8]

The sociability myth derives from the wish to see the flea market as an especially desirable place to spend one's time. Vendors chat about how "nice" most customers are and how they enjoy talking to them. Another vernacular describes the market as having "good vibes," where everyone is "doing his thing" and having a good time. Economic exchange is seen as incidental to social pleasantry. Buying is "finding nice things;" selling is "performing a service" or "sharing with others one's own pleasures." The hip may play at being free souls, even to the extent of giving away "freebees" if the impulse occurs. The question "What can you afford?" replaces the more abrasive "What will you offer?" More conventional types adopt a genteel manner and appear to conduct their business as incidental to the maintenance of a "gracious" manner. The sociability myth influences the conviction that one is having a good time or, more specifically, a good day and thus helps to gloss over the ordinary details of tedium, toil, and poor sales.

Finally, we have "character" tales (Goffman 1967, p. 214 ff.) where individuals recount their reaction to pressure or temptation. Occasionally, one hears stories of benevolence, where profits are sacrificed to some larger value or impulse. Such is one story told by a dealer who was offered (by a friend) an innocuous piece of silver for five dollars. He paid this sum, then handed over fifty dollars more saying that the piece was eighteenth century and worth over two hundred.

More commonly, stories of character deal with "facing down" a particularly pugnacious or obnoxious person, of showing him his "place." Outwitting such a person is highly prized and may take the form either of a verbal thrashing or the achievement of financial gain. The following story is representative of both points:

> I had just bought a pair of vases at a house sale. At the flea market a guy came by and wanted to buy them, but not at my price. I wanted sixty dollars, and he offered first fifty and finally, after a half an hour's haggling, fifty-five. Even though I had paid a lot for the vases I still wouldn't sell, probably because he had acted too pushy. Wouldn't you believe it if a dealer didn't walk up while the guy was still there and pay my price! That was one enjoyable sale.

[8]This function of myth seems common to gambles and therefore related to the psychology of gambling. See Goffman's more general discussion of "adaptations" to risk (1967: 174–181).

Stories of such personal exploit, however exaggerated, suggest that flea market encounters may be cast in a heroic mold as a trial of character, and even as an expression of one's power and freedom.

Summary and Conclusions

Market myths are not pure fabrications, for they are composed of events, however idealized, that are familiar to flea-market habitués. These myths express most pointedly what people think the flea market is all about, what one seeks to accomplish, and how it is expected to happen. The drama of the market involves its participants in a series of trials and contests, of purchases and sales, where the outcome is measured objectively by the yardsticks of profit and loss.

The flea market generates action. People play the entrepreneurial game for all it is worth, share in the excitement of trying to outguess the market and outwit one's neighbor. Though flea-market vendors are reluctant to specify their usual profits, it is clear that anticipation of a "good day"—that is, high profits—is the main source of their ambition and labor. Whether one is playing for small or large stakes, the same intensity of effort exists. For the market functions fundamentally in the same manner as the high risk, fateful enterprises described by Goffman—it provides participants with a sense of risk, uncertainty, consequential chance—and thus produces vivid experiences usually absent in ordinary social life.

References

Anderson, N. 1961. *Work and Leisure.* London: Routledge and Kegan Paul.
Belshaw, C. 1965. *Traditional Exchange and Modern Markets.* Englewood Cliffs, N.J.: Prentice-Hall.
Burch, W. 1965. "The Play Worlds of Camping." *American Journal of Sociology* 70 (March): 604–12.
Dalton, G., ed. 1967. *Tribal and Peasant Economies.* Garden City, N.Y.: Natural History Press.
De Grazia, S. 1964. *Of Time, Work and Leisure.* Garden City, N.Y.: Doubleday Anchor.

De Vincenzo, R., ed. 1971. *Curios and Collectibles: A Price Guide to the New Antiques.* New York: Dafran House.

Geertz, C. 1972. "Notes on a Balinese Cockfight." *Daedalus* 101 (Winter); 1–38.

Goffman, E. 1967. *Interaction Ritual.* Garden City, N.Y.: Doubleday Anchor.

Khuri, F. I. 1958 "Etiquette of Bargaining in the Middle East." *American Anthropologist* 70 (August): 698–706.

Mauss, M. 1954. *The Gift.* London: Cohen and West.

Mead, G. H. 1934. *Mind, Self and Society.* Chicago: University of Chicago.

Rosengren, W. 1971. "The Rhetoric of Sojourning." *Journal of Popular Culture* 5 (Fall): 298–314.

Sahlins, M. 1965. "On the Sociology of Primitive Exchange." In *The Relevance of Models for Social Anthropology,* ed. M. Banton. London: Tavistock.

Shanin, T. 1971. *Peasants and Peasant Societies.* London: Penguin.

Smelser, N. 1959. "A Comparative View of Exchange Systems." *Economic Development and Cultural Change* 7 (January): 173–182.

Uchendu, V. 1967. "Some Principles of Haggling in Peasant Markets." *Economic Development and Cultural Change* 16 (October): 37–49.

PART TEN
Bureaucracy and Power

The organization of social interaction is an integrating theme of this book. One form of organization, the bureaucracy, has become more and more pervasive in American society. Bureaucracies have the following attributes: they are governed by a set of abstract rules supposedly applicable to all the persons who come under their scope; relationships among members are characterized by impersonality; and they are organized according to some hierarchical principle. Bureaucracies may be political, such as the Democratic party; religious, such as the Methodist church; or economic, such as General Motors Corporation. In its fully developed form, in what we can imagine as its ideal state, the bureaucracy is a smoothly running, efficient mechanism for arranging complex work tasks. In the bureaucracy there are no favorites, promotions come to those best qualified for the job, and those at the top will look after the affairs of all in a fair and judicious fashion.

Underlying all this organization is power and authority. Power is simply the ability of one person or a group of people to influence the actions of others. Authority is legitimate power. Whenever the persons being influenced perceive that influence as correct or the way things should be, we are talking about authority. Authority is much more stable than power. It can be thought of as transformed power. Power can be transformed in a variety of ways: by reference to the past, by believing in the magic high qualities of the individual leader, or by believing in the "appropriateness" of the abstract rules.

All formal organizations rest on some form of transformed power. The most salient form in modern society is abstract or bureaucratic authority. However, descriptions of the actual workings of organizations illustrate that they rarely function according to the ideal conditions they define for themselves. More often we discover that the official face of the organization is different from its "real" face. An organization may feign democratic values or participation in decision making and actually operate on coercive power. An organization may operate on informal agreements worked out over long periods of time by workers or lower authority personnel only to find the stable applecart overturned by the serious enforcement of bureaucratic rules previously ignored. Pressure groups, majority interests, and the unsatisfied needs of minorities can foster corruption and usurp basic values of the organization.

The formal organizational setting provides the opportunities necessary to observe power at work. It is an arena limiting the kinds of interactions that can take place. Yet as we shall see, the limitations often have surprising impacts on behavior, values, and the resolution of problematic occurrences.

33
Informal law

One aspect of power involves the ability to settle disputes. Judges have great power in American society for this reason, as do juries and boards of appeal. But power is not always formalized in such positions or groups. In this article Spencer MacCullum demonstrates that informal law exists in a modern shopping center and that procedures exist for settling disputes. The informal processes described here can be considered similar to others that help maintain the social order and restore social relationships in society.

Dispute Settlement in an Urban Supermarket
Spencer MacCullum

An impressive development in modern American land tenure has been the postwar rise of professional property management. Besides this, there has been a proliferation of new forms and functions of the multiple-tenant income property. Types of the latter that have become familiar in the landscape since the war include shopping centers, marinas, industrial and research parks, medical clinics, professional and office centers, mobile-home parks, real estate complexes for which Rockefeller Center was an early prototype, and some of the new "planned communities."

From *Law and Warfare,* ed. Paul Bohannan (New York: Doubleday, 1967). Reprinted by permission. This paper is based on research by the writer which included a preliminary field survey of thirty-five shopping centers in California in 1962, under an NIH grant through the Department of Anthropology of the University of Chicago. The appended cases are taken from a group of forty-five cases collected at the time.

As a landlord-tenant arrangement, the multiple-tenant income property represents a land-tenure pattern of a kind we are used to thinking of in terms of peasants and feudal institutions and of absentee aristocracy battening on the land. But in the present case, the landlords are modern, efficient firms, specializing in property management for income on invested capital. From a structural viewpoint, nevertheless, these organizations are indeed akin to the landed estates and manorial organizations of antiquity, in which the internal public authority derived mainly from the proprietary land authority. They are truly "little communities" in modern garb, for to some extent they are modern counterparts also of village communities organized on the kinship tie, in which the land-distributive function was an attribute of the public authority, such as there was, vested in the chief or headman of the group.

The point I wish to make in this chapter is simply that the multiple-tenant income property can be viewed in its internal organization as a community of landlord and tenants. Of the many forms, the shopping center is sociologically most interesting because of the complex relations among its members. This complexity derives especially, but not by any means solely, from the need for joint promotions on which the center characteristically depends because of its locations away from downtown where there is sufficient "natural traffic" to sustain stores. While neighborhood centers are narrowly specialized, the larger shopping centers—containing from fifty to two hundred merchant tenants and a mixed composition of land uses, including professional and office buildings and even motels and apartments in the same plan of development—begin to resemble communities as we are accustomed to thinking of them.

Pospisil (1958, p. 274) has pointed out that we need not think of there being one system of law in a given society, but that each subgroup has its own.[1] Following this idea and inquiring into the law of the shopping center as a community of landlord and merchant tenants, we find an intriguing situation: the legal system of a shopping center is composed of two parts, a written part and an unwritten part. For the totality of the leases in effect at any given moment in time is the written, formal law which defines the respective rights and duties of all parties, merchants and landlord alike. The employed personnel of the individual business firms within the center do not come directly under this jurisdiction

---

[1] "Many ethnographers assume that a given society has a single legal system. They either neglect legal phenomena on the subgroup levels or project these phenomena into the top society level and make them consistent with it. Instead of accepting this smoothed-out picture of a single legal system in a society, the writer suggests recognition of the fact that there are as many such systems as there are functional groups. The legal systems of families, clans, and communities, for example, form a hierarchy of what we may call legal levels, according to the inclusiveness of the respective groups."

but are subject to the rules of their respective organizations. They belong to the shopping center community not in their own right but through their respective employers, as the members of the domestic groups making up a village community might be related to the polity through their respective "patresfamilias" and not in their individual rights. Case 3 below illustrates an appeal to lease law, and Case 4, the hierarchy of legal levels in the center.

The informal law on the other hand develops outside of the leases and consists of a body of rules and understandings, bylaws as it were, governing behavior in the center. Case 5 suggests one of the ways in which such law may develop, as does Case 4.

An important problem of shopping-center administration is writing effective leases. One of the requirements of an effective lease is that it consist with the existing leases—the rest of the body of written law— and also with the unwritten law of the center. A general development in the shopping-center lease has been a movement away from the traditional form of lease which defined a narrow dyadic relationship, specifying what the two parties would do for one another and leaving it at that, toward the lease becoming a conscious instrument of social policy in the shopping center as a community of merchants. Increasingly, it has been developing lateral extensions, as it were, citing positive obligations of the lessee not only to the landlord but also to the other merchants in the center. Clauses requiring a tenant to participate in the merchants' council, spend a minimum percentage of gross income on advertising and a portion of this in council-sponsored media, coordinate his minimum opening hours with those of other merchants, enforce the center parking rules among his own employees, and so forth, are becoming standard items in shopping-center leases.

If the shopping center is thought of in this way as an autonomous community of landlord and merchant tenants, then many suggestive parallels come to mind between its law and the law of primitive communities. The emphasis in both is toward resolving differences and preserving social relations, and neither is fundamentally concerned with rules and penalties.

One of the most fruitful areas for study, however, may be the problem of writing effective leases, since it is here that we confront the problem of the relation between written and unwritten law, and perhaps also the problem of boundaries between law and custom, on a manageable scale and, incidentally, without a language barrier. Moreover, the recent growth of these new forms of organization on the land—truly estate forms of urban land tenure—appearing de novo in the bare space of twenty years, affords unusual conditions for studying institutional emergence and change. For the anthropologist, moreover, it offers a natural opening to the study of contemporary society.

Cases

Case 1   The Case That Turned Around

Informants. Shopping-center manager, former promotion director, succeeding promotion director; consultant from an outside promotion firm who attended meetings of the board of directors of the merchants' council after the resignation of the promotion director.

Facts. Each year the baker had made a five hundred-pound cake for the center's birthday anniversary sale. The new promotion director thought the baker charged the merchants' council too much for his cake. He told the baker that and asked for a specific bid on the following year's cake. When the baker failed to give a price, the promotion director obtained a cake at a low price from a baker firm in another city that operated a chain outlet for ready-baked goods as a concession in the supermarket in the center. At a council meeting after the anniversary sale, the baker was irate. He said the arrangement had been "rigged" and that he had been unjustly accused of charging too much for his cake. He said his cake was better quality. He charged that the promotion director had been disloyal to the merchants in the center by going "off the mall."

Outcome. The promotion director publicly asked the baker for his friendship and was refused. The baker withdrew from the council and stopped paying dues. Within a year the promotion director had resigned under diffuse pressure from the council. The baker still did not return. Shortly afterward, the council directors decided to feature a cake again at the next birthday anniversary sale and to ask the baker to provide it.

Comment. The former promotion director's account differed from the other accounts on the point of whether he had "gone off the mall" or whether there were, as he recounted it, "two bakers in the center." (The center manager's story: "We went outside and got another baker . . .") He thus contrived to avoid the issue of disloyalty on a technicality and cited more fundamental reasons for his inability to get along with the merchants, of which he said the baker's withdrawal and refusal to pay dues was only a symptom and a further aggravation. Among his reasons, he cited: (1) tension in the center over a leveling off of volume gains over the past year due to new discount stores in the area and a natural tendency for a center's growth to slow around its seventh year;

(2) the structural problem of his being employed directly by the council instead of by the landlord, so that every merchant felt he "owned a piece of" the promotion director; and (3) that he was not temperamentally suited to the job.

He predicted the problem with the baker would be settled by a delegation from the promotion committee of the council going to him and saying, "Frank, we like your cake best and want to have it, to hell with the cost. Will you make it?" And Frank would say, "Well, I'll think it over." Two months later, just prior to the writer's leaving the field, this seemed to be the way events were developing; the promotion committee had decided to ask the baker to bake the cake, without making a point of price.

The succeeding promotion director suggested that a further element in the baker's stand may have been that it gave him a chance not to pay dues. He quoted the baker as once having said to him, "Promotions don't help bakers."

Case 2   The Case of the Shopping Carts

Informant.   Shopping center manager.

Facts.   A supermarket's checkout area faced onto an arcade of shops. On more than one occasion, boys bringing in shopping carts from the parking lots made up lines of carts that partly blocked access to shops in the arcade. Several of the merchants spoke to the manager of the center about it.

Outcome.   The manager took the problem to the food-store manager and questioned him in detail about what could be done. Together they worked out a different system of stacking the carts and decided upon various areas of the store where excess carts would be stored when not in use. The manager of the center then spoke to the other merchants, telling them something had been worked out, and suggesting they be lenient with the food-store manager, pointing out that often it is not the manager but employees who make the difficulties.

Comment.   The center manager emphasized that problems are handled in a face-to-face manner when they are still small. He said the management could do this because they spent so much time with the tenants that they learned the characteristics of each person. He said, "Just so they know you're doing something, it doesn't matter what you do. The merchants have got to feel that their interests are being looked out for."

Case 3 The Case of the Window Full of Slippers

Informants. Shopping center manager, promotion director.

Facts. A shoe store had an exclusive to sell shoes in the center. The ready-to-wear shop therefore had an express clause in its lease forbidding sale of shoes. The shop bought a lot of colorful, mule-type slippers of many different kinds and filled a window full of them. The shoe-store man did not make a point of going to the manager of the center, but he met him on the street, walking casually, and said, "I see they're selling shoes next door. I didn't think they were supposed to do that." The manager said "I'll chase the lease up and see what I can find out." He talked to the manager of the ready-to-wear shop, who said, "Oh no, these aren't shoes. They're boutique." The center manager went to his office and "let it cool off a bit . . . probably it was two hours." In the meantime, he looked for *boutique* in the dictionary and did not find it. He went to the shoe store, then back once more to the ready-to-wear shop, talking the thing down rather than inflaming it. The ready-to-wear man, appealing to the professionalism that is stressed in the shoe business, said it really was not a shoe because it did not have to be fitted. It was not customized. He said, moreover, that he had a tremendous stock.

Outcome. The center manager went to his office, and then, after a while, went back to the manager of the ready-to-wear shop and "just sat down with him." He said, "This is a borderline case; you're asking me to define something the dictionary hasn't defined. I think the thing to do on this is to compromise. Instead of filling the window and making a specialty item of it, just put two or three pairs in the window as you would an accessory. Then you won't look like a shoe store." He allowed him to keep his stock and sell it.

Comment. The center manager said, "We don't let those things go quickly. We let them cool, go slowly on them." Commenting further on how cases usually come to his attention, he said, "The grapevine is faster than your ears . . . I'm one of the last people that ever gets a complaint. About ninety percent of the complaints I get are indirect. Somebody says 'So-and-so's been beefing about that.'"

Case 4 The Case of the Obstinate Nurse

Informant. Promotion director.

Facts. Despite warnings placed on the car by the security guard, the nurse employed in a doctor's office in the center continued to take up valuable parking space, parking at the curb only twenty feet from the doctor's office instead of in the parking area designated for tenants and personnel. The nurse told the center manager and the council of merchants that it was none of their concern. The landlord advised the doctor by letter that if further violations occurred, he would have to leave the center. The doctor spoke to his nurse. She continued parking at the curb.

Outcome. When she had received three more warnings, the center manager sent a letter to the doctor requesting the premises at the end of the month. The doctor asked if he could stay if he dismissed his nurse and was told he could. He dismissed her reluctantly. He said she was a good nurse.

Comment. The promotion director said it thereafter became the unwritten rule in that center that any employee who accumulated three parking warnings (I did not think to ask over what period of time) would be dismissed.

Case 5   The Case of the Manipulated Merchants

Informant. Shopping center manager.

Facts. The manager of a major store in the center, while not a director on the merchants' council, was active on its advertising committee. He proposed at a weekly meeting that all the merchants hold a five-day flower show on the mall, during which they could put out "throw-aways" advertising the specials they would run during that week only. The other merchants liked the idea and began to develop the plan. Just before the flower show was scheduled to open, a small merchant learned from a newspaper-space salesman that the major was coming out with a big newspaper section at the same time as the show. The small merchant went to the center manager with this information. The center manager called the large merchant, who confirmed it. On the day that the "throw-aways" on the flower show were put out announcing the individual merchants' specials, the big store announced a major, week-long sales event that overshadowed the merchandising of the rest of the stores in the center.

Outcome. Everybody talked about the incident, but it was never brought into the open. The consensus was that the big store had conceived the idea of the flower show only to augment its own major promotional effort with advertising monies and specials put out by the other stores. All the merchants felt bad about it. They recognized there had been no lease violation and that all the stores were free to spend their own money for promotion as they liked, but they objected that the major had not told them about his plans so they could have geared their activity to his. Fortunately, everybody did a good business that week.

While the incident was never brought up in any kind of meeting, the informant said an understanding was arrived at with the merchants that the center management would assume responsibility in the future for knowing what promotions were being planned by the major stores, so that this could not happen again. Asked how he could do this, the informant said he and his staff ask the major merchants what they are planning, when they are coming out with circulars, and so forth.

"Do you ask them this in meetings?"

"No, just when we see them. We make it our business to keep informed about their advertising and promotion plans." The manager is able to do this because he is continually in touch with his tenants. He reported a Rotary Club organized entirely within the center; fifty-two merchants meet together every week.

"We're very close here. It's just like a little town. Now, at lunch today I talked to seven of my tenants. . . ."

References

Pospisil, Leopold. 1958. "The Kapauku, Papuans and Their Law." Yale University Studies in Anthropology 54. New Haven: Yale University Press.

34
The Life of an Organization

Organizations have a metaphoric life. They are born, they pass through stages, and sometimes they die. As long as we remind ourselves that we are referring to a collective entity that emerges out of many individual interpretations of social reality, we can increase our understanding of organizations by employing this metaphor of life. In this article John Maniha and Charles Perrow provide us with a clear description of cycles in the life of one organization. We see it change, redefine its purpose, and develop into a viable collectivity. All this is cast against the backdrop of an aggressive environment. We follow the interaction between the reluctant organization and the aggressive environment.

The Reluctant Organization and the Aggressive Environment
John Maniha and Charles Perrow

Organizations are usually defined as rational systems for coordinating the efforts of individuals towards a goal or goals. Increasingly, attention has been focused upon such topics as informal goals, the succession of goals, adaptation to the environment, intended rationality, and so on.[1] The nonrational, informal, and adaptive aspects generally appear with

From *Complex Organizations and Their Environments*, ed. Merlin B. Brinkerhoff and Phillip R. Kunz (Dubuque: Wm. C. Brown, 1972). Reprinted by permission.

[1] For a representative sampling see Philip Selznick, "Foundations of the Theory of Organization," *American Sociological Review* 13 (1948); 25–35; David Sills, *The Volunteers* (Glencoe, Ill.: Free Press, 1957); Herbert Simon, *Administrative Behavior,* 2nd ed. (New York: Macmillan, 1957), especially the introduction; and James D. Thompson et al., *Comparative Studies in Administration* (Pittsburgh, Pa.: University of Pittsburgh, 1959).

511

growing institutionalization, as Selznick persuasively argues.[2] But implicit in this view is the assumption that organizations start out as rationally designed instruments with a charter directed toward a clear set of goals designed to fulfill some social need. The distinctively sociological analysis is relevant when the compromises and affective networks of history have accumulated and fleshed out the structure and processes of the organization. We would like to present one case history where an organization had every reason not to be born and had no goals to guide it. It was used by other organizations for their own ends, but in this very process it became an organization with a mission of its own, in spite of itself, and even while its members denied it was becoming an action group.

The organization under study is the Youth Commission made up of nine private citizens appointed by the mayor of a city of some 70,000 persons. The origins and first year of the commission were reconstructed from structured interviews with most of the principals concerned, within and without the organization, the minutes of the commission, documents and letters in their file, and newspaper accounts. In the second year the meetings of the commission were observed, and interviews were held with the heads of other agencies, public officials, and private citizens involved in or concerned with the affairs of the commission. All commission members, except one who had moved away, were interviewed at length at least once.[3] The account is basically historical, starting with the community environment, the specific origins of the commission, its search for a role, its utilization by other groups, and finally, its emergence as an organization with an action role.

Setting

Collegetown considers itself a progressive community with few major problems. As the mayor once put it, when speaking of youth problems, "We've always known about the '5 percent' of the kids who go bad, but we've always felt that Collegetown had only 2 percent." Much of this image comes from the view that not only does the city have a large

[2] Philip Selznick, *Leadership and Administration* (New York: Row, Peterson, 1957).
[3] The commission agreed to serve as a research site for a seminar paper in organizational analysis, with the chairman hoping thereby that the role of the commission in the community might be clarified. J. Maniha conducted the field work, while C. Perrow had primary, though not exclusive responsibility for the framework of the analysis and much of the writing.

percentage of well-educated professional citizens—university professors, scientists, and engineers—but that it draws these citizens into government through the use of semiofficial commissions. The commissions are made up of a cross-section of the community elite—wealthy landowners, the business elite, representatives of the leading Protestant churches, university people, and sometimes representatives of the new electronics and aerospace industries. Commissions informally share responsibility for legislation passed by the city council and serve as sounding boards of elite public opinion on some of the issues upon which the council should act.

Some commissions are noncontroversial as, for example, the group of seven citizens formed to advise the council on how Collegetown could, according to the mayor, retain its "character . . . by trying to strike a balance between progress, as defined by growth, and the traditional character of our community." The Citizens Recreation Commission at the time of the study was somewhat more powerful, since it influenced the allocation of recreation resources. The Human Relations Commission, dealing with more explosive issues such as civil rights, minority housing, and zoning, had been forced into a controversial role by the pressure of liberal organizations. The Youth Commission started out innocuously enough, but by the end of its second year was making headlines and was even accused by members of the Human Relations Commission of invading their strife-ridden domain. In view of its origins, the change was significant.

Origins

The formation of the Youth Commission was not prompted by any dramatic evidence of need in the area, nor by demands of agencies dealing with youth, citizen groups, or political groups. Several cities in the region were reported to be forming youth commissions but generally in response to dramatic evidence of problems. During the preceding administration, a small group had looked into the problems of youth and made at least one report to the city council, but it received no publicity and little could be learned of its activities.

The idea of forming the Youth Commission came from a councilman who was a candidate for reelection. He initially explored the idea with his friends, some of whom were prominent in youth affairs, and while they agreed there might be some value in it, reportedly they expressed concern that the service might be a duplication of existing facilities. The director of the YMCA had a more explicit caution. He recalled that he told the councilman that he "thought it was a good idea but expressed the hope that the commission would not be an action group." The councilman used the proposal as a campaign plank during the election. Surprise was expressed by workers in both parties when, following his reelection, he continued to pursue the idea. He presented it to the council as an ordinance, which then required two readings and a vote. One member of the council characterized the atmosphere at the first reading as apathetic. The ordinance passed and came up again one month later for final action. At this point another councilman, a retired businessman and past chairman of the United Fund and Community Chest, proposed that the word "commission" be changed to "committee"—a term connoting less stature and influence. His proposal was defeated, and with the second councilman registering the only nay, the ordinance was officially passed, again apathetically.

The official goals of the charter were sufficiently straightforward to confer upon it the broad responsibility of appraising conditions and influences affecting youth, evaluating existing services, and recommending to the council measures which it could take "to promote the best interests of children and youth in the city." It was to report to the council every four months, advising the council of current developments relating to youth. Just how the commission was to go about its tasks was not spelled out. It was noted in the charter that it "shall not undertake or carry out youth projects," but this was followed by the ambiguous qualification "though after specific request therefrom may render such assistance as it deems appropriate to other agencies supporting youth projects or actions." What "appropriate assistance" might be, or the scope of support, was apparently left to the commission to decide. They decided quite early; indeed, by the time the members were selected other agencies had, in effect, decided for them.

Forming a Reluctant Organization

As soon as the ordinance was passed, the town newspaper informed the public of the "appraising, evaluating, and recommending" goals of the commission. The mayor immediately received queries from the heads of agencies concerned with youth. They wished to know what was to be appraised, who was to be evaluated, and whether this was not a duplication of existing services. It appeared that the autonomy and integrity of some twenty-nine existing agencies were threatened. The commission was not the mayor's idea, and he attempted to assuage their fears. His nine appointments to the commission can be interpreted in this light:

1. *High-School Principal*—The group's first chairman. He was head of the city's only public high school, which served about 2,000 students and held a very visible position in the community. He was highly respected by all the commission members for his knowledge of youth problems and his candid and forthright approach. The high school had been a focal point for some disturbances in the past and thus had a more than usual interest in youth problems.

2. *YMCA Director*—Representative of one of the organizations most conscious of public relations. He was a friend or acquaintance of the mayor and several councilmen as well as most of the other heads of agencies serving youth in Collegetown. The YMCA had also had problems with juvenile disturbances on its premises and had been criticized for this in the past.

3. *Catholic*—Athletic coach at a Catholic high school. He rarely came to meetings and took almost no part in them. He was interested in pursuing his sports activities with youth and working with them on a face-to-face basis and felt the commission should be talking with the youth of the community. In an interview, he said, "I was asked to be on the commission because they needed a Catholic. There aren't a lot of us here, but enough to be represented."

4. *Negro Woman*—She also recognized why she was appointed and was frank about it. She belonged to a great many other organizations, including the Human Relations Commission, and was a friend of the mayor and several powerful families in Collegetown. White leaders depended upon her to be prudent about the race issue, and she was in great demand for organizations requiring a Negro representative. Vocal elements in the Negro civil-rights movement did not feel she spoke for her race, and she in turn did not strongly identify with the Negro community in Collegetown.

5. *Junior-High-School Teacher*—A son of the mayor. His access to city hall was utilized by the commission in technical matters, and he may also have informed his father about developments in the group. He did not appear to find the connection between his relationship to the mayor and his commission membership awkward.

6. *Protestant Minister*—Four of the eight other members of the commission belonged to his church. The minister clearly represented organized religion and Christian morality, reminding members, for example, that even so-called unenforceable laws must be observed. He can be seen as the link between the commission and the powerful Collegetown Ministerial Association.

7. *Physician*—Professor of public health at the university. He was

elected chairman at the close of the commission's first year. He was interested in the welfare of youth and was also acting chairman of a statewide health organization dealing with children. The presence of a physician would ordinarily be a requisite of such an organization.

8. *University-Faculty Member*—In physical education. He belonged to a great many service groups and was active in many phases of community work. He was very interested in the affairs of the commission and probably the most vocal member of the group. But his role was mainly that of a public-spirited citizen and a concerned father of an adolescent. He was also at the same time the chairman of the Citizens Recreation Commission.

9. *Nurse*—She replaced another woman who moved away and who had been president of the Women's Auxiliary of the Junior Chamber of Commerce and, as secretary of the group, was said to have played almost no role in deliberations. Her replacement, the nurse, was also promptly made the group's secretary. She said she was appointed to the commission because "they needed a housewife." Her role was subordinate, she rarely spoke at meetings, and she admitted to being awed by the other "strong members who are authorities on youth."

The appointments, then, covered two of the powerful agencies most involved with youth—the high school and the YMCA—and added representatives from four other obvious fields: religion, recreation, medicine, and housewifery. Two minority groups were included: a Negro and a Catholic. The ruling political party was represented at least by the mayor's son and initially also by the representative from the Junior Chamber of Commerce. It can be assumed that most of the members were in sympathy with the political party in office. None of the many authorities in delinquency from the university, such as social workers, sociologists, or psychologists, were included, nor was a representative of the major Negro youth organization, which had programs similar to the YMCA. Any of these might have urged a more active role for the commission.

At the organization meeting of the group, the mayor discussed the implications of the creation of a group to study youth problems in a city which prided itself on the lack of such problems. He said he was "not sure" Collegetown had any youth problems, but if it did he "certainly wanted to know about them." He would also cooperate in any way he could with the group, and if the commission needed anything to let him know. One member recalls that he mentioned stamps and envelopes. He then explicitly advised them to move very slowly and cautiously in order to allay the suspicions of several agencies. He concluded by expressing his admiration for the fine group of public-spirited citizens he had chosen and appointed the high-school principal as chairman.

The First Year: Protecting the Minimal Role

"Goals appear to grow out of interaction both within the organization and between the organization and its environment."[4] In the case of the commission, much of the salient environment was built into the organization—representation of the two largest youth organizations in the city, and of the city administration. The high-school principal and the director of the YMCA immediately became the key personnel in the commission. They were instrumental in defining a no-action study group role for the commission at its first meeting. The goals of the commission had been clearly set forth in the charter—appraise, evaluate, and recommend—but appraisal, or more accurately, "listening," became the only operative goal.[5]

During its first year, and for some months after, the agency invited the heads of the major youth agencies in the city to describe the program and problems of their agencies. Each presentation was followed by a polite question-and-answer period. The presentations of the agencies appear to have been optimistic and self-satisfied, and the questions of the members were innocuous. Even so, some of the members felt that the agencies minimized their problems. For example, the head of the county health agency announced that there were almost no health problems among the youth in the city, and that this could be attributed to the fine cooperation between private physicians and his department. Several commission members, not particularly prone to gloomy views, privately debunked the statement. They had enough contact with juveniles to know that many poor children suffered from inadequate health facilities, and even the mayor was reportedly surprised when informed of the presentation. But the head of the agency was not questioned about this in the discussion session.

It was a commission member, the minister, who tested the reluctance of the commission to become active. Assigned to report on what the churches were doing with youth, with a panel discussion of his report by a group of ministers to follow at a later session, the minister stated that, in fact, the churches were doing virtually nothing and deplored the fact. The report was quickly tabled, and the panel discussion canceled. One commission member, a member of the minister's congregation, said, "We decided the panel should be postponed until further study could be made of the report. Of course, it never was. The report would

---

[4] James D. Thompson and William J. McEwen, "Organizational Goals and Environment: Goal Setting as an Interaction Process," *American Sociological Review* 23 (1958): 28–29.

[5] On the concept of "operative goals," see Charles Perrow, "The Analysis of Goals in Complex Organization," *American Sociological Review* 26 (1961): 854–66.

have set up barriers." The minister subsequently played a minor role at the meetings.

More informal means were used to allay the suspicion of groups. The YMCA director, a self-proclaimed listening post in the town, informed the chairman that the head of the Juvenile Division of the Police Department was suspicious of the role of the commission. This led to an informal meeting, and in the commission's first annual report, the commission supported the Police Department's request for more personnel.

Sensitivity to public criticism characterized the two dominant men in the commission in its first year, the principal and the YMCA director, and concern with the image of the town became a preoccupation of the group. The high-school principal set the tone of cautious procedure for the commission. The high school was occasionally the scene of vandalism and delinquency, and he was sensitive to potential criticisms. In the second year he was involved in a direct controversy with the local newspaper, which, he claimed, was placing the school in an unfavorable light by publishing accounts of delinquency by high-school students—he argued that they could just as well have been identified as Collegetown youths or the children of certain families. He felt the school was being made to look like "a training school for punks." The YMCA director also had similar experiences in which his organization was criticized for lack of supervision during its functions. He took on the role of seeing that no one was misquoted, misinterpreted, or otherwise compromised in dealing with the press. Another member was quite concerned that Collegetown had a reputation among other cities as being a "hoody town." All agreed with the statement of one member that "throwing these accusations and sensational terms around indiscreetly can give our town a bad reputation that will stick for years."

During the first year several formal and informal attempts by relatively weak groups were made to enlist the help of the commission in meeting problems related to youth. The commission resisted these attempts on the grounds of the no-action policy made explicit by the two dominant members and shared by others. For example, a local Protestant minister tried to get the commission interested in doing something about all-night parties after the senior prom at the high school. The minister was referred to the PTA since his proposal was "beyond the role of the commission, because we are not an action group." A more constructive role for the commission was sought by the head of the City Recreation Board, who attempted to enlist the commission's aid in keeping city recreation facilities open on school nights. Although the commission did not refuse to consider the proposal, it ignored it, and no formal action was taken on it, even though a member of the Citizens Recreation Commission was on the Youth Commission.

At the end of the year the Youth Commission was required to submit an annual report to the city council. Perhaps in keeping with the commission's minimal role, it had only had a few carbon copies made. To the surprise of the members, there were a number of requests for copies from agencies and citizens following the announcement of the report in the newspaper. The report was then mimeographed and distributed to those who requested it. The interest probably reflected both a concern with problems of youth by the citizens and a concern with the role and recommendations of the commission. The report, however, did much to allay the suspicions of the agencies. It was noncontroversial and minimized youth problems. It contained a few minor recommendations and was full of praise for the work the community youth agencies were doing, given the limitations that were beyond agency control. The report reaffirmed that the commission was "fully cognizant of its legal limitation to require action on its recommendations by any agency, civil or legal body. The commission's prime responsibility is to bring to the attention of the community and the several responsible agencies, through its report to the city council, the results of its findings and its recommendations for the alleviation or resolution of problems and issues of the youth of Collegetown." The report ended with a section on proposed plans for the coming year, one of which reads, "Make a more detailed analysis of the role of the Youth Commission."

The distribution of mimeographed copies of the annual report marked the end of the first phase of the commission's development—the study-group role—and the beginning of its second phase, involving an action role. The annual report was more than a symbolic calendaring of a new year; it stirred interest in the group by others in the community, allayed suspicions, and prompted criticism. At the same time, the term of the high-school principal as chairman expired, and he did not wish to serve as chairman for another year. A new chairman was elected, the public-health physician. This, it turned out, was a fateful decision. The physician differed from the other members in not having a local constituency—he did not represent the schools, the YMCA, the recreation department, Catholics, Negroes, or housewives. He might be seen as representing physicians or the university, but neither of these was involved, as an organization, in community youth affairs. Without a constituency, the physician could act as a free agent. He alone seems to have played the role of member of a commission rather than a representative of some interest group. In fact, at the end of the second year, he remarked that he was not so sure that the YMCA director and the high-school principal really ought to be on the commission: "They have difficulty separating their roles as director and principal from their roles as commission members. They often speak and act in terms of their own organizations and not the commission." As a corollary of the physician's role, he did not have great public visibility and was able to move inconspicuously in informal negotiations with groups.

The Emerging Action Role

There was nothing to indicate that the Youth Commission would do more than continue its role as a study group in its second year. Because it existed, however, it was there for others to utilize. As the head of the Juvenile Division of the Police Department put it, "The commission can do a lot to help all agencies. We all need support. People listen to them because their opinions carry weight and prestige."

There were some who urged the commission to take a more active, constructive role. In the early part of the second year, they asked an expert in juvenile delinquency and related community problems from the university to address them. He exhorted them to make an aggressive and sincere effort to attack the city's many youth problems. Members replied that this was "not the commission's role," but the faculty member then read them the official goals as stated in their charter and reminded them that their role was to appraise, evaluate, and recommend programs. Furthermore, he reminded them that other organizations in the city, like the Human Relations Commission, had not let their official charter goals stand in the way of the development of an aggressive approach to community problems. The commission appeared unmoved.

Shortly after this, the commission invited an official of the State Youth Commission, which had no affiliation with the local one, to address them on youth problems. He praised their annual report but then told them that they should seize the opportunity created by good feeling and the interest in the commission to forge ahead with some kind of constructive program. Again, the members listened but did not discuss these exhortations nor apparently take them seriously at the time.

The commission continued its study role but was pressed into a more active role by the city council itself. A well-publicized brawl broke out between a group of high school youths and students from the university. Publicity in the newspaper, letters to the editor, letters to the mayor and city council, and direct pressure upon the council from some of the citizens, who protested the lack of control by the police, demanded some kind of response. The response was an ordinance drafted by the city attorney, which would give the police power to arrest those whom they suspected of being about to cause a disturbance. The mayor and the council were reluctant to handle the ordinance from the start. Casting about for a device to suggest action while delaying any, the council seized upon the commission. As one councilman said when he was asked why the commission had been brought into the matter, "We didn't know what to do with the ordinance and needed more time to think about it and test out more opinions." A joint meeting between the council and the commission was called.

The meeting illustrated both the ambiguous role of the commission and the apprehensions which some council members had about its goals. The high-school principal began the discussion by stating frankly that he did not know what the council expected of the group and was waiting for positive leadership from the council. All evening the council and mayor solicited opinions from commission members about various aspects of the youth problem: Could we use a dragstrip? What sort of problems do the schools have? Are youth at the YMCA hard to control? Do you think the police juvenile division needs more men? The commission members gave their opinions and attempted, in some cases, to speak for the community at large; but several times they sought from the council a definite statement of purpose for their organization. None was forthcoming. Indeed, the councilman who had voted against the commission, felt that he should warn the commission to proceed slowly and be very careful about recommendations. He feared that "half-baked schemes" might be proposed by the commission. "Just because something worked in another city, doesn't mean it will work in Collegetown," he added. Finally, the mayor asked the commission to make a recommendation on the proposed ordinance and submit it to the council.

The commission met, but there was little consensus at first. The YMCA director was immediately concerned about public opinion and, in effect, admitted that a no-action role was no longer feasible. "We have to recommend the ordinance. If we don't and it's not passed, the first time something happens we'll be blamed for it. Anyway, the ordinance won't do any good, but if they think they need it then give it to them." But some other members felt the ordinance was potentially threatening to civil rights. The principal was not present but sent a letter stating that he was against the ordinance because it was unconstitutional. Finally, the new chairman reluctantly formulated a compromise agreeable to the YMCA director. It met its obligation to the city administration by recommending passage, but qualified its support by adding that it should be passed only if some means could be found to protect civil rights, and that other so-called unenforceable laws were attended to.

Opposition to the ordinance from groups concerned with civil liberties eventually caused the mayor to postpone action indefinitely. Although the newspapers gave prominence to the recommendations of the commission, its members did not feel that they had been compromised by the administration's decision to postpone action. Most of them, when interviewed, said that their actions as an organization were not especially noticed by the community.

The next group to seize upon the potentialities of the Youth Commission was the United Fund. This organization had originally been suspicious of the Youth Commission. Following the issuance of the commission's annual report, the planning committee of the United Fund asked the principal of the high school to discuss the commission and its role with them. This meeting apparently allayed many suspicions since, shortly afterwards, the head of the United Fund wrote to the commission regarding the meeting saying, "You have focused for this committee what the committee already knew and was concerned about; and you have done it with a realistic appreciation of the limitations we have in the face of so exacting and imperative a task and, finally, you have pointed the way to our working together." The planning committee of the United Fund decided that it would be beneficial to have a discussion comparable to that held with the high-school principal on a communitywide basis. A seminar was proposed which would be cosponsored by the United Fund and the Youth Commission. This proposal was made to the YMCA director, suggesting that the new chairman of the commission was still not visible or believed to be a powerful member. The YMCA director and the principal decided that the commission should not cosponsor the seminar because they were "not an action group" and so informed the United Fund. They rather casually informed the other members of the request, and the group agreed with their action. All agreed, however, that the commission should at least go on record as actively supporting the project, though it could not cosponsor it.

Less than three months later, at least partly through the leadership of the new chairman of the Youth Commission, the commission found itself cosponsoring the seminar. The proposal received favorable publicity in the press, which commended the commission and the United Fund for this constructive and positive step.

The city council and the United Fund were both influential agencies in the community. So was the Probate Court, and the third and even more significant line of action that engaged the commission stemmed from this source. A judge from the court, who was an officer in a statewide group promoting a project concerned with protective services for juveniles, met with the chairman of the Youth Commission and urged him to look into the project, which involved setting up protective services for children, which fell outside the jurisdiction or responsibility of existing youth agencies. For example, a community agency could be established to assume responsibility for the prosecution of parents of abused children. The initial step would be a survey of the community resources to see if a protective-service agency was needed. At the urging of the judge, the commission met with a representative of the statewide project. During the meeting, the judge stated frankly that he saw a real need for the program and would like to see the commission sponsor it. Whatever their individual feelings, the commission members must have found it difficult to turn down a request from this influential source.

The commission was now pressed to explore the role of recommending to other agencies a study by an outside group, which would assess the effectiveness of agencies in the community and might propose yet another agency to fill in the gaps. The implications of perhaps finding such a need were not lost upon agency heads. There would be implied criticism of existing facilities. A new organization might be created which would upset the balance of power and the accommodative division of labor existing among some twenty-nine community agencies and affect the distribution of United Fund resources. At a joint meeting of the agency heads, some sought to avoid the responsibilities and the burdens that such an organization might exact from them, and others attempted to place themselves in a position where they could have a share in its control. At the conclusion of our field work, agency heads had only agreed to confer with their respective organizations to see if approval would be given for a study in which they would have to cooperate, and even this agreement was reluctant in many cases.

By this time—the end of the commission's second year—meetings were lively and participation was more enthusiastic. This change had begun when the antibrawling ordinance had been discussed and quickened further during the planning of the seminar. A good deal of excitement was now generated in connection with the protective-service project. As one member put it with enthusiasm, "We are about to commit ourselves." The YMCA director characteristically saw the project as "a major test for the commission since it involves an expenditure of a lot of money and other responsibilities." While it certainly seemed as if they had compromised their hard-earned nonintervention reputation, the action implications of the project appeared to have been lost upon most of the commission members. In final interviews, all members (except the chairman, who recognized the action role implicit in current developments) affirmed that the commission should not be an action group nor should it be granted any more formal powers than it had. They affirmed that the group had no authority to go to any agency with plans, and that they had merely to keep themselves informed and await requests from others for their advice and information. The mayor's son summed it up well:

> Working with a lot of different groups as we are, groups like the churches, the city agencies, and private agencies, all of which are separate and autonomous, the city really can't give us any more power than we already have. All must work cooperatively and without force with these separate groups. We can only study the situation and wait for others to ask our opinion.

The study-group role was even pressed anew by some members in the final interviews. One said, somewhat wistfully, "We haven't talked to all the agencies yet." Another complained, "We haven't talked to the kids yet."

A postscript to our study was provided just one year after the end of the field work. A newspaper story reported that a survey initiated by the Youth Commission and the Probate Court had found that "at least 1,350 children in the county are known to suffer from neglect by their parents or guardians." The mayor, in summoning the commission, councilmen, judges, and police department to a meeting, stated again his belief that only about 2 percent of the youthful population were in trouble with authorities, but he stressed that, "The community must take constructive action; it must stop dividing itself."

The chairman of the Youth Commission, who had been unanimously encouraged by members to continue in office another year, was reported to be contacting those in charge of welfare matters in the state "to seek possibilities for state support for a protective service here." Even more significantly, the commission was also "considering the addition of a staff person to coordinate the work of all involved groups." The role of action and controversy, which had been so predictably rejected by the carefully selected members of the commission, had been embraced.

Discussion

There are many conclusions on organizational analysis to be drawn from this modest analysis of a modest organization. For one thing, not all organizations start out as rationally designed instruments directed toward a predetermined goal specified in their charter. As obvious as this may seem, there has been little attempt to explore the origins of organizations in these terms. Such an exploration immediately confronts one with the influence of the environment upon organizational behavior—a point analyzed systematically by Selznick from the beginning of his work[6] but still receiving only scattered attention in its own right.[7]

Other organizations constituted the most significant part of the environment in this case. The vicious rivalry and conflict that can occur between agencies has been described by Miller in his "Interinstitutional Conflict as a Major Impediment to Delinquency Prevention," and there are echoes of his distressing analysis here.[8] Agencies everywhere seem to fear the loss of their autonomy and invasions of their domain. In a rare admission of problems on this score, the mayor of Collegetown noted that the community "must stop dividing itself." But the surprising thing is that the Youth Commission survived at all, threatening, as it did, the domain of other agencies. The formal powers of the second chairman, as a free agent without a local constituency, may have proved decisive here, though we are unable to document this point. Perhaps even more important was the fact that while most active members had constituencies they sought to serve, the organization itself, as an organization, had none beyond that of youth in general. Were it given a specific task in its charter, for example, to study or promote racial integration or recreational facilities or health services, it would not have been as available for supporting ordinances, seminars, or protective services.[9]

But the significant generalization is related to the power that inheres in the very fact of an organization's existence. An organization can be a tool or weapon[10] to those outside of it as well as those who direct it. The uses to which some community organizations are put may be minor, as when they merely indicate "something is being done" about a problem even if they are expressly designed to do little beyond providing that indication. But a greater potential exists. A formal organization

---

[6] Philip Selznick, *Leadership and Administration;* also *TVA and the Grass Roots* (Berkeley: University of California Press, 1949).

[7] See, for example, Sol Levine and Paul E. White, "Exchange as a Conceptual Framework for the Study of Interorganizational Relationships," *Administrative Science Quarterly* 5 (1961):583–601. Eugene Litwak and Lydia Hylton, "Interorganizational Analysis," *Administrative Science Quarterly* 6 (1962):395–421; and Thompson and McEwen, "Organizational Goals."

[8] Walter B. Miller, "Interinstitutional Conflict as a Major Impediment to Delinquency Prevention," *Human Organization* 17 (1958):20–23.

[9] We are not inclined to attribute the survival of the commission to crises such as the brawl or a growing awareness of real problems. Mounting concern is always present, particularly in retrospect. Every few years an opportunity such as the protective-service project presents itself, but unless it falls within the province of a group that already exists, the opportunity may not even be perceived by most observers.

[10] This word is borrowed from Selznick who uses it in a much more dramatic sense in *The Organizational Weapon* (New York: McGraw-Hill, 1952). It has more general utility than has been recognized.

is visible and has an address to which communications can be sent; it has a legitimate, official area of relevant interest;[11] and it can speak with one voice, amplified by the size and prestige of its members and allies. It is equipped to be used for organized action even if its members wish to avoid action, as was the case with the Youth Commission. Reluctant as it may have been, the commission had no choice but to exist for some time, and within a short time organizations turned to it as a source of support for their activities, exploiting the potential derived from its presence and broad purview, despite its self-imposed operative goals of merely existing and "listening."

All organizations can be used for purposes that go beyond their normal goals. In the process of meeting their goals and surviving, they generate power which can be put to uses that are independent of the achievement of normal goals. The potential power of a business firm is being utilized when it is a source of testimonials, sponsorship, or support for political, social, or economic activities that are unrelated to its basic task of providing goods or services. When the American Medical Association supports the farm organizations in their relentless war on daylight-saving time, or takes a stand on the treaty-making powers of the presidency, its power as a medical group is being used by other groups. When organized labor is drawn into a political camp or liberal groups used by "front" organizations[12] or when a PTA is used to spearhead political reform or when an organization seeks to have its prestige claims validated by appropriate groups in an effort to control their dependency upon the environment,[13] existing tools are being activated and used by others.

Although such use of an organization often has no significant impact upon the organization, it can shape the organization and even constitute an unacknowledged or unwitting goal for the organization. Elsewhere, this has been labeled as a "derived goal"—derived from the normal activity of the organization and not essential to that activity.[14] Initially, the Youth Commission wished merely to exist and to provide a polite and

---

[11] An organization powerful in its own right becomes, moreover, like the physician, a generalized wise man wielding influence over a variety of areas. See the example of the American Medical Association mentioned in the next paragraph.

[12] Philip Selznick, *The Organizational Weapon*.

[13] Charles Perrow, "Organizational Prestige, Some Functions and Dysfunctions," *American Journal of Sociology* 66 (1961):335–41.

[14] Charles Perrow, "Organizational Goals," in *International Encyclopedia of the Social Sciences*, rev. ed., ed. David Sills (New York: Crowell-Collier, 1968). *Derived goals* are distinguished from *system goals*, which relate to system characteristics of the organization, such as its emphasis upon growth, stability, risk, etc., and from *product goals*, which relate to the type and characteristics of the goods or services produced, such as the emphasis upon quality, quantity, variety, etc. Derived goals may, in time, become system or product goals.

sympathetic hearing to all agencies. But this was a weak and vulnerable mission in the face of demands from powerful groups, and the uses derived from its existence became the open and acknowledged goals of the commission. This, at least, appears to be the significance of the newspaper report at the end of the third year. The organization was raising funds and hiring a staff and thus would grow in the face of a presumably hostile environment, and it would pursue such services as overseeing the activities of other organizations and conducting and coordinating protective services. The width of its province—matters affecting youth—and the existence and legitimacy of its machinery for investigating, validating, and organizing made it an available organizational weapon and transformed it.

Though its goals were changed by others, it need not be a captive of others. Presumably, among the possible options open to the once reluctant organization, after its third year of existence, is the one of becoming a reasonably viable and powerful central agency in the community, concerned with youth problems, free to utilize other agencies in the environment aggressively, even including the Probate Court.

35

The Structure of Power

The level of social power is frequently tacit. In our everyday lives, we are not aware of how decisions about land and resource utilization affect us. In fact, most of us probably believe that large corporations have little real impact on our personal, informal lives. We take for granted that our surroundings will remain stable enough for us to use our background knowledge. In American society a part of the background knowledge we all assume is the ideology of self-determination. However, at times, something out of the ordinary that calls into question our assumptions about self-determination and the constancy of our surroundings may occur. Such strategic events reveal "the way things really are." Sociologically, these events uncover the arrangement among the decision-making components of the society, isolate who or what actually has power, strips away the façade of individual determination, and shows how this power indirectly and directly affects our daily existence. Harvey Molotch discusses the oil leak in the Santa Barbara harbor, focuses on the chronicle of events surrounding this strategic event, and in the process, describes how the leaking oil leaked information on the structure of power.

Oil in Santa Barbara and Power in America

Harvey Molotch

More than oil leaked from Union Oil's Platform A in the Santa Barbara Channel—a bit of truth about power in America spilled out along with it. It is the thesis of this paper that this technological "accident," like

Reprinted from Harvey Molotch, "Oil in Santa Barbara and Power in America," *Sociological Inquiry* 40 (Winter 1969) by permission of the author and publisher.

This paper was written as Working Paper No. 8, Community and Organization Research Institute, University of California, Santa Barbara. It was delivered at the 1969 Annual Meeting of the American Sociological Association, San Francisco. A shorter version has been published in *Ramparts*, November 1969. The author wishes to thank his wife, Linda Molotch, for her active collaboration and Robert Mallen, reporter for the *Santa Barbara News Press*, for his cooperation and critical comments on an early draft.

all accidents, provides clues to the realities of social structure (in this instance, power arrangements) not otherwise available to the outside observer. Further, it is argued, the response of the aggrieved population (the citizenry of Santa Barbara) provides insight into the more general process which shapes disillusionment and frustration among those who come to closely examine and be injured by existing power arrangements.

A few historical details concerning the case under examination are in order. For over fifteen years, Santa Barbara's political leaders had attempted to prevent despoilation of their coastline by oil drilling on adjacent federal waters. Although they were unsuccessful in blocking eventual oil leasing (in February 1968) of *federal* waters beyond the three-mile limit, they were able to establish a sanctuary within *state* waters (thus foregoing the extraordinary revenues which leases in such areas bring to adjacent localities—e.g., the riches of Long Beach). It was therefore a great irony that the one city which voluntarily exchanged revenue for a pure environment should find itself faced, on January 28, 1969, with a massive eruption of crude oil—an eruption which was, in the end, to cover the entire city coastline (as well as much of Ventura and Santa Barbara County coastline as well) with a thick coat of crude oil. The air was soured for many hundreds of feet inland and the traditional economic base of the region (tourism) was under threat. After ten days of unsuccessful attempts, the runaway well was brought under control, only to be followed by a second eruption on February 12. This fissure was closed on March 3, but was followed by a sustained "seepage" of oil—a leakage which continues, at this writing, to pollute the sea, the air, and the famed local beaches. The oil companies had paid $603,000,000 for their lease rights, and neither they nor the federal government bear any significant legal responsibility toward the localities which these lease rights might endanger.

If the big spill had occurred almost anywhere else (e.g., Lima, Ohio; Lompoc, California), it is likely that the current research opportunity would not have developed. But Santa Barbara is different. Of its seventy thousand residents, a disproportionate number are upper class and upper middle class. They are persons who, having a wide choice of where in the world they might live, have chosen Santa Barbara for its ideal climate, gentle beauty, and sophisticated "culture." Thus a large number of worldly, rich, well-educated persons—individuals with resources, spare time, and contacts with national and international elites—found themselves with a commonly shared disagreeable situation: the pollution of their otherwise near-perfect environment. Santa Barbarans thus possessed none of the "problems" which otherwise are said to inhibit effective community response to external threat: they are not urban villagers (Gans 1962); they are not internally divided and parochial like the Springdalers (Vidich and Bensman 1960); nor emaciated with self-doubt and organizational naiveté as is supposed of the ghetto dwellers. With moral indignation and high self-confidence, they set out to right the wrong so obviously done to them.

Their response was immediate. The stodgy *Santa Barbara News-Press* inaugurated a series of editorials, unique in uncompromising stridency. Under the leadership of a former state senator and a local corporate executive, a community organization was established called "GOO" (Get Oil Out!) which took a militant stand against any and all oil activity in the channel.

In a petition to President Nixon (eventually to gain 110,000 signatures), GOO's position was clearly stated:

> With the seabed filled with fissures in this area, similar disastrous oil operation accidents may be expected. And with one of the largest faults centered in the channel waters, one sizable earthquake could mean possible disaster for the entire channel area. . . .
> Therefore, we the undersigned do call upon the state of California and the Federal Government to promote conservation by:
> 1. Taking immediate action to have present off-shore oil operations cease and desist at once.
> 2. Issuing no further leases in the Santa Barbara Channel.
> 3. Having all oil platforms and rigs removed from this area at the earliest possible date.

The same theme emerged in the hundreds of letters published by the *News-Press* in the weeks to follow and in the positions taken by virtually every local civic and government body. Both in terms of its volume (372 letters published in February alone) and the intensity of the revealed opinions, the flow of letters was hailed by the *News-Press* as "unprecedented." Rallies were held at the beach, GOO petitions were circulated at local shopping centers and sent to friends around the country; a fund-raising dramatic spoof of the oil industry was produced at a local high school. Local artists, playwrights, advertising men, retired executives, and academic specialists from the local campus of the University of California (UCSB) executed special projects appropriate to their areas of expertise.

A GOO strategy emerged for a two-front attack. Local indignation, producing the petition to the president and thousands of letters to key members of Congress and the executive would lead to appropriate legislation. Legal action in the courts against the oil companies and the federal government would have the double effect of recouping some of the financial losses certain to be endured by the local tourist and fishing industries while at the same time serving notice that drilling would be a much less profitable operation than it was supposed to be. Legislation to ban drilling was introduced by Cranston in the U.S. Senate and Teague in the House of Representatives. Joint suits by the city and county of Santa Barbara (later joined by the state) for $1 billion in damages was filed against the oil companies and the federal government.

All of these activities—petitions, rallies, court action, and legislative lobbying—were significant for their similarity in revealing faith in "the system." The tendency was to blame the oil companies. There was a muckraking tone to the Santa Barbara response: oil and the profit-crazy executives of Union Oil were ruining Santa Barbara—but once our national and state leaders became aware of what was going on and were provided with the "facts" of the case, justice would be done.

Indeed, there was good reason for hope. The quick and enthusiastic responses of Teague and Cranston represented a consensus of men otherwise polar opposites in their political behavior: Democrat Cranston was a charter member of the liberal California Democratic Council; Republican Teague was a staunch fiscal and moral conservative (e.g., a strong Vietnam hawk and unrelenting harasser of the local Center for the Study of Democratic Institutions). Their bills, for which there was great optimism, would have had the consequence of effecting a "permanent" ban on drilling in the channel.

But from other quarters there was silence. Santa Barbara's representatives in the state legislature either said nothing or (in later stages) offered minimal support. It took several months for Senator Murphy to introduce congressional legislation (for which he admitted to having little hope) which would have had the consequence of exchanging the oil companies' leases in the channel for comparable leases in the underexploited Elk Hills oil reserve in California's Kern County. Most disappointing of all to Santa Barbarans, Governor Reagan withheld support for proposals which would end the drilling.

As subsequent events unfolded, this seemingly inexplicable silence of the democratically elected representatives began to fall into place as part of a more general problem. American democracy came to be seen as a much more complicated affair than a system in which governmental officials actuate the desires of the "people who elected them" once those desires come to be known. Instead, increasing recognition came to be given to the "all-powerful oil lobby"; to legislators "in the pockets of Oil"; to academicians "bought" by Oil; and to regulatory agencies which lobby for those they are supposed to regulate. In other words, Santa Barbarans became increasingly *ideological,* increasingly *sociological,* and in the words of some observers, increasingly *"radical."*[1] Writing from

---

[1] See the report of Morton Mintz in the June 29, 1969 *Washington Post.* The conjunction of these three attributes is not, in my opinion, coincidental.

his lodgings in the area's most exclusive hotel (the Santa Barbara Biltmore), an irate citizen penned these words in his published letter to the *News-Press:*

> We the people can protest and protest and it means nothing because the industrial and military junta are the country. They tell us, the People, what is good for the oil companies is good for the People. To that I say, Like Hell! . . .
> Profit is their language and the proof of all this is their history (*SBNP*[2] Feb. 26, 1969, p. A-6).

As time wore on, the editorials and letters continued in their bitterness.

The Executive Branch and the Regulatory Agencies: Disillusionment

From the start, Secretary Hickel's actions were regarded with suspicion. His publicized associations with Alaskan oil interests did his reputation no good in Santa Barbara. When, after a halt to drilling (for "review" of procedures) immediately after the initial eruption, Hickel one day later ordered a resumption of drilling and production (even as the oil continued to gush into the channel), the government's response was seen as unbelievingly consistent with conservationists' worst fears. That he backed down within forty-eight hours and ordered a halt to drilling and production was taken as a response to the massive nationwide media play then being given to the Santa Barbara plight and to the citizens' mass outcry just then beginning to reach Washington.

Disenchantment with Hickel and the executive branch also came through less spectacular, less specific, but nevertheless genuine activity. First of all, Hickel's failure to support any of the legislation introduced to halt drilling was seen as an *action* favoring Oil. His remarks on the subject, while often expressing sympathy with Santa Barbarans[3] (and for a while placating local sentiment), were revealed as hypocritical in light of the action not taken. Of further note was the constant attempt by the Interior Department to minimize the extent of damage in Santa Barbara or to hint at possible "compromises" which were seen locally as near-total capitulation to the oil companies.

---

[2] *SBNP* will be used to denote Santa Barbara *News-Press* throughout this paper.
[3] Hickel publicly stated and wrote (personal communication) that the original leasing was a mistake and that he was doing all within discretionary power to solve the problem.

Volume of Oil Spillage

Many specific examples might be cited. An early (and continuing) issue in the oil spill was the *volume* of oil spilling into the channel. The U.S. Geological Survey (administered by Interior), when queried by reporters, broke its silence on the subject with estimates which struck as incredible in Santa Barbara. One of the extraordinary attributes of the Santa Barbara locale is the presence of a technology establishment among the most sophisticated in the country. Several officials of the General Research Corporation (a local R & D firm with experience in marine technology) initiated studies of the oil outflow and announced findings of pollution volume at a "minimum" of tenfold the Interior estimate. Further, General Research provided (and the *News-Press* published) a detailed account of the methods used in making the estimate (Allan 1969). Despite repeated challenges from the press, Interior both refused to alter its estimate or to reveal its method for making estimates. Throughout the crisis, the divergence of the estimates remained at about tenfold.

The "seepage" was estimated by the Geological Survey to have been reduced from 1,260 gallons per day to about 630 gallons. General Research, however, estimated the leakage at the rate of 8,400 gallons per day at the same point in time as Interior's 630 gallon estimate. The lowest estimate of all was provided by an official of the Western Oil and Gas Association in a letter to the *Wall Street Journal.* His estimate: "Probably less than 100 gallons a day" (*SBNP* August 5, 1969, p. A-1).

Damage to Beaches

Still another point of contention was the state of the beaches at varying points in time. The oil companies, through various public relations officials, constantly minimized the actual amount of damage and maximized the effect of Union Oil's cleanup activity. What surprised (and most irritated) the locals was the fact that Interior statements implied the same goal. Thus Hickel referred at a press conference to the "recent" oil spill, providing the impression that the oil spill was over, at a time when freshly erupting oil was continuing to stain local beaches. President Nixon appeared locally to "inspect" the damage to beaches, and Interior arranged for him to land his helicopter on a city beach which had been cleaned thoroughly in the days just before but spared him a closeup of much of the rest of the county shoreline which continued to be covered with a thick coat of crude oil. (The beach visited by Nixon has been oil stained on many occasions subsequent to the president's departure.) Secret servicemen kept the placards and shouts of several hundred demonstrators safely out of presidential viewing or hearing distance.

Continuously, the Oil-and-Interior combine implied the beaches to be restored when Santa Barbarans knew that even a beach which looked clean was by no means restored. The *News-Press* through a comprehensive series of interviews with local and national experts on wildlife and geology made the following points clear:

(1) As long as oil remained on the water and oil continued to leak from beneath the sands, all Santa Barbara beaches were subject to continuous doses of oil—subject only to the vagaries of wind change. Indeed, all through the spill and up to the present point in time, a beach walk is likely to result in tar on the feet. On "bad days" the beaches are unapproachable.

(2) The damage to the "ecological chain" (a concept which has become a household phrase in Santa Barbara) is of unknown proportions. Much study will be necessary to learn the extent of damage.

(3) The continuous alternating natural erosion and building up of beach sands means that "clean" beaches contain layers of oil at various sublevels under the mounting sands; layers which will once again be exposed when the cycle reverses itself and erosion begins anew. Thus, it will take many years for the beaches of Santa Barbara to be completely restored, even if the present seepage is halted and no additional pollution occurs.

Damage to Wildlife

Oil on feathers is ingested by birds; continuous preening thus leads to death. In what local and national authorities called a hopeless task, two bird-cleaning centers were established to cleanse feathers and otherwise administer to damaged wildfowl. (Oil money helped to establish and supply these centers.) Both spokesmen from Oil and the federal government then adopted these centers as sources of "data" on the extent of damage to wildfowl. Thus, the number of dead birds due to pollution was computed on the basis of fatalities at the wildfowl centers.[4] This, of course, is preposterous given the fact that dying birds are provided with very inefficient means of propelling themselves to such designated places. The obviousness of this dramatic understatement of fatalities was never acknowledged by either Oil or Interior —although noted in Santa Barbara.

At least those birds in the hands of local ornithologists could be

---

[4]In a February 7 letter to Union Oil shareholders, Fred Hartley informed them that the bird refuge centers had been "very successful in their efforts." In fact, by April 30, 1969, only 150 birds (of thousands treated) had been returned to the natural habitat as "fully recovered," and the survival rate of birds treated was estimated as a miraculously high (in light of previous experience) twenty percent (cf. *SBNP* April 30, 1969, p. F-3).

confirmed as dead—and this fact could not be disputed by either Oil or Interior. Not so, however, with species whose corpses are more difficult to produce on command. Several observers at the Channel Islands (a national wildlife preserve containing one of the country's largest colonies of sea animals) reported sighting unusually large numbers of dead sea-lion pups—on the oil stained shores of one of the islands. Statement and counterstatement followed with Oil's defenders arguing that the animals were not dead at all—but only appeared inert because they were sleeping. Despite the testimony of staff experts of the local Museum of Natural History and the Museum Scientist of UCSB's Biological Sciences Department that the number of "inert" sea-lion pups was far larger than normal and that field trips had confirmed the deaths, the position of Oil, as also expressed by the Department of the Navy (which administers the stricken island) remained adamant that the sea animals were only sleeping (*Life* June 13, 1969, July 4, 1969). The dramatic beaching of an unusually large number of dead whales on the beaches of northern California—whales which had just completed their migration through the Santa Barbara Channel—was acknowledged but held not to be caused by oil pollution. No direct linkage (or nonlinkage) with oil could be demonstrated by investigating scientists (*San Francisco Chronicle* March 12, 1969, pp. 1–3).

In the end, it was not simply Interior, its U.S. Geological Survey, and the president which either supported or tacitly accepted Oil's public relations tactics. The regulatory agencies at both national and state level, by action, inaction, and implication had the consequence of defending Oil at virtually every turn. Thus, at the outset of the first big blow, as the ocean churned with bubbling oil and gas, the U.S. Coast Guard (which patrols channel waters reguarly) failed to notify local officials of the pollution threat because, in the words of the local commander, "the seriousness of the situation was not apparent until late in the day Tuesday and it was difficult to reach officials after business hours" (*SBNP* January 30, 1969, pp. A-1, 4). Officials ended up hearing of the spill from the *News-Press*.

The Army Corps of Engineers must approve all structures placed on the ocean floor and thus had the discretion to hold public hearings on each application for a permit to build a drilling platform. With the exception of a single *pro forma* ceremony held on a platform erected in 1967, requests for such hearings were never granted. In its most recent handling of these matters (at a point long after the initial eruption and as oil still leaks into the ocean) the Corps changed its criteria for public hearings by restricting written objections to new drilling to "the effects of the proposed exploratory drilling on *navigation or national defense*" (*SBNP* August 17, 1969, pp. A-1, 4). Prior to the spill, effects on *fish and wildlife* were specified by the Army as possible grounds for objection, but at that time such objections, when raised, were more easily dismissed as unfounded.

The Federal Water Pollution Control Administration consistently attempted to understate the amount of damage done to waterfowl by quoting the "hospital dead" as though a reasonable assessment of the net damage. State agencies followed the same pattern. The charge of "industry domination" of state conservation boards was leveled by the state deputy attorney general, Charles O'Brien (*SBNP* February 9, 1969, p. A-6). Thomas Gaines, a Union Oil executive, actually sits as a member on the state agency board most directly connected with the control of pollution in channel waters. In correspondence with complaining citizens, N. B. Livermore, Jr., of the Resources Agency of California, refers to the continuing oil spill as "minor seepage" with "no major long-term effect on the marine ecology." The letter adopts the perspective of Interior and Oil, even though the state was in no way being held culpable for the spill (letter, undated to Joseph Keefe, citizen, University of California, Santa Barbara Library, on file).

With these details under their belts, Santa Barbarans were in a position to understand the sweeping condemnation of the regulatory system as contained in a *News-Press* front page, banner-headlined interview with Rep. Richard D. Ottenger (D–NY), quoted as follows: "And so on down the line. Each agency has a tendency to become the captive of the industry that it is to regulate" (*SBNP* March 1, 1969, p. A-1).

The Congress: Disillusionment

Irritations with Interior were paralleled by frustrations encountered in dealing with the congressional establishment which had the responsibility of holding hearings on ameliorative legislation. A delegation of Santa Barbarans was scheduled to testify in Washington on the Cranston bill. From the questions which congressmen asked of them and the manner in which they were "handled," the delegation could only conclude that the committee was "in the pockets of Oil." As one of the returning delegates put it, the presentation bespoke of "total futility."

At this writing, six months after their introduction, both the Cranston and Teague bills lie buried in committee with little prospect of surfacing. Cranston has softened his bill significantly—requiring only that new drilling be suspended until Congress is convinced that sufficient technological safeguards exist. But to no avail.

Science and Technology: Disillusionment

From the start, part of the shock of the oil spill was that such a thing could happen in a country with such sophisticated technology. The much overworked phrase, "If we can send a man to the moon . . . " was even more overworked in Santa Barbara. When, in years previous, Santa Barbara's elected officials had attempted to halt the original sale of leases, "assurances" were given from Interior that such an "accident" could not occur, given the highly developed state of the art. Not only did it occur, but the original gusher of oil spewed forth completely out of control for ten days and the continuing "seepage" which followed it remains uncontrolled to the present moment, seven months later. That the government would embark upon so massive a drilling program with such unsophisticated technologies was striking indeed.

Further, not only were the technologies inadequate and the plans for stopping a leak, should it occur, nonexistent, but the area in which the drilling took place was known to be ultrahazardous from the outset. That is, drilling was occurring on an ocean bottom known for its extraordinary geological circumstances—porous sands lacking a bedrock "ceiling" capable of containing runaway oil and gas. Thus, the continuing leakage through the sands at various points above the oil reservoir is unstoppable and could have been anticipated with the data *known to all parties involved*.

Another peculiarity of the channel is the fact that it is located in the heart of earthquake activity in that region of the country which, among all regions, is among the very most earthquake prone.[5] Santa Barbarans are now asking what might occur in an earthquake: if pipes on the ocean floor and casings through the ocean bottom should be sheared; the damage done by the Channel's *thousands* of potential producing wells would be devastating to the entire coast of southern California.[6]

Recurrent attempts have been made to ameliorate the continuing seep by placing floating booms around an area of leakage and then having workboats skim off the leakage from within the demaracated area.[7]

---

[5] Cf. "Damaging Earthquakes of the United States through 1966," Fig. 2, National Earthquake Information Center, Environmental Science Services Administration, Coast and Geodetic Survey.

[6] See Interview with Donald Weaver, Professor of Geology, UCSB, *SBNP* Feb. 21, 1969, pp. A-1, 6. (Also, remarks by Professor Donald Runnells, UCSB geologist, *SBNP* Feb. 23, 1969, p. B-2.) Both stress the dangers of faults in the channel, and potential earthquakes.

[7] More recently, plastic tents have been placed on the ocean floor to trap seeping oil; it is being claimed that half the runaway oil is now being trapped in these tents.

Chemical dispersants, of various varieties, have also been tried. But the oil bounces over the sea booms in the choppy waters; the work boats suck up only a drop in the bucket; and the dispersants are effective only when used in quantities which constitute a graver pollution threat than the oil they are designed to eliminate. Cement is poured into suspected fissures in an attempt to seal them up. Oil on beaches is periodically cleaned by dumping straw over the sands and then raking up the straw along with the oil it absorbs.

This striking contrast between the sophistication of the means used to locate and extract oil compared to the primitiveness of the means to control and clean it up was widely noted in Santa Barbara. It is the result of a system which promotes research and development which leads to strategic profitability rather than to social utility. The common sight of men throwing straw on miles of beaches within sight of complex drilling rigs capable of exploiting resources thousands of feet below the ocean's surface made the point clear.

The futility of the cleanup and control efforts was widely noted in Santa Barbara. Secretary Hickel's announcement that the Interior Department was generating new "tough" regulations to control offshore drilling was thus met with great skepticism. The Santa Barbara County Board of Supervisors was invited to "review" these new regulations—and refused to do so in the belief that such participation would be used to provide the fraudulent impression of democratic responsiveness—when, in fact, the relevant decisions had been already made. In previous years when they were fighting against the leasing of the channel, the supervisors had been assured of technological safeguards; now, as the emergency continued, they could witness for themselves the dearth of any means for ending the leakage in the channel. They had also heard the testimony of a high-ranking Interior engineer who, when asked if such safeguards could positively prevent furture spills, explained that "no prudent engineer would ever make such a claim" (*SBNP* February 19, 1969, p. A-1). They also had the testimony of Donald Solanas, a regional supervisor of Interior's U.S. Geological Survey, who had said about the Union Platform eruption:

> I could have had an engineer on that platform 24 hours a day, 7 days a week and he couldn't have prevented the accident.

His "explanation" of the cause of the "accident": "Mother earth broke down on us" (*SBNP* February 28, 1969, p. C-12).

Given these facts, as contained in the remarks of Interior's own spokesmen, combined with testimony and information received from non–Interior personnel, Interior's new regulations and the invitation to the county to participate in making them, could only be a ruse to preface a resumption of drilling. In initiating the county's policy of not responding to Interior's "invitation," a county supervisor explained: "I think we may be falling into a trap" (*SBNP* April 1, 1969).

The very next day, the supervisor's suspicions were confirmed. Interior announced a selective resumption of drilling "to relieve pressures." *(News-Press* letter writers asked if the "pressure" was geological or political.) The new tough regulations were themselves seriously flawed by the fact that most of their provisions specified those measures, such as buoyant booms around platforms, availability of chemical dispersants, etc., which had proven almost totally useless in the current emergency. They fell far short of minimum safety requirements as enumerated by UC Santa Barbara geologist Robert Curry who criticized a previous version of the same regulations as "relatively trivial" and "toothless"[8] (*SBNP* March 5, 1969, p. C-9).

On the other hand, the new regulations did specify that oil companies would henceforth be financially responsible for damages resulting from pollution mishaps. (This had been the de facto reality in the Union case; the company had assumed responsibility for the cleanup and advised stockholders that such costs were covered by "more than adequate" insurance.[9]) The liability requirement has been vociferously condemned by the oil companies—particularly by those firms which have failed to make significant strikes on their channel leases (*SBNP* March 14, 1969). Several of these companies have now entered suit (supported by the ACLU) against the federal government charging that the arbitrary chang-

---

[8] Curry's criticism is as follows:

"These new regulations make no mention at all about in-pipe safety valves to prevent blowouts, or to shut off the flow of oil deep in the well should the oil and gas escape from the drill hole region into a natural fissure at some depth below the wellhead blowout preventers. There is also no requirement for a backup valve in case the required preventer fails to work. Rembember, the runaway well on Union Platform A was equipped with a wellhead blowout preventer. The blowout occurred some 200 [feet] below that device.

"Only one of the new guidelines seems to recognize the possible calamitous results of earthquakes which are inevitable on the western offshore leases. None of the regulations require the minimization of pollution hazards during drilling that may result from a moderate-magnitude, nearby shallow-focus earthquake, seismic sea wave (tsunami) or submarine landslide which could shear off wells below the surface.

"None of the regulations state anything at all about onshore oil and gas storage facilities liable to release their contents into the oceans upon rupture due to an earthquake or seismic sea wave.

"None of the new regulations stipulate that wells must be cased to below a level of geologic hazard, or below a depth of possible open fissures or porous sands, and, as such, none of these changes would have helped the present situation in the Santa Barbara Channel or the almost continuous blowout that has been going on since last year in the Bass Straits off Tasmania, where one also finds porous sands extending all the way up to the sea floor in a tectonically active region—exactly the situation we have here."

[9] Letter from Fred Hartley, President of Union Oil, to "all shareholders," dated February 7, 1969.

ing of lease conditions renders channel exploitation "economically and practically impossible," thus depriving them of rights of due process (*SBNP* April 10, 1969, p. A-1).

The weaknesses of the new regulations came not as a surprise to people who had already adapted to thinking of Oil and the Interior Department as the same source. There was much less preparation for the results of the presidential committee of "distinguished" scientists and engineers (the DuBridge panel) which was to recommend means of eliminating the seepage under Platform A. Given the half-hearted, inexpensive, and primitive attempts by Union Oil to deal with the seepage, feeling ran high that at last the technological sophistication of the nation would be harnessed to solve this particular vexing problem. Instead, the panel—after a two-day session and after hearing testimony from no one not connected with either Oil or Interior—recommended the "solution" of drilling an additional fifty wells under Platform A in order to pump the area dry as quickly as possible. The process would require ten to twenty years, one member of the panel estimated.[10]

The recommendation was severly terse, requiring no more than one and a half pages of type. Despite an immediate local clamor, Interior refused to make public the data or the reasoning behind the recommendations. The information on channel geological conditions was provided by the oil companies; the Geological Survey routinely depends upon the oil industry for the data upon which it makes its "regulatory" decisions. The data, being proprietary, could thus not be released. Totally inexplicable, in light of this "explanation," is Interior's continuing refusal to immediately provide the information, given a recent clearance by Union Oil for public release of all the data. Santa Barbara's local experts have thus been thwarted by the counterarguments of Oil-Interior that "if you had the information we have, you would agree with us."

Science was also having its nonneutral consequences on the other battlefront being waged by Santa Barbarans. The chief deputy attorney general of California, in his April 7 speech to the blue-ribbon Channel City Club of Santa Barbara, complained that the oil industry

> is preventing oil drilling experts from aiding the Attorney General's office in its lawsuits over the Santa Barbara oil spill (*SBNP* Aug. 8, 1969).

---

[10]Robert Curry of the geography department of the University of California, Santa Barbara, warned that such a tactic might in fact accelerate leakage. If, as he thought, the oil reservoirs under the channel are linked, accelerated development of one such reservoir would, through erosion of subterranean linkage channels, accelerate the flow of oil into the reservoir under Platform A, thus adding to the uncontrolled flow of oil through the sands and into the ocean. Curry was not asked to testify by the DuBridge panel.

Complaining that his office has been unable to get assistance from petroleum experts at California universities, the deputy attorney general further stated:

> The university experts all seem to be working on grants from the oil industry. There is an atmosphere of fear. The experts are afraid that if they assist us in our case on behalf of the people of California, they will lose their oil industry grants.

At the Santa Barbara campus of the university, there is little Oil money in evidence, and few, if any, faculty members have entered into proprietary research arrangements with Oil. Petroleum geology and engineering is simply not a local specialty. Yet it is a fact that Oil interests did contact several Santa Barbara faculty members with offers of funds for studies of the ecological effects of the oil spill, with publication rights stipulated by Oil.[11] It is also the case that the Federal Water Pollution Control Administration explicitly requested a UC Santa Barbara botanist to withhold the findings of his study, funded by that agency, on the ecological consequences of the spill (*SBNP* July 29, 1969, p. A-3).

Except for the deputy attorney general's complaint, none of these revelations received any publicity outside of Santa Barbara. But the attorney's allegation became something of a statewide issue. A professor at the Berkeley campus, in his attempt to refute the allegation, actually confirmed it. Wilbur H. Somerton, professor of petroleum engineering, indicated he could not testify against Oil

> because my work depends on good relations with the petroleum industry. My interest is serving the petroleum industry. I view my obligation to the community as supplying it with well-trained petroleum engineers. We train the industry's engineers and they help us. (*SBNP* April 12, 1969, as quoted from a *San Francisco Chronicle* interview.)

Santa Barbara's leaders were incredulous about the whole affair. The question—one which is more often asked by the downtrodden sectors of the society—was asked: "Whose university is this, anyway?" A local executive and GOO leader asked, "If the truth isn't in the universities, where is it?" A conservative member of the state legislature, in

---

[11] Verbal communication from one of the faculty members involved. The kind of "studies" which Oil enjoys is typified by a research conclusion by Professor Wheeler J. North of Cal Tech, who after performing a one week study of the channel ecology under Western Oil and Gas Association sponsorship, determined that it was the California winter floods which caused most of the evident disturbance and that (as quoted from the Association Journal) "Santa Barbara beaches and marine life should be back to normal by summer with no adverse impact on tourism." Summer came with oil on the beaches, birds unreturned, and beach motels with unprecedented vacancies.

a move reminiscent of SDS demands, went so far as to ask an end to all faculty "moonlighting" for industry. In Santa Barbara, the only place where all of this publicity was occurring, there was thus an opportunity for insight into the linkages between knowledge, the university, government and Oil and the resultant nonneutrality of science. The backgrounds of many members of the DuBridge panel were linked publicly to the oil industry. In a line of reasoning usually the handiwork of groups like SDS, a *News-Press* letter writer labeled Dr. DuBridge as a servant of Oil interests because, as a past president of Cal Tech, he would have had to defer to Oil in generating the massive funding which that institution requires. In fact, the relationship was quite direct. Not only has Union Oil been a contributor to Cal Tech, but Fred Hartley (Union's President) is a Cal Tech trustee. The impropriety of such a man as DuBridge serving as the key "scientist" in determining the Santa Barbara outcome seemed more and more obvious.

Taxation and Patriotism: Disillusionment

From Engler's detailed study of the politics of Oil, we learn that the oil companies combat local resistance with arguments that hurt: taxation and patriotism (Engler 1961). They threaten to take their operations elsewhere, thus depriving the locality of taxes and jobs. The more grandiose argument is made that oil is necessary for the national defense; hence, any weakening of "incentives" to discover and produce oil plays into the hands of the enemy.

Santa Barbara, needing money less than most locales and valuing environment more, learned enough to know better. Santa Barbara wanted Oil to leave, but Oil would not. Because the oil is produced in federal waters, only a tiny proportion of Santa Barbara County's budget indirectly comes from oil, and virtually none of the city of Santa Barbara's budget comes from oil. *News-Press* letters and articles disposed of the defense argument with these points: (1) oil companies deliberately limit oil production under geographical quota restrictions designed to maintain the high price of oil by regulating supply; (2) the federal oil import quota (also sponsored by the oil industry) which restricts imports from abroad, weakens the country's defense posture by forcing the nation to exhaust its own finite supply while the Soviets rely on the Middle East; (3) most oil imported into the U.S. comes from relatively dependable sources of South America which foreign wars would not endanger; (4) the next major war will be a nuclear holocaust with possible oil shortages a very low level problem.

Just as an attempt to answer the national defense argument led to conclusions the very opposite of Oil's position, so did a closer examination of the tax argument. For not only did Oil not pay very much in local taxes, Oil also paid very little in *federal* taxes. In another of its front-page editorials the *News-Press* made the facts clear. The combination of the output restrictions, extraordinary tax write-off privileges for drilling expenses, the import quota, and the 27.5 percent depletion allowance, all created an artificially high price of U.S. oil—a price almost double the world market price for the comparable product delivered to comparable U.S. destinations.[12] The combination of incentives available creates a situation where some oil companies pay no taxes whatever during extraordinarily profitable years. In the years 1962–66, Standard of New Jersey paid less than 4 percent of profits in taxes, Standard of California, less than 3 percent, and twenty-two of the largest oil companies paid slightly more than 6 percent (*SBNP* February 16, 1969, p. A-1). It was pointed out again and again to Santa Barbarans that it was this system of subsidy which made the relatively high cost deep-sea exploration and drilling in the channel profitable in the first place. Thus, the citizens of Santa Barbara, as federal taxpayers and fleeced consumers, were subsidizing their own demise. The consequence of such a revelation can only be *infuriating*.

The Mobilization of Bias

The actions of Oil and Interior and the contexts in which such actions took place can be reexamined in terms of their function in diffusing local opposition, disorienting dissenters, and otherwise limiting the scope of issues which are potentially part of public controversies. E. E. Schattschneider (1960, p. 71) has noted:

> All forms of political organization have a bias in favor of the exploitation of some kinds of conflict and the suppression of others

---

[12]Cf. Walter J. Mead, "The Economics of Depletion Allowance," testimony presented to Assembly Revenue and Taxation Committee, California Legislature, June 10, 1969, mimeo; "The System of Government Subsidiaries to the Oil Industry," testimony presented to the U.S. Senate Subcommittee on Antitrust and Monopoly, March 11, 1969. The ostensible purpose of the depletion allowance is to encourage oil companies to explore for new oil reserves. A report to the Treasury Department by Consad Research Corp. concluded that *elimination* of the depletion allowance would decrease oil reserves by only 3 percent. The report advised that more efficient means could be found than a system which causes the government to pay $10 for every $1 in oil added to reserves. (Cf. Leo Rennert, "Oil Industry's Favors," *SBNP* April 27, 1969, pp. A-14, 15 as reprinted from the *Sacramento Bee*.)

because *organization is the mobilization of bias.* Some issues are organized into policies while others are organized out.

Expanding the notion slightly, certain techniques shaping the "mobilization of bias" can be said to have been revealed by the present case study.

1. The Pseudoevent

Boorstin (1962) has described the use of the pseudoevent in a large variety of task accomplishment situations. A pseudoevent occurs when men arrange conditions to simulate a certain kind of event, such that certain prearranged consequences follow as though the actual event had taken place. Several pseudoevents may be cited. *Local participation in decision making.* From the outset it was obvious that national actions, vis-á-vis Oil in Santa Barbara, had as their strategy the freezing out of any local participation in decisions affecting the channel. Thus, when in 1968 the federal government first called for bids on a channel lease, local officials were not even informed. When subsequently queried about the matter, federal officials indicated that the lease which was advertised for bid was just a corrective measure to prevent drainage of a "little old oil pool" on federal property adjacent to a state lease producing for Standard and Humble. This "little old pool" was to draw a high bonus bid of $21,189,000 from a syndicate headed by Phillips (*SBNP* February 9, 1969, p. A-17). Further, local officials were not notified by any government agency in the case of the original oil spill nor (exept after the spill was already widely known) in the case of any of the previous or subsequent more "minor" spills. Perhaps the thrust of the federal government's colonialist attitude toward the local community was contained in an Interior Department engineer's memo written to J. Cordell Moore, assistant secretary of Interior, explaining the policy of refusing public hearings prefatory to drilling: "We preferred not to stir up the natives any more than possible."[13] (The memo was released by Senator Cranston and excerpted on page 1 of the *News-Press.)*

Given this known history, the Santa Barbara County Board of Supervisors refused the call for "participation" in drawing up new "tougher" drilling regulations, precisely because they knew the government had no intention of creating "safe" drilling regulations. They refused to take part in the pseudoevent and thus refused to let the consequences (in this case the appearance of democratic decision making and local assent) of a pseudoevent occur.

[13]Cranston publicly confronted the staff engineer, Eugene Standley, who stated that he could neither confirm nor deny writing the memo. (Cf. *SBNP* March 11, 1969, p. A-1.)

Other attempts at the staging of pseudoevents may be cited. Nixon's "inspection" of the Santa Barbara beachfront was an obvious one. Another series of pseudoevents were the congressional hearings staged by legislators who were, in the words of a local well-to-do lady leader of GOO, "kept men." The locals blew off steam—but the hearing of arguments and the proposing of appropriate legislation based on those arguments (the presumed essence of the congressional hearing as a formal event) certainly did not come off. Many Santa Barbarans had a similar impression of the court hearings regarding the various legal maneuvers against oil drilling; legal proceedings came to be similarly seen as ceremonius arrangements for the accomplishing of tasks not revealed by their formally stated properties.

2. The Creeping Event

A creeping event is, in a sense, the opposite of a pseudoevent. It occurs when something *is* actually taking place, but when the manifest signs of the event are arranged to occur at an inconspicuously gradual and piecemeal pace, thus eliminating some of the consequences which would otherwise follow from the event if it were to be perceived all-at-once to be occurring. Two major creeping events were arranged for the Santa Barbara Channel. Although the great bulk of the bidding for leases in the channel occurred simultaneously, the first lease was, as was made clear earlier, advertised for bid prior to the others and prior to any public announcement of the leasing of the channel. The federal waters' virginity was thus ended with only a whimper. A more salient example of the creeping event is the resumption of production and drilling after Hickel's second moratorium. Authorization to resume *production* on different specific groups of wells occurred on these dates in 1969: February 17, February 21, February 22, and March 3. Authorization to resume *drilling* of various groups of new wells was announced by Interior on these dates in 1969: April 1, June 12, July 2, August 2, and August 16. (This is being written on August 20.) Each time, the resumption was announced as a safety precaution to relieve pressures, until finally on the most recent resumption date, the word "deplete" was used for the first time as the reason for granting permission to drill. There is thus no *particular* point in time in which production and drilling was reauthorized for the channel —and full resumption has still not been officially authorized.

A creeping event has the consequences of diffusing resistance to the event by holding back what journalists call a "time peg" on which to hang "the story." Even if the aggrieved party should get wind that "something is going on," strenuous reaction is inhibited. Nonroutine activity has as its prerequisite the crossing of a certain threshold point of input; the dribbling out of an event has the consequence of making each of the revealed inputs fall below the threshold level necessary for nonroutine activity. By the time it becomes quite clear that "something is going on" both the aggrieved and the sponsors of the creeping event can ask why there should be a response *"now"* when there was none previously to the very same kind of stimulus. In such manner, the aggrieved has resort only to frustration and a gnawing feeling that "events" are sweeping him by.

3. The "Neutrality" of Science and the "Knowledge" Producers

I have already dealt at some length with the disillusionment of Santa Barbarans with the "experts" and the university. After learning for themselves of the collusion between government and Oil and the use of secret science as a prop to that collusion, Santa Barbarans found themselves in the unenviable position of having to demonstrate that science and knowledge were, in fact, not neutral arbiters. They had to demonstrate, by themselves, that continued drilling was not safe, that the "experts" who said it was safe were the hirelings directly or indirectly of Oil interests, and that the report of the DuBridge panel recommending massive drilling was a fraudulent document. They had to document that the university *petroleum* geologists were themselves in league with their adversaries and that knowledge unfavorable to the Oil interests was systematically withheld by virtue of the very structure of the knowledge industry. As the SDS has learned in other contexts, this is no small task. It is a long story to tell, a complicated story to tell, and one which pits lay persons (and a few academic renegades) against a profession and patrons of a profession. An illustration of the difficulties involved may be drawn from very recent history. Seventeen Santa Barbara plaintiffs, represented by the ACLU, sought a temporary injunction against additional channel drilling at least until the information utilized by the DuBridge panel was made public and a hearing could be held. The injunction was not granted, and in the end, the presiding federal judge ruled in favor of what he termed the "expert" opinions available to the secretary of the Interior. It was a function of limited time for rebuttal, the disorienting confusions of courtroom procedures, and also perhaps the desire to not offend the court, that the ACLU lawyer could not make his subtle, complex, and highly controversial case that the "experts" were partisans and that their scientific "findings" follow from that partisanship.

4. Constraints of Communication Media

Just as the courtroom setting was not amenable to a full reproduction of the details surrounding the basis for the ACLU case, so the media in general—through restrictions of time and style—prevent a full airing of the details of the case. A more cynical analysis of the media's inability to make known the Santa Barbara "problem" in its full fidelity might hinge on an allegation that the media are constrained by fear of "pressures" from Oil and its allies; Metromedia, for example, sent a team to Santa Barbara which spent several days documenting, interviewing, and filming for an hour-long program—only to suddenly drop the whole matter due to what is reported by locals in touch with the network to have been "pressures" from Oil. Such blatant interventions aside, however, the problem of full reproduction of the Santa Barbara "news" would remain problematic nonetheless.

News media are notorious for the anecdotal nature of their reporting; even so-called think pieces rarely go beyond a stringing together of proximate "events." There are no analyses of the "mobilization of bias" or linkages of men's actions and their pecuniary interests. Science and learning are assumed to be neutral; regulatory agencies are assumed to function as "watchdogs" for the public. Information to the contrary of these assumptions is treated as exotic exception; in the manner of Drew Pearson columns, exception piles upon exception without intellectual combination, analysis, or ideological synthesis. The complexity of the situation to be reported, the wealth of details needed to support such analyses require more time and effort than journalists have at their command. Their recitation would produce long stories not consistent with space requirements and make-up preferences of newspapers and analogous constraints of the other media. A full telling of the whole story would tax the reader/viewer and would risk boring him.

For these reasons, the rather extensive media coverage of the oil spill centered on a few dramatic moments in its history (e.g., the initial gusher of oil) and a few simple-to-tell "human interest" aspects such as the pathetic deaths of the sea birds struggling along the oil-covered sands. With increasing temporal and geographical distance from the initial spill, national coverage became increasingly rare and increasingly sloppy. Interior statements on the state of the "crisis" were reported without local rejoinders as the newsmen who would have gathered them began leaving the scene. It is to be kept in mind that, relative to other local events, the Santa Barbara spill received extraordinarily extensive national coverage.[14] The point is that this coverage is nevertheless inadequate in both its quality and quantity to adequately inform the American public.

5. The Routinization of Evil

An oft-quoted American cliché is that the news media cover only the "bad" things; the everday world of people going about their business in conformity with American ideas loses out to the coverage of student and ghetto "riots," wars and crime, corruption and sin. The grain of truth in this cliché should not obfuscate the fact that there are *certain kinds of evil* which, partially for reasons cited in the preceding paragraphs, also lose their place in the public media and the public mind. Pollution of the Santa Barbara Channel is now routine; the issue is not whether or not the channel is polluted but *how much* it is polluted. A recent oil slick discovered off a Phillips Platform in the channel was dismissed by an oil company official as a "routine" drilling by-product which was not viewed as "obnoxious." That "about half" of the current oil seeping into the channel is allegedly being recovered is taken as an improvement sufficient to preclude the "outrage" that a big national story would require.

Similarly, the pollution of the "moral environment" becomes routine; politicians are, of course, on the take, in the pockets of Oil, etc. The depletion allowance issue becomes not whether or not such special benefits should exist at all, but rather whether it should be at the level of 20 or 27.5 percent. "Compromises" emerge such as the 24 percent depletion allowance and the new "tough" drilling regulations, which are already being hailed as "victories" for the reformers (*Los Angeles Times* July 14, 1969, p. 17). Like the oil spill itself, the depletion allowance debate becomes buried in its own disorienting detail, its ceremonious pseudoevents and in the triviality of the "solutions" which ultimately come to be considered as the "real" options. Evil is both banal and complicated; both of these attributes contribute to its durability.[15]

The Struggle for the Means to Power

It should (although it does not) go without saying that the parties competing

---

[14]Major magazine coverage occurred in these (and other) national publications: *Time* (February 14, 1969); *Newsweek* (March 3, 1969); *Life* (June 13, 1969); *Saturday Review* (May 10, 1969); *Sierra Club Bulletin; Sports Illustrated* (April 10, 1969). The last three articles cited were written by Santa Barbarans.

[15]The notion of the banality of evil is adapted from the usage of Arendt 1963.

to shape decision-making on oil in Santa Barbara do not have equal access to the means of "mobilizing bias" which this paper has discussed. The same social-structural characteristics which Michels has asserted make for an "iron law of oligarchy" make for, in this case, a series of extraordinary advantages for the Oil-government combine. The ability to create pseudoevents, such as Nixon's Santa Barbara inspection or controls necessary to bring off well-timed creeping events, are not evenly distributed throughout the social structure. Lacking such ready access to media, lacking the ability to stage events at will, lacking a well-integrated system of arrangements for goal attainment (at least in comparison to their adversaries), Santa Barbara's leaders have met with repeated frustrations.

Their response to their relative powerlessness has been analogous to other groups and individuals who, from a similar vantage point, come to see the system up close. They become willing to expand their repertoire of means of influence as their cynicism and bitterness increase concomitantly. Letter writing gives way to demonstrations, demonstrations to civil disobedience. People refuse to participate in "democratic procedures" which are a part of the opposition's event-management strategy. Confrontation politics arise as a means of countering with "events" of one's own, thus providing the media with "stories" which can be simply and energetically told. The lesson is learned that "the power to make a reportable event is . . . the power to make experience" (Boorstin 1962, p. 10).

Rallies were held at local beaches; congressmen and state and national officials were greeted by demonstrations. (Fred Hartley, of Union Oil, inadvertently landed his plane in the midst of one such demonstration, causing a rather ugly name-calling scene to ensue.) A "sail-in" was held one Sunday with a flotilla of local pleasure boats forming a circle around Platform A, each craft bearing large antioil banners. (Months earlier boats coming near the platforms were sprayed by oil personnel with fire hoses.) City-hall meetings were packed with citizens reciting "demands" for immediate and forceful local action.

A city council election in the midst of the crisis resulted in the landslide election of the council's bitterest critic and the defeat of a veteran councilman suspected of having "oil interests." In a rare action, the *News-Press* condemned the local chamber of commerce for accepting oil money for a fraudulent tourist advertising campaign which touted Santa Barbara (including its beaches) as restored to its former beauty. (In the end, references to the beaches were removed from subsequent advertisements, but the oil-financed campaign continued briefly.)

In the meantime, as a *Wall Street Journal* reporter was to observe, "a current of gloom and despair" ran through the ranks of Santa Barbara's militants. The president of Sloan Instruments Corporation, an international R & D firm with headquarters in Santa Barbara, came to comment:

> We are so God-damned frustrated. The whole democratic process seems to be falling apart. Nobody responds to us, and we end up doing things progressively less reasonable. This town is going to blow up if there isn't some reasonable attitude expressed by the federal government—nothing seems to happen except that we lose.

Similarly, a well-to-do widow, during a legal proceeding in Federal District Court in which Santa Barbara was once again "losing," whispered in the author's ear:

> Now I understand why those young people at the university go around throwing things. . . . The individual has no rights at all.

One possible grand strategy for Santa Barbara was outlined by a local public relations man and GOO worker:

> We've got to run the oil men out. The city owns the wharf and the harbor that the company has to use. The city has got to deny its facilities to oil traffic, service boats, cranes and the like. If the city contravenes some federal navigation laws (which such actions would unquestionably involve), to hell with it.
> The only hope to save Santa Barbara is to awaken the nation to the ravishment. That will take public officials who are willing to block oil traffic with their bodies and with police hoses, if necessary. Then federal marshals or federal troops would have to come in. This would pull in the national news media (*SBNP* July 6, 1969, p. 7).

This scenario has thus far not occurred in Santa Barbara, although the use of the wharf by the oil industries has led to certain militant actions. A picket was maintained at the wharf for two weeks, protesting the conversion of the pier from a recreation and tourist facility to a heavy industrial plant for the use of the oil companies.[16] A boycott of other wharf businesses (e.g., two restaurants) was urged. The picket line was led by white, middle-class adults—one of whom had almost won the mayoralty of Santa Barbara in a previous election. Hardly a "radical" or a "militant," this same man was several months later representing his neighborhood protective association in its opposition to the presence of a "Free School" described by this man (somewhat ambivalently) as a "hippie hotel."

Prior to the picketing, a dramatic Easter Sunday confrontation (involving approximately five hundred persons) took place between demon-

---

[16] As a result of local opposition, Union Oil was to subsequently move its operations from the Santa Barbara wharf to a more distant port in Ventura County.

strators and city police. Unexpectedly, as a wharf rally was breaking up, an oil service truck began driving up to the pier to make delivery of casing supplies for oil drilling. There was a spontaneous sit-down in front of the truck. For the first time since the Ku Klux Klan folded in the 1930s, a group of Santa Barbarans (some young, some "hippie," but many hard-working middle-class adults), was publicly taking the law into its own hands. After much lengthy discussion between police, the truck driver, and the demonstrators, the truck was ordered away and the demonstrators remained to rejoice their victory. The following day's *News-Press* editorial, while not supportive of such tactics, found much to excuse—noteworthy, given the paper's long standing *bitter* opposition to similar tactics when exercised by dissident northern blacks or student radicals.

A companion demonstration on the water failed to materialize; a group of Santa Barbarans was to sail to the Union platform and "take it"; choppy seas, however, precluded a landing, causing the would-be conquerors to return to port in failure.

It would be difficult to speculate at this writing what forms Santa Barbara's resistance might take in the future. The veteran *News-Press* reporter who has covered the important oil stories has publicly stated that if the government fails to eliminate both the pollution and its causes "there will, at best be civil disobedience in Santa Barbara and at worst, violence." In fact, talk of "blowing up" the ugly platforms has been recurrent—and is heard in all social circles.

But just as this kind of talk is not completely serious, it is difficult to know the degree to which the other kinds of militant statements are serious. Despite frequent observations of the "radicalization"[17] of Santa Barbara, it is difficult to determine the extent to which the authentic grievances against Oil have generalized to a radical analysis of American society. Certainly an SDS membership campaign among Santa Barbara adults would be a dismal failure. But that is too severe a test. People, especially basically contented people, change their world view only very slowly, if at all. Most Santa Barbarans go about their comfortable lives in the ways they always did; they may even help Ronald Reagan to another term in the state house. But I do conclude that large numbers of persons have been moved, and that they have been moved in the directions of the radical left. They have gained insights into the structure of power in America not possessed by similarly situated persons in other parts of the country. The claim is thus that some Santa Barbarans, especially those with most interest and most information about the oil spill

[17] Cf. Morton Mintz, "Oil Spill 'Radicalizes' a Conservative West Coast City," *Washington Post*, June 29, 1969, pp. C-1, 5.

and its surrounding circumstances, have come to view power in America more intellectually, more analytically, more sociologically—more *radically*—than they did before.

I hold this to be a general sociological response to a series of concomitant circumstances, which can be simply enumerated *(again!)* as follows:

1. Injustice

The powerful are operating in a manner inconsistent with the normatively sanctioned expectations of an aggrieved population. The aggrieved population is deprived of certain felt needs as a result.

2. Information

Those who are unjustly treated are provided with rather complete information regarding this disparity between expectations and actual performances of the powerful. In the present case, that information has been provided to Santa Barbarans (and only to Santa Barbarans) by virtue of their own observations of local physical conditions and by virtue of the unrelenting coverage of the city's newspaper. Hardly a day has gone by since the initial spill that the front page has not carried an oil story; everything the paper can get its hands on is printed. It carries analyses; it makes the connections. As an appropriate result, Oil officials have condemned the paper as a "lousy" and "distorted" publication of "lies."[18]

3. Literacy and Leisure

In order for the information relevant to the injustice to be assimilated in all its infuriating complexity, the aggrieved parties must be, in the larger sense of the terms, literate and leisured. They must have the ability and the time to read, to ponder, and to get upset.

My perspective thus differs from those who would regard the radical response as appropriate to some form or another of social or psychological freak. Radicalism is not a subtle form of mental illness (cf. recent statements of such as Bettelheim) caused by "rapid technological change" or increasing "impersonality" in the modern world; radicals are neither "immature" "underdisciplined," nor "anti-intellectual." Quite the re-

---

[18]Union Oil's public relations director stated: "In all my long career, I have never seen such distorted coverage of a news event as the *Santa Barbara News-Press* has foisted on its readers. It's a lousy newspaper." (*SBNP*, May 28, 1969, p. A-1.)

verse. They are persons who must clearly live under the conditions specified above and who make the most rational (and moral) response, given those circumstances. Thus, radical movements draw their membership disproportionately from the most leisured, intelligent, and informed of the white youth (Flacks 1967) and from the young blacks whose situations are most analogous to these white counterparts.

The Accident as a Research Methodology

If the present research effort has had as its strategy anything pretentious enough to be termed a "methodology," it is the methodology of what could be called "accident research." I define an "accident" as an occasion in which miscalculation leads to the breakdown of customary order. It has as its central characteristic the fact that an event occurs which is, to some large degree, unanticipated by those whose actions caused it to occur. As an event, an accident is thus crucially dissimilar both from the pseudoevent and the creeping event. It differs from the pseudoevent in that it bespeaks of an authentic and an unplanned happening; it differs from the creeping event in its suddenness, its sensation, in the fact that it brings to light a series of preconditions, actions, and consequences all at once. It is "news"—often sensational news. Thresholds are reached; attentions are held.

The accident thus tends to have consequences which are the very opposite of events which are pseudo or creeping. Instead of being a deliberately planned contribution to a purposely developed "social structure" (or, in the jargon of the relevant sociological literature, "decisional outcome"), it has as its consequence the revelation of features of a social system, or of individuals' actions and personalities, which are otherwise deliberately obfuscated by those with the resources to create pseudo- and creeping events. A resultant convenience is that the media, at the point of accident, may come to function as able and persistent research assistants.

At the level of everyday individual behavior, the accident is an important lay methodological resource of gossipers—especially for learning about those possessing the personality and physical resources to shield their private lives from public view. It is thus that the recent Ted Kennedy accident functioned so well for the purpose (perhaps useless) of gaining access to that individual's private routines and private dispositions. An accident such as the recent unprovoked police shooting of a deaf mute on the streets of Los Angeles provides analogous insights into routine police behavior which official records could never reveal. The massive and unprecedented Santa Barbara oil spill has similarly led to important revelations about the structure of power. An accident is thus an important instrument for learning about the lives of the powerful and the features of the social system which they deliberately and quasi-deliberately create. It is available as a research focus for those seeking a comprehensive understanding of the structure of power in America.

Finale

Bachrach and Baratz (1962) have pointed to the plight of the pluralist students of community power who lack any criteria for the inevitable *selecting* of the "key political decisions" which serve as the basis for their research conclusions. I offer accident as a criterion. An accident is not a decision, but it does provide a basis for insight into whole series of decisions and nondecisions, events, and pseudoevents which, taken together, might provide an explanation of the structure of power. Even though the local community is notorious for the increasing triviality of the decisions which occur within it (Schulze 1961, Vidich and Bensman 1958, Mills 1956) accident research at the local level might serve as "micro"-analyses capable of revealing the "second face of power" (Bachrach and Baratz 1962), ordinarily left faceless by traditional community studies which fail to concern themselves with the processes by which bias is mobilized and thus how "issues" rise and fall.

The present effort has been the relatively more difficult one of learning not about community power, but about national power—and the relationship between national and local power. The "findings" highlight the extraordinary intransigence of national institutions in the face of local dissent but more importantly, point to the processes and tactics which undermine that dissent and frustrate and radicalize the dissenters.

The relationship described between Oil, government, and the knowledge industry does not constitute a unique pattern of power in America. All major sectors of the industrial economy lend themselves to the same kind of analysis as Oil in Santa Barbara. Where such analyses have been carried out, the results are analogous in their content and analogous in the outrage which they cause. The nation's defeat in Vietnam, in a sense an accident, has led to analogous revelations about the arms industry and the manner in which American foreign policy is waged.[19] Comparable scrutinies of the agriculture industry, the banking industry, etc., would,

---

[19]I have in mind the exhaustively documented series of articles by I. F. Stone in the *New York Review of Books* over the course of 1968 and 1969, a series made possible, in part, by the outrage of Senator Fulbright and others at the *mistake* of Vietnam.

in my opinion, lead to the same infuriating findings as the Vietnam defeat and the oil spill.

The national media dwell upon only a few accidents at a time. But across the country, in various localities, accidents routinely occur—accidents which can tell much not only about local power but about national power as well. Community power studies typically have resulted in revelations of the "pluralistic" squabbles among local subelites which are stimulated by exogenous interventions (Walton 1968). Accident research at the local level might bring to light the larger societal arrangements which structure the parameters of such local debate. Research at the local level could thus serve as an avenue to knowledge about *national* power. Sociologists should be ready when an accident hits in their neighborhood, and then go to work.

References

Allen, Allan A. 1969. "Santa Barbara Oil Spill." Statement presented to the U. S. Senate Interior Committee, Subcommittee on Minerals, Materials and Fuels, May 20, 1969.

Arendt, Hannah. 1963. *Eichmann in Jerusalem: A Report on the Banality of Evil.* New York: Viking Press.

Bachrach, Peter and Morton Baratz. 1962. "The Two Faces of Power." *American Political Science Review* 57 (December): 947–52.

Boorstin, Daniel J. 1961. *The Image.* New York: Atheneum.

Engler, Robert. 1961. *The Politics of Oil.* New York: Macmillan.

Flacks, Richard. 1967. "The Liberated Generation." *Journal of Social Issues* 22 (December): 521–43.

Gans, Herbert. 1962. *The Urban Villagers.* New York: Free Press of Glencoe.

Mills, C. Wright. 1956. *The Power Elite.* New York: Oxford University Press.

Schattschneider, E.E. 1960. *The Semisovereign People.* New York: Holt, Rinehart and Winston.

Schulze, Robert O. 1961. "The Bifurcation of Power in a Satellite City." In *Community Political Systems,* ed. Morris Janowitz. New York: Free Press of Glencoe, pp. 19–81.

Vidich, Arthur and Joseph Bensman. 1958. *Small Town in Mass Society.* Princeton, N.J.: Princeton University Press.

Walton, John. 1968. "The Vertical Axis of Community Organization and the Structure of Power." In *The Search for Community Power,* ed. Willis D. Hawley and Frederick M. Wirt. Englewood Cliffs, N.J.: Prentice-Hall, pp. 353–67.

PART ELEVEN
Social Change

Sociologists of different theoretical persuasions have proposed ideas about the nature and course of social change. They all begin from the premise that society and its components are not constant. Some feel that the changes are cyclical, others that they depend upon the survival value of particular innovations; still others place emphasis on the impact of technological inventions. No sociologist or social theorist can unerringly predict the future. Either our theories are inadequate or understanding of the past is biased by our current concerns.

Throughout this book the negotiated and transitory nature of social reality has been emphasized. Sometimes explicitly and sometimes implicitly we have discovered that social scenes change, that they do not have the same meanings for all concerned, and that their past is remembered in a variety of different ways. All of this means that directions for the future character of social life are only partially determined by the past. There is always an element of the unanticipated and the invented. However, we can capture the changes in snapshot fashion. We can string our snapshots together, ascertain trends, and even see a past phenomenon unchanged in a new context.

From a descriptive point of view, we must be careful not to interpret and prejudge the future solely in terms of the past and the present. We need to refresh our "innocent" way of looking at the world through the eyes of others so that our own ways of interpreting the world do not blind us to the present as well as the future. We may believe, for example, that the urban community is a lonely, isolated place, filled with desperate, aimless people moving from job to job, job to joblessness, and remain blind to new manifestations of community in the city.

We are members of the society we study, and we understand what we observe as members. Although we attempt to "see" with the newness of an outsider or a newcomer, although we doubt what we see and assume an attitude of "watching and wondering," we may still be influenced by our own preconceptions. When discussing social change, it is of utmost importance to retain our capacity to be surprised. The broad theoretical questions of whether modern society actually results in alienation, whether feelings of community and neighboring occur, are largely outside the scope of the following descriptions. However, as before, we can point out that we need to see the change for what it is in advance of our assessment of it. More critically, we need to retain a posture that allows us to observe and understand what we see.

The following articles describe social scenes in which change has occurred. They help give us a sense of process and time, constant features of all social life. The first article demonstrates that a social process, neighboring, can endure many changes and emerge in an altered yet viable form. The second shows how the history of a single activity reveals many different and often opposing meanings for that activity. The final selection explores attempts to preserve and use the past according to our present definition of the values of items from the past.

36
New Kinds of Neighbors

The meanings we attribute to those who live around us, the actions we expect of them and ourselves, have undergone changes in recent years. Sometimes we think these changes have meant a diminishing of the importance of the neighbor. However, the research reported here indicates that a clear and describable phenomenon of neighboring exists among middle-class males in the American society. These men have rather well-defined notions of what a good and appropriate neighbor is, and these notions are related to other segments of their lives. A change in the meanings of any given aspect of social life does not necessarily imply stress or normlessness. Accurate descriptions of the phenomenon are required in order to assess this question.

The Function of Neighboring for the Middle-Class Male

Ruth Hill Useem, John Useem, and Duane L. Gibson

Introduction

The popular literature on man in a modern urban civilization presents the image of persons divested of enduring social ties, caught between conflicting pressures, and vulnerable to a depersonalized social world. This imagery of man accommodating to a new kind of human environment needs careful appraisal before it can be assumed that structural tensions have a one-to-one relationship with tensions experienced by indi-

Reprinted from *Human Organization* 19 (Summer 1960):68–76, by permission of the authors and the Society for Applied Anthropology.

viduals or that the passing of older norms have left vacuums.

In a society characterized by the nuclear family, high mobility, urban habitats, and subtle types of social stratification, how does a reasonably "normal," successful man put together the varied facets of his life and maintain his equilibrium? To examine this problem, an empirical study was made of the social and cultural resources of contemporary American society which are available to and used by middle-class men in coping with and preventing stress.[1] An earlier report[2] dealt with the stresses and resources in the world of work; the present one is concerned with the patterns of neighboring which have significance for the mental health of the male.

The data for this paper were secured in open-ended interviews with seventy-five men holding middle-management positions within bureaucratic structures, ranging between twenty-five and fifty years of age, currently residing in the Midwest, all having family responsibilities—seventy-four of the seventy-five are married, the one not married has children from a previous marriage residing with him, and seventy of the seventy-five have children. The group is highly mobile both geographically speaking (60 percent have lived in their present neighborhoods less than two years) and occupationally speaking (60 percent have held their present occupational role less than one year, 88 percent less than three years).

In exploring the meaning of their residential areas with the men of the sample, we found some illuminating material on the definition of the neighborhood and neighbors, the cultural norms and principles of neighboring, the ways in which these are resources or sources of stress, the extent to which the neighborhood serves as a network of personal support in lieu of that traditionally supplied by extended kin, and the way in which the neighborhood helps or hinders a man in establishing his self-identity in contemporary life.

Neighbors and Neighborhood: A Distinction

In research on neighborhoods, particularly urban neighborhoods, some confusion has been precipitated by defining neighbors as people who

[1] Supported by a grant from the National Institute of Mental Health, United States Public Health Service, administered by the Social Research Service of the Department of Sociology and Anthropology of Michigan State University.
[2] John and Ruth Useem, "Social Stresses and Resources Among Middle Management Men," in *Patients, Physicians and Illness,* ed. E. Gartly Jaco (Glencoe, Ill.: Free Press, 1958).

live in a neighborhood or, the reverse, that a neighborhood is composed of neighbors.[3] Perhaps this confusion arises from the fact that a rural neighborhood was composed of one's neighbors, but changes in the spatial arrangements of, and social relationships between, people have meant that these terms are no longer coterminous. At any rate, we shall use here the definitions of neighbors and neighborhood which emerge from the data gathered from our sample.

Neighbors, as designated by the men of our sample, are the adult occupants of households in close proximity to themselves. Each man conceived of himself and his wife as the center of his neighbors; and thus those immediately surrounding him are denoted as "my" neighbors, "our" neighbors, or the people living "next to us." Such persons are usually spatially and visibly accessible to the man and his wife. This would imply that, unless there is ecological separation of a small number of home units from other units, each contiguous household in a densely settled area will have an overlapping but slightly different set of neighbors.

Neighborhood is used by our informants in two ways. One is to refer to the locality of one's close neighbors; when so used it is either clear in the context of their discussion, or the term is modified by some adjective such as my "immediate" neighborhood. The second and more common usage is to refer to a geographical area distinguished by the characteristics and style of its inhabitants, including the type and arrangement of their housing. The crucial item in delineating the neighborhood in this sense is not the number of people but the "reputation" of the neighborhood—what it is known for. In the present trend toward large, residential settlements of persons similar in social and economic status and living in homes of comparable size and arrangement, the neighborhood can be composed of thousands of residents and coincide with a section, development, subdivision, school district, political entity, etc.

To keep these two meanings clear, we shall call the first the immediate neighborhood and the second the larger neighborhood, remembering

---

[3]See, for example, Paul Wallin who found that, although the interviewees were instructed to define a neighbor as a person living "within one block in any direction from the block where you live," the sample utilized a more restricted definition of neighbors. Wallin assumed that the interviewees were also restricting the definition of neighborhood. "A Guttman Scale for Measuring Neighborliness," *American Journal of Sociology,* 59 (November 1953):243–246. Peter Mann has helped to clarify this point by observing that: "The people who inhabit [neighborhoods] should therefore be called neighbors, but here, at once, a problem arises. In ordinary conversation, if we refer to our 'neighbors,' we normally mean a small number of people who live very near to us; rarely would we mean from five to ten thousand people living in the same neighborhood unit as ourselves." "The Concept of Neighborliness," *American Journal of Sociology,* 60 (September 1954):163–68.

that for some few who live in an isolated settlement of a few homes, the two senses of neighborhoods may be synonymous.

Neighbors and the larger neighborhood have different although related functions in the lives of the men of our sample, and we shall take them up separately.

Three Aspects of Neighboring with Neighbors

There are three distinguishable but interrelated aspects of neighboring—the cultural norms of neighboring, the overt behavior between neighbors, and the individual's emotional assessment of both the norms and the overt behavior.

By *cultural norms* we shall mean here what Goffman calls "rules of conduct."

> A rule of conduct may be defined as a guide for action, recommended not because it is pleasant, cheap or effective, but because it is suitable or just. . . . Rules of conduct impinge upon the individual in two general ways: directly as *obligations,* establishing how he is morally constrained to conduct himself; indirectly, as *expectations,* establishing how others are morally bound to act in regard to him.[4]

The *overt behavior* between neighbors includes "manifest neighborliness,"[5] that is, behavior which is in keeping with the cultural norms, acts which are in the form of violations of the rules (feuding with one's neighbor, for example, is interaction between neighbors but is not an expression of the rules), and behavior which falls under other rules (for example, close friendships).

The third aspect of neighboring is the *meanings* which both the norms and the overt behavior have for the individual. He may feel satisfaction in his neighboring relationships or he may feel stressed; he may be aware of the norms but dislike conforming to them; he may feel stressed by not being able to conform to the norms, etc. This is an important dimension, for it is only persons who feel stress or experience satisfaction.

---

[4]Erving Goffman, "The Nature of Deference and Demeanor," *American Anthropologist,* 58 (June 1956):473–502. This is a very insightful article, and the authors are indebted to it for a number of provocative leads.

[5]See: Peter Mann, "The Concept of Neighborliness," p. 164. Sylvia Fleis Fava, "Suburbanism as a Way of Life," *American Sociological Review,* 21 (February 1956):34–37, states, "Thus, neighboring is defined operationally as the practice of certain folkways."

We shall try to keep these three threads woven together in the following discussion.

Underlying Principles of Neighboring

There are subcultural variations in the specific content of behavior which is enjoined by the social rules of neighboring, but underlying all these variations are several basic principles which the men recognize implicitly or explicitly as the yardsticks by which overt behavior is assessed.

1. Neighboring should be *categorical.* That is, obligations should be felt towards and certain types of behavior expected from any person who is an instance of the category "neighbor." Persons living close by the individual are classifed as neighbors whether or not close personal interaction, or for that matter any personal interaction, exists. Thus it is possible to say, as the men do, "I just moved in two months ago and have not yet met my neighbors" or "I don't do anything with my neighbors" or "Regardless of who the person is, if he were a close neighbor, I would feel free to ask him for help." Children are not categorized as neighbors because these obligations and expectations are not applied to them; they are classified by some such terms as "my neighbor's children," or the "neighborhood kids." There are cultural rules for children in neighboring relationships, but they are different. Aged parents likewise are not considered neighbors but "my neighbor's parents."

2. Neighboring should be *symmetrical.* Neighboring is presumed to be between persons who are equals—at least in their status capacity of neighbors. Sometimes persons will underplay or overplay their other statuses in order to maintain the fiction that "they are just like their neighbors." One of the men described it thus:

> I'm much better off than my neighbors. I have this big, old house with quite an acreage around it; the other houses around me are nice, new ranch houses; but they're the kind foremen and junior executives just coming up have. They're not younger than me necessarily, but younger in business ways. I am sure there are many people in our neighborhood that *don't know that I make any more money than they do.* They just think he's the guy that gets out and mows his lawn on Sunday afternoon *like everybody else.*

Neighboring should be symmetrical also along sex and age lines. Thus, neighboring occurs male with male, female with female, couple with couple, family with family, or female with young child(ren) with female with young child(ren).[6]

3. Neighboring should be *reciprocal.* This is closely related to the principle of symmetry. To some extent, neighboring relationships are reciprocal to the particular person ("If our neighbor has helped us out, we would do it in turn for him"), but neighboring relations are also reciprocal to persons as instances of the category "neighbor." For example, a person feels obligated to help a neighbor who has a death in the family, whether or not he has had such experience in his own family—"That's just being nice people."

Resource and Stress

When those who categorize each other as neighbors meet the conditions of symmetry and reciprocity, agree on the substantive rules of neighboring, and act overtly in keeping with the rules, patterns of neighboring are resources both for the prevention of and alleviation of stress for the individual.

If, however, the conditions of symmetry and reciprocity do not obtain between those categorized as neighbors, or if there is not agreement between neighbors as to the substantive expectations which they have of each other, or if overt behavior deviates from expectations, or if obligations are fulfilled but are considered onerous, or some combination of these, neighboring precipitates stress in the individual.

On Being a Good Neighbor

The cultural norms of neighboring can be stated in answer to the question, "What is being a good neighbor?" in contrast, say, to being a good friend or a good colleague, etc.

---

[6]The one interesting exception to this mentioned by several of the men was that of a relationship established with a neighbor widower. Such widowers were often included in parties for couples which the men gave and were occasionally invited to family dinners (a rare occurrence with other neighbors). In these cases the relationship was asymmetrical. As we shall see later, close neighborliness is primarily female initiated; and since widowers do not have this avenue of inclusion in the social network, special efforts were made to involve them by social acts not ordinarily expected between neighbors. No mention was made of widows for, if they existed, it is presumed that they were seen when the husband was not present and fell into the category of "female with female" and hence, the husband was not involved.

Emergency Aid

A good neighbor is one who can be *counted on for help in times of crises*. Giving aid in an emergency is one of the most compelling obligations which one has to anyone in the category of neighbor.[7] Ordinarily, however, these obligations are performed "spontaneously" and unthinkingly. The most common of these emergency circumstances are accidents, sudden illnesses, births, deaths, and breakdown of mechanical equipment, particularly automobiles.

Help is limited to *action* (to be sure given in a friendly and sympathetic manner) and is confined to meeting the emergency directly or meeting the ongoing demands of the family (caring for children, preparing food, emergency nursing aid, etc.). It does not involve lending money or giving advice or even knowing all the details of the emergency situation. Sometimes overt aid is not needed, but the neighbor is expected to at least offer to "do something" ("Let me know if there is anything I can do").

However, the actions called for are limited to a period which can be labeled an emergency. If, for example, an illness persists, the neighbor is expected to routinize the need and make arrangements for it. It is alright to push the car once for a neighbor whose car battery is dead, but then it is expected that he will either get it charged or get a new one and not call on his neighbor day after day.

> Assume that something happened, say, to my wife which necessitated hospitalization or something like that. I think the neighbors, *for a matter of a day or two,* would step in and take over the children in a very friendly way *until such time as arrangements could be made,* like having a nurse or a relative come in.

Although the male may receive many benefits, a large share of the actual emergency aid is carried out by the wives. Men will be expected, if they are home, to provide transportation in emergencies, do chores connected with the outside of the house, help repair mechanical appliances, or make arrangements for their repair (e.g., call a plumber if the neighbor husband is out of town and the sewer is stopped up). Most of the aid extended in critical situations, however, is connected with picking up the wife's responsibilities, and this is done by neighbor women. The man, however, feels that if his wife has performed these acts, he in a sense has performed them. As unwittingly stated by one man:

---

[7]This is a reflection of the general cultural pattern found in Western society, and particularly in American society, that proximity to persons involved in critical situations obligates the individual to offer aid. This is quite in contrast to India, where such obligations are not felt to the same extent. Even in the United States, these obligations are not as compelling in urban situations.

If somebody dies in the neighborhood, *we* cook pies, take care of their children, everything else, sure. My wife is very good, to a fault. (Would you say that your wife does most of these things?) What can I do except offer to drive somebody?

Ninety-five percent of the men feel they can depend on their neighbors for emergency aid in unexpected situations which precipitate disruptions in the normal routine of family life. Knowing they can rely on neighbors is an important resource for men who spend the major portion of their daytime hours (and for some, evenings, occasional nights, and weekends) away from their families. Especially is this true for the American family which is separated from extended kin and has in the home for many hours of the day but one adult, the wife, upon whom falls the major share of family responsibilities. In this sense, the pattern of emergency aid is a resource which prevents stress from arising during the time the male is performing his occupational role. He can be at work without having the worry of his family on his mind, and he is less likely to be interrupted in the performance of his occupational duties. The pattern is also a resource which is utilized for the alleviation of stress when it is translated into manifest neighborliness during actual emergencies.

To say that reliance on neighbors is a type of crisis insurance does not mean that men necessarily recognize this function explicitly. People live their culture rather than intellectualize it. As put so aptly by one of the men:

That's a funny thing, you know. I've never thought of neighbors along the lines that you've been questioning me this morning. For example, when my wife was on the verge of going to the hospital, several neighbors came over to volunteer their help. They said that if we were caught in the middle of the night before we could get hold of the nurse, they would come in and take care of things. Four or five neighbors volunteered their help. I said before that I don't do anything with my neighbors, which is true, I don't. But they're very good neighbors, very friendly; and in an emergency I am sure that I could count on them. But I just never thought about it in quite that way before.

There were four cases of men who do not rely on their neighbors in times of crises. Two felt they could but would not want to. One is a man who has members of his wife's extended family residing near them. ("I suppose we could go to our neighbors, but we wouldn't. My wife has a brother in town, and her parents are living here.") The other is a person who feels he could not fulfill the condition of reciprocity. ("I feel I could, but I certainly would not want to. We have young children, and we live in a neighborhood of people much older than ourselves;

and we would not be able to reciprocate.") The other two cases are instances which do not meet the principle of symmetry, for both rent living quarters in immediate neighborhoods of homeowners. One is stressed by this fact, for his wife feels all alone with the children, whereas the other is not stressed, for he is without children and finds anonymous living quite satisfactory. (Those who rented in all-rental or predominantly rental neighborhoods felt they could rely on their neighbors in emergency situations).

Mutual Aid

A good neighbor is one with whom *mutual-aid* patterns can be established. In emergency aid, time is of the essence, and anyone in the category of neighbor can be called upon for help and should be rendered assistance. In mutual aid, time is less imperative, and greater selectivity is exercised in choosing among those persons labeled neighbors as to with which ones mutual-aid patterns are established. In other words, the selection is less categorical, and more emphasis is put upon the relationship being symmetrical and reciprocal to the particular person.

> You can ask them to watch the kids *if you can watch theirs,* get something from the store *if you've done the same for them.* The same things you're willing to do for them, you can ask them to do for you.

With whom mutual-aid patterns can be established and the substantive content of the patterns vary with a number of factors. In general, the lower the socioeconomic status, the earlier the couples are in the family cycle and the newer the neighborhood, the more extensive are the patterns of mutual aid; the higher the socioeconomic status, the later the couples are in the family cycle; and the older the neighborhood, the more the patterns of mutual aid are confined to protecting the property investments of the neighbors.

We are not interested here in delineating the full range of the variations, but several instances will illustrate the point. New neighborhoods of young couples with young children and modest incomes have a number of "do it youself" programs which require the cooperation of more than one man to get the jobs done. The men aid each other in solving their common problems of maintaining homes—painting houses, building garages, seeding lawns, putting in shrubbery, etc.

> There's not a lot of running around together socially, but out there [new suburban development] if one's got a job, we all pitch in and do it together. I've helped them paint the inside of their houses, and they've helped me. When we needed fences, why we all pitched in and put up the fences. If I'm fixing something at the house and

need a little help on it, why I've always gone to them to see if they can give me a hand on it—and they usually do. And it's the same with them. If they've got something they need help on, they come to one or another of us.

All the men with young children who lived in this type of immediate neighborhood mentioned the common mutual aid which went on between their wives with respect to child care, e.g., babysitting for each other.

In contrast with the above are older neighborhoods of higher-income status and people later in the family cycle. In such areas the home and lawn problems either have already been taken care of or the men pay to have such jobs done, and hence, these projects do not become the source of neighborly cooperation. However, they do have mutual-aid patterns of "keeping an eye on" each other's properties, particularly during vacations. This mutual-aid pattern is commonly symbolized by the phrase "the neighbor we leave our key with."

If those who fall into the category of neighbors meet the pinciples of symmetry and reciprocity, mutual aid patterns are established which are a resource for enabling families to fulfill their functions. All but seven of the men have established some mutual-aid patterns with particular neighbors. Four of the seven who did not have any mutual-aid patterns were renters in homeowner areas, two had recently moved into neighborhoods and had not yet established relationships, and in one case both the man and his wife worked and had little interaction with neighbors in any sphere. Only two of those who did not have mutual-aid patterns, however, felt stressed by their absence.

Of the sixty-eight who reported some type of mutual-aid patterns nine still experienced stress because, although they could depend on their neighbors for some things, they could not establish some desired mutual-aid relationship. These fell into two groups—those who were not symmetrically related to any neighbors in the family cycle stage (e.g., a couple with young children none of whose neighbors had young children) or in socioeconomic status (e.g., being considerably above the neighbors in income level and wishing to establish a different set of mutual-aid patterns consonant with that income level).

Borrowing

A good neighbor is one from whom one can *borrow* and to whom one can *lend*. The men gave us little information concerning the borrowing which goes on among women neighbors, although most mentioned that it does exist. For males, borrowing is confined to items connected with male-oriented activities around the home—tools, ladders, lawn equipment—and follows the principles of symmetry and reciprocity; you should not borrow unless you have an equivalent item to lend. For example, if a man in the neighborhood "has everything" and the other men have modest amounts of equipment, borrowing will be between those having modest holdings and not from the man to whom you can lend nothing, for it is impossible to reciprocate.

Items which are borrowed are those for which the person has only one time or occasional use and not things which are required regularly, unless some informal arrangements have been made for the exchange of large items. Items should be returned immediately after their use, and in good condition (perhaps better condition than they were in when borrowed, but at least not worse).

Nothing should be borrowed which, according to the standards of the neighbors, should be within the income bracket of people who live in that type of neighborhood. Paint brushes and lawn mowers are borrowable items in a neighborhood of young people just getting established, but they are not borrowable in established upper-income neighborhoods. If a person cannot afford the equipment that goes with the type of neighborhood in which he is living, the men feel that he shouldn't be living in that neighborhood.

As in emergency aid and mutual aid, borrowing is a resource for meeting family needs—particularly for young couples just establishing their homes. Only four of the men were nonborrowers and all four were renters in predominantly home-owned areas. The most commonly mentioned source of stress for the men in this area was neighbors who broke the rules of borrowing by borrowing too often, too much, and by not returning in good condition. This was not, however, a major source of stress for the men of the sample, for they reported that they took indirect steps to "put a stop to" such borrowing.

Perimeter of Privacy

Good neighbors *respect the privacy of each other.* Around each neighbor there is a perimeter of privacy (having both spatial and psychological dimensions) which should not be invaded. One man states: "We have a very congenial group of neighbors; they mind their own business." What is a neighbor's own business or the zone which is considered inviolable varies with a number of factors of which the most important are male-female, socioeconomic status, stage in the family cycle, stage in the occupational world.

All the men recognized that their neighboring relationships are quite distinct from those of their wives. Although the males spend a small segment of their lives with their neighbors, many of the daytime activities of the distaff side are centered in the neighborhood. Wives are likely to be more personally involved with each other, i.e., their perimeter of privacy is less. The men point out that "there's a lot of stuff going on in the daytime when I'm not there" and "what I talk about [with my neighbors] and what my wife talks about are two different things." When the male comes home, the wife's perimeter of privacy shifts to a family perimeter (e.g., women who visit in each other's homes during the day do not visit each other when the man is at home). "I occasionally see the neighbor lady running out the back door when I walk down the street."

The immediate neighborhood is a major resource to the man to the extent that his wife feels satisfied in her neighboring relationships with other women. The man does not need his neighbors to perform his main occupational task, but women, especially young mothers with young children on modest incomes, do need their neighbors for mutual aid and mutual psychological reinforcement. Female neighbors are expected to fulfill many of the needs of the woman for primary group interaction; if these are not met, the woman is thrown on the husband, and he, in turn, becomes stressed.[8] This may in turn reverberate into his effectiveness on the job, for his energy is not released for concentrating on what he feels is his primary role, nor can he feel relaxed and revitalized when he comes home to a wife unhappy in her neighboring relationships.

Typical of those who feel stress in this area are the following:

> We recently moved, and [my wife's neighboring relationship] is the only sour note in our moving. It didn't bother me particularly to move out of A, but it did my wife, although I had been in A as long as she had been. In fact, for a time I began to think I was being unfair to the point of cruelty because she was very unhappy, and still is, at being separated from a close group of women with whom she was associated.

> Our neighborhood is very old. I think it's one of the things that bothers my wife about living there; there are no young wives in the neighborhood. She puts a lot of pressure on me to take her back to her family [who live in another city] on weekends, and she wants me to try to get a job there so she can be near her family. I don't know what I'm going to do.

To say that the wife's perimeter of privacy is different from the male's does not say, of course, what the male's is. Neighboring between males is primarily an outdoor, daylight activity. In a north temperate

---

[8] Whyte implies that the visiting patterns of new suburbia are extensions of the "organization man"; our data would indicate that these patterns are the outgrowth of the needs of wives and children and the stage in the family cycle, rather than the direct needs of the organization man for self-expression. William H. Whyte, Jr., *The Organization Man*. New York: Doubleday Anchor Books, 1956.

climate, this means that men get together usually on weekends in the late spring, summer, and early fall months when they are performing male-oriented home activities—mowing the yard, gardening, painting, etc.

Although there is some variation by social class, for the male, occupational life and family relationships are sacred; they are within the zone considered private and are not open for conversation with neighbors. Common topics of conversation are those which do not infringe on the privacy of the neighbor and which are thought of as male interests—sports, weather, lawns, cars, house improvements. Rated high as a conversation piece is the "crabgrass," which gets more mention than any other single item.

Most of the contacts between males are made while they are standing up ("we holler across the fence at each other," "when people are out we call people by their first names and windbag with them") although they occasionally may end with a small gathering sitting down together outside "with a bottle of beer." In neighborhoods of young people, the contacts are increased when on mutual-aid projects.

Special note should be made of the significance of containing the man's occupational life within the perimeter of privacy. Confidences are not exchanged in this area, and what the man does at work is "his own business" which should be respected as being private. The higher the person is in his managerial status, the more important it is to segmentalize neighboring relationships from business relationships and the more there is need to make certain that a man's off-work activities do not reverberate into the occupational sphere of his life. For example, the occupational relationship between two men relatively low in an organization might not be seriously affected if they do not get along together or if their wives are feuding with each other in the immediate neighborhood, but for men whose main business is the organizing of men's occupational arrangements, such conflicting roles in the neighborhood might seriously hamper their on-work duties.

And yet the higher the status of the executive, the fewer the appropriate neighborhoods in which he can live and the more likely he is to reside nearer to persons that he contacts in the course of his business world. Especially is this true in smaller cities. For this reason, the restrictions against penetrating the occupational life of one's neighbors are tighter in upper-class neighborhoods than they are in neighborhoods composed of men of lower managerial status—although even here they exist. This taboo applies to the women as well as to the men. Women are expected to not carry tales about their husband's occupational role beyond the confines of the home.

Particularly to be avoided is living next door to —that is, having as a close neighbor—a person with whom one is associated closely in an occupational role.

One further note on the perimeter of privacy. To some extent the psychological privacy is translated into spatial terms. The least private, and hence the area in which one is most accessible to one's neighbors, is the yard surrounding one's house.[9] Entertaining on this semiprivate, semipublic property is considered less an invasion of privacy, and hence less personally involving, than entertaining within the house. At backyard cookouts each family may contribute part of the fare, and in a sense they are entertaining each other on "neighborhood property." The next most accessible spaces are porches and doorsteps. Neighbors will drop by to sit on the porch or stoop who would never drop by to visit in the house.

Similarly, within the house there are different definitions of space privacy. Parties in the recreation room are not as personally involving as are parties in the living section of the house. If a man, for example, has the only recreation room in his immediate neighborhood, this may become the gathering spot for the annual Christmas party; but the neighbors who come do not feel that they have to repay this party, for it is in an area which is defined for this occasion as semineighboring public. Meals at the family dining table constitute an invasion of privacy; and we found no cases where neighbors, when acting in the status capacity of neighbors, exchanged dinners with each other. Bedrooms are never entered by neighbors in the ordinary course of neighboring relationships, although there would be exceptions made in times of crises or emergencies.

Greatest stress in this area of privacy maintenance is found among men who cannot translate their conceptions of privacy into spatial terms. They know that their neighbors know their business even though both they and their neighbors act as though they could not hear or see what went on within the sphere of privacy.

---

[9]There is a cultural variation of this. In southern California, where considerable family living is carried on outside in the patio, the backyard is defined as being as private as the house; and this fact is often recognized by building fences, or walls, or having tall shrubbery which shuts off the backyard from the neighbor. If a person has a right to be in the backyard, then he also has the right to wander on into the contiguous part of the house without knocking. The frontyard, however, is still semipublic. In Western India, the significant perimeter is the wall of the compound which encloses both the front and backyards. If a person has been given permission to invade the privacy of the front gate, then he may step on into the house without indicating that he wishes to invade privacy. In other words, in the Midwest the point of challenge is the front and back doors; in southern California it is the front door and back gate; and in India it is the front and back gate. There have been some changes in the Midwest as greater emphasis has been put on summer living in the backyard, and patterns have not yet jelled as to whether one is or is not accessible to neighbors when eating in the backyard. In many Midwest communities there are prohibitions concerning the height of the fence which can be erected, i.e., the degree to which you can cut off a neighbor from his rights to semipublic living.

Friendly—But Not Friends

Good neighbors are *friendly* with each other—but *they are not friends*. Under certain circumstances, persons who start out in the category of neighbors may shift over to a friends basis; in such cases the perimeter of privacy becomes less—both spatially and emotionally. Friends can "run in " without prearrangements, and more of the personal details of life are exchanged. However, only four of the men had neighbors whom they also counted as friends, and with whom they interacted under another set of norms. The rest mention that their wives count some neighbor women as friends, but that they do not.

What are considered "friendly" relationships? It might be stated thus: immediate neighborhoods composed of children-bound, housebound, couples who are in modest circumstances have a number of friendly social activities which take place within the immediate neighborhood. The higher the socioeconomic status of the neighbors, the later they are in the family cycle, the more likely is the immediate neighborhood to be the place where the family lives as a separate unit and recreational pursuits are pursued outside the immediate neighborhood.[10] The following excerpts serve to illustrate the contrast:

> [*A* lives in a new suburban development of young couples.] I live in a very friendly community. We talk about sports, hunting, fishing, and so forth and attempt to make plans for a hunting trip. Sometimes the men will get together to watch the children while women go off to the movies or have one of their showers. And we talk about homes, naturally. You see, everyone down there has just bought a new home, so they're interested in home furnishings and decorations, and what they're going to do—are they going to build a garage, and what kind of grass are they going to put in, and so forth.
>
> [*B* lives in an older neighborhood of large homes and, as he puts it, the men hold "responsible positions in business or industry or are professional people—doctors and lawyers."] My contacts with my neighbors are coincidental because it so happens I belong to a club that three of our neighbors do. I see them over there quite frequently; but as far as being a real visiting type neighborhood, I don't think we are. People generally stick pretty much to themselves out there.

Children, however, do not stay young and neither do these men

---

[10]Although we do not have any strictly lower-class neighborhoods, evidently this generalization does extend downward. Gottlieb points out that persons in upper-income levels go out of their neighborhoods to cocktail lounges, but lower-class areas have taverns located in their midst and draw their clientele from a restricted geographical area. David Gottlieb, "The Neighborhood Tavern and the Cocktail Lounge: A Study of Class Differences," *American Journal of Sociology* 62, (May 1957):559–63.

remain static in their socioeconomic status. If they move their household as fast as they change their family or socioeconomic status and can, therefore, establish symmetrical and reciprocal friendly relationships with their neighbors, stress does not arise. However, for many of the men of our sample, their occupational mobility (and consequently their expectations for neighborly relationships) outstrips their geographical mobility, and they find themselves with neighbors considerably below themselves. ("I didn't make more income when I went there, but now I am probably more successful than most of the people living there.")

So long as they remain with a particular set of neighbors, there is a strain to be consistent with the norms of the neighbors. ("I have advanced beyond most of them, but I've tried not to let it show or let it interfere.") If the disparity becomes too great, however, and if they no longer wish to maintain the fiction that they are "just like their neighbors," stress does occur.

> I want more room in the house; I want land around it. I suppose there is what you would call snob appeal of wanting to live in a bigger house and in a neighborhood with more people of a comparable income bracket than I'm in now. I bought this house when I was making $200 a month, and it wasn't too ambitious a project. But we have outgrown it financially and socially as well as the physical space.

Tne following instance summarizes some of the changes:

> We had much closer social relationships in the neighborhood we lived in before. When we moved into that neighborhood, we had one youngster and another on the way. Most of the couples that moved in were our same age with youngsters coming along, too. And we were all just getting started on our careers. We formed a very close neighborhood unit. Where we are now we are pretty much on our own. Our oldest girl is fourteen, and most of our neighbors are a different age than we are. We go back for social relationships with our old neighbors; the only thing is that they, like us, no longer live in the old neighborhood. They're scattered all over in different suburbs. Some of them live in other cities, and we may look them up on our vacation, or I'll drop in to see the family if I'm in their city on business.

Other Expectations

Not all rules of neighboring apply to personal interaction. Good neighbors show respect for each other by the *condition in which they keep their property* and the *manner in which they act within their sphere of privacy*. What is expected of neighbors and the obligations felt toward them varies with the reputation which members of the immediate neighborhood wish to maintain, but in any case the rules are both symmetrical and reciprocal. For example, expression of regard for neighbors may take the form of keeping the house in good repair, the lawn mowed, the garage door closed.

Although neighbors are expected to respect the privacy of their neighbors and although what goes on within their family life is their own business, deviations (e.g., bickering spouses, noisy parties, immoral conduct, slovenly housekeeping) from whatever are the norms of the neighbors do become topics of conversation, particularly between women neighbors who in turn relay these items to their husbands.

However, respect for privacy is shown by not openly acknowledging the deviation to the offender himself or herself. Neighbors should not "tell off" a neighbor or call a deviation in behavior to the attention of the deviant directly.[11] The assumption is that the person should be sensitive to the patterns displayed around him and should control his own behavior. It is, in part, because of this rule that the men are quite aware of the occasions on which others deviate from their expectations or on which their own perimeters of privacy are invaded, but they are not similarly aware of the occasions on which their own behavior affronts their neighbors.

A highly sensitive area in the sphere of privacy is child-rearing practices. Theoretically, how neighbors raise their children is "their business," and yet the way in which children are raised does indicate the regard in which you hold your neighbors. Children, particularly of preschool and primary-grade age, within a neighborhood are dependent upon each other for playmates, learn from each other, and set standards for each other.

If neighbors have common patterns of child rearing, neighbors feel reinforced. If, however, they do not, the men experience stress. Typical of the men who feel stressed is the following:

> The thing I don't like about our neighborhood—and frankly I want to move when I can afford a little better, which shouldn't be too long now—is the philosophy of this neighborhood; it's how quick can I get my kid out of school so he can work in the factory and bring in more money. We plan to send our children to college. God

---

[11] It may be that this rule applies only to middle class and above. Lower-class neighbors may be more blunt in their expressions, but we have no data to either affirm or deny this possibility. The rule against calling attention to deviations directly to the deviant is part of a more pervasive American cultural pattern. Students from India studying abroad claimed that the British were quick to tell them when they were not conforming to British customs, but that Americans would neither tell them their faux pas nor explicitly state the cultural rules they were breaking. See Useem and Useem, *The Western-Educated Man in India* (Hinsdale, Ill.: Dryden Press, 1954).

knows we are not snobs, but there has just got to be a feeling of common interest. Those kids are nice and everything, but they get their philosophy from their parents, and it conflicts with the philosophy that ours get from us. There are plenty of areas around here that have more or less areas of mutual interest with us, and we are planning to move.

The Larger Neighborhood

When asked to "describe the neighborhood in which you live," all of the men employed the larger neighborhood as their reference and used one or more of the following items: one-half used a specific name ("X hills," "R subdivison");[12] almost one-half used social class ("upper-middle class" "middle-class") one-third employed some adjective with a class meaning ("good neighborhood," "not fashionable at all," "nice but deteriorating"); one-fourth used price range of homes—particularly if they resided in either a new development or in an upper-income neighborhood ("$8,000 to $10,000 homes," "$20,000 homes and up"); one-fourth indicated the age of the neighborhood ("new development," "older neighborhood"); one-fifth referred to the occupations of the household heads ("hourly rated people," "junior executives," "professional people"); 6 percent referred specifically to the age of residents ("younger couples," "older people"). There was a scattering of responses such as size of lots, availability of public services, degree of ruralness, etc.

It is significant that not one of these men described their neighborhoods in terms which would refer to the tone of interpersonal interaction, e.g., friendly, cooperative, people interesting to talk to, although these terms were employed when referring to neighbors. Larger neighborhood reputation evidently has a different function in the lives of these men than has interpersonal relationships with neighbors.

The reputation of the larger neighborhood which the resident shares indicates to some extent the type of person he is. In American culture, an individual cannot call attention directly to his achievements, but rather must seek our respect indirectly. Self-esteem is built upon a number of facets, and neighborhood reputation is one of these which a man uses to identify himself both to himself and others. He becomes an instance

---

[12]We suspect that an even higher proportion would have used a name to communicate the type of neighborhood in which they lived had the interviewers been from the same city and therefore knowledgeable about the reputation which a name would convey. To be sure, there are some larger neighborhoods without a specific name.

of the reputation which the larger neighborhood has, i.e., he is the type of person who lives in that type of neighborhood. If the man's self-image is consistent with the neighborhood reputation, he gains a sense of satisfaction; if, however, there is disparity between what he would like his self-image to be and the meaning which the neighborhood reputation conveys to others, he feels stressed.

A related aspect of self-image to which the reputation of the larger neighborhood contributes is his conception of himself as a provider for his family. Part of the reputation of the neighborhood is based on the type of services provided for the members—schools, churches, transporation facilities, shopping areas, etc. The man sees himself as the provider of the neighborhood setting, with its attendant facilities for his wife and children.

> I needed a larger house, but there was also a desire to associate with a better neighborhood, although the neighborhood we lived in before was not a low-class neighborhood. There are so many advantages that I could see that the children would get out of the new neighborhood with their associations in school.

New developments of families in the early part of the family cycle witness greater activities for the establishment of neighborhood reputations than do older developments of families with children later in the life cycle.

> We have a small homeowners association down there [suburban new development] which has been set up to try to promote the area and improve it and its relations to the city. We have a parents club in connection with the school, and a number of other very active organizations—all of which are because the neighborhood is new, because there are so many young couples in it.

Generally speaking, the more urban and anonymous the situation, the greater weight the neighborhood reputation has as a symbol of status, for the man has fewer other avenues for gaining respect (i.e., he is not known personally for what he is to others). Also the higher the socio-economic status, the more the man's social activities take place outside the immediate neighborhood, and hence the greater the need for having a neighborhood identity which conveys to people outside the neighborhood the type of person he is. Especially stressed in this area are those who have risen fast occupationally but who have been unable to purchase homes in neighborhoods commensurate with their new status.

The reputation of the larger neighborhood is the setting within which relationships are established with close neighbors—for it is presumed that neighbors will share the characteristics of the larger neighborhood. In this sense, one picks his close neighbors by picking the reputation of the larger neighborhood. Residents of the larger neighborhood are considered somewhat interchangeable, and the assumption is that an individual could live any place in the larger neighborhood and expect to establish comparable neighboring relationships with close neighbors.

None of the organizations in which these men were employed put direct pressure on their people to live in particular neighborhoods. Those lower in occupational status categorically denied that where they lived ("as long as it was decent and respectable") had any relevance for their career. Those higher in occupational status felt that the reputation of their neighborhood was irrelevant for their selection for advancement (which they felt was based solely on their competence on the job), but that *after* they had advanced in the organization there was or would be some informal expectations by others (both those higher and lower than themselves) for them to live in neighborhoods with reputations commensurate with their higher positions. However, the men felt this pressure to move as one which was self-imposed rather than imposed by their organizations.

Résumé and Implications

The analysis of the evidence collected in this field study suggests the need for further empirical work on the functional significance of emergent social groupings in modern American civilization. The findings herein depicted obviously do not hold for other segments of American society or for other societies, but they do invite comparisons to highlight their significance.[13]

1. The *nuclear family* in all societies is dependent upon other social structures for fulfilling its functions of socializing and educating the young, for psychological, social, and economic support of its members. In most societies, a major structure which has been and still is used is the extended kin group, although many other groupings, such as caste and ethnic enclaves, have performed these functions.

The nuclear family of the segment of American society we have under consideration is a small unit without much of the network of social support supplied by extended kin. This lack of kin support is due to a number of factors of which the most important are: a) the wide geographical dispersal of kin (only two of our sample had members of

---

[13]We are indebted to William F. Whyte for a number of pertinent suggestions in this section.

their wives' extended-kin group near enough to call upon for aid—and these two did use this resource); and b) the wide divergence of the men in their occupational status and style of life from other members of their kin—successful, individual upward mobility removes the men not only georgraphically but also socially and psychologically from kin members. The men of the sample reported that they had "little in common" except shared memories of childhood with their fathers, mothers, and siblings.

2. The *self-identity* of this segment of American society stems primarily from the occupational role, and this status position is the pivot for assessing the relevance and appropriateness of extended family, neighbors, schools, churches, friends, and style of life. Viewed worldwide this is a rather unique development, for in societies which are characterized by primary self-identity growing out of family membership, class, or caste status, the work role is chosen or entered into because of its appropriateness for one's family, social class, or caste status rather than the reverse.

Viewed in this light, the residential neighborhood has become, for upwardly mobile men stripped of kin and whose values stem primarily from the work role, the locus for working out the supporting framework for the functioning of their nuclear family and the basis for entrance into other supporting institutions of church, school, clubs, etc. The high preoccupation of the men with the social and status characteristics of their neighbors and neighborhood is understandable, for it stems from their need to have consistency and mutually reinforcing life segments. Residential neighborhoods in other areas of the world which do not serve these purposes also do not precipitate such concern for socioeconomic status on the part of their members. For many neighborhoods in the American South (which include widely divergent social classes) this has become a relatively recent preoccupation since school facilities have been equated with residential areas. In India a major concern with residential living is not socioeconomic class so much as caste or community, for the extended kin is the source of support for "untouchables," Brahmins, Parsees, Anglo-Indians. With the emergence of non-caste-oriented activities and the breaking up of the joint family in India, there are developing in urban centers certain neighborhoods not unlike those described in this paper, although not as yet with as clearly defined cultural norms for interaction.

Residential mobility, so characteristic of this segment of American life, is not then per se a stressful process leading to anomie, as it has sometimes been claimed, but is actually a resource for occupationally upwardly mobile men; for moving enables them to activate the supporting neighborhood functions appropriate for their changing occupational role. If the men can meet the cultural norms of neighboring based on categorical designation, symmetry, and reciprocity, neighbors and neighborhoods become limited but tangible resources; if the men and their families cannot meet these norms, they become a potential source of stress.

The findings of this study indicate that there are social strengths inherent in modern American life which help to sustain the individual and his family in the routine stresses of daily living, and that there are resources built into ordinary social groupings which provide persons with means for coping with and alleviating stresses in a complex world. There have been shifts in functions from one institution to another and the development of new activities to fulfill new needs precipitated by modern urban American civilization.

37
A Changing Social Scene

When people participate in social interaction, they often can recognize meanings and actions that form patterns or configurations. Some sociologists call these patterns *scenes*. Once a scene has been identified, its characteristics and history can be described. Irwin focuses on surfing as one such scene but points out that the processes and stages he relates may be found in any social scene. The four stages of a scene are: (1) articulation, (2) expansion, (3) corruption, and (4) decline. Irwin writes a social history of one scene by providing us with a rich description of the stages for the surfing phenomenon.

Surfing: The Natural History of an Urban Scene
John Irwin

In 1907 an Hawaiian swimmer and surfer traveled to the coast of southern California to introduce surfing—the traditional and royal sport of his ancestors—to the United States. Slowly the sport caught on. At the beginning of World War II, there were about five hundred regular surfers, most belonging to seven surfing clubs in southern Califcrnia. Then the war intervened, and the majority of these surfers were pulled away from their favorite leisure time activity. During and after the war, a new phe-

From *Urban Life and Culture* 2 (1973):131–160. Reprinted by permission. The present report draws upon my M. A. study of surfing, *Surfers: A Study of the Growth of a Deviant Subculture,* University of California, Berkeley, 1962. See also the materials scheduled for publication in Peter K. Manning, editor, *Deviance and Change,* Prentice-Hall, forthcoming, 1973.

nomenon started to grow. Surfing changed from the leisure time activity of athletic, beach-oriented southern California young men into a total, unconventional lifestyle which eventually involved thousands of youths.

The history, like the sport itself, is exciting. But that is not our primary interest here. This history has special sociological interest because it seems to be the prototype of a series of collective movements which have swept through American youth since World Wall II. Surfing was one, perhaps the first and perhaps the archetype, of a series of "scenes" which have taken shape, involved thousands before they soured, then declined. We will be examining this history with the aim of producing a model of scene evolution which will lend understanding to this important contemporary phenomenon.

The Scene

Briefly, the concept of the "scene" refers to a configuration of behavior patterns which is well known to a group of actors. Formerly, in its major folk usage as in the phrase, "make the scene," it referred to the ongoing behavior of some collectivity at a particular location and time.[1] The scene was where the "action" was (Goffman 1967). Presently, it has lost its definite temporal and locational dimensions and refers to a set of patterns followed by some collectivity of actors at various times and locations in their day-to-day routines. In the current folk version, which will concern us here, the scene varies from a set of patterns surrounding a particular component, to a total lifestyle which embraces most facets of the actors' lives. For instance, in a book on contemporary youth culture, Simmons and Winograd refer to the emerging "drug scene."

> The drug scene is a central plaza of happening America. It is the main ring, the granite cornerstone with a bronze plaque, the center of what's happening universe. It is the crossroads for conflicting ideologies [1967, p.86].

They are speaking here of a set of patterns related to a major component in the lives of the contemporary youth. In other uses, such as a news story about a young hippy who, after being given a general discharge from the army, "had come back to California to join up with

---

[1] J. I. Simmons and Barry Winograd (1967, p. 172) have offered a definition of this version of *scene:* "The whole of a setting and the action occurring within it. Includes both the physical setting and psychological mood and refers to the total organism/environment/activity. Is analogous to the scene of a play with props, staging, actors, and script."

The Scene and dabble in mysticism, drugs, and communal living," the term refers to a total lifestyle (Real 1968). Furthermore, as revealed by the capitalization of the scene in this quoted sentence, there are minor scenes, and there is *The Scene,* the latter being generally recognized as the most popular at a particular time.

We must take this popular folk concept and spell out the major dimensions of the phenomenon to which it refers in order to make the concept useful to us. (1) Referring now to *The Scene*—that is, to the dominant genre—the most important distinguishing feature is that it is *explicitly recognized* as a lifestyle by a large group of people. This distinguishes it from other very similar sociological concepts such as "subculture" and "behavior system" which may be entities recognized only by social scientists. (2) Participation in most scenes, and certainly *The Scene,* is *voluntary*. This is strongly suggested in the metaphor and points to an important dimension in the collective phenomenon. People, as they have come to recognize scenes and participate in scenes by their use of the metaphor, indicate that they can participate voluntarily. (3) The scene is a *noninstrumental system.* Though participants may join into collective goal-oriented enterprises, the scene members can and do interact together in an orderly fashion because they share a set of meanings, understandings, and interests and not because they have to cooperate to attain some goal. The source of cohesion, then, is the shared-meaning world or shared patterns of the scene and not goal attainment and other attendant social-system problems. (4) *Commitment* to scenes and especially *The Scene* is highly variable. For some it is a permanent way of life; for others it is a passing fad. (5) The scene supplies its members with an important *identity.* Persons who surf think of themselves and are referred to as surfers. This identity does not refer to their position in some social system, such as an occupational or family role, but to a category in the meaning world, the system of beliefs and values of surfing.

History of the Surfing Scene: Articulation

Members

Surfing passed through four distinct stages: (1) articulation, (2) expansion, (3) corruption, and (4) decline. In the initial stage of any scene—articulation—a group of actors piece together a new lifestyle. For this to occur, a group of persons who share some interest or some activities must have free time and freedom from other commitments. In the case of surfing, this condition developed when World War II swept most of the conventionally oriented surfers away to the armed services or war industry. Consequently, the conventional surfing clubs were disbanded, and the boards, the waves, and the beaches were left to a few younger surfers whose orientations to surfing and society were quite different than that of the older surfers. Many of them were "outsiders" to most groups of youths of their own age. If they went to school (several of them didn't), they did not participate in the high-school social systems. They were, rather, totally committed beach boys who had fastened themselves to the older surfers. The war produced a discontinuity in their socialization into the surfing world. While they were learning the sport and spending most of their time at the beach, they had not been accepted into many facets of the older surfers' lives—such as the club, family, and occupational activities.

Moreover, when World War II ended, it supplied surfing with large numbers of potential members. There were many returning veterans who were not ready to pick up civilian life, which, after the intensity of the war, seemed dull and meaningless. In addition, many civilians were experiencing a letdown and a reluctance to return to the "petty pursuits" of civilian life. Consequently, after 1945, there were multitudes of postwar disaffiliates who turned to unconventional lifestyles, such as the beat life, hot rodding, motorcyclying, *and* surfing.

> When the war ended . . . Boom, we were back in the environment. It was devotion—like seeing a girl again . . . like I'm never gonna leave! Anyway, after the war we plunged into this thing . . . gave ourselves over to it entirely. I think it was because we had spent four or five years in war and we had survived. And it had all been bad. Now there was no question about what had us by the throat. It was the ocean. Everything else was secondary [Rochlan 1964].

Elements

In order for the articulation of a scene to occur, in addition to a group or segment of people who are relatively free from other commitments, there must be some basic material—patterns, forms, traits—out of which a scene may be constructed. In the case of surfing, there were at least two important elements present. First, there was wave riding (as contrasted to "surfing" which refers to a broader configuration of traits and patterns) which served as the focusing activity and the central component in the configuration of patterns which emerged.

Wave Riding. Wave riding was able to serve as a central focus for these postwar disaffiliates and as the foundation of the emerging lifestyle, in part, because the action of wave riding was both exciting and demanding. To understand this, we must examine the mechanics of the sport itself. A wave is ridden by first paddling a surfboard in the direction of the shore and letting the wave catch up to one just when it has become steep enough to cause the board to slide on its face. A certain minimum paddling speed must be achieved to start the sliding movements and then the wave must afford a steep enough surface to keep the board sliding. The wave, as it travels through the open ocean as a ground swell, is not nearly steep enough to offer this type of slope. It only becomes sufficiently steep when it moves into shallow water and the bottom interferes with the normal deep-water wave action. This interference eventually leads to the wave "breaking." The wave becomes ideal for sliding (that is, when it reaches its steepest form) just before it breaks.

At some locations, with the proper swell, the surfer is afforded a minimum time to paddle into the sliding motion, stand up, and turn the board away from the location of the break and start across the face while just staying to one side of the breaking portion of the wave. This is called "making" the wave. The surfer makes the wave when he completes the whole process of getting up, turning to one side of the break, and staying just in front of this break until either the wave "flattens out" or he chooses to pull out of the wave by "kicking out" or "riding out the top." These are the bare essentials of wave riding.

In the early years, just "making the wave," that is, accomplishing the essentials of riding a wave described above, was the central focus of surfing. Making a wave in some locations with certain types of waves requires considerable skill, physical conditioning, and nerve. When the conditions are right, it is intensely exciting and challenging. The challenge is there because of the uncertainty. Each time the surfer "takes off" on a wave, it is uncertain whether he will succeed. A great deal depends on his judgment in selecting a makable wave, on his sense of timing in catching it just in the right spot, and on his skill in board maneuvering. And even with a maximum of these abilities, there are always moments when the outcome is totally uncertain. This type of activity has the capacity for deeply involving many individuals. It is similar to gambling, bullfighting, and other types of "action," where there is some risk to person or reputation (Goffman 1967).

In early surfing, besides repeatedly meeting the recurring challenge of a particular surfing spot, there was the additional constant search for new challenges—that is, new surfing spots which afforded new types, perhaps larger, waves which were more difficult to make.

The Beach. The beach itself was the second basic component that contributed to the articulation of a new lifestyle. The beach in southern California has, for decades, been a location where persons spend enjoyable days engaged in pleasant activities—for example, swimming, sunbathing, and volley ball—and avoid the strains and drudgery of routine urban worlds. Of course, to many it has been no more than a vacation or weekend spot. But to others, and there have always been individuals living this second theme, it has represented a way of life with a slower pace, a life closer to "nature," free from mechanization, responsibilities, commitments, and drudgery. Southern California beaches, like those of the South Seas, have long been a setting for the "beachcomber." Thus, the nonproductive, barefooted, beach-hoboism tradition was already present in southern California beaches and supplied some of the source material for the emerging surfing style.

From these two basic components—wave riding and beach life—the groups of wartime and postwar disaffiliates pieced together an almost total lifestyle which I will refer to as "classical surfing." Two essential dimensions of this period of articulation must be emphasized. First, the involvement of the participants was intense. The early surfers felt strongly that they were engaged in something meaningful and exciting. Second, there was a great deal of experimentation, innovation, and spontaneity. Many surfers were involved in experimenting with new patterns, relationships, and techniques in board design, wave riding, and other activities.

The Meanings and Dimensions of Classical Surfing

Surfing. In the style which emerged, many of the dominant meanings and dimensions were related to the central activity of wave riding. These may be divided into two main clusters. The first was surfing as the challenge—that is, the array of activities and meanings related to finding bigger or more difficult waves and new surfing spots. The search began in California but, soon after World War II, moved back to Hawaii. First a few small groups of surfers made the isand expedition. They rediscovered the north shore of Oahu, where the waves in the winter sometimes reached thirty feet and were considered unsurfable by the contemporary Hawaiians. One by one, spots were discovered where very large waves break. These waves were attempted and finally ridden succesfully by the California explorers. Each year the groups which made the winter trips were more numerous, and the Hawaiians themselves quickly joined the new trend and began riding the larger waves.

The second cluster of meanings related to wave riding itself was "going surfing." Going surfing, besides lots of wave riding, meant hours or days passed on a remote beach away from the "ugliness" of civilized life. The ocean was closely related to the meaning of this aspect of surfing. It was more than just the locus of waves. In part, the waves were merely manifestations of something more profound. It was the ocean that presented a primeval way of life and force—the complete antithesis of a too mechanized, too routinized, too tame civilization that physically ended at its boundaries.

Going surfing, in its more elaborate form, was the surfing expedition—a planned surfing trip which lasted several days or more. It may have been a short trip of a hundred miles or less down the coast to "trestles"—a surfing spot near a railroad trestle south of San Clemente, California—or a trip to the islands for a stay of several weeks or months. Importantly, besides a lot of surf, it promised hours spent at the ocean, perhaps doing nothing but watching others surf, completely away from the conventional "rut."

The expedition fulfilled a very special function in the development of the surfing subculture. Beliefs and symbolic systems that emerge in a given scene do so out of the interaction of the participants in their common activities. In the case of the surfing scene, this process reached its optimum intensity in the surf expedition, with its complex of activities that were "surfing." Camping at some remote beach away from civilization, surfing a maximum number of hours daily, cooking and eating meals at the beach, spending the hours in between surfing, watching, and discussing surfing: all these things were "surfing," condensed into a limited time and space so that the interaction was intense. The surf expedition, therefore, fulfilled a function that is important, if not essential, to all scenes; that is, it supplied the location and the circumstances for the intense interaction between participants that is necessary for the articulation of the scene.[2]

The Surfboard. In the continual search for conditions that presented the recurring challenge and in the surfers' attempts to develop better techniques of wave riding, experimentation with the surfboard was a dominant activity, and most of the core members of the incipient surfing scene were involved in it. What they were trying to develop was a board which would turn and travel faster and would "hang into" a steeper wave—that is, cross diagonally on the face of a steep wave without skipping down its face. As a result of these efforts, the modern surfboard emerged. It was first made of balsa, and then polyurethene foam and covered with fiberglass and synthetic resin. It was much lighter than the older board—twenty to thirty-five pounds as compared to eighty or

[2] This idea was suggested to me by David Matza.

more pounds. It was smaller and had a deep fin—skeg—at the tail which served to keep it travelling in a straight line. There were, and still are, many variations on this basic board design, but all variations have the basic qualities of relative lightness, small size, and the deep fin.

Besides the activities related to board experimentation, securing a board, keeping it in repair, and transporting it were all activities which demanded some of the surfer's time and some alteration in his life routine. Individuals either constructed their own boards, which required craftsmanship and knowledge of materials, or bought new or used boards, which were very scarce. And the surfer had either to own or have access to some vehicle which was capable of transporting the board.

Besides the cluster of activities relative to securing, caring for and transporting the surfboard, the board itself was a very important symbol to the surfer. It was an object of beauty which was decorated in a variety of ways. More importantly, it was the cherished symbol of the surfer's central activity to which he was devoted and which he often displayed quite proudly (on the top of his auto and close to him while he loafed on the beach).

The Beach. The beach was another central theme to the surfer. It and the ocean (the meanings of which were intermixed) had special significance as representations of a natural, primeval force and the location of natural, uncomplicated, responsibility-free existence. Beyond this, the beach was the actual location of the great majority of his activities.

Before, after, or between wave riding, the surfers spent many hours together on the beach, perhaps sitting in the sun, perhaps around a fire, warming up after becoming well chilled in the water. During these periods they talked, usually about surfing. If a group contained some strangers, information was exchanged about experiences, about different surfing spots and different surfers. If others were still in the water surfing, the group on the beach would watch and criticize the rides. On days when there was no surf, surfers still spent many hours on the beach, lying in the sun or beside fires, waiting.

> We used to sit down there at Malibu just looking at each other and asking when it (the surf) was going to come up. We'd even call up Hap Jacobs and ask when the surf was going to come up—he was supposed to know because he made surfboards [Rochlan 1964, p.12].

In addition to spending their days there, surfers very often also slept at the beach, especially when they were on a surfing expedition. Most commonly they slept in an automobile, the station wagon and the panel or pickup truck being especially suited for this function. Sometimes, cars which had been converted to board carriers had also been modified to afford a flat area where a mattress could be thrown. But very often there were more than one or two surfers to each car, and many had to spend the night in sleeping bags on the sand, waiting for the break of day. Many surfers spent long periods, often the entire summer, in this fashion—sleeping in their cars or on the beach, or perhaps on the lawn or floor of a friend's home.

The beach was also the significant determining factor in the surfer's choice of clothes and styles of personal grooming. Through the years, the surfer's dress has been a variation on traditional beach clothing. After the war, light- or dark-blue sailor pants were popular. These would be worn with no shoes and a T-shirt, an Hawaiian flower shirt, or no shirt at all. Later, Bermuda shorts or blue Levi's and T-shirts with no shoes became the style. After 1955, huaraches, tennis shoes, and Mazatlans (sandals from Mazatlan, Mexico) were worn. The hair was grown long and left to hang down, uncombed, on the sides. Beards were common. To some extent, the surfer resembled the beachcomber.

Comedy. Comedy was quite prominent and its major form involved the behavior of the "character."[3] The character is one to whom the qualities of jester or buffoon are imputed and one who accepts this definition. The character role may be assumed purposely by the individual or may merely be imputed to him because of attributes which he is seen to possess but which he did not originally intend to be taken as comical. Further, an individual may either have only limited areas in which his role is that of a character—a few ways that he acts in jest—or his total role may be that of a character. For instance, a surfer may wear a bizarre hat. In doing this, he assumes a little bit of the character properties, although in other regards, he may be more serious. Another may not only wear outlandish clothes but also perform many acts which have the quality of jest. He is a complete character. Both types were replete in surfing.

An incident occurring at a surfing spot in Hermosa Beach provides an example of consciously portrayed character behavior.

---

[3] An analysis of a social type which is related to the "character" appears in an article by Arlene K. Daniels and Richard R. Daniels (1964). The "fool," like the "character," makes fun of conventional norms, but the two types differ in the function they perform for the group and their prestige in the group. The fool serves the function of boundary maintenance. He, through his flaunting of the norms, clarifies for the group some of the ambiguous and conflicting areas in the normative structure. The character wins pleasure for all by flaunting the norms of the group, something all members of the character's own group wish to do. The character, therefore, has much more prestige than the fool.

> I remember one Easter Sunday afternoon I was sitting at 22nd Street in Hermosa, and all of a sudden I heard this congo drum, with somebody screaming "Has the Lord God come to thee?" I looked over the wall an there was Mike Zutell with an eight foot cross and he had his yellow terrycloth bathrobe, he had this beard that looked like the real thing. He had a pair of shades on and a beret and sandals and was carrying a bottle of Thunderbird and he had a loaf of bread in his pocket. He walked down the Strand and stopped at 22nd Street, and he served Communion to us all. People on the beach couldn't believe it [Rochlan 1964, p.16].

Another incident which reflects the character aspect in the routine of a group of surfers was related to me by a surfer. In his words:

> A group of Windansea surfers in about 1953 got Nazi costumes somewhere (SS uniforms with boots, hats, insignias, etc.) and attracted attention to themselves by directing traffic in downtown La Jolla. Following this incident, Nazi salutes, swastikas, and phoney German accents enjoyed a brief popularity throughout the San Diego County surfing community.

The surfing character, then, is a person who makes a spectacle of himself in the eyes of conventional society but remains unashamed and unabashed. When he does this, he is not performing for conventional society (it isn't necessary for outsiders to see the acts, though it becomes more convincing when they do), but for his own reference group who are able to derive from his act a great deal of amusement. Their pleasure comes from seeing him being ridiculous by conventional standards of propriety and not caring.

Expansion

When a configuration of patterns took shape and a relatively cohesive lifestyle began to appear, the expansion of surfing started to accelerate. Immediately after World War II, it was growing at a slow but steady rate, simply because the *sport* was fascinating to youth and young adults who came into contact with it. The numbers coming into contact were not large in the 1940s since most surfing spots were remote and boards were hard to secure; yet some did, and the sport grew steadily. And in the early 1950s, as the scene developed and the modern surfboard appeared, the growth rate increased. The scene now had the added attraction of offering a lifestyle to potential members. Moreover, the new, lighter, and more maneuverable board allowed "beach break" (the type of wave which breaks at sandy beaches) to be ridden, and since most populated beach areas are on sandy beaches, more people were witnessing the sport and the lifestyle. Thus, between 1950 and 1955, more and more surfing was taking place on populated beaches, and more persons saw the sport and the lifestyle and enlisted in the scene.

After 1956, surfing entered a new phase of expansion. Its growth began to accelerate rapidly. Figure 37-1 shows the estimated population growth of surfing.[4]

FIGURE 37-1. Estimated population growth of surfing in southern California, 1945-64

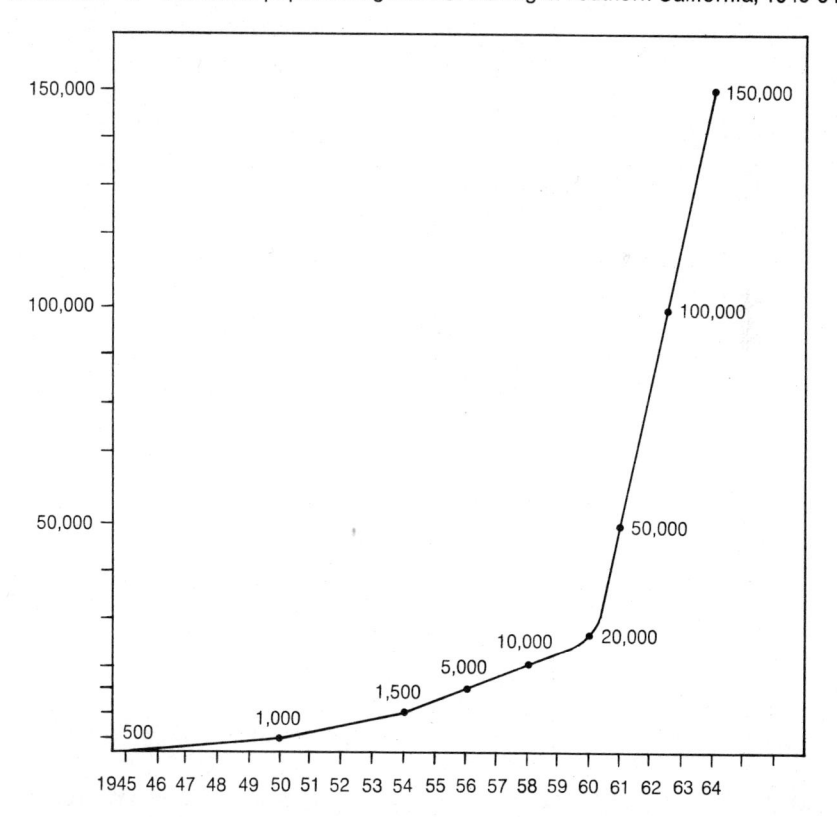

[4]These approximations were made by David Stern, who gathered data on surfing for several years. It must be emphasized that it is impossible to make accurate estimates of the number of surfers at any particular time, and these approximations are crude. However, David Stern did take into consideration the only piece of "hard" data here; the relative number of surfboard sales by some of the major manufacturers.

This rapid acceleration stage was precipitated by the media. Actually, the first media personnel to disseminate information about the scene were a few participants who made surfing films to show to small audiences of fellow surfers. In 1954, one of these rented several high-school auditoriums in the Los Angeles beach areas and showed his latest film, his most ambitious effort, to small audiences of surfers and other interested persons. He made a small profit on this film. Other surfer-filmmakers rapidly followed. The pattern in all these sixteen-millimeter films was the same: color shots of surf in California and Hawaii and a live narration by the filmmaker. The films were shown in rented high-school auditoriums in beach towns from San Diego to San Francisco, before audiences of active surfers, their friends and families, and other youths, mainly of high-school age, who were becoming interested in surfing. Surfing movies became a hit. The audiences and the number of towns in which they were shown grew rapidly.

A large portion of the shots in each film were of a few highly skilled surfers, and these men instantly became well known to the surfing community in general. Some films even featured surfers who had been sent on expeditions to Hawaii by the filmmaker for the specific purpose of filming them at various spots. Thus, each film tended to generate a small group of celebrities for the growing population of surfers. It now became possible for many youths to receive the same recognition and admiration for surfing that had previously been available only to the high-school football team. This added to its appeal.

In their propagation of surfing, "amateur" films were greatly assisted by a Hollywood production, *Gidget* (1957), which was a story of a young girl's summer experiences with the surfers at Malibu, California. Also at this time several newspaper and magazine articles about surfing appeared and added to the growing interest in the sport.

In the summer of 1960, one of the filmmakers introduced the first surfing magazine—*The Surfer*—and this was quickly followed in succeeding years by *Surfing Illustrated* (Winter 1962), *Surf Guide* (Summer 1963), and *Petersen's Surfing Magazine* (December 1963). These magazines carried on the work of spreading surfing to even more initiates. The magazines in fact reached an even wider audience than the "amateur" movies, since they were sold in all parts of the United States, including the Midwest.

The movies and magazines not only spread interest in the sport, they also began an initial inculcation into the patterns of surfing. This was accomplished in the films by the running commentary of the live narrator, who used the surfing argot and described surfing patterns to the audiences. Furthermore, most of the movies filled in breaks between surfing shots with comedy skits which revealed some of the dimensions of the surfer's perspective. The magazines imparted surfing patterns in jokes, in the descriptions of the surfing world in captions accompanying pictures, and in editorials and stories.

The appearance of surfing music added yet another facet to the media contribution to the growth of surfing. Surfing music had its roots in the surfing films. As a background to the films, producers dubbed in recorded music of various types—for example, classical, jazz, rock and roll, and folk. However, rock and roll, and folk music, with a heavy use of electric guitars, seemed best suited to enhancing the visual sequences. This music, then, became associated with surfing, and several rock and roll musicians in southern California quickly converted their style to catch the growing surfing trend. They emphasized electric guitars, wrote songs with surfing themes, and labeled themselves surfing bands. The phenomenon caught on in 1962 and 1963, and surfing music became popular throughout the United States. This in turn accelerated even more the growing interest in surfing.

A second factor which greatly accelerated the expansion of surfing in Southern California was surfing's relationship to the existing social organization of the adolescent community. Typically, the first surfers from any high school were from a particular section of the high-school social system. This system in Los Angeles, according to a description of Herman and Julia Schwendinger (1962), tended to have three strata. There were youths of the upper stratum who were the most popular in the system and who were labeled "soshes," from their "socializing" behavior; youths of a middle stratum who had patterns similar to the soshes, but who were excluded from most of their activities and were considered to be less popular and less prestigious; and finally, youths of the lower stratum who were variously labeled "bads," "vatos," and "esses." For the most part, the Mexican-American youths were in this stratum. Blacks, however, tended to have an independent system with their own three strata. The Japanese were integrated into the central system with members at all strata. (These were [and are] the only significant racial and ethnic contingents in the area.) There was also a residual category of youths, the "outsiders," who appeared to be quite a large proportion of the youths of any given high school, but who did not participate or occupy a position in the social system.

Without entering into a complete description, for the purposes of this paper, let me point out the following salient features of this system. First, the criteria for establishing a position in these strata was largely "popularity," that is, how well known, liked, and respected one was.[5] The proportional sizes of each stratum of a single social system located

---

[5]James Coleman, in his study of nine high schools in Illinois, discovered social systems which have important similarities to the systems described by the Schwendingers, Coleman found an elite group, which he labeled "the leading crowd" and which had criteria of admission similar to systems discovered by the Schwendingers (Coleman 1962).

at a particular high school varied, as did the clarity of the boundaries between the categories and the degree of crystalization of the system. These variables are related to the class and ethnic composition of the community where the high school is located. The group which possessed the least amount of the prestige was typically the intermediate strata. This group was oriented toward the high-sosh group but did not have the attributes for success in it.

Surfing penetrated this system by first enlisting a few low-status members, either outsiders or low soshes. These persons formed a small cohesive and visible group who insulated themselves from the particular high-school system. Surfing offered them an identity to embrace and to hold up to the other dominant identities of the system—the soshes and the bads—and a chance to display many of the attributes that were admired at both levels such as courage and physical prowess. The alienation from the high-school system of the first high-school-age surfers is revealed in the following statement of an early surfing style setter:

> When I went to school, damn near everything was organized. Little-league baseball, stoop-tag, the three major sports . . . everything was concocted around the buddy system. They never left you alone. But with surfing I could go to the beach and not have [to] depend on anybody. I could take a wave and forget about it [Dora, 1963, p.7].

Typically, after surfing achieved a small foothold in any high school, it rapidly enlisted a large proportion of the intermediate stratum. Surfing gave them a new identity within the high-school social system. They developed a degree of cohesion similar to that of the soshes and the bads. Like them, the surfer in the high-school social system had a uniform and special spots on and around the campus that were his "hangouts." At many schools the "surfers" came into conflict with the lower stratum, whom they labeled "hodadies" or hodads," since the latter felt pressured by these former "nobodies," "weirdos," and "rejects," who were now making claims to some importance.

The surfing identity, however, since it had the prestigious advantage of receiving increasing recognition, approval, and disapproval from the greater community, tended to win out in some high schools. It not only enveloped the entire intermediate stratum but chipped away at the lower and upper strata. And in some schools, surfers became the dominant group.

The most important effect of the penetration of surfing into the high-school social system was the swelling of the surfing population in a very short period. Up to a certain point in its progress in a given teenage community, surfing only nibbled steadily at the potential population. But once it had become recognized in the greater community and once the high school surfers had reached a certain number and were identified as a prestigious group, in a matter of weeks (usually the first weeks of summer when the whole school was becoming increasingly beach minded), the number of youths who identified themselves with the surfing group multiplied rapidly.

Corruption

As surfing expanded rapidly, the influx of new members precipitated its corruption: by first increasing competitiveness and invidiousness in the relationships between surfers; by then smothering the spontaneity and experimentation which had been an important aspect of the behavior of the earlier surfers; by initiating a period of bizarre deviant behavior which brought reaction from the greater community and curtailment of surfing activities; and finally, by resulting in the dilution or disappearance of the original surfing patterns.

This sequence of corruption began when surfers began viewing newcomers to their scene as nuisances and threats and openly defining them as unwelcome pariahs. This negative perception of the newcomer first emerged because increased numbers of surfers were becoming a very real problem. Ideally, only one surfer should ride each wave (two, if the wave can be ridden in both directions, left and right). When there are over a few surfers, say five or six at a surfing spot, surfing becomes more dangerous and less enjoyable. Furthermore, beginning surfers were seen as particularly bothersome and dangerous, since they got in the way and frequently lost their surfboards—the major source of danger in surfing. Consequently, from 1958 on, a growing disapproval of newcomers characterized surfing. Beginners were labeled "kooks," connoting lack of skill, stupidity, and complete repulsiveness.

The rapid influx and the derogation of the newcomer enhanced the already intense competitiveness and invidiousness in surfing. Surfing had already become somewhat competitive because of the emphasis on skill. Wave-riding styles, which were steadily improving, shifted from "making waves" to "hot dogging," a surfing style characterized by sharp turns, "walking," "nose riding," and other radical maneuvers. Status in the scene was established entirely on the basis of surfing skill. This single status criteria had been greatly advanced by the surfing films with their creation of surfing celebrities.

The competitiveness and invidiousness were intensified as it became harder to maintain a known position in the surfing world. When the scene was small, most surfers knew one another, or at least most surfers in a given locale knew one another and knew each other's position in the surfing skill hierarchy. But when, in a short period of time, thousands of surfers poured into a particular locale, a surfer often or usually found himself among strangers. He had to prove his rightful position over and over again. This alone enhanced the invidiousness.

The loss of community and the derogation of the flood of newcomers resulted in a period of extreme competition for legitimacy in the scene. Surfing skill was a sure way to prove this. But, as noted, it often had to be proven over and over again. Demonstration of other scene patterns —use of the argot, the physical accoutrements, and the grooming styles— were another way. Except for the few well-known, highly skilled surfers, however, everyone's authenticity was problematic.

Concern over one's own authenticity in a mushrooming scene served to stifle spontaneity and experimentation on the part of most scene members. For those for whom both authenticity as an actual member and relative status position were problematic, it was unsafe to take a chance and experiment with new patterns. It was much safer to learn carefully which particular patterns were "authentic" and follow these. Of course, there never is consensus on patterns in any scene, and attempting to locate the central patterns is a never ending and somewhat impossible task. But it was seen as better to keep trying and play it safe, than to be spontaneous and risk being viewed as unauthentic or even a kook. Only the secure leaders of the scene could introduce new patterns. Then when introduced, most others followed. The scene became conformist, unspontaneous, and highly invidious.

Conspicuous Display

The invidiousness, the competition, and the derogation of the newcomer led to the corruption of the scene in an even more radical manner. Newcomers, drawn to the scene because of its intrinsic appeal, because of their search for alternate, prestigious lifestyles or for whatever reasons, discovered that they were pariah "kooks" simply because they were newcomers. The desire to become authentic, therefore, was intense. To become fully authentic, however, meant acquiring considerable surfing skill and this required at least a year of hard work. A year or two is a long time as a pariah, and many searched for means to usurp authenticity. They did this by attempting to learn the other attributes of the scene quickly and display them conspicuously. Even this is difficult, since some of the patterns of the scene, such as the full surfing perspective, took a considerable time to master. But this did not deter them. Many newcomers, in an attempt to establish their authenticity, made considerable effort to display immediately what they thought were the scene attributes. This resulted in the surfing scene taking a radical turn towards the bizarre and deviant. The process here is interesting and has been repeated in other scenes; so let us examine it closely.

The newcomer approached the scene from the audience. Most of his information about the scene had come through the media and other secondhand sources. He had not had the close contact with the authentic scene members or the experiences which were required to know the scene—that is, to know its perspective and its more subtle authentic patterns. The information about the scene carried to the audience, especially by the media, was biased in the direction of the deviant and bizarre, because mundane, routine, and conventional matters do not make good news. Furthermore, outsiders to surfing had recently discovered some activities which were seen as undesirable and unconventional. Some of these were perfectly "conventional" activities when performed in the remote surfing spots, but when surfing moved to the city—that is, to populated beach fronts—were out of place. For instance, in the remote spots, surfers were very careless about changing their clothes and were nude while changing from street clothes to swim suit or the reverse. Such "carelessness" on a large scale on a public beach has a more "deviant" connotation. Likewise, fire building on remote beaches is quite normal but on a public beach, perhaps in front of an expensive home, is minimally a nuisance and, at times, illegal. Surfers' parties were much like any youth party. The surfers drank, made noise, and occasionally seduced girls. But when their numbers multiplied and the parties occurred more frequently and in populated beach towns, it appeared from the outside that there was one continual debauch. Thus, the image of surfing which formed in the minds of the conventional community and was conveyed in the media was characterized by deviance and abandon. And this was the image which was fresh in the minds of newcomers as they entered surfing and which generated the behavior patterns which they displayed conspicuously and which, in so doing, they carried to new extremes.

In this way, the spirit of the irresponsible, untrammeled, uncomplicated life of surfing was converted by newcomers, in their rush for "authenticity," to the spirit of complete abandon, or more accurately stated, to the spirit of conspicuous display of abandon, characterized by the purposive staging of abandon to an external audience—the outer community. The trend spread throughout the ranks of the surfers and a great many surfing patterns during this period were largely determined by a purposive desire to display disregard for the standards of conduct of the conventional society. There is a twist here on the former deviations of surfers, these being determined by other factors and only incidentally resulting in disregard for standards of conduct. In a way the purposive abandon was an extension of the comic aspects of much of the surfers' former activities, but it was now directed toward the outgroup and was more expressive of antagonism toward it although its comic quality was still very strong.

For instance, many forms of exhibitionism evolved first because of their power to amuse the surfers, and only secondly because of their ability to antagonize the audience and therefore display abandon. A story which is typical of many stories that were circulated and enjoyed immensely by the surfing community in this period involves a small group on a morning surfing excursion to Malibu Colony. This surfing spot is located in front of a row expensive view-homes, and the surfers, in a hurry to get into the water, took off their clothes and started putting on their trunks. A middle-aged woman yelled from the balcony of one of the homes above for them to stop displaying themselves in such a manner. The surfers stopped putting on their trunks long enough to yell "get fucked" and other vulgarities and shake their penes at the lady, after which they continued to dress for surfing and proceeded into the water. The lady called the police, but when they arrived, there were many surfers in the water, and identification was impossible.

A unique and bizarre maneuver, which became prevalent in this phase—the "brown eye"—had the qualities of conspicuous display of abandon. The maneuver was a variation on a surfing move, the head dip. The latter was done by bending in the middle while facing the walled section of a wave being crossed. The "brown-eye head dip" was accomplished by pulling the swim trunks down while bending over, revealing one's backside to those on shore. The "brown eye" was carried out of the water and became a common act in public places. In 1959 and 1960 in the beach towns in the Los Angeles area, cars passing by with a youth's bare posterior framed in the side window were a common sight.

As mentioned before, the building of fires also took on a quality of display of abandon. Not only did the surfers start fires on beaches where fires were not permitted, they also burnt almost any material in the area. For instance, many picket fences around houses near surfing locations served as fire wood. Several shacks near remote surfing spots were burned. Likewise, lifeguard stands and the pilings of a railroad trestle were lighted but put out before the trestle was burned.

Parties became notorious for their abandon. Extreme drunkenness, sexual promiscuity, fighting, and physical damage to the houses were the marks of a good surfing party.[6]

---

[6]For a good description of a surfing party after the corruption of surfing see Tom Wolfe (1968, p. 31).

Styles of personal grooming were another important aspect of this display of abandon. Extremely long hair, old oversized suits and overcoats, oversized surfing trunks, and other passing fads of dress all had, besides the comic strain, a strong strain of abandon.

Another trait, one that reveals more antagonism than most of the others, became quite common in surfing. This was the use of Nazi symbols, which became popular in the Los Angeles area after they were introduced in a series of comedy breaks in a surfing movie. In the movie, between shots of wave riding, scenes of German soldiers marching and then a comedy skit with surfers dressed as German soldiers were shown. Soon after this, the Nazi symbols started appearing in the surfing groups. There were surf boards with large swastikas painted on them, and many swastikas painted on cars, walls, and flat surfaces near surfing spots. Next, swastika and iron cross amulets appeared. No surfer that I have questioned has indicated any clear knowledge of the significance of the symbols in the historical context of Nazi Germany or any commitment to an ideology related to fascism. It seems likely that the symbols became important to the surfers merely because they had great potential to antagonize outsiders and further express the surfers' attitude of alienation toward conventional norms.

The promiscuous female appeared in surfing at this time. Formerly, female surfers were mostly confined to girl friends of surfers (which wasn't really a role in surfing but part of the surfers' other roles), or a female beach athlete who participated in the sport as a sport. In the phase of consicuous display of abandon, female surfers or at times non-surfers attached themselves to the group and participated in the deviant activities of the surfers. These females were often sexually promiscuous, and the ones that actually surfed matched the males in the deviant acts in and out of the water. They invented the "bare tittie" to match the "brown eye," that is, the removal of the bathing-suit tops while riding the waves. Some of them became notorious for their public executions of "brown eyes" as well.

Another deviant activity which arose in this phase was thievery. The first manifestation of this was shoplifting in markets. Surfers have big appetites and not much money, and shoplifting, as many a small grocer located near a surfing spot could testify, became a trademark. While thievery was not a direct expression of effrontery, it certainly had an element of this in it, and the attitude of abandon undoubtedly facilitated or justified stealing for the surfers.

Surfboard stealing was the next form of thievery to emerge. For the most part this was carried on by youths who had backgrounds in organized stealing and who turned to surfboards when they recognized the profit potential in them. Surfers did steal surfboards but not to the degree that such activity can be considered typical among them.

During the early 1960s, the abandoned character of surfing behavior, ironically, became the trademark of surfing to the greater community, especially in Los Angeles and San Diego County. For the majority of the population, the surfer was just another type of delinquent. Where shortly before it was unknown, it was now well-known for its bizarre and abandoned behavior.

Decline

From 1960 on, surfing grew so fast that the original scene could not maintain its integrity. First it became more and more competitive and invidious, stifling the inventiveness, the spontaneity of the scene. Then, because of the reaction of the newcomers to disparagement, it became increasingly bizarre and abandoned. Finally, the influx of newcomers was so great that it lost the distinctness of its original patterns entirely. New members came in too rapidly to acquire more than a semblance of the scene characteristics. Surfing became peopled almost entirely by "pseudosurfers," that is, surfers who were viewed by more permanent members of the scene as phonies who had neither knowledge nor commitment to the classical patterns of surfing and who were involved mainly because it was the "in" thing. For all intents and purposes, the original surfing style passed away shortly after 1960, even before its period of greatest size. This is probably true of all scenes; that is, the patterns of the original scene virtually disappear while it is still growing. In the case of surfing the "pseudos" took over and surfing was quite different for several years.

The "Pseudosurfer"

Essentially, the "pseudosurfer" was the high-school youth described earlier, who embraced surfing as an identification relative to his particular high-school social system. Surfing as an activity had only secondary importance to him. In fact, it was very often the case that he never actually did any surfing. He became a "surfer" by associating himself with the surfing group in his high school and by displaying the identifying dress—tennis shoes, huaraches, white T-shirts, Pendleton shirts, white Levi's, and long hair (perhaps peroxided), left to fall down on the sides and just brushed back slightly so as to keep it out of the eyes.

This category of surfer varied somewhat from high school to high school, since he was much more strongly oriented to his high-school set than to the surfing community and drew heavily in the patterns of its system. From the high schools that had a large lower stratum, a large proportion of "hodads" were drawn into surfing and a rougher-hewn surfer emerged. He was labeled "grub" or "hodad" surfer by those of his contemporaries who were trying to outlive their unruly past. The "hodad surfer" kept up the activities of conspicuous display of abandon, and added several traits of his own. One of these was more systematic stealing, such as stealing off beach blankets while sun bathers were in the water or had gone after food. Another trait unique to the "hodad surfer" was fighting. Surfers had previously rarely engaged in fights, but among the "hodad surfers," emerging as they did from a group which valued it, fighting was common.

Residues

After 1964 the number of surfers, pseudo- and otherwise, started declining rapidly. Many old-time surfers dropped out because of the corruption of the scene. The pseudos left because their numbers became so great and their image as phonies so widespread that surfing ceased to be prestige-winning for high-school youths. Moreover, another scene—the hippie scene—was emerging and started winning away many of the members of the same segments who were drawn into surfing.

Though it died as *The Scene,* surfing did not pass away completely. It deposited important residues which will remain for many years. It left the sport of wave riding advanced to a high level of sophistication. In addition, many of the nonsurfing patterns diffused into other youth scenes. The long hair of the surfers was one source of the hippie hair style. Surfing music was a link to acid rock. And the casual dress, the nomadism, and the antiemployment patterns of surfing influenced the hippie scene.

Besides the residual patterns, there were residual surfers. Many of the more serious surfers during the period of corruption and decline tried to counter the dominant trends by establishing formal organizations. The clubs which had been important before World War II returned in the early 1960s. In 1963 one surfing magazine listed sixty-five clubs in California. In 1961 a group of older "serious" surfers organized the United States Surfing Association. Their purpose was to improve the conduct of surfers and the image of the sport. By 1963 the membership of the USSA had reached three thousand.

The clubs and the larger organization enhanced a growing contest phenomenon in surfing. There had been "paddle board" contests before World War II, and after the war, yearly contests were held at Makaha in Hawaii. In 1959 the first postwar California contest was held at Huntington Beach. From then on, the contests proliferated, stimulated by the growing organizational structure. The effect of this was to create a large number of "professional" surfers and their followers who are committed to surfing as an organized, competitive sport, somewhat like bowling and golf.

Another important residue is a large and perhaps still growing group of surfers who yet cling to old surfing patterns. This group became quite small after 1962 but has grown since. Of course, the excitement, the vitality of a new emerging lifestyle is missing. However, wave riding is still exciting and surfing remains a way to turn one's back on conventional society. Furthermore, there are occasional new developments in wave riding which ingest some of the old excitement, such as a recent radical change in the size of the surfboard—from an average of ten feet to an average of six feet—and a change in wave riding emphasis—from "nose riding" and "trimming" to "total involvement," a style which entails turning more and riding closer to the broken part of the wave. This new tendency is more than just a change of emphasis in wave riding, however. The notion of total involvement "splashes" over into other areas and actually reflects a renewed commitment and involvement in surfing. So it appears that classical surfing is experiencing a small resurgence, a new-classical phase.

Summary

The processes which shaped the various stages of surfing were not unique to surfing but seem to be found in the organization and growth of any "scene." In the first stage, in the articulation of the scene, a group of actors, usually at some definite location where frequent face-to-face interaction occurs, fit together a set of components into a new subcultural configuration. This configuration involves a perspective and patterns for behaving which make up a relatively total world view and lifestyle. For this to occur, two conditions must exist. One, there must be a lull in the lives of the group of actors. That is, they must have relative freedom from commitment to other perspectives and lifestyles and freedom from time commitments to other activities. Secondly, there must be some focusing interest or interests and the basic components out of which to construct the lifestyle and the perspective. If these are present and the articulation occurs, there is a period of intense activity, experimentation, and spontaneity, when the scene actors are caught up in the excitement of the new emerging lifestyle.

The second stage, expansion, is precipitated by the discovery of the scene by outsiders. If the scene has appeal, that is, if it offers a somewhat cohesive and total lifestyle which has some intrinsic excitement and perhaps special excitement to some audience, it will begin to draw in new members. This process may be greatly accelerated by the atttention of the media, who in recent years have found unconventional walks of life highly salable journalistic items.

When the scene is highly publicized and begins to grow, the influx of new members generates change. First, it increases competition and invidiousness because growth brings loss of security of one's position in the scene. Second, the influx is seen as threatening to the activities of the oldtimers, and the newcomers are defined as undesirable, low-status persons, thus increasing the anxiety relative to most members' positions in the scene and further increasing competition and invidiousness. Third, some of the influx of newcomers, in trying rapidly to establish their authenticity, display conspicuously what they believe to be dominant scene attributes. Usually, however, these are the most bizarre elements learned only through media presentations, and as a result the scene veers towards the bizarre and deviant. Self-consciousness over authenticity stifles experimentation and spontaneity. Most members feel compelled to play it safe and follow the leaders in changes of patterns. The scene becomes extremely conformist in nature with a few leader style setters and many insecure followers.

Finally, the influx of the new members is so great that the central patterns, meanings, and understandings of the scene cannot be maintained. The scene becomes diluted, splintered, and distorted. Most of the members are only peripherally affiliated and are seen as "phonies," "pseudos," or "plastics." Many of the older members drop out or at least withdraw temporarily. The exterior conception of the scene changes from appreciation, with some concern over deviance and bizarreness, to recognition of its corruption and loss of authenticity and finally, to vehement derogation. And in the end, even the late arrivals, who are no longer able to earn prestige by membership in a scene which is now viewed as defunct and who were never immersed enough in its actual patterns to learn to enjoy it, drop out.

References

Coleman, J. 1962. *The Adolescent Society.* New York: Free Press.
Daniels, A. K. and R. Daniels. 1964."The Social Function of the Career Fool." *Psychiatry* (August): 219–29.

Dora, M. 1963. "Mickey Dora, the Angry Young Man of Surfing." *Surf Guide* (October).

Goffman, E. 1967. "Where the Action Is." In *Interactional Ritual*. Garden City, N.Y.: Doubleday.

Real, J. 1968. Article in San Francisco Chronicle (November 9): 8.

Rochlan, D., Jr. 1964. "Malibu, of Characters and Waves." *Surf Guide* (November).

Schwendinger, H. and J. Schwendinger. 1962. "The Insiders and the Outsiders." (Unpublished).

Simmons, J. I. and B. Winograd. 1967. *It's Happening*. Santa Barbara, Calif.: Marc-Laird.

Wolfe, T. 1968. *The Pump House Gang*. New York: Farrar, Strauss and Giroux.

38
Modern Reasons For Preserving the Past

Social change has impact on the entire structure of the society. It affects the personal lives of the members of the society. The modern society is characterized by change. Each new model of a car, a refrigerator, or even a can opener introduces "improvements" intended to change last year's version into an outmoded, undesirable item. Individuals must cope constantly with new, imposed meanings for everyday materials with which they live. One way of coping, one way of preserving an idealized and personally meaningful account of the past, is to collect the outmoded relics of an era. In this way the collector appreciates history and at the same time uses it for his own purposes. Armin Sebran tells us of three such types of persons.

Fear and Loathing in the Mass Society: The Strategic Negotiation of Social Change

Armin Sebran

We are standing behind a corrugated steel barrier at a demolition site. A caterpillar-orange utility van is parked in the roped-off street intersection. Atop the van a loudspeaker booms: "Five minutes from zero-hour and counting. All unauthorized personnel must leave the area or remain at their own hazard." We do not move. We look at the massive brick and granite train station sitting like some giant roller-coaster dinosaur

This article was written especially for this volume.

in the middle of a tar pit that has been dug around it. The train doesn't stop here anymore.

"Spectators please clear Grand Street," drones the electronified voice. A siren begins to wail. "10-9-8-7-6-5-4-3-2-1-zero. Destruct." There is an explosion. Nothing seems to happen. Then the earth begins to tremble. The terminal shudders, vibrates, and shatters. She's coming down. "It took eighteen seconds," says the next day's newspaper account. Smoke and rubble crumble into Grand Street. The siren slows to a stop. It is amazingly still and quiet. Nobody talks; nobody even whispers. There is an uneasiness in the crowd.

A little man sneaks inside the barricade. He picks up a brick from the debris. He looks at the brick and brushes the dust away. The brick has a date etched onto it: 1933. He touches the brick, and a tear runs from his eye. He tucks the brick beneath his coat and walks hurriedly to his car, looking back only once to see what can no longer be seen. He tells himself: "Don't look back." He drives off Grand Street, and we lose him in the distance. Who is he? He is a collector. What is he? A man on the street collecting the markers of social change.

In this study a typology is used as a technique for describing the relationship between social change and its impact on persons and groups. We focus on change in the mass society. Change in the mass society is continual, a major feature of the society itself. Every technological innovation, every new machine or new device, renders the one it replaces obsolete and, therefore, "useless." The reason for the item is determined by the technological use to which it is put. When the thing no longer has such a use, it becomes a collectible item.

The collector is the topic of this study. His life revolves around the task of deciding the meaning of rapid and sometimes incomprehensible change. Change intrudes upon his life, and he sees it as a force that must be reckoned with. He is a consumer in the mass society, but he does not simply respond to the meanings of objects imposed by the technological mode of production. He constructs his own meanings for objects that have lost their original use. He works within existing milieus, but his own being has its special form.

Collectors can be typed according to their motives for collecting. These motives may range from monetary gain to metaphysical ideals of the value of the past. There are many collectors and many motives for collecting. In this article three are described: the true collector, the collector as decorator, and the collector as camp vampire. This typology is based on a collection of motives and behaviors. It will in time become lifeless and archaic. For the moment, it will serve us and we will define its use-value.

The True Collector

The motive that defines the possible courses of action for the authentic collector is his desire to complete a set of objects. Collecting and filling in his set of objects is a driving passion with this type of person. In the course of this enterprise, he may have other motives that determine what is relevant about the object and his plan for it. He may want to be the progenitor of the object to succeeding generations. He may wish to preserve and guard these artifacts against damage and destruction. The true collector will use these objects to structure his sense of presence in the world of his contemporaries or in the world of his predecessors—a world from which he has been alienated by the continuous passage of time.

The collector is a consumer. The items chosen for collection tend to be mass-produced articles whose use-value has been altered by technological change and time. Their scarcity is due to loss of numbers and by damage to their quality. The true collector does not collect a one-of-a-kind object because he cannot create or recapitulate its origin and history. There is little available social knowledge distributed through the culture concerning items that are unique. The collector provides a social history for the mass-produced article as it moves through time from one milieu to another, from one meaning context to another as its value is redefined. Collected objects move through history like immigrants moving from rural Europe to New York City, becoming strangers to their origins. They are like technological refugees. The collector gives the wandering object a home among others of its kind.

The collector, to some extent, may want to enhance himself publicly by the use of these objects as prestige items. The true collector, however, is not concerned with such status motives except in a marginal way. It is the completion of a set, the collection of a realm that means everything to him. It is this quest that legitimizes the buying, spending, traveling, searching, bargaining, scrounging, and badgering necessary to complete his set. It is a slow and demanding process, with each acquisition adding an increased urgency to the task. In the collecting game the collector utilizes a logic of completeness and scarcity. He uses the logic of completeness in ordering his plan to fill in the set. "I have got to get that one to finish this series!" He uses the logic of scarcity in determining his methods, priorities, allocation of resources, and timing in achieving his goal of completion.

The true collector is very much involved with his objects. He acts to preserve their integrity and to prevent any changes from their original form, content, or physical condition. He will order the objects, count them, list and describe them for his records, and correspond with others who collect or have knowledge about the objects. He thinks of himself as a professional, seeking out and gaining expertise about the handling, care, rarity, scarcity, and monetary value of the objects. He is a competent member of the world of collectors. He takes special interest in the quality and detail of his find. He draws on theories about its mode of production; he knows the tales, folklore, and scandals that are involved in the history of the object. When the collector finds the artifact, it is not ordered; it is out of place and time. As a part of his collection, the object again will be placed within its proper context.

In this age the collector is most of all a mass man. The importance of his life, of his social and work product, is tiny in terms of the imposed relevance of a technological era and the programmed anonymity of a homogenized culture. He seeks to establish his unique presence, to acquire a personalized looking glass in which he can find and place himself in the universe. The true collector sees simplicity in the world. A part of him wishes to return to an earlier time of romanticized simplicity—the reconstructed world of his parents or grandparents—but he is not naive to historical reality. He understands something of the destruction and violence of the past and present. He knows how the objects he collects have come to be merely artifacts, shadows, hollow forms, so he celebrates their origins. His politics aside, as a collector he is a conservative. He challenges the world to surrender that which it has taken from him; he will guard it and conserve it.

Portrait of a True Collector

It is 1:30 A.M. There is a single, glaring bulb shining out from the chrome pedestal lamp above the round, oak dining table. The table is covered with obscure pamphlets, tabloid-sized newspapers consisting solely of ads upon ads, mimeographed lists, handprinted lists, magic markers, felt-tip pens. There is a green depression glass ashtray with a cigarette burning its way down to the filter; the air is thick with smoke. A vintage drugstore fountain glass bearing the familiar Coca-Cola logo is filled with Coca-Cola. Occasionally, he takes a break to go to the refrigerator and pour another glass of Coke. The Coke glass has a good feel to it; it is more rightly American than any other glass.

To the outsider the piles of papers covering the table appear undecipherable. They can't be found in the average bookstore or on the magazine rack. They won't arrive at the mailbox with book club offers and junk mail. Yet these papers are a map to America, an America that the collector knows has vanished and that in some ways he wishes could be reborn.

The pages of the newspapers are filled with numbers in columns with still other columns with abbreviations, codes, and special titles:

      Shadow V.1, #8   Fn. 12.00

      G. Lantern 77   mint 1.25

      Uncl. Scrooge 6   vg 4.50

More books and pamphlets are stacked around the room. Their covers display elaborately designed art work. Inside are illustration panels taken from popular stories from the "Golden Age" of comics. The tales are fantasies drawn from the culture's stocks of knowledge: funny animals and bug-eyed monsters, jungle thrills, deeds of valor, swords and sorcery, gun molls and gangsters, super heroes, super villains, front line combat, backstage romance, spaceships, men from Mars, and horror—crypts of horror, tombs of horror, vaults of horror. Other pamphlets and tabloids are filled with commentaries, analyses, original stories, and reports regarding this four-color world of fantasy and adventure. The collector reads them all. These publications give him information about where he can obtain more tabloids, pamphlets, and most of all—clues to the discovery of his wanted treasure: the prized comic book.

He is a comic collector, a comic-book fan. He knows the history of the industry, its captains and creators, and what kind of changes in the industry will affect the quality and quantity of the materials he collects. He knows more about this wonder of mass production than the average man knows about the auto industry when he buys a car. The collector explains that the creation of a comic book is a team effort, depending on the skills of the editor, the writer, the penciller, the inker, the layout man, the colorist, and the letterer. He says that this is perhaps the only artwork in the history of mankind that reflects a joint venture for the creation of an original piece of work that is then put on the presses and mass-produced. He believes it is one of the unique inventions of both American fantasy and industrial life.

The collector is reading a comic now. It is one of a half-dozen new issues that he bought today. They were books that he had been expecting because he subscribes to a monthly digest that lists all upcoming issues. Title, characters, story synopsis, and newsstand release date, it's all there and in advance, in this *TV Guide* of comics. He knows that new comics are delivered to the stores on Thursdays. Each Thursday they arrive without fail—and so does he. This way he can select the perfect copies. Crumpled edges, loose bindings, and a sloppy printing job are no good.

As he reads an issue, he is careful not to bend the covers or fold the pages. He turns first to the letters page, the fan page, his page. What was the verdict on the previous issue? Oxford, Ohio, liked it. Columbus, Georgia, hated the new artist; Austin, Texas, concurred. One letter is obviously from a younger reader; the editors have included it as an inside joke. The collector approves. He likes the letters page. His complaints, praises, and earnest suggestions have been printed there before.

Another comic arrived today by mail, an older one, but one could not tell by its physical conditon. He examines each page carefully, reading from cover to cover. He smells the comic book. It has a strange, hoary smell. To the collector it is a wonderful smell, part age, part toil, part the sweat of American history and industry. It is the smell that comes from a comic book that encapsulates an era in the stereotyped images of a nation and the caricatures of its enemies, whether they be the Japanese monkey-faces of World War II or alien beings in flying saucers, threatening to annihilate all civilization. To the collector the comic book is a mirror of the America that is part dream and ideals, part nightmare and technology. The comic book is part humor and part pathos. The collector feels all of these things as he reads.

A finger traces carefully over each column and line in the advertising section of a "fanzine," or a for sale list. A red felt-tip pen circles possible offerings that will need further research and scrutiny. A hefty soft-cover book, the price guide, fifth edition, sits like an old Bible at his elbow. Occasionally, he picks it up and thumbs through it until he finds what he is looking for. It tells him something about the value of the book he is considering purchasing. His set is not complete. This decision may take him one step closer to completion. Can he ever find the book in better condition, at a better price? . . . He has decided: "I must have this!" He clears a portion of the table and writes, enclosing a check for the purchase of a Green Lantern comic. The "run" is now complete.

The Comic Convention

The collector is a part of a collectivity separated by geographical location, occupation, and financial status. Its members are the custodians of the American ethos, the nightwatchmen of the fantasy warehouse. Next month the collector will be going to a comic convention a hundred miles from his home. This will be a time of exhultation. He will talk and joke with his peers as he searches from table to table. Comics will be bought and sold, the body of social knowledge will be shared and increased, transmitted and transformed. Venerated guests—the artists, writers, and creators from the industry—will make their triumphant entries. In this setting the comic character and its creator merge into a single identity, a separate reality constructed and ordered out of the projected images of the audience.

The comic convention serves several purposes. It reinforces the collector in his work and opens up new frontiers for exploration. It demonstrates to the collector that he is not alone, that there are others who believe in the world of imagination, who believe in the ideology and aesthetics portrayed by the comic book: that intelligent life exists on other planets; that beneath the facade of the mild-mannered reporter lives a Superman ready to defend the greatness of our cities, the integrity of our institutions, the honor of our women; that good must inevitably triumph over evil!

Most comic-book collectors lead quiet, even reclusive, lives, yet as a group they celebrate and ritualize the joy and spontaneity of fantasy. The collectivity is diversified, but they gather together in convention halls, in basement rooms, and attics with a single, driving motive—to share specific social knowledge so that the individual collector can succeed in the enterprise of collecting.

The Imposed World and the Fantasy World

Collecting comics is not seen as a "hobby" by the true collector. It is a way of knowledge. The comic collector uses the social meanings contained in the comic as an overlay that helps him to gain insight into the world of everyday life. Fantasy is predicated on a knowledge of the given, the world as it imposes itself on each of us. This world is sometimes nostalgic and sentimental, sometimes exaggerated and grotesque. Most often it is neither black nor white, only a dull, routinized gray. To the collector, his comic books form a map and index of this imposed world. Through his collection he can see himself and, through the creative aspect of collecting and reading his comics, impose himself upon a larger landscape, a fantastic and metaphysical one. This is the strategy by which he grounds himself in time, in history, and in the everyday world. The collector is a mass man, who like the creations in the comics, seeks to find his place within the world where he has a name, an identity.

He clears the table and switches off the light. With his new additions in hand, he descends the basement steps. Stacked along the pine wood shelves against the concrete walls are the carefully arranged products of his enterprise and the maps of his world. Each is neatly sealed in an air-tight plastic bag. All are stacked by title in order of their creation. He stares in wonderment. There it is: The Collection.

The Collector as Decorator

The decoration of lifespace involves a form of propaganda. It is a carefully staged performance for the benefit of spectators. Thus, the decorator is part set-designer, part prop-manager in the Hollywood studio of the home. Home decor serves as a prop in performances that vary according to the demands and expectations of a particular scenario. When decor is called in question, rather than abandoning the performance, the decorator merely changes the props and continues. The collector as decorator continually resets the stage for the dramaturgical production of routine daily life.

The decoration of the home also is a form of propaganda for the self. Nothing is more decisive to understanding the decorator than to see the way in which she materializes a self-image in the coordination of commonplace items in the home. What we call "vogue decor" encompasses the essential characteristic of a link between the self and the maze of systems in which it is enmeshed. This characteristic is instant variability, the quick change characteristic, in a word—stretch.

The traditional notion of conformity does not apply here. We are talking about permutability, i.e., the ability of the self to negotiate within imposed change. This change occurs in a milieu where the direct manipulation of consciousness by the industrial-technological propaganda machine is an everyday fact of life.

Collecting for Decoration

She is married, divorced, single. She is a career girl or a housewife. Her kids go to the day-care center, or she has no children. She is up early this morning, and she's in a hurry. She goes to the mirror and throws off the football shirt she slept in and forgets her dream of Kris Kristofferson. She slips on a $6.00 pair of designer bikini pants, a copy of Frederick's of Hollywood that she could have mail-ordered for $2.99. She shoots into her blue jeans, buttons her pink-satin, pearl-studded cowboy shirt, and hops into her expensive therapeutic shoes. She runs to the kitchen, swallows half a dozen vitamins—A through E. It's going to be a big day for self-improvement and decoration: aerobics for the body, ceramics for the soul, and consciousness-raising classes for the mind. She punches seven digits into her phone: "Pearl, be by to pick you up at nine." They are off to the flea market.

They are at the flea market looking over some turn-of-the-century postcards that she may purchase for decoupage. Behind the vendor's table, set on some chairs, are a couple of old, unfinished printer's boxes.

These rectangular boxes have rows of smaller boxes within them. Ms. Decor knows these boxes are getting hard to find and spends $40.00 for one. Soon she will convert this into a "memory box" by filling the little boxes with curios, photos, miniatures, and relics, some precious, some very common. She has seen these boxes in *Vogue, House Beautiful, Cosmopolitan,* and *Psychology Today.* Some of Ms. Decor's friends have these boxes, and they sometimes talk about them. Pearl remarks, "They're so cute, and really easy to put together and hang." She has made one memory box already; so she knows just what she will need for this one.

Ms. Decor moves to a stall where the vendor is selling dried plants: bean stalks, pussy willows, and corn stalks. There are some little vials shaped like the old pharmaceutical bottles. They contain such rare items as chick peas, soy beans, Indian corn, kidney beans, and peppercorns. These things are "very natural" and will bring a little of the farm into the home. She knows that being natural is very "now," so she purchases some for her memory box.

She moves on to a booth spread with buttons, souvenirs, memorabilia, and collectible items. With her glossy fingernail she pushes through all these. She finds a miniature of a Coca-Cola bottle. This little bottle of Coke will take a prominent place in the memory box because it is a symbol. Coke is a tradition, Coke is a way of life, Coke is youth, Coke is action. She buys a JFK campaign button and a Goldwater button that tend to neutralize each other as if to say: "Of course I know politics, but I don't want to argue with anyone."

At another booth Ms. Decor purchases a brass miniature of a cow, an enamelized miniature of a chicken, an old brass thimble, a small sea conch, a broken lute-shaped music holder from an old clarinet, and three miniature liquor bottles. Moving to a booth covered with a variety of different kinds of rocks, she buys several pieces of turquoise and a more expensive piece of Utah shale with a trilobite fossil on it. She is pleased when she buys a miniature of a light bulb. She also purchases a Vail ski patch (she had forgotten to save hers from last winter's vacation), and a small airline bottle opener with a well-known logo. She pays for two old coins and a cheap pendant with her sign of the zodiac on it. At a corner table where a man is hawking Astroturf, she acquires a small three-by-two-inch piece and adds this to her collection. This is her final buy for her memory box. Tomorrow, Ms. Decor finds that the entire memory box—technologically co-opted and institutionalized—can be bought as a unit at a local department store. But this does not matter. Her arrangement of the items in the box conveys information about how she wants others to perceive her. The box's total message is, "I am modern, yet sentimental."

Ms. Decor stops at a booth where they are selling ready-made boards, presanded and squared, some cut in hexagonal shapes, others in octagonal shapes, beveled and chamfered. She purchases a few, as well as Gesso and Elmer's glue and some polyvinyl lacquer. They are also pushing and selling rubber rollers, brushes, and emory and sandpapers. This is the world of decoupage, one of the many craft worlds Ms. Decor revels in. With these tools she can recycle the past quickly and efficiently. Her craft objects can be used to decorate, but she can also give them to her friends and her boss as tokens of her creativity.

She will also visit another booth and procure some precut patches for her quilting and at another table, yarn for her needlepoint. She will buy some ceramic pots for her many plants and cacti. Examining some old rattan and wicker furniture, she decides it is too worn and not as nice as the new imitation imports.

The next day Ms. Decor will talk about her finds at the office. The girls will reassure each other that there is an outside world. They are not merely working girls. They are not merely divorcees, wives, or single girls. These are women of leisure, of culture, with an appreciation of horticulture, nature, the crafts, and the arts. Ms. Decor is helping to keep America beautiful. She is not just a person—she is a personality. She is not just an anonymous urban dweller but an artist keeping America alive in the heart of the modular living center.

Conspicuous Elimination: The Garage Sale

Ms. Decor has purchased some items she decides she cannot use. These items are either shelved or recycled through the middle-class marketplace by means of the weekend garage sale. The garage sale enables Ms. Decor to rid herself of junk and to do it with a bit of flash. The garage sale functions as a social occasion. It involves planning and, in many instances, combining her salable items with those of her friends. It is considered a conspicuous mode of elimination that reflects one's mode of consumption. "Oh, you're having a garage sale?" "Yes, we simply have too much junk around the house, but it's too good to give to the Goodwill."

The objects from the garage sale make their way through some mysterious underground railway from station to station, from flea market to home, from home to garage sale, from garage sale to antique store, from antique store to attic, from attic to auction, from auction to flea market. Though the price of the fare may change and the timetable be altered, the trip continues. Sometimes the objects travel first-class, and their status is high; sometimes they travel by coach, and their status drops. They go from pauper objects to middle-class objects to elite objects—but not necessarily in that order.

The Decorator's Lifespace

Now we must examine Ms. Decor's lifespace, since it is the focus of her intent. Her apartment is done in antiseptic magazine modern. What is not wood is chrome and smoked glass. There are terrariums and hanging plants, lucite cubes, boxes, lights, and blocks sitting in carefully regulated symmetrical spaces on the flat planes of the tables. The walls are white, and everything appears as if it were against a motion picture screen that is being flooded by white light. This helps to carry across the feeling that all objects are staged. The lucite cube with a single, blonde, straw flower is a world in itself, an ecosystem of dead plastic.

The furnishings are a smooth mix of Honeywell naturalism and Euell Gibbons' cybernation. It would seem that anyone would be at peace here, but nobody is. The stage takes up so much space that there is little room for the actors. The apartment is a giant chrome-and-glass incubator that has the immediate effect of sterilizing any object, organic or inorganic, threatening to contaminate it. A few grains of dust on a lucite cube are the most visible signs of an outside world. The apartment is hermetically sealed and air-conditioned. The diffuse overhead lighting and illuminated lucite blocks add to the incubator mood of the place.

History seems bottled, and the digital clock appears to be making up time as it goes along. Space is organized in such formal geometry that the room either seems impossibly large and impersonal (like the layout of an airport waiting room) or impossibly small, forcing the occupants to huddle together on the floor or on cushions in order to perform the most simple social exchanges and ceremonies, like sharing a single oversized community ashtray.

The meaning of the ashtray is very important to a room where very little else is mobile. It becomes the focus of attention in opening ceremonies and rituals performed in the room. Magazine modern is so narcissistic that the excuse of sharing an ashtray may be the only connecting link between the occupants of the room. Ms. Decor thinks it's wonderful, stylish, efficient, and malleable—with enough stretch to handle a multiplicity of entertainment scenarios.

The Collector as Camp Culture Vampire

The collection and recycling of the past may serve the motive of enhancing the self. The collection of objects style the collector in an image that facilitates his social interactions and defines his situation. This type of collector likes to be part of the action; he likes to be where the action is. The collected objects are part of the action scene.

The items collected are chosen according to whether they are judged as having style or not. This collector has acquired a sensibility that enables him to label objects. In turn, labeling and possessing these items produce the style and image of the collector. The collector as *camper* is an aesthete. *Camp* is a game of labeling, indexing, and utilizing objects (including people) in order to affect a social consequence that insures the image, status, and prestige of the camper. The items in the game may change, but the rules of the game are determined by a social sensibility that defines which new objects are eligible for the game. Objects receive points or high status if they fit the definition of being camp and achieve low or zero status if they do not. The game is essentially binary; objects are either "in" or "out." They meet the social definition, or they do not. The collector as camper masters this game so that he can be socially successful.

Since social definitions change, items that are labeled camp also change. There is a continual transformation of cultural objects from the ordinary and the mundane to the exaggerated, the zany, the faddish, the camp. When the use-value of an object ceases, the object is then redefined and labeled as camp. When the object has served its purpose in the camp game, it returns to the ordinary and banal.

The Social Grammar of Appearance

You don't see him. You don't see her. You see THEM. THEM are not a couple, THEM is a phenomenon. He's Ike, she's Mike, see them on their tandem bike, wonder what they'll do tonight?

In the parking lot of the flea market, we see Ike and Mike. They are both wearing Levi's and polo shirts emblazoned with the symbols of their favorite culture heroes. Dangling from *her* neck is turquoise jewelry, and dangling from *his* wrists are turquoise bracelets. They are both wearing platform shoes. Ike and Mike typify a new type of sexuality called "nouveau vague." In the grammar of appearance it is difficult to tell which is the boy and which is the girl.

In the flea market, they go from table to table and booth to booth. They are trying on some old hats from the twenties, the thirties, the forties, the fifties, the sixties. Ike picks one out and tries it on, then Mike tries it on. They both like it and are laughing. They buy it. The price of the item is irrelevant, 29¢ or $29.00. At another booth they are looking at purses. Mike picks out a gaudy gold lamé purse. Ike moves to another table and looks through some watch fobs and lapel pins. He buys a lapel pin that is a green Heinz pickle from the 1929 World's Fair. He finds a brass belt buckle inscribed with the visage of the grand imperial wizard of the Ku Klux Klan. He calls Mike over. "What do you think?" "What is it?" she says. "It's a genuine belt buckle from the Ku Klux Klan," he says, looking at the vendor for confirmation. "Well, what do you think?" "I think it's great." They buy it.

They are at another booth, rummaging through some old clothing. Mike buys a thin, silver-lamé belt. Ike buys a white silk scarf. Mike is looking at a short jacket made of muskrat fur. "What do you think?" "Nope, don't think so." "Nope, some homicidal ecology nut is likely to go off his rocker if he sees it." The muskrat jacket is thrown back on the pile.

They speak of their game in a binary language, a sort of yes-or-no wink of the eye, a tilt of the head. They constantly flash amazement, on-off, off-on. It is a perpetual oscillation of judgment: it's in, it's out, it's in, it's out. They point a lot at objects and at people, and where others might think it rude, they continue to point. They are pointing at half a Vietnam veteran in a wheelchair; at an old black man with a cane and a straw cotton picker's hat; at a postcard of a dwarf dressed in Edwardian costume; at a Maxfield Parish magazine cover; at a circus poster of the Great Kharmi swallowing swords, eating fire, charming snakes. As they point they appear calculating within their binary code, thumb up, thumb down, on-off, yes-no.

They move to a booth where a jolly turquoise giant, with the appearance of one of Omar Khayyam's court eunuchs, hawks Indian jewelry. His head is bald—his eyes flash like the enormous lapis lazuli ring on his pinky. He is telling them about turquoise, its shape, its form, its weight, its market value. "Beware of phony imports from Hong Kong, Seoul, and Nationalist China." His arms are wreathed in snake-coiled bracelets of Mexican silver and turquoise. Ike and Mike are tilting out of their platforms, their jaws are dropping. They buy, by the pound, rings, bracelets, earrings, necklaces, pendants, whole uncut and unpolished hunks of the stuff. They stash it in their leather pouches and in the purses and the hats they've bought.

They move on through the flea market picking oddities and beaming to each other their approval or disapproval, looking for confirmation from each other that their choices are "right" and "now." The polarity of their objects is reversible; they pick objects the same as they pick tango partners or personal vibrators. It's a zero; it's an ace. It's a knockout; it's a drag. It's camp; it's a bore. It rocks; it bombs. It makes it; it doesn't make it. And the vampire says, "I think is zis von I vant." They start to take another turn around the flea market. but you can see by a lack of spark in their eyes and a slowing of their gait that they are growing bored. This is very bad. They are ready to leave.

After they leave, they walk down to the funky record store, Cay's Corner. Ike fingers through the stacks and dividers and comes up with an album, Lou Reed's "Berlin." "What's it about?" asks Mike. "Don't know, must be about what's happening in Berlin," says Ike. "Oh," says Mike. "It has a good review in *Rolling Stone.*" They buy the record. They also pick up tickets to next weekend's rock concert. On the way out they stop and stare at a life-size cardboard cutout of Leon Russell outfitted in white and turquoise country and western clothes. Mike says, "Nice duds!" "I wish we could find something like that at the flea market." Ike retorts, tongue in cheek, "Maybe next time."

They walk down a couple of blocks to the Beautiful Day Cafe where they purchase grain burgers and a smoothie—a wholesome yogurt drink. Ike and Mike have been vegetarians for two weeks now. The cafe is filled with restaurant-blend people. Appropriate greetings are exchanged. They speak to the right people; the right people speak to them. After drinking Pero, an ersatz coffee, they get up, pay, and leave.

Later in the afternoon, Ike and Mike go to visit a friend in the lower end of town, an older residential section. They are greeted by Claudius, a middle-aged man who reinforces them with a little Coke. Claudius has his hair sculptur-kut. His hair does not move; it flashes and glints because it has been transformed into gold by some sort of metallurgical process. Claudius is a collector. He collects mostly fine-art items, porcelain statues, cut glass, and old copies of magazines like *Esquire, Show* and *After Dark.* Claudius serves his guests some sarsaparilla lemonade and gives them some of the old magazines to look through. They converse with Claudius about his house and furniture. Although they don't know much about social history prior to the last space shot, they feel mellow as they browse through the cultural flotsam with Claudius. They come to Claudius because he is an available mentor in the sensibility that is so important to their lives. He has been around a long time and has seen things come and go. Claudius brings out one of his prize stag movies, "Both Ways Now," and as the sun sets over the wicker furniture on the veranda and the Tiffany lamp glows in the corners of the room, the scene is definitely blue. Ike and Mike feel real "laid back," "real mellow," just as does their inspiration, Claudius. Claudius resides in a mellow world. Mike and Ike collect mellow objects, mellow friends, and mellow experiences.

Culture Vampires and the Penny Arcade

It is night. Ike and Mike are fully loaded with their buys of the day. They drive downtown to a highrise where there is a promise of good times. Their day has been only a prelude to the party. It is a weekend like any other weekend. Everyone will be there: Claudius, the girls from the local head shop, some younger members of the university faculty, a few local artists and a few people from the media, some young married couples from the ranks, mostly social workers, junior attorneys and computer programmers, plus one or two bisexual medical technicians, an Ethiopian foreign-exchange student, and the owner of a local gay bar. They are all there, and they have all brought their collections: they are themselves a collection. There are rumors of the appearance of the coterie of a rock star who lives in the city, of a spiritualist, and of a self-proclaimed witch who exorcises demons while dancing scantily clad over a lava lamp.

The mood of the party is nouveau vague. They are wearing their collections, decked out in clothing that will have a half-life of one evening: feather boas, heavy leathers, forties' hairdos, cabaret makeups, satin suits, Hawaiian shirts, gold-lamé torreador pants, Cuban heels, turquoise-dyed snakeskin boots, flapper purses of chain mail with deco insets, 1950s pegged jeans, cowboy shirts, western belts, plastic belts, no belts. Twenty-four-karat coke spoons; fancy hash pipes made of seashells, stone, and glass; roach clips that range from medical hemostats to a clip made out of a human finger bone: everybody is pointing, everybody is scoring, everybody is mellow. The room is an arcade where the game is played and the points are scored.

Mike and Ike are mixing, showing their Heinz pickle and their slouch hat. They trade compliments with other collectors of their genre. They feel relieved; they feel right. They are making points, and the game feels good. Mike is "simply taken" by a tortoise-shell hairpiece another couple found at the flea market. Ike is drawn to a corner where everyone seems to be wearing Lauren Bacall scarves and Bogart cravats and the men are opening art-deco cigarette cases and smoking Luckies and Camels. He shows them his scrimshaw pill box on the pretense of offering them a Quaalude, the mellow pill of the evening. Somebody is playing an antique accordian, and somebody is dancing a tango, and somebody is reading palms. The air smells sweet of incense and grass. Nobody gets huffy. Nouveau vague demands a condoning coolness. It is not camp to be uptight. Anything goes if it is done with a little style and not too much seriousness.

There seems to be a lot of turquoise in the room, pounds of turquoise; a strip-mined New Mexico and Arizona must be right here in this high-rise apartment. Ike and Mike think the Navajos are wonderful people and must be doing very well.

They are juicing Tequila Sunrises and the latest pop wines along with the beers that are most difficult to find in the area. Lots of juice. It is part of the collection brought to the party by the collectors. It is part of the mood. They live in an ionized atmosphere of the now. They are the fireflies of the mass culture, collecting its magic dust and bringing it here where it can be seen, felt, touched; where it can transform a routine evening into a bacchanal.

With bent wrist and Midas touch, they transform the mundane into the magical, into the mysterious blood that is the continual nourishment of the culture vampire. And here at their party is their feast of blood in the collection of objects and people. They move in a type of café society that can transform a Greyhound station into a French salon and a penthouse into a truckstop.

All objects and events are recycled through the recyclotron of the camper's lifestyle in order to throw off and smash the mass-culture object and create a new element with the rarity and half-life of a moment. They can be seen as linear accelerators throwing a stepped-up pulse into the mass of mass culture. Next week's treasures lay ahead like an unknown element on the periodic chart, waiting to be discovered and labeled. The items they have brought with them are no more than universal nutrients for their social alchemy. With their totems, their amulets, their icons, and their beads, they can transform the banal into the exotic, the exotic into the banal, and the He into the She and the She into the He. They siphon the blood from the past so that they might survive the present. Tomorrow they must hunt again for the next night's sustenance.

The party breaks up slowly. People leave one by one, two by two, three by three. The construction and successful negotiation of their social roles have been founded on a shared social reality expressed in the artifacts and mentality of the camp scene. The party is a scenario that permits the actors to play out their roles in a socially legitimate manner. But like the vampire, they must always return to the confines and controls of their everyday situation. They must subjugate their camp sensibilities to the demands, the priorities, and impositions of the larger reality.

The party is over. The exotic becomes commonplace again: the collection wears and ages before the first rays of the sun. The mysteries of midnight give way to the paralyzing realities of mass man in a rapidly changing technological society.

References

Gass, William H. 1970. *Fiction and the Figures of Life.* New York: Alfred A. Knopf.

Schutz, Alfred. 970. *Reflection on the Problems of Relevance.* New Haven, Conn.: Yale University Press.

Sebran, Armin. 1974. Excursion in Ethnomethodology and the Common Sense World. Masters thesis, The University of Tulsa.

Sontag, Susan. 1966. *Against Interpretation and Other Essays.* New York: Farrar, Straus and Giroux.

Thompson, Hunter S. 1973. *Fear and Loathing in Las Vegas.* New York: Popular Library.

Wolfe, Tom. 1969. *The Electric Kool-Aid Acid Test.* New York: Bantam.